Profiles of Sport Industry Professionals

The People Who Make the Games Happen

Matthew J. Robinson, EdD
Associate Professor of Sport Management
York College of Pennsylvania
York, Pennsylvania

Mary A. Hums, MA, MBA, PhD
Associate Professor of Sport Administration
University of Louisville
Louisville, Kentucky

R. Brian Crow, MBA, EdD
Assistant Professor of Sport Management
Hampton University
Hampton, Virginia

Dennis R. Phillips, MAT, DPE
Graduate Coordinator, Associate Professor
Coaching and Sport Administration
University of Southern Mississippi
Hattiesburg, Mississippi

AN ASPEN PUBLICATI
Aspen Publishers, Inc
Gaithersburg, Marylan
2001

D0967680

Library of Congress Cataloging-in-Publication Data

Profiles of sport industry profesionals:
the people who make the games happen / Matthew J. Robinson ... [et al.].
p. cm.
Includes bibliographical references and index.
ISBN 0-8342-1796-1
1. Sports administration--United States--Case studies. 2. Sports
personnel--United States--Interviews. 3. Sports executives--
United States--Interviews. I. Title: Profiles of
sport industry professionals. II. Robinson, Matthew J.

GV713.M335 2000
796'.06'9--dc21   00-040605

Orders: 800-638-8437
Customer Service: 800-234-1660

About Aspen Publishers • For more than 40 years, Aspen has been a leading professional
publisher in a variety of disciplines. Aspen's vast information resources are available in both
print and electronic formats. We are committed to providing the highest quality information
available in the most appropriate format for our customers. Visit Aspen's Internet site for
more information resources, directories, articles, and a searchable version of Aspen's full
catalog, including the most recent publications: **www.aspenpublishers.com**
Aspen Publishers, Inc. • The hallmark of quality in publishing
Member of the worldwide Wolters Kluwer group.

Editorial Services: Joan Sesma
Library of Congress Catalog Card Number: 00-040605
ISBN: 0-8342-1796-1

Printed in the United States of America

1 2 3 4 5

Matthew J. Robinson
To Lynn and Cullen, my reasons for being
and to Mom and Dad for always being there.

Mary Hums
To all the students I have served during my teaching career.
Thank you for everything you taught me.

Brian Crow
To all those aspiring to positions in sports,
may you realize your dreams.

Dennis Phillips
To the three girls in my life whom God has so richly blessed me with:
my wonderful wife Lenora and my children Paige and Abbey,
for their unconditional love, support, and motivation each day.

To
Herman Hums
in loving memory.

Table of Contents

Contributors

Robertha Abney
Associate Athletic Director
Slippery Rock University
Slippery Rock, Pennyslvania

John L. Allen
Chief Operating Officer
Cincinnati Reds Baseball Club
Cincinnati, Ohio

Damon Andrews
Sports Anchor/Reporter
WBAL-TV 11
Baltimore, Maryland

Anne Sander "Sandy" Barbour
Athletic Director
Tulane University
New Orleans, Louisiana

Jeffrey W. Beaver
Executive Director
Charlotte Regional Sports Commission
Charlotte, North Carolina

Robert R. Bender
Recreation and Fitness Manager
Sea Pines Resort
Hilton Head, South Carolina

Brian R. Britten
Manager, Public Relations
Toledo Mud Hens Baseball Club
Toledo, Ohio

Susan C. Brown
Associate Professor
Flagler College
St. Augustine, Florida

John J. Cicero
President/Chief Executive Officer
Greater New Orleans Sports Foundation
New Orleans, Louisiana

Marc C. Connolly
Senior Writer/Producer
ABC Sports Online/ESPN.com
New York, New York

P. Scott Douglas
Promoter/Director of Media
Louisville Motor Speedway
Louisville, Kentucky

Derek M. Eiler
Vice President of University Services
Collegiate Licensing Company
Atlanta, Georgia

André L. Farr
Chairman/Chief Executive Officer
Black Sports Agents Association
Los Angles, California

Nancy M. Gonsalves
Manager of Paralympics
Salt Lake Organizing Committee for the
    Olympic and Paralymic Winter Games of
    2002
Colorado Springs, Colorado

Kimberly Sue Grant
Tournament Director
Firststar LPGA Classic
Dayton, Ohio

Victor S. Gregovitis
Vice President of Marketing and
    Broadcasting
Pittsburgh Pirates Baseball Club
Pittsburgh, Pennsylvania

Charles S. Harris
Commissioner
Mid-Eastern Athletic Conference
Greensboro, North Carolina

James A. Haynes
Marketing Coordinator
Palm Beach County Sports Commission
West Palm Beach, Florida

Jennifer L. Heppel
Director of NCAA Legislative and Eligibility
    Services
Big Ten Conference
Park Ridge, Illinois

Dennis R. Howard
Professor of Sport Marketing, Academic
    Coordinator
University of Oregon
Eugene, Oregon

Connie Hurlbut
Director, Basketball Operations
Women's National Basketball Association
New York, New York

Khalil Johnson
General Manager
Georgia Dome
Atlanta, Georgia

Robert F. Kanaby
Executive Director
National Federation of State High School
    Associations
Indianapolis, Indiana

Kyle Kirousis
Senior Events Coordinator
Alamodome
San Antonio, Texas

Brian L. Laubscher
Sports Information Director
Washington and Lee University
Lexington, Virginia

Richard V. Ledford
Athletic Director
North Hall High School
Gainsville, Georgia

Mark S. Levin
Assistant Director of Research
National Football League Players
   Association
Washington, DC

Susan T. Liebenow
President/Co-owner
L & T Health and Fitness
Falls Church, Virginia

Robert A. Lombardi
Associate Executive Director
Pennsylvania Interscholastic Athletic
   Association
Mechanicsburg, Pennsylvania

Oliver Luck
President and CEO
NFL Europe
Frankfurt, Germany

Joshua Mohlmann
Director of Service and Support
REDA Sports Express
Easton, Pennsylvania

Robert A. Mullens
Senior Associate Athletic Director for
   Internal Operations
University of Maryland
College Park, Maryland

Mel Narol
Attorney
Pellettieri, Rabstein and Altman
Princeton, New Jersey

Bradley C. Petty
Assistant Director for Recreational Sports
North Carolina State University
Raleigh, North Carolina

Susan Michelle Pollio
Event Coordinator
Churchill Downs (racetrack)
Louisville, Kentucky

Jeffrey S. Price
Vice President of Sponsorship and Events
MasterCard International Inc.
New York, New York

Jady H. Regard
General Manager
Louisiana Ice Gators Hockey
Lafayette, Louisiana

John Patrick Ringwald
General Manager
K. H.E. Fitness Inc./Hatfield Athletic Club
Hatfield, Pennsylvania

Tim C. Roberts
General Manager
ESPN Regional/Oregon Sports Network
Eugene, Oregon

Tracy Y. Royal
Public Relations Manager
AND 1
Philadelphia, PA

Todd A. Sammons
General Manager/PGA Professional
Glenmary Country Club
Louisville, Kentucky

Laura L. Sawyer
Executive Director
Carolina Marathon Association
Columbia, South Carolina

William A. Sutton
Associate Professor and Graduate Program
    Director
University of Massachusetts at Amherst
Amherst, Massachusetts

Jody Swimmer
Owner
Swimmer Wellness Services Inc.
Lousville, Kentucky

John D. Swofford
Commissioner
Atlantic Coast Conference
Greensboro, North Carolina

Charles Lee Todd II
Vice President of Sports and Competition
Special Olympics International
Washington, DC

David Mitchell Wheeler
President/Chief Executive Officer
MAI Sports Inc.
Kansas City, Missouri

Anne Wilkinson
Fitness Coordinator/Assistant Facility
    Manager
Temple University
Philadelphia, Pennsylvania

Foreword

Powerful lessons come from stories. *Profiles of Sport Industry Professionals: The People Who Make the Games Happen* tells the stories of a diverse group of sport industry professionals. The sport industry job market is ultra-competitive. Learning from those who have broken into the field will give readers a "leg up" on the competition. Breaking in takes a clear strategy and a little bit of luck. Possessing a strategy will ensure that the reader is prepared for every opportunity that presents itself. Reading the interviews in *Profiles of Sport Industry Professionals* will provide insight and inspiration on how to create one's own path into the industry.

Profiles of Sport Industry Professionals: The People Who Make the Games Happen educates students and those contemplating a career change about the myriad of opportunities in the multi-billion dollar business of sport. That the individuals profiled are in various stages of their careers provides a realistic view of the opportunities and paths into the sport management profession. *Profiles of Sport Industry Professionals* also allays many sport industry myths, such as only former athletes or coaches are offered positions in the industry and the sport industry has just two segments: collegiate and professional sports.

Profiles of Sport Industry Professionals: The People Who Make the Games Happen will be a valuable supplement to *Principles and Practice of Sport Management*. The chapters follow the sixteen segments of the industry targeted by *Principles and Practice of Sport Management*. The combination of the two books will encourage students to learn about the various segments of the industry while discovering professionals working in those segments of the sport industry.

I congratulate the authors on making a valuable contribution to the sport management library. This is a book which will not sit on the shelf. It will be picked up again and again to provide insight for aspiring sports industry professionals.

Lisa Pike Masteralexis
Department Head
Associate Professor
Department of Sport Studies
University of Massachusetts
Amherst, Massachusetts

Foreword

Professors Robinson, Hums, Crow, and Phillips have written a lively, and useful textbook for students of sport management. As a facilities manager of major sports facilities, currently Giants Stadium, I am honored to comment on this timely text, which will surely open the eyes of interested students. When did you last see a newspaper headline proclaiming "No Sports Today" or surf your evening cable channels and not find a live broadcast of some sport? Not recently, eh!

Traditional academicians may consider sports management to be a "new" field. New or old, it is here—rapidly evolving and growing at a dizzying pace. The four major sports are expanding, with ongoing talk of further expansion. New sports are being introduced. College sports are increasingly viewed as and managed as businesses, rather than as "extracurricular activities". Some major college players are already millionaires as a result of signing bonuses and salaries earned in other sports. It seems only a matter of time until major college players will receive some compensation beyond tuition waivers and living expenses for their active roles in collegiate athletics. As the names of new stadiums indicate, Fortune 500 corporations are now entering this highly competitive and often lucrative field of sport. Indeed sport has become big business at its best.

The competition in sport goes way beyond winning or losing on the playing field. Young professionals vie for front office positions at both the club and league levels. Name almost any managerial or professional specialty and you can put "sports" in front of it: sport medicine, sport psychology, sport public and community relations, and so on. Competition for these positions is all the keener because seasoned professionals from other fields are seeking to enter the sport business along with bright, well-educated, and aggressive recent graduates.

This text offers profiles of 48 successful sport managers. You can learn a lot from these profiles. Practical advice on how to get into the sport industry includes: do not limit yourself to a single sport, league, team, location, or position; and optimize your chances of getting a good start in the business by interning during your undergraduate years in order to learn more about your own capabilities and about the business itself. Effective internships benefit both the intern and the organization. Consider an internship part of your investment in getting a good education, so compensation for your service should not be an issue.

I recently hired an intern from Professor Crow's Sports Management Program at Hampton University. This intern worked as hard, if not harder, than any other member of my staff. He assumed full responsibility for a number of diverse tasks that I assigned him. At times he faltered—and that's part of what internships are all about. But he learned a lot from a few mistakes. He never stopped trying, and he produced a lot for the organization. He was pursued by not one, but two NFL organizations and is now working for one of them in the marketing department. He made the most of a challenging opportunity. I have no doubt that one day he will be a successful sports executive. Note how many of the 48 executives profiled in the text got their starts as interns.

Not everyone is cut out to succeed as a sports executive. The challenges are unique—long hours, in season/off season rhythms, uncertainties regarding changes of ownership and CEOs, lots of travel, to name a few. It's a business that has more hard-luck stories than success stories. You can use this text to increase your chances of being one of the success stories.

William Squires
Vice President/General Manager Giants Stadium
Formerly General Manager Walt Disney Wide World of Sports
Director of Stadium Operations, Yankee Stadium

Acknowledgments

There are always people besides the authors who are instrumental in seeing a project like this through, and it would be a grave injustice not to recognize their efforts. We first have to thank the subjects. If not for their willingness to participate, we would not have a book. We cannot thank them enough for taking the time from their busy schedules to participate in the interviews and editing process. We found all of the subjects to be of the highest professional standards. Their insights and advice will surely prove valuable to the next generation of sport managers, but the authors themselves have already benefited from their interaction with the subjects. We all walked away a little better and a little brighter from our contact with you. Thank you!

Also we would like to recognize those individuals who played a role in conceptualizing the idea for the book. Those individuals are Dr. Karen Walton, Vice President of Academic Affairs at Allentown College of St. Francis de Sales; Johnson Bowie, Associate Director of Athletics at Drexel University; and Dr. Ellen Staurowsky, Associate Professor of Sport Management at Ithaca College. Their advice and input enabled us to turn an abstract idea into a concrete one.

Each author had his or her personal support units and collectively these individuals played an important role in the process. Mary Hums would like to acknowledge the efforts of Pat Dalton, transcriptionist; and Shannette Owens, administrative assistance; Dan Funk, Dan Mahony, and Anita Moorman for their professional support; and Judy Wright for her ongoing personal support. Dennis Phillips would like to acknowledge the efforts of his wife Lenora Phillips for transcribing and Dr. Jane Boudreaux, the Dean of the College of Health and Human Sciences, and Dr. Walt Bumgardner, Director of the School of Human Performance at the University of Southern Mississippi, for their encouragement and support. Brian Crow would like to thank Dawn Ellen Cline for her timely and accurate transcription; the HPER faculty at Hampton University for their support and encouragement; and his wife Francie and son Samuel, for their love, patience, and understanding. I would like to thank Roxanne Myers for her efforts in transcribing the interviews; Joy Sayles for her transcription and her administrative efforts toward the project as well as for her delaying her Winter Break 1999 to help get the job done; the Research and Publication Committee of York College for its financial support of the project; my colleagues in the sport management program including Pat Massa, Nina Grove, Rich Achtzehn, and Sue Sponsler for their friendship and support during the process; Dr. Brian Glandon, my department chair, for his friendship and for granting me a course reduction to work on the project; my students for encouraging me by asking, "How's the book going?", Bruce Springsteen, for his inspiration; Dean Barnard, Ed Jones, Gerry Siegel, and Bob Weirich for putting the idea of writing a book in my head more than 15 years ago; and my wife Lynn for just being herself.

Thanks must also go to the people at Aspen Publishers with a special thanks to Susan Beauchamp who believed in the project, Monica Hincken for her guidance, and the reviewers for their insights.

On behalf of my co-authors, thank you all. We could not have done it without you.

Matt Robinson

Introduction

The subjects profiled in *Profiles of Sport Industry Professionals: The People Who Make the Games Happen* do not appear on the front page of the sports section, nor do they appear in the highlight clips on the local news or ESPN. They are not household names; they do not have any major endorsement deals, nor do their faces appear on trading cards. Although they do not have the name recognition of Michael Jordan, Troy Aikman, Rebecca Lobo, or Jackie Joiner Kersee, they play a vital role in making the games we attend, watch on TV, read about in the newspaper, or participate in ourselves happen!

Profiles of Sport Industry Professionals enables the reader to go behind the scenes of the $213 billion sport industry to meet the professionals who create the world of sport. *Profiles of Sport Industry Professionals* provides the reader with the insights of individuals who make important decisions related to the governance and administration of college and high school athletics. Readers learn from an individual who manages a facility that hosted Olympic basketball games, the Super Bowl, and the NCAA Men's Basketball Final Four, and that also serves as the home field for a National Football League franchise. A sport marketing executive is profiled whose company spends millions of dollars annually sponsoring major league baseball and professional golf to strengthen brand awareness and loyalty in the marketplace. We get the insights of a major league baseball executive who has the responsibility of generating revenue through the sale of tickets, sponsorships, premium seating, and advertising on broadcasts so the team can meet its yearly payroll and operating expenses. The health and fitness and recreation industries are represented by a recreation professional who runs a state-of-the-art fitness complex and its programs on a major college campus as well as a manager for a for-profit fitness club. An events professional is profiled who organizes statewide road races and marathons in her position as an executive director of a marathon association.

The authors' mission in writing this text was to present an overview of the sport industry to enlighten people interested in pursuing a career in the sport industry. A common misconception about the sport industry is that it only includes professional or college athletics. The authors dispel this myth by segmenting the sport industry into 16 areas. The segmenting was based on a model of the sport industry presented in the Masteralxis, Barr, and Hums text *Principles and Practices of Sport Management*. The segments presented in *Profiles of Sport Industry*

Professionals are (1) high school sport, (2) intercollegiate athletics, (3) sport governance, (4) international sport, (5) professional sport, (6) sport marketing, (7) media relations, (8) event management, (9) facility management, (10) academics, (11) sport commissions, (12) legal aspects, (13) fitness, (14) recreation, (15) sporting goods, and (16) sport communications.

The authors identified three professionals in each segment listed above and conducted a case study interview with each individual. The subjects were forwarded questions in advance so they had time to consider their responses. The questions fell under four main categories: (1) career path/experience, (2) current position, (3) trends in the industry segment, and (4) future aspirations. In selecting the subjects to be profiled, the authors emphasized diversity based on demographic and professional variables such as age, gender, race, progression in careers, educational background, and experience. The authors were interested in presenting individuals who have reached the apex of their career in top-level management positions as well as individuals who were either just entering the industry or who have been in the industry and progressed into middle management positions. The authors believed individuals at these different points in their careers have different perspectives to share. Many worthy professionals were considered for the text, which led to the difficult decision of who to include.

Keeping the objective of offering a diverse group of individuals, the book includes a chief operating officer for a major league baseball team as well as an individual 2 years out of college who works in media relations for a minor league baseball team. The book also profiles an individual working with a licensing company who decided in high school to work in the sport industry, and it also profiles a former professional football player who spent more than 20 years as an investment banker before becoming the executive director of a major city's sport commission. Finally, the book profiles a woman who came of age when equal opportunities were not offered to women in sport, but today owns her own fitness and wellness company, and it profiles a woman who was a college ice hockey player and now oversees compliance for one of the most prestigious college athletic conferences in the country.

Each subject has a unique story of how he or she got to this point in his or her career. There are tales of sacrifice as well as of luck. There are stories of great successes as well as those of failure and disappointment. The subjects provided insights into different sport environments through offering career advice and strategies, detailing their job responsibilities, discussing the pressures and environmental factors with which they contend, explaining what they enjoy and do not enjoy about their position and industry segment, and sharing future aspirations while also predicting the future industry trends. The key to the success of the project was the subjects' willingness to not only participate but also to open up and to share their stories, insights, and advice.

The authors hope the readers of *Profiles of Sport Industry Professionals* will recognize the varied and diverse career opportunities in the sport industry, appreciate the experiences and skills that are essential to securing a job in the different segments of the sport industry, understand what the job responsibilities are in the different positions and segments of the sport industry, develop a strategy to secure a position in the sport industry, and understand the positives and negatives associated with a career in the sport industry.

Profiles of Sport Industry Professionals provides beneficial insights and advice for students interested in embarking on a career in the sport industry as well as an individual who is considering making a career change to pursue his or her "dream" career in sport. The book would also serve as an excellent text for an introduction to sport management class because of its overview of the career opportunities in the sport industry. The authors hope that *Profiles of Sport Industry Professionals* will play an important role in helping aspiring sport managers make their career dreams come true.

CHAPTER 1

High
School
Sport

INTERSCHOLASTIC ATHLETICS GOVERNANCE

SPORT AND ATHLETIC COMPETITION in American high schools has a long and distinguished history. The beginning can be traced to the turn of the century when most interscholastic athletic programs were small, unorganized, student-initiated and administered enterprises. Times have changed. High school sport programs are now the single most significant dimension in the entire sport enterprise (VanderZwag, 1998). More than 17,000 high schools are members of the National Federation of State High School Associations (NFHS), and more than 6 million male and female athletes compete in interscholastic competition (National Federation of State High School Associations, 1998).

Currently, interscholastic athletics operate at four levels: (1) the individual school district, (2) the athletic conference, (3) the state athletic association, and (4) NFHS. Each level offers career opportunities in administration, governance, and coaching.

The NFHS is the national service organization for high school athletics. The organization's role is to provide leadership and national coordination for interscholastic athletic competition in the United States by publishing playing rules for 16 boys and girls sports and providing educational services and programs for the 51 member state associations. The NFHS does not possess enforcement powers and its rules are not mandatory nor enforceable. The national office has an executive director and a staff that conduct the organization's day-to-day operations. Entry level positions at the national level pay between $25,000 and $35,000 a

1

year. Middle management positions pay between $40,000 and $60,000 a year, and upper level positions pay between $70,000 and $100,000.

State associations govern athletics in their respective states. These state associations have the power to establish rules and in most cases possess enforcement powers. The extent of these powers varies from state to state. The majority of the state associations exist for the purpose of providing uniform standards for athletic competition within the state. They offer state championships; ensure safe, fair athletic competition; promote good sporting conduct; and provide an environment emphasizing the participants' overall development.

A state association will have an executive director and a staff who run the day-to-day operations. The executive director is a hired employee who oversees the direction of the state association and is responsible for implementing the association's policies and procedures. Depending on the state, entry level positions with a state association pay between $35,000 and $45,000 a year. Associate executive directors can earn between $45,000 and $55,000 and an executive director can earn $75,000 or more a year. The rules governing athletic competition come from the members.

Membership in interscholastic athletic conferences is usually based on geographic location. In some instances school size and type (whether private or public) are considerations in conference formation. At the conference or league level, a board or committee consists of representatives from each member institution. The representatives who serve in the governance structure are usually principals or athletic directors from the member institutions. Each member institution has a voice in creating the legislation it will have to follow.

Even with a comprehensive governance structure, the actual administration of high school athletics is primarily conducted on the local level. Most policy and procedural decisions are made at the school district or school level (Covell, 1998). A school board or board of education is made up of individuals living within the boundaries of a school district with the authority to establish policies and procedures and allocate resources for all school district programs including athletics. The school board approves budgets, determines the feasibility and allocation or resources for building athletic facilities, votes on the hiring and firing of athletic department personnel, and votes to establish policies for the school district's athletic programs. The athletic director has the responsibility of implementing the policies established by the school board for the athletic programs within the district.

In the past the athletic director position at the high school level was usually a part-time position held by a teacher or a coach. As the scope of high school athletic programs has grown, it is becoming more common for high school athletic directors to be full-time administrators with degrees in sport management or related fields. It is also still common for a high school athletic director to coach one or more sports. The high school athletic director position is a very hands-on position, where the individual prepares budgets, hires and evaluates coaches, and acts as facility and event manager. The salary for a high school athletic director varies based on the school district, the responsibilities of the position, and the number of years of experience. The salary range can be from $25,000 a year to $75,000 a year.

REFERENCES

Covell, D. (1998). High school and youth sport. In L.P. Masteralexis, C.A. Barr, & M.A. Hums (Eds.), *Principles and practice of sport management* (pp. 243–274). Gaithersburg, MD: Aspen Publishers, Inc.

National Federation of State High School Associations. (1998). Available on-line at http://nfhs.org/NFHS.htm.

VanderZwag, H.J. (1998). *Policy development in sport management* (2nd ed.). Westport, CT: Praeger.

Robert A. Lombardi

Associate Executive Director
Pennsylvania Interscholastic
Athletic Association

Education:
B.S., HEALTH AND PHYSICAL EDUCATION,
EAST STROUDSBURG STATE COLLEGE

M.ED., EAST STROUDSBURG UNIVERSITY,
HEALTH AND PHYSICAL EDUCATION, 1982

PH.D., UNIVERSITY OF NEW MEXICO, SPORTS
ADMINISTRATION, 1994

Career Progression:
EXECUTIVE STAFF MEMBER, PENNSYLVANIA
INTERSCHOLASTIC ATHLETIC ASSOCIATION
(PIAA), 1988 TO PRESENT

PART-TIME FUND RAISER/MEDIA RELATIONS
EMPLOYEE, NEW MEXICO
ACTIVITIES ASSOCIATION, 1987–1988

TEACHER AND COACH, WAYNE HIGHLANDS
SCHOOL DISTRICT, MONSIGNOR MCHUGH
ELEMENTARY SCHOOL/ POCONO CATHOLIC
HIGH SCHOOL

Best piece of advice you received in regards to your career:

"Get your doctorate. It will give you more opportunities."

FRANK PULLO, PROFESSOR AT EAST STROUDSBURG UNIVERSITY

Best advice for someone aspiring toward a career in the sport industry:

"Get background in health and physical education or sport administration and work hard."

Quote by which you live:

"Take care of your health and fitness."

IT WAS DURING MY UNDERGRADUATE STUDY that I decided to pursue a career in sport. I majored in health and physical education at East Stroudsburg State College in Stroudsburg, Pennsylvania, and initially wanted to teach and coach at the high school level. As associate executive director of the PIAA, I am very much involved in high school athletics, but I am not involved in coaching. Rather, I am directly involved in the governance of high school athletics in the state of Pennsylvania. Along with my bachelor's degree I earned my master's degree in health and physical education from East Stroudsburg University. I have also earned a doctorate in sports administration with a minor in educational administration from the University of New Mexico. These educational experiences were very influential in reaching this point in my career.

After I completed my undergraduate degree I taught health, physical education, and science at Msgr. McHugh Elementary School in Cresco, Pennsylvania for 1 year. From there I taught at Honesdale High School from 1979–1981. When I was at Msgr. McHugh Elementary School, I was the varsity soccer coach and the junior varsity basketball coach at Pocono Catholic High School. When I went to Honesdale I coached freshman football, junior varsity basketball, and varsity volleyball. It was during this time that I started my graduate studies. In Pennsylvania a person needs a certain number of credits to get permanent teaching certification. To earn a master's degree it only was 10 to 12 credits more than the number of credits required for the certification. It made sense to me to earn a master's degree. I decided to take a year off from my position at Honesdale and return to East Stroudsburg as a graduate assistant to complete my master's degree. After I completed the degree, I returned to Honesdale from 1982 until 1986.

I could have taught at the high school level anywhere, but was interested in moving into either athletic administration or teaching at the college level. Through the advice of some of my mentors, I realized that if I really wanted to reach those levels the doctorate was essential. I feel fortunate that I received some excellent advice while I was an undergraduate and graduate student at East Stroudsburg University in regard to my career aspirations. These individuals gave me sound advice and they were outstanding role models because they were the epitome of first class teachers. These people included Dr. Frank Pullo who is now the dean of students at East Stroudsburg, Dr. Mary-Sue Balducci, Dr. Jim Chamberlain, who unfortunately has passed away, and Dr. Bob Sutton. Dr. Gene Stish, who has also passed away, is the one who encouraged me the most to pursue my terminal degree.

I did not do much career research when looking at master's programs, but I spent a lot of time researching doctoral programs. I looked at various doctorate programs throughout the country. I looked at Ohio State, Florida, Penn State, University of Nevada at Las Vegas (UNLV), Arizona State, and New Mexico. Some of the institutions did not offer a terminal degree in sports administration, and New Mexico did. Plus Dr. Balducci gave me some astute advice when she said, "Bob, you grew up in the East, so go West. You can make contacts out there and establish a nice network." I went to visit New Mexico in the spring of 1983 and spoke with a fellow named Bob Sweeney who was from East Stroudsburg University. I spent some time speaking to him and he sold me on the place. I also was able to attend the 1983 National Collegiate Athletic Association (NCAA) basketball final between Houston and North Carolina State on my trip. After the trip, I decided to enroll and I began taking courses that summer. I went to New Mexico for two summers to take courses and then I took an educational leave in 1986–1987 and an unpaid leave in 1987–1988 to be a graduate assistant to work on my doctorate.

Earning my terminal degree was a truly rewarding experience. I met incredible people and I also learned how to think critically and to analyze topics in more depth. I learned to look beyond the author's point of view. I use these skills on a regular basis in my current position. In my mind, there are two stages to doctoral work: (1) the coursework/comprehensive exams stage and (2) the dissertation stage. The first stage is about the acquisition of knowledge. The dissertation stage is about perseverance and determination. I have seen a lot of friends not finish the degree. It is difficult, but persistence pays. After completing my coursework, I was working part-time for the New Mexico Activities Association in fund raising and public relations while also working on my dissertation. For my dissertation topic I researched the effectiveness of athletic public relations programs in New Mexico High Schools. It was during this time that I was made aware of an opening with the PIAA through the Chronicle of Higher Education. I applied and, after competing with 65 other applicants and going through two interviews, I was hired in January 1988. When I accepted the position with PIAA I had completed all of my requirements except the dissertation. It was extremely hard for me to sit down and work on that project once I took the position at the PIAA. It was also difficult communicating long distance to advisors and I had an advisor who left my dissertation committee. It took me 6 years to finish it because of the workload at the PIAA.

Sometimes I think I should have continued on for my doctorate on a full-time basis right after I earned my master's degree rather than going back to teaching and coaching on the high school level, but financial and life considerations can get in the way of plans. I realize that the teaching and coaching were beneficial for the work I do now with the PIAA because both gave me a grassroots perspective and understanding of what is going on in high school athletics on a daily basis. Although my original intent in pursuing the doctorate was to either teach or to work in college athletic administration, I really did not view accepting the position with the PIAA—which is involved in high school governance—as a deviation in my career. As much as I was interested in teaching at the college level, I have always thought that I could go back after I had gained some experience in the field.

PIAA is a voluntary organization consisting of member schools and serves as a registry for interscholastic sport officials in the state. The governance of the association is conducted by the member institutions and is a representative type of governance structure. There is an elected board of 22 individuals. Of the 22, 18 are voting members and four serve in an advisory role. Of the 22, 13 come from the 11 geographical districts that make up the PIAA. Two districts have more than 75 high schools so they get a second vote on the board as decreed in the PIAA constitution. The 18 voting members include junior high school administrators, athletic directors, and principals. The four advisory members represent girls' athletics, the state department of education, school superintendents, and private schools. The board serves as the policy maker and the PIAA staff members are the policy regulators and enforcers. We at PIAA believe the system works and we understand that our office is responsible to its membership.

The NFHS is the PIAA's parent organization. It writes contest rules and the PIAA follows them pretty closely. NFHS also provides educational materials and services for state associations to assist them in training, policy making, and conducting general business. NFHS has a very different role than the NCAA has in college athletics. NFHS does not attempt to govern high school athletics in the country. In the case of high school athletics, what works in Pennsylvania may not work in Mississippi. States are culturally diverse and their programs are diverse so it would be an incredible burden trying to put all of the state associations on the same page. Writing contest rules and providing expertise in those contest rules are really NFHS's strong points. NFHS can help all states have a common thread in regards to participation and that is valuable. There has been talk of national championship tournaments for high schools, but at the NFHS convention in 1999 the states throughout the federation resoundingly voted the idea down. They do not want any part of it. The feeling is that hosting national championships is not really the purpose of high school athletics.

My main responsibility with the PIAA is overseeing the officials' program that involves recruiting, retaining, training, and assigning officials to inter-district and championship events. My duties also include serving as the tournament director for the state championship events in golf, cross-country, wrestling, baseball, softball, and soccer. I am also involved with all of the other state championships because I assign the officials for the 45 championships that the PIAA hosts for boys and girls to the different classifications. Also, on a daily basis I assist our member schools in the interpretation of the PIAA's rules, regulations, and policies.

There are several demanding aspects of my job. The first demanding aspect is the sense of responsibility I feel about being accurate when providing an interpretation of a bylaw or of the constitution to a member school or to an athlete's parent. I also feel an enormous amount of responsibility for ensuring that all 15,500 of our registered officials have the ability to get proper training materials. I assist the 470 local chapters in their organization. At times the officials are our best public relations and they also can be our worst. The thing about being an official is that it is the only job you are going to start and have to be 100 percent correct the first day and then improve. I believe good officials go unnoticed. We have to educate people that officials are part of the athletic experience that is an extension of the classroom. Whatever walk of life from which the officials come, they are part of the education process. By focusing on that, hopefully we can get away from the "Kill the umpire" mentality. Unfortunately, that mentality exists all over the country. The primary reason we lose officials is spectator abuse. In Pennsylvania, there is a state law that assaulting an official is a misdemeanor that carries up to a $10,000 fine and 5 years in jail. That is a deterrent, but I would like to work from the positive side where those problems could be defused through teaching officials how to handle confrontations and to act like an official, not just a referee. The difference is that a referee calls the rules and an official calls the game. Calling the game means dealing with the coaches, players, and fans. If an official has a little style and a good handle on the situation, he or she can create a situation where everyone wins.

The thing I love most about what I do is the people with whom I work and interact. We are one of the largest states in the country with probably the smallest staff. I view that as a compliment to the men and women with whom I work because I think we run as many programs and championships as anybody in the country and we do it with less people and resources. We do it effectively through the hard work of the people in our office. Also the officials, athletic directors, principals, and coaches are a pleasure with which to work. I am somewhat removed from the athletes but I do get to see high level competition at the state championships and that is a wonderful thing. It is a pleasure to see people in a positive atmosphere where spectators are applauding and kids are reaching their potential. It is a wonderful arena in which to be involved on a daily basis. The hard part is that there is always a winner and a loser. It is a shame, but some people do not realize that even though they might not have won that match it does not make them a loser. They are still winners. They are the second best group in a state with 1,300 member schools. That is nothing of which to be ashamed. At the moment they may not realize it but over time they certainly will see it.

When I look at my typical days I view them as being in a state championship mode and nonstate championship mode. A typical day in a state championship mode involves fielding questions about the policies and procedures of the tournament. It also involves site selection. For championships such as soccer or basketball we determine the sites of the next round after the completion of the previous round. Besides football, wrestling, and basketball, it is difficult getting sites to host state championship events. It is a lot of work for the people at a site to make a facility available. People are always saying, "Why don't you use this facility or that college?"

Often administrators and/or athletic directors do not want to host a state championship game. It is not lucrative to the institutions. PIAA pays a rental fee to the institution but a lot of logistics are involved. We had a basketball game 2 years ago where the school charged the PIAA a $500 rental fee but the school had sustained $3,000 of damage across the school lawn because people parked on wet grass. Other times a facility may already be booked. This is especially true in the case of college gymnasiums. Another reason not to host a state championship game is that athletic directors find it is another night of work and it does not really benefit their own program. If it is just a one-time event such as cross-country or golf, the event is selected far in advance but there are still questions about starting times, practice rounds, and registration.

The assignment of officials takes time for championship events because it is such an important decision. We want to assign the best officials but we still want to assign "new blood" to expand the officiating pool so more people have a chance to work the big games. It takes a fair amount of time to prepare the groups who will keep the time and score at the championship events. The basketball and wrestling state championships overlap and that is difficult. We begin planning for those as early as October and much work remains to be done in February and March to pull off those events. We call that "Hell Month" because we work practically every day including Saturday and Sunday from the second to last week of February to the end of the basketball championships in March. This time is stressful because on a given night we will have several sites going at the same time. I constantly worry during that time about someone coming into a game with a gun, club, or knife or an incident occurring either in the stands or the playing area. For the state wrestling tournament, 54,000 fans attend this 3-day event and I am concerned for each person.

Even when we are not in championship mode, there is no real down time. There are sport meetings at the end of each season and we host summer workshops for the sport groups that do not meet at the end of the season. At six board meetings each year policy issues are debated and determined. We attend the NFHS national meeting for continuing education. At the NFHS convention we network and share ideas, experiences, and knowledge with other state associations. We also host our annual state officials' convention. I secure speakers and handle registration as well as reservations for our speakers. We write curriculum for the sessions at the convention so our statewide rules interpreters have a guide to follow while working with the officials. We remain busy throughout the year. Planning is essential to keep these functions and events running smoothly. We cannot wait until the last minute. Planning has to be done in advance.

In my position all management skills are important. I am not sure if I could prioritize them. It all depends on the situation. Some days it is communication and defusing confrontation. On other days, it is organization and making sure all the i's are dotted and the t's are crossed. Some days a decision has to be made that involves critical thinking and leadership skills. Motivation is also essential. We need to motivate the officials' groups as well as the people who work our championship events. It is not boring here. It is also multifaceted. One day I can be working in the financial area, the next day I may be working with a corporate sponsor, and the following day I can be looking at the philosophical content of the organization in terms of the long-range strategic plan. I also find myself using personal, technical, and conceptual skills. For example, team wrestling as a state championship event just started in 1998, but that was a conceptual idea that we started 5 or 6 years ago. Not only did we have to establish bracketing but also we established qualifications standards and the process for how teams and sites would be selected. To put it all together required foresight. Another idea for the future is team golf championships. Again, a number of factors will have to be addressed.

We must contend with several external factors as a state governing body. We must deal with parents or schools reacting to a negative decision on eligibility and seeking court involvement. In past years people did not have the initiative to use the courts. The legal challenges to the state association are stressful for the organization. Some years we have more than others. Our executive director is in court minimally six times a year. He is often defending eligibility cases that have been made by our board of control. A misconception of the general public is that the people at the PIAA office make the rules. The fact that we do not make the rules is difficult to communicate to the public. The membership understands and the people involved in the administration of the district committee's certainly understand, but sometimes at the grassroots level people do not handle it well when a decision is adverse to one of their athletes. We are really the policy enforcers, not the policy makers. I believe a lot of parents have lost perspective in regards to high school athletics. They believe every student-athlete will play either on the national team or at the college level. I read a statistic from the NFHS that stated that less than 5 percent of the 6.3 million who participate in high school sports go on to compete at the college level. I would surmise that more students in this state receive academic scholarships than they do athletic scholarships. There is a big misconception about the availability of athletic scholarships.

State associations also encounter interference from outside organizations that have the desire to run nonprofit corporations that are volunteer associations of member schools. Along with the external factors there are internal ones. Many of the internal factors are sports specific as well as issue specific. There is a fair amount of dialogue about reclassifying, where the criteria for the class in which a school competes would be redefined. There has also been talk about expanding the state play-off system to get more schools involved in the playoffs. We also had a redistricting committee. The committee investigated changing the geographics of districts that would potentially have some schools competing in another district. The committee discovered that no one really wanted to redistrict. The districts wanted to keep their sovereignty and continuity. It is important for me to be knowledgeable of the organization and to have a firm grasp of the internal factors, so when I am asked to comment I can make an educated statement that will help the organization. Sometimes the statement made may not be good for a certain constituency but it is intended for the good of the whole organization.

When I look at the future of high school athletics, I see more high schools getting involved in corporate sponsorship. Many schools throughout Pennsylvania exclusively sell a certain soda or product. Nationally, high school athletic budgets are anywhere between 1 percent and 3 percent of the school budget. That figure is a small percentage to support the lessons learned on the playing field. Also, athletic programs are the first to be cut in a budget crisis. Because of the visibility of the athletic program, more schools try to secure corporate support for their athletic teams. Finally, corporate sponsorship is a better alternative to assessing mandatory fees for student-athletes. Corporate sponsorship is becoming common among state associations. The California state association has had Reebok sponsor its state basketball championship for a number of years with Reebok paying close to $1 million annually. Corporate sponsorship is a reality. The question is just how much a school or state association wants to be involved. We have some corporate sponsors but they are a bit more subliminal. For example, we have a sporting goods manufacturer furnish products or balls and a small dollar amount that we direct toward our nonrevenue sport championships. Our sponsorships usually involve products because the people who benefit are the athletes.

I think the biggest issue that high school athletics will have to contend with in the next few years is sportsmanship. The national federation has taken a leadership role and I see the state associations following that lead. Sportsmanship is critical. The poor sportsmanship displayed in the National Basketball Association (NBA), National Football League (NFL), and major league baseball can have a huge trickle-down effect. The more fights a spectator sees in a major league baseball game the more we see at our level. Some states have discussed eliminating the postgame handshake. In my opinion, they are throwing the baby out with the bath water. That should be stressed more than ever in the current environment. The advent of the technology and the advancement of the Internet will have an impact on how we will do business. Already we have teleconferences for some of our rules meetings. In the future, people will be trained at home rather than being sent to national sites.

The advice I would give a student who aspires to my position would be to get a solid educational background in sport management, health and physical education, or a related field. If one wants to continue beyond a bachelor's degree, a master's in business administration would help them greatly. If they are interested in pursuing a doctorate, then they should go back into the sport administration or management area. I think that would be a nice blend. Another avenue is to get a bachelor's in health, physical education, or sport management and then obtain a law degree. I think it is also important that a person has some experience at the grassroots levels. I think the strength of our office is that both the executive director and I were both on the sidelines as coaches and have also officiated. That experience gives us a very good handle on the heartbeat of the emotion as well as the thinking processes of both sides.

I am very satisfied with my job. In regard to pay, I think people can always have an issue with it, but I have no qualms. I think the package that our board gives the staff is equitable. In regard to workload, I sometimes think I should be two people. I work 27 weekends a year and have extended hours of 70 hours a week during championship time. I also try to be helpful to 470 officials' chapters and more than 15,000 officials. If my position had two people, one would run championships and the other would service the officials. As far as promotion opportunities are concerned, the nature of our organization does not offer a lot of promotion opportunities. We only have 12 people in our office including support staff. I have been already promoted from assistant to associate executive director during my tenure.

Although I think being the commissioner of baseball would be a good job, I am very content. I enjoy working at PIAA. I am not a job jumper. If someone from another organization approached me about an opportunity, I would be open for dialogue. Sometime down the road—just like anybody else—I would like to put my theories and philosophies to work for an organization. However, the right situation would have to present itself. I have declined opportunities over the years for a host of reasons. One reason is that my wife is an assistant professor of health and physical education at Millersville University. She is extremely bright and very capable. It is wonderful to see her go to work with a smile on her face. She loves to teach and she loves to be with students. Our 2-year-old daughter is active and healthy and it is great being able to watch her grow. My family is an important consideration. I have to admit that sometimes I think about teaching again because I could apply my experiences in the classroom and help some young people, just like so many teachers helped me.

Robert F. Kanaby

Executive Director
National Federation of State High
School Associations

Education:
SOCIAL SCIENCE/ENGLISH, JERSEY CITY STATE COLLEGE, 1961

SECONDARY READING SPECIALIST, JERSEY CITY STATE COLLEGE, 1968

60 CREDITS IN ADMINISTRATION, RUTGERS UNIVERSITY, LEHIGH UNIVERSITY

Career Progression:
EXECUTIVE DIRECTOR, NATIONAL FEDERATION OF STATE HIGH SCHOOL ASSOCIATIONS, 1993 TO PRESENT

EXECUTIVE DIRECTOR, NEW JERSEY STATE INTERSCHOLASTIC ATHLETIC ASSOCIATION, 1980–1993

TEACHER/ HEAD BASKETBALL COACH, BRIDGEWATER-RARITAN EAST HIGH SCHOOL AND UNION HILL HIGH SCHOOL, UNION CITY, NJ

TEACHER/FRESHMAN BASKETBALL COACH, JERSEY CITY STATE COLLEGE

J.V. BASKETBALL COACH, HOLY FAMILY HIGH SCHOOL, UNION CITY, NJ

TEACHER/ J.V. BASKETBALL COACH, ST. ANTHONY HIGH SCHOOL , JERSEY CITY, NJ

Best piece of advice you received in regards to your career:

"What you spend years building may be destroyed overnight. Build anyway."

Best advice for someone aspiring toward a career in the sport industry:

"Work hard, be persistent, and have faith in yourself always. Act in a responsible and honest manner and keep your self-respect and character above reproach. Make your career successful by making certain that sports contribute, in a positive way, to the quality of life in America."

Quote by which you live:

"Do unto others as you would have them do unto you."

I GREW UP IN A ONE-PARENT FAMILY HOME and did not get involved in sports as a participant until I was in the eighth grade. My older brother played sports in high school, but a very influential man in my life, Robert (Rex) Rekuc, first approached me about participating in sport. Under his direction, I fell in love with basketball and eventually had some success on my team at St. Anthony High

School in Jersey City, New Jersey. Upon graduating from high school and not being able to afford college, I took a job in New York City and I was asked to coach the junior varsity team at my high school. A year later I entered Jersey City State College and majored in English and social studies with hopes of obtaining a high school teaching and coaching position. I played college basketball for 4 years and was captain of my team while maintaining my coaching duties of the junior varsity at St. Anthony. Upon graduation from college, I had the unique opportunity to become the freshman basketball coach at Jersey City State College while still remaining a high school coach.

My first varsity head coaching position was at Union Hill High School, an inner city school located in Union City, New Jersey. Five years later, I became the head coach at Bridgewater-Raritan East, a brand new high school in Bridgewater, New Jersey. During this time, I continued to work on my education. I completed a master's degree to become a reading specialist and later obtained an additional 60 credit hours in administration from Rutgers and Lehigh Universities.

I was 32 years old when I received my first job as principal at South Hunterdon High School in Hunterdon County, New Jersey. I spent my last 2 years at the high school level at Hunterdon Central High School and moved from there to the executive director position of the New Jersey State Interscholastic Athletic Association. I spent 13 years as the director of the state athletic association in New Jersey. During that time, I became very involved with the National Federation of State High School Associations in terms of chairing a number of its committee programs and speaking extensively at meetings. Thirteen years later I was fortunate to secure the position I presently hold as executive director of the organization.

As I mentioned, "Rex" Rekuc had a significant impact on my life. He put together basketball leagues just to give the young men in the community some out-of-school experiences. I was a kid running the streets and he just grabbed me by the back of the neck one day and said, "You're going to be on the basketball team." I told him I did not play basketball and he said, "you're going to now." Eight years later I was captain of my college team. The thing that affected me most was that he really had a feel and a perception for basketball and for the needs of young adults. There were some things I used 3 or 4 years later that I had seen him do in terms of coaching eighth graders that were unique. For example, he used a wholesale substitution pattern, where he actually had two teams. It is used sometimes in professional basketball now with a different five on the court who have particular roles to play. I can remember him doing that 35 years ago on an eighth grade level. So I was blessed with a good person who taught me the elements of compassion for human beings and a love for basketball. Those two things have really affected my professional life because it is important to love what you are doing, whether teaching, administering, coaching, or playing.

Charlie Adams was an individual who was particularly influential on me. He is the executive director of the North Carolina Athletic Association. As I came into this particular work, he was already on the staff there. He was a visionary in state association work and has few peers across this nation. What struck me was that his basic philosophy of teaching and administering was similar to mine and we both believed the activities in our schools such as sports, speech, music, and debate serve a specific purpose.

The purpose is not only to teach the skills of the activity, but the spirit of the activity as well. Dedication to purpose, the importance of teamwork, and interaction with other races are the kinds of things that can emanate from sports. Sport can be the vehicle by which we can meet this nation's needs of developing productive human beings to take their place as good citizens. He and I have worked closely together over the years. Recently he served as president of the National Federation. Many initiatives that have been undertaken in these past 6 years have turned our direction toward these kinds of goals.

The state directors really have the opportunity to enjoy two vastly different worlds within the management of high school sports. On one hand, they have the opportunity to work with a tremendous number of positive volunteers in their member schools who assist in putting on various tournaments. In New Jersey, for example, we sponsored championship events in 32 different activities involving 178,000 young people. The state directors plan and see events take shape in which a team or an individual reaches the ultimate level of success, the state championship. They live in another world, too, though. They must administer the constitution and bylaws that are determined by their respective member states. They make decisions relative to young people's eligibility and teams' eligibility for tournament play. Sometimes they have to make some difficult decisions where teams violate rules and use ineligible players. When a violation occurs, it may mean a team has to forfeit six or seven contests that may eliminate it from participating in a state championship event. By the same token, it is the basic underlying tenets of fairness in competition and level playing fields that lead to those decisions being made.

Many skills are needed to perform well at the state director or national leadership position. Understanding the issues and trends is very important. State associations are undergoing some rather extensive changes. Almost exclusively they are nonprofit organizations. However, there is a need to develop programs that are more of a for-profit philosophy to support their programs. Planning and people skills are also very important. One must have the respect of those who volunteer and give their energy to your organization. The programs have to be constantly reviewed so they can be adjusted to move in directions to satisfy the changing times. Financial skills are also necessary because some of the state associations operate on multi-million dollar budgets, and the associations are subject to tremendous public scrutiny.

As an executive director, I work with many different constituents including my staff, athletic administrators within the schools, and principals because they are the educational leader in that school. State directors now, more than ever before, have to work closely with superintendents' associations, school board associations, and even the state legislature. Some of our associations employ full-time lobbyists to keep in touch with legislative bills that may affect sport programs.

NFHS is the national service and administrative organization for high school athletics and fine arts programs in speech, music, and debate. We serve 50 member state associations and the District of Columbia. We publish playing rules in 16 sports for boys and girls that are used by approximately 18,000 secondary schools. Our program outreach eventually extends to 6.3 million sports participants and 4.2 million in speech, music, and debate. To put those statistics in perspective, add all of the intercollegiate athletes in the NCAA, National Association of Intercollegiate Athletics (NAIA), and the National Junior College Athletic Association (NJCAA) and it would total about 400,000. It underscores the need for us to continue with our mission and purpose to make certain the activities fulfill an educational purpose, as opposed to just getting kids scholarships or moving them on to a higher level of play. NFHS has a staff of approximately 40 people and an annual budget of about $7.5 million.

NFHS has developed professional organizations for officials, coaches, spirit groups, and interscholastic athletic administrators. We also have professional organizations for speech, music, and debate instructors. We traditionally organize five major conferences each year, and the largest one is for athletic administrators. In addition, we hold an annual conference that about 1,200 members attend. We also hold a very select conference each spring for about 200 to 225 invited individuals who are in key leadership positions in coaching and officiating at our state associations. We also hold an annual meeting for all of the legal counsels of our member state associations. One of my own personal dreams is to host the first ever national student leadership conference for youngsters who participate in high school sports and activities in our schools.

I think the most challenging part of my job is to stay current with what is happening across the country. If we are going to fully serve our purpose, we have to effectively and proactively deal with the current issues and trends. During my career I have witnessed a definite change in the nature of sports in the country, not all of which has been positive. What happens on the professional level will eventually affect sports in some ways at all other levels. If we do not address several negative cultural trends in sport, then some time early in the 21st century we may find ourselves having to find an answer to the question "Are sports good for America?" It's a simple and short question, but one with profound implications.

A current trend in high school sports is the exodus of teachers from the coaching ranks. We have fewer and fewer individuals who see the youngsters every day in the corridors, in the cafeteria, in class, or in front of the school. More and more people from the community and people from other schools are taking those positions, and they do not have day-to-day contact with the students. Teachers look at the amount of time involved in coaching and say it is not worth it. Parental pressure, changing attitudes among young people, changing attitudes in society relative to sport, and the role of sports in our schools are some reasons why teachers think that coaching is not worth the aggravation.

Officials have many of the same problems, and the trends in officiating are similar to that of coaching. People who officiate do not do it for the money and that is something that has been said a hundred times before. People were willing to do it because it kept them close to the game, kept them close to young people, and gave them a level of exercise. With the taunting and the baiting, the potential for violence, and the fact that everyone thinks that they can do a better job, it is no wonder people are shying away from that needed profession. For young people to grow during their sport experience, a cooperative atmosphere must exist among the parents, coaches, officials, administrators, superintendents, and school boards. They all have a role in making certain that sporting events remain educational experiences for young people. What we are seeing, unfortunately, is taking on more of a professional connotation of the "win or else" attitude that implies "produce or you lose your job or incur our wrath." That connotation is making it more difficult to get people to pursue these career areas.

An important issue is the continuing need for us to become more sensitive to risk management. This litigious society continues to propel itself down a slippery slope that has led to more lawsuits. I think we have a responsibility to do more in the area of preparing our people in the area of risk management. I think that is further complicated because more people are getting into coaching that do not have an educational background. As a national organization we need to continue to highlight risk management education. Those are the kinds of things we address at our leadership conference.

Another important initiative is the need to build relationships and coalitions among various organizations who serve amateur athletics within a state and this nation. There is a great need for young people to understand the purpose of sports. Although it would be too naive to think that we are all going to find a common ground on every issue, I think those coalitions can appreciate each other's organizational philosophy and work together. I think it is necessary if we are going to keep amateur sports a positive experience.

Three years ago we committed ourselves to operate from a very basic premise concerning sportsmanship. The basic premise is this: no matter what you are, an individual, or a private, public, profit, or nonprofit organization, you have a responsibility to ensure every single experience should complement the core goal of creating a better America for future generations. We all have a responsibility to do that. The Ford Motor Company has the responsibility to make safe cars and treat its employees in a manner that contributes toward life in America. On an amateur sport level, our educational purpose and educational mission should maintain that everything we do with young people can make them more productive people. That is our job and our bottom line. As a result, we have centered on a theme called "Teaching Citizenship Skills for Sports and Activities." In conjunction with the NCAA, we convinced the National Interscholastic Athletic Administrators Association (NIAAA), NJCAA, and the U.S. Olympic Committee to become charter members in a new endeavor to reach this goal. We then turned to the four professional sport leagues—the National Hockey League (NHL), NBA, NFL, and major league baseball—and asked them to be a part of this coalition. They all came on board and in January 1997, for the first time in sport in America, we had those nine organizations represented on the same stage in New York City. We announced that we were going to launch the project called "Teaching Citizenship Through Sports and Activities" and called it the Citizenship for Sports Alliance. We just conducted a summit of 100 leaders in amateur sports this past June in Washington, D.C., and discussed sports in the new millennium. We have developed a curriculum that we add to every year. We introduce a new segment of it each December at our NIAAA conference. It is designed to be a manual with videos and suggestions that help coaches use those teachable moments each day to create better human beings.

We have an extensive coaching education program. In addition, through the NIAAA we have instituted nine leadership training courses on risk management, compliance with the Americans with Disabilities Act (ADA), Title IX, legal issues, the purpose of athletics, and teaching citizenship through sports curriculum. Last December we had 700 athletic administrators take one or more of these courses before our conference. This year we expect more than 1,000 athletic administrators to take these courses. We also take that same concept of coaches' education and apply it to officials' education. We have a trained national faculty in soccer. We will start with soccer, volleyball, and basketball. We have trained a national faculty in soccer for officials and the officials' training materials will be unique. The materials will cover X's and O's to make officials more proficient, but will also include a core component to teach the official's role in the educational process of young people as they work with them on the interscholastic competitive field.

We have worked closely with Cedric Dempsey of the NCAA and think we are advocating the same messages for interscholastic as well as collegiate young people. Being next door to the NCAA facilities in Indianapolis will enhance our communication and working relationship. One core reason we decided to move from Kansas City was to allow us to restructure this organization. For the past 21 years, we have been involved in the print industry. It is no longer practical to be involved in a print industry, but we will remain in the publishing business. We could not remove ourselves from the print industry without moving locations because about 26,000 square feet of our building was involved with the warehousing and print shop operations. So we now out-source our print operations in Indianapolis, allowing us to down size the organization from a size as well as a staffing standpoint. We also out-source our equipment center, which is one of the largest equipment centers for officials' gear in the United States. We sense a community that is interested in the educational things we care about, and we have many more opportunities to develop programs within Indianapolis and Indiana than we had before.

Several other issues continue to be important for the future welfare of amateur sport in America. We issue study upon study that shows that youngsters who are involved in sports and athletics do better academically than those who are not. So it is typical then to say a marginal student needs this particular kind of experience to enhance his or her educational experience and productivity, but we cannot permit participation because he or she is not producing. I personally see a middle ground of having strong academic requirements for participation, but by the same token, to have strong support programs within a school district, school system, and a state as a whole to help those who struggle academically.

Many issues exist from the academic side, including home schooling. If our member state associations have not had to deal with it, they will be dealing with it within the next 18 months to 2 years. The proliferation of not only home schooling, but also charter schools and voucher plans creates a growing situation that is gaining bipartisan political support and will become increasingly important. There is increasing pressure for young people in those educational programs to participate in regular school programs.

The budgetary and finance issues continue to be critical challenges in education and sport. States have greater surpluses now than in the past 20 years, but that money does not seem to be filtering down to education. Funding will remain a critical issue because funding may be up, but programs are up, and participation is up, and the needs within those particular programs are greater. The old issue of ADA and the entire issue of seeing to it that the programs are of the best quality from the risk management standpoint will increase the pressures for funding on those bigger programs. Although we are in a tremendous economic upturn in this country, the need for resources remains a problem. More superintendents now come from a business background. There are more athletic administrators whose duties are being given to assistant principals who at the same time are handling other things such as bus transportation and discipline. This nation is in a serious crisis in terms of finding people who even want to be principals. Fewer individuals see being a principal as a pinnacle position. These factors will affect our programs.

There are a couple of things that I still want to do. I probably never will retire. When I leave this position, I may want to get back into teaching a course or two. I have a great deal of experience that might be useful to some of the young people starting out in this industry. Writing intrigues me. As far as this position is concerned, I think we still are at least 5 years from being where I personally feel we would like to be. Some great needs exist and I hope we can say that the economic future of this organization is set and complete, and the foundation will be able to support the educational initiatives of the future.

Another goal of mine is to put together a student leadership conference. My goal is to bring 25,000 to 30,000 young people together each year for a 2–3 day leadership conference. We will educate them and send them back to our nation's schools as good role models with the right message to really make an impact. My dream is to see sport in this country at every level contributing toward a better America.

If someone wants to go into this business and really make a difference and an impact they need certain personality traits. The first necessary trait is a searching personality. By that I mean life has to be a search. It cannot be limited to gaining possessions or positions. You must never be satisfied with something that can be done a better way.

Finally, ability is not enough. We see that in sports more than anywhere else. You can be the greatest basketball player in the world, but if you are a poor excuse for a human being, it really does not matter. Ability that brings achievement without purpose is diminished and ineffective—in sports and in life. To attain the greatest level of success, the best thing that somebody can say about your life is that you were both competent and compassionate.

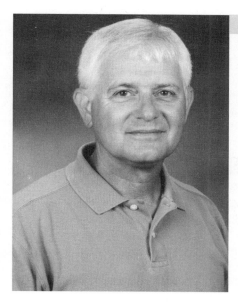

Richard V. Ledford

Athletic Director
North Hall High School

Education:
B.S., HEALTH AND PHYSICAL EDUCATION,
UNIVERSITY OF TENNESSEE, 1966
M.S., SPORT ADMINISTRATION, UNIVERSITY OF
SOUTHERN MISSISSIPPI, 1999

Career Progression:
ATHLETIC DIRECTOR, NORTH HALL HIGH
SCHOOL, 1998 TO PRESENT
ASSISTANT FOOTBALL COACH, NORTH HALL
HIGH SCHOOL, 1994–1998
HEAD FOOTBALL AND TRACK COACH, RABUN
COUNTY HIGH SCHOOL, 1986–1992
HEAD FOOTBALL COACH AND ATHLETIC
DIRECTOR, STOCKBRIDGE HIGH SCHOOL,
1981–1986
HEAD FOOTBALL COACH, ATHLETIC
DIRECTOR, JUNIOR VARSITY GIRLS BASKET-
BALL COACH, M.D. COLLINS HIGH SCHOOL
ASSISTANT FOOTBALL COACH, HEAD TRACK
COACH, CROSS-COUNTRY COACH, LAKESHORE
HIGH SCHOOL

Best piece of advice you received in regards to your career:

"Be happy, be loyal, or be gone."

COACH CHARLEY BROWN, 1966

Best advice for someone aspiring toward a career in the sport industry:

"Be prepared for the time factor (long hours) and work for the right reason—the kids. That individual athlete is the "why" of your job. Also remember daily that you are not the position. You occupy a position that someone else will eventually occupy."

Quote by which you live:

"We'll do something, even if it's right!"

I GREW UP IN NORTH CAROLINA and went to Lincolnton High School where I played football, basketball, and ran track. It was a small school and I had the chance to play on the varsity basketball and football teams in the ninth grade. It was an easy decision to get involved in sports. I came from a pretty athletic family of seven boys and one girl. Out on the playground we had our own team sometimes. One older brother was an all-state football player and an outstanding baseball player. Another older brother was great in basketball and baseball. Another brother two years younger than myself was outstanding in basketball. My biggest goal was to be active in sports both in high school and college. I was impressed by my high school football coach because he had previously coached one of my brothers, and he had a great deal of influence on me. It was at an early age, around 14, when I decided I wanted to teach and coach in high school.

I went to Gardner Webb Junior College and had the opportunity to participate in football and track. Some good advice came from one of my coaches, Melvin Ruggles. I wanted to walk on at Carson Newman to be a part of a college football program. He told me to forget football because of my size. He thought I would make a very good teacher and coach in high school, and should go to the University of Tennessee and get a quality degree in health and physical education. That degree helped propel me into the coaching and teaching job market. Coach Ruggles later became athletic director at Burke County schools and continued to influence a lot of people. Two other coaches that I learned a great deal from were Frank King and Von Ray Harris. Frank King was a fine person and taught me a strong work ethic and moral character. At the end of my tenth year in coaching I was sitting at the Atlanta Touchdown Club Jamboree where Coach King and Coach Harris were both being honored. One was the overall classification coach of the year in the state of Georgia, and the other was the Class AAA coach of the year in the state. As I sat there I thought, "Wow, I had 5 years with each of them, and they both had a real impact on my life."

School district recruiters came to the University of Tennessee during my senior year from various places and I received information from Fulton County Schools in the Atlanta area, as well as from a small school in northwest Georgia. I interviewed at both places and my heart was leaning toward the small school. I decided to accept a job at the larger school, however, because I felt that if I did not like the atmosphere, it would be easier to move down in size rather than to move up. I went to the Fulton County system and was very fortunate to be a part of a high quality athletic program at Lake Shore High School

My first job was as head track coach and assistant football coach in charge of defensive backs. I also doubled as defensive coordinator of the junior varsity team. I fell in love with the program and school and stayed there for 10 years. During the first eight of my 10 years, I coached three sports. It required long hours, high energy, and a great deal of time management. I was cross-country coach and defensive coach for varsity football during the same sport season. Apparently I juggled the schedule pretty effectively because we won two regional championships and one state championship in cross-country.

I went to M.D. Collins High School, also in Fulton County Schools, for my first administrative and head football coaching assignment. Everything was different when taking the reigns of a 3A football program. On top of that, it was my first experience as an athletic director. It was quite demanding. At that time, it was not unusual for athletic directors to be football coaches and eventually become principals. That trend seems to have changed over the years. At that time I think school boards were looking for people who had experience in the management and discipline of large groups of people, as well as experience with finances, budgeting, and scheduling.

After 5 years at Collins, I made a decision to accept a position outside Fulton County at Stockbridge High School, just outside Atlanta. I stayed there for 5 years as athletic director and football coach. In every position I have really enjoyed the people and every challenge has been different. At Stockbridge, I was the first athletic director of the school other than the principal. It was the first time the principal had relinquished the reigns to someone else and I felt privileged and honored. The athletic program really needed a change and more direct control from the athletic director. In addition to being the athletic director and head football coach, I was also the junior varsity girl's basketball coach and boy's baseball coach.

After several years at Stockbridge, I decided to move to the mountains of Georgia. I went to Rayun County in northeast Georgia. I had gone from a large school system with 17 high schools to a two high school system, and now to a one high school system. I realize in the career pursuit the idea in most peoples' minds is "bigger is better," and to get a position in the largest school system or school. For me, it has been more a matter of quality of life than the pursuit of status. I enjoy working with people and sometimes in the smaller school systems we can have more impact on the total situation. I stayed at Rayun for 6 years as head football coach and spent 5 years as track coach. The administrative situation was different because the principal was the athletic director, and it did not prove to be in the school's best interest because there were just too many responsibilities for him. After 6 years I experienced one of the more difficult things encountered in athletic careers—the loss of a job. The principal was released and the school board decided to make some major changes. Although it broke my heart, I left teaching and coaching and went into private business in 1992. I spent 2 years away from doing what I enjoyed the most. I missed it terribly and had a strong desire to go back. When I went back to my profession, I felt refreshed, more enthusiastic in my classes, and incorporated a lot of things I had learned over the years.

I am ready to start my 32nd year in the education profession. Some people go through a school system and stay there until they move up in the system to various administrative positions. Others continually move around from job to job, program to program, always looking for the best position and school. I do not think there is really a scenario to follow for advancement in the coaching and teaching profession in high school. Every individual is different and everyone has a unique career path. I certainly am atypical in one sense. I did postgraduate work in educational administration in the 1970s at Georgia State University, but I curtailed that after enrolling for my third summer because of the job offer for my first athletic director and head football coaching position. I wanted to stay in coaching and athletic administration rather than pursue my principal credentials.

At that time, schools did not compensate people for out-of-field master's degrees, so I discontinued the program I had begun. Years later, however, I found myself wanting to retool and upgrade my educational knowledge and skills. I wanted to have more options for the rest of my educational career. I was 55 years old when I decided to go back to school for a graduate degree.

I decided to attend the University of Southern Mississippi because I could finish my degree in two summers without leaving my regular job. The program in sport administration appealed to me because of the varied business and coaching backgrounds of the professors and the stimulating environment for learning. The graduate studies have given me the opportunity to explore a lot of new and different areas. I am still on a path to do what I came here for but my eyes have opened to the possibilities of working at various national organizations in sports administration. Some people call this the twilight of a career, and some of the graduate students call me the "Geritol Kid." I never look at retirement and instead prefer the word "re try ment" to describe "refueling" and "re-tooling" to do something different. I plan one more year in public education and then I will pursue several new ideas.

One idea is a proposal for a postgraduate football program. Three other programs exist in the United States similar to what I would like to start. I have an idea for a location and will be making a proposal in the near future. It is a dual plan. I call it a postgraduate football/academic program. It is an opportunity for young men who have been recruited to play college football but their Scholastic Aptitude Test (SAT) scores or grade point averages were not high enough to meet the requirements. My dream is that this type of program will be a place that will help prevent those young men from falling through the cracks in our educational system. A lot of athletes who are denied the opportunity to play college football will get a job and their life path changes drastically. However, if they have the opportunity to upgrade their academic skills while still enhancing their football skills, they can stay on a path to get their college degree.

I had a chance to participate in junior college football and it was a great experience despite my lack of size. Some players get their education, increase their academic skills, and then go to a senior college and complete their football eligibility. Most of the players who go to a junior college however, are not playing their dream. They are not playing at the level they want to if they have been recruited originally by a scholarship-offering institution. The route to major college athletics through the junior college costs a player 2 years of eligibility. Going into a postgraduate academic program, an individual could play college level football and upgrade his academic skills, but not lose any eligibility.

Teaching and coaching are both demanding and time consuming if you are committed to doing an excellent job. They are both full-time jobs, particularly when your sport is in season. Effective time management is crucial to success. I taught physical education for most of my career. I also taught world history and

Georgia state history at times and really enjoyed it. My favorite subject to teach, however, is health. I was hired in 1994 at North Hall High School. I currently teach health classes and weight training, and last year I became the athletic director. In our four high school system, I am the only athletic director who is not an assistant principal and who also coaches. The job of athletic administrator has changed dramatically over the years. To have the time to accomplish those tasks, I was placed in charge of the traditional in-school suspension (ISS) program for three periods a day. Because I am in the ISS program, I am able to stay by the phone—which rings constantly—and by the computer so I can communicate with other people.

The most demanding part of my job is the lack of time. I was in New York City recently and saw some taxis that had "off duty" signs on the top. As athletic director, it seems you never find the "off duty" hat to wear. When I have time to go to lunch I am typically stopped along the way at least four times by people needing help or wondering when I would finish the task they asked me to do.

One of the biggest responsibilities of my position is handling the finances. I try to make the right decisions on where to place the money, determine where we can get more money, and always assume the role of guarding the till. I cannot end the school year by saying we do not have much money. I have to end the school year with an adequate surplus so I feel confident going into the next year. Salaries are paid by the county system. We do have a percentage supplement basis for our coaches. It is in writing as to what they can expect to get and all of the supplements have a cap; there is a percentage but there is also a cap to keep coaches from making too much money. I feel the key in finances is not the coaching salaries but in how we can adequately provide things each team needs—uniforms, quality, safe equipment, reconditioning, officials' compensation, and security. For example, it costs $9,000 to $10,000 a year to have law enforcement officers at each of our activities.

There is no such thing as a typical day or typical week in high school athletic administration. I walk in and feel as if 20 ropes are tied to me and everybody is pulling. The one rope pulled the hardest and quickest is the direction my day goes. Every day I have a list of priorities for things I want to accomplish. I try to leave gaps for all of the other things that can become priorities. I never know who is going to be on the other end of the phone when it rings. It could be someone congratulating me for something, someone wondering why the coach made a certain decision, an angry parent complaining about their child's playing time, or even the athletic booster club president needing information or help.

We have 11 booster clubs in our program, and they are all active in fund raising and volunteer service to make our programs first class and successful. I have always liked the umbrella booster club for the entire athletic department, but I did not create this program. I inherited the program and it had a lot of separate entities as far as booster clubs and it has worked very well for us. Basketball, wrestling, tennis, cheerleading, band, and the cross-country team each have their own booster club.

It takes many skills to become a successful high school athletic administrator. It takes more personal skills because the primary resource of any sport program is its people. Athletic directors who do not have people skills do not last long in sport administration or coaching positions. We communicate and interact with athletes, coaches, parents, officials, faculty, student body, school administrators, school boards, and superintendents. I have to be able to relate to a diverse group of people and assume many different roles in the process.

This past spring I had the opportunity to take a management theory and practice course at Vernal University in Gainesville, Georgia. We did an in-depth assessment of our management and leadership skills and how we perceived ourselves as managers. I made copies of the instrument and gave one to my principal, one to a coach with whom I work directly, and another with whom I do not have much contact. What I found to be true was that all three of their assessments matched up with my own assessment. This made me feel very good that how I perceive myself is how I come across to other people. I have a participatory management style. As a leader, I cannot walk abreast of everyone; somebody has to step up. However, I cannot be so far out in front that I lose touch with those following behind. I try to be at least a step ahead of them so I can map out the way. Often a parent or community member has a problem with a coach's decision and the athletic director has an opportunity to stand between the critic and the coach. If it is an attack on a coach, then it is not a personal attack on me; therefore, I can use a more tactful and less defensive approach. I am a good defuser of negative emotion, and it turns out well most of the time. I have had opportunities to sit down with a coach and parent, or coach, athlete, and parent to try to solve problems. The one that really needs to come out the winner is the student because if they do not come out with a positive experience, then we have failed somewhere along the way or the student is just not doing his or her part.

Coaching and sport administration can be a stepping stone to other administrative positions. I think that there is more of a trend now to go away from head coaches being athletic directors because they might have a conflict of interest and do more for their sport than other sports. The pay supplement for head football coach or head basketball coach in my school system is much better than the athletic director. The pay scale is not in line with the authority and responsibility of the position. I am in a position to make recommendations or make changes. The athletic director's supplement is 5 percent whereas the head football coach's supplement is 17 percent and the head basketball coach's supplement is 15 percent. The football coach has a 12-month contract whereas the basketball coach has an 11-month contract.

Most athletic director contracts are 10-month contracts. I think some school systems are still in the 1960s as far as the athletic director's role and do not realize the extent of the responsibility. I think the athletic director's position should be a full-time position with a 12-month contract. Many things need to be done in the summer. I cannot wait until the fall to order fall and winter sport equipment and uniforms. It has to be done during the previous winter for fall and previous spring for winter. Most things except for the spring sports have been ordered by the time I close out the school year. During the fall we start ordering for spring. I complete forms that are required by the county and the state. Summer is a busy time with July 1 and August 1 deadlines involving coaching assignments and eligibility lists.

The world of interscholastic sports has changed greatly over the course of my career. I think one of the biggest things is just "more." Back in 1966 when I started, there was football, basketball, baseball, track, and I think we had tennis and cross-country. There was not much more than that. My current high school offers 15 sports programs and 62 coaching slots. We have 892 participants in the high school and middle school. We have more than 600 contests per year. So it has really grown over the years. Title IX has caused a lot of the growth and change. Just this past year we added a volleyball program. We have girl's softball, dance, middle school cheerleading, ninth grade, junior varsity, varsity, and now competition cheerleading. Our cross-country, track, and soccer programs for girls are very strong. Volleyball, for instance, has been fairly expensive to start. We have had to build another gym to accommodate the needs for increased sport teams, practice, and competitions.

It has a domino effect in growth and expansion of interscholastic sport as each sport now has its own tournament. Along with the growth come additional responsibilities for the athletic administrator. In our second year in volleyball competition, we now host the area tournament and I serve as tournament director. We have at least one major event for each sport per year. The successful teams make the playoffs and that adds many more events to the schedule. All of this means a lot of nights and weekends at work. Sometimes I feel like I am married to my job. I do not try to make every contest. Sometimes I may pick up two innings of a baseball game, 10 minutes of a soccer game, and go watch a little bit of a tennis match and then go home. I do not try to stay at every contest until it ends. If there is only one thing going on, I can do that but on some days there are three or four events simultaneously. Stress and long hours can be difficult at times. The day-to-day demands of the job and tight time schedules create pressure for the athletic administrator. Everybody wants it done yesterday and they do not tell you until this morning. There is often very little support staff or technology help. The secretaries in the school do everything I ask them to, but my office is in another building so it is hard to communicate. It seems like I get right in the middle of planning, ordering, or having a discussion with a coach, and there are 10 interruptions and a new crisis developing. It is stressful. I try to manage that stress by constantly reminding myself that I cannot be all things to everyone and I just do the best I can. If I have to take some planning home with me, I do that—but I do it when the house is quiet and nobody is expecting other things from me.

We still have great participation even in the tough sports of football and wrestling where the demands are great. I still think we can demand a lot of kids. Some people have the opinion that kids are too soft nowadays. We cannot demand as much of them as we used to but I still believe you can if you show them why you are demanding it. I have always been someone who believes the question "why" needs to be answered before it is asked. I think that is a great motivational tool. I think the needs in high school sports are constant. I do think coaches need to have more preparation before getting into coaching today than ever before, especially in the area of litigation and risk management. In the age of technology there is no excuse to not be prepared for emergencies. With the criteria set for being certified in CPR and first aid and the technology available with 911 numbers, pagers, and cell phones, we should be prepared for emergencies.

The face of interscholastic sports will continue to change for the coach and athletic director. New methods must be incorporated with traditional ways of motivation and problem solving to handle the complexities of today's competitors and competitions. Despite all the pressure, stress, and demands of sport management and coaching, I believe there is still no more meaningful, satisfying, and influential job than working with young people in athletics.

CHAPTER 2

———

College Athletics

INTERCOLLEGIATE ATHLETICS IS ONE OF THE LARGEST and most attractive segments of the sport industry. Two governing bodies oversee the governance of intercollegiate athletics in the United States. The largest is the National Collegiate Athletic Conference with 937 active member institutions. The other organization is the National Association of Intercollegiate Athletics with 335 total. There are 318 National Collegiate Athletic Association (NCAA) institutions competing at the highest level, NCAA Division I. Of that total, 114 offer college football at the highest level, NCAA I-A. Along with the major college athletic programs, 393 institutions compete at the Division III level and 262 compete at the Division II level.

Division I athletic departments operate with budgets of several million dollars and generate revenues through television contracts, sponsorship agreements, ticket sales, fund raising, game guarantees, and post-season payouts and student fees. In most cases Division I institutions receive little if any money from the institution. The Division II and III environments are different than Division I. At these divisions athletic departments are viewed as any other department on campus and the majority of their operating budget is provided by the institution through tuition and student fees.

Division I athletic departments have large staffs that handle the responsibilities of various aspects of running the department. The leader of the department is the athletic director. The person in this top-level management position establishes the vision and mission for the department as well as the objectives for the overall department. The person also ensures the overall functioning of the department. Division I athletic directors can earn $60,000 and, in some instances, athletic directors at major Division I institutions make more than $100,000 a year. Associate athletic directors oversee several areas within the department. A common organization has an associate athletic director for external affairs. The areas that would fall under this individual could include media, public and community relations, marketing, ticket sales, and fund raising. The associate athletic director for internal affairs may oversee facilities and contest management, equipment, athletic training, student services, compliance, and the coaches. Within each of the areas there will be a director, potentially a staff, and clerical assistants. Associate athletic directors can earn more than $40,000 a year and as much as $70,000 depending on the size and the cost of living in an area. At the Division I level it is more likely that the coaches concentrate all of their time on coaching their respective sports and are free of administrative responsibilities.

At the Division II and III levels the athletic director position is more of a hands-on position. It is common for athletic directors at these divisions to also coach and possibly teach in an academic discipline. It is also common for coaches to have administrative responsibilities within the athletic department or to coach another sport. Division II and III athletic directors can earn anywhere from the mid $30,000s to more than $70,000.

In pursuing a career in intercollegiate athletics it is important that an individual understand the differences among the divisions and recognize the nature of the positions. To get involved in Division III athletics, the person may enter through the coaching ranks and move up from within. At the Division I level, coaching is not as much a prerequisite with the diverse nature of the athletic department. The trend in the hiring of athletic directors at the Division I has moved away from the hiring of former coaches to the hiring of individuals with marketing, legal, and/or fund-raising backgrounds. Intercollegiate athletics is an exciting and growing area of the sport industry and it appears it will remain a viable career option well into the 21st century.

Robert A. Mullens

Senior Associate Athletic Director for
Internal Operations
University of Maryland

Education:

B.S., ACCOUNTING, WEST VIRGINIA
UNIVERSITY, 1991

M.S., SPORTS ADMINISTRATION, WEST
VIRGINIA UNIVERSITY, 1993

Career Progression:

SENIOR ASSOCIATE ATHLETIC
DIRECTOR FOR INTERNAL OPERATIONS,
UNIVERSITY OF MARYLAND, FEBRUARY 1999
TO PRESENT

ASSOCIATE ATHLETIC DIRECTOR FOR
ADMINISTRATION, UNIVERSITY OF MARY-
LAND, MAY 1998 TO JANUARY 1999

ASSISTANT ATHLETIC DIRECTOR FOR
BUSINESS, UNIVERSITY OF MARYLAND, MAY
1996 TO MAY 1998

SENIOR BUSINESS MANAGER, UNIVERSITY OF
MIAMI, DECEMBER 1995 TO APRIL 1996

BUSINESS MANAGER, UNIVERSITY OF MIAMI,
APRIL 1995 TO NOVEMBER 1995

ASSISTANT BUSINESS MANAGER,
UNIVERSITY OF MIAMI, JANUARY 1994 TO
APRIL 1995

INTERN, UNIVERSITY OF KENTUCKY ATHLETIC
ASSOCIATION, JULY 1993 TO DECEMBER 1993

GRADUATE ASSISTANT, WEST VIRGINIA
UNIVERSITY ATHLETIC DEPARTMENT,
SEPTEMBER 1992 TO JUNE 1993

Best piece of advice you received in regards to your career:

"Maintain your integrity and gain respect by doing
what is right in every situation."

JAMIE POLLARD, ASSOCIATE AD/CFO, UNIVERSITY OF WISCONSIN

Best advice for someone aspiring toward a career in the sport industry:

"The sports industry is ever expanding so it is vital to prepare
yourself as an expert to compete against an increasing pool of
highly qualified professionals."

Quote by which you live:

"A man reveals his character even in the simplest things he does."

JEAN DE LA BRUYERE

WHEN I WAS AN UNDERGRADUATE at West Virginia University (WVU) I began working as a student in the athletic department because I was awarded a work-study scholarship. Looking through the choices of where I could be placed, athletics popped up and I was fortunate enough to be placed there. Although I was not interested in sports information, I wanted to work in athletics and as a student employee I got to see a lot of different aspects. That is when I first started thinking about sport as a career. When I finished my degree in accounting I decided to go to work for a Big 6 accounting firm. About 6 months into my career there I decided I would enjoy working in the business side of sports. Nearly a year out of college I made the decision and commitment to go for a career in sport.

I then looked at several options of how to get into sports. I had a great job at Ernst and Young but wanted to make sure I could transition into sport without causing myself too much debt or detriment. Initially I started looking at jobs to just transition directly into sport but found that to be very difficult. That is when I decided to pursue a master's degree, and I decided to do that for two reasons. The first reason was I wanted an advanced degree in sport administration, and the second reason is I could gain some valuable work experience in athletics while building a network.

After researching graduate programs with sport administration curriculum, I visited the three programs I deemed the best: Ohio University, the University of Massachusetts (UMass), and WVU. All three programs had solid coursework, but WVU offered opportunities for quality work experience as a graduate assistant within the athletic department. In addition, WVU had a Paciolan computer system-teaching lab in the program, which was another feather in that program's cap. I was offered a graduate assistantship with the assistant athletic director for finance and administration at WVU and decided to attend the master's program. It is a 1-year program that requires an internship.

Craig Walker, the assistant athletic director, was a great mentor and willing to teach and answer questions whenever asked. Learning the daily operations of an athletic business office as well as building a quality network of contacts were the significant rewards from my graduate assistantship. My educational experience in WVU's Graduate Sport Management program was diverse. Studying areas from marketing to ethics provided me with extensive knowledge needed to excel in the marketplace. More important, however, was the relationship with my fellow classmates. With a small class of 12, we worked closely as a group to achieve the goals we set. These relationships have turned into lifelong personal and professional friendships.

My internship at the University of Kentucky (UK) came about as a result of my working relationship with Craig Walker. As noted earlier, he was a great mentor who was willing to assist wherever he could. I learned of the UK opportunity and approached Craig for his assistance. He immediately contacted UK and sold them on my abilities. As the intern for the senior associate athletic director, Larry Ivy, I did just about everything—whatever they needed me to do. We focused more on internal operations because that was my background. I had agreed to do a 1-year internship in UK's Athletic Department, but was fortunate enough to get a job offer after 6 months, so I only spent 6 months as an intern at UK.

In December 1993 I was fortunate enough to interview and accept the position of assistant business manager for athletics at the University of Miami in Florida. That opportunity came about through preparation. My experience and skill set matched Miami's need for an assistant business manager. The university was looking for somebody with an accounting and auditing background to come in and help their business office. I was a perfect fit, and it was a great place for me to start my career. Again, Craig Walker from WVU and Larry Ivy from UK were willing to push my candidacy with their counterparts at Miami. It was a nice match and fortunately I was there for 2–1/2 years. In that time there was some turnover that created some opportunities for me to expand and grow. I was given progressively more responsibility until at the end of my time there I was the senior business manager.

From there I was offered and accepted a position at the University of Maryland as the assistant athletic director for business in May 1996. Upon arriving at Maryland, I focused on gaining as much experience as possible. Again, I was fortunate to work for people (Jamie Pollard and Debbie Yow) who were willing to reward hard work and loyalty with additional responsibility. I always made both people aware of my goal to gain as broad an experience as possible. Fortunately, I was included in many facets of the athletic operation at Maryland and given a chance to prove myself. I was the assistant athletic director at Maryland for almost 2 years and then was named interim associate athletic director for administration. I was the interim for several months and then named to the position permanently. Since then the department has done some restructuring and I was named senior associate athletic director for internal operations at the age of 29. I was fortunate that a position became available when I was ready to accept greater responsibility.

I was very focused on the specific area of sport I wanted to enter. To get in the business I knew I was going to have to use my financial background. I had an accounting degree. I had a year's experience working as an auditor for one of the largest accounting firms in the world. Plus sport was my true passion so I was pretty focused. I did not do a lot of career research, but when I worked at West Virginia I learned more what it was like to work in a collegiate athletic business office. That is what I have always wanted to do, or at least that is how I wanted to make the transition into the business.

Both education and experience have helped me greatly in my position. The accounting degree was phenomenal, obviously, as well as the work experience at Ernst and Young. The master's degree helped because it enabled me to broaden my horizons. Within that degree program there is a finance piece, a marketing piece, a research piece, an ethics piece, and a technology piece so it was a little broader education. I would say my education and experience both benefited me, but in different ways.

If students want to continue their education at the graduate level, I would recommend that if they are going to get a master's in sport administration to go somewhere other than their undergraduate institution. The need to get some different viewpoints from different educators. If I was giving someone personal advice I would say go for a master's in business administration. They can still have some tie to the athletic departments at the institution they are attending.

The only obstacle I have encountered—and I do not know if it is an obstacle, it is just a choice I made when I entered this business—is that I have moved a lot. I welcomed the opportunities, but it is not the most stable situation. In order to advance quickly, you have to be willing to move in a sport career.

Craig Walker was a mentor. He was the assistant athletic director for business and administration at WVU when I was a graduate student. He really introduced me to the inner workings of an athletic business office, and I think he was a mentor because he was a clear communicator and he was very detail oriented and had his coworkers' respect. My second role model was the person who hired me at Maryland. His name is Jamie Pollard, and he was the associate athletic director for administration when I arrived. He has unbelievable vision and an ability to communicate with people and analyze and evaluate information. He is just an outstanding leader.

Today my ultimate goal is to become the athletic director at a major NCAA Division I institution. I am not discouraged yet. I know that those are highly sought after positions and few in number, so it is a challenge. I would not say it is discouraging. I know the odds of getting one of those positions at a major institution are small, but that is why I have done everything I can to prepare myself in case that opportunity presents itself.

My main responsibilities include being the chief financial officer of a 25-sport, $25 million budget. I am also the athletic director's right-hand person, and I oversee all internal operations. Anything that happens internally, including ticket operations, flows through my office. I directly supervise five sports and indirectly oversee 13 other sports that report to someone who reports to me. That is how I spend most of my day. As the chief financial officer, I compile and monitor the department's annual budget and long-range forecasts. I also serve as the department's primary contact with the President's Legal Office, the Office of Budget and Fiscal Analysis, the Comptroller's Office, and the University of Maryland Foundation. I represent the director of athletics on various departmental, campus, and community committees. I work hand-in-hand with the athletic department in the negotiations of a wide range of contracts on behalf of the department (coaches contracts, nonconference men's basketball and football contracts, multimedia rights contracts, apparel contracts, etc.). I serve as a member of the administrative team handling various departmental issues including Title IX compliance and our new field house project, among others. I interact regularly with key donors, fans, alumni, and friends of the program at athletic events, department functions, luncheons, and socials to promote the mission of Maryland Athletics. I work with the athletic development and marketing staffs to establish and monitor aggressive revenue goals to assist the department in balancing the operating budget and securing a sound financial future.

Ten employees report directly to me, including five head coaches. Of them, only one is younger than me. I would not say it has been an issue. It is kind of difficult for me at times, but I think that because I have proven I have a lot of integrity, am competent, and because I am going to do what is right every time, people respect me. I am a very strict planner. In meetings, I always have an agenda and stay on course to accomplish the meeting's goals while keeping everyone focused on the task at hand. I allow input from everyone, but make decisions when things begin to move in a circle.

I would say the most demanding aspect of this position and what I spend the most time doing is trying to balance a budget in college athletics and find new ways to do so. Providing the resources to be a major Division I, 25-sport, competitive program is a challenge. For example, we are building a $90 million arena. I have been involved since the beginning of the project. The money comes from various sources, one of which is athletics, so I have been a part of the team that laid out the business plan for that arena. I am not deeply involved. I am not the point person but my involvement mostly has been on the financial end, creating the business plan of how the university will pay for the arena. I have to determine how we are going to pay for the increased operations of such a facility. My greatest challenge is trying to provide everyone the resources that they need to succeed. That is just a tremendous daily challenge. Everyone busts their tail and everyone works so hard that I want to see them have everything they need to compete with the top schools in their sport.

The most enjoyable aspect of my job—which has been new to me—is I get to at least travel to the conference championships and spend time with student athletes because I supervise coaches. The students are a lot of fun and that is why we are in this business. I would also say at the same time it is enjoyable to find a way financially and operationally to help coaches achieve something. The five sports I supervise directly are wrestling, women's soccer, men's soccer, men's golf, and women's golf.

The least enjoyable aspect of the position is probably crisis management. Student-athlete issues, player/coach problems, student-athlete citizenship issues, or any kind of crisis management situations are difficult because they take so much time and everything is always urgent. I can write a "to do list" and then get that big curve ball right in the middle of the day that needs to be addressed immediately. The handling of that matter is crucial to success in this business.

A typical day for me consists of at least three or four meetings ranging from a budget meeting to a campus committee. I meet with my coaches biweekly so I am always in tune with what is going on with them, and I try to visit the other units I supervise, the ticket office and the business office, daily. We are always setting budgets or reviewing budgets or deciding on next year's ticket prices as well as developing and reviewing any kind of new policies. I travel, as I mentioned, at least to the conference championships. Depending on the time of year we do exit interviews with the senior student-athletes. We do any financial surveys that come into the office. I usually attend events. I also spend quite a bit of time with the athletic director. I would say my typical workday recently has been from 8:00 in the morning to 7:00 at night.

I am definitely satisfied with my compensation package, and I am very satisfied with the content of my work. I am very satisfied with my working relationship with the athletic director, and I enjoy my coworkers. I have had tremendous advancement opportunities. I cannot complain about that. Overall, the job is outstanding.

The field is getting to be more and more technology-oriented. We went live with our network in 1998 so we are starting to share files and send files via e-mail. Computer skills are very important, especially for someone trying to enter the field now because I am continually learning and I did not have to know this before. The only report writing I really do is monthly financial projections or budgets. Those are between the athletic director and myself. We also send out a monthly accounting statement to every unit head or coach in charge of a budget.

The most important strategy I incorporate within my management style is trying to do what is right every time. I want to make a decision that I can sleep with at night. I try to be consistent and insightful, and I try not to make any knee-jerk decisions. I try to think about things a little bit so that if it is an emotional decision I can settle down and decide. I am very organized and a clear communicator. I am very supportive and a big believer in positive reinforcement. I remain very calm and consistent in tense situations. I firmly believe in providing my staff the resources and autonomy to do their jobs, allowing for greater job satisfaction and growth. I think people who work for me would say I am fair, honest, and very hands-off. I am a perfectionist to a point but I do not tell those who report to me how to do everything. They know what the expectations are for the end result.

I definitely incorporate participative management. I always seek more information and typically will—if it is a major decision—call other institutions, particularly conference institutions, for input. I like to have a lot of data. My goal is to encourage employees to be problem solvers, not problem identifiers. Once the issue is identified, my staff and I discuss the situation and the range of possible solutions and their effects. We all give our two cents and then reach a decision we all agree to implement. As long as people have their say, I believe they feel comfortable in supporting the decision.

People who want to get into college athletic administration need to be honest and trustworthy. Others, especially coworkers, need to believe what they say. Obviously, they need to have integrity. I think they must have clear goals and expectations and provide constant feedback, whether it is good, bad, or indifferent. They need to be involved and loyal to coworkers.

I really believe in three basic principles. I think people need to have a strong work ethic, be willing to learn, and be loyal. I really do believe in those things. I place a high value on the internship experience. Obviously the intern would prefer that it be paid, especially if they bring some special skill to the table, but I think the work experience is very important. People apply for jobs here who have a wide variety of skills and experience. We get resumes from teachers to lawyers with 10 years of experience for just about every position. Everyone is trying to get into this field. I think in the future prospective employees are going to need some special experience to differentiate themselves from others.

Although this is not a new trend, college athletic departments need more revenue than ever. In the future, new revenue streams—at least at the University of Maryland—will not come from cigarette or beer advertising. I can assure you of that. Everyone in the department, obviously, is making sure we have a workable gender equity plan. The big trends here are making sure the gender equity plan works, the budgets are balanced, and we have created innovative revenue streams. With the success of the Women's World Cup, we plan to approach corporate sponsors and offer them another opportunity to be a part of the success of the women's athletics teams at Maryland. Obviously, the Women's World Cup reached an entirely new market that was virtually untapped.

I refer to history when I conceptualize because I always value what happened in the past. I am fortunate to work with someone who has a great vision so I lean on her vision to conceptualize what I think we need to do to get to where she wants us to be. I draw from everyone working here also because there are people here who see things differently. I want them to share the way they see things with me.

I think technology will be crucial, but I still think students will need to have all of the people skills. I am on-line. I need to be on-line just so I will not be blown away in the workplace. But those tools cannot replace people skills; they must be used to enhance work relationships. As I have moved up, I am more removed from the day-to-day business operations so I rely less and less on my technical skills, which is interesting. At first that was a little bit uncomfortable. I rely so much on personal skills now. In crisis management it does not matter if I can add two plus two. How I communicate with people becomes the important skill. I use fewer technical skills on a day-to-day basis, but rely on them heavily when dealing with big budget items. I work hard on the budget, but I do not do the day-to-day debits and credits.

I think I am always looking for new things from the athletic director. I am always looking to be involved in any type of situation and I am fortunate to work for someone who allows that. I am always looking to take on any new challenge within the department. Everyone thinks of a person working in internal operations as a bean counter, but occasionally I will go to a development outing to see what it is like or just to pick somebody's brain. I want to know what is happening everywhere because eventually, if I am going to be the athletic director, I will be managing it all.

When I first got here we were about $7 million in debt. First, let me say I was not the one who worked out the debt elimination plan. I came here and helped implement it. They had laid all of the groundwork. I am not going to take any credit for what Debbie Yow and Jamie Pollard laid out because they went to the administration and took on some heavy hitting things. They looked at things such as how much revenue student fees were generating. They went to different areas on campus to lobby for support for athletics. They got the University System of Maryland to agree to tuition waivers for anybody with a special skill, not just for athletics, but also for musically gifted students or a theater student who is gifted. If an out-of-state student on full scholarship comes to Maryland, the department that is paying the scholarship only has to pay the in-state rate. That is a big savings. This year that will probably save us about $750,000 to $900,000.

In a clever way Debbie Yow has increased sponsorship. Although some people may think our basketball arena looks like an outfield fence at a minor league ballpark, we were not afraid to explore new corporate sponsorship opportunities. Corporate sponsorship has more than doubled since she has been here. She has a fund-raising background and is very aggressive in that area.

The Office of Civil Rights has been here, so, in conjunction with our legal office, we developed a plan for Title IX implementation that was very aggressive. We decided when we would match participation rates and how scholarship dollars would be spent. It was a 5-year plan of ramped-up scholarships for the women and in some of the cases we were holding the men flat and we even had to reduce some of the men's scholarships, although I think that happened just in the first year. For the fiscal year 2000 all of our women's teams will be fully funded with the exception of one, women's golf, and that is because it is in its first year. To meet our Title IX demands the original 5-year plan stated we would fully fund all of the women's sports that we currently had and that would do the job. As we got closer we recognized that was not going to balance out to meet the participation rates so we went ahead and added women's golf.

Thirteen sports are available for women and 12 are available for men. Men's and women's indoor track, outdoor track, and cross-country count as three sports each. We will be extremely close in participation rates. Scholarship expenditures are moving in the right direction. At the end of next year, Fiscal Year 2000, we hope everything will be just as we planned. Our plan went from a 5-year plan to a 6-year plan for financial reasons. We had to take the last year and divide it up so that at the end of Fiscal Year 2000 we will be in full compliance.

We think we are very aggressive in our approach to Title IX. We report to our athletic council once a year on our plan. We have direct input and work very closely with the President's legal office. We believe in it and work very diligently to make sure we are in compliance.

This is a beautiful business. The one thing I gain from it is how people get to work in a field that represents their passion. It is hard work. I mean everyone views this as fun but it is hard work. Eleven-hour days are not easy. It does not matter what you are doing but people are very passionate about their work and they love it. That is one outstanding thing. Everyone told me I would never make any money or would not be challenged, and that is all hogwash. I love it. I would not change it for the world.

I will measure my success by looking back to see if I did exactly what I wanted to do. I will look back and say I did what I wanted to do and I busted my butt and was the best whatever, even if I am the best senior associate athletic director I could be.

Robertha Abney

Associate Athletic Director
Slippery Rock University

Education
B.S., PHYSICAL EDUCATION, SOUTH CAROLINA STATE UNIVERSITY, 1980
M.ED., ATHLETIC ADMINISTRATION, UNIVERSITY OF PITTSBURGH, 1982
PH.D., ATHLETIC ADMINISTRATION, UNIVERSITY OF IOWA, 1988

Career Progression:
ASSOCIATE ATHLETIC DIRECTOR / ASSOCIATE PROFESSOR, SLIPPERY ROCK UNIVERSITY, 11 YEARS

Best piece of advice you received in regards to your career:

"Follow your dreams and never give up." My parents.

Best advice for someone aspiring toward a career in the sport industry:

"Follow your dreams and never give up."

Quote by which you live:

"Do the right thing and do things right."

I FIRST DECIDED ON A CAREER in sport after experiencing a national championship in basketball at South Carolina State College. It is now South Carolina State University. We had finished the game and were celebrating. I recall, of course, those very exciting and joyous moments. But I did take the time to stop and ask the questions, "What is next? Where do I go from here?" At that time and during that particular phase of my life I really had reached the highest level. We did not have professional women's teams in the United States so as a female I had really experienced the top level of participation in collegiate sport.

That is when I first started to think there was more, and then I really started to focus. The celebrating, it was almost like this is it; I had reached the end. The next day I remember still trying to answer that question—what is next? I began to try to think about and pursue avenues where I could still be involved in sport, an area

I really enjoyed and loved so much. I knew I would not be participating, but I could possibly pursue other avenues such as athletic administration or coaching.

High school was an interesting experience because, as I am from South Carolina, segregation was very prevalent. My parents took it upon themselves to basically challenge the system and placed my sisters and myself in the white school system, which was located across the railroad tracks. During those times, the railroad tracks acted as the divider for the black and white communities. It was at that school where I was really introduced to competitive sport. Because our facilities at the black school were terribly inadequate, we did not have sport teams. We did not have a gymnasium. Attending school, across the railroad tracks, was a totally different academic and social experience. It was in this school system that I really began to compete in athletics.

After high school, I attended South Carolina State College. I majored in physical education and minored in biology. After completing my bachelor's degree, I attended the University of Pittsburgh as a graduate student. My coach at South Carolina State College had attended the University of Pittsburgh. He recognized my abilities as a student and an athlete and highly encouraged me to complete an application to pursue my master's degree at the University of Pittsburgh. From the University of Pittsburgh I then applied to the doctoral program at University of Iowa. During my master's degree defense I was asked if I planned to continue my education or pursue a terminal degree. At the time I was trying to complete the master's defense and had not considered furthering my education. Therefore, my response was no. One of the professors, Jane Clark, challenged me by saying, "If you decide to further your education, please stop by and see me. I know the ideal place." She told me the ideal place was the University of Iowa in Iowa City, Iowa, and that is how I began to pursue my doctoral degree there. I believe at the time the athletic administration academic program at the University of Iowa was ranked as one of the top programs in the country.

I think my career path was pretty normal for the time frame when I pursued the degree. It was different in that I had gone from kindergarten straight through to a Ph.D. with no work experience in between other than being a graduate assistant, teaching assistant, research assistant, or administrative assistant. Other than that, it was school all of the way through, nonstop, from kindergarten through to my doctoral degree.

I came to Slippery Rock University in 1988. The University of Iowa held a women's sport conference every summer and often graduate students planned and organized the entire conference. I was assigned this task one year, and Dr. Ann Griffiths, who at the time was a dean at Slippery Rock, attended that conference. I met her and we talked about my goals, career opportunities, and Slippery Rock University. We continued to communicate over the years and when I completed my degree, a position in physical education and athletics was available at Slippery Rock University. I applied and here I am 11 years later.

The exploration of my career varied. I talked to Dorothy Richey, who at the time was the first African American woman athletic director in the country. I met her during graduate school when she came to speak to one of my classes. I was the only African American woman in that class, and I spoke to my professor about my aspirations and desires to become an athletic administrator. I had not seen any African American women in this role so it was somewhat discouraging, but for me it was still a challenge to continue.

When Dr. Richey spoke to our class that was all I needed in terms of motivation. I remember that after the class I walked Dr. Richey to the parking lot trying to find out as much as I could. I received her number, business card, and through the years continued to talk with her about pursuing a doctoral degree and a career as an athletic administrator. Because I saw one African American woman in this position it was enough to say this dream could actually become a reality. It can be discouraging, as an African American woman, when you do not see other African American women in positions as athletic administrators. I often wondered if this dream/goal could actually be a reality. I was always encouraged to pursue my dreams by my parents, grandmother, and siblings. Knowing Dr. Richey was functioning in that capacity, I knew I could realize my dream.

I had several mentors and role models during my career development. Elizabeth Bandy, my high school coach; Lyman Foster, my collegiate coach; Dorothy Richey, whom I mentioned before; and Christine Grant, the former Association of Intercollegiate Athletics for Women President and Women's Athletic Director at the University of Iowa. They were extremely instrumental in my career development. My parents and siblings were instrumental in providing emotional and financial support. It was difficult for my parents to provide career guidance, but emotional support, financial support, and the basics I needed to really be motivated to pursue this dream definitely came from them.

I have encountered several obstacles in my career. These obstacles include such things as race, gender, inhospitable environment, age (too young), tokenism, burden of being the official minority spokesperson, lack of support groups, lack of cultural and social outlets in the community, and alienation. African American women who aspire to top administrative positions face a number of obstacles that make it difficult for them to achieve at the highest professional levels. Both racial and sexual discrimination are burdens African American women must bear in career development and in American society. The "double jeopardy" adds to the difficulty of African American women who are seeking career advancement. Often the double jeopardy prevents African American women from formal networks and informal networks in which social relationships could possibly generate career benefits.

I was never discouraged about achieving my career goals. My parents and mentors always supported my goals and always encouraged me to achieve them. While at Iowa, I was in an environment where all of my major professors were women and they served in leadership capacities nationally and internationally. They strongly encouraged, prepared, and to a certain degree expected the students to pursue leadership positions and roles. Also, there was a strong support system among the graduate students within the department and many of the students were aspiring to be athletic administrators. I would not have done anything differently.

Currently I am an associate athletic director and an associate professor in the physical education department. As an associate professor I teach courses in the sport management program. Those courses consist of sport marketing, management and leadership in sport, and organizational theory. I also teach several physical education activity courses.

Administratively, my responsibilities include coordinating the scheduling of athletic contests, day-to-day operations of several sports, maintaining sport accounts, promotions, and monitoring Title IX and Gender Equity compliance. We are an NCAA Division II program with 22 single-sex sports and one co-ed sport. In addition, I am specifically responsible for the daily operation of several sports, including men's and women's soccer, men's and women's tennis, softball, cross-country, men's and women's swimming, field hockey, and volleyball. The daily operation includes assisting or working with the coaches to address any concerns they may have regarding their team or student athletes. I am involved in event management. I am usually available to make sure everything is going okay on the day of the event. I usually try to attend most, if not all, of the home athletic contests.

I also manage the sport accounts. These accounts contain funds generated from donations and fund raising. Deposits and payments are processed through these accounts. I also process purchasing requests. If the coaches want to purchase any merchandise or equipment, the request is submitted to my office for review and approval. Once the merchandise has been received, I process the request for payment. I am involved with the promotion of athletic contests and events and I help to monitor compliance. As the senior woman administrator, I am involved with any gender equity issues within the department.

I really enjoy what I do. I enjoy the challenges, the people, and most of all I enjoy the student athletes; watching them mature, grow, and develop over the 4 or 5 years is very rewarding. I cannot really say I have a normal day in athletics because I may have a plan of what I am going to accomplish on a particular day, but there may be an incident that changes my plans for that day. I enjoy the management and leadership aspects involved in administering an intercollegiate athletic program. Sport administration is a very challenging and exciting profession. I have lots of variety. There is something new and different all of the time. There are very few routine days.

The very long hours are challenging for me. I will find myself working 7 days a week because we will have activities on Saturday and Sunday. I try to attend all home contests so that means I am coming in 7 days a week and that can be very demanding. My salary and the hours I work do not compare. I really try very hard to keep things in perspective. I make time for me and try to work out every other day. Even though I may find myself working 7 days a week, I still try to find time either in the afternoon or early morning before I go to work to do something I enjoy.

In this job I definitely have to have leadership skills. Interpersonal, conceptual, and technical skills are essential. Motivational skills are also necessary. One has to be visionary and be able to see the big picture, and also have a plan as to where the department needs to be in 5 to 10 years. I must be also be able to perform various managerial functions such as planning, organizing, communicating, staffing, controlling, and decision making. I also need good fiscal management skills because I have to monitor, assess, and allocate your financial resources. Being an efficient and effective leader is very essential to the department's success.

My dominant management style would be participatory or democratic with my secondary style being autocratic. I do have a tendency to be analytical and want to include everyone in decision making. I want to make sure I am doing the right thing *and* doing things right. If someone wanted to get into intercollegiate athletics I would definitely encourage her or him to pursue a degree in sport management because we are seeing a change in the experience and educational backgrounds of the individuals entering the field. At one point coaches were being promoted into these positions. That is no longer the case. Currently, position announcements are seeking individuals with sport management backgrounds as well as several years of experience in the area. I would also encourage the individual, especially a female, to not only get the sport management degree, but also to pursue avenues in terms of networking and to become involved professionally in various organizations. I would also encourage that individual to volunteer, do an internship, and even while doing the internship or after completing the internship, continue to volunteer. I think those things are critical for an individual pursuing or wanting to get into college athletics because it is a challenge to get into the area. Although things are changing, there are sill individuals who have been in coaching and athletic administrative positions for a very long time. It is one of those careers where those in the position have a tendency to stay. I have been in this position for 11 years.

Whether it is a Division I, II, or III institution, you must be prepared to work within a political environment. Division I may be a more political environment, although I think in all the divisions or within any organization, politics exist. Division I institutions are more business oriented. Be ready and prepared to work within that type of environment. Ten years from now I think intercollegiate athletics will have more of a business focus in terms of the individuals in managerial positions. As I mentioned earlier, we will not see coaches managing the department; there will be individuals with backgrounds in accounting, management, marketing, economics, and other areas such as law, communications, public relations, and fund raising.

I do think it is critical that students are involved in fund raising because funds are very limited within most athletic departments. If they are thinking about athletic administration, fund raising is critical for program's survival. In most instances, athletic administrators must generate funds for scholarships, equipment, and facilities. They may be within a department where the financial resources are limited. In a small town, for example, everyone, not only the athletic department, but everyone within the university is targeting the few businesses and individuals for funds. We have to develop creative ways to go beyond your geographical location and try to obtain funds. I have not been extensively involved in fund raising, and that is something in which I would like to have more experience. At Slippery Rock that is the responsibility of the head coaches and athletic director. In looking toward an athletic directorship, students are clearly going to need some experience in fund raising

African Americans seeking these careers need to persevere. Preparation is essential. Be prepared to meet and overcome the obstacles and challenges of obtaining a career in the profession or sport management related fields. When they have successfully obtained a position, it may be a situation or an environment where they are the only African American within the organization. Establish meaningful networking relationships and support systems during the collegiate years, internship, and volunteer experiences. Really and truly, there is a place for them, but they are definitely going to have to be prepared, competent, confident, have strong drive, and be determined to reach their goals.

I would hope one trend in intercollegiate athletics would be to focus more on diversity within the athletic department in not only gender equity, but also racial equity. The number of coaches, athletic administrators, managers, and chief executive officers is not proportionate to the number of African Americans on the playing fields and courts. Many sport organizations and athletic departments have little or no diversity among the staff members and administrators. Minorities are not in positions where they are operating, administering, or managing the organizations, departments, or athletic programs. I would hope there is an increased sincere effort toward making these offices more racially as well as gender diverse. The implementation of Gender Equity and Title IX will become more evident and there will be more equitable programs for men and women. There will continue to be a lot of opportunities within intercollegiate athletics because of society's love for sports. We are going to have sport within society, colleges, and universities for a very long time.

My next goal is to become an athletic director at a college or a university. Ultimately I would love to work at Division I, but it will probably first be Division II because I do enjoy the Division II philosophy. I enjoy Division II because we still basically provide broad-based programs and maintain the philosophy of student-athlete, where academics is first and foremost in the student athlete experience.

I believe I have achieved a level of success in my career because I have achieved or attained my first goal to become an athletic administrator. Even at the Division II level, I really do not know very many other African American women holding this position. It is something I always wanted to achieve. I would have to say I might be somebody's role model because of the correspondences I have received. I usually receive calls from African American women who are pursuing their degrees and often call just to ask questions, share experiences, receive advice, or express concerns. Sometimes I receive letters from students who have read one of my articles about African American women in sport. If their number is available, I will call to encourage and ensure them that the goal is reachable. I let them know they can call me and talk to me because I was in their shoes at one point. I probably have a very good idea as to what they are experiencing. If at any time they need to talk about what they are going through, or any type of situation, I say please give me a call. They are usually so appreciative. Some of the individuals I have never met. I have just talked with them on the telephone.

Anne Sander "Sandy" Barbour

Athletic Director
Tulane University

Education:
B.S., PHYSICAL EDUCATION, WAKE FOREST UNIVERSITY, 1981
M.S., SPORT MANAGEMENT, UNIVERSITY OF MASSACHUSETTS, 1983
M.S., MANAGEMENT, J.L. KELLOGG GRADUATE SCHOOL OF MANAGEMENT, NORTHWESTERN UNIVERSITY, 1991

Career Progression:
ATHLETIC DIRECTOR, TULANE UNIVERSITY, JUNE 1996 TO PRESENT
SENIOR ASSOCIATE ATHLETIC DIRECTOR, INTERNAL OPERATIONS, TULANE UNIVERSITY, JUNE 1995 TO JUNE 1996
ASSOCIATE ATHLETIC DIRECTOR, TULANE UNIVERSITY, AUGUST 1993 TO JUNE 1995
INTERN PROGRAMMING AND PRODUCTION DEPARTMENT, FOX SPORT NET-CHICAGO, SUMMER 1990
ASSISTANT ATHLETIC DIRECTOR, INTERCOLLEGIATE PROGRAMS, NORTHWESTERN UNIVERSITY, JULY 1984 TO JULY 1989
DIRECTOR, ATHLETIC RECRUITING SERVICES, NORTHWESTERN UNIVERSITY, AUGUST 1982 TO JULY 1984
ASSISTANT FIELD HOCKEY AND LACROSSE COACH, NORTHWESTERN UNIVERSITY, AUGUST 1982 TO JULY 1984
ASSISTANT FIELD HOCKEY AND LACROSSE COACH, UNIVERSITY OF MASSACHUSETTS, AUGUST 1981 TO JUNE 1982

Best piece of advice you received in regards to your career:
"Be passionate about what you are doing. Find a way to give it meaning."

Best advice for someone aspiring toward a career in the sport industry:
"Get a broad-based education and as much practical experience as you can. Volunteer for everything and anything."

Quote by which you live:
"Every morning in Africa, a gazelle wakes up. It knows it must run faster than the lion or it will be killed. Every morning a lion wakes up. It knows it must outrun the slowest gazelle or it will starve to death. It doesn't matter whether you are a lion or gazelle; when the sun comes up, you'd better be running."

I GREW UP AS A YOUNG LADY in the 1970s being very active in sports, both as a participant and as a fan. I was the third daughter of a career naval officer who loved sports. He played a little college baseball and desperately wanted a child who would share his interest and be a fan with him. I certainly grew up in that environment and played a lot of different sports at the school level as well as in the summer. I even tried to play Little League baseball during the late 60s and early 70s, but the rules did not allow girls. I could run faster, jump higher, and throw a baseball farther than the young boy next door, who made the team, yet I could not play because I was a girl.

I decided that I really wanted to coach and teach at the high school level. I thought I was going to college to further my education, get a teaching certificate, and the credentials, knowledge, and training to return to the high school level to become a successful teacher and coach. My undergraduate studies were done at Wake Forest University in North Carolina. Once I got to college and participated as a varsity athlete in field hockey and basketball, I said to myself, "I really like this." It was exciting and challenging, and it was at that point that I decided the college level was where I really wanted to be. I was only thinking in terms of a coaching and teaching career, and did not consider administration at that time.

Following graduation, I was a little tired of going to school, and like many young people, wanted to make a living in the real world. However, I made what I consider now, in hindsight, to be a very fortuitous decision, which was to go straight to graduate school and get a master's degree as soon as I could. In 1980–1981, sport management was just beginning to emerge as an academic discipline at the University of Massachusetts, Ohio University, and a few other schools. I chose the University of Massachusetts at Amherst because I believed it was the pre-eminent program in the country.

I had a wonderful year there obtaining a great education, great training, and valuable exposure to a number of people in the industry, as well as having an opportunity to become Pam Hixon's assistant coach in both field hockey and lacrosse. We played in the national finals in field hockey the first year of the NCAA championships. We lost to the University of Connecticut, but won the national collegiate championship in lacrosse. I walked out of UMass with a second place national trophy and a national championship trophy, and I was extremely excited about coaching. To complete my degree requirements I accepted an internship at Northwestern University in Evanston, Illinois. It was supposed to be a 13-week summer internship; however, we timed it so that I could be there during the fall semester and also be an assistant coach to Nancy Stevens in field hockey. My internship was administrative in nature and I was going to work for the departmental recruiting coordinator.

I arrived at Northwestern in mid-August 1982 and began my coaching and internship duties. After only about 2 weeks on the job, I was informed that the recruiting coordinator I was working for was taking another job. They offered a nervous, 22-year-old female with very little money in her pocket a chance to become the recruiting coordinator on an interim basis for the entire year instead of just the 13-week internship period. The pay was only about $500 a month, but I accepted the job immediately. Instead of spending 9 months I spent the next 9 years at Northwestern. The recruiting coordinator position was a tremendous opportunity for me because recruiting is the lifeblood of any athletic program, and the process involves everything from admissions to financial aid to compliance and regulations. In addition, much of the job was working with football, and for a 22-year-old female, the opportunity to get into the middle of what is going on in a Big 10 football program was invaluable.

I continued to coach both field hockey and lacrosse for 3 years. We had some success. We won a few Big 10 championships, made some NCAA appearances, and made Final Four appearances in field hockey, which was a thrill for me. The ambition of being a head coach was not a big issue to me. I could still be happy as an assistant coach because I enjoyed working on a daily basis with the student-athletes so much.

After a few years I was told, not asked, that I had to choose between being an administrator or coach when I was offered the position of assistant athletic director for intercollegiate services. It was made clear that I could not do both. It was a very difficult decision; however, I chose the administrative side. It was a hard transition to make, and I would occasionally sneak out the back door of my office to watch practice, but it obviously was the right move for me. My athletic administrative career has just continued to grow from that point.

I spent 7 years as a full-time employee in administration at Northwestern. During that time, I continued to evaluate the industry, to identify trends, and to determine which tools were needed to be successful in the future. I decided I needed some additional training, and that opportunity presented itself at Northwestern. At the age of 30, I decided to go back to school full-time and pursue a master's of business administration degree at Northwestern. Athletic administrative jobs are nowhere close to being 9:00–5:00 jobs. The best people in this industry are those that do not look for 5:00 or the weekend for their "break" (it does not exist), so I knew that I had to be a full-time student if I was going to do it the right way.

I resigned my full-time position and worked as a graduate assistant in academic services from 1989–1991, until I finished the MBA. I began looking for work in 1991. Many attractive opportunities existed but I chose the one that best fit my background. I attended Wake Forest as an undergraduate and I spent 9 years at Northwestern. Both were private, academically prestigious institutions trying to get it done in NCAA Division I-A athletics. Kevin White, the director of athletics at Tulane at the time, offered me a job as the associate athletic director for compliance and I jumped at the opportunity to go to Tulane and to New Orleans. The job responsibilities were another step up for me. I spent 5 years learning new areas of management within the athletic department. In April 1996, Kevin went to

Arizona State to become its athletic director. I was named the interim athletic director for 4 months until September 13, 1996 when I became the director of athletics for Tulane University.

In an industry that I do not think has a norm, the career path I took was probably typical for individuals in my age group. I think my generation is probably one of the last that includes the coaching part in the progression, and I happen to think that it is a very important part. It is not essential to have been a head coach for 15 or 20 years, which was typical of the generation before me. The past generation of athletic directors included retired coaches. Although I certainly do not advocate that, I do think that having some understanding of what it is like to have the pressures of a coach is important for any athletic administrator. It is important to have the actual knowledge and experience, but it also establishes credibility with coaches. I think it is important for coaches to believe that the administrator they are asking to solve a problem has some empathy and understanding for the situation. Now I also think the reverse is true and important. I believe coaches who have had some administrative or business experience tend to have better relationships with their administrators.

My sisters and mother were role models for me in a more personal way than an athletic way. My sisters are 12 and 14 years older that I am. They are from a generation that did not have the opportunities I had in athletics. Role models for me are an interesting mix. Given the time frame in which I was growing up, and even into the early years of my professional career, most of the people that I aspired to be like in this career track were men. I was very fortunate to have high quality coaches who were women throughout my college career in both field hockey and basketball. Also the director of the physical education program and assistant athletic director at Wake Forest, Dot Casey, always encouraged me to do whatever I wanted to do and become whatever I wanted to become. In my early coaching career, I learned a great deal from Coach Pam Hixon at UMass, who is as competitive a person as I have ever met. Most women in my age group were accused of not being very competitive, but she taught me that it was okay and required for success in this business.

As I reflect on the administrative side of the profession, the first athletic director I ever worked for was a very bright gentleman named Doug Single. He was only 29 years old, but he was very innovative and creative and I learned the importance of those traits. Ted Leland was the man who hired me for the internship position at Northwestern. Ted is now the athletic director at Stanford University. Ted has always been someone that has followed and been extremely supportive of my career, and someone who I have relied on frequently for advice. Kevin White is somebody who gave me a chance to get back into athletics at a time when I had taken a career risk by stepping out of athletic administration to get my MBA. He brought me back in at a very high level and then gave me significant responsibility. Kevin has always been a great mentor to me professionally and personally. I believe him to be at the elite level in this business.

I have had a number of female role models, yet Phyllis Bailey, a member of the senior women's administrative group of the Big 10, really stands out for me. That whole group was so good to me when I became the senior women's administrator at Northwestern at the age of 24. They taught me what I did not know—which was a lot—and it was Phyllis in particular that took a great interest in me. I think Phyllis was interested in making sure that the next generation of women had more and were capable of making the advances that were due to us. I remember my last Big 10 meeting when Phyllis asked me, "Okay kid, what do you want to be when you grow up?" I told her I did not know yet; I was 29 at the time, and I did not know yet. She said, "Well, okay, that's all right. But when you do figure it out, let me know because I want to help you get there." I think that is the really great message of the industry for women. It is not that women have not had the talent. Women have not had the opportunity to show off that talent. If you do not have a Doug Single, Ted Leland, or Kevin White who gives you the opportunity to get the experience, to take on the responsibility, and show you can do it, then you are not going to get hired into that next level.

In terms of training and skills for this job, I would not say that you must have an MBA. I think that the actual training and the educational information with the MBA were useful. I also think it was doubly useful for me because I had worked for 7 years. I would encourage any student to go out and work for a couple of years. I think in terms of skills, it gave me a whole different toolbox. I got a master's degree in sport management from UMass, and the marketing class, sport law class, and all of the other classes were specifically focused in sports. The MBA program at Northwestern, however, was a much broader focus on general business skills such as marketing, finance, organizational behavior, and human resources. It made me think about how I could translate what had been done in the traditional world of business to the nontraditional world of intercollegiate athletics. To be successful in today's athletic department, we must create additional resources and additional revenue sources. The only way to do that is to break that paradigm and apply the business principles in new and creative ways.

The job description and responsibilities of my position as the director of athletics are really to oversee and coordinate all functions, responsibilities, and activities of the intercollegiate athletic program at Tulane University. We are divided into internal and external operations. My senior associate athletic director on the external side oversees all of what are considered to be our external activities. Areas such as media relations, radio and TV broadcast properties, revenue production activities, marketing and promotions, ticket sales, corporate sponsorships, and advertising all are considered to be external operations. Our development or fund-raising area, actually because of its importance, does not fall under the senior associate; it reports directly to me. It is an external function. Our ticket office also falls under the revenue area or revenue production. On the internal side, there are things that would be germane to the actual programs themselves. An associate athletic director is in charge of internal operations that include the weight equipment and training rooms, and a number of our sport programs. Some of our sport programs report directly to me. We have an assistant athletic director for compliance and our student services operation. Game management is another internal area because it is related to program management.

The Green Wave Athletics Association, an athletic foundation for development, is a part of athletics. We have an associate athletic director who is in charge of fund raising. The interesting thing about development, which either does or should take up a majority of my time and my effort, is that people give out of trust and a developed relationship with others. Those relationships take time to develop and you have to be patient and invest in them. I like to think our entire athletic department personnel, whether internal or external, are ambassadors of our program from either a fund-raising standpoint or a public relations standpoint.

The most enjoyable part of my job is the time that I spend with our student-athletes. The time I spend congratulating them on success and helping them solve problems is very rewarding. I was the senior associate athletic director for internal operations before I became the athletic director, and the biggest difference between those two jobs is the time available to concentrate on and spend with our real central core mission, which is our student-athletes. In the mix of all we do, it is easy to lose track that this is really about the student-athletes, and all of our decisions should reflect that priority. We do exit interviews, as most universities do. The NCAA requires interviewing a certain number and cross-section of graduating seniors; however, we interview them all. I enjoy that a lot, because they come in and tell me what a great experience they have had and that is very gratifying.

I think the biggest challenge and frustration is what I do for a living is everybody else's hobby. If I was a chemical engineer, there would not be a community of 1.2 million people that would know a lot about being a chemical engineer, or even think they would know a lot about it. However, because I work in sports, there is this whole segment of the population who think they know a lot more than I do. That is challenging. Actually, a lot of great ideas are out there and a lot of different ways to get the job done, but we do not have the time, resources, or personnel to do them, and sometimes people get angry when we do not try their idea. The other challenge is trying to go somewhere without being identified as the athletic director of Tulane. Sometimes that is great if we are having a great year; however, it is not so good when we have a losing season. I got trapped in a taxi with an irate taxi driver my first fall when we were not doing very well in football. On the 15-minute drive to the airport, he screamed and yelled about what was wrong with Tulane football and how I needed to fix it. I was a captive audience.

Unfortunately, a typical week may have me out of town a couple of days. I serve on a number of NCAA committees that require travel, but I am also out of town for conference business, development business, and traveling with a team during the competitive year. The in-town days typically include a breakfast with a university administrator, a potential or current donor, or somebody in the business community. Then there are a number of meetings to conduct to plan for upcoming events or initiatives, and then hopefully an opportunity to make some phone calls, return some phone calls, and get to some correspondence before a luncheon of the same nature as the breakfast. During the afternoon, it is much of the same; however, at some point some type of crisis management will be needed. Somebody is going to walk in the door and will need an answer or to talk about an issue. Despite all of the structured meetings and planning, I have got to leave room for "stuff" to happen because it will. Unfortunately, in this business there really is not a down time. Summer is a different pace than the rest of the year because we do not have the athletic events, but the workload really is no different. It is a time to recharge your batteries, but there is still a lot of work.

Stress is related to the constant on-the-job pressure, and that is probably one of the few surprises of the job. I thought I was well prepared for this job; however, the visibility of the position and the pressure of always having to be "on" is more than I had expected. I consider myself very customer-oriented, and wherever I am or whatever I am doing, I am aware that I represent Tulane University. I am sure people deal with stress differently, perhaps with exercise, the arts, hobbies, reading, traveling, and so forth, but I need to learn to compartmentalize my personal time away from the job. I enjoy reading and watching movies for entertainment. I have a boat and some golf clubs but they are neglected right now.

As far as my management style is concerned, I like to hire good people and let them do their jobs. I try to provide direction and then let them go. I think I am stuck between hands-on and hands-off, which may be a good thing. I certainly know that there are times when I have a definite idea about how something should be done, and if it is not done that way I get upset. I am a relatively new manager with a lot of things to learn, but I am improving. I probably need to learn to communicate better under stress and in stressful situations. I think that hopefully I am perceived as a manager that will tolerate errors of omission as long as you work hard, but I do not want errors of omission to occur.

Many skills are needed to perform successfully in this job. The ability to convey a message in verbal and written form is so important. People ask me the skills they need to get a job in this field. Speak well. That is it. What I do for a living is not brain surgery and by communicating my message in writing and verbally, I have gone far in this business. As far as technology goes, I am a "tweener." A lot of athletic directors have never been updated on computer technologies. It is unbelievable the number of fans and university administrators who communicate by e-mail. There are pros and cons to e-mail. The e-mail has just become another form of correspondence that needs to be answered and it can become overwhelming. People expect instant, immediate responses from e-mail, and when I am traveling a lot it is not always possible. In some things I do not have the technical expertise or time to pursue, such as web site development, and for those things I hire people. It occasionally can be frustrating to have nearly 80 employees performing about 60 different tasks, and a booster asks why a certain thing was on the Internet site and I have not seen it. Overall, however, technology has been a wonderful thing that we need to learn how to use to our best advantage.

I think that intercollegiate athletics is headed to a real point of decision making. The rich are getting richer, and the poor are getting poorer. Institutions as a whole are being faced with quantifying the value of their intercollegiate athletics. If it is a $10 million bill, is it worth $10 million to the university? I am not going to pretend to know the answer, and it is probably different at different institutions. We are going to get to the point where those institutions that have the capability of generating huge amounts of revenue will not want to bother with those at the other end of the spectrum. A huge difference exists between the most prosperous NCAA Division I-A schools with budgets of $45 to $50 million and the lower end schools with operating budgets of $12 to $15 million. That is a four-fold difference, and at the poor end of the spectrum schools are scratching and clawing to try to compete with the rich. I think time will only exacerbate the problem, and some hard decisions will ultimately have to be made. There may be a realignment of institutions with like philosophical beliefs and values, with 40 or 50 of them forming a new alliance for competition. Some think that the entertainment and business aspects of big time athletics will create a sort of semiprofessional atmosphere where the athletes become contract-based employees of the university. I just cannot see that happening and I hope it does not happen. But I think there will be a philosophical emergence of like-minded colleges in some sort of agreement for competition.

I think many of the issues such as gender equity, gambling scandals, revenue production, television contracts, and so forth all boil down to money. Even the debate about academic integrity, I believe, is rooted in money. If there was not the incentive, the pressure to win, draw fans, and to get TV exposure, there would not be the pressure to compromise academics to get a high profile athlete.

Gender equity is also about finances. I do not think there is any man or woman who would argue that women should have their fair share of participation opportunities. The problem is that there is not enough money to do what we are doing now and increase these opportunities for women. The Title IX debate is really about resources. I think the issue of the next decade will be what is the value of intercollegiate athletics to educational entities, and can or will those institutions foot the bill? Some have suggested that everyone adopt an NCAA Division III philosophy of no scholarships to cut costs and save money. However, a Division

III program can cost even more than a Division I program because they have limited opportunities for revenue.

As far as my future career goals go, I believe I am challenged in my current position and have no desire to look elsewhere. When I entered this profession in 1982, I said I wanted to become an athletic director. Little did I know that it would only take about 15 years to do it. There are a number of challenges here to deal with, and one of the reasons I like this business is that no day or year is ever the same. I love what I do, and unless the face of intercollegiate athletics was to change drastically, I see myself in athletic administration for a long time.

An example of how things can change very quickly, however, is the success of Tulane football and the undefeated season with Coach Bowden in 1998. Football drives the economic train of the athletic program. The success of football happened so quickly that it caught us all by surprise. It was not a 3–4 year thing. It did not build or progress. It just arrived. We are just now beginning to reap the full benefits of our recent success. One of the natural events that can follow a program's success is the transition of coaches. You are going to have good coaches who will be successful and sometimes you are going to keep them and sometimes they will view your opportunity as a stepping stone. In the 8 years I have been at Tulane, we have only lost one extremely successful coach, and that was Tommy Bowden. We have been able to retain successful coaches in baseball, men's and women's basketball, women's golf, and men's tennis and track, each of which has achieved national rankings and respect for their programs.

We have benefited financially from the recent outstanding football season. Direct as well as indirect revenue streams have been affected. Despite the short turnaround, we have seen an increase in season ticket sales. Our season ticket sales were up 66 percent this past year, and we expect a similar jump for the upcoming year; however, the numbers are still small. We have suffered through 10 years of losing football, and even a 12–0 season does not bring it back immediately. We have a growing base of support, and our donations to athletics as well as the university as a whole are up significantly. Admissions applications to the university were up 6 percent. I received calls from all over the country because of the positive publicity generated from the football success. Tulane had major feature articles for about six straight weeks in *USA Today*, including a sports cover shot. We also had two articles in the *Los Angeles Times* and one in the *New York Times*. The full extent of that kind of positive publicity is hard to measure and occurs over an extended period of time. Have we raised the standard of success to a new level? You bet. Last year we won six conference championships and I am proud of that accomplishment. I have contributed to the success, but it is not something that Sandy Barbour has accomplished alone. Our recent success is the result of a coordinated effort on the part of an entire staff and begins with work done by those of us who laid the foundation during the early 1990s.

For a young woman getting into this business now, the future is very bright. Currently a dozen female athletic directors are at the NCAA Division I-A level. The total for NCAA Division I is in the 30's, which includes I-AA and I-AAA. When I was named the director of athletics 3 years ago, I was the fifth, and of those four who preceded me, three of the four had occurred within 18 months. We have gone from one to a dozen in about 5 years. I have been asked if I consider myself a role model for women in this career track. I try not to think of it in that way because that is a lot of pressure. I think that each of us should be proud of our achievements and strive to do the best in our jobs. Taking on the pressure of "carrying the flag" for women in this business is only counterproductive. I think today young women getting in this business have a lot more role models than ever before. Women have paved the way, shown it can be done and done well, and now help others achieve their aspirations.

Lots of obstacles still exist for women in athletics, however, and one of them is that the constituency groups that I deal with are predominantly male. I have not experienced a lot of difficulty but there is the subtle and there is the overt. In a business setting, as a stereotype, men relate better to men talking about sports and women who are in sports relate better to women. I feel comfortable in a group of men playing golf, talking about what is going on in the department, and I have experienced little if any overt opposition. The other good news is that this generation of student-athletes has a more equal representation of women and men. As they grow up and become professionals, women will control a bigger piece of the pie. That is good news for female administrators. I see nothing but positive trends for the future. It does not mean that challenges are not still there; you just have to prepare yourself to face them.

CHAPTER 3

International Sport

AS THE BORDERS OF THE WORLD continue to shift and disappear because of improved technology and communication, the sport marketplace is becoming more global. Sport managers need to be aware of the place of sport in the global marketplace, the opportunities that are available, and the skills needed to be successful in this ever-changing industry segment.

Many careers are available in international sport organizations. The Olympic Movement is the most widely recognized part of international sport. Sport managers work with every aspect of event management from securing corporate sponsorships to organizing international media coverage. The Olympic Movement encompasses National Olympic Committees (e.g., U.S. Olympic Committee, Japanese Olympic Committee), Organizing Committees for the Olympic Games (e.g., Salt Lake City Organizing Committee for the Winter Olympics 2002, Athens Organizing Committee), International Federations (e.g., International Baseball Association, Federation Internationale de Football), and National Governing Bodies (e.g., USA Baseball, Judo Canada). Sport organizations also are available for people with disabilities. Organizations such as the Paralympic Games, Wheelchair Sports USA, or Special Olympics, all need sport managers to work in various capacities. These organizations provide exciting opportunities for preparing athletes for international competition. Numerous U.S. leagues are making efforts to build support in other countries, as illustrated by National Football League (NFL) exhibition games in Mexico, National Basketball Association (NBA), and Major League Baseball (MLB) exhibition games in Europe, and MLB postseason All-Star Games in Japan. Licensed products for many of the "Big 4" are on sale in German department stores such as Karstadt as well as stores in Japan and Australia.

Sport marketing has also taken on international importance. Global companies such as Coca-Cola and United Parcel Service (UPS) use the Olympics and other sporting events as international marketing tools. Sport marketing companies are active around the world, including companies such as RSL Marketing (United Kingdom), Real-Marketing (Germany), Asset (Greece), Sponsorium International (Canada), as well as IMG, ISL, and Advantage International. These companies must deal with issues such as ambush marketing, merchandise licensing, and sponsorship contracts as they vary across national borders and legal systems.

Sport managers working in an international setting need a variety of skills. First and foremost, sport managers must develop a keen sense of cultural awareness. For example, something as basic as a business lunch may have a totally different dynamic in another country. As Americans, we are often casual and pay little heed to protocol, but knowledge of protocol is essential in other countries or we appear disrespectful. Who may sit at or near the head of the table? When may women speak and will they be listened to? Knowledge of the "pecking order" is vital so one does not speak out of turn or address the wrong individual. There is also a difference between "eating" as we do in the United States as opposed to "dining" in other countries. Knowledge of basic customs and manners in other countries is critical in gaining the respect of your international peers. Also, although being bilingual is not required, it is a valuable advantage. Learning a few basic phrases in other languages greatly enhances your interactions with others.

Anyone working in an international setting must be prepared for extensive travel. Although international travel offers great opportunities to visit other countries and cultures, it is far from glamorous. A person must become accustomed to long flights, multiple time zones, and odd schedules. Sport managers need to make sure their passports are current and always check to see if a visa is needed to visit or work in another country. Learning how to be a comfortable international traveler will help maximize the enlightening experience of meeting and working with people of different cultures. The varied cultures and countries will also have an impact on the salaries of those in international sport. In the case of international governing bodies salaries will be determined by which country an individual works and they may be paid in the currency of the country in which the organization is located. Whatever the culture may be an aspiring sport manager can expect to make the lower $20,000s in American currency for entry level positions. Middle level management positions or director positions would pay in the range of $40,000s to $50,000s, and leaders of these organizations can earn upward to $100,000 in some instances.

The sport world is becoming more and more global. Sport managers need to be aware of the relationship of the sport industry to the international marketplace and be prepared to work in this exciting and challenging environment.

Oliver Luck

President and CEO
NFL Europe

Education:
B.A., HISTORY, WEST VIRGINIA UNIVERSITY, 1982

JD, UNIVERSITY OF TEXAS LAW SCHOOL, 1987

Career Progression:
PRESIDENT AND CEO, NFL EUROPE, 1996 TO PRESENT

GENERAL MANAGER, RHEIN FIRE OF DUSSELDORF, 1995

DIRECTOR OF EUROPEAN OPERATIONS, NFL, 1993–1994

GENERAL MANAGER, FRANKFURT GALAXY, 1991–1993

Best piece of advice you received in regards to your career:

"Work hard, take risks, and be honest."

FRED SCHAUS, FORMER ATHLETIC DIRECTOR, WEST VIRGINIA UNIVERSITY

Quote by which you live:

"A man of genius makes no mistakes. His errors are volitional and are the portals of discovery."

JAMES JOYCE

MY CAREER PATH, BY DEFINITION, is going to be a little bit different than most students who read this because I was a professional football player in the NFL. Obviously, playing National Collegiate Athletic Association (NCAA) Division I college athletics and being in a professional league for a while, I was exposed to the business side of sport, although it was not something I focused on at the time. It gave me a much better understanding of the sport business overall because it can be argued that the most important piece of sport business is the athlete, the capital investment of the team owners. I made a conscious decision to get into the sport business in 1990 when I was 30 years old. I had a law degree and had practiced law for a couple of years. After a few years with a law firm in Washington, D.C., I had an offer to join the NFL to help build one of the teams in the World League. I made that decision in 1990.

From a student's perspective, I believe outside experience is a great teacher. I heard the Commissioner of the NFL, Paul Tagliabue, speaking to business students at West Virginia University in 1997, say the best advice he could give young students entering the sport business was to do something else first. Whether it is marketing, sales, or law, do something else first because those skills are all transferable into the business of sport. In a sense that advice has worked for me as well, even though I did not consciously plan it that way. I practiced law for a couple of years and then decided a career in sport business looked infinitely more interesting than a career in the legal business.

Another lesson for students is that often there are easier and quicker ways to get involved and move ahead in an organization by being outside the headquarters or home office. That is one of the reasons I progressed so rapidly. I went to Germany in 1990 to become the general manager of the Frankfurt Galaxy franchise and was the manager there for a number of years. I was also the general manager of the Rhein franchise we started in 1995. After our 1995 season I became president of the league and that has been my position since the summer of 1995.

I graduated magna cum laude from West Virginia University with a degree in history in 1982. (Editor's note: Luck was a Rhodes Scholar finalist, National Football Foundation Scholar, and a two-time GTE/CoSIDA Academic All-American.) Personally, at that time I had absolutely no career plan in mind, be it in sport business or anything else. Toward the end of my college career I became aware I had an opportunity to play football professionally. In addition, I planned to go on to law school, not necessarily with the goal of being a lawyer but because I thought advanced education was worthwhile. Luckily enough I was able to marry the two. I played quarterback for 5 years with the Houston Oilers and at the same time attended the University of Texas Law School and earned my law degree. I spent the fall and winter in Houston and spring and summer in Austin.

Obstacles exist in every profession, and professional football is no exception. The biggest one we faced in Europe was that we were a true start-up organization. When we started the Frankfurt Galaxy franchise and the other franchises in Europe at that time, hardly anyone knew about American football. It was a very exotic sport. Obviously, soccer holds the sporting passion for Europeans. It was fascinating because we would either make it on our own or fold. It was a real clear line. Even though we had the NFL involved, we were really 99.9 percent on our own as far as making the franchise work. Selling tickets, selling sponsorship, taking care of the players when they were in Europe, developing media contacts, developing broadcast partners, and finding simple things such as a practice field and housing for the players were all part of our responsibilities. It was a true start-up, which made it challenging.

At the same time it also made it immeasurably more exciting and satisfying because we accomplished so much with a really small staff, many of whom are still working for us. As difficult as it may be to believe, more than 50,000 people attended the fifth home game of the 1991 season, our first season. It blew us all away to realize how quickly we made it work. To summarize, the major obstacle was the start-up nature of the organization. Start-ups are by nature risky, the potential benefits are great, but the risks are increased. We could have fallen flat on our faces. That might have been the end of my sport business career.

The language barrier was not an obstacle for me. I spoke German and my mother is German, so I grew up with the language and culture. I had been to Germany a number of times before coming here professionally. I had credibility as a former NFL player, as a German-speaking American, and because I have an understanding of the German culture. That was a huge benefit getting this organization up and running in the first couple of years. I am a strong proponent of sport professionals being bilingual. It is the best thing a student can do to enhance his or her career. There is no other skill that is as beneficial. I do not care if it is a computer skill or whatever it is—no other skill is as valuable as a second language. The NFL is becoming more active globally, and I guarantee it is the same way in the NBA, MLB, and the National Hockey League (NHL). I do not hire anybody unless they are bilingual. Students do not think of knowing another language when they are in the sport business, particularly when they are in the United States. The U.S. market is big, but the single best thing a student can do is to learn another language.

Pete Rozelle was a role model I had as a player, even though I did not really pay much attention to the business side of sport. He did a phenomenal job of moving the NFL to where it is today. He was a genius in the sense that he recognized the power of television in professional sport and influenced the way Americans consumed the sport product. Bill Veeck was another role model for me as a kid. Growing up in Cleveland, Bill Veeck was—at least for my generation—still somewhat of a legend. I learned about him doing crazy stunts, even though he was really more active in the 40s and 50s in building up the Indians. He became a role model as I moved to Europe and we started doing the same types of things. We market our game as much more than a game. It is really a way of life. We do lots of crazy things that would not be done at a soccer game. I have used lots of Bill Veeck stories trying to teach our European employees about promotions.

One of my favorite Veeck stories is how he changed baseball's attitude toward female fans. He wanted to attract more women to Indians games so he conducted some research and one of the things he found was that women traditionally said they had a hard time seeing the ball. So he turned the lights off at night games and they played it with a fluorescent ball. It is great stuff. Apparently at one point 50 to 60 percent of Cleveland Indians fans were female. We cannot do the exact same things that Veeck did, but it is the general concept we emulate. We try to copy the attitude he brought to sport and apply it to our league.

For example, we took the fourth leading goal scorer in German soccer league history, a guy who is 50 years old, and made him a kicker in the league. He has been our place kicker for the past 4 years. Kickers can be 50 or 60 years old. We have tried to take that sort of attitude. We take the sport seriously but at the same time we have fun with it. People are not going to live and die with American football in Europe like they live and die with soccer so we can afford to have fun. It is a great way to get in the newspapers and get publicity.

I have been in Europe for almost 10 years, running various clubs here and then running the league for a while. My number one goal is to stay in the sport business. I find it very interesting. I enjoy it more than I would any other business. I am working for ultimately the best sports business organization in the country, the NFL, so I have no desire to really leave. Obviously, I am interested in getting promoted into more responsible positions in the NFL but those things happen with time if they are meant to happen. Certainly, I would imagine I would finish my career 25 to 35 years from now still involved in the sport business.

Currently, I am the president of the NFL-Europe. I did not say league because we actually have two different organizations. We have the "league business" with our clubs and at the same time we have what I call the "NFL business" representing the NFL in Europe with TV rights and various other opportunities. I am responsible for both aspects of the operation. Our most important function involves TV because it is the bread and butter for sports. We sell both NFL and NFL-Europe League rights worldwide. For example, we may work in Europe for broadcast rights, or work with the NFL people in New York to sell NFL Europe league rights to Mexico, Canada, Japan, or other markets where we think we can create some value. We are responsible for all league operations and all the licensing and merchandising operations over here for both the European league and the NFL; all commercial activities and sponsorships; and development of the game on the ground level, which goes beyond just our teams and involves working with the amateur football organizations in Europe to try to develop the game at a grassroots level in Europe.

We have 30 employees at the league level and approximately another 65 to 70 people at the team level. About an average of 11 employees work at each one of the six clubs. We have no outside equity and no outside ownership.

Two things are demanding in my position, as I presume they are for any manager. Number one, I have many different functions and responsibilities. I deal with TV rights and broadcasts, football development, the commercial part, licensing, and public relations. Every day I am juggling five or six different balls, all of which need to fit together somehow. We have a TV partner we want to get involved with our commercial partners, and we want support for both from a public relations standpoint. I am trying to juggle all of these different balls and there is never enough time to focus long enough on one particular function. I try to make sure the balls that may fall to the ground are the least important ones.

The second biggest challenge we have in Europe is dealing with different cultures. Europe is coming together slowly. We talk about a united Europe, but the Germans are still as different to the Spanish as the Canadians are to the Mexicans. The differences are apparent in everything. We try to come up with a strategy for Europe and then adapt it to the Germans, to the Spanish, and to all countries and nationalities we reach. In every one of our countries we have a different marketplace status. In some cases we are competing against sports such as rugby. Everywhere soccer is a factor. We try to figure out how "European" we can be and how much we have to adapt to the local culture.

One factor related to managing cultural differences is managing employees from different cultures. The Spanish have a different attitude about life and work than do the Germans. It involves simple things such as vacation time and different labor laws in their countries. The Germans are very American in the sense that when there is a business meeting, they get right down to business—five minutes of small talk and then get right to the point. They say, "What do you want, and what do you want to accomplish?" "This is what I want and this is what I want to accomplish." "Can we reach this?" "Do we have a common ground?" "Let's try to build a relationship." The Spanish, however, might get to that point after the fourth meeting. There are classic cultural differences we deal with every day that are time-consuming and challenging.

Trying to motivate employees takes time but it is very enjoyable. I have found that motivating a German employee is different from motivating a Spanish employee. I can push the Germans around a little bit if they have not reached their goal. They will get pumped up and excited about it, want to prove that they can do it, and they are very proud of their product. It is a highly developed nation, whereas the Spanish react a little bit differently. The Germans have a much different view of American culture than the Spanish or the English or the French. The French would like to ban the English language. The Germans want more of it. I just heard an English word that had been Germanized the other day. I was shocked. There are many cultural differences that people need to recognize.

I do several different things on a daily basis in season. I travel a great deal and put out a lot of small fires. With six teams in Europe, each having 45 to 50 players and several coaches, the usual problems can occur with bringing young American men to Europe. We do a good amount of public relations during the season, work with a lot of media, spend time with our sponsors during the season, and entertain potential new sponsors during games. It is a short, 11-week season for us, but it is a very intense time. Obviously, a lot of operational work has to be done.

Out of season we are—in a sense—a lot more relaxed. We are able to sit down, strategize more, and have long conversations with fan groups, focus groups, and the media to determine what we can do better. We develop strategies and tactics and spend a lot of time training our employees. We hire as many Europeans as we possibly can. We want to hire local people and spend a lot of time teaching in the off season, particularly new people or people who have only been working for 6, 7, or 8 months.

I have been very satisfied in this position, and have learned a lot. It has given me the chance to move up the food chain a little bit and get more responsibility. I work with good, friendly people. The challenge I see, as I compare the NFL as a multinational organization to virtually every other multinational, is that the NFL is very new in international business. Being in Europe for 10 years, basically our circle of friends is composed of American expatriates working for General Motors (GM), Opal, International Business Machines (IBM), or brokerage houses. When I was sent to Europe, I think I was the first NFL employee sent outside of the United States to work. No plan was in place like at GM or Merrill-Lynch where they prepare their expatriates to work overseas. Those companies may have 500, 1,000, or 2,000 people working in a given country and provide training and support including cost-of-living adjustments, expatriate packages, and tax ramifications. Such companies' employees also know how long they will live there. For example, many employees have a 2-year or a 3-year stay. Those benefits exist for employees of companies who have hundreds if not thousands of people overseas. That is not the case with the NFL because, only in the past 2 years has an international division in New York been set up to try to manage operations outside of the United States. That is a negative for a lot of employees, including myself, because we literally make up the rules as we go along. As far as repatriation packages, there is no plan in place at the NFL because it is a very new business form for us.

If I could change anything, it would be to tell people to stop talking and get to the point. In Europe, there is a dose of cultural sensitivity where the Spanish may present something differently than the Dutch. So one needs a good bit of cultural sensitivity and patience. At the same time, we are running a business and have got to see results. It cannot take me all day to accomplish a task such as getting a manager. I wish that there were 4 or 5 more hours in a day so we could really accomplish everything on time. At the same time, I find myself constantly encouraging our people to get to the point, summarize better, be more efficient, and be more productive. Whether it is dealing with a current sponsor or trying to put a sponsor deal together, I try to move it along as fast as we can, tie up loose ends as early as possible, and move on to the next project. That makes each team and all of us as a league much more efficient and productive. It involves having some cross-cultural training, cultural sensitivity, and a good deal of old fashioned patience. At the same time we need to know when to say that is enough, there is confusion here, and this is the way we are going to do it. I need to have people be very clear with what they want to accomplish and make sure they stick to the plan and can actually complete it. It is keeping their feet to the fire but constantly pushing them along.

Many external things ultimately have an impact on us. In our business, we kicked off the old league right in the middle of the Gulf War, so we all had political concerns. We were not necessarily worrying about player safety or about terrorists per se, but about general attitudes toward Americans. All of a sudden we realized over the years that we are identified really as more than a sport, we are sort of an American export. We stand for the United States and really promote the red, white, and blue in an allegorical sense. We wave the flag figuratively speaking at all of our events, and a lot of the entertainment and amenities are American. We serve spareribs at football games as opposed to bratwurst and potato chips or whatever they serve in Germany. We realize that to maintain a successful long-term business we are ultimately dependent on how the U.S. culture—be it film, music, or sport—is accepted around the world. The Germans, thank God, have a good, healthy relationship overall with the United States and with American pop culture. The French have a much more difficult relationship with U.S. culture. One segment of French society would like to limit the number of American films that can be shown. They are worried—and rightly so—about losing their French culture and the value of the French language. We are very much tied in with the image the United States has as a nation around the world. It is different in each country. It is different going from one European country to the next. Obviously, it is totally different in Japan, Mexico, or Southeast Asia.

My employees probably would describe me as someone who has a good bit of patience and understands the European culture. I have heard from a lot of different employees over the years. They say, "We're glad you're running this operation because you're half European and half American. You can understand our position while at the same time obviously understand what Americans want out of this organization." I think most of them would probably describe me as a bridge between the two cultures, although there is not a European culture. It is so varied within Europe. At least I am a bridge back to the United States where I can more or less understand what the Europeans are dealing with and how they think and their concerns. I can relate that to what my boss and the people I report to in New York ultimately want to have happen with the league.

I report directly to the President of NFL Enterprises. There are two business units: NFL Properties and NFL Enterprises. The whole international business is settled under NFL Enterprises along with the Internet, NFL Films, and some other areas. We probably only have 3, 4, or 5 percent American employees. The rest are European.

When talking about the globalization of American sport, we first have to define American sport. The only truly American sport, from my perspective, is American football. Basketball has been an Olympic sport since I think the 1930s. The NBA has a significant number of foreign players, predominantly Europeans, but the sport has been popular in China for decades. Nobody notices it because nobody notices anything that goes on in China. Baseball is the number one sport in Japan, Central America, and Cuba. Ice hockey, at least in the colder climates, is a worldwide sport. That points out, I think, both the opportunity as well as the obstacle for American football. Basketball cannot do what we do with the game on the ground level outside of the United States because there already is a game on the ground level outside the United States. There already are very strong basketball leagues in Italy, Spain, Yugoslavia, Astoria, Germany, and England, and so forth, with players who are actually pretty good. Ice hockey faces the same problem. Successful ice hockey leagues exist throughout Sweden and Russia and throughout northern Europe as well as in Canada and other places. The same is true for baseball in places such as Japan and Korea. Major league baseball could not create a league over there because one exists. They would have an inherent conflict with drawing fans away from the local leagues.

American football may be the only truly distinct American sport that can go almost anywhere outside the United States and establish a league from the ground up. Again, risks are involved. It is a lot of work. Sometimes one cannot always make the right steps because nobody has done it before. We have the ability to come in when people are literally just discovering the game. Compare that again to the NBA trying to go into Italy where a basketball league has existed for 60 to 70 years with its own teams, its own brands, and so forth. The Italians would just say "Well the NBA is a U.S. thing but the NBA has nothing to do in Italy." For our American football organization it is certainly been both a challenge and obstacle. I think the clear trend overall is that sports are becoming more global.

We certainly plan to expand. We will need to expand in a couple of years. I can envision an 8- or 10-team league in 10 years with two separate divisions, play-offs, and a championship. I would like to imagine that the NFL, as a U.S.-based league with 31 or maybe 32 teams, having a stronger position in Europe. Instead of only an hour-long game summary being shown on German TV or Spanish TV, we would have a live game with a good number of viewers. Some people are as passionate about whether the Redskins win or lose as they are about whether Manchester United wins or loses. In many of our markets, we are behind a decoder or a pay-TV system like a Showtime or an HBO. We need to develop enough of a fan base in England to move off Sky to get down that channel where the BBC is showing a NFL game on the weekend at 7 PM in prime time.

The Internet and World Wide Web have changed how we do business. There is more access to information than when I lived in Europe 10 years ago. I had to call somebody at home to find out the Monday night football score. For example, I was interested in a game this morning. When I woke up the game had been over for a couple of hours. I just got on the Web and found the score and game report and how Brian Griese played last night. Information is much easier to access, which generally is a good thing. I do not see any real negatives to that. I think the Internet is going to change our business even more once the technology is readily available to watch an NFL game on the Internet. I should be able to sit at home in a couple of years and have the broadband capability to plug in whatever numbers and watch the Oakland Raiders play if that is the game I want to see.

I think the real challenge of the Internet is for everybody to learn how to use it efficiently in the financial sense. The real impact I think we are all going to see is that the Internet removes political borders. There is broadband capability now. You could be anywhere, the top of the Himalayas, for example, with a mobile phone and a modem and watch an NFL game live if that plan were in place. It is a result of how TV, which has been the engine driving professional sport in the United States and in Europe, can work hand in hand with the Internet to maximize revenues. Revenue enhancement is the most important thing to make all games and sport even more available to people. That is going to be a continual process. Who knows...maybe in 20 years some new invention will change the face of sport.

With respect to job opportunities, I think information technology is the place for growth. The NFL has people on the IT side trying to figure out how to best use the Internet. I think there is a lot of general job opportunities because of globalization. The keys there are language skills and cultural sensitivity.

Over the past 10 years I have been most proud of taking a true start-up, where I was literally the first employee, and turning it into something with stability. People are buying season tickets, games are being broadcast, and the media are writing about us. Having that start-up opportunity was the most satisfying thing I have done. I suppose the lesson for students is that if they do have a chance, particularly when they are young and not so tied down, to look into start-up opportunities. It is a good thing to do if the opportunity arises.

I will say a couple of things to people aspiring to a career in sports. First, if you have an opportunity to do something unusual, do it. Everybody thinks they are going to work for the NFL, the NBA, or professional teams. I think they can learn a lot more with smaller organizations such as minor league baseball or the Continental Basketball Association. At the end of the day they have done the same things people do in the big leagues. It is really just the number of zeroes after the comma that is the difference, but the same concepts are in place. They would be better off, early in their career, trying to do one of two things. Either go to work for a smaller organization and learn the requisite skills, or work for a corporation outside of sport. Believe me, if they do a good job in the minor leagues, people in the big leagues will notice.

The second option is to not necessarily get hung up on working for a sport organization right away. A lot of the skills learned as a brand manager at Proctor and Gamble or working for any of the big blue chip corporations are transferable to sport. Spending 3, 4, or 5 years learning basic marketing, sponsorship, organizational, public relations, or television skills will prepare you well for the sports world. This is the advice of Paul Tagliabue, the commissioner, so it must be good advice. They can help themselves by moving outside of the sports world, developing skills, and then making more of a lateral move into a sport organization.

A third thing I would say to people is no matter position they are in, everything they do from the first minute they get into the job is being measured. I am ultimately responsible for the hundred or so people we have here, keeping them happy with a career path and promoting or firing when necessary. It dawned on me I am not even 40 but everything I do is being watched and measured. Students need to try as hard as they can, ask as many questions as necessary, and try to do the best job possible. Be very proud of your work product no matter how insignificant it may seem because it all adds up at the end of the day when people are making decisions about promotions. It is common sense, but every new job in a sense, is a try-out for the next job. It is similar to when a coach asks an athlete, "What have you done for me lately?" Do not rest on your laurels. If you can look at it as if every new job is really nothing more than a try-out for the following job, I think that keeps in perspective how important it is to work hard. At the same time, enjoy life, do not be a workaholic knucklehead, go home at 7 PM, and really try to do the best you possibly can. At the end of the day all you have are your reputation and your work product. They are very closely linked. That is ultimately how people get promoted or—in a lot of cases—passed over.

Nancy M. Gonsalves

Manager of Paralympics
Salt Lake Organizing Committee for
the Olympic and Paralympic Winter
Games of 2002

Education:
B.S., FINANCE, BOSTON COLLEGE, 1985
M.S., SPORT MANAGEMENT, UNIVERSITY OF
MASSACHUSETTS AT AMHERST, 1992

Career Progression:
MANAGER OF PARALYMPICS, SALT LAKE
ORGANIZING COMMITTEE, 1999 TO PRESENT
ASSISTANT DIRECTOR/GAMES OPERATIONS,
UNITED STATES OLYMPIC COMMITTEE,
1991–1999
RESOURCE CENTER & PROGRAMS ASSOCIATE
DIRECTOR, WOMEN'S SPORTS FOUNDATION,
1988–1990

Best advice for someone aspiring toward a career in the sport industry:

**"Gain as much practical experience as possible. Pick an internship
where you would want to work full time and then work as if you
are a permanent employee."**

Quote by which you live:

**"Be brave. Even if you are not, pretend to be.
No one can tell the difference."**

I KIND OF FELL INTO MY CAREER by chance, like a lot of people did. I
went to Boston College from 1981 to 1985 as an undergraduate majoring in finance and fully expected to become a loan officer or a chief financial officer
someday. I was also a student athlete and played field hockey and lacrosse. Those
in the Boston area will remember it as the Flutie years, the Flutie frenzy. Boston
College was inundated with media requests and did not really know how to handle a Heisman candidate. Being involved in sports and having friends on the football team, I helped out when I could in the sports information office. Simultaneously our basketball team went to the NCAA Sweet Sixteen that year, and the ice
hockey team went to the NCAA Final Four. It was really exciting being around
the media crush. All of a sudden it dawned on me that while I was preparing for a
degree in finance, all these people had jobs in sport. Although it was just a college

experience for me, I realized this was another path to pursue. I started getting the inkling that I wanted to pursue a career in sport after college.

In the back of my mind I had this sports thing, but it really was not anything concrete. It was just kind of an idea that subconsciously floated around in my head. I went to work in sales for Pitney Bowes and hated it! I soon started sending out letters blindly and went through the Sport Market Place and to see what was available. I had no experience related to it. My first job in sports was an internship with the Women's Sports Foundation in New York City. I heard about it through a friend of a friend who knew one of the founding members. I did the internship for 3 months and it became a full-time job. I was there for 2 years until I decided I did not want to stay in New York City.

Then I applied and went to graduate school at the University of Massachusetts-Amherst (UMass). The master's degree was a 1-year program. It appealed to me because I already had a job in the sport industry and I did not want to leave for 2 or 3 years and then try to get back into it. It was like a sabbatical versus eliminating myself from the field. I also had ulterior motives to go back to school so I could do an internship with the U.S. Olympic Committee (USOC). It is a great intern program, but only students could participate. So I became a student so I could get into USOC as an intern. In retrospect, it worked out just like I planned; however, in hindsight it is ironic or amazing that it actually did happen that way. My internship at USOC became a full-time job for 7 years.

On my resume I have a number of different titles at the USOC including intern, special projects coordinator, and games manager. Then I became disabled games and operations manager. From 1997 to 1999, I was an assistant director in games operations. I left there in April 1999 to work for the Salt Lake Organizing Committee for the Olympic and Paralympic Winter Games of 2002.

I guess my career path was normal for the industry in the sense that I got started through internships. Everyone has a different way of getting into the industry. It is very important to do an internship to get a foot in the door. Networking is essential. I got the internship at the U.S. Olympic Committee because one of my references was Mickey King who helped form the Women's Sports Foundation. Mickey also used to be a coach and professor at the Air Force Academy in Colorado Springs and she was an Olympic diver. When my eventual boss was looking at the intern candidates he was really busy that summer at the Pan American Games. All he had was this reference for me from Mickey. Because he knew Mickey and he was referring Nancy Gonsalves, he figured she must be good. That was how my foot got in the door. I think that is normal in the sport industry.

Here is an important message: do not take your internship just to finish your degree. I actually did not get offered the USOC internship until late summer after graduate school. They asked if I wanted to defer to the fall and I said yes, but I took another internship with Golf Digest that summer. I could have gotten credit and graduated then. When the Golf Digest internship was ending, I received the call from USOC asking if I was still interested in a fall internship. I just registered again at UMass for the fall semester and did my paperwork based on my internship at USOC. The Golf Digest job had the potential to turn into a full-time job, too. I declined it to do the internship with USOC because that is where I really wanted to head. I get so frustrated when I hear of students who take an internship to do something to get it over with because they really should do their internship where they want to work—and then work as an intern as if they already have the job.

In my internship at USOC I became involved in some real projects. When my internship ended it was December 1991. USOC was on its way to Albertville, France for the 1992 Winter Olympics and then Barcelona, Spain for the Summer Games. My boss realized no office staff would remain so he asked if I would stay through the Olympics. Of course, I said yes! My contract was expiring when the Barcelona games occurred yet I was already working on ticket packages for the 1994 Lillehammer Games as a contracted employee. It was one of those situations in which I was the only one who knew the job duties so I was given full-time status. Most of the people at USOC who are 20 to 30 years old came through the same internship path.

The Women's Sports Foundation was a great experience because it opened a lot of doors. In my job I got to talk to people. I did the whole International Hall of Fame research and election as one of my projects. I talked to the national governing bodies and USOC several times a year to get candidates and do research and also in some other areas. I dealt with college sports. I went down to the Super Show and worked a booth for the Women's Sports Foundation. I was exposed to many different areas. I was most enthused when I was either dealing with USOC or talking to an Olympian. I think that goes back to being a female athlete. For me the Olympics was the highest I could ever go in my sport, and so when I was talking to someone involved with the Olympics I always just thought it was extremely thrilling.

When I did research for the Hall of Fame and talked to each of the national governing bodies, the people who generally helped me were the media interns. That is how I got to know that USOC had the internship program, that sport management careers exist, and sport management degree programs exist. At the Women's Sports Foundation, the Hall of Fame event culminates in our big fundraising dinner every year, which is a wonderful dinner honoring women in sports. It is a huge production and it is a gala affair. A lot of the times I did the housing and accommodations for the athletes. That also started me down the path of logistics and operations and event planning. It is 15 years later and I am still doing housing and accommodations, logistics, operations, and meeting planning!

I think that being female, although it is not necessarily always an obstacle, sometimes is. When I am sitting in a meeting, I subconsciously look around the room and count how many females are there. With the Salt Lake Organizing

Committee I still notice it, but at some meetings there are more women than men, which is encouraging. However, when the International Olympic Committee and the International Paralympic Committee are in for a visit, the number of women in management drops off considerably. It is still a man's world out there for the Olympics. This could be a negative because they need to expand on the women's sport program. I know the U.S. women athletes are the ones who bring home most of the Olympic medals!

For my age, I definitely look about 4 to 8 years younger than I am, which is a slight hindrance. One of the coaches I dealt with on the phone leading up to the Paralympic Games got to Nagano and needed to find Nancy Gonsalves. He saw this woman in her 50s who does our games records and thought she was me. When I went up to him and said, "Hi, I'm Nancy Gonsalves," he just looked at me. He was kind of overwhelmed as it was his first games, and he thought there were children running this event. He had a completely different mental image of the stature of the position. He told me all this later only because he realized I was very capable and competent to do the job and knew what I was doing. It was actually sort of amusing.

My job description is a little nebulous now. The mission of the Salt Lake Organizing Committee is to organize the Olympic and Paralympic Games. These are the first Olympic and Paralympic winter games to be fully integrated. Although the Paralympics follow the Olympics, historically, these have been separate organizations. The Paralympics used a lot of the same facilities, but it was a different organization. At SLOC we are fully integrated. Everybody has responsibility for both games. For example, our Village planning has to incorporate the Olympics and the Paralympics. Everyone who has signed on realizes it is not just a 30-day event, but a 60-day event.

Now, that's the theory. The reality is the Olympics are overwhelming. It is huge! The Paralympics are not really understood. Most people planning now think the Paralympics are the same thing as the Olympics, only a quarter of the size. It is not true because in some areas it is less and in some areas it is probably more. I am trying to get each function, such as security, information technology, the Village, or medical, up to speed on its Paralympic role. In September 1999 we hired a managing director. I was hired to be number two before number one was identified because I brought a lot of experience with USOC, which also functions as the National Paralympic Committee in the United States.

At USOC I worked in the International Games Preparation (IGP) division. I thought it was the most important division. We took the U.S. team to the Games. Our group, along with other people, organized the logistics, operations, tickets, accommodations, and housing for the U.S. team at an international, multisport competition. We sent the U.S. team and then staffed it for the World University Games, the Olympic Games, the Pan American Games, and now the World Youth Games. In 1994 we added the Paralympic Games, when USOC also became the National Paralympic Committee. In 1995 I was given the job to head up the planning for the Paralympics. In retrospect, that was good because it forced me into situations in which decisions had to be made with little or no input from others. I planned things how I thought they should be planned. I developed relationships with the different disabled sport organizations. I handled selection criteria, ticketing, and housing. In that year leading up to the Games I spent 2 weeks in Atlanta every month handling Paralympic duties.

I had to learn the language of the disabled community, which has a whole different set of acronyms. I had to correspond with the International Paralympic Committee on certain issues. Although USOC was new to the whole movement, we were more advanced than a lot of countries. We were pretty far advanced because we wanted to bring the same level of staffing and professionalism to the disabled athletes as we did for the Olympic teams.

I knew from friends at the Salt Lake Organizing Committee that if I wanted to go to Salt Lake I could—and I wanted to do it. I thought it would be a natural career step. I had never worked for an organizing committee. I have always been on the client end. I did not want the managing director's job, which was advertised. However, it was a consensus that I would be a great number two, and number one would come on board in the fall. I have had my frustrations here because the Paralympics is somewhat unknown and misunderstood, and sometimes I wonder if I am just running in the wrong direction. I realize on most days I know what I am talking about. I know what I do know is valuable.

The best part of my job is the exposure. Disability sport is a hot issue because the Amateur Sports Act was rewritten to include more rights for athletes with disabilities. I serve as a resource. But again, I even learn that I know more than I think I know. I have learned so much from doing it.

I took the job at Salt Lake to grow and challenge myself. These days I find myself making a presentation to the Veterans Administration or talking to different school and community groups. It is enjoyable getting out to make such presentations. But the down side is that the Paralympics are second to the Olympics and always will be. I have to constantly remind people that our job is to put on both Games. These are deserving athletes. We need to address the issues if we are going to take on the job. No one is intentionally leaving it off, but it is hard every day to be the one to say, remember the Paralympics! It is going to take another year or so of constant reminding. People need to keep thinking about both games.

The Olympics are special, but we are under the microscope nationally and internationally. Anything that is said can and will be in the newspapers the next day. I cannot talk about work at a restaurant because someone may hear me. Everyone is very much aware of what it is. When I sit on an airplane, the person next to me can say "I'm an accountant" or "I do this..." or "I'm a sales person." When I say I work for the Olympics, the next 2 hours of the flight is all about the Olympics. It is fascinating. People are really drawn into it. Everyone has Olympic memories and moments.

The amount of work and travel are disadvantages to this job. It is not all great. Everything is under public scrutiny. I can imagine how a celebrity feels. Every day we are in the newspaper. We have pressure from the sponsors and the international community. They do not necessarily do business the way we do it. Their interests are different.

The Salt Lake Organizing Committee is fully exposed to public scrutiny, especially since the scandal broke out in 1998. Now everything is open and public. We have to generate more and more reports to the U.S. Department of Justice. We are totally open and we still have to plan and organize the event and meet our budget. We are not going to make everybody happy. We have an added responsibility to Utah citizens because the games will be held in their state. We want to leave a legacy that is positive so Utah citizens have a lot of input. But at the same time, it is a worldwide event, not just Utah's event. Utah just happens to be the location. We try to involve the community in a lot of positive ways and give the citizens the legacy, but a lot of criticism exists. Historically, every Olympics has encountered negative public opinion leading up to the event.

In this job I must handle multiple tasks simultaneously. Prioritizing those tasks that need my attention is critical. There has to be trust between people because everything is built on relationships. For me, honesty is a top priority. We are an international organization, and we are inviting the world to come to Salt Lake City. We must have cultural sensitivity and diplomacy. We have to understand other countries' timelines, their thinking, their cultures, and how they conduct business. International and cultural awareness are critical.

I would tell an aspiring sport management student who would like to have a job like mine to learn and volunteer. Get as much practical experience as possible. There are a lot of other activities they should sign on to do. Try to do as much as you can because people remember when you are kind to them. People say to me, "I remember you, you drove me to the airport." I may have picked up 20 people, but I only picked them up once. We have great conversations. When I am in a car for 25 minutes with someone I will talk and find out a little bit more about them. People came up to me when I started to get involved with the Paralympics and say "I remember you from the Women's Sports Foundation when you came to the annual meeting in Dallas." People keep resurfacing. I am working with people here at the Salt Lake Organizing Committee who I worked with before. One woman and I worked together years ago at the USOC as interns. I met a colleague who works down the hall from me when he was executive director of the State Games in Massachusetts. He has pursued a different road, but we are both in the same place now. We knew each other 15 years ago. I would say an intern should interact with people. Although the sporting world is getting bigger, it is still pretty small and very competitive. Get to know people because you are bound to see them again.

International sport is growing in different ways. A lot of it is made for television. This is what the X Games are all about. The Goodwill Games are still going. There are now the Transplant Games and Senior Games. It is going a little bit more beyond traditional sport, but I think there is obviously a place for the traditions. The Olympics are not going to go away. It is going to change, and it has changed with the professionalism and whatnot, but I do not think anyone is going to get tired of it. There are so many new sports trying to get on the Olympic program.

The awareness of the Paralympics is growing. I think we can sense it now just from the marketing of the Games. Just in general commercial sponsorship there are more disabled people in advertisements. I think disability is just one more part of our culture. There is a huge market of disabled people. Someone once said we are all just temporarily able bodied. Anyone at any time could become a disabled person. I think corporate sponsors are just starting to realize that disability touches many people. I think people with disabilities are becoming more mainstream. We see it in our schools, where students are more accustomed to having classmates with disabilities because of inclusion.

Creativity is going to be important in international sport. How can we create these events that people want to see and want to participate in? Technology has changed how we deal with a lot of things. The Internet has made it easier to communicate to some of the developing countries. It is faster than the mail and it is quicker with photos and other items. With cable TV, people have much more access. I am not going to say there is an over-saturation, but it is going to hit a point. I think we do have to be careful. Take figure skating for example. It used to be when figure skating was televised, it was the Olympics or a national championship. Now you do not know what is real or what counts anymore, or whether the event is just an exhibition. If it is competition, what does it mean? Does it mean the world championship or does it mean nothing? Is it just exhibition? The Olympic symbols are the most recognizable sport symbols in the world. The Olympics are understood everywhere. I think it just gets fogged up a little bit. It is getting cluttered by how many sports and events are being manufactured.

I think career opportunities are going to expand in international sport. There is the whole grassroots level, the national governing bodies, the elite programs, and programs from juniors on up. People are getting creative in their funding, so certain sports are growing. Snowboarding and beach volleyball came on the scene really fast. Are they going to stay? They are planning on it as far as I know. I think employment opportunities are available and this is just the amateur side of things. Hockey and baseball are expanding internationally. American football exists in Europe. Rugby is huge, and that is going to eventually come back to our way.

Women's basketball and soccer are popular, too. These sports are not just U.S. creations. Some of them have started and gotten popular in Europe and Australia and then come to the United States. We are not necessarily the lead on all these events in sports. A lot of Americans and people I know work for American football in Europe or World Cup Soccer. Those are all different opportunities. They are not just the Olympics. World Cup Soccer—for women and men—is very popular.

One reason I stayed at USOC for 8 years is because as I grew up, I thought it would be neat to be involved with the Olympics. It was a dream. For me, it was the ultimate when I landed my position at USOC. It was great, although I might not have set out concretely on paper to do it. The reason I do not know where to go next is because I never thought of it. Knowing Salt Lake was going to be the last probably big organizing committee for 12, 15, or maybe 20 years—if I was going to go that route—I was going to have to do it now. And again, here I am, guaranteed unemployment in 3 years. But I took this job to round out my experience. When it is over I will have broad Olympic experience from working on the organizing committee side, as well as the NOC perspective. I have got Olympic background, and I have done ticketing, housing, and Paralympics. Maybe someday I can start a consulting business. When the next host cities are selected and planning begins, they will come to our games and deal with my colleagues and me. I do not necessarily want to work for the Athens, Greece 2004 Summer Games or the next winter Games, but people have parlayed the Olympics into a nice consulting business. Organizers might go and look at someone's plans, and ask their opinion. Why reinvent the wheel each time? Because we are the first fully integrated winter Paralympics, people are going to look at what we did to see what works. Maybe I will consult for them on a certain project, but the travel would be grueling. This is an industry where people will bounce around from position to position. People who are in Sydney right now worked in Atlanta, and some will probably be working for SLOC by December 2000 because it is a very special thing. Then those people will go on to Athens, and then the next one, and so on.

I am glad the Olympics, the Paralympics, and amateur sport in general are getting more recognition because they do not necessarily think they come to the forefront of people's minds when considering a career. The opportunity exists if you want it.

Charles Lee Todd II

Vice President of Sports and Competition
Special Olympics International

Education:
B.A., MANAGEMENT, NICHOLS COLLEGE, 1972

Career Progression:
VICE PRESIDENT OF SPORTS AND COMPETITION, SPECIAL OLYMPICS INTERNATIONAL, 1995 TO PRESENT

DEPUTY DIRECTOR, SPECIAL OLYMPICS INTERNATIONAL, 1994–1995

WINTER SPORTS MANAGER, SPECIAL OLYMPICS INTERNATIONAL, 1989–1994

CROSS-COUNTRY PROGRAM DIRECTOR, UNITED STATES SKI TEAM AND UNITED STATES SKI ASSOCIATION, 1988–1989

NORDIC PROGRAM DIRECTOR, UNITED STATES SKI ASSOCIATION, 1985–1988

EASTERN NORDIC PROGRAM DIRECTOR AND NATIONAL YOUTH SKI LEAGUE DIRECTOR, UNITED STATES SKI ASSOCIATION, 1983–1985

Best piece of advice you received in regards to your career:

"Don't let size of the salary determine your future."

TONY CLARK, FRIEND AND COLLEAGUE

Quote by which you live:

"I like the dreams of the future better than the history of the past."

THOMAS JEFFERSON

I PROBABLY FIRST SUBCONSCIOUSLY decided to work in sport when I was a senior in high school. I say subconsciously because I was raised in a very sports-oriented family. My uncles and my father played semipro and pro baseball, and my parents exposed me to various other sports. In high school I always gravitated toward sports and in college I probably spent more time skiing than I did in the classroom!

I graduated from business school in December 1972. After spending the winter skiing, I started a small environmental landscape company that reshaped and brought land back to be used for wildlife habitat. In doing that I met a very interesting individual. He was a former marine captain and Harvard MBA graduate who started a sporting goods store outside of Boston called the Lincoln Guide Service and the Charles River Canoe Service. This individual took two sports I happened to love a great deal, bicycling and cross country skiing, added a third, canoeing, and managed a retail store that sold high-end bicycle and ski equipment and eventually canoes. He took advantage of the booming recreation movement just starting in the United States around 1974. That was the era of the kickoff of the health fads. He said to me, "I want you to come on board because you know a lot about the environment and sports and you love to cycle and ski, so would you manage my shop?" I started there and we added components of environmental education, technique education, and bicycle maintenance. Then we added bicycle tours as part of our program, including tours all over New England and Canada. We did ski tours to Norway and Scandinavia in the winter. During that same time, one of my uncles produced theater and he got me involved in theater. Theater looked very much as the same line as event production. We had to have schedules, rehearsals, and eventually there is a deadline when the curtain goes up. It is the same way with sports event management.

So, in a nutshell, my career path really was decided when an individual got me involved in sports that I loved and in an area where I could diversify. I think that was the catalyst that really gave me the incentive to stay in the business. It was a great deal of fun. Most people go into it because they love sports and they can talk it. I think in many instances people probably start off doing it because they love it, not because they can earn a huge salary.

It has always been one of my philosophies that change is good as long as it is somewhat seamless. In the retail business, the ski touring business, and the bicycling business, I would go to a lot of trade shows as a buyer for our shop. That is where I started to network. One person I met who intrigued me was an individual named Tony Clark. At the time Tony ran one of the more prestigious country inns in central Vermont. Growing up, my family spent 50 percent of our time at our farm in Vermont and 50 percent of our time at our house in Lincoln, Massachusetts, so I had roots in Vermont. Tony owned this very posh country inn located outside of Middlebury, Vermont that had a well known cross-country ski center. I was meeting with Tony there and had taken along my future wife, who is a Dartmouth graduate and former cross-country skier at Dartmouth. She and I were both really intrigued by Blueberry Hill. I went down and after another summer of working on bicycling—probably a 3-year stint with the bicycling cross-country business in Massachusetts—we decided we needed a change.

We moved to rural Goshen, Vermont, with a population of 100. There we ran the cross-country ski center where I basically started my management roots because at that point we had to hire ski staff. We developed the books. We did all of the buying. We were fully immersed in it. At that time it was only about a $100,000-$200,000 operation on the skiing side. We added cross-country skiing from inn to inn where we would cut trails and use them for skiing from inn to inn down the ribs of the Green Mountains in Vermont. As we started to do that we were always being creative and innovative. We also had some very talented people who would come through, and many guests who were wonderful. At that point the United States Ski Association came to us and asked if we would put on a major long distance ski race, and we agreed. We took on the race the first year and put together the logistics.

Because the ski business is really seasonal, although, I could stay and work during the summer, the Appalachian Mountain Club had come to us through contacts we had and asked if we would run one of their climbing lodges from May to October. We said this is something really neat for both worlds because we like the outdoors and we like hiking. I think it expanded my management skills quite a bit simply because of hiring people with a whole new skill set and high school kids and working with volunteer committees through the Appalachian Mountain Club and putting on a lot of educational seminars. I was really getting my feet wet in the world of volunteerism. We complemented that with the cross-country ski business and did that for 3 years. Going into the second year of running the ski race, the United States Ski Association felt we did a good job. I had hired some pretty good staff, and my wife was racing on the U.S. Cross Country Ski Circuit. They said, "If we paid your way and flew you from event to event, would you go to these major events around the country and basically be our seal of approval and help run these series of long distance races basically from Maine to California?" I did that while still running the ski shop. It's easy to see how a network gets larger and larger.

After the third year the ski association came back and said, "We'd like to hire you if you would want to make a move to our eastern office in Vermont where you would oversee the development of Nordic skiing in the east." This entailed bringing more people, especially youth, into the organization, reviewing the competition program in the east as well as taking on continued duties of running the race circuit. At that point I had become so enamored by events that I said, "Okay, it's on to another transition." I think that it is a huge part of what makes a good manager. If you decide to move on, you need to make that decision so the people you are leaving really understand that it is not only best for you but also it might be best for the future of the organization you are leaving.

I ended up at the Eastern Ski Association Office, and did everything I just described. As typical of the sport world where there is a lot of movement, the national director of the Nordic program decided to take a new job. The boss who was overseeing me was given a new position with the U.S. Ski Team and Ski Association and he asked, "Would you come along and be the national director?" So we relocated again out to the U.S. Olympic Committee Training Center in Colorado Springs and I oversaw the national program. At that point I started to get heavily involved in international competition because we were starting to work a lot with the International Ski Federation. We were organizing and marketing international events. I started to really get my feet wet internationally. We were not only bringing in teams to the United States, but also traveling outside the United States to the various federation meetings held on a biannual basis. The U.S. Ski

Association Ski Team then reorganized and we moved with that merged organization to Park City, Utah. I stayed for a year-and-a-half managing the entire U.S. Ski Team, U.S.A. Nordic Program, directing all of the international teams as well as the daily domestic program. It was now more than 10 years of just being in skiing and I felt I needed a career change that would bring me back to the east coast. All during the time I had been working in skiing I had also done some work for Special Olympics, purely on a volunteer basis. I helped write one of their first skiing manuals. I helped run some of their events, and I really enjoyed working with the Special Olympics athletes.

A couple of people here at Special Olympics had heard of me and had recommendations that I was a good hire. I came back here and spent a day interviewing. Mrs. Shriver (the founder of Special Olympics) personally asked me to come on and direct the International Winter Sports Program. So I left the U.S. Ski Team, but in their infinite wisdom, or maybe it was my infinite lack of wisdom, they said, "We've got to have you as a volunteer." I stayed on with the U.S. Ski Team in various capacities over the past 10 years, and am now on the executive committee of the board of directors of the U.S. Ski Team. I chair the cross-country committee, and am the assistant competition venue manager for the 2002 Olympics for Cross Country.

In my 10 years with Special Olympics I have progressed from overseeing all of the winter sports for Special Olympics to being the deputy director of international programs. In this position I oversaw all of the programs we developed outside the United States and made sure they were in compliance by establishing boards of directors and correct budget procedures, putting together proper staff and proper curriculum, and expanding their programs to reach as many athletes as possible. At International Winter Sports I oversaw six sports. I had branched out from skiing into figure skating, speed skating, and hockey.

I moved from the winter sports position to the deputy director position about 7–1/2 years ago. At that point I really was missing event management. I really wanted to get back into it, and I was actually being courted to go back to the U.S. Ski Team. I was just on the verge of making that decision when there was a reorganization at Special Olympics. They brought in a new chief operating officer, who, in turn, brought in a new chief executive officer, Tim Shriver, the son of Mr. and Mrs. Shriver. They came to me and said, "We don't want to lose you, we want you to continue on. What would keep you here?" I said, "If I could oversee and be the point person in running our world summer and winter games I'll stay." At that point they said, "You've got it," and they put me in a department where I oversaw those events.

There has been growth in my career path including growth in my responsibility by size of event, dollars, and number of athletes. A year-and-a-half later we did another internal reorganization and merged the coaches' education department with the department I ran and I became the chief of both departments.

Everything that is sports related including coaches' education, training, event management, or relationships with international and national governing bodies is now all under one umbrella.

I feel it is very important to maintain the other side of one's career—we will call it the volunteer career path. The volunteer career path, married with the U.S. Ski Association and the Ski Team, allowed me to be involved with international governing bodies and national governing bodies to see how they worked. I travel all over the world for the Ski Team and do Special Olympics on its behalf. I am involved in international meetings on both sides, and I think I have a wider scope in the decision-making processes with my staff simply because I can share my perspective; for example, I can say, "Well look, this is the way we have done it in Sweden in skiing," or "This is how the clock system works in Norway," or "This is in fact how the Japanese manage an event." It allows us in Special Olympics, being so multinational with 150 nations, to understand how best to invigorate and motivate people. I look at the two career paths and I really stress that in your personal life if you love sports, look at the volunteer aspect of it as well and—it is neat. I can truthfully say that when I hire here, I am looking for someone who has a broad range of interests and volunteering is a good way to show it.

If I would have done anything differently it was at a couple of points. When we were living in Vermont and running the country inn, I had a wonderful job offer to be the senior vice president of the Boston Shakespeare Company. That is one of those things we all experience where I had to go for a long walk, literally flipped a coin, and the coin landed for skiing. I do not know if I would have done much else other than perhaps when I was with the U.S. Ski Association, and as I mentioned, when we moved from Colorado to Park City, there was a merger. If I would have made a different decision I may have been the executive director of the U.S. Ski Team.

I have not experienced many obstacles. There have been "lulls" in my career path. When I hit an area where the lull has occurred and the challenge is not there and I polished my resume, luck has been that the organization started to change or make a move. Every time these moves have come—and I think this is true probably in many people's careers—it has been in that window where you have probably gone through the challenges of the position and seeking a promotion.

I did have some role models. One interesting one is my wife. She is an avid outdoors person, graduated summa cum laude from Dartmouth with a degree in English, but pursued her career as an engineer. She now has her own firm. She has helped educate me on how to make a more clear and concise product, which is vital when we are communicating to many of our international programs in English as their second language.

One of my mentors was Mike Farny, who combined sensitivity to the environment with a "can do" attitude. Another mentor of mine was Howard Peterson, who was just a step above me in skiing and became the executive director of the

U.S. Ski Team. He had a brilliant business mind. He understood everything about budgets including how to read them, how to set a percentage back on them, and the planning process. Through mentoring and working with him on a personal basis I was probably getting the equivalent of an MBA and being paid for it.

Another mentor of mine is Jim McCarthy, an attorney, who is the chair of the board of directors of the U.S. Ski Team. He brought more logical thinking to the organization in terms of breaking things down into components and analyzing how best to set goals tied to the mission and vision of the organization. Two other mentors are Tim Shriver, my chief executive officer, who brings the political dimension and demonstrates how to deal with people in a positive manner; and his father, Mr. Shriver, who models how to do things professionally with a smile in a humble way.

The vision and the mission of Special Olympics are to provide sport training and competition for people with mental retardation. I oversee a staff of 16 in the office and I have an expanded staff outside of the office in each of the regions around the world.

I was given the task of redesigning and restructuring the department. I looked at basic components of sport management from an international standpoint and from what I have learned from international governing bodies. I broke it down into first the World Games—a World Games division within the department. The World Games division basically oversees the huge events in North Carolina, Anchorage, and Dublin. Then I put in a second component that includes all competition below the World Games level. We have everything from the Mediterranean Games to regional games to the Peace Games between Israel and Palestine. These other events are multinational in flavor. The third division oversees coaches' education. I have tried to model that using a National Governing Bodyformat where there are various levels one can achieve, and each level has tiers of competency, not only for athletes but also for coaches. We develop our own training materials, but do it in conjunction with materials coming from the sports governing bodies. We have a tracking system that is basically a certification system that we now are driving in house through our technology system. A fourth component is extra programming that includes: Unified Sports, where athletes and their partners without disabilities compete equally on teams; NATP, which is a motorized activity program for our athletes who are severely retarded; and Women in Sports, which has expanded womens' programs in Special Olympics and also is involved in womens' sports in general. Those are the four key components of the department I oversee. Then I have a wing that oversees our technology, including a games management system and a volunteer management system. These systems run the games and also schedule and register and coordinate with volunteers.

The best part of my job is the whole oversight of these major competitions because of the diversity and challenges. One phone call can be about a contract with ABC. The next phone call can be solving a parent's problem or delegating how to solve a parent's problem. A third phone call may involve analyzing rule infractions and rule enforcement before the games. Creating crisis management and risk management plans are exciting and big challenges. We are fortunate at Special Olympics. Although we watch every cent, unlike some sports organizations we do not have to struggle for funding. We do not have to spend 90 percent of our time on fund raising. We can spend maybe 30 or 40 percent of our time raising money and the rest doing a superior job of servicing our clients—our athletes. We are very visionary. Both the Shrivers and our Chief Executive Officer Ken Shriver as well as the marketing department recognize that for us to be a leader in the nonprofit world—and from my standpoint a leader in the sports world—we need to be visionary and innovative.

Part of stress management means having to just "chill out" and think "I've got another life," "I've got to buy some time," and "I've got to recharge my batteries." My staff is pretty good at stress management. The only time we do have stress is when we get a new game situation because we constantly deal with crisis management, which is true of any event. I try to leave the job here when I go home. I think that helps with stress management.

I probably travel 150–180 days a year. Probably a good 50 percent of that has been international to every continent and that is very stressful. We do not travel business class and we do not stay in luxurious hotels. But in all cases I am relatively well taken care of when I get there. I usually have people who are really appreciative that I came and really step forward, whether it is with translators or greeting me at the plane. I have spent a tremendous amount of time in China, and I actually am no longer intimidated by a country where I cannot read the signs or understand the language. Part of it is that I have traveled a lot for 20 years. I do not look at travel as an addiction, and I am not sure if it is a perk. Some trips are a perk and some trips are not. I do see travel as an integral part of making the job as diverse as it is and part of why I have stayed. The travel has opened up a whole new world for me.

I think in this position that people skills, listening skills, and decision making are essential. The people skills are critical. My management style is a lot of one-on-one with my staff. Whether it is with our administrative assistant or the assistant vice president of our department, I will sit with them and although they know I am the boss, they also know I am a friend. I think the combination of the two works well in management. That is where I feel one-on-one interaction is important. In my management style I tend to think it is very important to listen and to reward whether individually or at staff meetings, commending good ideas, recognizing great planning, or whatever. But then I have no fear in saying "Okay, I think this is the way we're going to go and in fact, we are going to go this way, let's march."

From a management standpoint, I do not readily jump into decision making until I feel comfortable with the decision that needs to be made. My style is to first sit back and listen, and when I feel comfortable then I make a decision. I want to make a decision that rewards people and gives a concrete objective that we can target together. Part of management is trust. I really put a lot of trust in my staff. I try to convey that to my staff and in turn I think they put a lot of trust in me. I will help them in any way if something goes wrong. I have been very loyal to the organization and it really has enhanced my career path.

When dealing with people from different countries I have to listen more. In dealing with the Middle East I really have to be firm, but also I have to listen and take input. I found in China and Japan in particular where people are sensitive yet have their own cultural style and know where they are going, you know that perhaps the decision you brokered at a meeting probably is only half a decision. You have to adjust. In Europe, I call it European democracy. If the vote is eight to one, but if the one is the key person then usually it is the one that wins because that is the power vote.

Whenever I travel overseas I have to be concise and speak slowly and not in acronyms, slang, or anything else. That is crucial. For example, in skiing when I give a lecture and talk about Alpine skiing, we have skiers who want gates on Thursday morning. More than likely the simultaneous translator will translate "gate" not as a bamboo post stuck in the snow, but as a "gate" that a cow goes through. You must be very conscious of the words you choose. Once when we opened up Russia up for Special Olympics I gave a speech. The Soviet Union still existed and I had this giant Lenin looking down on me, over my head, and I gave this speech with simultaneous translation. Suddenly I realized as I was speaking that I may have been going too fast. The big tip off for me was I told a joke that I thought would work, and when I came to the punch line and there was absolutely no laughter, and I just looked out at people with headphones on and said, "Well, I blew that one." I kept going and about 2 minutes later there was this huge, warm laughter.

The worldwide economy affects what we do. The U.S. economy is great now and our programs are very strong. They have a lot of money and financial backing behind them. But when we go out around the world we find others' greatest need is money. I try to use my budget that is fairly sizable in ways where I can help people outside of the United States. Special Olympics has huge name recognition here in the United States. When we get outside of the United States it has low name recognition, so we fight that battle as we raise funds in other countries.

No matter what national or international governing body meeting you attend, the people are anywhere from 50 to 70 years old. Those people are automatically going to be moving out. I hope to still be employed in the sport world after the 2002 Olympics either with Special Olympics or somewhere else that is another seamless move. I know I probably will not be in skiing because it is time to bring in new blood. At my last meetings with the International Olympic Committee and with the International Ski Federation in Europe, people were biding their time.

Although it may be our biggest nemesis, technology could be our biggest plus. It may be as simple as what we have seen in cycling. In cycling road bikes were very popular until the mid 1980s and then mountain biking came in and became more popular. Almost 90 percent of the bikes sold today are mountain bikes whereas 25 years ago they were road bikes. Snow boarding is very popular now. I think the sport managers of the future have to recognize not only technological innovation, but also trends within the industries.

Internationally over the next 10 years I would say career opportunities will increase. International sport is where I see the career opportunities expanding in companies like International Management Group, not necessarily just agents, but event management. Events such as the X Games, the Outside Life Games, and the Goodwill Games happening on international levels. I think where corporations are looking for new and hopefully innovative events to sponsor that the money will be there. You are really looking more at event management but with the events tied to public relations and promotion, it satisfies corporate sponsor needs with marketing images and so forth.

I guess the way I look at success is that every morning when I go to work I really want to go to work, and I really want to be here, and I want the job. Sure, there are some times that I did not want to be here but for the most part no matter where I worked I have always wanted to get to the job and was challenged by it. I guess I measure it simply by a happy thermometer. I have really enjoyed it.

One of these phrases you always hear is that you cannot fire a volunteer. Well, you can but it is always difficult, and so the challenges in working for a volunteer organization are unique. The reality is that every organization is staff driven. Here with Special Olympics and with the U.S. Ski Team in the end it is staff that makes things happen. The reality is that for a volunteer organization to succeed it must be staff driven. If not, it becomes committee driven, and committee driven organizations are destined to fail.

The first and foremost challenge is finding the volunteers. We tend to be fairly good at finding volunteers at Special Olympics. The second challenge is educating the volunteers and then putting them in a situation where they will succeed and feel rewarded. I think many volunteers do so partially out of the goodness of their hearts because it is Special Olympics and partially because they may not be rewarded in their daily job. They may not be in a management role at their company, but as a volunteer they can chair a committee on figure skating. In Special Olympics that opportunity exists for volunteers. Obviously the difficulty is that volunteers not only burn out, but also they only have so much time to give. You really have to be sensitive in recognizing the burnout factor and a volunteer's time. Various statistics indicate that the average person will volunteer approximately 9 hours a month. We have volunteers who come 5 days a week. We have others that give an hour a week. We need to know that and then make sure the volunteers can succeed.

I believe in 10 years I may be "retired." I have always loved working outdoors and working in the environment. I will be involved—probably on a volunteer level—in some type of environmental work that would allow me to be outside. I still have work aspirations, and occasionally I am solicited and I have declined offers to be either a corporation's chief executive officer or chief operating officer. I have thought about working outside of the sport world for a large nonprofit organization such as the Audubon Society or the Sierra Club. I would not exclude running a company or a national governing body within the sport world. I certainly would look inside or outside the sport industry if opportunities existed.

CHAPTER 4

Legal Aspects of Sport

The legal aspects of sport are far reaching and significant. Wong and Masteralexis (1998) stated that the legal aspects or sport law can be viewed from three different perspectives. The first perspective is the application of existing laws to the sport setting. The second perspective is the creation of laws at the state and federal level to regulate sport. Wong and Masteralexis (1998) cite that 26 states have laws that regulate the activities of sport agents. The third perspective is the creation of rules, regulations, and procedures that govern sport organizations.

Although possessing a law degree is not required to work in the sport industry, understanding the law is an important skill. A sport manager will encounter legal questions and issues on a regular basis. As far as possessing a law degree, many top-level managers with professional sport teams and leagues and college athletics directors hold law degrees. The degree is useful as these individuals are involved in million dollar negotiations involving player contracts, sponsorship agreements, naming rights deals, as well as issues related to collective bargaining agreements. In these instances an expertise in the law is required beyond just a basic understanding.

Many organizations also retain the services of law firms that have lawyers with an expertise in sport. Attorneys with a specialty in sport law can also represent those plaintiffs interested in seeking damages from sport organizations for issues related to tort, contract, administrative law, or constitutional law. An attorney can receive 25 percent to 35 percent of any damages received in a civil suit.

The law degree is a degree commonly held by sport agents. Sport agency has expanded as a career orientation in the past 25 years. Sport agents represent professional athletes in the major sport leagues as well as on the major tours such as golf and tennis. They also represent professional and college coaches. The player and coach contracts of today are complex legal documents in which such terms as salary, bonuses, deferred income, guaranteed income and roster sports are negotiable (Masteralexis, 1998). The sport agent has expanded responsibilities beyond the contract negotiation including marketing the athlete, negotiating endorsement contracts, planning finances, conducting career and postcareer planning, resolving disputes, offering legal counsel, and providing personal care (Masteralexis, 1998).

The sport agent field is a competitive field where the competition to sign clients is fierce. The competition has an impact on what agents are paid to represent athletes. Agent fees are often based on a percentage of the athlete's compensation (Masteralexis, 1998). The agent will take anywhere from 2 percent to 6 percent of the negotiated contract. If an athlete signs for $2 million for one year, the agent who receives 4% will be compensated with $80,000. As far as negotiating marketing and endorsements deals, agents charge anywhere from 15 percent to 33 percent (Masteralexis, 1998). This means that the salaries of those in the agent field are varied. Those with many clients or those with a few high paid clients can make millions in a year. An agent with only a few minor league or fringe major league players could be making less than $50,000 a year.

As the sport industry continues to grow so will the importance of the legal aspects of sport. The understanding of these legal aspects is a minimum requirement to work in the profession, and expertise in the form of a law degree is an excellent credential to hold for those aspiring to a career in top-level management or as a sport agent.

REFERENCES

Masteralexis, L.P. (1998). Sport agency. In L.P. Masteralexis, C. Barr, & M. Hums (Eds.), *Principles and practice of sport management* (pp. 243–274). Gaithersburg, MD: Aspen Publishers, Inc.

Wong, G., & Masteralexis, L.P. (1998). Legal principles applied to sport. In L.P. Masteralexis, C. Barr, & M. Hums (Eds.), *Principles and practice of sport management* (pp. 87–116). Gaithersburg, MD: Aspen Publishers, Inc.

Mel Narol

Attorney
Pellettieri, Rabstein and Altman

Education:
B.A. POLITICAL SCIENCE, DICKINSON
COLLEGE, 1972

M.A., POLITICAL SCIENCE, RUTGERS
UNIVERSITY, 1974

J.D., OHIO NORTHERN UNIVERSITY COLLEGE
OF LAW, 1976

Career Progression:
PARTNER, PELLETTIERI, RABSTEIN AND
ALTMAN, 1989 TO PRESENT

ASSOCIATE AND PARTNER, JAMIESON, MOORE,
PESKIN & SPICER, 1977–1989

HONORABLE JOHN A. MARZULLI, SUPERIOR
COURT OF NEW JERSEY, 1976–1977

LAW CLERK, HANSON, PANTAGES, SELLAR
AND ZAVENSKY, 1975

OFFICE OF PUBLIC DEFENDER, LIMA, OHIO
1975–1976

Best piece of advice you received in regards to your career:

**"Always be conscientious and apply the law to seek a practical
solution to problems."**

Best advice for someone aspiring toward a career in the sport industry:

**"Sports law is an amalgam of many substantive legal areas topped by a
sports gloss. It is therefore very important to have a broad based liberal arts
and legal education focused on critical thinking."**

Quote by which you live:

"Self-criticism is the highest form of patriotism."

WILLIAM FULBRIGHT

**(This means that one should continually be critical of himself or
herself and of those projects in which he or she is involved to
always try to improve in a creative, practical matter.)**

I OFFICIATED HIGH SCHOOL BASKETBALL during college and later while
I was in law school. During my last year in law school I worked on an independent study project with a fellow student, Stewart Dedopoulos, who also was a
basketball official. We did some research on officiating. We found back then, in

1976, that there was almost no literature in the field, and only a few reported court decisions dealt with referees' rights and liabilities. We wrote the paper for school and both graduated from law school. The following year we were solicited for a subscription to a new publication called *Referee Magazine*. We decided to try to publish our paper as an article to see if there was any interest. There was no real research on officiating, and we thought this was a way we could lend our expertise as both officials and lawyers. We wrote a piece that *Referee Magazine* published. That started my whole involvement in sports law, specifically officials and the law.

I have the original letter I wrote to the publisher of *Referee Magazine* back in 1977. It said, "Here are some ideas for future articles, what do you think? Would you be interested?" He wrote back and said he had no idea what I was talking about. Twenty years later I still write a regularly featured law column for the magazine. It is kind of funny—we always laugh about it—but it shows how things have grown and how all areas of sports have become so sophisticated now that lawyers are involved in every facet of sport.

I have an undergraduate degree from Dickinson College in Carlisle, Pennsylvania. I have a master's degree in American Government from Rutgers University, and my law degree is from Ohio Northern University. There was a time I debated between a career in sports journalism and one as a lawyer. I was very involved in sports journalism as the sports editor of my high school paper, and later I worked on the Dickinson College newspaper for three years. I was going to graduate school in journalism but instead decided to go to law school because I thought I could do both by staying involved in journalism as a lawyer, which fortunately I have been able to do.

My first involvement with law was in the area of the rights and potential liabilities of sports officials. From those early articles sprang inquiries from officials who had legal questions in New Jersey and nationally because *Referee Magazine* was read by people around the country. Originally I represented officials who were sued or suits involving a claim that a player was injured during a game and it was the official's fault because of poor field conditions, poor weather conditions, or inadequate control of the game. On the other side, officials who were injured or had been physically assaulted would call me for representation. At the same time sports officials' organizations contacted me to find out about the business side of sports. Should they incorporate as an association? What were their rights and responsibilities as an organization? Should they become a nonprofit organization? The first few years I spent a lot of time in that area of sports law, and then I became involved with the National Association of Sports Officials. Back in the early 1980s I served as a member of the board of directors of that group, which is now the parent group for all officials in all sports at all levels around the country. I became chair of its board of directors in 1983 and served as a board member for 8 years. I still serve as the association's legal counsel.

From the many connections I made from writing and presenting on officials, people started asking me to speak around the country. I did, and still do, a great deal of public speaking on officials' rights, but also sports and the law, sports and society, and issues involving youth, high school, and college sport. College conferences called with questions because many of the issues were similar. Officials, coaches, and administrators face very similar issues. From that exposure and from making the contacts through articles that continued in *Referee Magazine*, I wrote articles for other athletic and general interest magazines and newspapers. My contacts broadened and eventually some of the NCAA Division I college conferences contacted me. That was probably 15 years ago. Most of these college conferences were on the east coast. They wanted to know whether I would represent them as legal counsel to deal with NCAA issues and the business issues of running a conference including liability, insurance, and marketing issues. Conferences were just starting to deal with television and sponsorship issues. I made an intentional switch to not exclusively deal with officials, but to deal with the broader aspects of sport business and litigation at the amateur level. I have spent most of my time in that area of litigation and business, mainly at the amateur level, and not very much at the professional level; although I have had matters and cases involving professional sports.

It is very hard to decipher an exact percentage of time I spend dealing with sport issues. It certainly depends on the time of the year. At the beginning of the basketball season, I am very busy with college conference issues so more of my time is spent there. Other parts of the year I spend less time on that. It also depends on what issue comes forward. The other part of what I do is business and employment law and litigation. I would say my workload is equally split between the two disciplines of (1) sports law and (2) business and employment law and litigation. They complement each other because a lot of the things I do in the sport field are really business or litigation kinds of issues. There is one difference. I always say that when applying the general principles of law to the sport world, there is a special gloss on top of the general principles of law that applies specifically to sport. In the tort area, general principles exist, but on the sport side, different standards and principles get integrated into what is usually done in torts. One of the key recent issues that has seen a lot of litigation is something I have written about and litigated: the appropriate standard of care in player vs. player injury cases. The trend is away from simple negligence and toward a necessity for an injured plaintiff to show that the other player acted with reckless disregard to recover monetary damages in a civil lawsuit.

An obstacle I faced early in my career was the lack of interest and understanding of sports law. A lot of people would say, "What is sports law?" or "What are you talking about? There is no such thing as sports law." It is kind of interesting to look back because when I was in law school there was one sports law textbook that was used at law schools because there were very few courses. That was the bible of sports law for a long time. Over the years as sports grew with television and other media sources, lawyers got more interested. Lawyers who were traditionally representing teams or doing tort litigation in any field suddenly began doing things in sports and started calling themselves sports lawyers. The field of sports law started to grow with the growth of the economic and media sides of sports. It was a hurdle to convince the public that sports law was going to be prevalent in the future. There were going to be a lot of interesting legal issues for me to be involved in. It did relate to my other practice, but it was a little different. That was somewhat of a hurdle, not only for me, but also for a lot of people. They were more like I am, that is, working in the traditional law firm setting.

I do not think I had any role models in terms of my career. Nobody really comes to mind. The only thing I can say is that my dad was a lawyer for 55 years. His famous line when I told him I was getting involved in sports was, "When are you going to become a real lawyer?" I tell that story at a lot at presentations. It took him probably 10 years to understand that part of my law practice.

Currently I am a partner in a 35-person, full service, civil practice law firm. My role is as a partner in our business law and litigation group, which is made up of about 10 attorneys. We do all types of business law and litigation. One segment of that, of course, is the sports law field, so our sport law clients are included in that segment. I am also in charge of three associates who work with me here at the firm. I am the only sport law person with my firm. Depending on the matter I will call on different people to work with me on sport matters. If it happens to be a tax matter or a real estate matter, I will call on one of the other attorneys who has expertise in that area. If it is a case that I am going to handle myself, sometimes one of the associates would work with me on the case.

I think the most difficult but also the most challenging part of my job is the diverse issues. On any given day I can deal with a sport case, a question of tax exempt status for a sports entity, an employment matter or discrimination matter for an official, or a television marketing contract that is worth millions of dollars. At the same time, on the nonsports side, I can be in court doing business or employment litigation cases, going to conferences with the judge, and handling telephone calls. It is the diversity of the subject areas that I am involved in that I enjoy. My wife is a family lawyer, all she does is divorce law. It is a very narrow field of law. I am involved in many fields of law and apply them to the sport or business world. It is pressure packed because I jump from one area to another, and I must be on my toes all day trying to think differently.

The stress level is extremely high, not only because it is law, but also because of my other duties. It takes a lot of time during the day, evenings, and weekends to be a good administrator and take care of all of those things, as well as try to be a good and creative lawyer that thinks strategically. Today's clients are very time sensitive and want things right away. If there are a hundred clients who want time, and everyone wants it right away, you have got to work very hard. It is very demanding. I do not think people understand how much pressure it is to be a good lawyer and at the same time be involved in civic, community, and professional groups. I enjoy my involvement with the civic, community, and professional groups. I am also on the executive committee of the New Jersey State Bar Association and am on track to become President in 3 years.

Every weekend I am at the office or at home catching up on cases or with my heavy involvement in the New Jersey State Bar Association. There is a lot of work I do now on weekends. People do not really understand that being a lawyer is so paper and pencil (and computer) intense and involves so much written communication. Everything must be in writing. I cannot just rely on phone calls like my father did when he was practicing law. Everything now has to be memorialized because you are doing so much and so is the other attorney. Without that people forget what they said and what they did and the client wants to see something concrete. You have to document everything. Lawyers have to digest, understand, and convey back to a client a tremendous amount of written materials. Reading is probably the most time-consuming task for lawyers. I read every day from the time I get to the office in the morning at 7:30 AM until about 6:00 PM, and then after dinner when I am at home I read. The ability to digest all that information is a real skill to hone over one's career.

I never have a typical day. It is very different each day. One day I can be in court all day. Another day I may give a speech in the morning and the afternoon I am in court, then I work on a brief late in the afternoon, and at night I review an associate's work product to go out to a client the next day. Each of these activities could involve different subject areas.

I like the variety in my job and I really love the sport side. The sport side is very visible, and that visibility increases the pressure, especially at the college level. Many times what I do is novel or gets out to the public or is in the public eye. That adds a lot of pressure. It has to be done right. The sports cases are the great and fun parts in terms of my practice.

A standard by which I have lived my personal and professional life is self-criticism. I, personally, ask the people who work with me to be constantly critical, to look at what we are doing and try to do it better. Always think of something that has not been done. Do not continue to say "Well, that is what the law is," or "That's what the document says." Think about what it is you can do to move it to the next step and try to be creative in some way to assist a client or society.

In this profession, critical thinking skills are very important. Those skills come from my very strong liberal arts education at Dickinson College. A hallmark of a liberal arts education is critical and strategic thinking. I am very much a strategic thinker. When I do something key in a case I think about how it will appear in court someday in the future. If it is a contract negotiation or advice to a client, after I write it I ask myself, "What is the reaction going to be to what I wrote?" Yesterday I was at a meeting of college presidents for one of the Division I conferences I represent. In each meeting we prepare a legal report of what we are working on. I know what they are looking for now, but I also have to try to decide in my mind strategically what they want at the next step. I am very careful about that, and I try to tell people who report to me to plan, be conscientious, and think strategically about problems.

If someone is thinking about a job like mine the first thing I would tell them is to look for a niche, look for something that has not been done before. That is what happened to me because no one was focusing on officials. Still today hardly anybody does to the extent I do. Look for a niche. Look for a real slant on an area of interest to you. Then write about it by going out and meeting people in the field. The Sports Lawyers Association has been very helpful to me and to a lot of young people who want to get into the field. Meet people in the field, talk with them, and do whatever possible in that field. What is important is building the relationships and networking. Find the people and build the relationships. Then if you have a niche and you can write something, try to get published. I know an attorney in Washington who is a noted sports attorney. He started the way I did. He wrote an article while he was in school about cable television and sports. Back then people did not know anything about cable television, much less about sports on cable. He had done some work on it, was interested in journalism, and within a few months one of the professional sports teams called him to talk with him. He was in his early 20s. That is how his career started. He found his niche.

Even in college athletics there were very few people 10 years ago who spent any time representing college athletic conferences. If most college athletic conferences, even NCAA Division I, had lawyers, they used them very sparingly. It is only with the growth of the economic side of Division I sports that colleges are consulting attorneys more for the planning of the athletic events, marketing, sponsorship, contracts, television, and the Internet.

A hot topic in sport law now is the area of sports torts. That is, when will the court system allow a sport participant who is injured in a sporting event or related to a sporting event to sue in court? There has been a real societal trend and court trend away from allowing people to sue for injuries sustained during a sporting event. That is an area I personally get involved in litigating and writing about, and I agree with the court trend. When I say sport participants I mean officials, coaches, or fans. There is a real trend away from allowing lawsuits in that venue unless there is some specific conduct, what is called the reckless disregard for the other participant or gross negligence. I think that is a good trend because otherwise any time anybody is hurt connected to a game they can make an argument that someone was careless or negligent and therefore they should be able to sue. That would have a serious, chilling effect on athletic participation and drive up the cost of participation tremendously because of insurance costs. It does not just apply to the players. There is a trend also with regard to suing officials. For example, many states now have laws saying an official can only be sued for something he or she did during the game that caused an injury if the official was grossly negligent. The same principle is being applied to coaches in many states. That is a trend that started probably in the early 1990s, and it remains. I believe 14 states have now adopted this theory of saying things that happen on the field or in the arena should stay there because you accept some responsibility by participating in sports. However, they draw the line and indicate that if it is reckless, then you should be able to recover. That is a hot button issue now in sport. I think other areas include licensing, Internet, television sports, and protection of and bundling the rights to maximize the economic gain for clients.

When I do contracts now there are clauses in them that say we own the rights anywhere in the world. One of my clients is a very large sports marketing company, and we do contracts with colleges or conferences where he owns the rights to the X, Y, or Z university sports program. In the contract it now must stipulate that he owns those rights worldwide on any medium. If he wants to sell advertising on the Internet he has the right to do so. I knew nothing back in the 1980s about television and sport or the Internet and sport and very little about the marketing side of sport. I have learned through my clients and by getting involved, reading, and attending seminars. It is a learning process in a new field such as sports that is constantly growing. When a problem presents itself that I know very little about, I must learn the field through intense reading before I can actually give the clients what they need.

As far as trends in the next 10 years, lawyers have to learn a lot more about technology in sport. It is an issue in terms of college and professional sports, and lawyers are not up to speed on the laws of technology. Little law exists in the whole area of the new media of technology. I think career opportunities in the sport law field are great. More opportunities exist now than ever before. I think one opportunity is in sport insurance. I do not think lawyers have gotten involved much in how to write insurance, what events should be insured and how, and then handling the interpretation of the events, especially with international events.

In the future I really want to continue to practice law in the traditional way I practice it now. I would also like to go back into teaching a sports law course. I taught the sports law course at Seton Hall University for about 10 years. I have not done it for about 3 years, and I would like to get involved again. I think I am beginning to be successful. I have been very fortunate to be involved in a number of organizations, especially the New Jersey State Bar Association. I am beginning to feel like I have made a dent and tried to carve out my niche. Maybe when I can do that at a fuller level and make an impact on legal principles and society I will be more successful.

An issue I have examined over the years, and one that sport managers need to be aware of, is assaults against officials. Back in 1986–1987 stories of assaults against officials were often in the news. Many officials were being assaulted, and I represented a number of them. The thought came to my mind that there needs to be some deterrent. In doing some research I found there were state laws protecting educators, firefighters, and police officers from assault. If someone assaulted one of those kinds of people there would be a more serious penalty because they were authority people, and society wanted them to be respected. Therefore, if you punched an officer in the mouth you were going to jail for a longer period of time than if you punched a citizen in the mouth. So I created a piece of model legislation on assault and officials and got the National Association of Sports Officials to promote it around the country. For the past 13 years, I have been very involved in promoting and moving that legislation around the country. Now I believe 14 or 15 states have passed that model law in some form. If someone assaults an official it is either a felony in certain states, which requires a longer jail time and a substantial fine, or it is a high misdemeanor, which requires a substantial fine and maybe some jail time, as opposed to a very minor offense, which was the way it used to be treated. I am very proud of my involvement because even though we hear about assaults on officials we have heightened the awareness about this whole issue. Back in the 1980s officials would not come forward because they were fearful if they complained about being assaulted that they would not be assigned any more games. We have raised that consciousness to where officials now think they are professionals. Something happens when they can step forward and say, "I've got this problem. I'm going to use the legal process if necessary to protect not only me, the official, but also the game, because if we don't keep doing this it will get worse and worse." In the 1990s we saw the violence increase again.

I think violence has increased for a couple of reasons. The economics at stake is one reason. Even at the lower levels, say high school, parents push kids and kids push themselves for college scholarships. Today college scholarships are worth $30-$40,000 a year. If they feel someone is responsible for their child's sport-related injury and impeding on their progress, they are going to go after them. If they feel they are not doing as well as they can in the sport and they are frustrated, they look to sue somebody. That somebody is usually the neutral person out on the field, or on the ice, or in the arena—the official—so there is more aggression toward that person. The second reason is in general in society there is aggression toward authority, and sports is no different. There is just so much more intensity in sport, and therefore more opportunity exists to have aggression occur. There is also the media side. We can see when plays happen or mistakes occur. We see them replayed over and over again, and that causes people to criticize officials. When officials make the call, one team or 50 percent of the players are unhappy every time. The official becomes the target. It is never the player's fault, it is always the official's fault. That is what we are hearing still despite our strong belief that society and sport go together in a very appropriate way. Some people have taken sport maybe a bit too far at the younger level. Officials educate and teach as well as control the game, and we have lost some of that. This issue continues to bother me because I speak about the role of parenting kids in society and the officials' role here. We still fight the issue that the official is not the target. The official is present to ensure the participants have a safe, educational, and athletic experience.

When I reflect back on my career I think I might be a little different than some people. I am a traditional lawyer in a traditional firm but doing some sport law. When most people hear sport law they think of the people who are agents representing players. More people are doing sport law now in traditional law firms because they represent clients who are athletes, coaches, sport organizations, teams, leagues, schools, colleges, etc. I repeat what I said before. The key to success is to be self-critical, conscientious, and find your niche and then go out and get after it.

André L. Farr

Chairman/CEO
Black Sports Agents Association

Education:
B.A. HISTORY, UCLA 1992

Career Progression:
THE BLACK SPORTS AGENTS ASSOCIATION, CHAIRMAN/CEO

HOUSE OF BLUES SPORTS, PRESIDENT, CEO

STANLEY AND ASSOCIATES, DIRECTOR OF CLIENT SERVICES

UCLA ATHLETICS, SPORTS MARKETING ASSISTANT

Best piece of advice you received in regards to your career:

"I don't know the key to success but I know the key to failure, and that's trying to please everybody."

BILL COSBY

Best advice for someone aspiring toward a career in the sport industry:

Make sure it is your passion before your pursue it.

Quote by which you live:

"It is far better to walk a race and finish than it is to run as fast as you can only to discover you're running in the wrong direction."

MY NAME IS ANDRÉ FARR and I am the chairman and chief executive officer of the Black Sports Agents Association (BSAA) based in Los Angeles, California. I got into the sport business as an agent because many of my family members have been or currently are professional athletes and I was curious about the business side of sport and entertainment. Once I negotiated a pretty lucrative deal for my little brother, DeMarco, who currently plays for the St. Louis Rams. Also, I was chosen to head this initiative, the BSAA, to bring more African Americans into a prominent position of representing athletes.

I went to the University of California at Los Angeles (UCLA) as an undergraduate. While at UCLA, I majored in history and communications and was a 4-year varsity football player. I was very involved in entertainment promotion. I promoted concerts and parties at UCLA and got my feet wet in the entertainment capital of the world. As I grew in the entertainment production practice, I learned the different nuances of producing shows and getting along with entertainment people, and I also got to see the business aspects of entertainment. I learned that being behind the scenes would help me be prosperous longer and it is a much easier road emotionally than being in front of the camera or on the field.

After pursuing those interests, the opportunity to help rewrite the script of a movie called "The Program" just sort of fell in my lap. Once I did that we flew to South Carolina to film the movie and I was hooked. I said, "This is definitely what I want to do." Once I graduated from UCLA I did not even consider any offers to play professional football. I went directly into the business working for my uncle, Mel Farr, who is a highly respected and successful black businessperson. I worked for him for 2 months and got an offer to become a partner with Jerome Stanley, an agent who had just negotiated the richest contract in NBA history at that time for Reggie Lewis. He wanted me to help him start to bolster his football business. I signed with him and stayed there a year and a half. We ended up signing Keyshawn Johnson, the number one pick in NFL draft overall in 1996. Then I became the chairman and CEO of BSAA.

The decision to major in history helped me tremendously because one thing I have always believed—and I believe it now even more—is that history repeats itself. We really cannot know where we are going unless we know where we have been. The study of American history and business history will help students tremendously in the business world. Predictions from many business experts have come to light today in terms of technology, business structure, and financial indicators. I have benefited from the lessons I learned in college. Also, I think college in general teaches some form of discipline. Students learn how to balance several projects and classes every semester to meet various deadlines. I learned more about research and how research could be used to my advantage. But the most important thing that college life taught me is that life is not based on one quarter or one semester. Students may not have a great semester, for example, in the first part of the year, but the second part of the year can be completely different. There is always an opportunity to finish up real strong. That is something that I have carried over in my businesses. Sometimes things will slow up. Things may not go well early, but there is always tomorrow.

I invested a great deal of thought and research into my career development. In sport management, it is a little bit more difficult to do career exploration because people are not that open in terms of teaching, and there are not a lot of schools that offer the degree. Only a few business management programs offer sport management degrees. I was fortunate because my family has been and still is involved in sports and we have a tremendous number of contacts in sport management, athlete representation, and entertainment. I learned under the tutelage of Jerome Stanley and other agents. I learned from practical experience that this is definitely what I wanted to do. I have done a lot of on-the-job learning and development, but not in the traditional sense of doing an internship with a team or league and then advancing from there. I have been fortunate to take advantage and capitalize on the network that was available to me.

Early in my career, I also headed up the Sports Division for House of Blues. That position came along right at the time I was about to wrap up my term with Jerome Stanley. Keyshawn Johnson basically wanted to have a draft party, and I was in charge of that party for our firm. I did not particularly like the way the House of Blues management was handling the party, so I demanded to see the owner. One of the employees said—sarcastically I guess—"He's here, would you like to meet him?" I said absolutely. We met, and a 2-minute conversation turned into a 3–1/2 hour conversation. From that conversation the House of Blues Sport Division was born. It became a division of House of Blues that promoted sport through radio and television, sold merchandise, and had live music performances associated with sporting events.

I owned 51 percent of the entity and House of Blues owned the other 49 percent. That was an amazing experience for me. It taught me a lot about partnering with a corporation that was big enough to be on the national radar screen with regard to Wall Street and initial public offerings. It also taught me how to deal with publicity and how to deal with the expectations of national media. I also learned how to deal with branding, licensing, and merchandising. It was an incredible experience. It was something I would not trade. I was with House of Blues 2 years, from the time I was 25 years old until I was 27. After that I became the chairman of BSAA.

There are some obstacles that I have faced as my career progressed. When I was with Jerome Stanley, I always wanted to include entertainment in our sport practice. He was interested, but it was not a priority for him. That was an obstacle because he was the owner of the business so basically I could only make suggestions, and not just go out and do what I thought was best. With House of Blues, it started out great because the founder of the House of Blues backed all my ideas for the Sports Division. The major obstacle, however, was that the corporate types came in, did a corporate takeover, and got rid of him. They did not see the vision. They basically cut all divisions except for one. I think we had nine divisions at the time and House of Blues Sports Division was one of them. We were probably one of the only profitable divisions in the company outside of the live music acts. Dealing with the corporate side and people who only focus on the bottom line and have no vision was a major struggle for me. It also let me know that the next time I get involved with a major corporation, I will make sure I keep total control of the creative process. That is the way I operate most effectively.

The major struggle with BSAA was dealing with agents because it is such a highly competitive business. A lot of the agents simply did not like or trust each other. To bring agents together collectively to form a more stable foundation was difficult. I tried to establish a way to create more opportunities and profitability for African American agents. Once I gained the trust of the agents and they started to see that I did not want anything from them and did not plan to do anything bad to them, they embraced BSAA and me, and we have grown.

An obvious role model for me is Mel Farr, my uncle, who is just a tremendous success in business. He was a success on the field for the Detroit Lions for many years. He has influenced me in many ways, but particularly because of his staying power. He is an incredibly focused individual, and he shows me every day that if I stay focused on a goal, continue to move toward that goal, and not be daunted by any obstacles that sooner or later I will succeed. Mel Farr is a great testament to that because in 1979 his whole empire was bankrupt. I am happy to say in 1998 his companies grossed almost $600 million. He is a testament to the staying power of focus. I take that example and try to run with it.

Ray Anderson is another person who impresses me and whom I admire. He is a tremendous success as an agent and attorney based out of Atlanta. He represents Dennis Green, the Minnesota Vikings head coach; Tony Dungy, the Tampa Bay Buccaneers head coach; and several players. Ray is just a stand-up guy. He is an honest person. He has shown me that honesty, perseverance, character, and integrity are the main ingredients to success in life. It may not come quickly, but it will definitely come. Jesse Jackson is another person who has positively influenced my career. Jesse Jackson is one of the people who actually brought together BSAA. He thought that the number of athletes being represented by African Americans was far too small compared with the number of African American professional athletes. He thought there was wasted revenue that African Americans were not controlling so he brought the agents together. We took it from there and ran with it. Jesse Jackson is a visionary. He is someone who can see problems and communicate how they can be solved or at least provide the pieces of the puzzle that need to be put together. He is a man respected worldwide and he has had a tremendous influence on me.

Some of my role models have nothing to do with sport. For example, Don Cornelius, the founder of Soul Train, has an office downstairs from me. His staying power is tremendous. Quincy Jones has been a great influence on me. Bill Cosby is another role model. I am a person who likes to study people, see what they do, take positives from them, and put it together and make it my own. That is what I really try to do. I learn a lot from not only the professionals who have been in the business for many years, but also from students. I am always learning. I think life is one big classroom.

My ultimate goal in life is to be at peace with myself and be content with how I live my life. My ultimate goal is to know that I fulfilled what the Lord has put me on the earth to do. My business goal is to make as much money as possible in the sport and entertainment world and to establish entities that become institutions that would flourish, with or without my help. I want to employ as many people as possible that are passionate about sport and entertainment.

My main responsibility is to continue to grow the organization and to create more opportunities for minorities in sport. Currently, we have about 1,496 members. Some of my everyday responsibilities are dealing with my board of directors to ensure a clear path to accomplish our goals. I counsel our new members to give them a clear path on success in the sport industry. That success could be in many different categories, such as sport management, publicity, entertainment, and so forth. I guess one of my most difficult tasks is helping agents negotiate contracts. Agents will call me in the middle of the negotiating process and ask my advice in terms of what questions they should ask and how they should negotiate a player's contract. BSAA is used as a large information bank because I know the details of nearly every contract being negotiated at any given time. I know which player is being offered what amount, for how long, and how the contract is configured. I share that information with the agents, giving them a little bit more leverage in the negotiation process.

A large part of our business is to produce an annual convention, special events, workshops, and seminars. When I have time, I speak at different colleges and universities. In 1997 I spoke at 26 law schools and in 1998 I went to about 15 schools. We are trying to increase that to around 25 again. That is basically what the job entails.

The most demanding aspect of my position is the amount of time I spend doing my job or some aspect related to it. I am the conduit between the many different aspects of this business, but for me to be able to take a vacation for 2 or 3 weeks is almost unimaginable at this time. Things would not move for 2 or 3 weeks. The time commitment is the most demanding part of being the person in the top position of an organization. I would like to grow this organization to where I can delegate a lot of that responsibility, but it is hard to delegate trust. When people only trust me to make key decisions, it gets pretty difficult to delegate. I guess with more success growth, I will have a little more leeway to do that.

The most enjoyable aspect of this job is seeing people accomplish their goals. I get tremendous satisfaction from seeing young students wanting to be agents knowing nothing about the field. They may have been trying for years to get into the business and have not had the opportunity. No one would afford them an opportunity to work as an intern or learn about negotiating. I enjoy seeing those people go through our whole program, sign their first athlete, and negotiate the contract. Just to see the joy on their faces is tremendously rewarding. Sometimes they do not actually stay in the business, but the fact that they had the opportunity to try is gratifying. It truly is a joy to see that. Seeing a young agent come around, get certified, and sign a player, even if it is a minimum wage contract, is exciting.

To see the look on their face and the confidence that is in them because now they know they can do it is great. They realize athlete representation is a skill that needs to be developed. Once they go through it, that is the greatest thrill.

I usually get to the office at about 8:30 AM during normal times of the year but when we have special events I get here about 7:00 AM Basically, the first thing I do is listen to messages, and there are always a lot of either voice-mail or e-mail messages. I try to answer as many of those as I can in the morning. Before I call people I always read the sports page, the *Los Angeles Times*, and the *Sports Business Daily*. I read the *Sports Business Journal*. I check a lot of electronic news sources to make sure that everything is the way I left it the day before. I check to see if any changes occurred that I need to be aware of and to make sure I am staying abreast of what is happening in the sport world. I return calls in the morning, and I may have meetings with potential sponsors who want to partner with BSAA. I may have a meeting or two with agents in person. I am constantly on the phone with one of my board members. At some point during every day I talk to at least one of them.

About midday I may start to write an article for our newsletter. I will write an article for a newspaper like *USA Today* or the *Los Angeles Times,* and after lunch I work on my contract negotiations. That takes me to the end of the day around 6:00 or 7:00 PM At the end of the day I leave myself notes as to what I need to get back to the following day.

My job requires a tremendous amount of travel. I spend more time traveling than I do in the office. I travel for speaking engagements and special events. I travel to meet with different agents about the business or about opportunities for our association and for our members. I have been traveling out of the country a lot now currently seeking out some of these opportunities. Looking at my typical day, it does not seem like I have a lot of time to receive phone calls, but I get about 200 phone calls a day. During events such as the annual conference, football or basketball meetings, the NBA draft, or the NFL draft, that 200 number is very, very low.

As chief executive officer, I manage the association, which means the buck stops with me. I am the person ultimately responsible for the association's finances including payroll, office expenses, advertising budgets, and all other aspects of running a successful business. Also, I have to be somewhat of a counselor/referee for my employees because the work environment is very competitive, just like the business. I like to keep it fun, exciting, and youthful, but discipline is essential for everything to work correctly. I am also the encourager and the person that has to reprimand my staff. There are 11 employees. Ultimately the board does have the final say in major decisions, but I do vote with the board. I have been fortunate to have a board that follows my lead, has a tremendous amount of respect for me, and believes in me. Whenever I really want to make something happen I have not had a problem with my board.

A major external factor that affects my business and BSAA is any kind of salary cap adjustment. Salary cap issues, agent issues, collective bargaining agreement issues, or anything that will affect an athlete or an athlete's pay basically affects the agent and the agent's pay. That affects my business. Any time someone is laying down legislation that would put a ceiling on the amount of money an athlete may earn, it affects my business.

The negative perception of agents does not really affect the business too much because people who are in the business understand the negative perception, but it does not necessarily affect them. I hear a lot of jokes about lawyers and how negative and unscrupulous lawyers can be. But when someone is in trouble, needs to go to court, and needs someone to defend them, who do they call? A lawyer. It is the same thing in this business. Athletes have to use agents if they are going to get the best contract. Just because a negative stereotype of a few agents exists does not mean all agents are that way. With BSAA, we have cleaned up the active agents, and I think we have raised the bar on people's perception of agents. That negative perception does not really affect my job.

I guess the greatest stress I face is the number of hours I put into BSAA. I may work 12 hours at the office and then go home and talk on the phone some more. I am always thinking about ways to make the business better and ways to create more opportunities, so I guess the greatest stress comes with being away from my family. A family needs undivided attention and I long to be able to give that. But I also know the incredible weight on me in regard to moving this association forward so I try to balance the two. I am a planner, so I plan that I am going to retire from the day-to-day operation of this business at the age of 35. I am 31 now, so I have just about 3–1/2 years left and then I will not have to do this day-to-day.

I always try to encourage what I call executive decision making. Everything that comes into the office does not need to pass my desk for approval. I want the employees to make their own decisions, once they have learned what kind of decision I would make. If they would make a different decision than I would, it is because they have a different capacity to actualize a solution to the problem. Some people process things differently. I do not have a problem with people processing things differently as long as we get the same result within certain parameters. Those parameters include no cheating, no lying, and always operating with integrity. Until my employees get to the experience level where I am comfortable and they are comfortable with making their own decisions, I tell them to make the decision they think I would make. Then let me know what those decisions were. That is how I grow an executive. I do not hold their hand. I have to let them go out and make some mistakes. I let them know they made a mistake. The worst part about making mistakes is making the same mistake twice. They need to learn from each and every mistake. I, too, have to learn from mistakes.

To a student who wants to become an agent, I would recommend they join BSAA and learn the correct way to negotiate contracts, recruit players, and become a business manager. To aspire to be in my position, first of all I would not wish it on anybody, but I would say they need to have a passion for three things: sports, entertainment, and business.

The trend I see in the industry is capping of player salaries. I think that trend is going to continue for all leagues, although salaries are still going to be enormous. The biggest area for growth potential in sport for athletes is going to be through sponsorship and endorsement dollars. The players who understand marketing, imaging, and branding will take advantage of a market that spends in excess of $90 billion a year event sponsoring and sponsorship endorsement. Astute business people will see opportunity in trying to merge sport with sponsorship dollars. That is where I see the biggest growth potential.

The Internet and Web business are just incredible and will continue to grow. About 40 percent of new members of the association come through our Web site. I have never spoken to them on the phone. It is an incredible tool, an incredible vehicle to grow a business. I use it extensively to write. I put my writing on the Web site each quarter and it has been just great for us. I think it will continue to grow not only to disperse information but also to sell merchandise.

I honestly think there are not enough people aspiring to positions in sport. What people must understand is that there are sports with professional athletes who do not have an agent. Different aspects of sport are controlled by people who have no knowledge of tomorrow's technology or where the opportunities lie. I think we need to have more people preparing themselves to be sport professionals because not only is there a need to represent athletes and negotiate contracts, but also a huge gap will exist to fill in terms of sponsorships. Right now to successfully represent an athlete with any kind of marketability requires about seven people. I have seen one agent and an assistant try to do it. The more the industry grows, the more people start to grasp where the profits lie, and where new revenue streams are, the greater the need for people who are passionate about sport and also have an understanding of the sport business.

I think companies are going to see the power in athletics. Studies show that athletics and athletic teams go into the emotional fiber of a society. There was a study of New York Giants fans that found that when the Giants won, those employees who followed the Giants did tremendous at work during the week. They had higher spirits and were more productive at work. But when the Giants lost, they were a lot less productive. Even their sexual drive went down. It is amazing how fixated fans are with their teams. Once corporations start to understand that sport is the very fiber of society, they will pay more attention to sport professionals who can align them with the right sport teams and athletes.

In the sport industry I think negotiating is always going to be the number one skill a person needs. Knowledge of business management principles is the second skill sport managers need. Being able to write is essential in business. That is one thing my uncle and I speak of all the time. I think writing is a lost art form. Someone who wants to succeed must be able to write and put ideas down on paper. If they cannot, they run the risk of not passing on the knowledge they have gained. Once something is down in writing, it is amazing how many people believe the same thing and will follow the thought process and turn it into profit.

The best advice I can give to students is this: It is far better to walk a race and finish than it is to run as fast as you can and discover that you are running in the wrong direction.

Mark S. Levin

Assistant Director of Research
NFL Players Association (NFLPA)

Education:
COMMUNICATIONS, TEMPLE UNIVERSITY, 1986

Career Progression:
ASSISTANT DIRECTOR OF RESEARCH, NFLPA,
1993 TO PRESENT

MEMBER AGENT COORDINATOR, NFLPA,
1989–1992

PUBLIC RELATIONS ASSISTANT, NFLPA,
1986–1989

Best piece of advice you received in regards to your career:

"Always try to improve on what you did the day before."

FRANK WOSCHITZ, DIRECTOR OF NFLPA RETIRED PLAYERS

Best advice for someone aspiring toward a career in the sport industry:

"Be patient, pay your dues, and with hard work you'll achieve your goals."

Quote by which you live:

"Treat others the way you'd like them to treat you."

MY NAME IS MARK LEVIN, and I am the assistant director of research for the National Football League Players Association (NFLPA). I was an undergraduate at Temple University in Philadelphia, Pennsylvania, from 1982–1986 majoring in radio, television, and film with an emphasis in public relations. I started as an intern in the NFLPA Public Relations Department in the summer of 1985 between my junior and senior years. I came back for winter breaks and spring breaks during my senior year. I got the position because of a contact I made. I knew the director of the public relations department, Frank Woschitz. His son David and I went to high school together.

After graduating in 1986, the USFL Players Association, which at the time was headed by Doug Allen, was in the same office as the NFLPA. They were familiar with me and had me cover the USFL/NFL antitrust trial that occurred during the summer of 1986. Basically I just sat in on the court proceedings every day and reported back over the phone and through written correspondence in a journal I was keeping as to what went on each particular day of the trial. When that trial was over, which I believe was some time around September, I went back to Washington, D.C. and started working on a full-time, temporary basis. I went on a temporary assignment at the NFLPA working in the public relations department, which also handles membership for retired football players who are members of the NFL Retired Players Association.

My full-time, temporary status lasted for about a year until the middle of 1987 when I was hired permanently. I actually started by sharing my duties between the public relations department and the mailroom. I worked in that capacity for a couple of years and then was relieved of the mailroom activities for about a year or so and worked full-time in public relations. Around 1990 or 1991 we had de-certified as a union and there were some cutbacks in staff and changes that occurred at NFLPA. For me to continue to be employed at NFLPA I had to move to the legal department to deal with the certification of player agents. I handled all of the certification of player agents for probably 3 years and then was named assistant director of the research department, the position I currently hold.

As the assistant director of research I am the contact person for all the agents and the players for salary information, advice on the rules of the collective bargaining agreement, and advice on the salary cap and free agency. I am the person an agent calls to get advice on contact structure, length of contract, negotiating methods, and fair market value for his or her particular client. I help the agents who are representing draft picks get their clients signed and help the players make as much money as possible.

The term "research department" is something of a misnomer, but it has been around since the early 1980s. It has kept that name, although the scope of the department has changed a lot over the years, especially since the advent of the salary cap in 1993. I am the assistant director and there is a department director, another manager, two administrative assistants, and a couple of interns every semester. So, we still do get involved in "research projects," but the research department basically is the department agents call to get economic data, economic analyses, economic trends of salaries by position, by team, and by starter versus nonstarter depending on when the player entered the league. We have that data, on a consistent basis, all the way back to 1982.

My role in the department is to be the main point person for actual negotiations. The department director, Mike Duberstein, is involved in that to some extent, but he is more involved in taking the data I get from the agents and using that to do the economic analyses. He determines what is happening salary-wise and economically with franchise sales, designated gross revenues, shared revenues, and related issues. Everybody reports directly to Gene Upshaw, the executive director of the NFLPA. There is a hierarchy here, but the working environment is very informal. I sometimes go to Gene directly with an idea or suggestion. There is obviously a hierarchy and Gene's in charge, but everybody is on a first name basis with everybody. We employ, if you include our for-profit marketing subsidiary called Players, Inc., probably in the range of about 65 people. If you do not include Players, Inc., it is about 40 people.

With regard to changing anything educationally or career-wise, I probably would have gone to law school. I completed a 4-year degree, but when I was coming out I had no intention of getting into this side of the business, the representation and the salary side. I was strictly interested in public relations and the special events aspect of sport. By the time I got switched into the legal department and then the research department I did not have the motivation or financial wherewithal to go back to school. If I knew coming out of college right away about getting into the representation side of business and the economics side of business, I would definitely have gone to law school.

I have always been around sports. In high school I was a sports editor for my high school newspaper in my junior year and coeditor of the entire paper in my senior year. When I went to college I wanted to get into broadcast journalism and sports broadcasting. I wanted to be the next Howard Cosell in those days. I was switching between newspaper writing, public relations, and sports writing, but definitely knew I wanted to do something in sport. As I graduated from Temple I was applying to public relations and other non-sports related firms in Philadelphia, but I just did not get any job offers. I always knew I had my contact at the NFLPA, and I was not really that worried about it because I always knew I could fall back on this at least on a temporary full-time basis. I was very fortunate to be at NFLPA at the right time and do a very good job because I have been retained and have worked my way up.

I did not really have any other meaningful, full-time work experience. This is the only place I have ever worked. I have not had any other job other than small jobs while in high school. While I was in college I wrote a newsletter for one of the departments, the Department of Health and Physical Education at Temple University. I did all that on a weekly basis and wrote one article for the school newspaper, but I had to work small jobs to earn some income so I never had a whole lot of time to do a lot of extracurricular stuff while I was in school.

One of the most important things I can say is how critical it is to have good communication skills. I think everybody should take some type of speech communications or public speaking class. I do not necessarily think they have to get much into the journalistic side of things, but schools offer business writing classes or public relations types of courses. It is something that is important. I also think everybody should take economics. If students are interested in getting into the representation side of the field or anything to do with the big bucks that are being earned by athletes and owners, I think they need some finance classes. Statistics certainly would not hurt either. I have more or less learned as I have gone along. I did not take any of those classes in college other than the communications coursework, and I wish now that I had.

We have hired interns from a wide range of educational and experiential backgrounds. We have hired people who have been a part of a sport administration program, like at George Washington University, we have hired law students, we have hired law graduates, and we have hired undergraduates who are just interested in sports. There has to be a genuine interest in the representation side of things or the legal side of things in football. They have to know football. They have to at least know a little bit about the sport and the business of football. Hopefully they express a genuine interest in wanting to get into the field. We have had many people who started at NFLPA and wanted to become an agent and then after they work here for a summer they change their minds. Our internship periods are 90 days and interns get to know some of the agents over the phone or in person and they see the type of stuff they have to go through, such as recruiting and babysitting some clients. They see a lot of the "dirt" that goes on and they realize the last thing they want to do is become an agent. In that sense I think the internship is very helpful. We have had a lot of interns go on to be agents, work for other agents, work for the NFL Management Council, and then go on to work for teams. At least three people work for NFL teams as the main negotiators who started off as interns either in the research or the legal department.

Frank Woschitz, who gave me the opportunity as a public relations graduate, is a role model. He is the director of public relations at NFLPA and director of the Retired Players Association. He taught me a lot about public relations, communications, your conduct in a business environment, and loyalty to the company you work for—things you do not necessarily learn from a textbook. I have always admired him professionally and personally. He has a great family, is a family man, and is a real good guy. Also at NFLPA I admire Richard Berthelsen, General Counsel; Tom DePaso, Staff Counsel; and Gene Upshaw, the Executive Director. I particularly admire Gene because he came from a poor background in Texas and became a first round pick of the Raiders and then got involved with the union while he was playing. After retiring from playing, he was an elected official at the union and eventually became the executive director. He has come from way down the bottom of the ladder all the way to the top as one of the most important people in sport, in my opinion. He has overcome the stigma of being a "dumb jock." I think he has overcome a lot of criticism, especially when the new collective bargaining agreement was reached in 1993. A lot of people criticized him that when he sold the players out, he did not know what he was doing. A lot of racial tension was created with that. He does not let any of that really bother him. He is only out for one thing and that is to do what is best for the players. He represents 1,800 players and cannot please every one of them. I think he has done a great job pleasing the majority of players. I think it is quite admirable. He is a great guy to work for, too.

As far as my future plans, honestly, at this stage I do not know. I would not be surprised if I stayed at NFLPA for a long time. It is a great job and a great place to work. The thought of becoming an agent has crossed my mind every once in a while. I have had some interest from agents who wanted to hire me but the right opportunity has never come up. I do not necessarily know if that would be a step up in my career. Going to work for a team as a negotiator is a possibility. As long as there is football, a labor agreement, a salary cap, and individual contract negotiations, I could stay here for a long time. Job security is not a big concern with me right now.

Talking to agents who think they know everything is probably the worst part of the job. But seriously, the most demanding part of my position is just knowing the collective bargaining agreement, at least the portion of it that deals with the salary cap and free agency system. I must know many rules well enough to recite off the top of my head. I am always rereading things in the collective bargaining agreement and always getting opinions from the legal department because I am not a lawyer. I am constantly on the phone. The summer is very busy for me. That is when players are negotiating their contracts. Right when free agency opens up in February it is very busy. During the season, it is not so busy.

Overall, I think having knowledge of the system and knowing how to be honest with an agent about his client's worth without insulting the player or insulting the agent is important. I need to be very diplomatic about it. There are times where I have, depending on who the agent is, given advice. Leigh Steinberg does not call NFLPA for advice because he does not need it. His office calls just to get economic and salary information. Other agents who do not represent as many players will call for my advice in addition to the raw salary data. I learn just as much from agents, I think, as they do from me. I can use that information to talk to the next agent. It is sort of like a circle of information. The flow of information is circular with me in the middle of the circle. If agent A calls in and gives me some information, I can give that to agent B. Agent B gives me some information so I might give that back to agent A. They are competing against each other only when it comes to recruiting.

Anything they can use to make the players' deal better, whether that comes from me or from another agent, they are going to want to use it. Remember, if the player makes more money, then the agent makes more money, and they can use that the next time they are recruiting. They can say to their next recruit, "Look what I did for this player." "I got him $300,000 to sign when everybody else around him was getting $250,000." Now, he is not going to tell the player how he got that extra $50,000 or even if he had anything to do with it. When it comes to recruiting, the agents do not want to do anything with each other. But when it comes to negotiating the contract, I think 90 percent of the agents realize it is in their best interest to not communicate directly with one another but communicate through me so there are not a whole lot of secrets. The more information that is available, the more money the player makes—and if you want to look at it from the most selfish terms—the more money the agent makes.

I like everything about my job. The perks are nice. I enjoy just being involved in the sport world and football and meeting the players. Getting to go to games is great. I also take pride in knowing I am making a difference, even though on the grand social scheme of things football is not as important as teaching kids to read, helping teachers, or being a doctor. Knowing I am making a difference in a player's life and helping him earn a better living is very satisfying to me.

Our typical day goes from 9:00 AM to 5:30 PM, but rarely am I out of here at 5:30 PM. Some times of the year I am here until 8:00 PM, but I never leave before 6:00 PM. On a typical day the first thing I do is enter in the transactions that occurred in the league the day before. We get a copy of the waiver wire from the NFL Management Council. To help make all those transactions in the computer we have a customized software package where I can terminate a player's contract or add in new player contracts. The computer then calculates the effect it has on that team's salary cap. I did not develop the software. I am almost computer illiterate. We hired a company, told them what we needed, and they designed it for us. It works great most of the time. It gives continuous updates of how much salary cap room the club has to sign players. It calculates how all of the signing bonuses a player gets are prorated over the length of the contract. The computer can do that automatically for us. We do not have to write it on a piece of paper and divide it out by long hand. I do all that data entry in the morning and then the rest of it is basically responding to phone calls and talking to agents about their particular deals.

Right now the biggest thing going on is the draft. It is a little slow now because the majority of the draftees will not get their deals done until July, right before training camp. An agent will call and say, "Mark, this is what Jacksonville's offered me, what advice do you have?" With the draft, every team has a finite amount of money to spend on its rookies and everybody knows that amount. The negotiation is not so much over the portion of the pie that the player is going to get, but it is the structure of the contract, the size of the signing bonus, and the length of the contract. Where a player is drafted dictates the makeup of the contract. If a player is drafted outside of the first or second round, he is going to get a minimum base salary and the agent is just negotiating some incentives and the size of the signing bonus.

I do not like to refer to it as slotting, but basically that is what it is. There are times when a player can jump a slot or two, but in 90 percent of the draft player A makes a little bit more than player B, player B makes more than player C, and player C makes more than player D. That does not necessarily mean that player A's contract is a better contract than player D's because it depends on the structure. Player A could have signed a 5-year deal and player D signed a 4-year deal and that player is an unrestricted free agent 1 year earlier. It might be a better contract even though he may have sacrificed some money up front. Those are the types of topics I discuss with agents on a daily basis.

I also review contract language outside of the boilerplate language of the standard player contract. There are addenda that teams want players to sign for various things. For example, there are addenda for signing bonuses, workout bonuses, roster bonuses, clauses against injury protection, and more. Just through working here for so many years, again even though I am not a lawyer, I know what good language is and what bad language is for a football player. I can help advise them on the language. Basically, a lot of times an agent will just call to run something by me and use me as a sounding board to sort of reaffirm what they are already thinking—that the deal is a good deal. If I say, "Hey, that sounds like a pretty good offer, I would probably go for it," more often than not they say, "Yeah, that's what I wanted to hear, that's what I was thinking anyway."

The pay structure at NFLPA is not so great, but the perks and benefits make up for it. As far as advancement goes, it took 6 years for me to get into middle management where I am now and I have been in middle management for 6 or 7 years. Am I going to get to that next step? I do not know yet. It is something I think about. It is something that becomes a little bit more important as I go on year by year here but I do not know. I am more concerned about the money. I would sacrifice a job title for more money. The benefits, such as health benefits and our employee pension, are what keep a lot of people here for years. There are many people that stay here for years once they get to management. We have some people who have been here for more than 25 years. A lot of it is timing, luck, and being a very good worker, but we have got a number of people at NFLPA who started as interns. I did. I would say we have at least six or seven other people who started as interns that are working in some capacity here.

I do not directly supervise, so I do not have a management style. Instead I will describe what I look for in an employee manager. I want someone who comes to work on time, takes initiative, and is not waiting around to be given a task. Employees, especially new or young employees, should ask, "Hey is there anything I can do?" That is the way I was when I was support staff. My management style is pretty laid-back and easy-going. I think that is one of the things I need to work on, but again, it sort of comes with the informal atmosphere here at NFLPA. There is a hierarchy here but everybody works together. Everybody stuffs envelopes if it has to be done.

I think my boss, the director, would say that I am a very hard worker, very good at what I do, very conscientious, and very loyal. I hope that is what he would say. Loyalty means a lot here. People want to move up very quickly. That is human nature to want to grab things very quickly and move up the corporate ladder, but I found people that pay their dues for a couple of years end up benefiting in the long run.

I think if one wants to go into athlete representation, salary cap, or labor relations in sport, a law degree would definitely be a huge help. It is obviously not a necessity, but I think it would be a huge help. If you are not going to be a lawyer, you should have a strong business background in marketing and negotiations. Take courses such as public communications, finance, statistics, and economics if you are not going to pursue a law degree. We have a lot of agents who are lawyers and certified public accountants. If you are going to represent players you have to know tax law. You do not have to be a tax lawyer but you have to know a little bit about whether it is in a client's best interest to defer money or take it all up front. Or if they should get a residence in a state that does not have a state income tax like Florida, North Carolina, or Washington. Those are all things that can save players hundreds of thousands of dollars.

Take Tim Couch, for example. His contract has been negotiated. It was officially signed when he established residence in Florida. He is getting a $12 million signing bonus, none of which can be taxed as state income. Of course, federal income tax cannot be avoided, but the state is not going to levy a tax on it because there is no state income tax in Florida. These are the types of things that good agents need to know. I think it is important to know the sport. Being a former player is not a necessity, but knowing how the game is played, knowing the rules, and knowing the star players is important. You would be surprised, but there are potential interns who I interview that come in not knowing the first thing about football. Not that it means they are not going to be a good intern, but I think it is important if somebody like Warrick Dunn calls that he gets special treatment. A person working here needs to recognize the name Warrick Dunn.

As far as player representation goes, I think there is going to be a lot of consolidation. There are big companies, like SFX. I think it will become more difficult for the individual practitioner to make a huge inroad in team sports. David Falk sold his company. Even though he is still the one in charge, it is owned by a parent company now. They have picked up a couple of other sports representation firms and actually there is another article in *Sports Business Journal* about them going after Randall and Alan Hendricks who are major baseball agents. I think there will be a lot of consolidation on the representation side of things.

From the union standpoint, I am not sure. I do not think there is really any trend. The unions will be busier as we expand with more members but I think we are in pretty good shape. When the collective bargaining agreement is due to expire in the year 2003—well, it actually could expire a year earlier—is there going to be a continuation of the collective bargaining agreement or is it actually going to come to an end? If it comes to an end, is there going to be a work stoppage? In football that is at least 3 years down the road. We are preparing for that as a union. We are establishing a fund of money for players to use in case there is a work stoppage, whether it is a strike or a lock out. We are always thinking that far down the road.

A lot of other industries face recessions and face cutbacks. I would be very surprised if a recession ever occurs in the sport world. I think people who have some discretionary income are going to spend it on entertainment and a large part of entertainment these days is sports related.

In football, we discourage players negotiating their own contract. We have about 950 agents certified right now. In football, I do not think we will see rookies negotiating for themselves. It does happen as the player gets on in his career. Players who have been around 8 or 9 years sometimes represent themselves unless they are superstars. NFL teams are prohibited from dealing with an agent who is not certified. They can deal directly with a player. For a majority of football players, we think trained professionals should pay a maximum of 3 percent to let them do their job. They should concentrate on making the team. I do not think you will ever see the majority of players representing themselves in football unless the NFL somehow turns to a system, such as the NBA, where there are minimum and maximum salaries.

The 3 percent maximum fee is one of the rules set by our board of player representatives. This is truly a player's association. The board of player representatives and the executive committee set the rules of how we conduct our business. They set our budget, set the rules on the agents, determine what we are going to negotiate for in a collective bargaining agreement, and set the priorities for negotiations. They approve everything. Gene is the administrator for what the board mandates.

To become certified, there is a $1000 fee, an application to be completed, and then the application needs to be approved. If the application is approved then the applicant is sent an invitation to a mandatory 2-day seminar. At the end of the second day, there is a 3-hour written exam that requires a 70 percent passing score. The agents pay $1,000 annually to maintain the certification. NFLPA is by far the most stringent of the associations in certifying and disciplining agents. Agents do not have to have a client to become certified. It is not like baseball where a player must be on the 40-man roster. Whether an agent has a client does not matter to us. We do not help an agent get clients. We do not recommend one agent over another. We will tell a player or his family if there is a complaint about an agent, but we will not tell a player he should sign with Tom Condon over Leigh Steinberg, for example.

A large percentage of the players are controlled by a small percentage of agents. I would say probably 400 agents, nearly half of all certified agents, do not have any clients. There are about 20 agents or companies that represent more than 30 players. That means 20 agents control close to 600 players. A third of the league is controlled by 2 percent of the agents. We have 110 agents who have five or more clients, including the previously mentioned ones. More than 10 percent of the agents have five or more clients. In football, that is not a lot of clients unless one of them happens to be Barry Sanders or something. If an agent has a player making a minimum salary of $175,000 and he gets 3 percent, he only makes $5,200.

Anyone interested in athlete representation should consider doing more than one sport, unless they work in an individual sport such as tennis or golf. There is a lot of money to be made in tennis or golf because they are not regulated. It is something that I would tell somebody going in sort of blind without any strong foothold with clients already. Being an agent should be treated like any other type of small business venture; give it a good 4 or 5 years to get started. If after 4 or 5 years you still struggle, cut your losses and get out because you are not going to make it. It is no different than any other business. Unless an agent has some type of "in" with a high caliber player coming into the draft, a new agent is going to concentrate on the athletes who are projected to be late round picks and the athletes who do not get drafted. They take their chances for the first couple of years, hope somebody sticks, and then word of mouth can mean a lot. We have agents who started 10 years ago with no clients and maybe had two or three athletes after 3 or 4 years who are now representing 14 or 15 athletes. Now, none of them are superstars, but the agent is still making a decent living.

I was very fortunate; however, I work hard. I do a good job. Everybody says it is who you know, which is true, but it is also what you know and how you perform that keeps you in the business. Who you know gets you in; what you know keeps you there.

CHAPTER 5

Professional Sport

THROUGHOUT THE 20TH CENTURY, four sports became established as the major professional sport leagues: Major League Baseball (MLB), the National Football League (NFL), the National Basketball Association (NBA), and the National Hockey League (NHL). Professional sport does not stop with the "Big Four." More than 792 franchises are in the major league and minor league levels competing in six different sports (Masteralexis, 1998). There are also professional tours in men's and women's golf and tennis as well as tours in more diverse sports such as beach volleyball, rodeo, motor sports, and ice skating. Since the creation of the Cincinnati Red Stockings professional baseball club in 1869, professional sport has become an integral part of the sport landscape in the United States. Professional baseball became the first established professional league with the creation of the National League in 1876. The National League set a precedent because it was an owner-controlled league in which the players were employees. All other professional leagues that have followed have imitated this model.

The opportunities to work in the professional sport environment are better than the chances of playing professional sport. In the case of an NBA franchise, there will be 12 players and a coaching staff of several individuals. In the team's front office will be individuals responsible for marketing the team, selling tickets, advertising and sponsorship, conducting public and community relations, and managing the facility. A person interested in working in professional sport would enter in one of these areas and advance. A career aspiration of many is to reach upper-level management positions. In most cases, these upper-level management positions are divided between the business side of the organization and the sport side of the organization. For example, a vice president of sales and marketing oversees all aspects of revenue generation for the organization. A general manager or a vice president for baseball operations oversees all baseball-related matters such as scouting, player development, and contract negotiations. A team president in turn oversees both aspects of the organization and establishes the overall vision for the organization. Entry-level positions pay as low as $20,000. As one advances in the organization the financial rewards increase. Marketing, ticket sales, and public relations directors can make more than $40,000 a year. Top executives with professional organizations can easily make more than $100,000 a year. To reach that point, however, a person has to have the desire, pay the dues of the position, persevere, and realize the financial rewards will come from personal growth and making valuable contributions to the success of the organization. Along with the career opportunities with individual teams there are also league offices responsible for day-to-day operations of the league and its members. The team owners govern the league by creating policies and rules of operations both on and off the field, and the league office carries out the owners' directives.

Not all career opportunities are at the major league level. Established minor leagues exist in baseball, hockey, basketball, and soccer. NFL also has NFL Europe, a player-development league that plays in the spring in Europe. The front offices of minor league teams are smaller so the staff members wear many different hats. The pay scale in minor league sports is lower because the revenues are not as great. Entry-level positions can be less than $20,000 a year, but the potential exists to earn more than $75,000 a year as a general manager of a minor league franchise.

Career opportunities are also available with the various professional tours. Numerous Professional Golf Association (PGA) and LPGA tournaments occur each year. Hundreds of volunteers work the week of the tournament, but the tournament staff works year round to prepare for the tournament. Entry-level pay for positions on the golf tour can pay in the low $20,000s, but again as responsibilities increase so does the pay. Tournament directors can earn more than $60,000 a year. Opportunities are also available to work for both the LPGA and PGA in the golf industry. The same opportunities exist in tennis.

The competition for jobs in professional sport is tough. Those who have the desire as well as the dedication and perseverance will have the greatest chance of success to secure a career in the field.

REFERENCES

Masteralexis, L.P. (1998). Professional sport. In L.P. Masteralexis, C.A. Barr, & M.A. Hums (Eds.), *Principles and practice of sport management* (pp. 275–306). Gaithersburg, MD: Aspen Publishers, Inc.

John L. Allen

Chief Operating Officer
Cincinnati Reds Baseball Club

Education:
B.S., ACCOUNTING, KANSAS STATE UNIVER-
SITY, 1974

M.S., SPORT MANAGEMENT, OHIO STATE UNI-
VERSITY, 1991

Career Progression:
CHIEF OPERATING OFFICER, CINCINNATI REDS,
OCTOBER 1999 TO PRESENT

MANAGING EXECUTIVE, CINCINNATI REDS,
1996–1999

CONTROLLER, CINCINNATI REDS, 1995–1996

DIRECTOR OF BUSINESS OPERATIONS, COLUM-
BUS CLIPPERS, 1990–1995

COLUMBUS CLIPPERS, UNPAID INTERN, JANU-
ARY 1990 TO MAY 1990

Best piece of advice you received in regards to your career:

"Do anything to get your foot in the door—sell yourself."

DALE ROHR, VP FINANCE, KANSAS CITY ROYALS

Best advice for someone aspiring toward a career in the sport industry:

**"It's so important to get your foot in the door even if it is not
directly your ultimate area of expertise."**

Quote by which you live:

"Do unto others as you would have them do unto you."

I ALWAYS ENJOYED SPORTS and wanted to get into sports from my youngest days. Being of the older generation and going on 50, when I was in college you could not major in sport management. I had an accounting degree from Kansas State University and went to work for the CPA firm Arthur Anderson Company in Kansas City, Missouri. I received a wide variety of business experiences that have been extremely helpful through the years. It was 1989 when I finally decided I was going to have to make this happen for myself—no one was going to invite me to come to work in sports. Late in 1989 I made the decision, did my home-work, and talked to several people in the baseball industry. My focus has always been on baseball. I have no desire to go into sport other than baseball. I interviewed with several people at the Kansas City Royals, where I was a 15-year season ticket holder. I did some informational interviews and research reading. I wrote to literally every team in professional baseball about opportunities, and I just did a lot of homework. I finally concluded the best approach for me was probably to get a master's degree in sport management and do an internship. After doing my research I decided the best place for me was Ohio State University. I applied at Ohio State and the program had fairly stringent entrance requirements, and I went through an interview process. I was concerned about my age because I was 40. Yet everything went very well throughout the interview process and the people were impressed that I would make a career decision to quit my job to get into sports. Strangely enough, during the course of the interview with Bill Sutton, one of the professors at the time, I told him about my interest for baseball. During the middle of the interview for graduate school he suggested I interview with the Columbus Clippers, the Yankee's triple A team in Columbus. During my sport management interview I also interviewed for an unpaid internship with the New York Yankees triple A team in Columbus. I was fortunate enough to get the internship and also be accepted into the program at Ohio State. That is how I got started—as an unpaid intern with the Columbus Clippers while working on my master's degree.

I think the way I got my foot in the door was relatively normal. Many people have been in the workforce for a few years before getting into sport, but I had been in accounting and business for almost 15 years. I see a lot of resumes come through my office where people have had other careers for 4 or 5 years and then pursued a career in sport management. I got very lucky and was at the "right place, right time" to get to where I am today as basically the chief executive officer with the Cincinnati Reds. It has been a very unusual career path, but a lot of fun.

I started out as an intern, and they treated me no differently. Although I had a number of years on quite a few of the people, they treated me the same. In hindsight it was great, because I did the same tasks as any other intern would do in the off season including mundane duties such as typing invoices, working with ticket accounts, and selling program ads. I did anything that needed to be done. Once the season started I sold hot dogs and programs, monitored the gates, and worked in the parking lot occasionally. I did all types of customer service related duties and I learned all facets of the operation. The minor league level is a little bit different, but a lot of similarities exist in dealing with fans.

The management figured out pretty soon that I knew a little bit about accounting and business with my background. As luck would have it, the director of business operations at the Clippers was making a career change and I was offered the job, and of course I said yes. I was still working on my degree and performing that job full time. That was in the summer of 1990. I graduated in June 1991, and then retained that position until May 1995. Again the importance of networking comes through because while I was with the Clippers there were three of us—Brad Kuhlman, Rob Butcher, and myself—who people called "The Three Musketeers." We spent a lot of time together and became very close friends both at work and away from the office. We always sat around and discussed how one of us would get there first and how he would help the other two get there eventually. Again, as luck would have it, Brad Kuhlman, who was the director of media relations for the Clippers, took a position with the Cincinnati Reds in March 1995 as an assistant in the media relations department. A few months later, Brad was walking down the hall one day talking to Mrs. Schott, who was the president and chief executive officer of the Reds. She was complaining about her current—and as she referred to it—bookkeeper who actually was the chief financial officer of the Reds. Brad mentioned he had a friend up in Columbus who was just an outstanding bookkeeper who she ought to contact. Again, being in the right place at the right time, I received a call from Mrs. Schott in May 1995, came down and interviewed, and was hired within a few days.

My career in the big leagues actually started in May 1995. I had the feeling when I got the position, "This is it, I've accomplished my goal. I am in the big leagues. I am the controller of a Major League Baseball team." I was so excited as I drove to accept my position as I anticipated the future. One year later I became the chief financial officer! Mrs. Schott reportedly made what we refer to in baseball as insensitive remarks in an ESPN interview and later in a *Sports Illustrated* article. At that time, during the previous 12 months I had gotten closer to Mrs. Schott. I had performed very well for her and communicated extremely well with her. I had done a good job for the Reds. At the time she decided she would accept her suspension from MLB so she had to appoint somebody to take control of the team. She immediately indicated it was going to be me. The MLB representatives and executive council members laughed because they did not know me. When they figured out I was the controller of the Reds they just did not think that it was going to work. But again, I got lucky when MLB said, "We'll give Mrs. Schott up to 60 days to go out and find somebody else to run the team. In the interim John Allen can be the managing executive for the Reds." On June 12, 1996, I was appointed interim managing executive for a period of up to 60 days. That was probably the turning point in my baseball career, the day I came back from the meetings. I came back and knew I had to make strong personal and career decisions. Mrs. Schott had specific ideas and thoughts on how the team ought to be run. I did not agree with many of her ideas. I knew when I came back I could do things as she would want them done or I could step up and exercise my judgment on how the team ought to operate. I chose the latter knowing that it was going to upset her and not help me with my career. But I thought it was the right thing to do and that it is a matter of integrity to do what you think is right and do the best you can. During those 60 days we made a lot of changes at the Cincinnati Reds front office, and people seemed to like it. Our attendance increased as a result of simple things such as doing promotions, getting the fans involved, and going to the fans for input. The very first day I was on the job I did a 3-hour radio show with our flagship station WLW. We asked the fans to call in to the show, tell me what the problems were, and what they wanted to see. I got some tremendous ideas, and I immediately implemented some fan friendly ideas and activities such as running the bases. A nice promotion we do on the weekends is called "Stand By Your Red" where we select kids from the stands to go out on the field with a player during the national anthem. We have a guest announcer where children announce the next batter at certain points during the game.

The promotion I am most proud of is an event called Celebration of Diversity where we went into the community, distributed free tickets to different socioeconomic groups, and invited them to the ballpark to enjoy a game. It was very successful. We had almost 10,000 fans take advantage of that one night. The Reds had somewhat of a negative reputation pertaining to diversity. I do not know whether it was warranted or not, but nonetheless we had that reputation and we needed to do something about it. Now it has become an annual event. As you study our socioeconomic base and the demographics of our fans, we do not draw well from the African American community. We try to reach them.

During that 60 days things were very well received. Attendance was up and MLB saw that this John Allen (Mrs. Schott's person) seems to be doing okay and he's a good one. Acting Commissioner Bud Selig and National League President Bill White both said, "If Mrs. Schott will approve him we'll go ahead and allow him to run the team for the remaining 2 years of her suspension. By this time Mrs. Schott was very upset with me and did not agree with the changes I had made. It came down to almost the 60th day and at the last minute she assigned me to drop the interim part of the managing executive title. In August 1996 I was appointed on a full-time basis for a 2-year period through the 1998 season.

I took over a team with a $47 million payroll and revenues of about $42 million. I think we had less than 20 scouts in the system, where other teams average 30, and our minor league teams had been decimated. We had a minimum number of prospects in the minor league system. I sat back and thought, "We'll finish 1996 with the team we have, and see how they perform." We were maybe three games out of first place when I took over. Unfortunately the team did not pull it off, and I do not remember how we finished that year, but we certainly did not win or make the play-offs. I had some decisions to make not only business-wise, but also baseball-wise. My term was to expire at the end of the 1998 season. We had done well and baseball made the decision to have the current management continue running the team. Mrs. Schott had some interest in selling the team, and basically it was decided that Mrs. Schott would sell the team and all of the sanctions would go away. In September 1998 my agreement was extended for a period of 90 days or until she sold the team, whichever came first. That ran through December 1998. In the six months before July 1999 she agreed to sell the team to one of her other limited partners in the ownership group. That limited partner had liked my performance and agreed to have me stay on with the team.

When I think of role models, I always liked Al Kaline who played right field for the Detroit Tigers. I am not very athletic. In Little League the kid who cannot catch or hit bats ninth in the order and plays right field. So I played right field, and I remember asking my coach, "Who is the best right fielder? Who should I try to emulate?" Roberto Clemente fans probably would argue this, but he said Al Kaline. I followed his career for years, and fortunately I did choose someone who exemplifies the game and is a tremendous person. I have met Mr. Kaline and we have kind of become friends. I saw him at the Baseball Hall of Fame induction in Cooperstown in 1999. We always look each other up if we are at the same events. It is a nice sidebar that I met this gentleman, and he is everything I emulated as a kid. This may sound corny but another one of my personal heroes was always my father. I am from a family of six kids. We did not have a lot of wealth or anything, but my father was always there. You hear stories today about families that are not together and so forth. My dad always was, and still is, supporting me. I think the world of my father and he taught me a lot of lessons in life by the way he worked and performed under somewhat adverse conditions, not having a lot of money, and raising six kids. We all went to college. We never wanted for anything. We did not have big fancy cars, but as far as the basics of life, just the companionship of the family that my dad kept together was great. I always admired the president of the United States. I always admired anybody who could run a country. Being from Kansas, Dwight Eisenhower, who was raised in Kansas, was my favorite president. Now that I am in baseball and I represent the Reds at the owners meetings, I have gotten to know all 30 owners and all of the major executives in baseball. Someone I respect who does not always get positive publicity and press is Bud Selig. He respects and understands the game. I think he takes some negative hits in the media, but he should not because he has a very tough situation. Baseball has been around so long that we are kind of stuck in our ways, and he is trying to make changes that are good for the industry and the game.

I think I am a role model or a mentor for people. When I go out and speak to people, especially young adults trying to get into sport management, I think they see this person who made it happen and went to the top. I always try to tell people my situation is extremely unusual. Few people go from being an unpaid intern to the chief financial officer and then the chief executive officer of a team in 6 years. It is highly unusual. I do not say that to be braggadocios, but when I talk to people they respect what I have accomplished.

I do a lot of radio shows, TV shows, call-in shows, and so forth. One night, Jim Bowden, our general manager, and Jack McKeon, our field manager, and I, on an off night after a road trip, were asked by one of the local stations to come on the air. We spent 3 hours talking to the fans about baseball, the stadium, and other things. They said, "John, the Reds are probably the only Major League team where the top three team representatives will sit down and talk to the fans for three hours on your off day." We enjoy talking to the fans. I think it is important because the fans are what it is all about. I guess my business background comes through because I am a firm believer that baseball in many respects is no different than any other business. I try to use the word customer as much as I do fan. They have to want to come to the ballpark. If you do not listen to your fans or your customers, you are not going to have success, whether you are a plumber, an attorney, or whatever. If you do not listen to your customer you are not going to succeed. I think that is critical. I try to respond to most of my e-mails. I get 20, 30, or 40 a day sometimes, and it is difficult and time consuming requiring long evenings sometimes, but we try to communicate and respond to all of the fans. I think that is very important.

I am unique because literally the past 3 years I have operated as the owner of the team and also as the chief executive officer. On most teams there is an owner, a president, and a chief executive officer. I function in both roles. When we get new owners I assume my title will change. We have not talked about that. I will have an owner to which I will report.

I am responsible for every department. It is not different from being president or chief executive officer of any major corporation in that I have department heads who report to me. I give them direction and guidance and so forth. At the Reds we have a lot of great employees. We have a tremendous front office including people who have been here a number of years. Once people get in this industry they tend to stay because they enjoy it so much, so there is not a lot of turnover. Most of my department heads have been here a number of years and know their job better than I do. It is a matter of coordinating their activities, listening, and giving suggestions as to how I think something else might work better. I have a director of season tickets, group sales, ticketing, marketing, media relations, and a traveling secretary. Jim Bowden, the general manager, runs the baseball operations with a very large department reporting to him. All those people report to me. I am pretty easy to work for, I think. I just expect everybody to do their job, they know what it is, and I expect results. I am more of a guidance counselor in that respect rather than sitting there and doing hands-on work. Certain projects arise where I need to be hands-on, but I prefer not to be hands-on because not enough time is available and these people can do it better than I can. They know their job and it is just a matter of trying to keep up with what is happening so I am not surprised. It sounds easy, but it is very time consuming.

Communicating with people is an important facet of my position. It is very important that I keep up with what happens in all departments. I do require those departments to communicate with me. I get very testy if something is happening and I am unaware of it. I need to know what is happening because of my role and because I interface so much with the fans and the press. I am the person the media contacts with any problems or complaints. It is important that I know what is happening so I do not embarrass myself and/or the organization.

If anything, I am probably too easy with the employees sometimes. Perhaps because of my background I am not a strict disciplinarian. I always want to believe the best in people, and I think sometimes that probably gets me in a little bit of trouble. But that is just my nature, the type of person I am. I spend a lot of time every day, going up and down the hall, and just talking to people, poking my head into a department to say, "Hey, what's going on? Are things going okay? Do you need anything?" I do not try to override the responsibilities of department heads, but I tell them I am interested in what they are doing. I never try to usurp the authority of the department head.

By far the worst part of my job is dealing with the media. I am an accountant, a business person. I never had any direct dealings with the media. I had never done a radio or a print media or been on TV. Then in June 1996 I was thrust into the limelight. I went from being a nobody in Cincinnati to being on Cable News Network (CNN), ESPN, and everything during the hearings regarding Mrs. Schott. Learning to deal with the media has been by far the most difficult. The best part is getting to be around the sport I love, which means being around the people in baseball. Some of the nicest people in the world are in baseball, not only in Cincinnati but also as I travel or as I meet people who work in the industry. I think the most rewarding part of this job is getting to do what I want to do and being involved in baseball. It is fun to come to work every day.

I think many of the management skills we use in baseball apply to any industry or any type of work. I focus a lot on communication. Communication is so important including not only outward, but also inward communication. A manager has to be a good listener. I deal with part-time people and full-time people, and I have to listen to them because they approach me with problems, suggestions, or ideas. I have to listen, respond, and communicate with them. Communication is a major tool in all industries, not just baseball. We have roughly 225 baseball players. They are all blessed with physical talent and athletic ability, from the rawest rookie in the minor leagues to the players who have made it to the Reds. All the players are very talented, and it takes a unique person to get to the big league level. Dealing with them is unique because you are dealing with a Barry Larkin or Greg Vaughn who make more than $5 million a year. They make more in a day than some people make all year. Then you deal with the people who clean the stadium who make minimum or a little higher than minimum wage. Dealing with all of the socioeconomic stratospheres is tough and that is not necessarily the case in other industries. Everybody has prima donnas within a company. We have many and they are important because our product is these 25 players and what they do. My career and success depend on 25 players ranging in age from 25 to 35 making an average of $1.5 million a year. You have to measure my success by the team on the field.

Sometimes this job can be stressful. I deal with stress by running. I try to run a couple of miles every day and just let my mind go. Sometimes at 4:00 or 5:00 PM I need a mental health break so I take the rest of the day off and go home. I have a very understanding wife who supports me and understands the pressure. She is always supportive. It is very nice to have a good family that will let you relax and take out your frustrations. My wife complains that I keep stress inside of me too much. I do not think so; I just do not talk a lot about it. I think stress is sometimes an overused term. I think people have to deal with themselves when things are not going right or they do not feel right, and they have to do something to adjust and to compensate. I guess that is stress, but life is too short to get wrapped up in all that stuff.

Be willing to do whatever it takes to get your foot in the door. Once you get the opportunity in sport, work very diligently, do anything you are asked, be aggressive, and network. If Brad Kuhlman and I had not been good friends and he had not recommended me to Mrs. Schott, then I would not have this position. Networking is vital. But again, you have got to get your foot in the door. Get that first opening, get that first opportunity, and take advantage of it regardless of the compensation or if it is not something you want to do long term.

I am beginning to see more corporate involvement in professional sport, and I am not sure it is all good. If it is handled properly it can be okay, as long as the integrity of the individual sport is maintained, whether it is football, baseball, or whatever. I think there will be more corporate involvement because of the dollars involved. From an ownership standpoint in baseball, you see less and less family ownership over the recent years. You see more and more media companies own teams such as FOX buying the Dodgers and Disney buying the Angels. You see more corporations getting involved because baseball has become the biggest problem in the professional sport industry because of economic disparity. That has been brought on because someone can go out and buy a team now with free agents. We saw that happen with the Marlins some years ago where they literally just went out and bought themselves a world championship. I do not know if the Dodgers would admit this, but to the average fan it looks as if they attempted to do the same thing in 1999 with their large payroll. Now in New York, I cannot say they are just going to buy a world championship. The players are paid well and they get what they need, but they also have a very strong farm system. If you are looking for players at the big league level, a Bernie Williams, a Derek Jeter, or the Yankees can look through the farm system and that is a tribute to them. Once they become free agents, they have the dollars to keep them. That is what I call home-grown talent. Because of those economics it is tough for the small market team. We do not generate the revenues to go out and buy those free agents. In the past, before free agency, regardless of revenues, teams were measured on what type of farm system they had. The prospects in the minor leagues were the measuring stick rather than economics.

I think job opportunities will be good for the person who can sell and market. On the baseball operations side I think it is going to continue the way it is now. People in baseball operations predominantly have been people who have played the game or have been involved in one way or another, either as a player or a coach. They continue to turn over. There is constant turnover with field managers, too. Almost every field manager has managed at least two or three other teams. The same is true for general managers and with managers and coaches at the minor league level. We have a couple of player-coaches in our organization. They are great kids, know and love the game, and although they do not have that natural ability to get to the big league level, they understand the game enough to turn them into coaches. I do not see a tremendous amount of opportunities on the baseball side, but on the business side anybody who can sell or market has a great opportunity. There are only 30 major league teams, 30 directors of stadium operations, and 30 directors of season tickets, and those are tough jobs to get because they do not turn over. The demand exists for people to sell and that is true at the major and minor league levels.

When I came to the Reds in 1995 there were rumblings that the NFL franchise here in town, the Bengals, wanted a new stadium. Fortunately the community leaders said, "If we're going to take care of the Bengals we also need to take care of the Reds." The new stadium is probably one of the more important functions I have been involved with as it concerns the organization's future health and I started from the beginning. In the fall of 1996 we got an issue on the ballot for the March election for a half-cent countywide sales tax. That half-cent sales tax went toward building two new stadiums, one for the Bengals and one for the Reds. At that point I was still the controller, and Mrs. Schott's approach on this was, "I'm not going to tell the voters how to vote. I'm not going to get behind this thing, nor am I going to go against it, and the Reds are not going to get involved." I questioned her judgment, but she was the boss and that was her position. All around me the Bengals, their players, and their fans were getting behind this grassroots effort to get the sales tax passed while the Reds just sat there passively. I found that very embarrassing, and did not think it was too wise from a business perspective, but my hands were tied. In March 1996 the sales tax passed by a tremendous margin. Now few communities can get any kind of tax passed to support one new stadium, let alone two new stadiums. When the tax passed the county representatives met with the Reds management. They said, "Let's start negotiating on a new stadium." For whatever reason, Mrs. Schott made the decision that the Reds would not negotiate at that point. She wanted to wait until the Bengals had completed their negotiations and then she would pursue a deal that was a little bit better than their deal. In my opinion, that was probably not the best move to make at that time. The Bengals went about their business, negotiated a very good deal with Hamilton County for their new stadium, and obtained their desired location. By June 1996, nobody at the Reds knew what was happening. Mrs. Schott was going to be suspended. I was on a 60-day interim and could not do much. It was not until after the 60-day interim period that the Reds could aggressively negotiate. By then the Bengals' deal was pretty well done. They had the location we wanted on the west side of the suspension bridge. We all sat down, saw what the Bengals did, and tried to negotiate something similar to that, but it just did not happen. The long and drawn out negotiations went from the Fall of 1996 until July 1997 before we came to what we thought were outstanding baseball terms, at least compared with other new baseball stadiums being built. The deal paled in comparison with what the Bengals received, but nonetheless we received a strong baseball deal and it was completed in July 1997. In May 1999, we signed the completed lease. We are now in the design phase of the new stadium.

The new stadium is important to advancing this organization. We talked about economic disparity. One of the ways the "small market team" can compete is to increase revenues. Unfortunately, I think many of our fans have the perception we will have all this revenue with a new stadium and be able to acquire a lot of free agents. That is not the case. We estimate that we will generate another $20 to $25 million in additional revenues. That sounds like a lot of money, but in today's economy it is not enough to chase every free agent. In our payroll in 1999, we exceeded the budget and were in the low 30s. If we decided to put that $20 to $25 million into payroll, it would increase to around $55 million. About six teams exceed that amount in today's dollars and they will have more revenue. The stadium is probably the most critical project in which I have been involved. I have been with it from day one through the lease negotiations and into the design phase. I gained a great deal of experience, but it is not something I would want to do again.

We will definitely sell the naming rights, probably for $40 to $50 million over 20 years. A lot of stories are written and a lot of things are said about naming rights. As you study it, you can break the numbers up. You get down to the pure naming rights number, and it goes all over the board. People do not like to give a number out, or they include this or do not include that, that type of thing. I am looking for the straight $30 to $50 million for pure naming rights and everything else would be on top of that.

Through fan surveys and open forums I have conducted, one thing is clear. A core group exists that could care less about cup holders, about a kid zone, about this type of menu, or whatever. These people just want to come watch good baseball and have a great season. However, some families and corporations want to use the stadium for entertaining. They want it to be a destination to do a lot of other things. You try to make sure you serve Joe Baseball Fan who does not want anything, and then you serve the family of four who wants to have the kids entertained a little bit in addition to seeing a ballgame. Trying to achieve that blend is difficult. We hope to have "neighborhoods" within the ballpark where those different things can be addressed to allow everybody to get a little bit of what they want.

Among our biggest challenges in baseball is the economic disparity. In 1990 this team won the World Series with a payroll at approximately $15 million. In 1995 we won the Central Division Championship and our payroll was $47 million. It tripled. Obviously during that 5-year period our revenues did not triple, and our attendance did not triple. Roughly 90 percent of our operating costs are related to the 25 players who suit up every day. Now the New York Yankees have a large TV rights deal. With the Reds, we have a local cable deal that nets us maybe 10 percent or less of what the Yankees receive. Their revenues are tremendously higher than ours so they can afford to have a $70 million payroll. It is impossible for us to match that. The fans see that and start comparing championships to payrolls. It is bad for the sport and the industry.

What is the solution? I have got to admit that if I was Barry Larkin or Sean Casey and someone said, "Hey, I'll pay you $10 million a year," I'd take it. In a heartbeat I would jump on it. I think it has to be a combination of the players' association, ownership, and baseball as a whole working together to find a solution. I hate to talk about problems and not have a solution, but I do not have a solution for this. I do not know the answer. Potentially some type of revenue sharing could be the solution, but with my business background I also understand free enterprise. If I pay a "gazillion" dollars to buy a franchise in a big market city, hey, so be it, then let me. Let me maximize my revenues because I would be taking the financial risk. It is a free enterprise system. I can understand Mr. Steinbrenner saying why should I give the small market team X millions of dollars as part of the revenue sharing and then some of them do not put it in the payroll anyway. That is a major problem. I talked earlier about Bud Selig and that is one of the reasons I admire him because he certainly understands the problem coming from Milwaukee, a small market team. I think he will make the tough decisions. When you have 30 teams, not all 30 teams will like the solutions, but we have to agree to something. That is the problem I deal with daily and worry about for the industry—income disparity and how we are going to survive it. We feel we have a written plan here at the Reds. It is going to all come through the farm system so we make sure we get the supply of prospects we need so when we lose a key player we have a replacement. Then we sprinkle the team with a few veterans or a couple of free agents who we can afford to keep and be successful that way. We must have the scouts out there we need to have the minor league system or it will never work. We must stay the course. I get a lot of that from the media near the trading deadline where people tell me to go out and get that starting pitcher. Well economically it is tough. If someone gives you a top-line starting pitcher, they will want one of your prospects in return. They are not stupid. We must have a plan and stick with it. I have to be thick-skinned because I know if I do not get the front line pitcher I will hear, "What a cheapskate he was!" It is not the cost of the new pitcher as much as it is what we have to give up in return.

When I got into sports all I wanted was to be in the big leagues doing something. I did not care how. It took me 6 years to get to the Reds initially as the chief financial officer, and I thought that was the ultimate position. I thought I had peaked there. I think I would have been very pleased to have that position for a long time. At this point, I could potentially see myself, if the opportunity was right, somewhere in MLB at the league level in some type of position. It is not something I am necessarily politicking for or have a vision on one specific job. I have learned about the industry, the people within the industry, and served on the executive committee of the National League for a couple of years. I could see the possibility of working at the league level in a role where I was involved with all of the teams within that league or within MLB. I am not seeking this position, but it is the next logical step if I choose to continue down that path. I am very happy in Cincinnati so to be here for 10 more years would be all right.

I am not sure I can say I am a success yet. We are not going to have the ultimate success until the Reds start winning. In July 1999 the team started to gel. When we rounded off a 10-game winning streak and were tied for first place, the fans started to come back. That is because they want a winner. I think my ultimate success personally is going to be when this team wins. The ultimate success is when you get that World Series Trophy and the championship ring. Then I will sit back and say that I have done it. I have accomplished everything I could possibly accomplish in this game and accomplished it as the managing executive.

Connie H. Hurlbut

Director of Basketball Operations
Women's National Basketball
Association

Education:
B.A., POLITICAL SCIENCE, UNIVERSITY OF
PENNSYLVANIA, 1983

Career Progression:
DIRECTOR OF BASKETBALL OPERATIONS,
WNBA, 1999 TO PRESENT

COMMISSIONER, PATRIOT LEAGUE, 1993–1999

IVY LEAGUE ASSOCIATE COMMISSIONER,
1989–1993

IVY LEAGUE ASSISTANT COMMISSIONER,
1986–1989

ASSISTANT COMMISSIONER, EASTERN COL-
LEGE ATHLETIC CONFERENCE, 1984–1986

ASA S. BUSHNELL INTERN, EASTERN COLLEGE
ATHLETIC CONFERENCE, 1983–1984

Best advice for someone aspiring toward a career in the sport industry:

"Anything is possible."

I WAS A POLITICAL SCIENCE MAJOR as an undergraduate student at the University of Pennsylvania and at that time I was more interested in career options related to political campaigns than a career in sport. At Penn, I played field hockey and lacrosse and for 2 years I headed the Women's Athletic Association, which was a women's sport advocacy group on campus. Through the Women's Athletic Association I had the opportunity to work with the athletic administration at Penn and that experience definitely sparked an interest. When an opportunity arose to do a 1-year internship with the Eastern College Athletic Conference (ECAC) the year after graduation, I was very interested.

The first year the ECAC conducted men's and women's championships was 1983-1984 so they were hiring an additional intern who was a female. I thought the position sounded like fun. The primary responsibilities were event management and sports information. I figured those experiences would provide a good background for me to get into public relations with a political campaign later in life. I took the position and loved everything about it. The working environment, the subject matter, the fact that it was sport, the engagement with both men's and women's programs, and the public relations angle made the position appealing.

Because it was the first year the ECAC was offering women's championships, a lot of decision making occurred. Decisions had to be made on which championships to conduct, how big the tournament fields would be, and whether there would be regional play. Also during that year a staff change created a situation in which no one was overseeing the interns. Without that supervision, Chris Ritrievi (the other intern) and I were given a fair amount of responsibility. Sometimes it seemed as if we were inventing things as we went along.

After the internship, the ECAC offered me a position as assistant commissioner with the conference. I accepted. By taking the assistant commissioner position, I had become more or less my own boss and gained more responsibilities. I was responsible for implementing and administering championships in 16 sports, producing and editing all publications, managing the two interns, and supervising the production and distribution of all conference publicity for the 243-member conference. I served as assistant commissioner of the ECAC for 2 years. I left in 1986 to become the assistant executive director of the Ivy Group. The idea of working with the Ivy schools was very appealing to me because I am an Ivy graduate. Also, it was a little bit more focused than working at ECAC. At the ECAC, about 250 schools were in the three divisions. With the Ivy League the focus is on the eight schools in the conference that share the same philosophies. It was much more specific. It was also beneficial for me because I moved closer to my home in the Philadelphia area.

When I started with the Ivy Group in 1986, my main responsibility was sport information and producing publications. This was about the time the NCAA started placing a lot more emphasis and responsibility on the conferences to administer rules compliance programs for its member institutions. I quickly became more of a legislative assistant for the league so I was handling interpretations of NCAA rules and random questions. Over time, I started doing more by representing the conference at meetings on rules interpretations and running rules seminars for the member institutions with less focus on sports information.

In 1989, the Ivy Group expanded its staff and I became the associate executive director. The league hired an assistant to handle the sport information. I began working more with NCAA in committee structures and with our schools on compliance. I was also involved with the Ivy Group Drug Education policy and managed the NCAA conference grant program. I had served in the associate director position for 4 years when the opportunity to become executive director of the Patriot League arose in 1993.

Being a commissioner of a conference was attractive to me. The Patriot League had been an eight-team Division I-AA football conference since 1986, and it became an all-sport conference in 1991. When the Patriot League was moving toward becoming an all-sport conference, we at the Ivy League office spent a lot of time sharing ideas with representatives from the Patriot League on how we did things. From my experience with the Ivy League, I was comfortable in terms of how the Patriot League operated and its direction. Given my background as an administrator at the Ivy League conference, I probably would not have gotten the opportunity to be a commissioner anywhere but at a conference that was similar to the Ivy League. It was intriguing to be the only woman commissioner of an NCAA Division I conference.

I think I felt a bit of pressure being the first female commissioner of an NCAA Division I conference, but I never thought my hiring was a gender issue and that speaks to the institutions and presidents with whom I was working. If it was not going to be an issue for them, it certainly was not going to be an issue for me. I have always thought that a lot of very talented men and women are in intercollegiate athletics. I have never thought being a women was a stumbling block. I have had the good fortune of working with administrators at institutions that were open-minded and fair, and it was never a hindrance to me that I thought could constrict my career.

I was fortunate to have the opportunity to work with Jeff Orleans, the executive director of the Ivy League before going to the Patriot League. He taught me a tremendous amount about creating an environment in which people strive and feel empowered. Jeff is also a "big picture" person and he helped shape the way I view situations. I learned the importance of considering every angle and all the information presented before making a decision. I found this to be invaluable when I managed an athletic conference. There were changes going from being an associate commissioner to a commissioner. I think any time you become the person in charge it is a transition. I found staff management issues a bit daunting. You never recognize those challenges until you manage a staff. I realized the importance of being responsive to people's needs and assisting them in doing their job.

As an executive director, I was an employee of the member institutions. The presidents hired me so I reported to them. Everyone knew this so it was easier to direct because I was performing a job that was defined by the member institutions' presidents. To be an effective commissioner of a conference you must act in accordance with the wishes of the member institutions. But it is also important for the conference to be recognized as an entity in and of itself. A lot of times what is good for individual members may not be good for the conference as a whole. I think you need to make sure people realize that and you must direct initiatives to benefit the conference as an entity as opposed to a group of individual members.

Here is an example of the "big picture" coming into play. For example, league members resist changing a tournament format because it would keep students out of class and cost each institution more. It needs to be stressed from the conference perspective that this enables the conference to be more competitive, aligns the conference with the current trend in the sport and that helps recruiting, while giving the conference additional exposure for our athletes and programs.

I enjoyed my experience as a commissioner. I put a lot of credit to that enjoyment to the people with whom I worked at the member institutions and the league office staff. It was a great group of people. There was a great deal of support for one another. It was a team-oriented environment. In that atmosphere you are working for the betterment of individuals and you feel good about it.

I had been at the Patriot League 5–1/2 years when I decided to go to the WNBA in 1999. At that time I was ready for a change. I had given thought to what I wanted to do next in my career and I was not sure whether I wanted to stay in sport. When the WNBA opportunity arose it made me realize how much I had invested in my sport career and wanted to continue with it. A friend told me that Val Ackerman, the WNBA president, was contacting people in college athletics for a director of basketball operations. The professional sport environment is completely different than anything I had been in before but I have a certain comfort level with the subject matter from my experience in the Patriot League and on the NCAA Division I Women's Basketball Committee.

I welcomed the challenge and I was excited about the prospect of being involved with something as new and national as WNBA. But as attractive as it was, it was not a slam dunk decision to take it. A lot of different factors that were primarily family-oriented weighed into my decision. Geography was one factor that made the position attractive. My husband, Steve, an associate commissioner with the Northeast Conference, had accepted a position as an athletic director at Fairleigh Dickinson University in Teaneck, New Jersey, which is outside of New York City. When I accepted the job with WNBA we moved to northern New Jersey to shorten our commutes. I had been commuting from our home in central New Jersey to the Patriot League Offices in Bethlehem, Pennsylvania, for those 5 years.

As director of basketball operations my primary focus is the game itself. I formulate the league schedule and oversee all aspects of our officiating program and all basketball events such as our pre-draft camp, veterans camp, and postseason tours. At the time of this writing I have completed my first season. The season is very tense. It seems as if I worked 24 hours a day, 7 days a week because of the league schedule. In season you never know what is going to happen that will require your attention.

I have three people who report to me including the supervisor of officials, the manager of basketball operations, and the assistant for basketball operations. The contact I have with officials is through the supervisor of officials. The manager of basketball operations works with statistics and game management personnel at all of the arenas. We have to make sure table operations run effectively. If a problem arises with the table operation crew at a game it is our department's responsibility to review it. It is our responsibility to check that every game meets WNBA's standards. For example, although we are not directly involved with marketing we are conscious of the league's sponsorship agreements. If an agreement indicates that a particular company's name is supposed to be on the towels on the benches we make sure those towels are there. As a league we have to live up to our agreements with our sponsors. To create a positive work environment for the department it is important to keep lines of communications open. We try to meet once a week to discuss what everybody has on their plate. From those meetings I can determine whether someone is getting swamped. Ours is a more cooperative working environment than a hierarchical one.

One of the more challenging aspects of my position is working with the league's officials to make sure they are prepared for the season. About half of our officials come from college women's games and the other half come from the Continental Basketball Association (CBA). The challenge our officials face is that our game is different from women's college basketball and the CBA. Our rules are different in terms of judgment calls and court management. We have training for 4 weeks before the season starts to get them into our mode. Then there is 10 weeks of the season. Our teams play a 32-game schedule and our officials get anywhere between 15 to 20 assignments during the regular season. The other challenge related to the officials is the league's rapid expansion. We started in 1997 with eight teams; in 1998 there were 10 teams; and in 1999 there were 12. There will be 16 in 2000. Each time the league expands we have to recruit more officials. In 1999 about one-third of our officials were new. A similar situation will be present in 2000.

In looking to the future I think the WNBA will continue to thrive and grow. If a women's professional basketball league can succeed, I have no doubt that it will be WNBA. There is a huge commitment from the NBA and its owners to make the league successful. Although there are comparisons made between the NBA and WNBA, I think most people watching our game understand the differences. It is the same game but some subtle differences exist in the way it is played. The league is showing signs of positive growth and longevity and I think that is pretty exciting for women's sport in general.

In 1983, I did not expect a professional women's basketball league to form when I started with ECAC, especially one that has existed for 3 years and attracts more than 10,000 people per game. When I consider my future career aspirations, I realize I have never done something to get me somewhere else. When I was at the Ivy League I was not there because I thought I wanted to be a commissioner. I was there because I enjoyed my job. Even when I was at the Patriot League, I did not look to move to professional sport. I do not normally plan in that manner. If you are good at something, you represent value to somebody. I have been fortunate and have worked hard, and my career path has been good. I know it is not over but I think my career has some highlights in it. I have had the opportunity to know a lot of people from many different areas and I have done a lot of different things. Even with the career highlights, I will define success in my career by ensuring that I maintain the proper balance between my family and my job. I think it is so easy to have that equation get out of kilter with more going toward career than family. It is a challenge to maintain your priorities and recognize where they have to lie. To me success will be making sure I am doing right in both spheres simultaneously.

Jady H. Regard

General Manager
Louisiana Ice Gators Hockey

Education:

B.A., PSYCHOLOGY, LOUISIANA STATE UNIVERSITY, 1992

M.ED., EDUCATIONAL PSYCHOLOGY, TEXAS A&M, 1995

Career Progression:

GENERAL MANAGER, LOUISIANA ICE GATORS HOCKEY, 1998 TO PRESENT

DIRECTOR OF MARKETING, ASSISTANT GENERAL MANAGER, MISSISSIPPI SEA WOLVES, 1996–1997

PUBLIC RELATIONS DIRECTOR, MERCHANDISE DIRECTOR, LOUISIANA ICE GATORS, 1995–1996

SNOW SKI INSTRUCTOR, KEYSTONE CO., 1992–1994

EQUIPMENT MANAGER, LOUISIANA STATE UNIVERSITY MEN'S BASKETBALL, 1989–1992

Best piece of advice you received in regards to your career:

"Practice patience and be a good listener."

Best advice for someone aspiring toward a career in the sport industry:

"Do what you can to get your foot in the door and once you are there do anything and everything to learn as much as possible."

Quote by which you live:

"There is only one boss: the customer. And he can fire everybody in the company, from the chairman on down simply by spending his money somewhere else."

SAM WALTON

MY INTEREST IN A SPORT CAREER CENTERED on my constant involvement in sports. The majority of the people involved in this business at one time in their lives expressed a huge interest in sports. They may have been an athlete or a spectator, looking in and wishing they were a part of it. They may have been a manager, a ball boy or girl, athletic trainer, volunteer coach, ticker taker, and so forth, but they definitely had a love for sport.

I participated in sports as a youngster. I played football at a very young age; however, I ended up concentrating on basketball in high school. I did have some measure of success and almost considered playing at an NAIA school, Spring Hill College, in Mobile, Alabama. I decided, however, to go to Louisiana State University (LSU) where I was involved as a manager with the men's basketball program for 3 years from 1989–1992. Shaquille O'Neal was there during that time so we were picked in the top 10 every year, and we sold out every night playing the likes of Duke and UNLV. I saw the marketing, promotion, crowd excitement, and entertainment aspects of sport and I loved it!

So how does someone from southern Louisiana end up in winter businesses like snow skiing and ice hockey? I guess I was just lucky. I always seemed to pick up sports pretty easily and skiing was one of those things that I did as a child on family vacations. I strongly believe if you have a passion for something and pursue it, you are going to be good at it. I moved to Colorado to fulfill a childhood dream of becoming a ski instructor. For 2 years, I was on the hill 6 days a week and absolutely loved it. I wanted to continue to do a variety of jobs in sport however. I coached at a basketball camp in France one summer, and I became a recreation director at a summer camp in Galveston, Texas, for several years. The common aspect of each of those jobs was that I enjoyed helping people enjoy themselves through sport. My progression in sport had been as an athlete, a manager, a ski instructor, camp administrator, and recreation director. Although that progression may not be unusual, what may be a little abnormal is how quickly I rose in the business side of professional sport.

My career climb in the world of professional sport, especially minor league pro ice hockey, has been a bit unusual. When I was living in Colorado, we had four guys living in a condominium and one of my roommates was a big hockey nut from Virginia. At the time, I was a ski instructor during the day and worked six nights a week as a bartender. I had one night off a week and it happened to be the night that a hockey game was on television. My roommate and I argued because I did not want to spend my one night off watching hockey on TV. I made him go to the nearest sports bar to watch the hockey games because I refused to watch. It is ironic that 5 years later I would be the general manager of an ice hockey team!

When I was finishing my master's degree at Texas A&M University, I found that there was a hockey team moving to Louisiana, specifically Lafayette in southern Louisiana, which is close to my hometown of New Iberia. As a child, I knew a girl from San Antonio, Texas, who told me all about how excited her city was about the new ice hockey team. I figured if hockey would work in San Antonio, it would certainly have a chance in Lafayette. I knew nothing about the game. I just wanted to be a part of the sport business. I thought I would at least give it a try and if it did not work out, I would go back to school and finish my degree in educational psychology.

I felt fortunate to get a job with the new Ice Gators franchise. I was working at home in southern Louisiana, in the sport business, with my family, and where I could go duck hunting. What a dream! I believe that my passion for the job and the location had a lot to do with my unusually quick career climb. I loved being a part of game nights. I liked being on the bus with the team. I liked being in the visitors' arena when we beat a team. I enjoyed going to seminars and meeting successful people who told me more about the business of sport. Although most people get promoted to jobs of higher responsibility and authority gradually, it is not normal to have the opportunity to progress as quickly as I did. I went from being a salesperson to public relations, to merchandising, to director of marketing, to assistant general manager, and general manager, all within about 2–1/2 years.

Things were not always easy in my career climb however. As I was learning the hockey business, I took a job working for the Mississippi Sea Wolves in Biloxi, Mississippi. I remember thinking to myself that things probably were not going the way that I planned them. The biggest problem was that my level of responsibility was not the level I wanted it to be. I was always the person that said, "Hey, put it on my back, let me take it." I had a great living situation and a very successful team. I was being paid well and there was a lot of interest in the community, but I did not have the responsibility I wanted. I did not think it was working out so I tried very hard to get a position with another hockey team in Greenville, South Carolina. I wanted to work for Carl Shear, a man who spent 25 years as an executive in the NBA who was the owner of the new hockey team. It was one of those situations, however, where I called several times, but never received a return call. In retrospect, however, it was a blessing because shortly thereafter I was offered one of the five best management jobs in minor league sports. I accepted the general manager's position with the Louisiana Ice Gators back in Lafayette.

I have faced several obstacles in becoming successful in the sport industry. One was a lack of educational training in my field to prepare me for what I would have to face each day at work. I had to undergo a great deal of on-the-job training because my educational training was not in the sport management field. Although my degree was in psychology, which may not translate into something very useful in the sport business, it represents the academic discipline that I was successful in at school. I think having more business courses to my credit or having practical business knowledge would have helped. I have considered returning to school to work on an executive MBA degree at night, but it is difficult with my job because I have a lot of night work. I believe it is something I will pursue at some point in the future because it would help legitimize my position as a sport executive.

Another obstacle was my age. I became the general manager of the Ice Gators at the age of 28. At the time, I was the youngest general manager in the country. Everyone I dealt with including the people in my office, my coach, the owners, accountants, marketing director, and sales director was older than me. It was very difficult to establish the level of authority and credibility I needed to succeed. I had to prove myself in everything.

As general manager of my team, I am responsible for all the day-to-day operations. I oversee two major areas: hockey operations and front office operations. Hockey operations includes overseeing the head coach, coaching staff, trainer, equipment manager, and about 22 players during the season. Front office operations involves supervising about 11 people, including the director of sales, director of promotions, director of tickets, two ticket representatives, a receptionist, director of marketing, director of player relations, director of media relations, director of community relations, and comptroller.

Day-to-day operations vary. About 85 percent of my day is planned during the first hour, and although I try to set an agenda for that day, rarely do I have the chance to take care of everything. Almost every day, an unplanned situation arises that needs immediate attention. Crisis situations may involve a player injury, worker's compensation, immigration issues, or expenses on the hockey side or front office side. Other crisis situations include hiring a new employee, developing a new marketing plan, developing a ticket plan, working with the director of sales, going on a sales call, or working on a television or radio deal.

Immigration issues are very commonplace in the world of minor league hockey. About 85 percent of our players are Canadian, and a small percentage of the rest are from European countries such as Czechoslovakia, Sweden, or Finland. I have a person in my office dedicated to dealing with immigration legal issues and paperwork. The players are paid on a work basis to come and play hockey—and only hockey—and you must abide by certain rules, dates, timelines, and paperwork.

I think the most satisfaction from my job is when we have 10,000 plus fans in Lafayette on their feet, screaming their lungs out for their team to win, and we come up with a 4–2 victory. On top of that, if we have had a very successful theme night, or a great promotional plan, I get satisfaction from watching the fans file out with genuine smiles on their faces. Delivering that kind of high quality entertainment is the best kind of feeling I get from this business. When it is over, it is all about that person walking out happy. When that happens, you know they will come back.

I think the most demanding challenge is to be innovative in creating better entertainment options for our fans. We have 35 games per year and we strive to sell out all of our home games. Lafayette has a population area of about 120,000, and the Cajun Dome seats nearly 11,123 for ice hockey. We have been fortunate enough to average 10,500 over the past couple of years. That places us third overall in attendance of the 110 minor league hockey teams in North America. We are very proud of those figures, but it is very difficult to continue to maintain or surpass that level. Our main challenge now is to maintain and expand the interest in our area. The newness of the product has dissipated so now we must use some grassroots initiatives to ensure we are tapping into the youth of the area and exposing them to this sport at a very young age. We have to develop programs where we go into parks, schools, and recreational leagues to put a hockey stick and hockey puck into some kid's hand so he or she can learn the game. In Lafayette we now have three full-time facilities dedicated to hockey 12 months a year, including two roller rinks and an ice rink. We have youth leagues and have developed a select team to play against other all-star type teams around the nation. We are about to start club teams at the high school level because we believe if we are progressive in developing outlets for the youth of this area, we will develop future fans for our team.

I am not sure there is such a thing as a "typical" day in my job. I do not travel a lot, but I try to travel as much as I can with the team. Some difference exists in the office climate depending on whether the team is in town or traveling. When the team is out of town, the phone does not ring as much and the pace seems to slow down a bit. For some reason, when we have a home game everyone has a quicker step, phones ring a little more, and everyone is on his or her "A" game. I try to get to work around 7:45 AM, make the coffee, and turn on the TV to catch up on the previous night's scores. On Mondays, we start with a marketing meeting for all of the staff at 9:00 AM. We review the past week and then discuss the upcoming week's projects. We have the meetings on Mondays so we can discuss the weekend games. In the summer we stay with that schedule so everyone is used to being in that routine for "game season." I schedule a lot of individual meetings with my different staff members and have an open door policy in my office. One minute a fan may walk in, another minute it might be a vendor, and another minute it might be a potential client we are signing to a sponsor deal. It goes that way all day long.

I am very fortunate to have a group of owners who are all local Lafayette gentlemen. I report to them monthly with financial updates. At the end of May and June, we do the yearly budget and we try to stay on top of the budget as much as we can. In our meetings, we not only discuss financial news, but also any other news pertinent to our community. They are very passionate about the success of the team and about the level and quality of entertainment we provide because their name is on the team and they are very recognizable in our community.

An outside company manages our Web site. The beauty of minor league sports, or sport in general, is trade—trade, trade, trade. We trade for company services with four season tickets. The person in charge of our site has to keep the statistics updated constantly and, unlike a lot of business sites, sports Web sites change every time there is a game. If there is a promotion; then there is a history of what happened before, and it is very important to stay up to the minute because the fans want to know. We have had fans working in the oil industry get transferred to Saudi Arabia and military personnel move to Germany, and the wonderful thing about the Internet is they correspond with us to tell us how much they enjoy keeping up with the team.

Most of the beginning administrative salaries in minor league sports are modest to say the least. I came in my first year with a master's degree and earned about $16,000. If you want to work in the hockey business, you must understand that initially it will be little pay and very long hours. My first job had some bonuses and incentives built into my ticket and sponsorship sales. My ticket representatives now are on salary at $14,000 per year, but they get a 10 percent commission on season tickets, 12 percent on group tickets, and 5 percent commission on mini plans. My director of marketing, director of media relations and community relations, and my youth hockey development people all make a base salary between $18,000 to $22,000 per year plus incentives. My director of marketing earns about $30,000; my director of sales makes about $30,000 plus 4 percent for old accounts and 8 percent for new accounts. He will make between $65,000 and $75,000. He also has a car and some other perks. My accountant is making about $30,000. A head coach in the East Coast Hockey League usually earns between $55,000 and $70,000, plus he has a home, a car, and an annual life insurance policy paid for him. Additional bonuses are based on attendance, divisional championships, play-off position, conference standings, and so forth. Most of our general managers are making between $45,000 and $60,000 per year. My base salary is $70,000, plus I get a golf club membership at a very nice golf club in Lafayette. I have a health club membership and a car provided for me. It is a nice package for a young person like myself.

To be a successful manager in this business, you must be a people person and a good listener. I believe you have to understand, first and foremost, the needs of the fan. I think you have to realize what it is like to be a fan. I think you have to feel out the parking lot and walk to the stadium. I think you have to go sit in the third level and experience what it is like to sit in the middle of the section and hear the fans during the game. I think you have to go to the restroom and stand in line. I think you have to experience what the fan experiences at the concession stand and at the souvenir booth. If you do not see the game as the fans do, you will not be able to meet their needs. We try to maintain communication with our fans through surveys, polls, and focus groups. Everyone in the sport business is trying to identify their fan base and trying to determine how to keep them attending the games. I have a personal management philosophy that says "if you don't know what you're doing, hire somebody that does." I have surrounded myself with very talented and smart people and am not afraid to admit that I do not have all the answers. I have been fortunate to hire excellent people who have made the organization and me successful.

Many other factors lead to success for a sport franchise. One is location. It is the truth for a football team, basketball team, hockey team, or any sports team.

You need good location. Once you pinpoint a city, you have to pinpoint what area is most accessible for your fans. When we started in Lafayette we attributed our success to a number of different factors. One, we are an oil-based economy, which was doing very well in the mid-1990s. We are a type of people who are passionate and social, and the Ice Gators became the social thing to do in Lafayette. Add to that a beautiful building, ease of entry and exit, and safety and people have an enjoyable experience and want to return.

I think hockey became popular in the south because hockey was not here. When Wayne Gretzky went from the Edmonton Oilers to the Los Angeles Kings, inline hockey boomed on the west coast and slowly worked its way across the United States. At the same time, minor league hockey is filtering down from the east coast and spreading its tentacles out across the midwest and south. Technology was developed to allow ice rinks to be built in pre-existing buildings, and then sports fans learned that the game never before played in their area has the physical play of football, the speed of baseball, and the fast-break action of basketball. Women and families love it. All of this action is happening at one time and before you know it, combustion!

Another reason ice hockey and most other minor league sports are so popular is the inexpensive ticket price. Hockey is a spectator sport that unfortunately does not translate well to television. You have to be there to get the feel for hockey. There is so much action away from the puck and that hurts us a little bit. We do not see the television revenues and NHL has to raise the prices because 70 percent of their income is at the gate. The rising salaries of NHL will continue to cause an increase in ticket prices that will pose a serious challenge for the future of hockey at the highest level. I will say that television has helped the south get a taste of hockey by covering inline hockey and NHL games on ESPN, ESPN2, and Fox stations.

As far as my future and where I want to be in 10 years, it is difficult to say. Five years ago, I would not have dreamed I would be where I am today! In 10 years I will be 40 years old and I may be at the major league level. I believe my first love for sports has always been college basketball. I do not know if I would be in the college basketball business, but basketball is a consideration. I have an affinity for football, too, although hockey has grown on me. The current president of the Nashville Predators used to be the president of the San Antonio Spurs. He has been very successful in a new sport in a new area, and I think the transition and crossover from one sport to another would be easy. You are dealing with the same ticketing, marketing, game, coaching, equipment, and entertainment issues. Right now, the main thing for me is to be the best I can at my current position and make the owners and board of directors happy. I want to make our team profitable and a part of the social fabric of our community while providing a source of entertainment that is not available elsewhere.

Where do I see hockey evolving in the future? It is interesting to guess where several of the major league sports will be in the future as some of the icons of the game retire. The retirements of John Elway, Michael Jordan, and Wayne Gretzky were a tremendous jolt to their respective leagues. Growing up, I did not know much about Wayne Gretzky, but I have read a lot about him now and I wish I was working in hockey when he was still playing. I wish I could have witnessed some of his amazing feats, like 200 points in a season! I am sure there will always be another player to carry the torch, but maybe not quite like him. I heard it said that the difference between Michael Jordan and Wayne Gretzky was that Jordan elevated the status of the NBA, whereas Wayne Gretzky literally carried the league on his back. He was the guy who brought the game over the border, exposed it to the United States, and is directly responsible for its expansion. His class and off-the-ice presence, just like Michael Jordan's, is very difficult to replace.

One particular area of management I love is the marketing aspect of this sport. As the entertainment dollar continues to be stretched, I believe creativity in marketing will be even more important. I get very excited when a new idea is implemented and it succeeds. We had an all-inclusive "70s" night last year that was a big hit. The staff dressed in 70s outfits, danced to 70s music, and we had 70s competitions. We did a first-rate NHL caliber job on a minor league budget, and it was exciting and fun and we also won the game! That was one of those nights where I look back and say, "Wow, this was a great night!"

The major leagues have the same problems that I do, and they have to be just as creative and aggressive. However, they have more marketing dollars and employee resources. An NHL team has a 65-person staff and I have 11. In some cases, we average more attendance than they do! That is amazing. However, not every promotion goes off without a hitch. One year we had a wedding on the ice; however, the couple got extremely intoxicated before they got married and the judge did not want to marry them. Ten thousand people in the building expected to see a wedding, so with much chagrin the judge finally relented and conducted the ceremony.

We start our marketing for the next year by late January when we send out letters for renewals on tickets. While preparing for play-offs we also prepare for sponsorship renewals and that carries us through the play-offs. The play-offs end suddenly and the "off season" begins immediately. We go back to selling tickets, re-establishing our relationship with customers and sponsors, and preparing for the new fiscal year. Late June and early July is a little slow, but in August we start thinking about training camp and the beginning of the season. Marketing never stops, and we try to capitalize on several types of special events. We are fortunate to have an NHL pre-season game in Lafayette. It is pretty exciting to have teams like the St. Louis Blues and the Colorado Avalanche play in our city. We do another big event in October called Roller Blade for Cancer. It is a 6-mile marathon with people on roller blades. The whole team roller blades with the general public. We had about 500 skaters last year and raised about $16,000. We can get people interested in roller blading and get them excited about the season by having the players sign autographs and skate with the general public. Mardi Gras is also a special time in Louisiana. Our population increases six-fold and nearly 600,000 people are on the parade route. We spend about $5,000 a year to be in one parade for one day because it is important to be in front of as many people as possible. The players wear their jerseys and they throw beads from our special float with a big alligator on it. We are very recognizable and it is just a lot of fun to be a part it.

I have been so fortunate to make a living working in the sport industry. The best way to get into professional sport is through sales. If you can succeed in selling yourself and your product, there will be a job for you. The best way to get started is by doing an internship for an organization. You can get some practical experience and learn the business by doing the work. We have had at least four interns become full-time employees in professional hockey and that speaks for itself. The world of minor league professional sport can be a job requiring long hours, great energy, and constant creativity, but the rewards are great.

CHAPTER 6

Facility Management

FACILITY MANAGEMENT INVOLVES THE APPLICATION of management principles to the operation and maintenance of athletic venues, namely stadiums and arenas. These principles include planning, organizing, staffing, financing, scheduling, marketing, controlling, and evaluating (Walker & Stotlar, 1997). Facility managers also need to be aware of risk management issues, have knowledge of legal terminology and contracts, and ensure compliance with the Americans with Disabilities Act. Sport facilities include public assembly venues such as stadiums, arenas, ballparks and racetracks, and participant facilities such as fitness centers, swimming pools, golf courses, tennis courts, and playgrounds.

According to the December 20–26, 1999 issue of the *Sports Business Journal,* sport facility construction accounted for $2.49 billion in 1999, with facility management and consulting accounting for another $5.74 billion. Developing funding sources for these new facilities has become increasingly complex, however, innovative financing techniques are continually being developed. One popular form of financing for both newly constructed and existing facilities is the sale of naming rights. Venues that house professional teams, minor league teams, and even college teams have benefited from the sale of naming rights. The most recent and most lucrative deal was struck in Washington, D.C., where new Redskins owner Daniel Snyder sold the naming rights to the existing 80,000 seat stadium to Federal Express for $205 million over 27 years (Shapiro & Clarke, 1999). Other teams have used naming rights fees to fund new venue construction, such as the Pittsburgh Pirates and PNC (Bank) Park, and the Los Angeles Kings, Clippers, and Lakers with the Staples Center. Another creative revenue source used to offset construction costs is the sale of Permanent Seat Licenses (PSLs) which guarantee the purchaser the right to buy season tickets for a particular seat over a specified time period. The NFL's Carolina Panthers sold 62,000 PSL's in 1993, which generated more than $100 million for stadium construction (Spanberg, 1996).

Career opportunities in facility management are varied and include marketing, public relations, booking and scheduling, operations, sales, and box office operations (Graney & Barrett, 1998). Facility marketing directors create marketing plans and coordinate activities with sponsors, promoters, and advertisers to facilitate increased attendance and exposure of the facility in general or a specific event. Public relations professionals deal with the media and public relative to events at the venue, including coordinating media coverage, distributing press releases, and arranging celebrity or athlete appearances. The booking or scheduling director solicits events and negotiates with promoters to host shows, sport events, or conventions, and the sales professionals on staff solicit partnerships with local, regional, and national sponsors and advertisers to offset the cost of event production and promotion.

The operations director supervises facility preparation for events by coordinating the changeovers that occur. For example, in a multipurpose arena with a basketball game scheduled for Saturday and a hockey game scheduled for Sunday, a significant amount of activity is required to get the playing surfaces properly prepared. The operations manager also directly supervises the housekeeping, maintenance, and operations staff. The box office director is often responsible for the sale of all event tickets as well as the postevent financial settlement.

The career opportunities in facility management are quite varied and often require long hours, but can be satisfying and financially rewarding. Entry-level pay in facility management ranges from $25,000 to $35,000 per year, middle-level positions salaries range from $35,000 to $60,000 per year, and a facility manager can earn up to $100,000 per year. These salaries vary based on the size of the facilities as well as the responsibilities of the positions.

REFERENCES

Graney, M., & Barrett, K. (1998). Facility management. In L.P. Masteralexis, C.A. Barr, & M.A. Hums (Eds.), *Principles and practice of sport management* (pp. 307–327). Gaithersburg, MD: Aspen Publishers, Inc.

Shapiro, L., & Clarke, L. (1999, December 26). Snyder: a matter of style. *The Washington Post.* Available at: http://www.washingtonpost.com/wp-srv/sports/redskins/daily/dec00/26/snyder26.htm.

Spanberg, E. (1996, July 22). PSL a valuable commodity. *The Business Journal of Charlotte.* Available at: http://www.amcity.com/charlotte/stories/1996/07/22/story2.html.

Sports Business Journal. (1999, December 20–26). *Sports business at the end of the millennium,* pp. 24–25.

Walker, M., & Stotlar, D. (Eds.). (1997). *Sport facility management.* Sudbury, MA: Jones and Bartlett Publishers, Inc.

Kyle Kirousis

Senior Events Coordinator
Alamodome

Education:
B.S. SPORT MANAGEMENT, UNIVERSITY OF
MASSACHUSETTS-AMHERST, 1997

Career Progression:
SENIOR EVENTS COORDINATOR, ALAMODOME,
APRIL 1999 TO PRESENT

EVENTS COORDINATOR, ALAMODOME, JANU-
ARY 1997 TO APRIL 1999

Best piece of advice you received in regards to your career:

"If there is something you truly believe in, go after it with your best effort. If you fail, you fail, but at least you won't have any regrets for not trying."

ANGELO KIROUSIS, MY FATHER.

Best advice for someone aspiring toward a career in the sport industry:

"A career in sport can be very exciting and a great experience, however be prepared to work incredibly long hours often without seeing much of the events you work so hard to organize. Remember you work when other people work, but you will also work when other people play."

Quote by which you live:

"Whatever the mind of man can conceive and believe it can achieve."

NAPOLEON HILL

THE FIRST TIME I CONSIDERED A CAREER in sport was after a meeting with my high school guidance counselor, Ed Gastonguay, during my senior year. At that time, I was interested in pursuing a career in business but I also had a strong interest in sports having been involved with them as long as I could remember. I knew realistically that I could not play sports forever, but I did know I wanted to work in some capacity on the business side of the industry. Finding a career combining my two interests sounded ideal, but I had no idea how to go about pursuing a career in sport. The meeting with Mr. Gastonguay proved to be very enlightening as he made me aware of two schools offering relatively new degree programs specifically geared toward the business side of sports. I researched the two sport management programs and ultimately decided to attend the University of Massachusetts at Amherst, where I graduated with a bachelor's degree in sport management in 1997.

When I was at UMass, I was in what was called the internship track, which meant I had to complete an internship to satisfy my credit requirement to graduate. At the time I was looking for an internship, I was mainly interested in pursuing a career in facility management because it seemed like an exciting and challenging work environment. However, to a certain extent, my adult interest in facility management was probably subconsciously influenced by a childhood fascination with stadiums and arenas. I will never forget the first time I went to places like the old Boston Garden, the Worcester Centrum, Fenway Park, and the Spectrum. I was in such awe. You would have thought I had just landed on another planet. I was captivated by the architecture, vastness, and details of these buildings. To be quite honest, I think in most cases I was actually more interested in the facilities than the events I went to see. Even today, it is a great treat for me to go to an arena or stadium I have never been to before.

When I was looking for an internship in facility management I wanted the opportunity to work in a venue that had hosted several major events. I wanted the chance to gain great experience and get actively involved in the organization and preferably live in southwest. I basically wanted to test myself at one of the premier venues in the industry and experience living in a different part of the country because I was ready for a change. For some reason the southwest had appealed to me for a long time. I was also motivated by the belief that my degree was my ticket to go anywhere I wanted to go in the pursuit of a career. So with my "no limits" attitude and pioneer spirit, I started contacting facilities in Arizona, New Mexico, Colorado, Utah, and Texas. In the beginning, I did not have much luck. Some of the facilities I called had no formal internship programs and the ones that did could not give me a commitment by the date I needed one. I was frustrated and began to realize just how difficult it was to get a foot in the door in the sport industry. I refused to give up, however, and came to the realization that I needed some help. I made an appointment with Howie Davis, my internship advisor at UMass, to get some direction. I explained my goal to him, the steps I had taken, and the fruitless results I had achieved. He then asked me if I had talked to Steve Zito, the general manager at San Antonio's Alamodome, about internship possibilities. Steve Zito was a 1985 graduate from the sport management program at UMass and is considered one of the most prominent and highly regarded members of the UMass sport management alumni network. Steve had expressed interest to Mr. Davis about having UMass students do internships at his facility. The only drawbacks for UMass students were that it was so far away and it did not pay a lot—pretty major obstacles for college students coming right out of school. Those two details did not deter me, however, because I knew this was the opportunity I had looked so hard to find and was willing to do whatever it took (within reason) to make it a reality. It was the internship that offered everything I wanted. The Alamodome was a major facility with an NBA team as its primary tenant. It hosted the Alamobowl every year and had hosted the 1997 Midwest Regional and the 1998 Final Four of the men's basketball tournament. Several concerts with top performers and many other major events also are held at the Alamodome. I thought to myself, "These people must be doing something right." But perhaps the most exciting part about the internship at the Alamodome was that it was in a part of the country where I wanted to live. After a summer of working long hours at a Coors beer distributorship, I saved enough money to finance my venture and drove 2,000 miles from home to start my career in San Antonio.

I learned four major lessons during the process of securing my internship. They are as follows: First, be persistent. The sport and entertainment industry is a very difficult one to crack. It may take making 50 phone calls and sending out 20 resumes to land an internship. At times it can be frustrating. It is important to stay focused and not get discouraged. For me the greatest satisfaction comes from achieving those goals I believe strongly in and work hard for. Things that come too easily always make me wonder if I could have done more. Second, remember the strength of an alumni network. A school's alumni network is an extremely valuable resource and its importance should not be underestimated or neglected. When I started looking for internships, I thought the noble approach was to compile a list of facilities I was interested in, cold call them to learn more about internship possibilities, and send out resumes. Going completely off on your own is a tough way to go and kudos to anyone who can be successful with this approach. However, always keep in mind that people want to help you and want to see you do well. You do not have to go it alone. The best decision I made when looking for my internship was to make that appointment with Howie Davis. I got more accomplished in that 45-minute session than I did with the countless phone calls I made to facilities across the country.

Third, do not set limits for yourself and do not listen to the naysayers. Always be open to new possibilities. Sometimes the greatest opportunities arise when we allow ourselves to think "outside of the box." If I had listened to all the people who told me I was "crazy" (and yes, there were many) for going to San Antonio—a place I had never been to and did not know anyone—I probably would still be back in New England haunted by the thoughts of what could have been if I only had the courage to follow my heart. Always remember the naysayers are often the ones who have their own fears about leaving a comfortable environment to pursue their goals and dreams and simply cannot relate to you. This is not a knock on them, but do not let their negative thoughts and comments influence you. Finally, if there is something you strongly believe in, go after it and make it happen. I think the following quote by motivational author Napoleon Hill is appropriate: "Whatever the mind of man can conceive and believe it can achieve." In my case, I knew I wanted to work in a "big time" facility and preferably live in the southwest. I also believed I could succeed in that environment if given the chance. This focus and confidence enabled me to pursue my goals and make them a reality.

Let me describe my workplace, the Alamodome. The Alamodome is a city-owned and operated multipurpose sports and entertainment facility located in downtown San Antonio. Completed in May 1993 at a cost of $182.7 million, the Alamodome has been debt free because of a sales tax on public transportation that was collected over 5 years. Since opening its doors, the Alamodome has become one of the most sought after venues in Texas for major sporting events, concerts, conventions, trade shows, and assemblies. During an average year, the Alamodome hosts about 110 events. In 1998 it was ranked the third highest grossing venue in North America and the sixth highest grossing facility in the world. It is the home of the 1999 NBA World Champion San Antonio Spurs (until the end of the 2002 season) and the annual Sylvania Alamobowl. It is the past and future site of the Midwest Regional and both the men's and women's Division I NCAA Final Four basketball tournaments. Its impressive resume also includes two Big XII football championships, a Billy Graham Crusade, and performances by groups and artists such as Pink Floyd, the Rolling Stones, Elton John, Billy Joel, Janet Jackson, Celine Dion, George Strait, and Garth Brooks.

The Alamodome is a very unique and impressive structure. Designed by the architects at HOK Sports, it is classified as a third generation domed stadium because of the cable system, which supports its 9-acre roof. It is basically the same engineering concept used in suspension bridges. For full-stadium events, such as football and monster truck shows, the Alamodome can seat up to 65,000 people. When set up in our arena configuration, we can seat up to 32,500 people depending on the event. For example, a family show such as Barney's Big Surprise could be manifested for about 10,000. The smaller, more intimate configurations are made possible by the use of curtain systems that can close off or hide seats not being used. For events that will draw more than 32,000, such as a Spurs/ Lakers game or a Ricky Martin concert, the curtain systems are not used.

When I started my internship at the Alamodome, my goal was to become actively involved in the organization, have as many different experiences as possible, and learn as much as I could in the 4 months I would be there. Because there was no guarantee of a full-time opportunity when I completed my internship, I wanted to gain extensive experience in a world-class facility, develop marketable skills, and strengthen my resume, at the very least. I became a sponge and absorbed everything that came my way. I became involved with several projects; wrote articles for *Between the Masts*, the official newsletter of the Alamodome; assisted the senior event coordinators with event preparations; and worked with the conversion crew to learn the intricacies of converting from one configuration to another. Then, about a month into my internship, a senior events coordinator left to accept a similar position at the Phoenix Civic Plaza, a convention center in downtown Phoenix. His departure allowed me the opportunity to take the lead in organizing various events from Spurs games and small concerts to meeting room events. This experience helped lay the foundation for my current position.

Toward the end of my internship, Alamodome management posted a job announcement for the vacant senior events coordinator. I applied for the position and subsequently ran into the first roadblock of my young career. Because the Alamodome is a municipal department of the City of San Antonio, all applications for city job postings are processed through a central human resources department. Human resources uses a certain selection criteria to select qualified applicants and then sends the information on the successful candidates to the department so interviews can be scheduled. For example, they may require 3 years of administrative experience as they did for the senior events coordinator position. Having just finished my internship, I came up just a "little" short of the city's 3-year requirement and therefore my application was not sent for consideration. I was devastated and confused. How could someone who did not know anything about facility management or how the Alamodome operates make the judgment on my future? That was the hardest thing to accept. I had successfully been doing the job for the previous 2 months, was familiar with the Alamodome and how events were produced, and knew the policies. Fortunately for me, people at the Alamodome saw my potential and commitment to the organization. They downgraded the position to an events coordinator to make it more feasible for me to comply with the city's requirements. This newly created position would allow me to gain more experience and be better qualified when the senior events coordinator was posted again in the future. I went through the application process again and was chosen as the successful candidate. I served as an events coordinator for a year and a half or so and then was promoted to a senior events coordinator, my current position.

I think my career path to this point has been logical and probably common for today's sport management environment. You hear of so many people who started as interns and advanced. I can cite several examples from my immediate work environment. Both the Alamodome and San Antonio Spurs have employees in upper management positions who started their careers as interns. I am a firm believer that an internship is a great way to get your foot in the door and show an organization what you have to offer, your strengths, work ethic, and commitment. Impressions made during an internship can be very influential to one's future with the organization.

There is not much I would do differently up to this point but, if I were to do my college years over again, I would have done at least one more internship. Things have worked out well for me having only done one internship, but it would have allowed me to get more practical work experience before I graduated. However, if that is my biggest regret about my career thus far, I guess I am not doing too badly.

As lucky as I have been to start my career at a high-profile facility like the Alamodome, I have been even more fortunate to work with and learn from a team of talented and experienced facility managers. To me, it is the people who make a facility first-class and successful. You could have the most state-of-the-art-building with all the amenities but that does not mean a thing without a top quality staff. On several occasions after shows, promoters have told me the Alamodome is one of the premier venues in the country and one they always enjoy returning to for a performance. In large part their reasoning had nothing to do with sight lines, production features, or video broadcast capabilities. It overwhelmingly had to do with our staff and how "great they were to work with." I cannot think of another place where I would have wanted to start my career. Several fine facilities exist, but I know I am part of a very special team so I guess I am slightly biased.

During my time at the Alamodome I have looked to three people as mentors. I respect them tremendously as professionals and more importantly for who they are. The first is Steve Zito, the general manager of the Alamodome who, as I mentioned briefly before, also graduated from UMass. With more than 15 years of facility and event management experience, Steve Zito is a revered figure in the industry. An active member of the International Association of Assembly Managers (IAAM), Steve is a talented manager and a creative problem solver. He also has an incredible work ethic and is well organized. On countless occasions I have gone to the administrative offices late (2:00 AM) after an event and he was working on memos, projects, or proposals. Steve was also instrumental in helping me land my first position at the Alamodome. Kevin Duvall, the events director, is another person I look to as a role model. He is responsible for "event development" or booking Alamodome events and negotiating the rental deals. When I first started at the Alamodome, Kevin was the events manager and my immediate supervisor. By working closely with him, I learned a lot about the sport and entertainment business. Kevin is a strong manager with exceptional organizational skills and to me he epitomizes the word "professionalism." He handles every situation with the same calm demeanor, a quality of his that I greatly admire. Kevin was another person who "went to bat" for me early in my career and was influential in my securing a full-time position at the Alamodome. Perhaps the person who was most responsible for my day-to-day development as an events coordinator was Terry Caven, who is now the events manager. Terry took me under his wing early in my career when he was a senior events coordinator and taught me a lot. With more than 15 years of diverse event production experience, Terry was an incredible resource. I was very fortunate to share the same office as him. He was always there to answer my questions. I am sure I drove him nuts at times, but I will be forever grateful for Terry's guidance and most importantly his patience. I sincerely hope that at some point in my career I will be looked upon as a mentor and be a positive influence in someone's life as these three men have been in mine.

As a senior events coordinator, I am the primary contact for event promoters once the events are booked. My job is to organize all of the event logistics, accommodate the promoter's needs, and delegate tasks to the various Alamodome departments or subcontractors. For each event I am assigned I create a document called a "prospectus," which outlines all of the unique details of the event and includes a departmental breakdown of everything needed to make the event a success. For example, if I were coordinating a concert, the operations section would include things such as stage size, number of chairs on the floor, what the conversion entails, room set-ups, and so forth. The engineering section would have information on electrical, HVAC (air conditioning), carpentry, and plumbing needs. The security section would contain information on first-aid locations, parking, and crowd control. The event staff section would list restricted areas, meet and greets, and special functions. This is just a sample of the items often found in a prospectus. The prospectus is a very thorough and comprehensive reference and becomes the "official" in-house manual of the event. Often it is about 10 pages but, for larger events like the Final Fours and Big XII Championships, it can be about 30 pages. It is a tremendous tool and makes it easier for all those involved because they have everything they need to know right at their fingertips.

Having said that, it is no surprise that the most important skill needed in my position—and any management position—is the ability to communicate effectively. It sounds like a basic principle, but often I think it is a dying art. I learned early that you can never be too thorough when communicating. You just cannot expect to tell someone something once and assume it will get done. Many times I will back up a conversation with an e-mail or memo. I also think having the ability to handle several things simultaneously is critical. On a typical day I need to budget my time so I can advance upcoming shows with promoters, attend meetings, respond to e-mail, return calls, work on other projects, be available to answer any questions from my supervisors or coworkers, and manage the many distractions that arise. Another very important skill is the flexibility to work with many different types of people and personalities. As far as my management style is concerned, I am still developing it but I think treating people with respect and being up front with them are important. Talking down to people and dropping tasks on them at the last minute does not warrant good results. I think the people I work with know I am very fair and approachable.

Organizing an event is the same regardless of the size or type of the event. The same fundamental steps must be taken to ensure the bases are covered. For example, for a concert some fundamental issues include helping plan the conversion, putting the event on sale, managing seat kills and relocates, accommodating stage size, adjusting for rigging and power requirements, and setting up rooms. I know each concert and event will have its own unique requirements but the fundamentals remain the same. The only difference is that for the larger shows or events the promoter's needs are greater and I interact with a lot more people. When the event is over I prepare a summary report of the event that serves as a valuable reference for the next coordinator who does the show or one similar to it. These postevent notes include any special event set-up information, any problems that occurred, and suggestions for improvement.

As I mentioned earlier, part of my job is to help plan conversions, which can be very challenging. Every Wednesday we have a conversion meeting and we discuss the conversions for the upcoming week and cover the details of each conversion. The Alamodome can be set up in about 25 different configurations and often the conversions need to be completed on tight timelines. At times I feel as though it is like a chess game. For example, we may have a Spurs game on a given night and a concert scheduled for the next day with a 5:00 AM load-in. To make it on time, the conversion would start immediately after the game. The first things to be struck are the court, goals, and seats around the court. The next step would be to push in some of our south seats and build a stage in front of the pushed-in sections. Depending on the concert, some additional seating might need to be done. This type of conversion is perhaps the most basic and common one. Going from a full stadium configuration to our arena set-up is considerably more labor intensive. Perhaps the toughest conversion we ever did was going from a "Woman of Faith" conference (an arena event) to the George Strait Music Festival, a full stadium event with doors opening at noon the next day. It was a real challenge to find ways to accommodate both groups and turn the building around in time. The last thing we wanted was to have either promoter think his or her event was short-changed in some way. Because George Strait was such a major production, they had to load-in 4 days before the show compared to the Woman of Faith event, where everything was set up the day before the event. We had George Strait on one side of the big curtain that divides the stadium and the Woman of Faith event on the other side. The Strait production had to stop with the load-in and sound checks during the Woman of Faith event and return when it was over. The production load-in and our conversion started right after the Woman of Faith event and continued through the night. At that point we still had some major seating work to do. We set up close to 10,000 chairs on the floor once it was cleared. The tremendous feat of getting everything ready for the noon doors the next day is a credit to the Alamodome's fine operations crew and the months of planning. Everybody knew exactly what needed to be done and their role in the process.

The most demanding part of my job is the hours. During our busy season (November through May), a 70-hour workweek is not uncommon and there are times, like during the Final Four, when I put in back-to-back 80-hour weeks. On the positive side, I accumulate what we call "discretionary hours" that I can take off at a later date. These hours are based on the number of hours I work in a month and accumulate throughout the year. I usually can take off about 4–5 weeks a year using my discretionary time, which is a pretty nice perk.

I would have to say the most enjoyable parts of my job are working with the people here at the Alamodome and meeting people of all different backgrounds. In my position I come across many types of people, from promoters, to stage-hands, to media, and in some instances celebrities, which keeps things interesting. I will never forget the time I went to an HBO production meeting when I co-ordinated an Oscar de la Hoya fight in 1997. I took my seat at a large table and was surrounded by executives from Top Rank Boxing and HBO. Shortly thereafter, George Foreman and Jim Lampley, the announcers for the fight, sat down in the two empty chairs next to me. It was quite an experience for me to see that aspect of the boxing business. I have watched boxing many times on TV, but being at that production meeting gave me a totally different perspective.

To this point I have been very satisfied with my experience at the Alamodome. I work with many wonderful people and have grown professionally and advanced. It is not about the salary now. Other factors are more important to me. I want to continue progressing and developing my management, organizational, and interpersonal skills. As long as I can do that, I will be happy. I know in time the money will follow.

With a referendum for a new county-managed arena recently passing, the prospect of the Spurs moving into another facility has become a reality. The San Antonio Spurs account for about half of the Alamodome's annual revenue, so with half of its primary tenant "walking out the door" at the end of the 2002 season, the Alamodome faces uncertain times ahead. The focus now is on finding creative ways to fill the 45+ dates that will become available once the Spurs leave.

If someone was aspiring to have a job like mine, the most important things are a willingness to pay your dues and a good attitude. Otherwise, the hours and pressures involved will wear you down. One of the most common stresses of my job is dealing with patron complaints, but it can also be very rewarding when the patron goes away happy as a result of your resolution. How you resolve a patron's problem could very well influence him or her wanting to return. It is also important to have interests outside of work and have balance in your life. Without them, I think you can burn out quickly as an events coordinator. The industry average for a person in my position is about 3 years.

I think the next step I would like to take in facility management is to be a booking manager for an arena. I would like to be the person responsible for attracting events to a facility and negotiating the rental deals. I could draw on my previous event management because I know the logistics of producing a variety of events and meeting the promoters' needs. It would enable me to learn a different facet of the industry and provide me with a new challenge.

Robert R. Bender

Recreation and Fitness Manager
Sea Pines Resort

Education:
B.S., SPORT MANAGEMENT, ROBERT MORRIS COLLEGE, 1991

M.A., SPORT MANAGEMENT, THE OHIO STATE UNIVERSITY, 1992

Career Progression:
RECREATION AND FITNESS MANAGER, SEA PINES, 1993 TO PRESENT

INTERN, COLUMBUS CLIPPERS AAA BASEBALL CLUB, 1991–1992

INTERN AND SUPERVISOR, RESORT RECREATION AND TENNIS MANAGEMENT, JANUARY 1991 TO AUGUST 1991

SUMMER CAMP COUNSELOR, SEWICKLEY VALLEY YMCA, JUNE 1990 TO AUGUST 1990

TICKET PROCESSOR, PITTSBURGH PIRATES, MARCH 1989 TO AUGUST 1989

Best piece of advice you received in regards to your career:

"Get as much work related experience as you can and start early."

DR. SUSAN HOFACRE, ROBERT MORRIS COLLEGE

Best advice for someone aspiring toward a career in the sport industry:

"Get to know as many people as you can in the sports industry and maintain those relationships."

Quote by which you live:

"Success...The difference between a successful person and others is not a lack of strength, not a lack of knowledge, but rather a lack of will."

MY NAME IS ROB BENDER and I am the recreation manager for the Sea Pines Resort in Hilton Head Island, South Carolina. I have been with the company for nearly 7 years. I attended Robert Morris College in Pittsburgh, Pennsylvania, for my undergraduate degree and attended Ohio State University for my master's degree. Both degrees were in sport management with an emphasis in business, management, and marketing. I graduated from Robert Morris in 1991 and Ohio State in 1992. The Robert Morris program focuses more on the business side of sports/recreation than on the programming side. This was a great benefit because it allowed me to gain skills in areas that were not just specific to the sport/recreation industry such as accounting, statistics, marketing, public relations, public speaking, and management. There were also classes specific to the sport/recreation field, but again the approach was more from the business aspect. The class sizes were smaller and allowed for discussion and questions. Because many of the graduates of the program worked in the area, we constantly had guest speakers who provided a wealth of practical knowledge. Additionally, this also allowed us to visit many different sport/recreation facilities and companies.

I had been involved in recreation and sports through junior high and high school, but was not sure what I wanted to do. When I finished high school I knew I wanted to go to college but was not exactly sure what specific career I wanted to pursue. I found out about the sport management program at Robert Morris. It appealed to me because I could major in something related to sports. Since I did not have the talent to be a professional athlete, the opportunity to be involved in sports or recreation in some capacity was exciting. The program at Robert Morris College is in the school of business.

The program at Ohio State University is in the department of physical education within the college of education. Fortunately the program at Ohio State was still structured similar to the one at Robert Morris even though it came under a different school. Both programs had strong emphasis on management, marketing, business, and accounting. There was also an emphasis on the practical side of sport management and recreation, which I thought gave me more opportunities than some of the typical recreation programs that tend to deal more with leadership training, children's programming, and team-building activities. Both programs provided an overview of true day-to-day operations. I thought this was a better opportunity to gain experience and learn about the behind-the-scenes aspects of program, facility, or event management and it gave students a lot more flexibility in their career choice. It also gave students the option that if they decided not to pursue a career in sports or recreation, they still had the management, business, and marketing background to pursue other jobs. The graduate program at Ohio State allowed for more in-depth learning about the business aspect of the sport/recreation field. Specific classes included sports law, international sports business, and facility and event management. Graduate studies require a great deal more research and project work. With the immense number of sports facilities at Ohio State numerous opportunities were available to gain practical knowledge about facility and event management, sports programming, and intramurals. Several of the department's faculty members were involved with the athletics and intramural programs, which again allowed for practical learning. Classroom learning is valuable but the knowledge gained by visiting facilities or events and meeting people who are in the field is invaluable.

The education, nurturing, and mentoring I received at Robert Morris were critical to where I am in my career. My experience at Ohio State definitely complemented that and allowed me to take the next step, obtain more practical experience, and learn a little bit more. I think both experiences were invaluable to my career.

I did a 4-month internship my last semester at Robert Morris and was fortunate enough to stay with that company for about another 4 months before going to Ohio State. My undergraduate internship took place on Hilton Head Island, South Carolina, with a private recreation company that provided services for various resorts, hotels, and facilities around the United States. I had the opportunity to be involved with facility and event management, recreation programming, and the hotel front desk. Just before the completion of my internship I was offered a summer position as the manager of a water park facility, in addition to supervising three recreation programs for various sized resorts. This was a wonderful opportunity having just graduated from college. My internship experience finally allowed me to use many of the skills I had learned about through coursework and research. More was expected of me than at a typical summer job in the sport/recreation field. I am not saying that as a negative because it was a definite positive.

I happened to be at the right place at the right time and everything fell into place. At Ohio State I did an internship while still doing my coursework with the minor league baseball team in Columbus, the Clippers. I was there for about a year and gained an invaluable amount of practical experience in the areas of customer service, facility and event management for large-scale venues, merchandising, and ticket operations. The hours are long and the work is not as glamorous as one may think—the glamour is for the athletes.

Working in professional baseball was a different experience than being in the resort field. Going through college and summer jobs I tried to do many different things within the sport/recreation field to get a good idea of available job opportunities. The more jobs I did within those internships gave me a much broader perspective on event and facility operations.

I obtained my current position, again, by being in the right place at the right time. I made a contact in Hilton Head when I did my undergraduate internship and a job opened about 4 or 5 months after I finished at Ohio State. Everything fell into place. I had done a lot of searching in facility management and event management and was interested in returning to Hilton Head because it is such a wonderful area with many opportunities. It was fortunate the way things worked out, but I was well prepared when my opportunity came.

I used my various contacts to assist in my job search, whether they were from the professional, public, or private sector of the sport industry. Additionally, I contacted most of the major indoor and outdoor sports facilities on the East Coast for any available positions. These tactics did lead to a few interviews and offers, but the contacts were the most helpful. My advice is to get to know as many people as possible and keep contact with them even if you are not currently looking for a job, because you never know when you will be looking for one.

As the recreation manager for Sea Pines, I oversee the year-round fitness center, bicycle shop operations, the department that handles golf tee time reservations, tennis court reservations, and reservations for various other activities. I manage the swimming pool operations, playground, nature tours, family activities, and all other special events. Sea Pines is a 5,000-acre resort on Hilton Head Island, the largest resort on the island, with 5 miles of beach, two marinas, an intercoastal waterway, a 605-acre forest reserve, four championship golf courses, and a world-class tennis facility. We host two nationally televised sporting events each year: The MCI Classic (men's golf) and the Family Circle Cup (women's tennis). Numerous recreation opportunities are available such as golf, tennis, nature tours, fitness, biking, kayaking, parasailing, fishing, riding wave-runners, dolphin watching, and roller-blading, as well as going to the beach.

The number of employees I directly supervise varies by the time of the year. In peak time, there are close to 30 people between part-time and full-time employees. I report to the director of sports, who reports directly to the company president. He oversees all golf operations, tennis operations, retail operations, and recreation. I do not see myself advancing to the director of sports position because of its emphasis on golf. I would need a strong background in golf and PGA certification. Although in the hierarchy it looks like the next step, I do not have the golf background to do that position at this point. Our company is getting involved in some new projects and expanding. Various things can happen and different opportunities can arise. I have been very fortunate because I have received greater responsibility and accountability for new departments each year for the past 6 years. Every year has been a new challenge.

I am responsible for many different recreational facilities. We have a fitness center offering aerobic classes, an equipment room, showers, and locker room facilities. Facility maintenance and risk management are important, particularly maintaining safe facilities. The infrastructure of the building, the equipment within the building, and the accessibility for our patrons is our main concern. We also operate three swimming pools. We have to work with our state department of health and environmental control and meet specific regulations. We set our own standards that exceed environmental concerns because we insist on safe, accessible facilities. We have a renovated playground. It was renovated because of the safety risks associated with playgrounds. Our equipment did not conform to current safety codes, and we made a huge investment in replacing that equipment with new equipment that meets current standards and safety codes. Obviously, safety training and risk management are a huge component of my position.

Most of what I learned about risk management was on the job. I talked with many other professionals in the business who had years of experience and heard about the lessons they learned. I also did a lot of reading on pool and playground safety, fitness practices, and other risk management manuals. Additionally, I have several certifications that have assisted me in compiling a risk management program including Aerobics and Fitness Association of America (AFAA) Personal Trainer, Certified Pool Operator, Certified Playground Safety Inspector, First Aid, and CPR.

Within the recreation field liability is a concern, whether in swimming pools, fitness centers, playgrounds, golf courses, or tennis courts. When people are out and moving around in new settings, the host venue and its employees must be very conscious of safety. We want to make sure the place looks inviting, comfortable, and clean. We continuously inspect, clean, and maintain our facilities. Some of it is more of an annual maintenance, and some of it involves a 2- 3-year project. We do a 5-year plan so we can keep track of what needs to be done annually to maintain our facilities in a safe, pleasant manner.

A lot of our programs, and especially our golf facilities, charge higher fees than many of the other resorts in the area, but the service we deliver is superior to other facilities. Our customers have the expectation that service is going to be outstanding, and they are willing to pay for it. They expect great course conditions, superior service, lessons, and a friendly knowledgeable staff. Service is something we reinforce constantly in training our receptionists, reservationists, and other staff. Service is what makes the difference between other golf courses and us. Our customers expect a certain delivery and we need to always fulfill that and have the best course conditions and best staff possible. We have been very fortunate to do so. Fifty-one percent of our business is repeat customers.

In the past 6 years I have learned many things that could not have been taught in a classroom. For example, in our geographical region, the contractors have more construction work than they can handle. Resorts, hotels, and individual residences are built here at a tremendous pace. Getting a contractor to do a job, stay on the job, and complete it on time is very challenging. We are constantly working with contractors and meeting schedules, which ties into the planning process. We realize that even though ours may be a 1-month project, realistically it will probably take 2 months to finish. When we work with contractors we need to be conscious of time frames and scheduling. Whenever possible, we plan our construction and maintenance around major events and the busy season. I definitely have learned more on the job and on a case-by-case basis in dealing with contracts and agreements.

The most demanding part of my job, and any job in this profession, is that I work 7 days a week, 365 days a year. Even when I have a day off there are still things happening that I am responsible for and need to have good people working them. I am very fortunate to have very good managers working with me and the bulk of our full-time employees have been with us for a while. We have some employees who have good backgrounds in recreation and resort management. The one downside and challenge is that the labor market here is very tight. Our unemployment rate is less than 1 percent and trying to find employees is very challenging. One of the biggest challenges our resort faces is hiring good qualified employees. What I like about my job is I do not even think of it as a job. I am fortunate to live on the resort so I am here every day of the year. It is a wonderful place to live, work, play, and recreate. There are not many things I dislike about my job.

A typical day involves getting here in the morning to make sure everything is running smoothly, all of the shops and operations are properly staffed, all the computers, telephones, and registers are working properly, and everything is set up for the rest of the day. Then I handle any problems, issues, or challenges that arise. For example, we are always involved in staff training. We continually revise our budget and plan and forecast ahead of time to make sure all of our needs are met. I meet with various department heads and our marketing department to make sure we are always cross-selling our activities and that everybody knows what programs and events are going on company-wide on any given day.

My work hours vary by season. During peak season I typically work about 50 hours a week over 5–1/2 days a week. In the off-season it is 5 days a week most of the time and more like 45 hours a week. Again, every week is different. It depends on who is on vacation, who is sick, what special activity is being conducted, what group is in-house, and many other factors. I perform many public relations activities such as talking with our guests and interacting with our customers. It is essential to determine what they like or do not like about the resort or our services. I always try to have a good feel for how the guests spend their time and we work to improve the experience for them. As far as the company goes, I have no complaints. Sea Pines is an excellent company. They offer great benefits and I am fortunate to have great people as coworkers and supervisors.

I am a very proactive person. Rather than reacting to situations and always being behind the eight ball, I try to anticipate problems and address them before they become unmanageable. Something unusual is going to happen every day. That is one of the best aspects of this job—no day is ever the same. If I can prevent a customer or guest from having a bad experience by proactively dealing with a problem, it is truly satisfying. Also, it is counterproductive and inefficient to always be dealing with problems. If we have a sound game plan for the common occurrences, we can handle them efficiently. We do a lot of planning and always have several back-up plans so the staff can focus on the event or project rather than worrying about some other factor. Unforeseen things can and do happen, and we deal with them on a case-by-case basis.

Because I tend to be a more proactive manager I am not stressed out very often. I try to anticipate and plan ahead to avoid those things. Again, being a 365-day-a-year operation there is no down time.

I would say my greatest stress is that there is always something happening. Many offices are open 9:00 AM to 5:00 PM Monday through Friday and Saturday and Sunday are off or employees leave work at 5:00 PM and are done. When I leave work, everything is still going on, even on weekends or my day off, so I am always on call and ready if needed. If someone described my managerial style, they would say I am extremely conscientious, very fair, a hard worker, honest, very supportive of my employees, and give 110 percent effort every day.

I am very fortunate that my supervisor is someone I definitely look to as a role model. He has been with our company for 15 to 20 years and I ask for his guidance and assistance. He has been very supportive.

I am still trying to figure out where I see myself in the future. I try to take everything one day at a time, yet look to the future. I enjoy the recreation field and the resort setting so I would like to continue to grow within that area. A tremendous number of opportunities exist in the resort field on Hilton Head Island, not just in recreation but also in marketing, management, business, sports, real estate, and lodging. I love this area so much, so I will try to continue to grow within the resort field and recreation. The company I am working for is a great company so I have no reason to think of moving somewhere else or looking for a different career path. I will just keep doing as good a job as I can here, continuing to succeed with the various departments and programs I have, and try to get involved with as many of the other departments within our company as possible. I would like to work more with our marketing, lodging, and accounting departments to learn how they function and to let people know I am eager to learn and advance within the company. Getting there will take a little bit of internal networking and continuing to learn more about the resort field as a whole, not necessarily just resort recreation.

One external factor impacting our business is the tourism industry. Obviously, the more tourists we have, the busier we are, and the more programs and staff we need. The flip side of that is if tourism is down it negatively impacts our programs. We are fortunate because Hilton Head as a whole and more specifically Sea Pines has continued to grow year after year. Every year we set new records for reaching capacity and attendance. We do not assume that it will happen all of the time. We work very hard to continue to have our guests return and try to get new guests to come here by focusing on our customer service, programs, and facilities.

Our industry is not recession proof. Before I got here in the late 1980s there was a real recession, and a change in the second homes tax laws affected the area. It hurt some of the property values. Tourism was down in the area. In the 1970s with the oil crisis people were not traveling as much. Gas prices were higher which had a big effect on travel and tourism. As far as being recession proof, we definitely feel recessions much later than a lot of other communities and resort communities but we never assume we are 100 percent recession proof.

One of the biggest trends now in the travel/resort/tourism industry is packaging. The cruise industry has brought a lot of that to the forefront. Cruise is such a huge tourist opportunity now and with everything all inclusive, customers pay one fee, get on the ship, and all recreation, food, and entertainment needs are provided. I see that impacting the resort recreation field more and more. I had a meeting with our director of sales about putting together some different packages that group all of our different activities together. I mean it sounds silly but look at McDonald's and Burger King with the meal deals and all the value meals and how they package different aspects together. It makes it easier for the customer to make a selection and there is a tendency to sell more product. If customers want to pay a la carte, they can, and if they want to pay as a package then usually there is some discount and better opportunities and experience.

With regard to technology, we try to adapt to current trends. Computers are a huge part of our day-to-day operations now and more work is being done on the Internet. We are doing more reservations within the lodging department through the Internet and e-mails than ever before. The Internet changed how we do our business, our marketing, and our reservations.

More recreation and sport opportunities will arise with the Internet because of the explosion in that communication medium. Exactly what that will happen is anybody's guess. Even with computers we can never forget the human element. Communication skills and dealing with a variety of people are critical to success. To succeed in this field, one has to be a very people-oriented person, which means being very supportive and able to motivate and train people. Good employees are ones who can deal with people and give them the service they expect. People have fixed incomes and when they decide to go on vacation they research it and make a decision based on the benefits a certain place offers. A huge part of those benefits is the service and the helpfulness of the staff. Having good qualified people to give outstanding customer service and providing safe, quality programs are critical to our success.

As I emphasized earlier, I would recommend that students get as much experience as possible. Learn as much as possible from professors and make as many contacts as possible. Do not limit yourself to a field you think you want to enter because you never know what other opportunities may arise or what type of contacts your contact has. Learn as much as you can, get as much experience as you can, and get to know as many people as possible.

I was fortunate in some of the work experiences I was able to enjoy. I worked at a YMCA, in the resort field, in the professional field, and at the collegiate level. Having worked in all of those different areas, a commonality of sports and recreation exists but each has its own specific aspects. To tie all of those together and relate them to the sport/recreation field was very beneficial. Get that experience, whether it is through volunteering, paid work, or an internship. Use some of the knowledge you are learning in class and put it to practical use.

I enjoyed working in professional sports through college and they were great summer jobs, but making it a permanent career did not appeal to me. I'm not saying I would not have necessarily pursued a career in that profession or that I would not enjoy it, but this opportunity arose and it was a better opportunity and has been extremely enjoyable. The world of professional sports is not all the glamour with the athletes on TV. Just like with any job, particularly in this field, there are lots of long hours and long days, but I find this work more rewarding than I did professional sports.

Khalil Johnson

General Manager
Georgia Dome

Education:
BEHAVIORAL SCIENCES, NATIONAL-LOUIS UNIVERSITY, 1991

Career Progression:
GENERAL MANAGER, GEORGIA DOME, 1989 TO PRESENT

DIRECTOR OF EVENTS SERVICES, GEORGIA WORLD CONGRESS CENTER, 1986 TO 1989

DIRECTOR OF SALES AND SERVICES, D.C. CONVENTION CENTER, 1982 TO 1985

EVENTS COORDINATOR, GEORGIA WORLD CONGRESS CENTER, 1977 TO 1981

Best piece of advice you received in regards to your career:

"Always remain teachable."

DAN GRAVELINE, EXECUTIVE DIRECTOR, GEORGIA WORLD CONGRESS CENTER AUTHORITY

Best advice for someone aspiring toward a career in the sport industry:

"Take on the hard jobs nobody else wants, volunteer for everything, and don't give up—no matter what."

Quote by which you live:

"Don't look back. Something might be gaining on you."

MY BACKGROUND FOR MOST OF MY WORKING CAREER has been facility management as opposed to sports facility management. I was at the Georgia World Congress Center on and off from 1977 to 1989 doing facility management work for conventions and trade shows. I secured my current position, as general manager of one of the finest sport venues in the world, through luck, hard work, and preparation.

I grew up in Brooklyn, New York, and I came to Atlanta, my father's original home, in 1976. In 1977, the Georgia World Congress Center opened and a friend of mine suggested that I try to find a job there. At that point, I had not zeroed in on a career. I was 24 years old at the time. The only job available at the Congress

Center was as a part-time set up person. Because it was kind of a "get your foot in the door" opportunity and a way to pay the bills at home, I took it. I worked in the convention set-up department for about 2 years in various positions, learning the general patterns of operation, developing relationships, and learning how the other departments worked.

Eventually, I became the supervisor of the department. I did that for a year until I had an opportunity to become the event coordinator. I went from wearing a uniform to wearing a shirt and tie. I went from "behind the house to the front of the house," and I was event coordinator for the Congress Center from 1979 to 1981. During those years, there were big shows in Atlanta but not as large as the mega-events we do routinely now. At that time the convention business was just developing in Atlanta. Big hotels were still new and the convention business community was just developing. Many young people were molding, shaping, and creating an industry. Camaraderie existed among the youthful managers. It was a fun time to be in Atlanta as it grew and developed a new image and reputation.

I was fortunate to obtain some operational background and experience that gave me a good sense of what it would take to get the work done. I became a fairly well informed service representative for the city and its conventions. Few jobs in the Congress Center existed that I had not done myself. I not only had the feel for the work, I had a feel for the people who performed the work. I think that has served me well and carried through to my position today.

I had an opportunity in 1992 to move to Washington, D.C. as part of the start-up team for the D.C. Convention Center. They were trying to get on the map and saw themselves in a similar stage as Atlanta had been in terms of a new building and trying to create a new energy. They wanted someone who had been working in one of the premium programs in the country at that time. The Congress Center was and still is considered to be one of the finest facilities of its type in the nation. I went to Washington as director of sales and services and was part of the group that opened the building. I was one of three people who had ever set foot in a convention center when it opened. I arrived there in time for the last 9 months of construction. That experience proved to be very fortuitous because I had some real start-up knowledge to bring to the process, and I learned about the construction process. Both served me well in the future.

In Washington, we used to joke about how we would sit in one of those planning meetings getting ready for start-up, and people would ask me, "Well how did they do that down in the World Congress?" I would say, "Give me five minutes and let me go check my notes." I would get on the phone and call the engineer back in Atlanta and say, "Walk me through that real quick." Then I would hang up, go back into the meeting with an answer, and suddenly I became an expert! I became familiar with not just a piece of the pie, but how the pieces were put together in the construction process and operations start-up process, and I think that was probably the most valuable lesson I learned in Washington.

Three years later, an opportunity arose at the Congress Center for a director of events services. The Congress Center had expanded while I was in Washington and had opened up its second stage of expansion. I had lunch with Dan Graveline, the executive director at the Congress Center, and we discussed the future of the convention business in Atlanta. Dan described the mega-shows coming to Atlanta and the need to have someone to help coordinate the large citywide users. He spoke of the possibility of the Democratic National Convention being held in Atlanta and also indicated that the Atlanta Falcons might get a new stadium downtown. He also said he had heard a rumor that somebody wanted to bid on the Summer Olympic Games. He did not know if any of these situations were going to happen, but asked me to come back on board and see what developed. Sure enough, all of the above mentioned events happened and I was fortunate enough to be right in the middle of it all.

When it came time to do a feasibility study on a new stadium for the Falcons, the Congress Center was asked to help create the design for the stadium. Dan asked if anybody was interested and it kind of fell in my lap because nobody offered to help. I worked with the program architect and provided input from a facility operator's perspective. It was a formal program for design. In doing so, I developed relationships with other stadium managers. The Falcons were kind enough to let me travel to away games with them to see other stadiums, learn about their preferences, and to find out what worked for the team and the stadium operators.

Before this the only experiences I had in sport were as a high school and college athlete. Although I did not have a stadium or arena background, I did have the general facility background. I had an appreciation and now a great love for the Atlanta Falcons. The leadership of our Authority, which came to be the developer of the stadium, wanted a general manager of the new Georgia Dome facility on board from the design and initial construction stages through completion. They wanted somebody who knew the design and would be able to manage it the right way. I was fortunate to have volunteered to work on the planning and program development of the facility so when the opportunity arose, I was in a position to be selected for the job. There was never any job posting because they looked in-house first, and I was the one who knew the most about the project at that time.

I was part of the Congress Center's core management team and came to understand how the Georgia Dome worked from the inside out. I understood from the operational as well as management perspectives how the building should be run and integrated into the overall campus. I worked with a design team and construction team for 3 years while the building was created. We opened in 1992 and have since exceeded expectations from a financial standpoint. Initially, we were fortunate to be awarded the bid for the Super Bowl and also the 1996 Summer Olympics. All of a sudden our venue was booked with premiere events and the event pipeline was very bright. We have been off and running ever since. We had another Super Bowl (2000), two NCAA Final Four basketball tournaments, Southeastern Conference (SEC) football and basketball championships, Atlantic Coast Conference (ACC) championships, indoor track, gymnastics, as well as other championships. We like to think we have become the "Home of Champions."

We do about 25–30 major ticket events a year, most of which are sports. We have high school and college football games, and the Heritage and Peach Bowls as well as all the Atlanta Falcons home games. We even housed the Atlanta Hawks pro basketball team for 2 years while their arena was being rebuilt. We do ticketed events that range in attendance from 20,000 people or less, to full sell-outs for more than 72,000 people. In addition, we have a variety of entertainment events such as motor sports and tractor pulls. We also facilitate a number of conventions during the year. For example, during the month of July, we hosted a direct marketing insurance company convention, a women's religious conference, and the Southern Baptist Convention. We have served nearly every denomination or religious order, and all of that is important business because it fills hotel rooms during typically slow periods. We perform a citywide function in providing a stage for large events that otherwise would not be held in Atlanta. Probably 80 to 85 percent of our business is repeat, which makes our job easier and indicates we are doing a good job.

I think I have the best job in Georgia, and I do not think anybody gets in a position such as mine without having tremendous amounts of support along the way. My parents encouraged and pushed me to work, so I started working Christmas holidays and summers when I was 13 years old. I toiled in factories, sold soap, and worked in a funeral home. An early influence in my life was the funeral director who taught me how to work hard. He made me sweep the sidewalks, vacuum, and set up chairs. He taught me to be respectful, and a lot of what I learned about how to serve was done right in that funeral home. He was a taskmaster who would not tolerate anything out of line, and his motto at that time was "We also serve who only stand and wait." I will always remember that. He exemplified customer service and was ready to help out if somebody needed it.

In Atlanta, a very influential man in my life has been Dan Graveline, the executive director of the Georgia Dome and Convention Center. He was an assistant director at the Los Angeles Convention Center in 1976. He was offered an opportunity to open the World Congress Center and moved to Atlanta about 3 months before the building opened. He arrived on site, quickly put an organization together, and established a performance standard and organizational culture that has become world-renowned. He assembled a group of top-notch people to make the Georgia Dome and Convention Center a success. At every key juncture in my career he has been a source of counseling. He told me I needed to go to Washington D.C. to learn things I could not learn in Atlanta. He also invited me to come back, so he is at the top of the list of people who have been supportive and given me direction.

I have been a manager since 1985, so I have weathered a few storms. A certain amount of patience in facility management has to be developed because it takes a while to learn how things operate. It then takes a longer time to convince people that maybe things could be better with some change. It takes a while for opportunities to open, and to move in, around, and up an organization. It is tough sometimes when you are 22 or maybe 25 years old to patiently look down the road. However, the ability to pace yourself and make calculated and bold moves at the right time is almost an art. Developing any art takes time and practice. That is the tough part.

Dan Graveline always provided opportunities for all of us to stretch out and learn things to help prepare us for future opportunities. For example, in 1996 when we were working the Olympics, Dan needed somebody to help work on the development of Centennial Olympic Park. We looked around the table and nobody raised their hand, so I was brought in as project manager, which was great fun. Fortunately, we hired an operating manager after the park was built. I did not run the park but I was involved in the design and construction and that is probably the most significant thing I will do in my career from a lasting perspective. The park will be here long after the Georgia Dome is gone. They will tear this building down in 30 to 40 years, but the park will be here 100 years from now.

My title is general manager. I work for the Georgia World Congress Center Authority, a nonprofit public corporation owned by the State of Georgia. If it was a private corporation, I would probably be called the chief operating officer. I am responsible for all the day-to-day management of the facility as well as the long-term financial projections. Dan Graveline, the executive director of the Authority, provides strategic direction for the Dome, Congress Center, and Centennial Park, and he also is responsible for the liaison with all elected officials. Dan is very involved in the day-to-day performance. I make sure our tenants are happy, the pipeline is full, and our staff performs in an efficient manner. We have about 130 people on our staff. That is upper middle in terms of staff sizes for domes and large stadiums. We perform all the core services and supplement them with outside contractors. We have housekeeping/set-up staff that we combined in one department called building services. We have an engineering group consisting of painters, electricians, plumbers, and utility people. We have a security staff who does the day-to-day safety and security management of the building. Then we have a small finance group that manages the finances and budget projections of our seat and suites leasing program and conducts all event settlements. We have a sales group responsible for our event booking program and also the executive club seat and suite leasing program. Event services is responsible for the customer interface for the events. We also have an executive services group that is basically our concierge group who takes care of our seats and suites customers.

These customers are very important to our long-term success, so we make sure we are set up to take very good care of these important folks.

We also have what we call "associates" or close partners. Our food service operation is an example of one of these. We own all the knives, forks, china, glass, silver, and kitchen equipment; however, a company manages the food and beverage operations for us. MGR is a small, local company that is part of our family. We also have a relationship with Argenbright, our crowd management company that supervises the ushers, ticket takers, and game or event day security. We have a merchandiser, FMI, housed on site. It is extremely convenient for us to communicate with all of these companies without going across town or across the country. Our management core and all of our related services are located on premises. That is a big plus for us.

Meetings are a big part of my workweek. We have weekly scheduled meetings with the senior managers of all the facilities on campus. We also have campus-wide operations meetings to be apprised of what each group is doing and how one event in the area may affect other facilities. Meetings are an important part of what we do, and we consciously try to make them regular, productive, and not spontaneous. We try to keep ad hoc meetings to a minimum because they could overwhelm us if we are not careful. I have three or four key meetings each week. Outside of these regularly scheduled meetings, the schedule varies according to the season.

The workday for a facility manager can be very long. When I worked at the Congress Center as an event coordinator, I worked from the breakfast to the banquet, each day, for as long as the trade show was in town. A Homebuilder's Association show is an example of a 4-day event requiring additional long days and nights for move-in and move-out. The hours in the Georgia Dome are somewhat seasonal, with the busiest part of the year running from August through March. If a major event is here, we try to be here the entire time. If you have 30,000 people in your house, a lot of staff and customers are very anxious for the event to go well. If the event falls on a Thursday night, a Saturday, or a Sunday, it makes no difference. During the football season, we are probably down to a day off per week. Some weeks we will do Saturday college games and Sunday professional games, so we may go 2 weeks or more without a day off. It is difficult to take time off during the regular workweek because the administrative duties can rarely wait. Our schedule is driven by our customers' schedule. On weekdays, unless there is a night event in the building, we usually leave at 6:00 PM. Some of the days can get pretty long, but when we have 60,000 fans in here screaming and yelling it is extremely exciting and we get caught up in the action too. At the end of the day, the adrenaline drops and we are definitely tired, but it is all worthwhile. At least it is for me, and that is why we are in this profession.

The most enjoyable parts of my job are the variety of events and responsibilities I have. One example is the process we engage in to land a big event. We work with a city-wide marketing team to put together a proposal, design and deliver a presentation, and then have a group like the NFL owners award the team The Super Bowl. It does not get much better than that. That is winning the Super Bowl for us.

We just bid on the Women's NCAA Final Four for 2003. We wanted to win that event because it is a great event with tremendous potential. Winning that bid was great because bidding is a very competitive process, and I like to compete. I am a "gamer," and I want to say, "Coach, put me in" when it is time to give a presentation or proposal, because I want to come out of the meeting with a win. I constantly work with very high quality people in these endeavors, and that is the other part of the job I enjoy. I have met tremendous people in all walks of life from our own housekeepers who work harder than anybody in the building, to company presidents, team owners, rock stars, and professional basketball and football players. The joy about this is they all bring something to the table and have something unique to offer. They are not all great people, but they all have something to offer and there is never a dull moment.

The technical skills in this job are not great, but you need to know some simple things. You need to be computer literate as well as have some basic understanding of electronics and heating/air-conditioning systems. A lot of this I learned from the ground up. For example, when I first started working, there was no Microsoft. I knew that if I was going to be involved in facility programming and working on budgets I needed to learn how to do spreadsheets, so I took a few days in the office and learned Lotus 1–2–3. I have taken that same approach to many things in my career. I work at something until I get it right.

Things change. I worked my way from the bottom up, and many of my peers got their foot in the door as a ticket taker or as an usher or stagehand. Now, colleges are producing people with the technical expertise I had to learn on the job. Students graduate with a conceptual understanding of what the business is and how the pieces fit together, things we learned by trial and error. The people we hire as event coordinators are often graduates with a masters in sport administration or sport management. They start their first day on the job with some of the knowledge it took me several years to learn.

Many challenges exist in the sport facility business, and privatization is a big issue in our industry. The issue is whether a private management group can do a better job at managing a building than a public group. Many factors are involved in this analysis, including unionization, existing employees' wage scales, efficiencies in marketing, and coordinating national sales activities. Neither public nor private management is necessarily superior in every situation. I think here at the Dome and Congress Center we have the best of both worlds. We are a public management team designed to have the flexibility of a private company.

I believe another key question for the future is what impact technology will have in terms of whether a fan can have a better experience away from the stadium than at the stadium. I think the market could segment into several areas. One is the high end—there could be an exclusive audience of basically long-term license holders for executive-level services, seats, and suites. That is where the new basketball arena is headed to a certain extent. All the suites and the luxury items are concentrated on one side of the building and the general population is kept outside these private spaces. Another potential segmentation suggests that those people outside the gated area are given less service, less amenities, and are dealt with more from the standpoint of security risks and bare necessities. We may even get to the same point as some of the soccer facilities in Europe are now, with moats separating the field and spectators, machine gun wielding police in the stands, and standing room only, with no seats provided in the general admission areas. There may also be a requirement for identification and background checks to get into the building.

The areas of the business segment that are growing today are auto racing and certain "gladiator games" like wrestling. The ticket prices for the traditional professional sport leagues are becoming so high that the general admission folks find it more difficult to afford to bring their families. In my mind, this trend could result in the stadium of the future having a greatly reduced seating capacity, with 2/3 of all locations reserved for luxury services targeted to the wealthy or corporate customers, and 1/3 targeted to the hard-core fans who have been there for generations.

We host wrestling in here and at the end of every wrestling match it is accepted behavior for the fans to throw beer cups into the ring. When you go to a wrestling match, you are not paying to see the wrestling match; you are paying to see the guy throw somebody out of the ring and watch him get beat up with a chair. Or you are paying to see the free-for-all, where three guys jump on one guy and beat him up. Well, where does it go next? I worry that this gladiator mentality can lead us down a very slippery slope of which none of us will be proud. We need to ask what role we play as facility managers in steering clear of such a fall.

Another important area we need to continue to address is social diversity. This applies to our work force, our events, and our communities. I happen to be the only African American manager of a professional sporting facility in the United States. I am not a torchbearer, groundbreaker, or anything like that. I have had a lot of opportunities and it is my job to give other people opportunities. Over the years I have been in many boardrooms and loading docks, and I have dealt with fair-minded people and some questionable characters in both locations. I try to treat people as individuals and hope they do the same for me. If they do, fine; if not, such is life.

Quite a few minorities get in the business and try to advance. For the industry to diversify at all levels, it must start with the education of school kids. Somehow we have to get them to understand that this is a valuable field employing a lot of people in different capacities and providing good entertainment opportunities to enhance a community. How do I convey the message, especially to African American youth? I talk to elementary school, middle school, high school, and college students and we try to employ a cross-section of interns in the various sectors of our operation. I try to impress on them that the hardest thing is to persevere through that rookie season because you must be patient and learn the trade. Once you have the qualifications and skills, the opportunities will be there "good Lord willing and the creek don't rise."

Lifelong learning is important, too. Education is a continuing process, whether you get it on the job or in the classroom. Most of our senior managers are part of the International Association of Assembly Managers, the industry's main professional organization. The association has a certification program, and I was one of the first 100 people to complete it. Although few people know about it, within our industry it shows we have demonstrated a certain level of knowledge.

We have to constantly read about the new trends and success stories in our field because it is constantly changing. The main publications concerning the business side are Street & Smith's new publication, *Sports Business Journal* and *The Sports Business Daily*. Those who want to focus more on the sport side should read *The Sporting News* and *Sports Illustrated*.

The field will continue to change, perhaps more rapidly in the next 10 years than ever before. Despite these changes, or maybe because it is changing so fast, I believe it will always be a profession that will offer a rewarding and fulfilling career. I am just glad to be a part of it.

CHAPTER 7

Event Management

ACCORDING TO GRAHAM, GOLDBLATT, AND DELPY (1995), sport event management is one of the fastest growing career paths in the field of sport management. Broadly defined, event management is "administration, coordination, and evaluation of any type of event related to sport" (p. x). Professionals involved in this field develop, plan, coordinate, promote, and evaluate events for full-service event management or marketing agencies, charitable organizations, not-for-profit companies, cities or municipalities, or tourism/hospitality groups. Specialized skills in personnel management, public relations and communications, vendor relations, concessions, operations, finance or accounting, ticket sales, and customer service are vital to success in planning, coordinating, promoting, and implementing a sport event.

Initially, sport organizations and sponsors exclusively used in-house (within an organization) event planners to develop and produce events, create sport programming, and review partnership opportunities. Professional event management companies began to appear in the 1960s and 1970s, enhancing and in some cases replacing in-house planners and promoters. Fully integrated companies such as International Management Group (IMG) can create an event that highlights athletes they represent, sell sponsorships and naming rights, and produce television and other media coverage of the event. These corporations accounted for more than $2 billion in 1999, according to a *Sports Business Journal* report (December 20–26, 1999). With the advent of the Internet, Direct TV, and other broadcast and media outlets, event planners can reap significant financial rewards through rights fees and other revenue streams created by their events.

On a smaller but no less significant level, grassroots events and programs require professional event management. These events, such as road races, 3-on-3 street basketball tournaments, and charity golf tournaments, emphasize active participation rather than spectatorship and are often marketed locally. For example, NIKE, Inc. has a grassroots basketball operation that produces local AAU

(Amateur Athletic Union) basketball tournaments around the United States as well as a high school All-America camp for both boys and girls. Although the events are coordinated through a central office, each local tournament has a director and operations staff that organizes and executes the event.

Several critical functions are involved in event management, including budgeting, risk management, tournament operations, volunteer management, hospitality, and event marketing. Budgeting, which is the process of developing a written estimate of revenues and expenses for a given time period, is essential for a successful event. Event organizers must develop realistic revenue and expense projections to ensure the event is financially feasible. Risk management is another function fundamental to the success of an event. Spectators, participants, and workers need to be made aware of and protected from the possibility of injury during a sport event. Risk management is the process of identifying potential risks and developing a plan to minimize or eliminate their impact (Ammon, 1997).

Tournament and event operations are a third critical area of event management. During the event, the operations team may follow a script, or schedule of activities, detailing the precise time and location specific activities are to occur. No matter how well scripted an event is, event planners must be flexible and prepared for nonscheduled events. Postevent operations include cleaning the venue and surrounding areas, final financial analysis, and return of sponsor signage.

Volunteer management is crucial to the success of a sport event. The number of volunteers is again dependent on the size and scope of the event and can range from a handful to several thousand people. Volunteer management involves two distinct responsibilities: (1) determining the number of volunteers necessary and placing them appropriately; and (2) soliciting, training, and managing them.

Numerous event marketing areas need to be addressed when promoting a sport event. Perhaps the most important are corporate sponsorships, as local, regional, national, and international event managers rely heavily on corporate funding to underwrite their events. Corporate sponsorship of events, teams, leagues, and broadcasts was estimated at $5.09 billion in 1999 (*Sports Business Journal*, December 20–26, 1999). Broadcasting on radio or television can lend credibility to the event as well as increased exposure for sponsors. Broadcast options include network television, cable outlets, local TV stations, and local or national radio.

Career opportunities in event management are varied and depend on the type of organization. When working for a sport marketing or management agency, entry-level positions can include client services, sales, hospitality, and business development. When working in-house for an organization, employees may be required to perform many operational or sponsorship related tasks because of the generally small number of employees. Those interested in full-time event management employment usually begin with an internship, yet valuable experience can be gained by volunteering at local, regional, and national sport events. Entry-level positions in event management pay in the low to mid $20,000s. Those aspiring to upper-level management positions in event management can anticipate making more than $40,000 a year or more depending on the nature and size of the events as well as the responsibilities of the position.

REFERENCES

Ammon, R. (1997). Risk management processes. In D.J. Cotton & T.J. Wilde (Eds.), *Sport law for sport managers* (pp. 174–180). Dubuque, IA: Kendall/Hunt Publishing Company.

Graham, S., Goldblatt, J.J., & Delpy, L. (1995). *The ultimate guide to sport event management and marketing*. Chicago: Irwin Publishing Group.

Sports Business Journal. (1999, December 20–26). *Sports business at the end of the millennium*, pp. 24–25.

Susan Michelle Pollio

Event Coordinator
Churchill Downs (racetrack)

Education:
B.S., SPORT ADMINISTRATION, UNIVERSITY OF
LOUISVILLE, 1999

Career Progression:
EVENT COORDINATOR-MARKETING DEPT.,
CHURCHILL DOWNS, JANUARY 1998 TO PRE-
SENT

COMMUNICATIONS INTERN-BREEDER'S CUP,
CHURCHILL DOWNS, AUGUST 1998 TO DECEM-
BER 1998

STADIUM OPERATIONS ASSISTANT, NEW YORK
YANKEES, MAY 1998 TO AUGUST 1998

ASSISTANT TO THE EVENT COORDINATOR, THE
EVENT COMPANY, MAY 1996 TO JANUARY 1997

Best piece of advice you received in regards to your career:

"Internship, Internship, Internship!"

DR. MARY HUMS, UNIVERSITY OF LOUISVILLE

Best advice for someone aspiring toward a career in the sport industry:

"Spend your time in college getting experience, even if you have to work for free. Being broke is no fun, but making money and being in high demand after college is worth all of the Ramen Noodle nights."

Quote by which you live:

"Real leaders are ordinary people with extraordinary determination."

MY FAMILY HISTORY IS VERY RICH IN SPORTS. My father has been in athletics all of his life. He is the associate athletic director at the University of Louisville and was a basketball coach/athletic director before coming to the University of Louisville. My brother has been a basketball coach in college and also in high school. There was not really a point where I said, "I definitely wanted to be in sports." I actually wanted to go into event management first. Sport has always been a great interest of mine because I had been around it so much. I knew sport and event management together would make a fantastic career, so that is what I decided to do.

I had two different majors before I became a sport administration major. It did take an extra year to graduate, but it was important for me to decide what I wanted to do and not get on the wrong career path. I did not want to major in something and then be afraid to change my major because I was going to have to stay an extra semester or so. Eventually I found out about sport administration, looked at the courses, and thought, "This is what I have been looking for."

There is nothing I would do differently; I would have to say that. I had four internships in college. I began in student government and in my sorority. I always coordinated and organized things. I found myself to be organized, a leader, and very influential. I would create events for the Greek system and student government. When I found out it was the 75th anniversary of the Greek system, I said we needed to celebrate. I soon found myself surrounded by events, organizations, and committees, many of which I initiated myself. Now, academically I have not always been the best student. I was not a straight A student, so I kept telling myself there had to be something related to what I was good at—organizing. I opened up the phone book, talked to different people in the community, and found out there was an occupation called event coordination. I called a place named The Event Company and told them I would break down boxes or do whatever they needed done for that summer. I did not ask for pay; I just wanted to work there so I could put it on my resume. At that point I was only a freshman and they hired me. I was literally helping them set up and tear down events. They did not do sport-oriented events. They decorated for parties, receptions, and groundbreakings. They did the Papa John's Cardinal Stadium groundbreaking, a Toyota dealership groundbreaking, and the Toyota Tenth Anniversary Party. Eventually I started helping with the weddings and smaller events that the owner did not have time to manage. It was a fairly small company, but they did very large events. That was my first experience. My second internship was with the University of Louisville Bicentennial Celebration. The University was celebrating its 200th birthday, and we had a whole year of events to celebrate. I worked for the event coordinator as her assistant. My third internship was with the New York Yankees and that was actually not with events, but with facility management. I learned more about the industry and some of the different things the sport industry entails. I also learned whether I would like to move for a job. That was a learning experience, personally and professionally. Finally I worked for Churchill Downs, where I was hired specifically to do the Breeder's Cup Press Party, which was a very large private party. There were 2,000 attendees and I was responsible for a $150,000 budget. Those were my four internships, so I had a lot of hands-on experience and had really learned. Although I did a lot of photocopying and stapling I also did a lot of important jobs that taught me the ins and outs of actually coordinating events. I probably would not change anything as far as what my path was at that time. I do not know many people who have had four internships. It was hard because of the pay, but it definitely was worth it.

Being a woman is sometimes an obstacle. Being a 22-year-old blonde can really be an obstacle. I am young, blonde, and pretty much happy most of the time. People can often misconstrue those qualities. Luckily, financially I have not had any major obstacles, although many times I have had to go to school, work at my internship, and hold a serving job on the weekends to afford to do my internship.

My dad was my biggest role model. He is two different people. He is Mike Pollio at work, and he is Mike Pollio at home. His interns would come up to me and say, "I don't see how you can stand having him as a father," but he's two completely different people. He taught me that just because I act one way at home does not mean I have to act that way at work or vice versa. He has also taught me not to get too "personal" with other people at work and to keep it professional. Sometimes that is hard when everyone is young, and they all want to go out on Friday and Saturday night. It would be very easy being the only woman who works there to gain a bad reputation. My dad kept me out of any awkward situations and taught me to remain professional and not to cross any lines. He has been my role model. Many of my teachers in school have been my role models. In our sport administration program, all of the professors have worked in the sport industry and they all have something noteworthy to say. At each of my internships I had incredible bosses who each taught me something different.

For example, at the Bicentennial Celebration, we had to work with committees all of the time. I was impressed by the way my supervisor would handle them with such grace. She would turn her ideas into their ideas. She taught me how to deal with people with grace and reverence. She was 30 but she looked like she was about 19. She was a blonde and she was even more bouncy than I was. She taught me how to deal with stereotypes and how not to be offended all of the time when somebody called me "honey" or "chick." Throughout my career I have had many role models who have all taught me different things, whether it was how to be organized, how to be professional, how to deal with people, or how to handle sponsors. I think anyone in my position can learn from other people if they open up and observe. It is a matter of taking off your blinders. I have two interns who are great, but a lot of times they do not notice the simple things, unless I point them out. I will say things like "When you do an event..." or "This is my theory with an event...", and I will just see them going "uh-huh, uh-huh," because they are not really listening. They are trying to get the job done because they want it on their resume, but if they would really listen they could learn a lot. When I was on the Student Activities Board, my supervisor taught me a lot of theories on event coordination that helped me throughout my entire career. She got me to look at myself and see what I needed to improve. It was my sophomore year, and I learned what I needed to improve in the next 3 years. She was a great role model.

I think I am a role model for my interns because "I've been there and done it." One of my interns works for Churchill Downs and another local sports organization. He works at night for the other organization and he does office work for us.

Sometimes he is so frustrated, but every day I tell him it will pay off in the end. I say to him, "I know you feel like you're doing grunt work, and nobody else would do it, but I've been there, and in the end it will pay off." I think I might be a role model for them without them realizing it.

There have been times when I was frustrated, too. I think the key is to have somebody you can talk to other than the people at work. It is important to have somebody else to go to outside of the company to vent, whether it is a friend, a professor, or a parent. I have watched people make the mistake of venting to the wrong person. Everybody gets frustrated in their job, no matter where you work or how incredible the job. The key is to handle it in a professional manner. When my intern vents to me about the other sport organization, that is fine because he might be indirectly asking for my opinion. If he starts venting to me about Churchill Downs that will probably cause some friction. It is important who you vent to if you have frustrations.

Let me describe my workplace. Churchill Downs owns a racetrack and then there is Churchill Downs the management company. I work for Churchill Downs the racetrack, and not Churchill Downs Management Company. They are separate entities. The management company owns Hollywood Park, Calder Race Course, Ellis Park, Hoosier Park, the Kentucky Horse Center, and all of the Kentucky and Indiana Sports Spectrums. Approximately 300 full-time staff are employed at Churchill Down's track. The management company only has 20 or so people. I work for Churchill Downs, the racetrack. I do all the logistics for the events our promotions manager creates. For example, if we create a chili cook-off, the promotions manager sends out all the information. Her job is to get the people to the event. I coordinate the event, make sure it runs smoothly, and make sure our patrons are happy. I coordinate all of our giveaways, festivals, and kids activities. We have something every week. Some people think of Churchill Downs and all they think of is the Derby, but there about 80 other racing days.

We have to think of ways to get people to come to the track. What is going to get them here? Betting, yes, some people have been betting for 50 years. But what is going to get a college student here? What is going to get a person who just moved into Louisville here? What is going to get a 50-year-old person who has never been to Churchill Downs here? We have to think of all these things. How can we get new people here? How can we get more people here? One of the ways is through our Junior Jockey Club, our kids' club. We try to create a family atmosphere at Churchill Downs. In other words, when the Derby is over, at the beginning of our spring meet, we need to keep attendance up. We cannot just say, "Okay, Derby's over, job's over, everybody gets to sit and rest." This is where my job comes in. It is our job to get people to the track every day. Now that there are riverboat casinos on the Ohio River we have major competition for the gambling dollars. How can we make our customers happy? One way is to have a T-shirt giveaway. On a given day, the first 10,000 patrons into the track get a free T-shirt.

If they wear their T-shirt later in the racing season they get into the track free on weekdays. Getting a free T-shirt gets them here that day, but telling them they get in free on weekdays with their T-shirt is a real selling point We do not give the T-shirts away at the door like you might see at baseball games. We give them a redemption slip at the admission gate. They have to come to the redemption center and fill out the slip with their name, address, and phone number. My job is to get the ushers and volunteers at the redemption center to make up the vouchers, and make sure the admission clerks are giving out all of the vouchers. There are a lot of little things to remember. Are there enough pens for people to fill out their vouchers? If I am sitting at a window and I am going to collect vouchers from 2,000 people, will I have a place to put my vouchers? When are the shirts going to arrive? Is there going to be someone there to receive them? I have to get all these boxes delivered to all of the different redemption centers and in the correct fractions. We need three fourths of them here and one fourth of them there. My job involves the small logistics. We take all of those redemption slips and create a database of 60,000 people. I also have to get a design for the T-shirts and order the T-shirts, all within my budget. We have more than $500,000 in event dollars. My job is not to create the event, but to plan it. When our season ends in June each year we spend 2 months doing profit/loss statements and checking attendance. I need to ask important questions. What are our suggestions for next year? Was it worth doing this event budget-wise? Did we spend more than it was worth? We spend 2 months reviewing these aspects. The following spring I am part of the team evaluating the events. Were they practical and were they worth it? Were the customers happy? Is there a simpler way to do it?

The best part of my job is that I get to see the end product. In other words, I get rewarded on an event-to-event basis. For example, I worked 2 months on the Kentucky Sampler. It is a very large event we do in our infield with music, crafts, food, equine demonstrations, and dancers. When the planning is over, I get to see the patrons walk around with smiles on their face. I get to hear people say, "Oh, this is wonderful, this is great!" I see the end product. I close it out and I start new. Whether it is a big event like the Kentucky Sampler or a smaller event like a giveaway, I get to see the end product and get to start over new. If I did not do something so well, I write it down, and the next year I will make it better. Sometimes I mess up and when I do, I know what to do next year, and next year will be better. I think that is the most rewarding part of this job.

As far as the worst parts of my job, I would have to say—and this is different from job to job, but I would say definitely at Churchill Downs—there is just so much physical work to do. I used to have a theory that if you were organized beforehand you would not have to do anything at all during the event. Now sometimes that works with major parties, very luxurious parties, or high profile parties, but on these day-to-day promotional events, it is just not the case. That idea does not really apply here.

Say we need an extra table. Should I call maintenance and say we need an extra table? Or should I walk in that closet over there, lift up the table myself, and bring it over? It would take a lot more time for maintenance to drive all the way down there. I do more physical work than I ever thought I would possibly do in any job. Sometimes there are too many trashcans in a certain place and we need more of them elsewhere. I have this huge pile of trashcans and I go in and see flies everywhere and garbage in them, but I just have to do it. I have had my interns almost in tears. They could not believe they had to do this stuff. I just kept telling them, "Somehow it will pay off, you don't think it will, but it will pay off." I think that is the worst, but it builds character, and I know I am not going to be dragging garbage cans all my life. I look at the vice presidents in the company and they are not dragging garbage cans. It is just part of the job; it is a matter of getting things done. When under pressure and things need to be done, it does not matter what is in that trash can. I guarantee I will pick it up and move it.

My work is definitely seasonal and varies from day to day. On Thursday or Friday, I set up for the event. When the season comes to a close there is more planning, sitting down, typing up agendas, typing up outlines, typing up time lines, typing up general descriptions of the events, and writing down ideas, suggestions, and budgets. I like that part, too. I would not want to only sit at the desk all of the time or only run around the track all the time either. I like both.

Derby is more operational. Derby promotes itself, so our job does not kick in until after Derby. We do have a Festival in the Field the Thursday and Friday before Derby. This is a huge event with concerts in the infield. We know the people are in town and we know the population has increased because it is Derby, but why aren't people coming to Churchill Downs on Thursday and Friday? Why are we waiting until Saturday? That is why we plan to get them here Thursday and Friday.

On Derby Day I just work with sponsors. I walk to their table and say, "Hi, my name is Susan, would you like to come down to the paddock area to walk around?" With my job I cannot ever be above doing anything. During Derby I can be called to do anything so I am not an event coordinator, I am just available to help out.

In reference to managing people, I would have to say for me the past 6 months have been the most difficult because I have always been an intern. I have never been up with the management people. For me managing two interns has been very challenging because we are the same age. I have a lot of pressure on me. I am new at the job. I really want to do it right, and my interns are really great, but they lose focus very easily. Things are not as important to them. Sometimes they think some of the things I want are dumb. I am a perfectionist. Sometimes during the event it gets kind of intense. It does not mean the promotions manager or I am mad. We are simply just being direct. I need to say, "Hey, those tables need to come over here." At times I do not have time for a friendly buffer. It is so hard to manage people, personally and professionally, because there can be so many conflicts throughout a day.

How do you motivate people? How do you make them understand that because a situation is intense it has nothing to do with them? My most difficult challenge has been learning how to manage people and how to talk to them without them thinking I am barking at them. At the same time, they are my age and I need to learn how to communicate with them. Sometimes I will forget to ask, "How was your weekend?" at 11:00 AM when they come to work. I will be so far into my day with a list of things to do that I forget. Learning how to manage people is so important. It is hard to get that experience before a certain age because you do not get the opportunity. If you ever get an opportunity to learn more about managing people, take advantage of it.

I had to learn the customer is always right, even when he or she is not. How do I talk to that person? My dad always told me to say, "I understand, I would feel the same way if I was in your position." It does not mean I am going to change anything for them. It does not mean I am going to help them. But I say I understand their feelings. I have to learn not to be frustrated because I hear five complaints one day. If you can deal with customers and if you can learn how to manage employees before you get out into the corporate world, you have got a great head start.

Planning and organizing are the keys in event management. You have to be organized and you have to be able to think ahead and troubleshoot. I have to look at an event from different angles. I have to look from an employee's perspective. What do I need? What do my employees need? What do the people above me need? I have to look at it from a patron's perspective. My interns and I will walk through the gates as if we are patrons and think of everything from a patron's perspective. One of the biggest skills you need is the ability to troubleshoot beforehand, look at what will happen, what you will need. You need the ability to fluctuate whatever it is you are doing and then go back in focus.

With organizing, I need to see the entire event from the beginning when I start with my budget to when I start my timeline. What date do I need to have these letters mailed? If you are not careful, it may be March 15th and those letters were due out 2 weeks ago. You cannot let those types of things happen. Some people are just not cut out to do event management. Some people are better at sales or other things. You really have to be able to look ahead and to be organized.

My way to handle stress is to vent to somebody other than people at work. I am an emotional person, very vocal and opinionated, and I work with five people who are very vocal and just as opinionated. It is very important to go to somebody outside the job. Again, I cannot stress that point enough. Every level has pressure from different angles, different types of pressure, but I just focus on the task, focus on the job.

I did not know what my management style was going to be because I had never managed. After a couple of weeks of working I sat down and said to my interns, "I didn't know this before about myself but now I do. During an event I'm stressed — it's intense. I just want you to know it has nothing to do with you." Even though I am happy and bubbly I am still very direct and I want to get the job done. I work a lot of hours, but I want to go home to spend time with my family so when I am at work I want to get it done.

I do not take an hour-and-a-half lunch because that is an hour more that I will be here away from my family so I am more focused and direct than a lot of people. It is important to communicate with your employees and tell them what your management style is. If it is direct and sometimes harsh or a little abrasive, you need to tell them. At times I will say, "How is everything going?" If I feel like their attitude is getting a little bit strange, I will say, "Is there something that I'm doing, or is there something that can be changed? Is everything okay? Let me know, because I do care. I'm so busy you might not think I do, but I do."

Event management has grown tremendously. Over the past 10 to 20 years people have come to realize there is more to a sporting event than the event itself. It is getting so competitive with the sponsorship dollars involved. We must have other things to attract people other than a basketball game or a horse race. I do think there is room to grow but I think the growth has an end. I think there is an upper limit. There has to be some limit on budget because I cannot spend $50,000 on an event that only brings in $20,000. I think there is definitely room for growth, but it will cap off eventually. I think promotions are never going to die. That is the nature of the industry.

Job opportunities are different because 10 years ago not many organizations had event coordinators. It would be interesting to see how many event coordinators there were in 1989 compared with 1999. My guess is it has easily quadrupled. Sport is becoming more of a business than sport or play. With the industry getting new jobs and new titles, event management is definitely an area of growth.

Customers have not changed too much; they have only become more demanding. I think customers today expect more because there are more events. Before there were just the races. Now people coming to the races want to know what are you going to give them for getting here?

I like the title of event coordinator. If anything, I would like to branch off to another type of event coordinator, more of an in-house event coordinator. I think my specialty is dealing with high profile events and V.I.P. events. I am very good at comfort. As part of my internship at Churchill Downs, I was responsible for the Breeder's Cup Press Party, for instance. There was one out in Hollywood the year before. How do you compare with a Hollywood party? You do not even try.

We had almost 2,000 people. We had 17 bars and 25 bartenders. I had 10 food stations and a huge shrimp station in the middle so our guests never had to stand in line and never had to go through a buffet. Seats were available for everybody. If a seat was not available, there was a place to rest their drinks. There were cocktail tables. There were cabs to take them home if they had too much to drink. There were attendants, including umbrella attendants if it was raining, and valet parking attendants. As you can see my specialty is comfort. I had the biggest compliment when a gentleman who was there came up to me and said, "This was the most comfortable party I've ever been to."

I think success in my mind is how much I have grown. I look back at how I have grown and I look forward and see room to grow. There is a saying that goes "When you think of yesterday with pride and tomorrow with hope, you can live peacefully today." I am happy I took the time in college to explore. I was not afraid to change majors or move to New York for 3 months. I may have been scared but I did not question myself, and I was never scared to explore different options. I have grown professionally and personally. I would tell sport management students to try to focus on the positive things and work to improve personally and professionally.

A factor that contributed to getting this job at Churchill Downs was my portfolio. For sport administration it is important to have a portfolio. I kept everything from every event, from fliers I made for events, fliers I made for my marketing class, pictures, etc. I kept the budget and attendance from every single event. I went to an art supply store, bought a portfolio, and created something where I had the headline and materials from the event. I started chronologically back when I was a freshman on a student government event and put a flier there. What I wanted to show in my portfolio was the diversity of things I can do. I put the name of the event, who was the event for, the purpose of the event, the budget, and the attendance. Numbers are great so I definitely had numbers. I used pictures or invitations to events. I did not want to mislead anyone during my interview so if I did not make the invitation in my portfolio, I did not indicate that I did. It is important to be very truthful. The best thing about the portfolio was it was great for answering questions. When the interviewers asked a question like, "How do you go about organizing an event?" I just opened the portfolio and talked about a specific event that grabbed their attention. It woke them up. We had a lot of interviewees for one position, and the interviewers were tired of hearing the same things all of the time. My portfolio stuck out in their mind. It separated me from everybody else.

As far as career advice, sport administration or working in the sport industry is a tough road either in an entry-level position or as the vice president. You receive more attention from the media than many other professions. In the sport industry you have to be prepared for ridicule and criticism. You have to be prepared for whatever you do to wind up in the newspaper. It is a complete microscope. If I am event coordinator and I say a certain jockey is going to be at the autograph session and he does not show up, that will be in the paper. You will be scrutinized by the public, your peers, and people above you. But at the same time, everyone is going to tell you, "You've got the best job in the world," so it is a catch twenty-two. It is a lot of pressure. You must be ready to deal with a lot of different things. There are so many different aspects to the sport industry and it is so different than other industries. Some companies focus just on marketing or just on advertising. In the sport industry it is all there. You basically have it all right under one roof.

I know I have a great job in the sport industry because at the beginning of the day I hear the national anthem. When I was with the Yankees they played it before every game. That really reminded me I had a good job. Sometimes people fall into the trap, and their job becomes just like any other job. They say things like, "I don't get paid enough," "I don't get enough recognition," "It's so hard to deal with the customers," or "It's just like any other job." But when I hear that national anthem every day I remind myself that this is the type of job I always wanted. This is the type of job hundreds of other people would like to have.

Kimberly Sue Grant

Tournament Director
Firstar LPGA Classic

Education:
B.A., SPORT MANAGEMENT, BOWLING GREEN
STATE UNIVERSITY, 1987

M.A., COMMUNICATIONS SCIENCE, WRIGHT
STATE UNIVERSITY, 1999

Career Progression:
TOURNAMENT DIRECTOR, FIRSTAR LPGA
CLASSIC, 1996 TO PRESENT

PROMOTIONS DIRECTOR, WRIGHT STATE UNI-
VERSITY ATHLETICS DEPARTMENT, 1989–1996

MARKETING DIRECTOR, DAYTON DYNAMO
PROFESSIONAL INDOOR SOCCER, 1988–1989

SPECIAL EVENTS COORDINATOR, RIVERFRONT
COLISEUM (CINCINNATI, OHIO), 1987–1988

Best piece of advice you received in regards to your career:

"Return all phone calls within one day of receiving them."

Best advice for someone aspiring toward a career in the sport industry:

**"VOLUNTEER for as many sport related organizations,
events, etc. as possible while in school to build not only your resume
but gain valuable experience and contacts."**

Quote by which you live:

**"Never, never, never lie in any business relationship. People will
respect you more when you always tell the truth even if it's not
what they want to hear!"**

I KNEW SINCE I WAS AN UNDERGRADUATE STUDENT at Bowling
Green University that I wanted a career in sport. I just never thought my career
would involve running a professional golf tournament. I had been involved in
sport as a participant and worked within the athletic department at Bowling
Green, but I did not know much about golf. I thought people who played were really old, like my dad! Five years ago, I decided I was going to start to learn to golf
only because my husband was golfing on the weekends. When there were golf
outings while I was working at Wright State University, I was the one who had to
sign people in, instead of playing.

In hindsight, I was glad I learned to play golf or I may not have been comfortable with the responsibility of running the Firstar LPGA classic. With that said, I do not think it is essential to be a good golfer or even to play golf, but it is important to understand the terminology and nuances of the game. It is also important to understand the passion people have for the game.

I am not sure the career path that has led me to be tournament director for the Firststar LPGA event is atypical of others in my position or others in the sport management field. First of all, this may sound strange, but I have never sent in a blind resume for any of the positions I have held. Either someone asked me to interview for a position or I met a person who asked if I would be interested in a position with his or her organization. I still had to interview for the positions, but the networking I did through my career created the interview opportunities. In each case, I performed well enough in the interview to secure the position.

The second point is I never had a certain goal or direction mapped out for myself. I have always been in the right place at the right time, and truly, getting the Firstar LPGA tournament position was another one of those experiences. I find that interesting because I receive calls from students who know they want to be involved in running a golf tournament as a career orientation while still an undergraduate. Despite this, I have bonded with every job I had and grew from each experience.

Bowling Green's undergraduate program introduced me to the concept of networking. As students we were required to participate in practicums where we had to put hours in at various sport organizations. Along with the required experiences, I became involved in as many things as possible. This was a great strategy because it looked good on my resume, I gained a lot of experience as an undergraduate, and it gave me more confidence when I went into jobs out of school.

We also had to interview professionals and finally participate in an internship experience. I did my internship with the Wright State Athletic Department in the fall of 1987. From that experience I met people who told me about an opportunity at Riverfront Coliseum, an indoor arena in Cincinnati that hosted sport and entertainment events. They needed someone to do group sales and marketing in the Dayton area because they drew people from Dayton to Cincinnati for concerts and events. At the same time, Wright State offered me an opportunity to stay on after my internship to be involved in marketing the women's athletic teams. As I was graduating from Bowling Green I had two great opportunities. I took the position of special accounts coordinator for Riverfront Coliseum in January 1988 because the job responsibilities interested me.

I was involved in generating group sales as well as servicing the corporate boxes. Servicing the corporate box customers involved securing tickets, invoicing the customers for the use of the box, and ensuring the customers had a positive experience while at the event. It was a great experience, but it involved the financial dealings of the organization, and I was not interested in this area.

Leaving that position lead to the experience I think launched me into my career more than anything else. I returned to Dayton in May 1988 to take a sales and marketing position for the Dayton Dynamo indoor soccer team. I was familiar with indoor soccer because I had done some work for the team in Toledo while at Bowling Green. The Dayton team did not have any money except to pay the players, so I was paid a commission on the sponsorship sales I made. I figured I would do it to gain some experience, but within 6 months I had the title of marketing director. I was still not being paid much, but it was an incredible learning experience. I did a little bit of everything including setting up half-time shows for the team, doing sales, and preparing the program. I had to do everything because there was no one else there to do it.

It would have been easier to be representing a more established organization. A sale was tough because the organization did not have brand recognition. I would knock on a door and say "Hi, I am working for the Dayton Dynamo" and they would think the Dynamo was an ice hockey team. It was a tough sell.

It is important in a career to recognize when it is time for a change and to determine what career opportunities are worth pursuing. I have been fortunate in that every time I looked for a career change an opportunity arose. For example, after a year, I wanted to move on from the Dayton Dynamo. I received a call from Wright State Athletic Department asking me to interview for a job. I had done an internship with them only 2 years earlier. Honestly, I thought my internship there as an undergraduate student was my real interview. I mentioned that and I still believe the internship is the best job interview. If an employer likes the performance of an intern he or she will find a way to hire the intern or find the intern a job with another organization.

In June 1989 I was named director of marketing and promotions at Wright State. I had varied responsibilities related to advertising. I sold the program ads, arena and scoreboard signs, as well as radio and television game sponsorship. I developed special events and game promotions associated with fund raising. I planned, organized, and administered community nights at Wright State basketball games and handled some media relations responsibilities. Those 8 years at Wright State were a positive experience because I honed my sales and marketing skills. I liked being involved in sponsorship sales.

College athletics is a great work environment and offers a lot of perks, but after 8 years with Wright State I was ready for a change. The downside of working in college athletics is the long hours and weekends. If you think about it, college contests are either in the evening or on the weekends. Athletic department employees work weekdays to prepare for the evening and weekend contests and then must attend the contests on those evenings and weekends. That is a lot of hours. The pay is not the greatest in intercollegiate athletics. I was reaching the burnout point with the position when the opportunity to be involved with the golf tournament arose in October 1997.

A friend made me aware of the position and asked if I was interested. Although I had no experience in the golf industry, I did have a wealth of experience in sales and marketing which were major aspects of the position. Now that I have been with the tournament for 2–1/2 years, I am not interested in having the schedule I did in college athletics. As much as I liked intercollegiate athletics, I like this environment better. It is low key for half the year and then crazy for half the year. The experiences I gained prior to this position were invaluable, and I would recommend those types of experiences for people interested in growing as professionals in the field. I have learned that any hands-on experience in any area of the sport industry can be transferred to other areas in the industry. I was in college athletics but now I am in golf but the sales and marketing skills are applicable. You just use your skills in a different environment.

All my work experiences have been beneficial in shaping me as a professional. This is partly because I was in relatively new positions, which gave me flexibility. This is also because I had more responsibility for a person my age than others in a similar position. I thrived on that because I am a self-starter and I like to challenge myself. This has been the same situation with the golf tournament. Although I am the tournament coordinator for Firstar LPGA Classic, I work for Riber Sport Management, a sport marketing company based in Cincinnati. Riber Sport has the contract to run the Firstar LPGA Classic.

My direct boss with Riber spends his time in Cincinnati and California. In 2–1/2 years I probably have seen my boss personally maybe 20 times. I talk to him on the phone maybe every 2 weeks. He has given me the freedom to do my job. I hired an assistant and my boss did not meet her for several weeks. Because I had the experience of making decisions and handling a number of responsibilities I can manage the freedom I have here, and I love it. To be honest, my coworker and I could get away with a lot of stuff—but we do not—because this tournament is a reflection on us and we do not want to see it fail. If we took short cuts or did not put our best effort forward we would get away with it for awhile, but not for very long. To succeed in this position, I need to work hard and be honest and ethical.

I have also been fortunate to work with some excellent role models. When I worked at Riverfront Coliseum, the vice president of marketing was in charge signage and sponsorship sales. I really thought he was great on the phone with people. I often listened to him and his conversations and sometimes he took me into meetings with him. They were incredible learning experiences. Just listening to Rich prepared me for when I was thrown into the sales and marketing position with the Dayton Dynamo. I make it a point with my interns to bring them in meetings with me so they could learn as I did from listening and watching.

Managing a golf event is very different from managing a professional sport team. In professional sport, the product is in front of the public for 6 months and numerous contests are held throughout the season. In a golf tournament we are only in the spotlight for a week with a 4-day event. Therefore, we must be very creative to keep the level of awareness high throughout the year. The media is not interested in talking about golf in the middle of the winter. It is focusing on the basketball or football seasons. We have to take proactive steps to remind them we are here. For example, I might decide that I had not talked to my key media people in awhile during the late winter or early spring, so I will send them a jacket and a sleeve of golf balls with a note wishing them a great golf season and saying I look forward to talking to them in the summer. Throughout the year we donate tickets to everybody and anybody who asks. We donate to the Boy Scouts, community events, and golf outings to name a few. That is another way to keep your name in front of sponsors' and spectators' minds.

We have established networking and golf seminars for businesswomen because there is a new market of women golfers. The seminar involves a luncheon with a guest speaker who describes how golf can be used as a networking tool and discusses business on the golf course. We also increase awareness by informing the attendees about how to use our professional golf tournament to entertain clients whether it is on the course, in the clubhouse, or in a corporate tent.

We have done several seminars and have incorporated them into some of our sponsorship packages. Every sponsor wants some unique twist. Another idea we have used is a golf walk. The tournament is held at a beautiful, private country club that is relatively new. Many people in the community have never seen it. We tied a sponsor into the event and people came out during the summer leading up to the tournament to walk either nine or 18 holes. (Nine holes is 2–1/2 miles and 18 holes is 5 miles). We had more than 500 people at the first walk last year and we are doing it again July 2000. The sponsor came in with a larger amount because they loved it so much. In both situations, we satisfied a sponsor while increasing awareness of the tournament.

We have partnered with two colleges in the area, Wright State University and the University of Dayton and have used their sport-marketing students. The partnership has allowed the students to develop a marketing plan for the tournament as well as a plan for recruiting and retaining volunteers. The other benefit of the partnership is I get a lot of college students who will work the tournament.

In running a golf tournament there is the time leading up to the actual tournament and the tournament week itself. The time leading up to the tournament is devoted to planning, organizing, and selling. We establish a timeline for the year leading up to the tournament and strive to reach the deadlines on the timeline. A typical day during nontournament is somewhat 9 to 5 with occasional dinners with potential sponsors and evening or weekend appearances at local events to help heighten the awareness of the tournament. It is a lot more relaxed than college athletics because that environment always involved weekends and evenings.

The majority of the nontournament week time is spent on sales calls to potential sponsors for the tournament or Pro-Am. We focus on sponsorship sales right up to the start of the tournament. You have to remain in contact with the potential sponsors. That can get hard, but it is necessary because they are not going to call and offer their money. A lot of time is spent on ticket sales. We do an early-bird discount from November until the end of May. This has been a success because a lot of people buy early to get the discount. In looking at the demographics of our ticket buyers, we found that 52 percent are women and 48 percent are men. It is pretty even and people may not realize it. I think we mainly attract golf fans. One of my goals is to get the nongolf fan out for the golf walk. If the nongolf fan saw the beauty of the course he or she may consider returning to the course. I have found that anyone who comes to the course and the tournament loves it whether or not he or she is a golfer. There is something to be said to about being at a professional event. It is great to see an athlete at the top of his or her sport. A lot of men do not come because they do not want to see the women. I tell the men that the LPGA players' games are closer to their games than the PGA players in terms of how far the women hit the ball and how close they get to the greens.

Tournament week is like nothing I have ever experienced in my entire life. It is total 100 percent chaos. No matter how organized you are, something will pop up. For example, the Port-O-Johns get delivered to the wrong holes or volunteers call to cancel. Questions come at you for 18 hours straight. The only thing that gets you through is knowing that on Sunday it is over. As a tournament coordinator you have to be adaptable and think quickly and adjust midstream. Many times there are factors to contend with that are beyond our control. For example, we had to cancel a Pro-Am day 2 years ago because of weather. People pay a lot of money to play in it and we plan all year for it, but the weather is uncontrollable and unpredictable.

To prepare for tournament week, we move into a temporary trailer on site at the country club about 2 months before the tournament. This way we can accept deliveries and be close to everyone involved with the event to make sure it is as organized as possible. Planning is essential to tournament week success. All of our planning leads up to the week before the tournament and the actual tournament week. At that time things are just going to happen whether you want them to or not. These skills, which honestly were not one of my strengths, have forced me to be organized because so many details have to kept together to ensure a smooth event. If everything is in place and the right people know what they are doing things will run more smoothly than if a plan did not exist.

Our hope is that all of our suppliers arrive and deliver on time. I have completed evaluation forms for companies that have worked our tournaments and I emphasize the necessity to deliver at the scheduled time, and when applicable pick up at the scheduled time. This is important because we try to get everything off the course the day after the event. The tournament is held on a private course and the course needs to get back to normal as much and as quickly as possible. It is imperative that companies remove their goods. On one occasion, a Port-O-John was left on the 18th hole. The people who live out there did not appreciate that in their backyard. On another occasion, copy machines were left in our temporary trailers and the trailers were going to be picked up whether the copy machines were removed or not. Planning is important, but those plans must be implemented effectively. Also, the companies we deal with must follow through with their commitments.

My main responsibility in running the tournament involves establishing and staying within the budget. The budget drives all of our decisions and enables us to prioritize. To develop the budget I need to estimate our revenue from ticket sales and sponsorship, our two main revenue sources, and then turn the estimated revenue into actual revenue through ticket and sponsorship sales.

To generate revenue through sponsorships, we have to cultivate and then satisfy the sponsors. The process of cultivating and satisfying the sponsor is challenging. Of the two, satisfying is harder to do. Cultivating potential sponsors is easy because I am passionate about our tournament and I enjoy trying to sell sponsorships and getting potential sponsors excited about being a part of the tournament. It is also important to identify the sponsor's goals and present the best way to meet those goals for overall satisfaction with the sponsorship package and experience.

Satisfying the sponsors can be the challenging part. Often a company buys a sponsorship package but no point person ensures the benefits of the sponsorship package are used effectively. We can do everything on our end, but if the sponsor does not use the benefits the sponsorship is not perceived as beneficial. For example, a company purchases a corporate hospitality tent, but does not send out any invitations. When no one uses the tent, the sponsor thinks it is not worth the financial commitment and decides not to renew the corporate package. We lose a sponsor and have to look for a new one. The challenge is to educate the sponsor on how to use the benefits of a sponsorship package. Other times we have no control over whether a sponsor returns or not. A company may have to make cutbacks and sponsorships are one of the first things to go. There is no way we can control or predict it but losing sponsorships hurts.

Measuring the worth of sponsorship is also a challenge. This is an issue any one who has dealt with sponsorship, especially in sport and entertainment, has to address. We fall short on measuring the worth because we do not always have great evaluation methods. Some sponsors base the decision on whether they had a good time at the tournament. If they go away feeling good about the experience of being a part of a professional tournament, they are satisfied. Other sponsors measure the bottom line and determine if they received a return on their investment. That is more difficult to gauge.

Our main sources of revenue are sponsorships and ticket sales. I would say 80 percent comes from the sale of sponsorship packages and 20 percent from the ticket sales. Based on the estimated revenues from the sponsorship and ticket sales we plan our expenses for the coming year. The $650,000 purse is a big chunk of the budget. Our other expenses are related to tournament operations such as renting bleachers, tents, and roping for the course. To minimize expenses we trade or barter for many of the services and products needed for the tournament. For example, we will trade tickets for the use of two vans during the tournament or provide a Pro-Am spot in exchange for $2,500 in radio advertising. We also receive ads in the newspapers as a trade. This is an effective strategy to minimize expenses.

I have a gained a new appreciation for what I spend money on by overseeing the budget for our organization. While working in an athletic department, I never knew where the budget stood. Now the budget is my responsibility. When I take people out to lunch I do not exceed my budget and try to spend less than the budgeted amount in case we do not meet our revenue goals. Along with the budget, I pay all the bills. I did not like the financial aspects in the past, but it has been a valuable learning experience.

The most demanding aspect of running an LPGA event is ensuring proper communication with all the parties involved. These parties include my superiors, volunteers, sponsors, and the LPGA. It is important to communicate with my boss about what we do and when we do it. We as a tournament must communicate with the LPGA because we have to do things under its guidelines. The LPGA gives us a manual to follow for advance week and tournament week. In the case of the title sponsor, they do not make their financial commitment and then sit back and not get involved. They want to know where you stand and what you are doing. There are also sponsors besides the naming sponsor who have questions and concerns. The Children's Medical Center, the tournament's benefactor, actually owns it and in a way is my boss. It is so important to be honest with all of these parties. If you are not, it will come back to haunt you. People appreciate it more when you say you are sorry for forgetting or missing a deadline. When you admit your mistake, people appreciate that more than if you make an excuse or lie. Balancing all these parties, keeping the communication consistent and honest, and making everyone happy are the greatest challenges.

A unique aspect of operating a professional golf tournament is that the staff is primarily volunteers. There are only two full-time staff members of the tournament. We rely on 650 volunteers who perform essential tasks associated with the actual operation of the tournament. A group of volunteers oversees parking and trash removal and another group ensures that water, fruit, and ice are on each tee box. Other volunteers are course marshals who oversee crowd control. Some of their duties include carrying the walking scores, staffing the leader boards, and reporting the scores from each green to the leader boards. Luckily, we have a great group of head volunteers and volunteer chair people. We have a flow chart of people who are involved with the volunteers. I always believe if I have a good attitude it will rub off on the people who are the volunteer chair people and in turn it will rub off on the other volunteers. The Children's Medical Center is such a great charity that people feel good about volunteering for the cause.

In turn, we do things for the volunteers. For example, we developed discount cards that can be used in the community and during the golf tournament. The volunteers have access to the clubhouse where nobody but major sponsors have access. The volunteers receive priority parking during the tournament while they are working so they do not have to take the shuttle. We hold pizza parties at the end of the tournament and provide snacks and drinks and other gifts for them during the week. Finally, we take every measure possible to communicate to them how much we appreciate their effort. The most important aspect in dealing with the volunteers is projecting a good attitude. It is amazing how far being positive and treating volunteers with respect can go. It is contagious. Unfortunately, it works the other way too. When people are negative and complain about what they get and do not get, it has a ripple effect.

In dealing with the volunteers and interns, I consider myself a hands-off manager. I give them a lot of flexibility. I encourage my interns to generate ideas for the tournament and to be creative. I am collaborative on decision making. I seek input before I make any decisions and I consult different people to get their opinions. When I make a decision I take responsibility for it, whether it is a good or bad decision. It is good to get advice and opinions so it can be an educated decision. I have also learned to delegate as a manager, because I cannot do it all. I have learned to trust those who work for me.

The most enjoyable aspect of my job is meeting so many different people. Sport touches everyone in some way. I deal with doctors, lawyers, and management people and I deal with people when they are talking about golf. I deal with them when they are in a positive mood. No life-threatening decisions are made here. Although things can be stressful it is not stressful when perceived in the bigger scheme of things. A great aspect of my position is that I meet people I probably would have never met. I have been in the office with the president and chief executive officer of a major company like Standard Register. That would not have happened if I did not have this job. These are people who play golf and love it. Because I have always been involved in sports and often deal with men I am not intimidated by these situations. I enjoy them. If I did not play golf, I would not have met all these people. I met the national president of Jacor Radio, which is now owned by Clear Channel, because we played in the same foursome in a golf outing.

What I have found interesting about being around golf is what you find out about people while playing golf. You may be entertaining a client, but golf is a great way to learn about people. In my mind the way a person plays golf is a microcosm of how they act. If people cheat or lie on the golf course, chances are they cheat or lie in their job or position. If a person is a risk taker on the golf course, he or she may be one in life. A person may be very methodical and hit short strokes. Also one person may have a short fuse and lose his or her temper whereas another does not let a missed putt affect his or her entire game. On the other side, you never know who is watching you on the course.

Being able to play golf is becoming a part of many business positions. Someone told me that a recent Bowling Green graduate received a job offer contingent on her learning how to play golf so she could use it to entertain clients. Golf can be intimidating for those who do not play, but it is an easy game to learn and it is a worthwhile investment of time.

I am satisfied with certain aspects of my position, but there are others in which I could be more satisfied. I am slightly dissatisfied with my salary although I have never done enough research to know what is appropriate. I have a lot of responsibility to run this tournament with little direction, but at the same time it is bit intimidating and a little scary. The amount of responsibility I have makes me slightly dissatisfied with my salary. Many jobs in sport do not pay well, but the trade-off is my job is to run a golf tournament and that is awesome. Many people would love to be in this position. I do not know whether they would be willing to take a pay cut. My husband, who is an assistant athletic director at Wright State, agrees there is a trade-off between work and salary. His salary is good but not great, but he gets perks such as tickets to sporting events and the opportunity to travel to different places with the teams.

What is interesting about my career promotion opportunities is that little potential for advancement exists because there are only two employees. However, I have been approached by some sponsors to work for them. I would have to leave the sport industry and I am not interested in doing so. I could take other opportunities in golf, but I am not interested.

I love the work content. I have one full-time coworker with whom I am so blessed because we get along. She is great. Actually, I was not scared about leaving the athletic department where people were around all the time. Luckily we click and it has really been great.

I think the golf industry and the LPGA tour are on the rise. Some statistics may say otherwise, but that is not what I have seen locally. Men, women, and juniors are getting into the game as players and they are becoming fans of the tours. As far as the LPGA tour is concerned, I think that the tour has done a great job thus far marketing itself, but I think they need to do more. We need a Tiger Woods of the women's tour—a media darling everyone wants to see play. It could happen because a lot of great players are coming out of college. The golf market and women's golf market will grow over the next 10 years.

When I consider my future aspirations, I would like to be self-employed. My job has given me a lot of responsibility and I could take those same skills, work for myself, and possibly make more money. I would enjoy consulting and teaching. I have always wanted to get expertise in some field and focus on it and golf may be it for me. Up to this point in my career, I have fallen into everything, so I have not followed a set plan. I have been lucky to have a career in sport and stay in the Dayton area. It would take a lot for my husband and I to leave this area because family is very important to us. If I am happy and content then I do not need to make a million dollars. I just want to keep the balance between a career and a family life.

Laura L. Sawyer

Executive Director
Carolina Marathon Association

Education:

B.S., SPORT ADMINISTRATION, UNIVERSITY OF SOUTH CAROLINA, 1992

M.S., SPORT MANAGEMENT, GEORGIA SOUTHERN UNIVERSITY, 1994

ED.D., SPORT MANAGEMENT, UNIVERSITY OF NORTHERN COLORADO, 1997

Career Progression:

EXECUTIVE DIRECTOR, CAROLINA MARATHON ASSOCIATION, 1998 TO PRESENT

ADJUNCT PROFESSOR, UNIVERSITY OF SOUTH CAROLINA, 1999 TO PRESENT

VISITING PROFESSOR, SPORT INSTITUTE, GRONINGEN, HOLLAND, 1998 TO PRESENT

ASSISTANT PROFESSOR, JAMES MADISON UNIVERSITY, 1997–1998

FITNESS COORDINATOR, UNIVERSITY OF NORTHERN COLORADO, 1996–1997

DIRECTOR OF EMERGENCY RESPONSE, MILE HIGH STADIUM (DENVER BRONCOS), 1996

FACILITY CONSULTANT, LOSS CONTROL AND AUDIT SERVICES, DENVER, CO, 1995

LIFETIME ACTIVITIES AND PROGRAM COORDINATOR, FLORIDA STATE UNIVERSITY, 1994

INTERN, UNIVERSITY OF SOUTH CAROLINA, ATHLETIC DEPARTMENT, 1992

INTERN, ALL PRO CHAMPIONSHIPS, 1991

Best piece of advice you received in regards to your career:

"Always inquire about positions and experiences that interest you because the cost of inquiring is usually only a postage stamp or a phone call. Not inquiring could cost a lot more in the long run."

DR. DAVE STOTLAR, UNIVERSITY OF NORTHERN COLORADO

Best advice for someone aspiring toward a career in the sport industry:

"Practice what you preach in your degree programs long after you graduate. Whether working on a research paper, professional project, practicum, internship, or in a job within the industry - ALWAYS OVERDELIVER!"

Quote by which you live:

"Knowledge and information will take you to exciting places but passion will make sure that you enjoy the ride!"

MY NAME IS LAURA SAWYER and I am currently the executive director of the Carolina Marathon Association and an adjunct professor of sport management at the University of South Carolina at Columbia.

I grew up being an athlete who was fascinated with two things: the entertainment industry and the sport industry. Even when I was not a participant, I was interested in what was happening in sports. I completely absorbed any information I could get through newspapers or magazines about sports entertainment, particularly the Disney organization. My social personality coupled with excellent planning and people skills has groomed me for a career in sport. My hesitation was that I did not know the outlets for careers in sports.

I left school in 1986 having completed only 2 years of general coursework. When I returned in the fall of 1990, I began to seriously look for a career field and came upon Guy Lewis and Peter Graham in the sport management department at the University of South Carolina. I was pleased to learn about the sport management curriculum and the many options available, including facility planning and event management. The more I began to find out, the more I was hooked. I also went to the career center to see if my personal attributes matched what I thought it would take in the field and they did. That is how I decided on a career in sport.

I did two internships while at the University of South Carolina. The first one I did was with All Pro Championships in Louisville, Kentucky, a merchandising company for large sport events including the Kentucky Derby and Churchill Downs. The company has also done the Super Bowl, the Belmont, the Preakness, and NBA Finals. When I was there I went to the 1991 NBA finals (Lakers vs. Bulls) for 2 weeks. I helped oversee eight satellite merchandising locations and learned about royalties, licensors and licensees, and the contracts it takes to maintain those relationships. That probably spurred my interest in sponsorship. I did a second internship at the University of South Carolina with Sid Kenyon and John Bolin, who were both in athletic facility management.

Then I went to Georgia Southern University to pursue my masters in sport management. I chose Georgia Southern mainly on the advice of the faculty at the University of South Carolina. Location was important to me at that time too. I was going to pursue a doctorate so I opted out of the internship and wrote a thesis in facility management. When I came home from Georgia Southern on weekends, I worked events in Columbia.

After Georgia Southern University, I spent 1 year at Florida State in the doctoral program. I headed up the Lifetime Activities program that encompassed about 25 instructors who taught 100 classes. I scheduled all of the activity classes within the program. It was a great experience from an administrative standpoint that included planning and a lot of paperwork. I organized evaluations from graduate assistants and received lesson plans, schedules, and budgets.

I wrote to the seven doctoral programs that existed at that time. I chose Florida State University after reviewing materials from the others. After a year there I transferred to the University of Northern Colorado specifically to study with Dr. David Stotlar because of his expertise in sport marketing and sponsorship. By that time, I had a strong interest in facilities, but had a budding interest in sponsorship. He wanted to capitalize on that interest. I spent about 2 to 2–1/2 years at the University of Northern Colorado and finished in 1997. Attending that program was clearly the best decision I ever made.

At the University of Northern Colorado, I did two really neat things. I served as the fitness coordinator for a recreation program that included 15 aerobic instructors and 10 personal trainers. I maintained budgets and planned and evaluated programs. I also worked for the Denver Broncos in Mile High Stadium. I helped Marcia Walker teach her facility management class and decided the students should talk to people involved in facilities management. During that semester, I met Gary Jones, the operations director at Mile High Stadium. He was in the International Association of Assembly Managers (IAAM). At that time I had written a couple of articles for *Facility Manager*, the trade publication, and I asked him to review them and we began talking back and forth.

At Mile High, I was the director of emergency response for a season. I handled all types of problems, from beer sales not getting turned off in the fourth quarter, to fan incidents, to crowd problems and ticket counterfeiters. I have always believed that if you are going to teach something you should do it. It was a way for me to practice what I was teaching. I wrote my dissertation while I worked for the Broncos at Mile High Stadium and coordinated the fitness program. My dissertation topic was corporate sponsorship and reasons for sponsorship cancellation by big sport organizations. It was a busy year as I began to look for teaching positions. I finished the dissertation before I left and took a faculty position at James Madison University for a year. I taught a variety of sport management classes there, then relocated back to Columbia, South Carolina, to be closer to my family.

I heard about a position with the Carolina Marathon Association, known for its reputation for producing quality events, including the Governor's Cup road race, the longest road race in South Carolina. It includes a half marathon and an 8K race and has been run for 27 years. Additionally, the association produces the Carolina Marathon, which includes a 10K run, a full marathon and wheelchair, youth, and corporate events.

I knew they were both big events and attracted elite athletes. Since 1995 the Carolina Marathon Association has hosted national championship events including the Olympic Trials for the women's marathon, the 8K national championships, and the marathon national championships. I also knew Dr. Russ Pate was at the helm. He was from the department of exercise science at the University of South Carolina. I spoke with Russ and learned that they were bidding on the 2000 Olympic Trials for the women's marathon and knew this would be wonderful experience in terms of event planning. The association has garnered long-standing sponsorship relationships in the community and has had some sponsors for 10 to 15 years. They needed to procure some new sponsorships because of the amount of money necessary to produce the Olympic trials. Someone was needed who could both maintain sponsorship relationships currently in the community and help procure some new money. This person needed good people skills because it is a nonprofit organization that is heavily dependent on volunteers.

I want to teach full-time again but I think I will always feel a need—even if it is on a volunteer basis—to work events. It can easily be done with my students producing an event but I need to be well versed in what I teach. Students in sport management do not understand all of the available outlets. They often enter programs and say they want to be an agent or work with a professional team. Those careers are fine, but they are not aware of nonprofit companies, event coordination, or facility management. They do not look for internships or jobs at Chambers of Commerce or Sports Councils.

Being a woman in the sport industry is not an obstacle. I have heard other women say sport is a "man's world," but that is true only to the extent we allow it to be. When I bring the correct competencies and requisite skills to the table people do not care that I am a woman. I have encountered people who did not expect as much from me because I was a woman, but it did not bother me. Regardless of who employs me, who asks me a question, who consults me for an answer, or who I teach, my responsibility is to do those things the best that I can.

My academic role model is clearly David Stotlar. He is an exemplary teacher and has conducted important research in the field. I have long been an advocate that research not only needs to contribute to the discipline but also needs to create answers for practitioners. Doing research for the sake of doing research is not the answer. We need to contribute to the discipline but also listen to practitioners and do the research they need done. That might be simple descriptive research or detailed statistical analyses. They may not know exactly what research they need done, and we can enlighten them that way. I think the gap between those practitioners and academicians needs to be bridged for both the academic side of sport management and the sport and entertainment industry to become more efficient and effective. I think David Stotlar represents that bridge. He teaches in a conversant way, and his answer to everything is that knowledge is not any good if you cannot do anything with it. He gave his students a very healthy respect for the theoretical and empirical side to our discipline but he also made us think about what it meant and what we could do with it. For those reasons, he has been my academic role model.

My professional role models are John Bolin and Gary Jones. John Bolin is the director of the Carolina Coliseum at the University of South Carolina. He introduced me to facility management. On a day-to-day basis he operates the venue that houses the basketball team and classrooms, hosts conventions and concerts, and performs every single aspect of it well. He knew the everyday things that he asked entry-level people to do, but also empowered his marketing and office managers. He knows what to delegate and how to let people be autonomous but is never too out of touch to answer a question from an entry-level employee. He is also excited about what he does and constantly preaches that facilities are a business of leverage and relationships. He taught me critical decision-making and problem-solving skills. I have spoken to his classes. He was very encouraging to students and discussed all of the different outlets and places for them to work. He has written many reference letters and bends over backward to accommodate the students.

My other role model is Gary Jones, the manager of Mile High Stadium. He summed up his job philosophy by saying there has never been a day when he did not want to get up and go to work. He began many years ago hanging Christmas lights for the city of Denver and ended up managing Mile High Stadium. He is willing to take people like me and find a place for them in his organization. I would have to be there 2 or 3 hours early on game day, and I would walk around and listen to him talk about sponsor negotiations, facility issues, and cost comparisons.

My job description reads as follows: The executive director functions as the chief executive officer of the association. The executive director is responsible for the day-to-day operation of the association and is expected to ensure that the association operates in a manner consistent with policies established by the board of directors, with state and federal regulations, pertinent to not-for-profit organizations, and with accepted business practices. The executive director represents the association in a wide range of settings and ensures that the association operates in a fiscally sound manner and functions to ensure that the programmatic activities of the association meet the highest standards. To summarize, I ensure that the Carolina Marathon Association operates in a fiscally sound manner, by preparing and managing an annual budget approved by the board of directors Keep the board of directors informed about our financial status at all times. I supervise the staff and recruit, support, coordinate, and reward volunteers, maintain regular and effective communication with them, and ensure that the staff assistants do their duties in an effective manner.

We have a volunteer base that ranges from 75 to 100 key volunteers. On the day of the Olympic Trials, we use about 2,000 volunteers. It is important to develop a relationship with volunteers. They are busy people with full lives, yet I have to get what I need from them to make the event happen. That is a very fine art of management. I deal with a variety of people who are emotionally invested in this event at different levels. Some people might be brand new whereas others have helped for 10 to 15 years. We have volunteers who might not have a family, have lots of discretionary time, and flood my desk with material. We also have volunteers who work 60 hours a week, have a number of children and full lives, yet I can depend on them. I have one in particular who cannot make meetings, but I can depend on him like I can depend on the sun to come up in the morning. If somebody does not need much leadership, I do not give it. I check to make sure the volunteers are progressing, but if they want autonomy, I let them have it.

I am very task-oriented. If you ask me to do something right now when we hang up the phone I will try to do it and make it happen right then. I try to keep meetings right to the point and less than an hour if possible. I am very people-oriented and very communication-oriented. My management style is trying to empower the people around me, even if I am the sole decision maker. I get input from my intern, my assistant, and the board of directors. My style is based on empowerment with a great deal of consultation.

For the people who flood my desk with material, I take the time to give them feedback because they took the time to write to me. I have established a healthy respect for my time and theirs with real allegiance to a hierarchy. I found out the hard way when I first started because I had a tendency to get too personal. I was spread too vertically and not enough horizontally in terms of the organizational chart. I always have time for people regardless of their level, but I try to have them ask questions in a hierarchical fashion.

One of the things I had to learn is that not everybody operates the way I do. I think management takes patience and knowing how hard to push how long to wait, and when to provide recognition, rewards, or reprimands. We produce a newsletter to keep people updated about meetings, the Governor's Cup, and the Olympic Trials. We also thank people. Although it is a very common business practice, some people forget to say thank you. It can go a long way in satisfying employees and volunteers to thank them and put their names in print.

My position also requires that I deal with sponsor signage. Sponsors pay a certain amount of money and in return expect certain things, like signage at press conferences announcing athletes. I make sure those sponsors are not forgotten because their money makes our events happen. I also write a combination of tax grants, including accommodations grants from the city and surrounding counties. There is a political element to my job, both in terms of police support on event days and in relationships with local counties and cities regarding their allocation of money for our event. I am involved in publication and promotion. We use direct mail to reach previous participants and new audiences. We also have to make nonrunners aware of our events. It is important to let them know about a street that will be blocked off so they are not held up in traffic on the day of the event. Some groups may want to sponsor an event or volunteer to help and they need more information. Those are all things to address at county and city hearings.

We also deal closely with USA Track and Field and the United States Olympic Committee (USOC). That adds another tier of restrictions and limitations. At the Olympic Trials, Carolina Marathon Association sponsors are third in line, behind USOC sponsors and USA Track and Field sponsors. The event may have national TV coverage, so we would have to switch out signage, take our sponsor signs down during the Olympic Trials, but leave them up for the other races. It is a jewel in our crown to have an event such as the Olympic Trials but it complicates the picture. The logo as well as the actual title of the Trials have to be approved. Every sponsor must be approved.

Our budget this year, including the Governor's Cup, Carolina Marathon, and the Olympic Trials is about $950,000. We are required to give $250,000 in prize money during the Olympic Trials and pay a $50,000 rights fee. It takes a lot of planning to operate day-to-day. We need prize money and the rights fee, and we also need to pay the bills. I am responsible for maintaining the relationships with our sponsors including providing signage at an event, putting their logo on our letterhead, mentioning them in all our news releases and newspaper articles, or inviting them to all of our press conferences, luncheons, and workshops. I emphasize regularly that we can not succeed without them and keep track of every mention that they get. I also try to identify new sponsors for our events and make sure all of our committees are working well. A perfect example is the Governor's Cup. We have a wonderful race director for that event. I show up at event committee meetings not to do their work but to make sure everything is on schedule. Often I sit back and supervise. Many people in this field are enthusiastic, energetic, and well organized, and they think it is easier to do the work themselves.

With the Olympic Trials, all the qualifiers are adopted by liaisons in town. A liaison may have three, four, or more runners to acquaint with the weather, training sites, and restaurants in Columbia. Local elementary school classrooms adopt our Olympic qualifiers and correspond with the athletes via e-mail. They send videotapes of their classroom and relate the Olympic trials to every subject within the curriculum. For example, if the qualifier is from California, the students learn about the climate in California. In math class, they may learn about running 90 to 100 miles a week and how many miles that is per day.

My typical day depends on the proximity of time to an event. Close to an event I come in at 5:00 AM and stay late, but there is a lot more energy. Farther away from the event I meet with committees on a regular basis to identify needs such as order quantities for food and drinks. We determine at what mile marker the sponsors will be placed and if we are going to have them at reception parties. We determine how many volunteers are needed, what streets to block off, how much money will be spent, what age categories will be awarded, where exactly our race applications will be disseminated, and many other issues. We look at how many monitors will be needed on the course, how many police officers, and who will be in the lead vehicles. As we get 2 months away from the race we begin ordering food and T-shirts and training the race monitors. We meet with the finish line director to know exactly how to disseminate the results, how the data will be entered into the computer, and where to put the split time clocks. A good event planner does not wait until the last week. A month out from the event we refine, revise, take care of any last minute details, and pray to the weather gods.

For the Olympic Trials we expect 173 qualifiers. All of those people hope to get one of three spots to go to the 2000 Olympic Games in Sydney. Our take on it is, for 170 athletes, or all but the three qualifiers, Columbia, South Carolina, is their Olympics. Our hospitality process, with the liaison program needs to be top-notch. We reserve an entire hotel to house the athletes and USA Track and Field officials. They are elite athletes so they expect to be treated as such. We must put on a quality event. We also have to take care of drug-testing protocol if athletes are tested after the trials. When an event ends we collect information and feedback and our committee members and volunteers critique the event. The most important part of evaluation is getting feedback from people in the city, the athletes, and the committee members. It is crucial that I get feedback directly after the event from my 75 to 100 key volunteers.

One of the things I stress to students is that the gap between entertainment and sport closes quickly. I always tell them they are not just looking for a job in sport but also they are looking for a job in the sport entertainment industry. A number of events need to be planned. Our graduates are just as qualified to plan entertainment events as they are to plan a road race, a football game, or a college event. I think the number of jobs will grow, but people seeking jobs must realize the number of outlets is growing horizontally and not necessarily vertically. Somebody aspiring to this position can build a great foundation while in school. Students should ask practitioners about their positions. I called people who managed facilities and asked them about their jobs, their likes and dislikes, and their perception of people in academia. I think networking has the negative connotation of just plain schmoozing. I see it as more of an informational inquiry. One of the assignments I gave students was to speak with somebody in the industry and ask about the job, a typical day, and the salary. Students need to understand a job before they know if they will like it. People who want to plan events need to work events and get on committees. I encourage people to go outside their comfort zone. Just wanting to work within one particular sport is narrow-minded. Someone may want to work in professional golf as an ultimate goal, but gaining event experience in different sports will broaden the experience base.

Ten years from now I will be teaching. I still want to plan events. A goal of mine has been to be a director of marketing in a facility. My original fascination for sport management started with buildings. I can get more excited in an empty building than most people would sitting on the 50-yard line at the Super Bowl. I love facilities and event management because they involve marketing, finance, personnel, and sponsorships. I want to remain as active as I am today.

In the sponsorship industry, my advice to students is to work real hard. I know a lot of people use that "work real hard," but to quote John Baldwin, one of my professional mentors, "sport management is clearly a business of leverage and relationships." Students cannot network enough. The biggest mistake they can make is to sit back and wait for a job to come to them. For every person who is not willing to do a volunteer internship somewhere in the sports field there is somebody who is willing. Clearly, sport crosses all personal, gender, age, racial, and cultural barriers. Most everybody has an opinion on sport. It is a competitive industry. If they are not willing to do what it takes, then somebody else will. Students can do things to leverage themselves, such as joining the North American Society for Sport Management (NASSM) or the International Association of Assembly Managers (IAAM). All those outside sources, in addition to texts like this, are valuable. It is not enough nor will it ever be enough to just understand theory and empirical concepts. Students have to apply it.

Research skills are also important. For example, if an internship supervisor asks a student's opinion about advertising expenditures, they need to find that information quickly. When a boss asks for your opinion, he or she is looking for what you can contribute, not just a definition. Students also need to volunteer at their college or with a team or YMCA or some sport organization. They will be surprised that once they have done a lot of volunteering, people will offer to pay them. The knowledge they have is worth a lot. It all comes down to leveraging yourself. Coming out of school I had a lot of experience, and that made me marketable.

Students also need to read *Sports Business Daily* and the *Sports Business Journal*, as well as every newspaper they can. Classes do not always require looking at other sport management textbooks in addition to the class requirement. In addition, they need energy, enthusiasm, and passion. I have never for half of a millisecond been sorry for choosing the industry. It is my goal now to contribute to the industry in a practical, theoretical, and academic way.

CHAPTER 8

Media and Public Relations

A MEDIA RELATIONS PROFESSIONAL has one of the most multifaceted positions in the sport industry. People working in the field need multiple technical skills and must be able to work with a variety of people both inside and outside the sport organization. Media relations can be defined as the concerted efforts to foster a mutually beneficial relationship with the media to attract attention for a sport organization in the print and electronic media. This is accomplished by making the sport organization more accessible to the media by providing services that make the media members' job easier. A positive relationship with the media is important because the general public's knowledge about a sport organization comes primarily from the media.

A media relations professional can have several different titles. In college athletics the title is sports information director (SID). In professional sport the title may be media relations director. In some instances, media relations responsibilities are combined with public relations so the title would be director of media and public relations. Along with different job titles, job responsibilities vary by environment. In college athletics, the sports information director is responsible for overseeing a variety of sports. In professional sport, the media relations director is concerned with only one sport.

Media relations professionals create a variety of materials in their jobs, including press releases, news advisories, fact sheets, game notes, game programs, Web sites, media kits, and media guides. Media relations professionals also are involved in managing home contests because they keep statistics, prepare the press table or press box, work with the opponent's media relations person, ensure the public address system works, update the record books after the game, and may

211

even be responsible for playing the national anthem. Media relations professionals also arrange press conferences to announce important news such as player signings, changes in important front office positions, a crisis situation, or plans for building a new facility. They also arrange press conferences after contests to make coaches and players available to the media. The media relations professional will also set up interviews for members of the sport organization with the media and, in some instances, may help prepare the person for the interview.

Career opportunities are available in the area of media relations. Every professional sport franchise has a media relations office and staff. In college athletics, there are sport information offices. At larger universities there will be staffs. The responsibilities are often broken down between high profile sports such as football and men's and women's basketball, and the nonrevenue sports such as swimming, track and field, and tennis.

Entry-level salaries in media relations in all environments are low. The entry-level position in college athletics comes in the form of an internship where the individual may make as little as $14,000 a year with no benefits. From these positions, individuals earn assistant positions that pay in the low $20,000s with benefits. Associate and sports information directors can earn $40,000 a year or more depending on the size of the institution. At smaller schools, sports information directors salaries can range from the mid $20,000s to $40,000 per year. The pay scale is similar in the professional sport environment.

In any environment, media relations professionals play an important role in their sport organization as they are the contact people for the media. If the media are provided with ample information the sport organization will receive maximum media exposure.

P. Scott Douglas

Promoter/Director of Media
Louisville Motor Speedway

Education:
LOUISVILLE SCHOOL OF BROADCASTING, 1976

Career Progression:
"MOTOR MADNESS" PLAY BY PLAY,
TNN/WORLD SPORTS, 1998 TO PRESENT

PROMOTER/DIRECTOR OF PR AND MEDIA,
LOUISVILLE MOTOR SPEEDWAY, 1996 TO
PRESENT

PROMOTER, ALTAMONT RACEWAY (TRACY,
CALIFORNIA), 1995 TO 1996

DIRECTOR OF MARKETING, LOUISVILLE
MOTOR SPEEDWAY, 1987 TO 1995

SPONSORSHIP DIRECTOR, KENTUCKY MOTOR
SPEEDWAY (WHITESVILLE), 1980 TO 1987

NEWS AND SPORTS DIRECTOR, WVJS RADIO/TV
(OWENSBORO, KENTUCKY), 1980 TO 1987

SPORTS DIRECTOR, WOMI RADIO
(OWENSBORO, KENTUCKY), 1977 TO 1980

Best piece of advice you received in regards to your career:

**"Never forget that racing's the bread and butter,
but we're in the entertainment business. Focus on the
entertainment whether it's with fans or sponsors."**

ANDY VERTREES, PROMOTER

Best advice for someone aspiring toward a career in the sport industry:

**"Just because you love the sport doesn't mean you can sell or promote it. If
you can master the business of sports you truly have the opportunity to go
to work everyday at a job you love."**

I STARTED DOING RADIO BACK IN THE MID TO LATE 1970S. I am the
Promoter at the Louisville Motor Speedway and previously was the director of
media and marketing. I have worked at the speedway for the 10 or 12 years it has
been open.

I went to a broadcasting trade school about a year out of high school and then
obtained a job in Owensboro, Kentucky, as a nighttime disc jockey. I was in
Owensboro for about 10 years and went through the normal progressions and
different shifts, and I ended up doing a lot of sports and running the news
department. I also did all of the play-by-play for Kentucky Wesleyan College
basketball and football. During that time back in 1980 Andy Vertrees bought a

racetrack down near Owensboro called the Kentucky Motor Speedway. He needed an announcer so I went there to meet him and I started announcing for him. I had never seen a stock car race. The announcer's job was more to entertain and not necessarily to worry about how many horsepower this car had or getting too technical. Andy was living in Louisville and realized he was not spending enough time on marketing the track so I also did all of his marketing and sponsorship duties. I started cutting my teeth there on $50 program ads and $300 billboards. I did this at the same time I was doing all of my radio and television work. In 1987, Andy and his partner decided to build Louisville Motor Speedway and they offered me a full-time job.

In 1995, I accepted an offer to help re-open Altamont Raceway in California. I promoted that racetrack for a couple of years. Then we just decided to move back. Jerry Carroll's group came and ended up buying Louisville Motor Speedway. Jerry Carroll's group is a group of private investors that is building the super speedway up at Galatin County by Cincinnati. It was going to be hard for them to walk in as outsiders and build the racetrack. Getting Louisville Motor Speedway, one of the most respected short tracks in NASCAR, and having Andy Vertrees, NASCAR promoter of the year, gave Jerry Carroll's group an "in" into the business.

I kind of stumbled into my career. I just always liked doing sports stuff. When I was a kid I always wanted to play sports, but I also used to love listening to the play-by-play announcers. To do an Indians or Browns game would have been a great aspiration, but you can work hard for 50 years and maybe never get that call. I had a chance to go to some little town in Missouri. The pay was not much, but I was going to get 150 play-by-play games a year. I declined the offer even though it would have been tremendous experience. You can do jobs like that for years and still not be the one who gets that certain job. Probably the biggest step was going back to broadcasting school and being very focused on what I wanted to do. I graduated from high school in 1974, took a labor job with the highway department for about a year-and-a-half, and just floated around. Then I found out about a school being run by the University of Louisville. It was basically one of these "three months over the summer learn the business" kind of things. I ended up getting a job out of it, and advanced from that point. I guess the most important thing was I got my foot in the door to get started in that business. That is why it is great for our intern, Robert Sexton, that the University of Louisville offers internships. He is doing everything right by aggressively trying to get in with companies like us and with race teams. He will end up working in this business. He is not just putting in his time, but he is making the most of his opportunity.

One of the things I really had to learn every day on the job was to deal with the media. Recent college graduates are already ahead of me with their knowledge of technology. Everybody in the promotions end of sport marketing has to fight the same thing. There is no easy way to do this. If you have enough money, you can buy 10,000 Beanie Babies to give away to spectators. That is going to work, but it is only one date. Unless you have something to sell and the right way to sell it, it does not do any good. A lot of this has to be learned on the job.

I have seen lots of people advance in the radio and television business, but few great jobs and few network anchor positions are available. A lot of reporters can barely pay their rent. They go back to school to get their master's degree after trying radio and TV a few years or they do something else. A lot of people who began in radio and TV are in different areas now because they found other ways to be more successful than trying to advance in radio and TV. I think I probably fall into that category. I love doing radio and television. I have done it part-time since I have been in this job. I have a Friday night show on TNN right now called Motor Madness. I go all over the country with them through the first quarter of the year when we are not racing on the weekends here, but I have always found that I make a better living in racing. Many short tracks are family operations, so many of the marketing and public relations people at racetracks have been children of the promoters coming up in the business, and they eventually run the business. Louisville is in the upper 10 percent of short tracks in terms of what we do, the number of races we run, and the amount of revenue we generate. Our staff is a little different than a lot of other short tracks. Yet we are nothing compared with a Lowe's Motor Speedway in Charlotte. Lowe's has a fleet of people doing what one or two of us do here.

There are about 1,000 short tracks in the country. You can pretty much go anywhere and find one. There are large numbers of dirt tracks. About 35 to 40 racetracks are in Kentucky. Only three are asphalt tracks and everything else is dirt. Anyone can go build a dirt track somewhere and put up some stands. If you can get the land and somebody who knows how to work the dirt, it is a whole different investment than building an asphalt track. Most of these dirt tracks run only on Saturday nights to get what local racers they can to come out.

Louisville Motor Speedway is the only NASCAR sanctioned track in Kentucky. NASCAR sanctions 100 tracks on its Winston racing series and Louisville is one of them. No other Winston racing series track exists in Kentucky. NASCAR tries to hand pick the better racetracks and then tie all of their races together on a national point system. Certain racetracks are chosen because of their reputations as high quality tracks. NASCAR is partial to asphalt tracks because that is more of what it does. A higher caliber of racing and more sponsorships are involved with asphalt tracks. NASCAR wants things that are going to look good because the track represents NASCAR. We pay a sanction fee to be a part of NASCAR, which averages anywhere from a thousand to a couple thousand dollars a night. NASCAR will not sanction facilities that are potential problems for its reputation. Over the years a lot of strange things have occurred. Promoters did not have a good name because it was perceived that they would screw the drivers over at any opportunity. That was not necessarily the case, but all it took was a couple occurrences and the image was created. When I went out to Altamont our main problem getting started was that previous fly-by-night promoters had ripped off so many sponsors. Those are the kind of things NASCAR does not want. A lot of it comes down to tracks that are versatile. We run an all pro race, a NASCAR truck race, and a Goody's dash race. That is why we are a NASCAR track.

The obstacles I face are mostly those in our business. To be successful we have to generate sponsorship dollars, get a lot of race fans in the stands, and put a lot of cars in the pits. Racing is just now expanding into being a mainstream sponsorship advertising vehicle. Louisville has done better than any short track in the country in terms of sponsorships. We have done tremendous numbers. We will probably do a million dollars in sponsorships this year for a short track and nobody else is doing the same. The location, quality of the track, and events we run are contributing factors to sponsorship dollars. Yet a lot of potential sponsors we call on are not interested. Some people have a misconceived notion about NASCAR and car racing. They have sort of the old stereotypes, although they are changing now. With the number of seats we have, we cannot afford to try and get the old roughneck 18- to 24-year-old who wants to come out and drink beer and get in a fight. We use off-duty police officers as security, and we do not tolerate anything in the pits or in the grandstands. We haul people to jail for violence or disorderly behavior. People realize quickly that we are strict. We have always had a nondrinking section. We do sell alcohol and make a lot of money from it, but also we have an area where alcohol is not permitted. From day one we tried to make this a family attraction and it has worked, but we have fought through those stereotypes. It is always amazing, even to this day, that people will come in for the first time and be amazed at how clean it is or how much fun it is to watch. I listen to some of the sports talk shows and they zero in on the stick and ball stuff, baseball, and football. Whenever somebody wants to talk NASCAR it is as if they are a lower form of life. Old stereotypes are tough to replace.

Andy Vertrees has been a mentor to me. I have been with him since 1980. I have learned about racing promotion from him. He is now the director of operations for the entire Kentucky Speedway/Louisville Speedway operation. His reputation is tremendous. Andy has the ability to see things a lot of us do not observe. Andy taught me the ability to see the big picture.

I cannot say I would have done anything differently at this point. The careers I have been in are especially experience driven. You just cannot walk in and promote a racetrack. I could have gained some extra experience in different ways. I had a couple of opportunities to work at super speedways that I turned down, and rightly so I guess. I wonder sometimes how that would have been different. I have always had the good fortune of enjoying what I am doing. I do not really spend every day looking for another job.

As the director of media at the speedway, my main job is to sell advertising and sponsorship. In addition, I organize any promotions at the racetrack, buy all of the media, market the races, and oversee all written materials. Frank Scott produces a lot of those materials because he is very computer literate and creative.

I assist with whatever is needed, especially taking care of clients. Most of my race night is spent in the VIP suite with our clients. I rarely go in the pits except to do a couple of things. I go in the press box for big events when needed, but I have people who handle it. My job on race night tends to be focused on sponsor relations. I also do a few show type things. I grab the wireless microphone and go on the track for whatever presentations or special events take place that day.

The best part of the job is landing a major sponsor. It is the excitement and the rush that anybody gets out of a great success in whatever job they do. To seal the deal is probably the neatest, most exciting part of it. Buying media is probably the most mundane part of it, and frankly, the part that gets on your nerves a little bit. For us it is buying radio. We do some newspaper and some trade stuff. One of the things we do is spend a lot of time looking at some alternatives not used before such as direct mail. We try to shake it up a little bit because certain things seem to be a little flat. I have been in this for 12 years so I know the market, although it is a mess with all the consolidating, buying, and breaking up of stations. It makes it difficult in some ways. We know what formats we want to use in this business. You have to find the dominant country music station because that is where we get our fans. We try to branch out and do some different things. We did a survey a few years ago on the crowd and 60 percent of them listened to WAMZ (country music) as their favorite radio station. That shows us where we should advertise to keep our fans. We still want more and new people, but racing and country music have gone together for a long time.

We examine the ratings and figure out what will work for us and experiment with our advertising. We did an experiment a few years ago with an easy listening station. It plays the soft music with good background referred to as "elevator music;" it is heard in business offices, doctors' offices, and lawyers' offices. We tried a different appeal. The station gave us a tremendous deal. We advertised all of the time but did not get anything out of it. It showed us that easy listening stations were not the media buy for racing. In advertising, that part is pretty simple. You add up, you look at that gate, and you see if you have anybody coming through the gate. It either worked or did not work. For us it either comes through the gate or it does not. It is pretty much that simple.

As a general rule we are a weekly short track. Our bread and butter is running Friday and Saturday night and we have 300 to 500 different competitors racing here over the course of a year. On Friday and Saturday night it is local racing. We always start qualifying at 6:00 PM and we race at 7:30 PM.

We have seven divisions that run weekly. Three of them are figure eight divisions. We have the late model stock car, which is like what NASCAR runs. Those are the most expensive cars around here and the best drivers. We have other entry-level divisions and feeder divisions that race street stocks and thunder trucks. The best-known driver is Chuck Winders, who has won 77 races here. He has raced here since the place opened. He goes on an all pro race occasionally, which is a regional touring series, but generally Chuck races here. A lot of guys in these pits hope they will get a break and step up. Frank Kimmel is probably one who has done that from here. He was our champion back in 1990 and may run the Winston Cup in a couple of years. Everybody in Winston Cup basically started at a track like Louisville. It is a hard climb up the ladder.

On race day the maintenance crew and some other folks are here early. Part of my responsibility is to come in earlier in the day and check things out. For the most part, most of the crew does not get in until about 3:00 PM. Everybody then starts answering the phones because if things are going well then our phones will be ringing. "What time does the race start?" "How much does it cost?" "What are you going to do if it rains?" Those are the questions we are asked. I like to get here early, look at the pits, see who is there, and look at what the cars are doing. That is another place where our intern Robert Sexton has helped. We send Robert to the pits every night to see if there is anything new we can feed to the media. The more work you can do for the media the better your chance of getting something. They are not going to come out and do a lot of it on their own.

Race days tend to be pretty similar, yet some variables exist. There can be a rain delay or a big wreck. Strange things may happen that cost us time or we may blow right through and get the show over by 9:45 PM. Then it is a matter of getting the results to all the media. Certain races are different because of their magnitude. When we do the race of champions, it is an all-day deal because the NASCAR Winston Cup drivers come in and so much is involved. We are not a huge staff. In this office there are basically five full-time people, although for a short track that is phenomenal. On race day anywhere from 75 to 150 people work. It all depends on what kind of crowd we will draw.

We start in April and run through the third week of September when it starts getting really cool. We create a major figure eight race for the end of the year. Then it is the off season. Everything is backed up earlier from a marketing point of view. It used to be we let the season get over. I remember when we were building Louisville Motor Speedway I was sitting there in late January putting together a deal with Pinkerton Tobacco Company to sponsor our Busch Grand National race. These days that money is already spent in January and February. Now I work on proposals for the next year in September and October, and discover I am actually late. We made our pitches in July and August 1999 to get the bigger sponsors we need for 2000. I get all of that done whether it is off-season or during the week so we can make it happen on race night.

Communication skills are needed for this job. We deal with the media. We try to sell our place and sell sponsorships. The ability to communicate is critical. You need an ability to sell. Even media relations involves the ability to sell. You try to sell ideas and sell your sport to the people who cover it. I would say communication skills would be at the top.

Organizing is essential for us, in terms of having the year planned in terms of what we will do, what events will be run, where the sponsorships will fall, and what media are bought. It is more managing my own time than anybody else's right now. Our staff is small and there is not a lot of support help. We have to manage and organize our own time to make sure the job gets done. If you wait too late it is hard to get ahead. It would be nice to have everything sold when the season starts, but it is impossible. One of our biggest revenue producers is selling hospitality tents for the NASCAR truck race. It is not a sales process, but it is an order-taking process. They tell us what they want. With everything that is happening we cannot wrap that up by April 1. It never fails. We have a billboard we thought was sold but is not sold. We decided to just "white" it out. You would be surprised that some people come to the races, see a white billboard, and then call Monday and ask, "Hey, you got that thing sold?"

Stress is part of the job. Stress is sitting here on Saturday night and not seeing anybody come through that front gate. Certain things are uncontrollable, including the weather. We work hard, we get everything set, and then all it takes is a change in the weather. One Wednesday night we scheduled an event, which is a risk for us to run a Wednesday night. We obtained a lot of promotions and thought we were set. Then a tornado came the day before and killed 43 people. The tornado was in the newspapers and the local weather forecasters said the tornado would hit us. Then a tornado is sighted 40 miles away, and what happens? We had nobody in the grandstand. We still had to run the event, because it was not raining. There was nothing we could do.

I believe in hiring good people and letting them do their jobs. If they do not do it, then I deal with it. They are accountable to me at the end of the day. They either do their job or leave. I do not like standing over top of people. That is not my style. I also believe in team effort. Everything cannot be done by one person—me or anybody else—so I need to get as many good people on my team as possible. I let them do their job and hopefully I am able to reward them enough to keep them doing it.

Tremendous opportunities exist in racing. You need to get an education and do an internship. Get your hands into it at any point you can, even if it is coming out and helping at the racetrack doing whatever they will let you do. I believe Charlotte probably has interns and young people they hire all of the time because the operation is so big. The internship gives you a great opportunity. You can get a lot through education. New tracks are being built all over and those tracks need people. NASCAR's popularity is booming. The future looks very healthy for motorsports.

I love this part of the country and I love the situation. I never know when it will change. I look forward to the opportunity to manage this racetrack. It has what I have been trained to do for 15 years. I can see myself still doing this for a lot of years. Future opportunities may exist with the super speedway outside of Cincinnati. In the next 5 years or so, I want to do everything possible to make this place as profitable as it can be. I am excited about the possibilities and opportunities here.

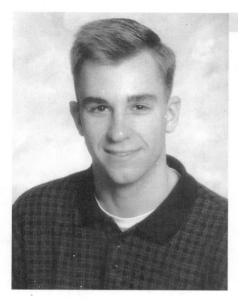

Brian R. Britten

Manager, Public Relations
Toledo Mud Hens Baseball Club

Education:
B.S., EDUCATION & SPORT MANAGEMENT,
BOWLING GREEN STATE UNIVERSITY, 1999

Career Progression:
MANAGER OF PUBLIC RELATIONS, TOLEDO
MUD HENS, NOVEMBER 1998 TO PRESENT
INTERN, TOLEDO MUD HENS, APRIL 1996 TO
SEPTEMBER 1996; JANUARY 1997 TO SEPTEM-
BER 1997; JANUARY 1998 TO SEPTEMBER 1998

Best piece of advice you received in regards to your career:

"Go out as a volunteer and gain experience."

DR. JANET PARKS, BOWLING GREEN STATE UNIVERSITY

Best advice for someone aspiring toward a career in the sport industry:

"Volunteer as much as you can for two reasons: you gain so much experience and you are able to meet different people."

Quote by which you live:

"Whatever is worth doing at all, is worth doing well."

PHILIP DORMER STANHOPE

I DECIDED ON A CAREER IN SPORT IN HIGH SCHOOL when I learned I could major in sport management in college. I met a sport management major and he explained to me what career opportunities were available. I had grown up loving baseball, so I decided to attend Bowling Green University to major in sport management and to pursue my dream of working in baseball. When I showed up at Bowling Green for my first semester in the autumn of 1995, I was not sure what I wanted to do in baseball. During freshman orientation, I expressed my interest in working in baseball to my academic advisor and a professor in the sport management program, Dr. Janet Parks. Dr. Parks told me to call Jim Konecny, who was a graduate of Bowling Green and was assistant general manager in charge of media relations for the Toledo Mud Hens Class AAA minor league baseball team. She suggested that I ask for an opportunity to volunteer with the team. I called Jim and he accepted my offer.

To be quite honest, I probably would have not thought of volunteering if it had not been for Dr. Parks' advice. My friends thought I was crazy to work for free, but I did it because I knew I could take the experience I was getting anywhere I went. Also, how can you knock someone for spending his free time at a ballpark? I immediately saw the benefits of getting practical experience. I can remember being in class and hearing the professor lecture on a topic such as motivation or communication. I knew some students were thinking that things did not work that way. For me, however, I would go to the ballpark and see the managers communicating with and motivating their employees. What I learned in class stayed with me because I had a chance to apply the lessons and see them in action. I can remember thinking to myself, "I guess those professors know what they are talking about."

Another lesson I learned was the importance of being responsible. College students live day-by-day and in most cases only have to worry about themselves. In the real world I discovered that people counted on me and I had responsibilities. I realized early on that if you do not take care of business then you are not going to be in the real world very long. A college student cannot understand this until he or she experiences it. We hire interns and they think working for a baseball team is going to be a big party. It is not a big party. Responsibilities have to be met for 7,000 fans to enjoy themselves.

As a student at Bowling Green I lived at home. My home was between Bowling Green and the ballpark. It was about 6 miles to the ballpark and 12 miles to school from my house. If I had to go from school to the park it was about a 20-minute commute. I never had a conflict between work and school. I budgeted my time so I would get my class work done and still put in quality hours with the Mud Hens. I had a very humbling beginning as a volunteer. The very first thing I did was work in the parking lot for the last month of the 1995 season. I returned as an unpaid intern in April 1996 and I worked the entire season. During that season, I was a jack-of-all-trades. I would work in the press box running the message board one night and be on the field organizing the in-between innings promotions the next night. I took the fall off and I returned to work in January 1997. Again I worked through the season. That season I began to focus more on media relations responsibilities. I assisted in preparing the media guide and program for the year and handled many media-related tasks during the season. I focused on media relations again during the 1998 season, and I realized the organization relied on me a great deal because I had more responsibility. After the season the manager of media relations left and I was offered the job in November 1998. This was interesting because I was not graduating from Bowling Green State until May 1999. The only requirement I had left was the internship I was required to complete in the spring semester. I arranged it so that my position with the Mud Hens would also serve as my internship. I treated my position as my job, but I still had to complete the requirements for the internship including completing a log and a few other projects. I was not a college graduate yet, but I had a job in the field.

I realize that many students have the perception that if they are good at playing a sport it guarantees them a position in the sport field. That is not the case. You must have the practical experience even if it is working in a parking lot. If a student is expecting to be handed an opportunity, it probably will not happen. The opportunities come to those who work the hardest. If I look at my college experience, what I did was more beneficial for my career than playing a sport. I was in the setting in which I wanted to work and I learned from different professionals who had the knowledge I desired. I learned a great deal from just watching and listening. I made my mistakes as an unpaid volunteer, and what I learned from those mistakes is the experience I have today. I think the biggest reason I was hired is because I showed the desire to learn. Many kids starting their college careers just want to have a good time. I showed up at the ballpark every day wanting to learn and to make a positive impact on the organization. The people with the Mud Hens also knew me from being around for 4 years. I was not a faceless person on a resume. I had demonstrated what I could do and they were comfortable with me. Fortunately for me an opportunity presented itself and I was in the right place.

I am 22 years old and already in the field, so I have not faced any major obstacles in my career aspirations. I am sure a lot of obstacles will arise in the future, but I realize it is important to remain positive and focused. Even during my time in school, I was positive and focused on my goals. Yes, there were times during a long home stand where I had to be at the park every night until 11:00 PM and I missed out on things my friends were doing. But after I thought about it, I realized my sacrifice would pay off in the future.

Being so young in the field I have been conscious of identifying mentors. The most important mentor has been Jim Konecny. He not only gave me my start, but also taught most of the things I know about the baseball business. The thing I admire most about Jim is his professionalism. He is very well organized and has excellent time management skills. Jim has many diverse responsibilities and he has the ability to get them all accomplished while paying attention to detail. Jim has mentored me in how to deal with the players and the coaching staff as well as the media. He has also shown me how to juggle all of the responsibilities associated with my position. Finally, he really assisted me in sharpening my technical skills such as writing.

My main responsibility as a manager of media relations is dealing with members of the print and electronic media. What surprised me the most were the demands made from the media. I did not realize those demands would be so time-consuming. The members of the media request interviews with the coaching staff and the players and they are also interested in other information pertaining to the team. For example, the franchise is trying to secure a new ballpark, so the media is interested in progress. During the season I provide the media with game notes every day. The game notes consist of about 12 pages of statistics with information and interesting facts on the game, our team, the individual players, and the opponent.

I also oversee several areas not directly dealing with the media. For example, I organize the baseball camps and clinics we host at the stadium and in the Toledo area. I also am involved in a speaker series we host at the ballpark. We bring in a well-known sport professional to give a talk. We also provide a buffet dinner and a ticket to the game to the customer. I also am involved in the club's community relations efforts. I set up appearances for players and the manager at hospitals and schools. We do not have to work with the players on how to deal with the media and the various publics. At the AAA level, the guys have been around for a few years so they know and understand their role. We have a lot of veteran guys on our club who have had been to the big leagues and they are down in AAA trying to work their way back. I think it would be a lot different if I worked with some rookie league where the players are right out of high school or college. Finally, I work with our manager so he can handle his numerous obligations in the community and with the media. Sometimes I feel like I am his personal assistant.

Although it is my responsibility to release information to the media, the decision on what information to release and when to release it is made by someone else. We had an instance when a major leaguer was going to be sent down to us. He had skipped right by us on the way up. In that case, although I knew it was going to happen, the Detroit Tiger organization, with whom we have our affiliation, made the decision when we would release the information to the media. In other instances, I will give the local newspaper a story so it can be in the morning edition, although it would not be officially announced until that day. I have to assess the situation and determine how I will handle it, but as I mentioned before, sometimes those decisions are out of my hands. Through experience and time, I now know the decisions I can make on my own and those that I have to review with my general manager. At the start I played better safe than sorry. Now I have a good feel for my boundaries. For example, I do not think my general manager wants me to consult with him on whether I should serve pizza or hot dogs in the press box, but I know he will have input on releasing important information. A lot of people coming out of college think they will have the autonomy to make those decisions and they will not. I discovered that when I worked here as a student.

My typical day when the team is playing at home lasts about 14 hours. I arrive about 9:00 AM. The first thing I normally do is download all the team statistics from our statistics provider, Howe Sports Data, for the visiting team. These statistics include a player's average in left and right situations and at home and on the road. I make copies of the statistics and distribute them to the coaching staff. After that I work on my game notes. The game notes are put together based on the statistical information I downloaded. I include statistics on everything imaginable in the game notes including players' statistics against right handers in different situations. We keep track of hitting streaks and nonhitting streaks. The reporters may need to know the information for a story or use it as filler. The two broadcasters from our local stations and visiting team's broadcasters use the information on the air either during the game or during the pregame show.

I try to get all that done by 1:00 PM because I know by 2:00 PM a lot of phone calls will come from the media. The TV people come into work about that time and they want to speak with someone or set up an interview to be aired on the 6:00 news. Writers will also call to confirm information on a story. Usually before the game I answer the phone and prepare the press box for game time. I actually get to relax a little once the game starts. We have an official scorer and a computer programmed as an automated score book. On a ground out to shortstop, he just plugs in 6/3 and moves on to the next batter. Two to three minutes after the game I have a box score printed out that is ready to be faxed to area media. I also send the game statistics via modem to Howe Sports Data and they in turn compile all the season statistics for all the minor leagues. If a media member has a question about something that happened in the game, I get whatever information he or she may need. From the box score I can update our Web page. I usually walk out of the park around 11:00 PM. It is a little bit more relaxing during the season when the team is on the road. I still do my game notes and update statistics, but I spend a fair amount of time addressing those details I did not have a chance to take care of when the team was at home. I also prepare for when the team returns home. When the team is on the road, it is more of a 9 to 5 day.

When our season ends in early September, I will wrap up everything from the season, and then in October and November we begin to think about the next season. December is a relaxed month because we attend the baseball winter meetings and enjoy the holiday season. January, February, and March are important months because we plan for the coming season. I prepare the program, media guide, and all the other printed materials related to our public and media relations efforts. Planning is especially essential for these major projects. I need to break the projects down into smaller projects with deadlines so that the projects are completed by the start of the season. Once the season starts it is a sprint to September.

The most demanding aspect of my job is trying to meet the needs of all the media. We deal with four local TV stations, the reporters from our local newspaper and the visiting team's beat reporter (if present), and radio broadcasters from our area and the visiting team's. The newspaper reporters are a bit easier to work with because they provide descriptions in their stories so they want quotes and statistics to support their observations. The TV people need people to interview and access to the field to film or request a backdrop for an interview. Both are easy to deal with but their demands are different. On occasion, a radio station or TV station from Cleveland will do a story. That makes things hectic because, in addition to my usual responsibilities, I arrange for these reporters to talk to a player or the manager for 10 or 15 minutes before the game. When TV reporters from Cleveland come I take care of them to the best of my abilities, but I try to keep my priority with the people who are here every night. I think the key to developing a good relationship with the media is respect. They have a job to do and are often working on a deadline and I try to work with them to meet their needs as much as I can to make their job easier. If the writers are looking for a story, I will give them ideas or statistics.

The thing I enjoy most about my job is that every morning I get up and I come to a ballpark and not many people get to do that. I think that is the reason why I have a passion for what I do. Baseball is in my blood. When I was a little kid, I dreamed of being a major league baseball player. As I got older, I realized I was not good enough to play in the big leagues, so the next best thing was to study sport management so I could have a career in professional baseball. I have a high degree of job satisfaction. My salary is not bad for an entry-level position. I know I am not going to get rich quick or anything like that, nor do I expect to. I knew that before I began. As I get more experience, I hope my salary increases and I make more money.

I am satisfied with my job; but if I become content and lose my desire, I want to find an opportunity to challenge me. Advancement opportunities exist in baseball. If the opportunity is not present in the organization in which a person works, then opportunities exist with other organizations. A lot of turnover occurs. People leave for better opportunities with other organizations, and some leave sports because they want to make more money or want more time to spend with their families. I like media and public relations and I see myself working in a major league team's media relations department. Opportunities exist for me to advance both in the minor and major leagues. If a situation arose where I was competing for a position with a major league team with an assistant director of public relations with another major league team, I think we would be equally qualified. I think the major league team would look at our qualifications. The person from the major league club would be more familiar with the environment, but I would bring more leadership experience. I would love to become a general manager or a scouting director of a major league ball club, but that is ambitious because not many of those positions exist. I am also very satisfied with the relationship I have with my coworkers. Everybody gets along in the office here because most of us are friends outside of the work environment and we care about each other succeeding. I also enjoy the interaction I have with so many different people in a day. I like to think of myself as a people person to some extent and I deal with TV and newspaper people as well as our players, coaches, manager, and even the fans who call our offices. Meeting and getting to know these people make the job fun.

A trend I see emerging in the media relations area is the increased role of the Internet in our efforts to reach the fans and make us more accessible to them. We have a counter on our Web page and we will average 45,000 hits over the course of a few months. For starters, the Toledo Mud Hens name is famous because of Jamie Farr's Klinger character on the TV show M-A-S-H, but most of the people visit the Web page for the statistical information and box scores. We list our game promotions and fans can order their tickets over the Web page. We also have a link to our souvenir store. It has led to an increase in sales and we have people on the other side of the United States wearing Mud Hen apparel. A sense of responsibility has come with establishing the Web page. Fans come to expect that the page will be updated consistently. Sometime I am so swamped that I do not update the Web page with a couple of roster moves. I get three or four e-mails informing me that I had not updated the roster in 4 days. Fans are information-hungry and we need to meet their needs as much as we meet the media's needs. I only see the Web taking on increased importance.

Currently, I do not have any real management responsibilities. I only oversee an intern who works in the press box during games. I do have aspirations to be a manager. I would like to be a hands-off manager. Most people are more inclined to take pride in what they do and they do not need someone looking over their shoulder all of the time. I believe in hiring good people and letting them do their job. I also think it is important to lead by example. If you expect a great deal from your employees, you should exert the same effort. When I do achieve that level, I think the people who would work for me would respect me for what I have accomplished. I have worked hard and sacrificed to forge a career in baseball. I know I would have trouble respecting a boss who had not done anything to earn it. I would have more respect for somebody that worked and sacrificed.

In my current position, my main focus is on my technical skills. Writing is the most essential technical skill. I write on a daily basis. During the season I write the game notes every day. I also write press releases both in-season and out-of-season. I write the program and the media guide. Students aspiring for a position in media relations should take journalism and writing courses and write every opportunity they can get whether it be for a college newspaper or a sports information office. Learning to write in the journalistic style teaches you to write in a concise manner. I also use some personal skills in interacting with my coworkers and the media.

I have not had the chance to use my conceptual skills as much. Our general manager is the person who thinks in terms of the big picture for the organization. I want to develop my conceptual skills and that will come with time and more experience. I recognize conceptual skills are going to be important if I plan on achieving my goal of advancing in baseball. An interesting aspect of working minor league baseball is that even though my main area is media, I also am involved in other areas of the organization. We are a small organization so we have to assist each other to get the job done. This has enabled me to be exposed to the other areas. In a larger organization I might not get that same opportunity. I would like to pursue an MBA to enhance my management skills. I believe these skills would also prove useful as I advance in an organization.

Career opportunities always will be available in media relations. Every professional sport organization has a department. Most departments are staffed with more than one person. College athletic departments have sports information offices. If someone is interested in working in minor league baseball, opportunities exist there as well. Minor league baseball is not a fad. It has evolved into an entertainment business and it offers more than the game. The giveaways, promotions between the innings, and the entertainment acts such as the Blues Brothers make it affordable, family entertainment. The demands and expectations of these media relations departments have increased as the number of media have increased. There are now 24-hour sports cable stations, Internet sites, and numerous sport publications seeking information to provide to their audiences. A major league team like the New York Yankees has more than 100 media members follow it during the season. Media relations people must provide information to the media. Finding a job in the sports field is difficult and moving in the sport field can be difficult because most jobs in sports are not publicized. When a position is open it is usually filled from within the organization or by someone who has been referred or knows the hiring official. The key to advancement is getting into an environment and making yourself known. Do a good job and people notice. When a job opens, people will then say, "I know someone who's doing a great job and I think he or she might fit in perfectly for you." That is how opportunities are presented.

Brian L. Laubscher

Sports Information Director
Washington and Lee University

Education:
B.S., SPORT MANAGEMENT, SLIPPERY ROCK
UNIVERSITY, 1995

Career Progression:
SPORTS INFORMATION DIRECTOR,
WASHINGTON AND LEE, 1998 TO PRESENT

ATHLETIC COMMUNICATIONS ASSISTANT,
LAFAYETTE COLLEGE, 1997 TO 1998

SPORTS INFORMATION INTERN, JAMES
MADISON UNIVERSITY, 1996 TO 1997

SPORTS INFORMATION GRADUATE ASSISTANT,
UNIVERSITY OF CALIFORNIA (PA), 1995 TO 1996

SPORTS INFORMATION INTERN, PENN STATE
ATHLETIC CONFERENCE, JUNE 1995 TO
AUGUST 1995

Best piece of advice you received in regards to your career:

**"Keep the faith." My parents gave me this advice when going
after jobs and trying to break into the business.**

Best advice for someone aspiring toward a career in the sport industry:

"Keep up with technology and its changes."

WHEN I ENROLLED AT SLIPPERY ROCK UNIVERSITY in the fall of 1991, I was not sure what I wanted to do for a career so I was undeclared for my first 2 years. I did not research any majors a great deal during those first 2 years. Instead I took my liberal arts classes and tried to decide what was of interest to me. A couple of friends on my dorm floor were sport management majors and they introduced me to the major. In speaking with them, it seemed logical for me to major in sport management because I had always been interested in sport. I decided it may be a good career.

Once in the sport management major, I was not sure what area of sport I wanted to pursue. At the beginning of my final year at Slippery Rock I had to determine where and in what area of sport I would do my 12-credit internship requirement. I did not know what to do. One of my friend's fathers was the sports information director at Slippery Rock. I had spoken to him about sports information and it sounded like an interesting field, so I focused on that area as I searched for an internship site. I secured an internship with the Pennsylvania State Athletic Conference (PSAC), the conference in which Slippery Rock competes. When I spoke with the PSAC sports information director, Steve Murray, he said it would be beneficial for me to get some practical experience before I came for the internship to get some familiarity with the field. To get that experience I worked hours in the Slippery Rock sports information office during my senior year. My first practical experience in sports information was keeping statistics at Slippery Rock University basketball games. The experience was not overly challenging because I am pretty knowledgeable in sports and I had kept statistics in the past.

My first real work experience in the field was the 3-month internship at the PSAC during the summer of 1995. The internship was very important since I did not have much experience and the Conference sports information director did not have much help. This enabled me to gain a lot of hands-on experience because he needed someone on which to rely. Strong writing skills are essential in sports information and Steve helped me with my writing and in preparing press releases. In sports information you write more than anything else. I think the most important aspect of the internship and the best part of being at a conference office was the networking opportunities. There are 14 schools in the PSAC and I had the chance to become acquainted with all 14 sports information directors in the league. I was able to network myself with those people. The internship experience was also an eye-opener for me because I never realized what time and effort was required to get the job done. For example, setting up for the football conference media day was quite an effort. Steve and I had to plan everything from a speaker to who was going to sit at what table to the program format. I was amazed at what it took to organize that event.

My main responsibility at the PSAC was preparing press releases. I did the softball and baseball conference report which involved preparing notes on the teams and compiling the leaders in statistical categories such as batting averages, fielding percentages, and earned run averages. I also prepared the monthly PSAC newsletter. The schools' sports information directors would send in releases on coaching milestones, records set by players and teams, or honors earned such as Academic All-American. I compiled that information and each month I laid out a newsletter and mailed it to each school. I produced the conference football and fall sports media guides, too.

In retrospect, the best experience for a college student interested in a career in sports information is not found in the classroom. It is the practical experience a student can acquire as a work-study or student assistant in the sports information office while in school. Because I did not have much experience in sports information before graduation, I think that held me back in the field earlier in my career. Nothing can replace the experiences of being in the office and actually doing certain tasks. The student also needs to develop computer skills. Desktop publishing is a large part of the job. For example, in my current position we use PageMaker, which is a desktop publishing program. I use it to do press releases, lay out game programs, and produce media guides. It is not an easy program to learn, so if a student can get experience with it he or she is ahead of the game. Also, computers are taking on even more importance with the Internet as an information resource in sports.

Sports information is a highly competitive field and I am very lucky to be sitting where I am today because of my lack of experience upon graduation. In most cases when a sports information office is looking for somebody, even as an intern, somebody with skills is needed. They are not interested in training someone in the basics. When I was finishing my internship with PSAC, I was applying for graduate assistantships and I did not get many responses. While attending a meeting of PSAC sports information directors, I had dinner with all of the sports information directors and happened to sit next to one from California University of Pennsylvania, Bruce Wald. I told him at dinner that I wanted to pursue sports information as a career. He had a graduate assistantship opening for the fall of 1995 and he said he was not looking forward to conducting a nationwide search for the position. He thought I would be great for the job. I interviewed for it and was offered the job. If I had not attended the league sports information directors meeting, my career in sports information may have ended that summer.

Going from the PSAC to California I learned that the institutional setting is very different from the conference office. A lot of day-to-day issues arise and little fires have to be put out at an institution. In the institutional setting, you receive and try to compile information while also trying to distribute it to as many media outlets as possible. At the conference office, the institutional sports information directors submit information so the conference sports information director can package it as conference information. The conference office is more about regurgitating information than compiling it. Also, from the conference perspective you do not work the games like you do as an institutional sports information director. I enjoyed going to the contests and working games while also getting to know the athletes. You miss that at a conference office.

Also, while I was at California, an opportunity arose to do some writing for the local paper, the *Valley Independent*. I viewed it as a chance to make some extra money. I had never written a story for a newspaper before, but they gave me a shot. The first game I covered was a high school football game where one team was the high school that Joe Montana attended. Also, the athletic director of the school was NFL quarterback Scott Zolac's father. This experience helped me develop my writing skills and also increased my understanding of the media. It made me understand what the media is looking for and what facts they include in their stories. It also gave me an appreciation for what they experience. A reporter's life is a lot like a sports information director. They do not work normal hours. I remember going home after that first game and I stayed up all night writing the story. I rewrote it like five times until I was comfortable with it, and then I went in the next day and typed it in the computer at the newspaper office. They liked the story and I told them I was up all night. They said, "Well you don't need to do that, just come in and write it the next day." The stories were not perfect but they had potential. The editors gave me some pointers on what to include in a game story and worked with me on some writing fundamentals. By the end of the year, I had improved tremendously because I was always writing.

The graduate assistantship at California was a 2-year appointment and I also worked on a master's degree in communications. After 1 year, I was not very happy. California was not the school for me. The master's degree program did not interest me, but getting my master's did. I came to a crossroads at that point in my career. I thought if I am fortunate enough to get a full-time position in sports information at a college then I would most likely get a tuition waiver at the college and I could work on getting my master's degree one course at a time. Even with the experience at California, I probably did not have enough to secure a full-time position. Others had done two or three internships and I had done the 3-month internship with the PSAC and the graduate assistantship at California. My experience just did not compare. Despite these obstacles, I started looking for full-time internships. I sent out numerous applications and was fortunate enough to secure an internship at James Madison University (JMU). I sent in a blind resume for the position that was advertised in the *NCAA News*. I did not know anyone there. My experience at the PSAC really paid off because Steve Murray, the PSAC sports information director, called and spoke to the people at JMU about my abilities. That really helped me get the job.

There was a huge difference going from California, a Division II school, to James Madison, a Division I school. The technology at JMU was more advanced and there was a lot more money to do publications. Also, at California, there was the head sports information director, another graduate assistant, and myself. At James Madison it was myself, a full-time secretary, three full-time sports information directors, and a person who prepared videos and produced the coaches shows. There were also more sports to cover. At California there were 14 sports and at James Madison there were 27. The volume of information generated at James Madison as compared with California was so much greater. Finally, the amount of exposure was drastically different. At California if we sent something out, maybe a newspaper or two in the area would pick it up and write a little story. If something happens at James Madison, say in basketball, and you send out a release, it is picked up by four or five newspapers around the state and goes across the AP wires and is picked up by newspapers out of state. It is much easier to get the media to bite on stories at the Division I level.

One aspect of the internship at James Madison I really loved is that the coaches respected me, an intern, the same way they respected the head sports information director and the assistants. That is not always the case. Some coaches view interns in a negative way. They say, "Well he's not full-time" or "He's just getting experience and he doesn't know what he's doing." When I was at JMU the basketball coach was Lefty Driesell who is quite famous in the world of basketball. I could talk to Coach Driesell and I did not feel like an intern and I never felt slighted. Also, while I was there the soccer team ranked second in the country and the head soccer coach, Tom Martin, was easy to work with. In developing a relationship with the coaches, it is important to demonstrate a strong work ethic. When coaches see you work hard to promote their teams, keep the statistics consistently, and are thorough in your work, they are going to trust you and treat you like a professional. The best way to develop a rapport is to show the coaches you care about what they are doing. Even if you are not covering a game, go to their game that day and show your support. Also, go to their office to talk to them about the season or recruitment. By demonstrating a genuine interest in their program, they will return the respect.

In July 1997, I left the intern position at JMU to take another internship position at Lafayette College in Easton, Pennsylvania. One major aspect of the move was money. At James Madison I made $900 a month, my rent was $300, and my car payment was $150. To put things into perspective, after I paid all my bills I had $60 a week for food, gas, and miscellaneous expenses. I loved James Madison and enjoyed being there and I would have liked to have stayed. JMU was such a large office. I received great experience helping out with football, basketball, and soccer, but the main sports I dealt with were women's tennis, gymnastics, and fencing. Those sports do not garner much media exposure. I thought I was ready for a position with more responsibility. I applied for mostly full-time jobs but I did not have much success. I had an interview at Georgia State for a position but I ended up as the second choice. It was getting late and I saw the internship at Lafayette. I knew a little bit about the position at Lafayette because a good friend of mine, Pat Farbaugh, was the sports information director at Bucknell, a school in the same league as Lafayette. Pat was the graduate assistant at Slippery Rock when I was there. Lafayette had a small office, with a head sports information director and two interns for 21 sports. I could work some sports that have more media exposure such as basketball and baseball. It paid $100 more a month and health benefits were included, which is something I did not have at James Madison. Although I thought I was ready for a full-time position, I accepted the Lafayette internship position.

I made a lot of financial sacrifices while at JMU and Lafayette. It can get difficult when you look at your classmates from college who are ahead of you financially. There were circumstances at James Madison where my car broke down and I did not have the money to fix it. I always found a way to get by, however. I was eating Minute Rice while my friends were spending their money. Those are the sacrifices one has to make to stay and advance in this business.

Probably less than 1 percent of people coming out of college get a full-time job in sports information. Of that 1 percent, the majority were 4-year assistants or work-study students who had proven themselves reliable at their institutions. They were in the right place at the right time when somebody stepped down. That is probably the only circumstance where a person coming out of college gets a full-time position in sports information. Every job has 70 to 80 applicants. A lot of people do internships.

I finally secured my first full-time position in July 1998 when I was hired as sports information director at Washington and Lee University (W&L) in Lexington, Virginia. I responded to an ad in the *NCAA News*. When I applied for positions while at Lafayette I considered mostly Division I schools. I only applied to two Division III schools, Wittenberg University in Ohio and W&L. I applied to Wittenberg because it had some pretty successful programs and I thought it was a place conducive to marketing an athletic program to the media. I applied to W&L because it was only an hour south of Harrisonburg, Virginia, where James Madison is located. I enjoyed living in the area while at James Madison, so I decided to send in my resume. When I interviewed for the job, I realized it just was too good of an opportunity to pass.

Going from Division I experiences at JMU and Lafayette to Washington and Lee, a Division III school was an adjustment. At W & L, there were a lot less coaches to deal with because many of the coaches coached two sports. Also at Division I more people are in the sports information office to assist in getting the job done. My full-time intern and I talk with one another about what is happening for the week and we plan. It is more of a team effort here between the two of us because I make the decisions and both of us do the work. At Division I, there is less interaction between the head sports information director and the assistants as to what is happening and what needs to be done. It is also a little bit more of a laid-back atmosphere at Division III, but even though we are a Division III school we run a Division I type operation. We have an enormous budget for a Division III sports information office. My assistant is a full-time intern and plenty of work-study students assist us. We develop media guides for every sport and we staff nearly every athletic contest. The expectations placed on the sports information office are pretty much the same as at a Division I school.

The main difference between Division I and Division III is in the media exposure. Whether it is right or wrong we do not get the exposure we would at the Division I level. Division I contests attract more spectators and more people are interested in the outcome. However, some of the best stories I experienced and best people I have met are at the Division III level. I think sports information jobs at Division I and Division III institutions are similar. However, more planning is involved at a Division I institution because so many people are involved, so many sports need to be covered, and so much information has to be handled.

At Division III, I have to do the nuts and bolts to get somebody to pick up a story on one of our athletes or teams. Our men's lacrosse team went to the NCAA tournament and was ranked #1 in the country at one point during the 1999 season but we could not get media coverage. If we competed in Division I with the same players and coaches we would have been ranked anywhere from #15 to #20. Because we play Division III lacrosse we cannot get exposure. To combat the lack of media exposure we use different methods to distribute information besides the newspaper. We put a lot of time and effort into developing and updating our Web site and we place an enormous amount of information on it. We get good feedback from the coaches, athletes, parents of the athletes, and the alumni. We have reached people just as well through our Web site as we could in the newspaper.

Up until the Washington and Lee position I had been an intern. In my position at Washington and Lee, I have managerial responsibilities. The transition was not an easy one. A lot of pressure goes with being an intern but I was not held accountable. If I did something wrong, it all came back to the boss. Now I am responsible for everything that goes on in this office whether I produce it or not. Having that responsibility was hard to deal with at first. I now have budget maintenance responsibilities and need to know what to spend my money on and when. Planning is essential. It is important to know when projects are due and what it takes to reach deadlines. The hardest thing for me to adjust to was my time management. Sports information is a tough field to be in as far as time. Sometimes there should be 27 hours in a day instead of 24 because there is so much to do and not enough time to do it. My best investment was a Day Planner to keep track of meetings and deadlines. I like being in charge and having the freedom to make decisions on how to do things. Before this position I was always told how to do things. Now I make those decisions.

When I assumed the position at Washington and Lee, I needed to know some history and expectations about my position. I did a great deal of evaluating during my first year. I had to determine whether I liked the way things were done or whether I would make changes. After evaluating, I decided to redesign our Web site. It contained a wealth of information, but some of the coaches wanted to see more pictures and graphics online. The Web site is often the first impression a recruit gets even before they step on campus. I wanted to improve some things but some good things were already in place. Washington and Lee has a good reputation in sports information. Brian Logue, the previous sports information director, was incredible. Following in his footsteps was a challenge. I want to keep many of the things in place, but I also want to make my mark. It would have been easy to do everything like it was done before but that is not me. I do not want to take the easy way. I want to try to do as many good things as I can and make a positive impression on people. It makes me feel good to make improvements that people will notice.

The hours are long in sports information. This is especially true while working at a school that has football. Football is one of my favorite sports and I do not know if I would want to be at a school without football. Football requires a lot of work for a sports information director. My work schedule during the fall means 8 to 10 hours a day even on Sunday. On game day I come in at 10:00 AM for a 1:00 PM game. I set up for the game and then cover the game. I make sure the media has what they need, set up the stat crews, and make sure everything is running smoothly in the press box. After the game I write the game stories, update the statistics, and then fax the information to various places. I am usually done at 8:00 or 9:00 PM. If there is a home game the next week, I begin to work on the game program and my game notes for the week on Sunday morning. The program must be at the printer on Tuesday, so Sunday, Monday, and Tuesday are all football. I cannot deal with a whole lot else. A lot of work is involved with football, but I enjoy it. A person's interests would determine if he or she wants to work at a school that has football. If someone wants a family and does not want long hours then he or she should not consider a job at an institution with football. If you are single and full of energy like me and want to do as much as you can, I recommend being at a school that has football. For somebody doing an internship, working at a school with football is a great work experience. For example, four or five different stories can be in a game program and three of them can be features. The sports information director often relies on interns to write a feature story for the game program, and the intern gets the experience of working with football statistics and setting up the press conference. Working football gives an intern a complete picture of the profession.

A typical nongame day during the school year means I arrive about 9:00 AM and leave about 6:00 or 6:30 PM. If it is a day in the fall or spring when a game is being played outside, I arrive about 9:00 AM and leave around 8:00 or 8:30 PM. If it is during the winter when sports are played inside and usually at night, I come in at 9:00 AM and leave at 11:00 PM. The hours vary from week to week and it depends on the sport. On average throughout the year, not including the summer or off season times, I average 50 to 60 hours a week, and sometimes it goes up to 70 hours a week. In the spring we have a year-end athletic banquet to give the outstanding senior male athlete award, outstanding senior female athlete award, outstanding freshman award, spirit award, and so forth. I compile the program, write the scripts for everyone, and schedule speakers. We also do year-end reports on each sport that contain the schedule, results, and interesting things that happened during the year including honors awarded and records broken. In May I wrap up the past year. In mid June to early July I begin planning for the coming year. We work on the fall media guides and update or revise the Web site. The summer is a more relaxing time. There are not as many deadlines to meet from week to week. During the year, week-to-week deadlines are a reality. During the summer, the deadlines for projects are usually in September when the years starts again. I try to enjoy the summer because the fall season means 10- to 14-hour days.

The role of the Internet is going to continue to grow in sports information. Already, we write a game story or a news release and e-mail it to a number of different people. On our Web page people can click on numerous links to receive information on all our sports. When we write a news release we put it on the Web and copy and paste it into e-mail so we can send it to our various distribution lists. People have information on our teams and outcomes of contests delivered to their home via the Internet. This technology is replacing the traditional method of faxing information or making phone calls. The e-mail system enables us to forward information to a newspaper so it does not need to be retyped. As huge an impact as the Internet has, some people are missing it. A lot of schools in our league do not have the technology. A lot of times it is not the sports information director's fault or even the athletic director's, but rather the school does not have the technology. The nice thing about working at W&L is when new technology is available we usually get it. I do not want to be left behind. I have seen some sports information directors who still use typewriters. They have not changed with the times. For somebody who has been in the business for 30 years a lot of change did not occur in the first 25, but a lot of change has occurred in the past 5 years. The changes will continue with advances in computers, scanners, and software. We are lucky to have resources to keep up with the changes.

Composing media guides is one of the main responsibilities of a sports information director. A good media guide contains pertinent information including the upcoming schedule; last year's schedule and results; university facts such as cost, enrollment, overall athletic program, success rate of a program, All-American student-athletes; and coaches' biographies and phone numbers. A recruit wants to see the coach's biography. It is a necessity to have players' biographies too, not particularly what they have done but their interests and background. At the Division III level, media guides are also recruiting brochures because we do not have as much media exposure. At the Division I level, a lot more is involved to give the media the information they seek. I think the extensive record sections, research, and more expanded biographies should be tailored to a recruit. If recruits can see that an athlete has a certain interest and where he or she has completed an internship, it helps them determine their fit on the team. Some basic things are fundamental including records. It is helpful for a recruit to compare their times with existing records. A number of things can be included but those biographies and records are the most important. Some schools use their Web site as the media guide. They tell the media and recruits to visit their Web site. I can see that becoming more prevalent. Coaches are not ready to make that move yet because they like tangible things they can send to recruits. Also, not everybody is hooked into the Internet.

Developing a good relationship with the media is very important for a sports information director. By developing a good relationship with a reporter based on trust, you can contact him or her if you have a good story. If the reporter has worked with you before he or she will trust your judgment on a good story. If you have a bad relationship with the media, the reporter will probably blow it off and think you are looking for something that does not interest him or her. The relationship also involves providing information when the reporter needs it. If the reporter gets a tip or responds to a news release and needs more information, you must follow up. If a reporter does not trust you he or she may contact the coach or the athletic director directly and that is not good. It is your job to deal with reporters. It is very important to develop a good and trusting relationship with the media.

I realized the importance of this relationship while I was at California. Bruce Wald, the sports information director, had a great relationship with the sports editor of *The Observer-Reporter* in Washington, Pennsylvania. The editor covered all our basketball games and enjoyed coming to the games and working with Bruce. We gave him everything he needed in a timely fashion to cover the game including game notes and statistics. He knew he would have a good story not only from what he saw on the court but also from the facts and figures provided by the sports information office. That experience carried on to James Madison. While I was at JMU, I dealt with a reporter who was not an easy person to work with. He had little patience and liked to write negative stories. I tried to do the best that I could for him by providing the best information and trying to build a rapport with him. I let him know he could come to me for whatever he needed. Dealing with a difficult person is good experience because it makes it that much easier when you deal with the opposite.

In my current position I use organizational skills to get the job done. If I am not organized, things sneak up and there is not enough time to get things done. Like I said, deadlines are very important, especially when you deal with printers who do your media guides and game programs. You cannot drop off a program on Friday for a Saturday game and expect it to be ready. Organizational skills enable you to handle projects that overlap. On Mondays, I look at the week through Sunday and determine what I need to do, when I need to start a project, and how much time it will require. I look at the upcoming contests and determine who will travel with a team and what home games will be covered. Organizing is a key part of the job.

It is also important to be flexible as a sports information director because many internal and external environmental factors affect your job. Requests are made by coaches for which I have not planned, but I want to be flexible. I know I will need something from them at some point so I want to help. I hope they make the same effort for me. For example, a coach will ask me to prepare a player's game-by-game statistics and fax it to an All-American committee for consideration. I may be doing three or four other things, but I fit it into my schedule. The coach will appreciate the effort to get it done and it prevents any flare-ups.

Although I acquired my full-time position, I challenge myself to grow as a professional. I attend the College Sports Information Directors of America (COSIDA) convention annually. At the convention a number of topics are discussed including handling certain professional situations better to using the latest technologies. Attending the convention is an opportunity to interact with my peers while allowing for professional growth. Right now I am not interested in finishing my master's degree but I want to do so eventually. The degree is important and, in a lot of cases, it means more money. It is something I think I have to do. I do not have to do that, but I want to keep improving myself.

I spent a great deal of time thinking about my future as I worked up to a full-time position. I am happy to have a full-time job and to have some financial stability and I would like to stay here for a while, but I will watch available opportunities. I am only going to apply for those things that interest me. Ever since I was at James Madison I have seen myself as a Division I person. That is not to say I do not like the job I have now, because I do. Yet Division I level is viewed as the top and it can be more exciting. It may be difficult for me to return to Division I after being at a Division III institution. I considered that when I came to Washington and Lee. Now that I am here I realize it is the right choice, but at the same time I would like to return to the Division I level again and be a head sports information director. The most logical next step for me would be to become an assistant at the Division I level. I would not apply for an assistant position where I would not have the sports I wanted. I want the responsibility of handling men's basketball, football, or baseball as opposed to nonrevenue sports. I cannot say when that will happen. If the right opportunity presents itself I may pursue it but otherwise I am content here.

The one thing I would change with my career is I would have gotten more involved as an undergraduate student. When I came out of school I did not have much experience. I was lucky to get the internship with the PSAC because the person was looking for help. He could not pay anybody so he took a chance on someone with no experience. He also did not have to pay me because I was doing it for credit. The PSAC internship gave me some experience to go to California. If I had spent 4 years as a work-study or a student assistant in the sports information office, I would have understood better what I was doing. Instead of people saying he only has 1 year of experience they could have said he has 4 years of experience.

You have to love working in sports information. Even with the sacrifices necessary before landing a full-time job, more sacrifices are associated with the position. If your friends go away on the weekend, you do not go with them. If somebody gets married on a Saturday of a football game, you cannot attend.

There have been weeks when my assistant and I have worked more than 40 hours by Wednesday. I am still early in my career and I am 26, but I see myself staying in sport information. If I get married and have a family, those priorities could change. My predecessor got out of the business because he and his wife had a baby. If that would happen, I could see myself doing something else. I do not know what field that would be because I have always focused on sports and this is what I have wanted to do since I graduated. I am happy doing it, so I do not know what else I would do at this point. Could the plans change? Perhaps later, but now I enjoy what I do.

CHAPTER 9

Sport Communication

SPORTS COMMUNICATIONS IS A MULTIFACETED, rapidly changing, highly complex, and critical part of the sport industry. Whereas excellent oral and written communication skills are important in most segments of the industry, they are the foundation of communications in sport. Advanced skills in computer and electronic technologies, news and feature reporting and writing, the ability to work well with diverse populations, statistical expertise, creativity in a variety of publications, and a thorough knowledge of a wide range of sports are all necessary skills for professionals in the sport communications field. A knowledge of advertising and broadcasting business principles such as market share, Neilsen ratings, designated market areas (DMAs), cost per thousand (CPM), cumulative audience over time, and return on investment (ROI) are also helpful.

Sport communications cover a wide variety of media relations and communication mediums. The electronic and technological mediums of radio, television, e-mail, and the Internet have revolutionized the ability to take the game to sports fans wherever they are. The increase in the volume and methods of communication transmission has helped the sports industry flourish internationally.

Technological advancements continue to change the role of the sport communicator. Fax on demand, digital technology, and especially the Internet have added instant information access. The development of individual player and team Web sites requires creativity, knowledge, and constant updates. Liberman (1999) reported that the three top online sports sites were ESPN.com, with 4,387,000 average unique visitors per month, followed by SPORTSLINE.com, and CNNSI.com.

Salaries in the sport communications area vary. It is a very competitive field and entry-level salaries are low in print and electronic journalism. As a person progresses through his or her career and moves to large media markets the pay will increase. On-air personalities for the major networks and major media markets can make more than $100,000, but those working in small markets can be paid in the low $20,000s. The same is true in the print media. Sportswriters for a small paper will make low $20,000s to mid $30,000, whereas those working for major metropolitan papers or a major sports news magazine will be paid higher. The future career seeker in this segment of the industry must be familiar with Web site development and stay abreast of the latest changes in communication technology.

REFERENCE

Liberman, N. (1999, November 15–21). Sports' Internet future: Growth. *The Sports Business Journal*, 2(30): 25, 38.

Tim C. Roberts

General Manager
ESPN Regional/Oregon Sports Network

Education:

B.S., FINANCE, UNIVERSITY OF OREGON, 1987

M.S., SPORT MANAGEMENT, WEST VIRGINIA UNIVERSITY, 1993

Career Progression:

GENERAL MANAGER, ESPN REGIONAL, APRIL 1998 TO PRESENT

REGIONAL DIRECTOR FOR ATHLETIC DEVELOPMENT, UNIVERSITY OF OREGON, JANUARY 1996 TO APRIL 1998

SPORTS MARKETING DIRECTOR, WEST VIRGINIA UNIVERSITY, NOVEMBER 1992 TO JANUARY 1996

INTERIM MARKETING DIRECTOR, UNIVERSITY OF CALIFORNIA AT IRVINE, JUNE 1990 TO JULY 1991

Best piece of advice you received in regards to your career:

"Status quo is not an option!"

MIKE PARSONS, ASSISTANT ATHLETIC DIRECTOR, WEST VIRGINIA UNIVERSITY

Best advice for someone aspiring toward a career in the sport industry:

"Get as much experience as you can, create opportunities for yourself, and work hard!"

Quote by which you live:

"Success—To laugh often and much; to win the respect of intelligent people and the affection of children; to earn the appreciation of honest critics and endure the betrayal of false friends; to appreciate beauty; to find the best in others; to make the world a bit better, whether by a healthy child, a garden patch or a redeemed social condition; to know even one life has breathed easier because you have lived. This is to have succeeded."

RALPH WALDO EMERSON

I DECIDED ON A CAREER IN SPORTS about 3 years after I graduated from the University of Oregon. I had a bachelor of science degree in finance and worked in the computer industry. I pretty much despised Monday through Friday.

I decided that if I was going to work for the rest of my life I better figure out what it was I had a passion for and wanted to do. It was intercollegiate athletics. At that point I made the decision to actively pursue a career in sport.

After graduating from Oregon in 1987, I worked in the insurance industry for a company in Portland for about 6 months. Then I was offered a position with a small start-up computer company in sales and marketing in southern California. I worked there for about a year and a half, but they had some severe financial difficulties. Around the same time I decided I wanted to go into sports. I started researching graduate programs in sport administration. During that time I took another job with a computer company, also in sales and marketing, and worked there until I entered the sports marketing profession.

My undergraduate degree in finance has helped immensely. The University of Oregon has a very well respected business school. That experience gave me a knowledge base and I am fortunate to have had private sector experience before entering the intercollegiate athletic field. Some of my colleagues would be well served to learn that the grass is truly not greener on the other side (the private sector). Sometimes a practical business approach is not well accepted in academia, but as more athletic departments are expected to become self-sustaining entities, a hard-line business approach must be adopted. The tricky part of athletics is continuing to serve the student-athletes, providing a healthy environment and the resources for success to the coaches, and maintaining fiscal responsibility. Athletic directors juggle those three balls on a daily basis.

When I decided I wanted to get into intercollegiate athletics, I had no idea what the field was about or how to make my goal a reality. I made a call to the PAC-10 office and spoke to a woman who said if I had not played at the intercollegiate level or did not know anybody in college athletics that I was barking up the wrong tree. After about a month and a half of pondering that statement, I decided that it was not true and started researching graduate programs. I spoke with Ken Winstead, who was at the University of Oregon, and he introduced me to the graduate program at Ohio University. That helped me expand my search into other institutions. I applied to several programs but was not accepted into one I thought would further my career. I worked as an intern the following year in addition to my full-time position to gain some experience. The second time around I was accepted at West Virginia University, among others, and offered a graduate assistant position in the athletic marketing department, which helped defer some of my costs. That made my decision of where to go to school pretty easy.

The situation at WVU is somewhat unique in that the graduate assistant position serves as an assistant director of marketing and promotions. That person coordinates promotions and does a lot of the ticket marketing. Rather than funding a full-time position, the department uses the 2-year graduate assistant position to fulfill all of those duties, so I was exposed to many things that I would not have experienced otherwise. West Virginia University is a major NCAA Division I athletic program, so I received hands-on experience in marketing and promotions and saw how other areas worked. For example, I worked closely with ticketing, the Mountaineer Athletic Club (development), and the Mountaineer Sports Network. I use much of the knowledge I gained there in my current position.

For me, West Virginia was the perfect classroom experience because practitioners rather than professors taught the courses. They are people who have to walk the walk, if you will. They teach what they actually do every day. They don't necessarily teach theory. They teach what works for them in their particular field. The Director of the Compliance Department taught the compliance course and the Assistant AD for Finance and Administration taught sport finance. He literally opened up the Athletic Department budgets so the students could get a really clear picture of how things work. On the broadcast side, the gentleman who oversees the Mountaineer Sports Network taught us about television contracts and how all of these things affected what the university was trying to accomplish. He also taught us about the radio network setup and how the game is delivered and about the athletic department's sales philosophy. For me that was the perfect scenario rather than theory-based education and teaching.

Prior to entering graduate school I had volunteered at the University of California-Irvine and worked there for a little over a year. The first 7 months I worked on a volunteer basis in development and the last 6 months in a paid role as the interim director of marketing. I was denied admission to Ohio University the first year I applied. I applied to more schools in the second year and I ended up going to WVU, but I had gained a fair amount of experience at UC-Irvine. I was not necessarily looking for an internship after I finished school. I was looking for a full-time job, which proved to be difficult. I went back to UC-Irvine and offered to volunteer some more so I could do something in athletics. During the time I was in graduate school, most of the development and marketing staff had turned over, including the athletic director. The administration at the time indicated they did not want any help, which shocked me. I did not have many contacts in the field, but I ended up working out a deal at Cal State-Fullerton, which was extremely short-lived. I worked there for about a week when Mike Parsons at West Virginia University offered me the sports marketing director position.

My experience at WVU was awesome. The department was stable financially but there was always a keen eye watching the bottom line. We could not just do something simply because it was a great idea; it also had to make financial sense. Some would probably argue that if it did not make financial sense then it was not a great idea in the first place. One of my duties at WVU included planning and administering ticket marketing campaigns, including season, single game, and group plans. I also organized and directed event promotions, including game-day schedules, public-address and message-board announcements, and entertainment and sponsored activities. I was responsible for cultivating and soliciting new season, single game, and group ticket sales throughout the state and developing corporate sponsor opportunities for the Mountaineer Sports Network by establishing strong personal contacts. I also was fortunate to oversee the procurement, installation, and sponsor sales for the athletic department's $1.4 million scoreboard project. Mike Parsons at WVU taught me the ropes of this business. Every day I use knowledge gained from working with him and often refer to notes from the broadcasting class he taught.

One of the things WVU does best is organize an event at football bowl games called the Mountaineer Fan Center. In its simplest form it is a place for fans attending WVU bowl games to congregate. The Fan Center includes many different activities that allow people to connect with WVU and the athletic department, locate old friends, and meet former players and coaches. I would be remiss if I did not mention Dave Satterfield while talking about WVU. Dave is the chief of staff for the University and was a great resource, and his friendship is one of the many things my wife Susan and I miss about Morgantown.

I was at WVU for a little more than 2 years and then was offered a position as the regional development director for the University of Oregon Athletic Department working in our Portland office. In that position I oversaw all annual giving coming out of the Portland area as well as special events related to funding scholarships. I gained fund-raising experience by working the development side of the business. Knowing that some day down the road I wanted to be an athletic director, I needed broader experiences than marketing and promotions exclusively. The regional development position afforded me that opportunity. I was there for about 2 years and was in a meeting with the athletic director discussing future plans and my future professional direction. He mentioned that the athletic department was exploring a partnership with ESPN Regional Television, and if things worked out he would like me in the role of general manager. Subsequently an agreement was reached about a year and a half ago, and I have been the general manager since then.

My role in the fund-raising position was not much different than the marketing positions because this is a people-oriented business. The only difference is that on the marketing/promotions side I deliver something, such as a promotion or a coupon opportunity in an advertisement so it is easy to go back and see what I promised, what we charged, and whether we delivered. On the fund-raising side we deliver intangibles such as tax breaks, priority seating, and a feeling of helping to support the scholarship fund. The only real difference was not having something tangible on the fund-raising side to give. It is all about selling, relationships, people, and following through with promises. My philosophy is to under-promise and over-deliver.

I probably learned more from Mike Parsons, assistant athletic director for external affairs at West Virginia University, than anyone in the business. I think he has a sound sales philosophy and a strong plan to run a network. Jim Schaus, former athletic director at Wichita State, who worked under Mike Parsons for 2 years, started a lot of what we do at the University of Oregon and with the Oregon Sports Network. Philosophically we are pretty much operating the same way WVU does because I believe in Mike's ideas on packaging and servicing.

My other role model is Tom Ford. He is a person whose name I saw in a newspaper article when he was hired as the athletic director at the University of California at Irvine. I walked into his office and said, "My name is Tim Roberts. I have no experience whatsoever in the intercollegiate athletics field. I think it's something I would be interested in, I'd love to volunteer, and if you don't have any work I'd love to have the opportunity to at least hang around and listen to people so I can hear what they talk about, how they talk, and what this whole business is about." He gave me a chance a long time ago and took a leap of faith to let me work in the development and marketing units with no experience. I appreciated his confidence.

I always respond in the same way when asked what is my ultimate goal—and I am asked that question frequently. It is to be the athletic director at the University of Oregon. The industry is changing constantly and I realize people change, but my conviction in that goal has remained unchanged. Will that opportunity present itself or will my thinking change? Time will tell, but Bill Moos (Oregon's current athletic director) is aware of my goal and serves as one of my mentors.

About the only time I have been truly discouraged about this career is when I read an article from the vice president of the University of Oregon. Our former athletic director, who was also the football coach, resigned his position to become the head coach of the St. Louis Rams. The vice president of the university, who oversees athletics, said the university would likely seek somebody for the vacant position in a less than full-time basis because it had worked in the past. Subsequently, when I heard that quote I told my wife, Susan, that it did not look like we would ever end up at the University of Oregon if that was the philosophy. That same vice president subsequently served as the interim athletic director for about 6 months and then quickly realized it was a full-time position. That has been the only small frustration I have encountered in my career path.

Currently I am the general manager of ESPN Regional and the Oregon Sports Network. We manage all multimedia rights for the University of Oregon athletic department, which includes radio, television, and corporate sponsorships. We handle expansion of the existing network, affiliate relations, game production, sponsor fulfillment, game formats, and so forth. The whole operation can basically be broken down into two parts: sales and production. On the sales side we have a very aggressive expansion plan and handle advertising sales for radio and television time, as well as signage, hospitality, promotions, and special events. On the production side the short answer is to say that we have mechanisms to record, track, and deliver everything we have sold. Shelly Canada, a former basketball player at Kansas, is our office manager and makes the whole operation run on a daily basis. Anyone wanting to get into intercollegiate athletics should use Shelly as a role model.

We work very closely with the marketing/promotions staff to make sure what we sell can be done. A couple of interns work closely with the department to ensure that promotions are run properly and that we are not making commitments that we can not meet. I am responsible for the daily operations of the ESPN Regional/Oregon Sports Network. We have four full-time employees and handle all sales related duties within the athletic department. The University of Oregon Athletic Department has a $28 million budget, and I manage a unit of that department with a budget of about $3 million. We work very closely with the ticket office, marketing and promotions, and media relations.

I have a dual role. My job is part sales and part management. Specifically, we have an office manager (Shelly) and two account executives, one in Portland and one in Eugene. I manage the office and the sales people, and I am actively involved in the sales process. I sell about a million dollars worth of ads and sponsorships a year and am ultimately responsible to ESPN Regional and the Oregon athletic department for the financial success of this project. I also manage affiliate relations with Shelly, the day-to-day operations of the office, and certain special events. More accurately, I service the larger clients and our two radio and TV stations that pay us an annual rights fee. I am actively involved in staying in front of those people.

In our larger markets, Portland and Eugene, our radio and television rights holders pay us an annual rights fee to be the exclusive broadcast outlet in those particular markets. That positions their stations as the place Duck fans listen or see Oregon teams in action. The stations tie themselves to the University and the athletic department, which allows them to use certain university marks. In return, the stations receive a specific amount of air time to sell locally. The easiest way to explain it is that the Oregon Sports Network retains 50 percent of the commercial time and the local stations retain the other 50 percent. We sell network spots, which means that what we sell will be heard statewide, and what the local stations sell will air only in their local market.

I report to Ralph McBarron who oversees all of our institutional projects. He is based in Charlotte, North Carolina, and he oversees Kansas, South Florida, TCU, and Oregon. I am actually an ESPN employee, but we are pretty autonomous in the west. We see him every 6 weeks or so. We have office space in the athletic department building, and for the most part we are treated like department employees with regard to special events and university functions. It is a nice set-up. We have the support and resources of a multinational parent company in Walt Disney/ABC, but we operate in the collegiate environment.

ESPN Regional's agreement with the University of Oregon is based on an annual guarantee with a revenue sharing formula that kicks in at a certain net revenue level. ESPN Regional takes on all the expenses of running the network and the sales process. We work directly with Oregon athletic director Bill Moos and associate athletic director Dave Heeke. In some respects we invent the relationship as we go. A contract is in place, but it cannot cover every scenario, so we work together to ensure that everyone's best interests are met.

There is no such thing as a typical day in college athletics. For example, in July we are in our sales mode so we sell our entire football and basketball inventory. Typically we bundle everything, so we put together a package including inventory for both basketball and football. We renew people that have been with us for several years as well as drive new business. Our greatest challenge is when all the radio and the TV inventory are sold, all of the signs are sold, and we still have X number of dollars to reach our revenue goal. We make up the difference by being a little creative in developing new opportunities. For example, we created a basketball event in the Portland Rose Garden called the Portland Jam. It is a men's and women's doubleheader played in December. We have a Friday night hospitality function for the teams, provide a tour of the NIKE campus in nearby Beaverton, provide gifts for each team, and so forth. We have taken it beyond being a men's and women's game. From the revenue side we developed a title sponsor opportunity and four presenting sponsor opportunities, and we receive net gate receipts from the event. In July I also place phone calls to follow up on various things, get in front of people, and renew expired contracts of some radio stations. Typically we do 3-year contracts so a few are due for renewal each year. During the summer I try to visit all 20 of our radio stations. In-season most of my time is devoted to getting the broadcast ready. We produce about 100 different radio shows a year, including men's and women's basketball games, football games, and coaches' shows. We also produce about 15 TV shows a year consisting mainly of live televised football and basketball games. In addition, one year we produced two Aloha Bowl specials from Hawaii that aired in the state of Oregon.

Those things keep us busy on the production side. We also fulfill our sales commitments in the summer. That involves implementing all the promotions that we developed, sponsoring hospitality, cultivating new sponsors, and enhancing relationships with our current sponsors. A lot of what we do is following through with what we developed in the current package.

If an event is a nationally televised game, we do not produce it. The PAC-10 television rights are held at the conference level. The primary rights holder is ABC Sports and FOX Sports is the secondary rights holder. If neither one of them picks up a particular game, the third tier package is owned by the individual schools and available for "local" telecasts. In our case "local" means the state of Oregon. The third tier package is our statewide package mentioned earlier which is produced by ESPN Regional/Oregon Sports Network. If it is FOX or ABC there is not as much for me to do on the TV side other than help coordinate the broadcast with those entities. I basically make sure they have everything they need to get the game on the air. Every stadium and arena has different nuances with regard to television camera angles, sound, and so forth so I usually attend a production meeting with those folks to help them learn that information.

If we produce the game I am in the production truck during the broadcast. We generally have a production meeting the day before the game that is attended by the producer, director, play-by-play and color commentators, and myself. We discuss story lines, what to look for, what players to highlight, and so forth. We also discuss the opening, halftime, and close of the broadcast, timelines, sponsored elements, and the like. Basically we decide what we want the "show" to sound and look like when we produce it live. Before the game I am in the truck overseeing the building of the sponsored elements and associated graphics, making sure we are delivering what we sold. When the actual game starts I answer any questions and generally monitor the telecast for any problems.

I generally work from 8:00 AM to 8:00 PM, and my schedule is a little more flexible and a little less structured in the summer. Basically every weekend from September through the end of March involves all the staff attending or working some event. I am either at a home or away football game every Saturday during football season. Then toward the end of football season, basketball starts. If I am not on the road doing a men's TV game, I am at home doing radio for the women. Throw in the need to be at a certain number of volleyball, wrestling, track, and softball events, and it can be very hectic during the academic year. A typical week includes a Tuesday operations/events staff meeting, generally three to five appointments with current or potential sponsors, a couple of Oregon Club Lunches (Eugene on Mondays, Portland on Thursdays), and a lot of coordinating for the upcoming game. I make sure our 20 radio partners have received the game format, verify that our flagship has all the correct spots for our sponsors, coordinate travel plans for the radio or television crew, and oversee the sponsor hospitality. We try to stay ahead of the game as much as possible and handle any curve balls thrown our way.

The most enjoyable aspect of my job is working in and being around intercollegiate athletics. I enjoy the events, the games, and being at my alma mater. I love college sports. Within that realm I enjoy the corporate marketing aspect of structuring deals that make sense for the University and for the corporate partners. The overwhelming reward, one that is sometimes lost in this business, is that we help educate young people who in some cases may not have otherwise had the opportunity to attend college.

Truly I do not know if there is a least enjoyable part. Some days are more stressful than others because everything does not run perfectly. We may have a radio broadcast where the lines go down and all of the spots do not get in so we need to make that call Monday morning and say, "Oh, by the way, here's what we're going to do." Maybe something did not happen exactly as planned and the sponsor is unhappy. This business has challenging aspects but there has never been a day when I woke up and said, "I don't want to go to work today."

For the most part I am satisfied with my compensation, and I am extremely pleased with the content of my work. I enjoy being around my colleagues and have a great relationship with my boss. I am also pleased and satisfied with my advancement opportunities. This position gives me great exposure in several different arenas. If something opens up in the athletic department, I am still very much in the mix so I could potentially jump back there. As ESPN Regional adds new properties an opportunity may arise for me to manage three or four schools in the west. Because I am in the ESPN/ABC/Disney family now, I receive job postings every week. If I decided to take a little different route those opportunities exist as well.

Managing people is probably one of the most difficult aspects of this job. My management philosophy is to hire good people and let them do their jobs. I do not particularly like to be micro-managed and therefore I do not micro-manage. I may need to give more attention to the management side and let my salespeople create new business. In the past 6 months I have learned a lot about management. I learned to ask my employees questions to develop a feel for what is going on in my department. Just because a red flag has not been raised does not mean a problem or issue does not exist.

I will never be the type of manager who tries to keep an eye on my employees and say, "I need to know where you are and what you're doing every minute of every day" and tell them how to do every little task. I give them my philosophy and tell them how I would handle a situation. I need to make sure we all are on the same page regarding our packaging and philosophy. How each person sells is up to him or her. They just need to know we are all representing the University of Oregon Athletic Department and if we jeopardize that relationship then we have problems.

Success on the athletic field breeds more listeners, more viewers, and drives more value on the network side of things. It also drives exposure. More people become aware of the program and the things we do. It opens up a lot of doors with the sales process. I have never picked up the phone and talked to somebody cold and heard, "You know, I'm not familiar with the University." People know who we are so on the sales side so it is not an issue of getting through the door. The door is always open because people want to talk about the Ducks. The challenge is convincing them of the value within the network. Many people still look at college sponsorships as support rather than as a media buy. Our job is to convince them that there is value and they are not just supporting the University of Oregon with this contribution. They must realize that they are making a buy into a corporate sponsorship program with a lot of value. The money does help support the athletic department but they get great value in return. When things on the field do not go as well, people tend to look for other ways to spend their money so we need to be as successful in as many areas as possible.

We have a good relationship with all areas of the athletic department. I have been on the development side of the department so I have no problem if corporations are not particularly interested in radio or TV advertising but want to support the athletic department. I send them to the Duck Athletic Fund so they can make a contribution. The same applies for the marketing and promotions office or the Duck Athletic Fund. If they encounter somebody who is interested in buying an ad or is sales-related, they send them to me. Some of what we do is a combination of several departments. I may structure a deal that is a $100,000 corporate sponsorship, $10,000 of which is a contribution from that company to the Duck Athletic Fund to directly support scholarships. We help each other in that manner.

My greatest stress is meeting our revenue goal. A lot of lead time is required to sell these packages. Once we get a commitment from an organization, the company still has to produce print media, radio spots, TV spots, and so forth. We cannot put things together 2 weeks before the first game. We have to actively keep a lot of people in the cycle year round and get in front of them during their budget times. Companies set budgets a year ahead of time so we position ourselves to ask them early.

I mainly use personal skills in my role as manager. A level of technical knowledge is needed but I think everything is based on the personal side. I sit in the TV production meeting and people use technical terms and I say, "Okay, I don't know how we do it, or if we can do it, but here is what I think we should do." I just lay out a picture and talk about games, who is hot and who is not, and what special features we need. My main task during the broadcast—because I know my radio and my TV people are pros—is to help them troubleshoot and give them any assistance. I make sure that everything that sponsors pay for is getting done so all of these sponsored elements are in the broadcast. In our production meetings questions arise about how a graphic element should look or how the sponsor logo should look. For example, if someone pays to sponsor the half-time statistics, what does that entail? Does that mean it is a half-time scoreboard show or a one-page graphic element with some statistics that we drop in? I do not have to know how to work the Chyron or Infinite machine and enter fonts and push buttons and switch from camera three to camera four. I just need to know what the look of the broadcast needs to be and that the sponsored elements are properly included. The technicians know I cannot do a lot of the hands-on broadcast components, but if I went in there as a jerk and had no personal skills, they would not respect me or my opinions, and they would do it how they wanted it done.

My best advice is to identify early on what you want to do. I hear people say, "I'm a huge sports fan, I'm interested in sports, and this is what I want to do." They think that because they love sports they will love this profession. That could not be further from the truth. I watch far fewer sport events on TV now than I ever have just because I live it every day. Students need to have a passion for what they do. We have heard it a thousand times. They have to be willing to work long hours for less pay than is available elsewhere. If someone truly is interested, he or she should get a good academic background and as much experience as possible. That is what employers look for when reviewing applications, whether for an internship, graduate school, or a full-time job. If one aspires to be an athletic director or something of that nature, most people in those positions have at least a master's degree. Do some research and determine what coursework is necessary to get the desired position and get as much hands-on experience as possible. When I interview prospective employees, I look for a sports-related master's degree. I look at experience as much as anything. If somebody knows they want to go into sport, I recommend a master's degree in a sports-related field. The University of Oregon has a wonderful program and I am also partial to West Virginia.

The best piece of advice for people who want to get into this field is if you are truly interested in sports, do not take "no" for an answer and or let anyone's ideas or perceptions—especially if they are negative—affect you. You will find out in a hurry that long hours and less pay are a reality but it can be rewarding if you have a passion for it. If you are not having fun, find something else to do.

I think the broadcast side will continue to evolve with the expansion of cable and other forms of media communication. Ten or 20 years ago cable was perceived as a minor player. The networks scoffed at it and assumed they would always be the major players. Now hundreds of cable stations exist. Many games are broadcast on cable networks. With cable networks expanding and with computerization, the face of sport and the way sport is delivered to the consumer is rapidly changing. I can be in Japan on the Saturday of a football game and log onto my computer and listen to the Ducks game. I can download highlights practically in real time. All of those things are opening up new opportunities not only for delivering the game but also for sponsors. Everyone is still trying to wrap their arms around the Internet and advertising on Web sites to see how much it is worth and how effective. I think the next big wave is how the Internet affects the delivery of the game and how games will be affected by money, national championships, and other issues. I hear that the top 50 or 60 teams will split off on their own and create a bigger pie to divide among themselves and leave a smaller pie for everyone else.

We have a 3-year contract with an outside company who does our Web pages. In turn, they sell advertising. We sell advertising. They get a percentage of advertising sales. I would expect that when this contract expires, we will develop our own Web site. Fortunately we are in a unique situation because of the partnership with ESPN and the athletic department. We will have the opportunity to have a direct link from ESPN.com to the University site. Obviously, ESPN.com is one of the highest profile sites on the net. We will develop our University site as an information area where people can obtain information about the Ducks, and it also is an opportunity to drive some sales. We will have corporate sponsorship opportunities on there. If I talk to somebody who has a company based in Georgia and he or she wants information, the Web site contains my sales presentation. I tell them to log onto the site and look under corporate sponsorships to see what we offer. In the meantime, I send a hard copy through the mail. It will change the response time we have with customers much like a fax did years ago, but this delivers it digitally, in color, and in the same format they will see when they receive our packet. I think the Internet and Web sites will add opportunities in the athletic department. I would not have a hard time approaching our athletic director and saying, "Bill, we feel strongly that we need to have a Web site as an element in sales next year but we need to dedicate somebody full-time to running and updating it." It may cost $35,000 to $40,000 a year but I could tell him that the return would be 10 times that much in the first year in advertising revenue. We will have some big questions to answer with this scenario. If the game is on ABC, will that game be simultaneously broadcast on the Internet or on Fox or some day the Oregon Sports Network? If so, what does that do to rights fees and how does it affect ratings? I can look at our radio broadcasts from last year and know the numbers from all of our stations. I can also go to our broadcast partner on the Web, Broadcast.com, and log onto our site and see how many people listened to our games on the Internet last year. When our games are broadcast on the Internet, the advertising that people bought for radio also runs. When I do postseason wrap-up with our advertisers, I can say, "Oh, by the way here's what we promised you, but we gave you bonus spots in these games and 35,000 people listened to all or some portion of the games on the Internet and your commercials played during those games." It raises some eyebrows. It is not a situation in which the impact is specifically measured, but it is an area in which advertisers are impressed with the numbers of people listening on the Internet.

Currently ESPN is looking to add one school per year. One year we added TCU. Other companies are involved in the same business. Host Communications is a competitor, and OSI (Outdoor Systems) has a marketing group formerly known as Premier Sports. They all do the same thing we do. Those organizations pursue properties more aggressively than we do. They get involved in bidding processes and Requests for Proposals (RFPs). The philosophy of ESPN Regional is to try to structure a partnership with universities that is a more personal than responding to an RFP. The margins are so small on a lot of those things that it is a losing proposition for a few years. Schools may make more money than they could with ESPN Regional, but they relinquish a lot of control. They have no say in what is being sold and how they are being represented, whereas with our structure probably a small amount of money is left on the table but the University is comfortable knowing it is well represented in the community.

I think the future will require the same skills that have always been necessary for survival. You must adapt to change and be willing to embrace new technologies and new ways of doing things. I think that is one of the greatest things Mike Parsons taught me at WVU. Status quo is not an option. Every year things were great and the numbers grew. Every year things had to get a little bit better. We had to change things a little bit to keep it interesting. You have to have people skills and a strong work ethic.

What would I like to do in 10 years? Ultimately I would like to be the athletic director at the University of Oregon at a boyish 45 years old. I will measure success in the future probably the same way I do now, by measuring my level of happiness. I like getting up and going to work every day. I am a results-oriented person but I would not be happy if the results do not merit what I do. My goal in life is very simple: to have fun. Fun for me is measured by spending time with my wife and son and friends as well as job success and career fulfillment. I am definitely having fun.

Damon Andrews

Sports Anchor/Reporter
WBAL-TV 11 (NBC)

Education:
B.A., RADIO AND TV COMMUNICATIONS,
EASTERN WASHINGTON UNIVERSITY, 1990

Career Progression:
SPORTS ANCHOR, WBAL (BALTIMORE,
MARYLAND), JANUARY 1999 TO PRESENT

SPORTS DIRECTOR, WPTY (MEMPHIS,
TENNESSEE), DECEMBER 1995 TO DECEMBER
1998

WEEKEND SPORT ANCHOR, KVEW
(KENNEWICK, WASHINGTON), 1994 TO 1995

NEWS EDITOR, KABC (LOS ANGELES,
CALIFORNIA), 1993 TO 1994

Best piece of advice you received in regards to your career:

**"Don't try to be anyone other than yourself.
Your personality is the best asset you have."**

TOM SPENCER, NEWS DIRECTOR, KVEW

Best advice for someone aspiring toward a career in the sport industry:

**"Shoot for the stars, but prepare to be grounded.
Hard work is you greatest dividend."**

Quote by which you live:

"Do unto others, as you would have others do unto you."

AS A KID WHEN SOMEONE ASKS YOU WHAT YOU WANT TO BE when you grow up, you really do not give it much thought. After all it was 1981, I was 13 and 20 seemed so far away. I guess that is why every school in America provides a standardized skills test to determine a profession you may be good at. For me the test score said it was a career in communications. With those results the seed was planted and I began to think of how communications would fit in with my love of Atari and sports.

In 1985, I began my undergraduate studies at Cerritos Junior College (CJC). While playing basketball for CJC, I was fortunate to receive an athletic scholarship to Eastern Washington University in Cheney, Washington. When I got to Eastern in 1987, I wanted a career in sports broadcasting. I had already got a taste of it in junior college and Eastern Washington had a department geared toward my choice of career. Life experience and classroom studies have played an equal part in my growth as an up and coming communications graduate. At CJC, I took several speech classes and was in student government. Our basketball team was ranked first in the State of California and we gained a great deal of attention. I have always welcomed the opportunity of being in the forefront, whether it was in athletics, student government, or in the classroom. By the way, I had now graduated to the love of Nintendo and sports.

Although I wanted a career in sports broadcasting I would not get the opportunity until an internship during my senior year. Remember, NCAA rules prohibit scholarship athletes from holding paying jobs during the academic year. So I had summer jobs. I worked for the City of Norwalk Parks and Recreation as a day camp counselor, as a shoe salesperson, and as a parking attendant at an amusement park. At the time I did not think those jobs would help me grow professionally since they were not directly related to broadcasting, but in hindsight they did. All of the jobs dealt directly with the public and refined my people skills. I was asked questions and had to respond accordingly and accurately. Lesson 1: Be prepared.

In 1990 I began a 3-month internship with KXLY-TV, an ABC affiliate in Spokane, Washington. Talk about baptism by fire! I did a little bit of everything. I shot video, wrote stories and edited videotape to be aired for the nightly newscast. Although I had done all these things in my college classes and for a cable sports show also college related, it was different doing it for all the people of Spokane to see. It had a profound impact on me. My internship required me to work on Friday and/or Saturday nights, which meant giving up a party night. That was tough for a college kid, especially when I was not getting paid for it. There were times that I did not want to go, but I did. Because I did I had the opportunity to interview a star player like Shawn Kemp, when he was with the Seattle Sonics. Such are the perks of TV, even when you are just an intern. There was a sense of responsibility here and the experience is one that I can directly point to that enabled me to get my foot in the door of sports television. Even though my internship requirements were completed in 3 months, I stayed on a short while longer because I enjoyed it. Note from Dad: "If you're interested in something then it ceases to be a job." Note to Dad: "Thanks for the advice."

Speaking of Dad, Fred Andrews is one of the best you can have and has been an inspiration to me. He started as a meter reader in Los Angeles when he was 18 years old. He worked his way up the ladder at the Department of Water & Power and retired as a department manager in 1993. He always told me that I could do anything if I put my mind to it. He also said to find a job that I liked so it would not seem like work. Because of his advice I chose to become a television sports anchor. My father's determination, persistence, and work ethic are part of me, and if it was not for his early encouragement I would not be where I am today.

After graduating from Eastern Washington University in June 1990, I began looking for a job. My resume included all of the skills and activities I thought a TV news director would find valuable. I plastered the West Coast from Seattle to San Diego with my resume. I was looking for anything. I wanted to be on air but I also knew I would not start at the top. My efforts landed me a job as a news apprentice at KABC-TV in Los Angeles, which is the second largest TV market in the nation. As a news apprentice I did everything that needed to be done. That included shuttling reporters to stories or live shots, ripping scripts, getting lunch, and even getting the general manager's car washed. It is not something I am proud of, but I stuck with it. The job experience and exposure were invaluable. In fact, the people I worked with at KABC continue to help me with my career today. Lesson 2: Never shut off the lines of communication.

I had enjoyed the high life of news apprenticing ("NOT!") for about a year and a half when the news director noticed I had editing experience from my college internship. The station needed an editor and I was in the right place at the right time. It was one of those sink or swim opportunities. After all, this was LA. For the first few months, several of the editing veterans helped me. I advanced quickly and occasionally filled in for the supervisors. This experience made me realize that editing was the next best thing to reporting. It was a great learning tool because I had to paint the picture of a story without sound. When you are good at that you realize how your voice should enhance the story rather than clutter it. TV is a visual medium and reporters must tell a story with the pictures and words. Video is what makes it unique from radio and print news.

I was cutting tape for the nightly newscast but I was still interested in sports. The editing supervisor put me on the Sunday night sports shift. The show was all about the NFL, NBA, MLB, and NHL teams in the LA area. I found myself looking forward to Sundays because it was for the most part uplifting. Although I enjoyed myself, I still thought that my true calling was anchoring. It was something I never acted on until Shelcy (my wife) stood behind me, encouraged me, and sometimes prodded me to give it a try. I was not going to get a job in a top 50 market and make the kind of money I made as an editor. I would most likely get a job in a small market and work my way up. Who knows if I ever would have left KABC had it not been for Shelcy. They say behind every good man there is a good woman and mine often leads the way.

I picked up a few tips from the reporters and anchors at the station about how to get an on-air job. Build a resume tape. When the reporters came back with a story they were going to put together I would watch and build my own version of the story. Born out of a bunch of old stories was my first resume tape. It was not flashy but I was getting my feet wet. Occasionally the news director would designate a day after the noon show for all the interns to build their own segment. We used the news set and computers to build a mini show. My sportscast was so... so... how do I say this... Bad! But it was good enough for a news director in Kennewick, Washington to see potential. Believe me, on that tape he had to look hard.

Move number one came in 1994. I left KABC for an on-air position at KVEW-TV in Kennewick. I was 26 and making a pretty good living editing in LA, and I threw it all away to make a salary worthy of a fast food fry chef. Follow your dream but get a bank loan first. I was the weekend sports anchor and Tuesday through Friday news reporter. The Tri Cities (Kennewick, Pasco, Richland) was market number 127 at the time, and the only reason it was that big is because it was combined with Yakima, Washington, which was about an hour away. During the week we did a regional broadcast with Yakima and the Tri Cities at 5:00 PM and then went local at 5:30 PM and 11:00 PM. On the weekends we had two shows on Saturday and no shows on Sunday. I don't know why. The job was hands-on. We shot and edited all of our own video and produced our own shows.

I do not regret leaving LA, but there were some very hard times. Shelcy is from the Tri Cities and her mother still lived there so we rented a room from her. That quickly changed to a no rent situation because of the vast wealth I accumulated. It was difficult to make ends meet. People bagging groceries were making more money. The only way we made it was from the generosity of Luisa McEachern, my mother-in-law, who helped us in so many ways it would be impossible to list each one. She supported us at times when we did not think we could support ourselves. That is the kind of lady she is and I am grateful to call her my mom. During this time I grew and matured because of the things my wife and I endured financially and the stress of a new job.

I came to KVEW in the middle of high school basketball season and had the challenge of getting through the Friday night wrap-up show. It was 10 minutes long, and I had never produced a show before in my life! I had to shoot three games, edit them, produce the line-up including graphics, and anchor the show. Because of the large geographic territory, people were shooting games for me in Yakima and then sent them via microwave to our station. Most of the time I did not see the video until it aired and when you are as green as I was that is a bad thing. As if that was not enough, the script or shot sheet was faxed to me by the same people who shot the video and sometimes the fax ink would run. That is what happened the first night. To say the least it was difficult to read. To add insult to injury I was not familiar with the names of the schools and players. Washington State has quite a few Native American tribes with unique names and pronunciations. That night was the worst TV night of my life. I stumbled through the entire 10 minutes. After the last highlight aired I turned to the camera and told the viewers: "It can only get better from here." I came home that night and asked my wife, "What have we done?" "Have I given up a great opportunity in LA for this?" The following week people who saw the show agreed that it was terrible but appreciated me for being honest and wished me well.

That first night did not go unnoticed by my two news directors either. Yes, I had two bosses because of the sister station set-up. After the first month on the job I received a letter from the news director of the Yakima station stating either I get better or they would make a change. I knew that I was terrible that night but give me a break. I walked on pins and needles for awhile stuck in another sink or swim situation. I began doing the backstroke. I started to feel more comfortable in front of the camera and four months later, people on the streets shouted my name and told me "good job." A year later, the same news director that sent the threatening letter told me he knew I could do it all along. My wife and family believed in me and they turned a rocky road into a smooth highway. Now I can look back and laugh at the experience but at the time no one was laughing, except for maybe the home audience. I realize everybody experiences struggles, maybe not to the extent that I did but you have to start somewhere and that was my beginning.

It took me about a year before I got my first offer from another station. KMBC in Kansas City flew me out and offered me a sports reporter job. It was a pretty big jump in market size but I was not quite sure if I wanted to be "just" a sports reporter. I wanted to continue anchoring so I called a friend in LA (one of the people at KABC) and he referred me to an agent to get some "professional" career advice. I sent the agent a tape. He called me back the next day and advised me not to take the job. He said my future was in anchoring. So I declined the job and signed with the agent. Five months later I accepted a job offer from WPTY in Memphis, Tennessee. I would be the sports director and this would be move number two.

I did not know much about Memphis or anything about WPTY except that it was a start-up news organization. It was a FOX affiliate and switched over to ABC Programming so a local news product was needed. WPTY was like college compared with the high school experience of KVEW. I took a step up in the sports teams and events that I covered. Memphis had the St. Louis Cardinals AAA franchise (The Redbirds), a minor league hockey team (The Riverkings), and arena football for a short time. On the college scene there was the University of Memphis, Mississippi, Arkansas, Tennessee, and Mississippi State. We lived in Memphis for 3 years from December 1995 to December 1998. The experience was invaluable and we met many people we will always call friends.

The next opportunity landed us in Baltimore. My first day on the job was January 1, 1999. I was the weekend sports anchor/weekday sports reporter at WBAL, an NBC affiliate. You usually have to move to advance as an on-air talent and this was move number three. When we left Memphis it was market #42 whereas Baltimore was market #22. The move brought a little more money, but more importantly it was a step up in the sports teams I would cover daily. I have now moved from college to graduate school. The move meant I would get to cover the Orioles, the Ravens of the NFL, and The University of Maryland of the Atlantic Coast Conference.

Looking back, my career path is fairly typical of most TV reporter-anchors, but I admit I was a late bloomer having started my on-air career at the age of 26, whereas most begin in their early 20s. However, I have more than made up for the lost time in the rapid climb up the TV ladder. Given the amount of competition for each position I have been fortunate to be in the right place in the right time. Usually two to three sports jobs exist per station and an average of four network affiliates (ABC, NBC, CBS, and FOX) exist per market. Competition is healthy and I have always competed, but I am just happy to be in the game because it is hard to get a job and keep it in a top 20 market. I am confident in my abilities so I do not look back; I concentrate on what is ahead by focusing on my daily duties. It is a pretty packed day as soon as I enter the station. From finding stories, covering events, and reporting on breaking news, I stay busy. My goal each day is to give the public a behind-the-scenes view of sporting events whether that means reporting on an Orioles game or doing a story on the hot dog vendor at that game. Free hot dogs are not included. You must be phone friendly in this business. The majority of my stories come by word of mouth, a tip, or a follow-up to something I've done before. Once all the information is gathered, then comes the fun part— putting it all together so that it tells a story that makes sense and grabs the viewer from start to finish, and that informs the viewer.

Personally, I am more of a human-interest type of person. I love to bring out the human element of a sports figure, whether in the pro ranks or the high school softball player next door to reveal a side of people through sports that viewers rarely see. You think you know somebody because you see him or her on TV competing, but that is just a small percentage of who that person is. Human-interest stories help show another side. I am proud of a few that I have done. One was on Ravens running back Errict Rhett, who is known throughout the NFL as a trash talker, but not in the conventional form. Errict just runs his mouth.... CONSTANTLY! He psychs out his opponent by his verbal barrage. Errict let me in on his style of verbal warfare, and the viewers loved it and so did the Ravens. It also helped me develop some relationships with the players, which is invaluable as the new guy in town who covers them every fall.

Anchoring is a little different because it is done live on the set. I write about daily events and games and I try to personalize each story by phrasing the story in terms that I use in everyday language. I do not try to be a comedian, but I do like to add humor when appropriate because I find things around me so funny. To me that is the beauty of television sports as opposed to hard news. You do not have to be a cookie cutter anchor to convey your point. In personalizing stories the goal first and foremost is to deliver the information quickly and correctly. Local sports is not given a ton of time in the newscast so each second is a precious commodity. News directors often look for someone who can get the point across without being timed on a sundial. Delivering the information in an entertaining way just adds to your value.

My day usually starts at 10:00 AM. Before I go out on the story I make beat calls to the area sports teams—Orioles, Ravens, University of Maryland—to make sure there is no breaking news. Most of the time I have some idea what I want to do the day before, so when I come in I can either go out on the story I chose or the assignment desk gives me one. From there the photographer and I go to the story location, shoot video of the event, get interviews, return to the station, and produce what I like to call the news jigsaw puzzle. My stories usually run in the 5:30 newscast at about 5:50 so my deadline is 5:15, but the absolute deadline is 5:45, five minutes before it airs.

Interviews and eyewitness accounts make the story, but wading through a ton of sound does not help you when you are under deadline, especially when your story will run only about a minute and a half. I try to ask only questions that I can use in the piece on camera. If I need any background information I ask them off camera and take notes. That helps me back at the station as well. Although sometimes I get to a story location and discover the story has changed or is not what I thought it was. Then you have to get as much information on camera to formulate the story angle. That happens more with breaking news than with a set-up story. Simplifying the angle also makes it easier to write and edit. I do not mind bragging when I say most sports people think well on their feet, so it doesn't take us long to write a story, which eliminates the pressure of a deadline. My process begins as soon as the photographer and I get into the car to return to the station. I start writing the story on paper so I can type it into the computer as soon as we get to the station.

The earlier I do it, the better as far as I am concerned. I try to schedule things before noon so I can take more time writing and thinking about how to put it together. A lot of times sports organizations help us because they know that in the long run it will help them in getting coverage. However, sometimes later is better. Just last year the Orioles were ready to introduce Mike Hargrove as their new manager. I talked to the O's media relations person and he was not sure when to schedule the news conference. Working with my executive producer I convinced the O's to make the announcement at 5:00 PM. It just so happened to be when our first newscast began. That allowed our station to lead with the story and toss it to me live so we could capture the moment as it happened.

After a full day of reporting I head out the door by 6:30 after the early newscast. On occasion I will stick around to help the weekday anchor by picking up sound from a late game or an interview The only other thing that can keep me past 6:30 is another story shoot. Just because I try to schedule stories during my work hours does not mean it always happens. There are times when I have to shoot the story for the next day at night, which is not all bad because I get ahead in the game.

An anchor day typically starts at 2:00 PM. I line up the 6:00 show, make more calls, and roll tapes on our video news feeds from NBC and CNN, our main source for video of national events. The assignment desk must know times and locations for local shoots, e.g., Orioles' games, local college hoops and or high school sports. Then I am on the computer writing stories and producing graphics for the 6:00 show. I get 4 minutes at the 6:00 and 11:00 newscasts to tell the day's events in the world of sports. That amount differs from station to station and market to market. Back in Memphis 5 minutes was not out of the question for a sportscast. During the weekdays at WBAL we get 2 minutes and 30 seconds.

The challenges that anchoring and reporting present are close to the same, formulating a story from start to finish. The only real difference is the ability to write it in a teleprompter instead of on tape, or in the case of a live shot from memory. For me, a live shot adds to the excitement of going out in the field. You have to remember the facts and present them in a way that makes sense and tells the story. It takes a while but once you get it down it can be an adrenaline rush, especially if you have an unpredictable live interview.

Things can go wrong and often do when anchoring. I can recall a show where my lead story was supposed to be fed in from our microwave truck out in the field at 10:00 PM. It did not happen that way. It turned out the photographer was sent to a fire and was not able to feed video until 11:10, and no one told me. On top of that something was wrong with the video feed in the truck so the tape he sent me was not airable. I did not find all this out until two minutes before I went on air. Seconds before I went on I told the producer to cut the lead story and move the other stories up in the line-up. This is not a world shattering event, but something you must deal with as a sports anchor. Sometimes video from our news feeds is delayed and we do not find out until the last moment. I adlib and hope everything turns out all right. Once you hit the seat, the studio lights go on and you have to gather some kind of presence and deliver the sportscast like it was any other night. My wife can tell by now when I am under some kind of duress but you must pull it off so the viewers do not see it. It is part of the job.

At the risk of sounding like a masochist, I love the rush of change at the last moment. I do not want it to happen every night, but when it does I just roll with the punches. Bottom line, in what other job can you talk about sports and get paid for it? I can't think of anything I'd rather do. I have been to major sporting events I would never have been able to see otherwise including the 97 Super Bowl between the Packers and Patriots and several college football bowl games. It is not just a job. TV truly is an adventure.

Through it all I have gotten to know the athletes that I cover on the job. Building relationships makes it easier to cover the athletes that people want to know. They feel more at ease with you and let you into their lives a little more. You walk a fine line as those relationships grow, because every story may not be complimentary toward a particular athlete. But if they know you personally then they should realize there was no malicious intent involved because you are just doing a job. It takes awhile to get to that point, but once you do it makes the job more enjoyable.

Talking to athletes can be an experience as well. One of my first interviews was with Wayne Gretzky back in Los Angeles. This was during my news apprentice days and I was out on a story with one of the reporters. He told me to go in there and talk to Wayne. My knees were shaking like an earthquake had just hit and I could barely spit out a sentence. Wayne was forgiving, but it took me awhile to get over the stage fright of interviewing a superstar. But once you realize they are just like you, it's not a big deal. Besides they have heard every question. The interview process is more intense when you start talking to pro athletes and coaches on a regular basis. As you can imagine after losing a big game, they are not in the mood to chat. You need some kind of game plan for questions you want to ask, how to ask them, and follow up with a related question. Above all else be prepared and ask with conviction. If you believe in what you ask, it is not a bad question even if they think so.

Several factors are considered when deciding what to put in a show and what ultimately goes on-air. The most important to me is interest. If people are talking about an upcoming, current, or past event, it is topical and most likely we will have something about it on that night's newscast. But we also have to weigh location, our resources, and the story's importance. Let me give you an example. If a big regular season high school basketball game is being played, but it is 45 minutes from the station, and we only have one photographer to split between news and sports, chances are we are not going to get that game. We will settle for a game of lesser relevance but closer to the station. We have to compromise to get something shot instead of nothing at all. Another example might be the University of Maryland's basketball team is playing in College Park, 45 minutes away, and the only way to get video is to shoot it ourselves. Regardless of the camera situation, we will most likely shoot the game. Both examples are a question of importance. The high school game affects fewer people; therefore it is less important. However, the Terps have a huge following and it is a game we must shoot. Each day I juggle our resources to get video of events people want to see. It is often an uphill battle if your sports department does not have its own photographer.

I think the future is hazy at best in the local sports scene. Stations all over the country are changing their views toward sports. Some think it is somewhat important, others see no value at all. Cable sports channels have had a direct impact on local sports broadcasting. The inventions of CNNSI, FOX, and ESPN have given news directors the false impression that everyone who is interested in sports watches cable sports only. Even I watch ESPN, but the "big boys" are not going to do the story of the girl from the local high school and her four championships in the state track meet. These are the stories that local news will always own. The Internet is also cutting into our viewership. Sports fans can get sports information just by clicking a mouse. That was not an option 10 years ago. If a person has the correct media players in a computer they can even get live coverage of a game. Many different ways exist to get sports news these days, but local news will always have its place because it is the one thing that helps a local station build its identity within a community.

I do not know what the future holds for me in this business but I will be an anchor or a reporter. Once it is in the blood you can not get it out. I plan to settle in a market where sports is important, where I can make a decent living, and where my family can be happy. I am interested in being a color analyst for televised games whether it is the NBA, NFL, college football, or college basketball. Diversification is what keeps you fresh and employed.

It has been a great experience being in the TV business. Few things can top it. You learn about others through each interview and story. They become a part of you. I define success in my career by its longevity as well as by whom I have touched. Since what we do is directed toward the public, I can easily measure my impact on the people who I have affected in a positive way. If they say, "Good story, or great job Damon," then I am reminded that it has never been about me being famous or anything like that—it is about the sports stories I tell and the people behind them that make it all possible.

Marc C. Connolly

Senior Writer/Producer
ABC Sports Online/ESPN.com

Education:
B.S., SPORTS INFORMATION AND
COMMUNICATION, ITHACA COLLEGE

Career Progression:
SENIOR WRITER/PRODUCER, ABC SPORTS
ONLINE/ESPN.COM, APRIL 1999 TO PRESENT

WRITER/PRODUCER, ABC SPORTS ONLINE, 1997
TO 1999

ASSOCIATE PRODUCER, ABC SPORTS ONLINE,
1996 TO 1997

COMMUNITY RELATIONS, WOMEN'S SPORTS
FOUNDATION, MAY 1996 TO SEPTEMBER 1996

MEDIA RELATIONS, CENTER FOR THE STUDY
OF SPORT IN SOCIETY, MAY 1995 TO AUGUST
1995

SPORTS INFORMATION DEPARTMENT ASSIS-
TANT, CORNELL UNIVERSITY, AUGUST 1994 TO
DECEMBER 1994

PRODUCTION ASSISTANT, PRIME NETWORK,
AUGUST 1994 TO DECEMBER 1994

Best piece of advice you received in regards to your career:

**"Life is mostly endurance, making it so important one
must be ready for those moments of joy."**

KEITH JACKSON

Best advice for someone aspiring toward a career in the sport industry:

"Good things will come if you work hard and always keep your passion."

Quote by which you live:

"Do or do not. There is no try."

YODA, THE EMPIRE STRIKES BACK

MY NAME IS MARC CONNOLLY AND I AM 25 YEARS OLD. My current position is senior writer/producer for ABC Sports Online/ESPN.com. From the youngest age I can remember, about 5 or 6 years old, I always said I would either be a professional athlete or a broadcaster. When I was older and knew I would not be on a baseball card some day I looked for a way to be a part of it all. For me it was always going to be as a broadcaster all the way until about my sophomore and junior year of high school. When I heard about this amazing program at Ithaca College where not only was there a sport management program but also a sports information and communications program, I pretty much focused on Ithaca. I was intrigued after learning that many of their graduates worked in marketing or in the front offices of many teams and leagues. Never did I realistically think I would be writing, but at least at that point I decided I wanted to get into professional and collegiate sports. Even though I knew some of my friends and teachers quietly doubted my decision, I was determined to work in the sport industry no matter how long the road. I never considered another profession.

Once I got to Ithaca I became involved in many things. I wrote for the paper, *The Ithacan*, and I did well. I wrote for the football team. It was exciting because the Bombers were the defending NCAA Division III national champions. I did some of the game stories as a freshman. I was the only freshman sports reporter to make the lead station at Ithaca, WICB, where I gave news updates. I was also on the talk show on Sundays. Between both of those activities, with classwork and being a freshman, it was just too much. My grades were not very good so I cut out the radio work and decided that was not for me. Even though I do not have much of a Boston accent, I had some sort of northeast tone in my voice that bothered me on the air because the people I tried to emulate had those perfect, Bob Costas-like voices. I gave good information and had some good interviews with players and coaches—which was a great learning experience for what I do now—but I did not speak clearly enough on a regular basis to be on the radio. They liked my work, but I was not satisfied with myself, and sometimes that is what is most important. I even stopped writing for the school paper thinking I did not have a career as a writer. I never thought I did because I was a slow deadline writer. It is funny because now I am known for my quickness on game days.

At that time I pushed a lot off my plate. By talking to my advisors and my parents I got into marketing, public relations, and that type of thing. I did fieldwork for the Cornell University football team in the fall of 1994 as a junior and it exposed me to all sorts of things. I was working with the sports information director, but at the same time on Cornell game days I worked for Prime Network. I worked with the legendary producer Chuck Howard, who won several Emmys at ABC Sports. I did pretty much everything. I worked for the broadcast sometimes and gave injury reports to Bruce Beck, who is now on TV every night as an anchor in New York City. I did not actually go on the air; I just gave them all the information. One day I did injury reports, and the next day I was on the sidelines letting teams know when they could come out from the locker room. Other times I compiled statistics in the press box or acted as a spotter. I was exposed the logistics of organizing an event from both the media side and the sports information side. Looking back, all this work was invaluable because, as a writer, I deal with sports information departments on a regular basis. It also heightened my interest in being a part of big events even though Cornell football is not a huge event comparatively. My first big break happened when I wrote a 40-page research paper with someone who actually works with me at ABC Sports. He was a year older than me. Our study looked at Native Americans and the impact Native American mascots have in sports. It was a comprehensive study that took a whole semester to complete. We contacted every NCAA Division I, II, and III school with a Native American mascot, as well as junior colleges and NAIA schools. We either interviewed their sports information director or asked the athletic department personnel to complete a three-page questionnaire. It was used by my professor and advisor, Dr. Ellen Staurowsky, and eventually caught the eye of Richard Lapchick at the Center for the Study of Sport in Society. The Native American mascot issue was something Richard had written about in columns for *The Sporting News* at the time. He tested me on my paper during an internship interview. I was offered an internship with the Center the summer between my junior and senior years of college, which set the tone for my entire career.

I started at the Center immediately after school ended that spring and was very excited to work on an educational initiative with the movie Hoop Dreams, an absolutely brilliant film. In my curriculum at Ithaca I had to not only view the film, but also write about and discuss it in classes like Social Aspects of Sport. I remember dragging my friends and my girlfriend at the time to the little independent theater in town to see the movie a bunch of times. Not only was I an avid moviegoer and sports fan, but also I understood and appreciated the ramifications behind it. This initiative was called Hoop Dreams and More. It was run by the Center for the Study of Sport in Society, and we worked in conjunction with the cast and directors. We created a playbook that was distributed to teachers around the country to use during a certain week in November 1995. That week ended up being kind of an official "Hoop Dreams Week" culminating in a big day when PBS broadcast the movie live at night. During the day at school, the teachers showed it and then they used the playbook to review many social and urban issues. Middle and high schools used the movie as a tool to talk about growing up and issues in urban life. It was a great way to convey a message to kids everywhere because Arthur Agee and William Gates were likeable and everyone could identify with them, regardless of class, race, or social status.

Whether it was about putting all of your eggs in one basket, hoping that you will be a professional basketball player, or the importance of education, family, or perseverance, people can learn several different lessons from the movie. In 12 different cities across the country the cast met with us to discuss the movie and use the playbook. About 500 kids came and we put together little celebrity basketball games with the Hoop Dreams people and some visiting professional ballplayers. In Boston we had Celtics great Jo Jo White and a couple of former Patriots and some of the people on our staff, like former Syracuse quarterback Don MacPherson who was the Heisman Trophy runner-up in 1987 to Tim Brown. We gathered the kids for a basketball tournament and then brought them into an auditorium, showed the movie, and broke into discussion groups. Usually we did it on the Northeastern University campus. The main one I was a part of was the first one there. We divided the kids into different rooms and the stars from the movie were there to talk not only about the movie but also about what they had done since and what they learned about it. Then we used the playbooks. For example, William might say, "You all know that part in the movie when the coach says this to me—has that ever happened to you? And how did you deal with it?" I found it to be an extraordinary way to reach kids, especially in cities. I was the media relations director for the whole operation. Any media that wanted to cover this event, get more information, or conduct interviews with William Gates, Arthur Agee, or anybody else in the movie, as well as Richard Lapchick, contacted me. I may have been in a little over my head at first because I had never done anything like it. The Center was a little bit understaffed. It is a nonprofit organization. It enabled me to take on great responsibility while still being in college. Overall it was an incredible experience. Getting involved that way on the other side of the media—made me think about being a writer. I thought about covering events and writing features because I always read what the local writers wrote about William and the program. I would constantly think, "Oh, I wouldn't have lead the piece like that" or "I'd have taken this angle."

What shaped my sports career path the most was working with the people I did at the Center, including Richard Lapchick and my immediate supervisor, Art Taylor. I mimic their actions to this day. I list Richard Lapchick at the top of my list of role models. I learned the most from watching him greet a person, talk on the phone, and write a letter. I try to fashion myself after him because of my enormous respect for him and his manner. The passion he keeps on a day-to-day basis is something I hope to have in 20 to 30 years. I still reread his books. It was great working for him in my first real professional environment. After the experience at Cornell and working for Richard, a lot of doors opened for me. I thank Richard for those opportunities. He is constantly listed in the "Top 100 People in Sports" and he went out of the way to help me. For example, out of the blue, he wrote a two-page letter to Ithaca College's president, James Whalen, whom he knew because they were both on the Knight Commission. Mr. Whalen then wrote me. It was kind of cool having our president write me a two-page personal note. It said that Richard was a close friend of his and how it made his day to get that letter because his students were a reflection on the school and ultimately him as president. It was an amazing boost to my confidence in the beginning of my senior year.

I knew there would be internships and other jobs. Most of the people coming out of Ithaca have a pretty good track record in the world of sports and return to campus to recruit students who did well. I was very careful throughout my senior year and worked especially hard at writing. I applied for graduate school at Ohio University, Ohio State, and West Virginia. They have the top graduate programs in my opinion. I went on interviews at all three and made the finals every time. My advisor, Ellen Staurowsky, told them I was one of our best, but I was not admitted into those schools and I was momentarily destroyed. I could not believe it because I thought I would be accepted. I had great references, did well in school, and I was coming out of a top school in the country for anyone looking to work in the sports industry. Looking back, I will admit that it put a chip on my shoulder. I still have those rejection letters and they drive me.

I had an internship with the Women's Sports Foundation, which was the best thing for me at the time. I went the day after the Ohio University rejection letter arrived and I will always remember that drive from Massachusetts to Long Island. I talked to myself the whole way. It was like a motivational speech after a blowout loss. I basically took the attitude of "OK, if that's the way it's gonna be, I'll just have to work 100 hours a week and live anywhere in the country under any conditions, because I won't bail out no matter what happens." I used the fact that I was the only man out of 30 women at the Foundation as an extreme case of my dedication because it put me in such a strange environment. It was a great place to work. It was the right place to intern because only 30 people work there yet they have a lot to do. There are people like Donna Lopiano, who is a legend in the industry. She is the president but I was around her all the time, working right with her and directly for her on many occasions. I would not have been exposed to situations like that in a big corporation. It was the same thing at the Center. Twenty people worked there and I worked directly with Richard.

The Women's Sports Foundation was another nonprofit organization and as the community relations coordinator I was the contact for 82 community action groups set up around the country by the Foundation. I kept in touch with those groups, sent materials to them, assisted with conference set-up and obtaining guest speakers, put them in touch with major women athletes, and helped them raise funds. I also wrote articles for their publication, the *Women's Sports Experience*. That was a great experience for me. I actually coached the softball team that summer and Donna Lopiano was my pitcher. She is probably the most famous softball player of all time, yet she was the one I gave the ball to and moved around the lineup. While I was working there, I actually got into Bowling Green State University with a fellowship. I was relieved and was ready to go there that January. At that point, I was in charge of all of the interns and was being paid a little bit more than when I started, which was next to nothing. I had a lot more responsibility and was going to do that through December and then go on to graduate school. Plus, I was working on the side with Ernestine Miller on a comprehensive book on women's sports that still has not been published. One of the women at the Women's Sports Foundation, Tracy Hawkins, got a job at ABC earlier that summer. I had worked for her. Once Tracy got to ABC, they were talking in a meeting about how they needed to add people quickly who knew what they were talking about and could write. Tracy brought my name up and said, "You know, this kid's only twenty-two, he's very young, but he majored in sport management and has more qualifications than people who are older, why don't we give him a look?" She contacted me the next day and I was ecstatic. I had an interview, but was not sure about my chances. It sounded like they wanted somebody older. They even said, "Hey, look, we're looking for someone with a bit more experience." Then I came in for a second interview. I knew I had nothing to lose. I was brought back one afternoon and was offered a position to begin immediately because college football had already begun. Tim Pernetti, now director of programming at ABC, wanted me on the staff because he knew I could write, was current on the college football season, was available right away, and would probably accept less money than someone older. I thought I was given a good deal.

I started here at the end of September 1996, just 3 months after I graduated. I moved from Long Island to New York City, where I still live. I was thrown into the fire immediately. At the time, we only had eight staff members and were publishing strictly on America Online (AOL). I was a junior producer. I covered college football on our college football area on AOL. At that point, only two people (including me) did the work for college football. It is amazing to think that now I have a staff of six employees for college football. I was doing everything from helping to make videos, doing interviews, writing pieces, to putting up recaps and coverage after the games. I did everything! I worked 80 hours a week, 7 days a week. I learned so much, not only about the Internet and computers but also about writing. After college football season I was asked to write a daily column, something new that needed to be done.

I was 22-years-old and started writing as a columnist, so I was pleased. It was an incredible learning opportunity because I had the freedom to try new things, whether they failed or found success. The first event I covered was the Super Bowl, which was great for me because I am a New England Patriots fan and they played the Packers. I was a little intimidated because I was down at my first Super Bowl in New Orleans, of all places. I learned a great deal there. I was there 11 days and spoke with many writers, including those I had admired for years at the *Boston Globe* and *New York Times* or people I met while interviewing a coach or player. I picked up many hints during those 2 weeks by talking to them, observing what they did, and studying how they covered the event. From that point I started writing every day under the pseudonym of Jocko. They wanted to have an old, weathered columnist who was a "fan's fan" rather than some punk kid, so I came up with the idea to use my dad's name, Jocko. They asked to see a picture of him, and when I showed them they kept saying, "Are you kidding? This is perfect." So, as weird as it sounds, I wrote as my dad at the start. My dad is this old former quarterback, point guard, and baseball pitcher. He is a big guy, and he fit the bill. It became one of the most popular sites on AOL, and my numbers were really good.

The number of people that came onto the Web site increased month to month until it took on a life of its own. I was relieved of my other duties and worked on the column full-time. Every day I reacted to what was happening and wrote a column in the first person, except it was really under the pseudonym of this person named Jocko. Not only did I write columns, but also readers were encouraged to e-mail me, so I received about 500 e-mails each day. It was crazy. I tried to return all the e-mails and I did fan pools. It got to the point that I was covering events. If the event was local, like that year at the Belmont Stakes when Silver Charm went for the Triple Crown, we had my dad go to the Belmont so we could take pictures of him there. I still cannot believe we did some of that stuff. In that first year alone I covered the Super Bowl, the Indy-500, the Belmont Stakes, the NFL Draft, the WNBA, Monday Night Football, college football, and college basketball. I also covered World Cup qualifying matches for the U.S. Soccer team because soccer was my best sport growing up and one in which I think I am an expert. I covered soccer using my own name, however.

Then in early winter 1998 I started writing mostly as "Marc Connolly" rather than "Jocko." We ended Jocko even though it was doing well because it limited me. I could not do a lot of things, because I was this older person. I couldn't be too hip in my references or analogies. I planned to write a lot for the World Cup so I stopped writing as Jocko in the summer of 1998. Now and then I would write a guest column as him but I covered the U.S. men's team all the way through the World Cup as myself. When late summer came, we started the Bowl Championship Series Web site. I became its main columnist, writing "Marc My Words," which I still do. I wrote a weekly column from August through mid January. It is at www.ABCCOLLEGEFOOTBALL.com on the Web and is now of the most popular college football sites anywhere. "Marc My Words" brought me some notoriety, I guess, at least from most of my peers.

I went to games and met people who read my columns. People out of the blue knew who I was and it was something that still floors me whenever it happens. As far as networking, it has been great for me. I received a lot of different job offers from newspapers and magazines at the end of that fall and right through the spring, yet I am still here. I give credit to my bosses at both ABC and ESPN for always upping the ante and giving me promotions to keep me. Seeing that type of commitment to my work means a great deal to me and I am loyal to both companies because of such treatment.

Not only did I write a column each week, but I was also ghostwriting for some of our announcers, including Keith Jackson, Brent Musburger, Jack Arute, Dan Fouts, and Lynn Swann. That was a great thrill for me. With Keith, we worked out a deal. We said, "Listen, we have somebody who writes for a living and will make it look good who will ghostwrite for you. All you have to do is speak with him for 20 minutes a week, then he will ghostwrite for you just like he was doing a book." I would call Keith and we talked about it and went over some things. Luckily, he liked me. We developed a pretty good friendship, where we would talk for about 45 minutes sometimes about life and other things besides football. He would talk about his grandkids and I would ask him about fishing and all his other hobbies. I was very proud to work with Keith last year because he is an amazing man. In addition, I did a lot of editing for our other writers. I probably covered about 11 games last year including the Rose Bowl, the Fiesta Bowl, the

Heisman ceremony, and most of the other big games that fall. I would like to think that I was one of the first writers on the Internet who had a regular beat and traveled to cover games the way they should be covered.

When that ended in January, I found out I won my first national award. Every year the National Soccer Coaches Association of America (NSCAA) chooses a best feature story for the year. It is a best feature story/game deadline, and the piece I wrote on Tab Ramos' comeback from knee surgery won. I received the award at a dinner at the National Soccer Coaches Convention in Philadelphia. I am still amazed because it beat out all of the stories from the World Cup. A lot of the top writers, in and out of soccer, from around the country were in France, so winning that award boosted my confidence. I do not talk about it much, but it is something I am extremely proud of, especially because I modeled my game after Tab Ramos when I was younger. I always wore No. 10, Tab's number. When he found out I won, I saw him at a media event and he congratulated me and signed a photo from the event I wrote about. I will always treasure that photo. Here is the man I admired as a soccer player growing up and to win an award with his name on it (the title was "Ramos Comeback Nearly Complete") was very special.

I covered college basketball all winter. A lot of my college football stuff last year started being picked up by ESPN.com on its college football area. As a result, many of my college basketball pieces were published on their site. I got a lot of readers because of it, which was great. Getting readers is all you can ask for when you write. ESPN.com by far gets the most hits of any sports site on the Web.

I also covered the Preakness and the Women's World Cup for ESPN.com one summer. I went to every game the U.S. women played including the final in Pasadena, California. I also covered the Tiger Woods/David Duval golf match on ESPN.com.

Ithaca College was great, and I like to help if I can. Dr. Staurowsky has given me students' phone numbers and I have called them and asked if I could help in any way. I talked to them and gave them advice. I know my classmates have done the same. Dr. Staurowsky and Dr. Blann are incredible people. They are both highly respected and hard workers. People at ABC Sports joke about the number of Ithaca graduates employed at ABC and ESPN. Three people in my department are Ithaca graduates. We are all proud of it. Many sport organizations know that Ithaca graduates are well prepared, and if one of our faculty members gives a strong recommendation, it is deserved. I think that is one of the reasons the program is successful.

Eventually I would like to move on to print, but not necessarily for a newspaper. I would like to write for a magazine doing features or columns like the back-page type of columnist Rick Reilly, one of my idols. I would love to be the back page writer. My best work has always been writing. I fashion myself after Reilly and Dan Jenkins, the writer Rick Reilly emulated. Those two writers are superstars to me. They are the Michael Jordans of sports writing. Realistically, I do not know if I could ever be a Dan Jenkins or a Rick Reilly, but it is my goal. For me, my future goals are not based on money or power. Call it simple, but I hope there will be a 12-year-old boy or a kid in college who asks someone every other day or once a week, "Hey, did you read Connolly this week?" To be on a name basis with readers everywhere is one of my goals. Another goal is to write a novel. If it comes up, I would love to do something like John Feinstein did in *Season on the Brink*, or what Darcy Frey did in *The Last Shot*. I want to expose something and bring an issue to light in the way they did.

The most enjoyable part of my job is game coverage. It is not so much being at the game, but the pressure involved. This sounds funny but as a former athlete I get the same feeling walking into the press box as I got walking onto the field. I really do. It is a rush. I have butterflies, but yet I have this "all right let's show them...time to go to work" type of attitude. The most enjoyable aspect is when I finish a pretty good piece and I know it will be viewed by a lot of people. That walk out of the stadium to my car when everyone has gone home, including the players, is one of the few times I pause, capture the moment, and feel good about myself for at least a minute. The rest of my waking hours I never seem to do that.

The least enjoyable aspect of my position is the lack of respect that sometimes comes because my work is on the Internet. Sometimes people think I am a young writer who does not know anything and is simply a computer person writing. The people who have seen my work and know who I am give me a tremendous amount of respect. The ones who do not and maybe just see an "online" attached or a ".com" attached to my work immediately have a preconceived notion of some techie sitting down in the basement writing on a Web page. This not only happens with the other journalists, but also with college sports information directors. It has gotten better over the past year and a half, however. Now when I say, "ESPN.com" or "ABC Sports Online" it carries more weight than it did 3 years ago because of the online explosion. Now we can call up on a day's notice and get an interview with Peter Warrick, Ron Dayne, or other big-name athletes without any trouble. That was not always the situation.

My typical day starts around 9:00 AM. I usually start by logging on to Sportspages.com. I have a link in there that is pretty cool. I usually read five or six different papers. I get a lot of information from the *Boston Globe*. I grew up in the Boston area so it is always one of those papers I read to get reactions from columnists like Bob Ryan or Dan Shaughnessy. I can read about some things that may not be on Sports Center or in *USA Today*.

From that point, if I am writing that day, if I have not had my interviews already then I am usually on the phone in the morning trying to line up an interview. If I am writing something that day, I may call a day in advance to try to get a player for the next day at noon so I can write my piece a day or two later. Then if I am writing I usually start around 11:00 AM. If something needs to be done by that day, and if the interviews are on time, I can usually finish by about 3:00 PM. Then I pass it on to an editor. We have a read-through editor first and then it is given to an editor who is good conceptually. He is a fellow Ithaca College graduate, Chris Corbellini. He understands how I write and he has helped me a lot. He knows what works for me and what does not work for me. A lot of times it ends up being collaborative. He will add to the story or delete some of it. He is excellent and someone I know will say to my face, "It works" or "You've had better days." Constructive criticism is important for what I do, so I always welcome and appreciate his honesty.

From that point it usually gets published and I look ahead for the next feature or next column. A number of meetings occur to discuss our game plan for an event. For example, for the Preakness we met about what I was going to write the following Friday and Saturday and what would be the best angle. I wrote a piece on Elliott Walden, the trainer for Menifee. When I do columns, I develop almost every idea. I may have an editor review it to see what he or she thinks but I have a lot of leeway.

During football season I work about 80 hours a week, especially with all the travel. Even during the times I am not working I spend a lot of time placing calls or working on my laptop in hotel rooms. I spend a lot of time on my cell phone. Outside of football season or when no huge events are occurring, I probably work 60 hours a week.

Advancement may exist if I want to get into management. I think I manage anyway because six people work for me. I have pretty much hit the top here as far as being a writer. My next move is either to another online site or another publication. Now that we are part of a new tracking stock, Go.com, and Steve Bornstein is our new president (formerly chief executive officer of ESPN, then president of ABC Sports and ABC, Inc.), our futures individually and as a group are very bright.

I like working for a network. It has been very enjoyable. I have had the best of both worlds and have done a lot of media things. At the same time I know how to organize an event and get involved in programming a little bit and see why certain shows/events/games get on television. Being here has its advantages, especially when I cover an event. I get TV credentials as well as media credentials, so it allows more access to me than other writers. For example, at the Heisman Trophy ceremony I was one of two writers in the room when Ricky Williams accepted the award. The rest of the national media were not on the same floor.

The growth of the Internet is truly amazing. When I first started here and told people my work was on AOL, they said, "What's AOL?" I would have to tell them America Online. Now most of the work I do is on the Web. It is amazing how many people—and not just my age either—use it as a tool and for enjoyment. My parents (my mom lives online) and people their age are Web savvy. Getting people online over a 3-year span is something we will look back on some day with wonder. I cannot imagine 10 years down the road. It is already becoming a part of our TV process. All of these TV projects are in the mix, with WebTV and others, so that access will be easy. Some day computer prices will be less expensive, almost like buying a telephone. It will take off! Once the expansion levels off, the sites that will remain are the ones with name recognition. That bodes well for ESPN.com as far as sports are concerned, especially with Disney behind us. Disney is into the Internet all the way from Michael Eisner down. They are excited to enter this whole initiative. In 10 years it will be a fabric of everyday life. Instead of walking into New York's hip coffee shops where they have online access, I picture walking into a diner in Yuma, Arizona, and getting online. That will help get everybody involved.

Just a couple of years ago, to use a computer required knowledge of a lot of coding and programming, but now programs are so easy that I learned a publishing program in 15 minutes. In a few years it will be very user-friendly. It will be like America Online where you can be a dummy and sign on and send e-mail. As far as working online, the skills required will not change that much. Creativity, an advertising background, being able to sell, and marketing savvy will be necessary for success.

The impact of the Internet is amazing. It has created a ton of new jobs for young people like myself who need a chance to prove themselves and how they can benefit a company. I may not have had a chance as a writer if online positions like this did not exist. I probably would be doing marketing or something related to it. Newspapers have to think differently now. They know these online sites will disseminate information to readers faster. I experienced this at the Preakness. I listened to these writers from the big dailies across the country who had to get things in to go on the Web site. They may not know how to even sign in online. Yet some of their stuff is getting online and *only* online in some cases because space is not an issue like it is in newspapers. If you only have 800 words a weekend going into the newspaper and the boss knows he or she can get another story from the writer because of his or her salary or duties, the boss will do that. I have seen newspaper articles go online a lot. The respect factor increases, especially if they see somebody from one of the network sites, such as ABC, ESPN, or Fox. We start to get respect from our peers, the sports information directors, and the leagues. Covering college athletics is great because college students are all online.

If I want to interview Donovan McNabb (former Syracuse quarterback), he will be more excited about talking to somebody from the BCS site or ESPN.com than he would to a daily that he does not get to read. Jobs are more competitive because people are going online. I have been lucky because I have had some offers for my online work, and I know some people in print have had offers to go online and make more money than they do in print. They had offers to go to some of the bigger Web sites to be the managing editor and also write a column and make a lot more money. I know some people who have made that move. At first the quality of online writing was not very good, but now they are hiring people out of school with journalism backgrounds and it helps the quality of writing. I know we only hire the top of the line journalism or sport management majors even for freelance positions.

I do not want to live in the city in 10 years because I do not want to be too hardened. I would probably like to move back to Massachusetts, perhaps to the Boston area, which is home for me. As much as I love New York City, I cannot picture raising a family here. There is nothing wrong with it, but it is not like the way I was raised. I want to still be writing. I would love it if I could live anywhere and e-mail my work to an office every day without going there. Being a telecommuter is goal of mine. I am pretty self-sufficient. I work very independently. Sometimes I come to my office and not talk to anybody and wonder why I commute because I do the work online. I hope by that point I will be good enough to pursue my dream of publishing a book, even if it is just for my family to read. I have always wanted to be published because of all the reading that I do.

I always had a lot of respect from friends and people I grew up with but a lot of people laughed at me when I said I wanted to degree in sport management. A lot of people still do because there is this notion that we go in and study Babe Ruth all day. People at college always made fun of my classes. My message is if you want to get into sports, just go for it. Work hard enough and do not get lazy in the summers. If you do not mind taking an internship and not making money it is worth it because there are many positions in sport. You just have to get in, suck it up, and make yourself indispensable to an organization. That is always what I tell people younger than me, even my sister and her friends, who just graduated from college.

It would have been easier to have another major. There were times I doubted myself because it was such a very small field. Sports information and communications were such narrow fields. Yet our degrees can be used in all walks of life. If I never went into sport as a career, I learned enough at Ithaca to pursue marketing, advertising, or information services at companies unrelated to sports.

CHAPTER 10

Sporting Goods and Licensed Products

THE SPORTING GOODS INDUSTRY IS A LARGE INDUSTRY segment encompassing a wide variety of opportunities and products. Within the sporting goods industry, products can be divided into several categories, including sporting goods equipment, athletic footwear, and sports apparel, as well as the area of licensed products. This industry segment has a rich history and continues to evolve from the sporting goods store on the corner to the fast-paced growth of e-commerce.

People working in sporting goods are employed in a number of settings. Jobs exist with major firms such as adidas, NIKE, Rawlings, or Easton. Sport managers with these companies can work as sales representatives or marketing executives. They could work specifically with sport lines, such as Rawlings Baseball Division or NIKE Golf. Opportunities are available in sporting goods stores, ranging from the small locally owned and operated store, to the one-stop-shopping big box locations like Sports Authority or Dick's Sporting Goods. Here there are job opportunities to own a franchise or work as a buyer who interacts with the before-mentioned major firms. In addition, the sporting goods industry has jumped onto the e-commerce trend, led by companies such as Reda Sports and fogodg.com. Sport managers here may be involved in securing new clients or designing Web pages. There are also specialized areas within sporting goods, such as the production of equipment for athletes with disabilities by companies like Flex-Foot or Quickie Wheelchair. This is also an area ripe for someone with an entrepreneurial spirit who may have a new product in mind, such as we have seen in the past with snowboards, aluminum baseball bats, or in-line skates.

The sale of licensed products is also a part of the sporting goods industry. These are products emblazoned with some type of logo or mark, whether a team name like the Atlanta Braves, a school name such as the University of Iowa, a NASCAR driver's image, or branded products that bear a company mark such as NIKE, FUBU, or Tommy Hilfiger. Again with companies that produce these types of products, there are jobs for people in marketing, sales, and design, as well as openings for those with a legal background interested in working with trademark and licensing law.

The sporting goods industry offers a little bit of everything in terms of career opportunities. One can work with small local companies or large multinational firms, focus on a single sport, work with licensed products, or be an entrepreneur. Depending on one's interest and skills, the job opportunities exist. In the sporting goods business in general, the front-line positions are in sales because most of the business is manufacturing. Most young sport marketing students would likely start in inside sales or marketing at a range of upper $20,000s to mid $30,000s. Advancing into a successful sales person would result in quickly getting to a six-figure salary after 2 or 3 years—that is, if the person is very good. It is more common for someone in the sporting goods area to make anywhere from $40,000 to $80,000 per year. For someone interested in working in licensing on a college campus, most of these positions begin in the mid $20,000s to lower $30,000s. Someone with 5 years of experience would likely earn in the upper $30,000s to upper $40,000s range, depending on the university.

Derek M. Eiler

Vice President, University Services
Collegiate Licensing Company

Education:
B.S., SPORTS MARKETING, BOWLING GREEN
STATE UNIVERSITY, 1993

Career Progression:
VICE PRESIDENT OF UNIVERSITY SERVICES,
THE COLLEGIATE LICENSING COMPANY, 1997
TO PRESENT

DIRECTOR OF UNIVERSITY SERVICES, THE
COLLEGIATE LICENSING COMPANY, 1995 TO
1996

UNIVERSITY SERVICES REPRESENTATIVE, THE
COLLEGIATE LICENSING COMPANY, 1994

UNIVERSITY SERVICES ASSISTANT, THE
COLLEGIATE LICENSING COMPANY, 1993

INTERN, WOOD COUNTY SPECIAL OLYMPICS,
1992

SUMMER INTERN, UNIVERSITY OF MICHIGAN
ATHLETIC DEPARTMENT, 1991

SUMMER INTERN, TOLEDO MUD HENS, 1990

Best piece of advice you received in regards to your career and from whom it came:

"If you cannot outsmart people, you can always outwork them."

DEBBIE ANTONELLI, FORMER OHIO STATE ATHLETIC MARKETING DIRECTOR

Best advice for someone aspiring toward a career in the sport industry:

**"Be willing to sacrifice short term rewards in order
to make long term gains."**

Quote by which you live:

The words of Desirada

I PROBABLY DECIDED IN JUNIOR HIGH SCHOOL that I wanted to be involved in sport management as a career. I was not a very good athlete, but I had a lot of interest in sports. The business side of sports always fascinated me. In high school, I wrote papers and did research about the business side of sports. I read a number of books about the careers of famous people in sports. I also participated in simple things like fantasy basketball leagues. All of these experiences got me interested in the management side of sports. At first, I also had an interest in broadcasting. When my dad was young he put himself through college as a sports writer. He used to tell me stories about going to great athletic contests and meeting many people who were involved with sports. But when I found out that an entry-level sports media job pays next to nothing, I decided that maybe broadcasting was not for me. Despite this, I remained focused on a career in sports.

Starting college at Bowling Green, I had aspirations to work in college athletics. Through my research, I realized my dream job was working as a marketing director in a college athletic department. I realized that an undergraduate degree was a definite prerequisite to start in sport management. I was a good student, but textbooks did not thrill me. I determined early on that I wanted to differentiate myself and make myself as marketable as possible. I decided to learn how to successfully market myself. I never worked for money in the summers. I would go into places and say, "I don't know if you have any money to pay me but I want to come in here and volunteer my services. I promise I will do a great job." There are not many people who will decline that kind of offer. I gave up short term dollars to gain long-term growth opportunities and experience that would help me market myself once I graduated from college. I made myself marketable by getting professional experience.

In 1991, the summer after my sophomore year at Bowling Green, I volunteered with the Toledo Mud Hens minor league baseball team. They had just hired a new director of marketing who was on a shoestring budget so he secured a staff of five or six volunteer interns for the summer. Fortunately, I was one of those interns. We did everything. I sold concessions and tickets, set up promotions, designed "Player Profiles" for the game programs, and wrote press releases. I even had the chance to dress up as the Mud Hen mascot one night. There could not have been a greater growth experience than that summer with the Mud Hens. I was thrown right in and given the chance to either sink or swim.

The following summer I volunteered with both the Great Lakes State Games and The University of Michigan Athletic Department. For the Great Lakes State Games, I was director of media relations. The Games did not have a whole lot of financial backing in the early stages, and they needed people. They basically said to me, "You're in charge of media. We don't know what to do, so you go figure it out." Through this experience, I learned more about media relations and sports information than I could have ever learned in a classroom. It was a great experience for a kid still in school. I had a real chance to be a "hero." I got the idea of being a "hero" from one of my professional mentors, Joe Napoli, the director of marketing for the Mud Hens. He always said that it is relatively easy to market the New York Yankees or Los Angeles Lakers. What kind of challenge is that? The real challenge is to join an organization where there is nowhere to go but up. It is hard for someone starting in a career to see that being able to turn around a bad situation can be where a person can leave his or her mark. Joe taught me this important lesson.

That summer I also volunteered in The University of Michigan Athletic Department. I grew up in Ann Arbor so I have always been a huge Michigan fan. The Department had already hired its paid interns for the summer, so they brought me in to be a "jack of all trades." I was primarily involved in event management for a major fund-raising event called the Hall of Honor Dinner. From the Michigan experience, I learned the importance of not falling prey to the saying, "We do it this way because we have always done it this way." On one specific occasion, we were pricing the costs of setting up the stage for the event. In the past, the cost for the stage was more than $11,000. I asked my supervisor if I could try to find someone to do it for a lesser price. He said campus union help had the first right of refusal, but he gave me the go ahead to see what I could do. I called around for 20 minutes and found someone to set it up for $3,000. What interns and students need to remember is that employers want them to think this way. They want you to uncover new opportunities. This experience taught me to challenge the status quo. Another important lesson I learned while at Michigan is that future college athletic directors are coming from the ranks of the people who can generate money. If you can market and sell, you will be in high demand. Today's athletic director spends his or her time generating dollars by calling on big donors and sponsors or putting together broadcast or Internet deals. The fastest route to the top spot in an athletic department is knowing how to sell.

Working for Wood County Special Olympics was another excellent learning experience during my time at Bowling Green. As a part of our academic requirements, we needed to complete a full-time internship for a semester. I chose to work for Wood County Special Olympics, which is located near Bowling Green. One of the best traits that you can ever learn in business is resourcefulness. Beyond any other experience, working for a nonprofit organization teaches you to be resourceful. In my role at Special Olympics, I raised several thousand dollars by hosting a 5-kilometer run. The community was behind the effort, and through good public relations, marketing, fund raising, and sponsorship programs, this event was a success for the organization. Although it was on a smaller scale, this opportunity gave me the ability to learn how to run my own business. From budgeting to purchasing to graphic design and event management, I did it all. The management of the Special Olympics organization was proud of this effort and I enjoyed interacting with many of the athletes in the program. If you can learn to be resourceful through working in a nonprofit organization, you will be more valuable once you start working in a for-profit organization.

Along with volunteering with sport organizations, I spent a great deal of time on career exploration while in college. I began this practice in high school. Rather than spending my lunch hour messing around in the hallways, I was at the career resource center trying to figure out what I wanted to do for a career. I searched CD-ROMs and databases in marketing, broadcasting, and media careers. In college, I did some research on careers during my freshman and sophomore years, but became more focused during my junior and senior years. I tried to keep a few hours open every afternoon to scan the *Sports Market Place*. This publication contains a wealth of information on contacts in the sports industry. The advantages of doing career exploration as a student is that you are "technically" not looking for a job. I developed my own database of organizations and contacts, and I started cold calling people from the database. I would call the contact person for an organization and say, "My name is Derek Eiler and I am an aspiring sports marketing person. If you have any time at all I'd love to spend five minutes with you on the phone and just get the benefit of your experience." I would try to build a relationship with the person rather than just firing off unsolicited resumes. I figured if I did send them a resume in the future, maybe they would associate my name with it. In eight out of 10 calls, people said they were not interested. However, two out of those 10 calls enabled me to become acquainted with some important people. Once we established a relationship, we would talk more frequently. They would tell me, "I heard about this job," "You'd be qualified for this," or "There's an opportunity coming up at this company." It was the start of my professional network.

My career exploration efforts, volunteerism, and development of a professional network led to my opportunity with The Collegiate Licensing Company. When I took the position at Michigan, I told the senior associate athletic director Fritz Seyferth that "I'll work for you for free this summer, but I would love to have a strong letter of reference at the end of the summer if you feel I have done a good job. Also, I would respectfully ask that you open your Rolodex and give me 10 names of people that you would be comfortable with me calling, using you as a reference point." At the end of the internship, Fritz gave me a great letter of reference and opened up his Rolodex. One name he gave me was Debbie Antonelli, who, at the time, was the director of marketing and promotions at Ohio State. I contacted Debbie and conducted an informational interview over the phone. An informational interview is a great "no pressure" way to build a professional contact. The fall of my senior year, Debbie visited Bowling Green and I spent some time talking to her. I also set up a time to visit her at Ohio State. From our meeting at Ohio State, she gave me the name of someone at the Collegiate Licensing Company (CLC) whom she knew from her prior job at the University of Kentucky (UK). While at Kentucky, Debbie worked closely with CLC on UK's licensing program. The contact that Debbie gave me at CLC put me in touch with the president of CLC. I sent a resume to the president, Pat Battle, and a few days later, I received a reply letter in the mail. The letter indicated that I should call him if I was ever in Atlanta. I called him and said I would be there in a few weeks to meet with him. I went to Atlanta and received an offer for an internship with CLC. I tried to play as much "hard ball" as a 22-year old could do and eventually, after a month of exchanging phone calls and letters, I turned the internship offer into a job offer. I packed up my car and headed south in June of 1993, one month after graduating from Bowling Green State University.

The Collegiate Licensing Company is a corporation that represents about 180 colleges, universities, bowl games, conferences, and other properties such as the

NCAA and The Heisman Trophy. CLC is responsible for signing license agreements with manufacturers and collecting royalties from licensed merchandise sales. CLC in turn pays the schools. Institutions like The University of Michigan or properties like The Heisman Trophy all have trademarks. Michigan has the block "M" and they have a trademark on the word Michigan and the image of a Wolverine. When T-shirt companies such as NIKE and Pro Player and video game companies such as EA Sports develop products with one of these logos, they must pay royalties. Royalties are typically charged as a percentage of their wholesale price. CLC licenses the school's trademarks, determines new ways of marketing merchandise, and ensures that bootleggers are not using the licensed marks without authorization. CLC operates very much like NFL Properties or NBA Properties in marketing and protecting the logos, intellectual properties, and trademarks.

CLC does not work with every college and university. The benchmark we use to determine whether we are interested in working with a university is $25,000 to $50,000 in potential licensing revenues. This benchmark is set to justify the time, expense, and resources it takes to start a licensing program with a university. Going lower than the benchmark makes it difficult for us to make money and for the university to make any money. We do have small clients that have very successful programs. These are typically smaller Division I colleges and universities. I receive sometimes two or three letters a week from junior colleges, Division III schools, or NAIA schools that I have to turn down respectfully. It just does not make sense to have a licensing program at a smaller institution. There is not enough retail demand for products of those universities. Protecting your trademarks is important, but starting a licensing program must be a sound business decision for the university and its licensees.

The benefit of an institution having a relationship with CLC is that there is a centralized focus. It is 180 universities all pulling in the same direction. The national buyer for a licensed product retailer in Dallas, Texas, does not have time to go out and deal with 180 schools around the country. They do have the time to deal with one organization that represents those 180 institutions. CLC represents Michigan, North Carolina, Penn State, and other larger and well-recognized universities so we offer a one-stop shopping approach. For an institution, it is not feasible to spend the money to hire a staff to replicate what we do. Schools are in the education business, not licensing business, so it is easier and more effective for them to hire CLC as a licensing expert to manage their program for them. The benefit for the manufacturers is when they pay their royalties to the licensor, rather than cutting 180 checks. We have 60 people on staff with 20 people in the licensing department that handles the relationships and the approval processes between the manufacturers and the universities. It is not an easy process but the manufacturers realize the benefits of working with one entity as they do when working with NFL Properties. We have systems and technologies to leverage the strength in numbers that we possess and the economies of scale that result.

When I came to CLC my title was university services coordinator. The position was a junior account manager. I had certain schools assigned to me by a university services representative that managed the accounts. It was my job to meet with them and get into the market and look for problems and opportunities for those schools. Next, I was promoted to university services representative for those schools when the representative was promoted to a director position in the company. I then took on the responsibility of developing more nonapparel opportunities like collectibles, trading cards, consumable products, and hard goods, and I gained the co-title of university services representative and marketing manager for nonapparel. In this position I spent about 15 percent of my time trying to find new dollars and new companies that could get involved and help us to sell more nonapparel products.

My next position at CLC was director of university services. At the time of the promotion, we probably had five university services representatives that all reported directly to CLC's president. We had about 45 people in the organization at that time and most reported to the president, so we put in a layer of managers for the first time in CLC's history. When I was promoted to director of university services, the remaining four representatives and coordinators started reporting to me. After about 2 years in the position of director of university services, which was then a division of the marketing department, the university services was established as its own department and I became vice president of the department.

In my position as vice president of university services, I oversee a staff of 13 people who serve as the main day-to-day contacts and account managers for the universities around the country. It is difficult to deal with 13 people and their day-to-day issues so we have three directors below my position. I now primarily deal with three people on a day-to-day basis. These three directors help to keep the department in unison. An effective manager has to be organized, diligent, and set a good example. The person also needs to stay focused on projects and provide direction for the department.

Although it may sound as if the road to my position was an easy one, I was discouraged at times and thought I was heading down the wrong career path. I felt this way about 3 months into my job with CLC. The management structure was not very rigid and organized and I did not receive much formal training. I remember one day asking, "What am I doing with my life?" I had packed up my car and moved to Atlanta. I had never lived in the south before. I had no idea what I was doing and no one told me what to do. I asked myself, "Why did I make this decision?" That night I thought a lot about it. The next day I came in and decided that I would just work hard and figure out what to do and how to get it done. The start of you career can be very frustrating. You are not making a lot of money and you have no vision of your future. From those times you learn to persevere. You also learn the value of hard work and that you have to "grab your own boot straps," pick yourself up, and make it happen. People are not going to feed you on a silver platter like in college or high school. It is up to you to figure out how things are going to get done.

Currently, four other departments are within CLC besides the university services department. The accounting department is responsible for accounting for and allocating all monies received on behalf of CLC. The legal and enforcement department enforces the trademark rights of the CLC member institutions and also approves and executes contracts. The licensing administration department is responsible for quality control, artwork and product approval, renewals, and customer service with manufacturers. If a person wanted to work for CLC, the licensing administration department would be the best department to start in because you learn about the core foundation elements of the business in licensing. The marketing department helps manufacturers, universities, and retailers expand the collegiate licensing business. Marketing has the promotions, public relations, and retail marketing divisions that focus on expanding sales for our universities and other members.

CLC is an organization that plays the role of an agent between the universities and manufacturers. CLC makes recommendations to the universities and then deals with the manufacturers for the universities. We may say to the University of Michigan or the University of North Carolina, "You do not need another T-shirt manufacturer. You have 20 companies making T-shirts. There is no need to divide sales up any further." Our recommendation would be to not license that company, but political factors sometimes come into play. The university might say, "Well this company is located in our town" or "It's an alum of the college, we have to be cordial to him/her." It becomes a political decision sometimes rather than a business decision. The NFL does not make decisions based on political factors so it has a leg up on the collegiate market. It is a challenge to deal with the politics in collegiate licensing, but you learn how to deal with the political influences.

Each of CLC's universities sets their own quality control standards. It is CLC's responsibility to enforce them. If Michigan does not want to license products in the color green because they do not want people thinking it is a Michigan State product, this is set in the standards. If the licensee submits for approval a Michigan product in green, we will inform the licensee that it does not meet the standards and it must be resubmitted in the colors set by the standards.

The enforcement side is more cut and dried. A lot of unlicensed manufacturers try to make a "quick buck." They create the products and ship them to nomadic bootleggers that go from the George Strait concert to the Super Bowl to the U2 concert to the NCAA Final Four and then the NBA Finals. The majority of the products come out of New York City, Dallas, Chicago, or Los Angeles, and they are shipped overnight to these nomads. We work with local police authorities to seize the bootlegged products. The authorities arrest and charge these people, and they also seize product, vehicles, and cash. Our legal department also helps to pass stronger laws to give us more strength in protecting universities through enforcement efforts. Enforcement is one of the most important benefits we provide universities and licensed manufacturers (licensees). Every year we seize thousands of products from the market, which creates a huge positive impact for those licensees that play by the rules. Through our enforcement efforts, universities have eyes and ears in virtually all 50 states. It would be difficult and expensive for a university to send their licensing director to the Final Four every year or to pay enforcement officers to look for unlicensed products all around the country. We can handle this very easily. CLC may have four schools that have agreements with CLC in the Final Four plus the NCAA, so we can really have a much greater impact.

While we stay busy year-round, there are two peak times in our business. One is in December, with the bowl games, and the other is in March when the NCAA Basketball Tournaments are played. For example, in 1998 we had done a month worth of work getting ready for either UCLA, Kansas State, or Ohio State to play in the Fiesta Bowl for the national championship against Tennessee. The scenarios that retailers and licensees thought were going to play out took a turn when Ohio State lost to Michigan State late in the season, Texas A & M then beat Kansas State, and Miami beat UCLA on the same day in December. All the work that we had done was useless. Not only was the national championship game impacted, but also all of the other bowls. Once the teams changed in the Fiesta Bowl, everything was realigned below and we basically had to start over again. Schools who thought they were going to one bowl were now going to another. We had less than a month to get new designs approved and new contracts signed. It was absolute bedlam trying to get ready.

External factors have a huge impact on our organization. In the case of Kansas State football, we worked for months and months, actually for years, believing 1998 was going to be the year in which they would compete for a national championship. We were planning promotions and new products for Kansas State, and then they lost a game that prevented them from going to the national championship game. The work we did with Kansas State was not completely wasted because Kansas State learned how to prepare for its next national championship opportunity. We will be even more prepared next time.

In our relationship with institutions that seek a national championship, we provide advice on which companies are best to work with. We will say, "Here's a great company that can do commemorative prints" or "Let's go to Coca-Cola or Pepsi-Cola and get a commemorative bottle deal done." We have represented 13 out of the past 14 NCAA champions in basketball and the past seven consecutive national champions in football. We provide the experience for an institution that has never been to a national championship. The challenge for our universities involved in the men's and women's NCAA basketball tournaments is that there is such a short sales window. It is 3 or 4 days between the time a team wins its conference championship and the first round games of the NCAA Tournament. Teams advancing to the "Sweet 16" also only have 3 or 4 days and the same applies to teams going to the Final Four. In the case of the "Sweet 16," manufacturers have to produce a shirt with all 16 teams on it and they are sold in the local areas of the teams as well as the regional sites. In this scenario, the royalties get divided 16 times by all the schools that appear on the shirt. Schools will see an increase in their general merchandise and they will receive great national publicity, but the direct revenue impact on the program is probably less than what you would expect. The tournament comes and goes before you know it. In regards to the Final Four, we try to project what teams will be there months in advance and get those schools prepared for the opportunity. Licensing is an ongoing process and we always want to have a stable foundation. In the case of a Cinderella team (Gonzaga in 1999) or a perennial contender (Duke), you can capitalize on these opportunities. For example, in women's basketball in 1999, everyone predicted that Tennessee would win its fourth consecutive NCAA title. Tennessee lost and Purdue won the championship. You just never know.

The most demanding aspect of my job is trying to control the uncontrollables. In our business, we attempt to determine what the next trends will be. "What will be the next popular product?" and "Where is the entire industry going?" are questions we must try to answer. Over the past 5 years the market for college merchandise has been flat. The market grew from 1981 up to about 1993 and it has been flat since then. The overall revenue has remained stable in the $2.3 to the $2.5 billion range (at retail). Revenues for the licensed sport products as an entire industry is around $13 billion. The reality is that the licensed product companies such as NIKE and Zephyr and retail chains such as JCPenney's look at licensed products as a whole category. So when a JCPenney buyer sees that Major League Baseball licensed products sales are down 40 percent because of a strike or that the NBA lockout has caused the buyer to cancel $200 million in orders, that has a negative impact on the licensed product category. Even though colleges are up 10 percent, the NFL may be up 5 percent, and the NHL may be up 20 percent, with the NBA being down 40 percent and Major League Baseball being down 60 percent, it makes the overall market down. A retail buyer thinks the sky is falling in and looks to get out of the category. We are tied to the success of the professional leagues and the leagues are tied to us. We would like for everyone to be healthy so the schools and the professional teams can make money and everyone is happy. The advantage we have is the passion for the collegiate experience and the loyalty that college fans have for their alma mater. Labor problems in the professional leagues have eroded some of their fan loyalty in recent years. Fortunately, this is not a problem for colleges.

In my position, I use a wide range of management skills to succeed. My position involves communication; personal, conceptual, and technical skills; strategic planning; decision making; and delegating. Another management skill that is important is the ability to deal one-on-one with people. About 90 percent of my time is dealing with those people who report to me, but I also deal with others inside the organization as well as clients. Management of your clients is vital. I try to help them adjust or set their expectation level. From a management perspective, I try to lead by example through hard work and through being extremely well-organized. Actions speak louder than words in management.

Face-to-face communication is vital to motivating your employees. Those reporting to you do not want to hear about a big deal by e-mail. They want to hear about it from you and be a part of things and be motivated by that personal interaction. This lesson is easier said than done. It is much easier to sit down and fire off an e-mail than to deal with someone one-on-one, especially if the situation is not a positive one. Strategic planning is also very important, yet very challenging in the licensed product industry. I can plan for 50 percent of what will happen, but for the other 50 percent, I have no idea what will occur. New schools may come along, the market may change, and staff may leave. These unforeseen occurrences in our business are difficult to predict. But it is important from the big picture perspective to always have some core goals and strategic plans to help you determine how close you are to achieving the goals.

Sixty percent of my job entails personal skills, 30 percent involves conceptual skills, and only 10 percent involves technical skills. The personal skills involve dealing with the people I supervise. I help them become better at their jobs. Conceptual skills involve trying to envision the "what if" scenarios. If we sign this university, what will the impact be? If we add a new service, what will the impact be on our universities? If we decide to raise prices, what will the impact be? I also try to project what the potential responses of clients will be to scenarios to prepare appropriate answers before being asked. Finally, conceptualization helps to organize the internal structure and direction for the company. CLC needs to know where it wants to be in 3 years and what it will take to get there. In my role, I need to help chart CLC's future.

Preparation and information are probably two keys to making good decisions. Another is "gut feel." Having access to information comes from being organized. By having organized information, you are prepared to think about scenarios and to make decisions about possible outcomes. Before making the final decision you have to ask yourself how you feel about a decision. Is there anything nagging me that makes me feel like we should not do this? If I have enough information and if my instinct feels right, I will make the decision.

From a management perspective, I always tell my staff to bring me solutions, not questions, if they want to advance. I am not saying questions are wrong, but I want them to come to me and say "Derek, I have a question and here are the four answers I have for it. I think that choice B is the best." Nine times out of 10 I am going to say, "Well you thought it out more clearly then I ever would have, you're right, go make that decision." Challenging and empowering your employees to approach you with answers instead of questions is how I like to manage them from a decision-making standpoint.

A person interested in working in this field can expect to work long hours. Also do not expect too much too soon. It is virtually impossible for us to hire any-body other than in an entry-level position because we are in such a niche market. The business relationships we cultivate and the services we provide are unique. CLC has 60 people that know service and know how to cultivate relationships. It would be very hard for someone to walk in here and start "doing what we do." So for somebody who has aspirations of being in this business, I would tell them to come in at the ground level, be willing to work for a few years at that level, and to learn, absorb, listen, and ask questions (and eventually provide answers). They need to gain as much knowledge as they can before they move up in the organization.

The way we manage licensing for universities is much different than the way the NFL or anybody else does it. The NFL has exclusive contracts and has the ability to make multimillion deals. The NFL tells a manufacturer it has the exclusive rights to produce the authentic apparel under the "Pro-Line" authentic label. That manufacturer is the only one able to make the official team jersey. We work with nonexclusive license agreements; therefore, our job involves more account management, account maintenance, and enforcement and not just closing deals. Nonexclusive means the University of Florida may have license agreements with a number of manufacturers that can create licensed apparel. Florida's athletic department may have a corporate supplier agreement with a company that produces the uniforms for the athletic teams, but the licensing is separate. In the collegiate market, NIKE deals with Michigan, North Carolina, and Duke or their respective athletic teams from a supplier standpoint. They then come to us to get the retail license to produce merchandise to sell at retail. Champion could make a Michigan jersey. The football team is not going to wear it because NIKE has those rights, but Champion, as well as a lot of other companies, produce Michigan jerseys and sell a lot of them.

I love being involved with college athletics in a private company. The demands are different from working in a college athletic department but plenty of benefits are associated with my position. I like the incentive of generating revenues for a for-profit company. I believe we have more resources than universities that are often hampered by bureaucratic policies and procedures. Many of the decisions they make are based on politics and not always on sound business principles. I also enjoy the travel part of my job. I grew up as one of seven kids, and a trip for our family was to drive an hour away and go to a petting zoo. With seven kids, you cannot afford to do more than that. With my position I have traveled to 42 of the 50 states. Another benefit is that my career requires me to keep up-to-date on the sports world. When I say, "I read the sports page for business," that is an honest to goodness statement. Whether or not UConn is winning has a real affect on our business. I read the transaction page every day to see who is going where within the college administration level because it is also important to our business. I have attended some great college games. I have been to big bowl games, the Final Four, the great stadiums, and the huge rivalry games. I have been very fortunate to experience these wonderful opportunities.

As far as job satisfaction, I am very satisfied with my current job. I seize opportunities and solve problems. By taking that kind of initiative, you grow professionally. I am also very satisfied with my coworkers. CLC is a young and energetic organization. Many on our staff are around the same age and that creates an enjoyable environment to work in from a teamwork and a friendship standpoint.

I have benefited from having mentors during my career and I recommend people entering the sports industry to acquire mentors. If you do not have good mentors along the way, it is hard to envision the type of professional you want to be. It is important to have multiple mentors because if you pattern yourself too much after one person, you will have a hard time building your own identity. In every professional relationship opportunities exist to absorb some of the good traits from every person you meet. If you meet someone who is good with people and who makes people feel good about themselves; you may want to grab a hold of that part of their personality. If you meet someone who knows how to sell, you may want to use their techniques. If you meet someone who is a dynamic public speaker, you may want to adopt their public speaking strategies. One of my mentors was Joe Napoli, the director of marketing for the Toledo Mud Hens. Joe was a very driven guy and he believed in what he did for the Mud Hens. The biggest thing I learned from him is that he knew that he could really make a name for himself by turning a loser into a winner. Another mentor, Fritz Seyferth at Michigan, always had a lot of balls in the air but when you met with him on a certain topic he was very focused on that issue. He blocked everything out and focused on making a decision. He also had a great deal of charisma. He was the kind of guy you just wanted to be around.

I am not quite sure where the licensed product industry will be in 10 years. A lot of volatility exists in the market. I would hope that colleges and universities continue to realize what can be achieved through market consolidation and synergy. Everyone being on the same team and consolidating into one organization is CLC's vision for the future. We are working toward that and have made a lot of progress in the past 5 years. Ten more years of hard work and I think we will have a shot of meeting that goal. Just recently the University of Miami (FL) came on board and in the past few years we have signed Penn State, Florida, Texas, Syracuse, Northwestern, Oklahoma, Texas Tech, Stanford, and Missouri. A few big schools conduct licensing on their own, but not many.

There is definitely growth potential in hard goods and upscale products. The problem is that apparel has always been the category that has driven the ship, but sales are hurting now. First and foremost, this can be attributed to fashion trends. Kids are wearing Timberland, FUBU, and Mecca and other crazy brands that have popped out of nowhere. What is "fashionable" is an uncontrollable factor in our business. If I could control it, I would have retired a wealthy man by now. The other factor is that after 15 years of people buying collegiate product, closets are filled with Alabama, Nebraska, and Florida State sweatshirts. The quality and selection of the products has increased over the years, so people will automatically keep buying collegiate products forever. We must have new ideas and creative designs to satisfy current customers and attract new ones. This is among our greatest ongoing challenges.

When I was in college I thought a great deal about my career aspirations, but I have not really thought about it recently. It may be because I love what I do. The Litmus test that I use is when I am on a plane and the person next to me asks me what I do. I say enthusiastically that "I am coming from a meeting at The University of Arizona, and now I am on my way to the Michigan/Ohio State football game." They then proceed to tell me that they are on a 12-hour flight back from Taiwan where they just closed a deal for 1 million widgets. All things considered, I am pretty pleased with where I am and that conversation on the plane keeps things in perspective. My quality of life is good, business is great, and CLC is a fun organization. I could work at CLC for the next 60 years. I would have a hard time going into the university environment after working in a private company for 6 years. I would like be an adjunct professor and that would probably be secondary to my current career. As far as growing as a manager, I have considered taking some evening classes in management and trying to broaden my financial and accounting skills. Professionally, I try to focus on gaining new experiences. I always tell my directors to take things off my desk because that will help them learn. I try to do the same with the president and chief executive officer of the company. I say, "Let me take that, because if I can free up your time, you can go do bigger deals and generate more revenues." Taking on new challenges is how I have grown professionally, but I still have a lot to learn. I have a clear vision about where we need to go; now we just need to work smarter and harder to get us there.

Joshua Mohlmann

Director of Service and Support
REDA Sports Express

Education:
B.S., SPORT MANAGEMENT, ALLENTOWN
COLLEGE OF ST. FRANCIS DE SALES, 1998

Career Progression:
DIRECTOR OF SERVICE AND SUPPORT, REDA
SPORTS EXPRESS, AUGUST 1999 TO PRESENT

KEY ACCOUNT EXECUTIVE, REDA SPORTS
EXPRESS, JUNE 1998 AUGUST 1999

Best piece of advice you received in regards to your career and from whom it came:

"Good things come to those who work hard."

MY FATHER

Best advice for someone aspiring toward a career in the sport industry:

"Dark Suit, Light Tie."

I FIRST STARTED THINKING ABOUT A CAREER IN SPORT in junior high school. I have been a sport enthusiast who played sports from age 9. I played everything: soccer, football, basketball, golf, tennis, and so forth. I earned 12 varsity letters in high school. I figured I would probably get a job in sports so I started looking at colleges early. I knew from an early age that I would go to college, so my main concern was to decide on an area of focus. When I started looking at colleges I wanted to stay relatively close to home. I looked at several colleges but none of them fit my needs. I chose Allentown College because it was close to home and offered a sport management degree.

I was too busy with sports and academics. Starting in college I was a computer instructor for kids in kindergarten through third graders, and I was a substitute teacher. My first sport-related activity outside of being a player was to coach. My brother is 7 years younger than I am. I coached his 13-year-old all-star team with my father. For 3 years during college I coached the freshman basketball team at my high school. I was co-director of a regional Babe Ruth league tournament. I did everything including scheduling, finances, door-to-door donor solicitations, coordination of umpires, and field maintenance.

My first internship was at my high school with the athletic director. I helped with scheduling and taught him how to use a computer. While I was there they started a women's soccer team and it needed a coach. My major task was to develop questions for an interview, call the people, and set up interview times. I sat in on the interviews and had a vote as to who was hired. Being a 19-year-old kid and helping to choose your high school soccer coach was neat. That internship provided great experience.

Next I interned at Lehigh University in the athletic office under Karen Adams, the associate athletic director. I worked with team rosters, did some budgeting, and attended every meeting she did. She taught me a lot. Then second semester, I interned at Lafayette College. I worked under the associate athletic director, Dr. Bruce McCutcheon. Unlike Lehigh, at Lafayette I did game and facility management for the basketball teams. I also attended meetings and helped with NCAA compliance.

I graduated from Allentown College in 1998. I immediately took a job managing a sporting goods store and hated every minute of it. I could not do anything right and hated working with the public. As that was going downhill I got a call from Scott Reda, the chief executive officer at Reda Sporting Goods. While I was in college I sent him a letter and a resume. He called me and said, "Why don't you come in and we'll talk." We had a laid-back interview, and he said, "If you want a job it's yours." On Friday I was managing a sporting goods store and on Monday I became a key account manager at REDA Sports.

REDA Sports Incorporated is broken into three divisions. The first division, REDA Sports Express, is a distributor for 65 of the leading sporting good manufacturers, including Wilson, Rawlings, and Easton. Our customers are the retailers, such as Sports Authority, Dick's Sporting Goods, or Sam's Sports Shop in some little town somewhere. We buy in bulk from Easton at discounts, add a profit, and sell the product to retailers. As a retailer, sporting goods can be purchased in two ways, either directly from a manufacturer or through a distributor. Buying directly from the manufacturer results in great pricing, but there are minimum orders. A small store would need to buy $5,000 worth of Easton bats to be able to buy from Easton. The small retailers cannot afford that, so they go to a distributor like REDA Sports. We have no minimum order requirement. We ship the same day so retailers receive orders within 2 to 3 days. Retailers will pay a little more to have the exact product they need in a couple of days. They do not have to pay $5,000 at Easton, $5,000 at Louisville, and $5,000 at Weston. A $15,000 bill would be spent on only three vendors. Reda has 65 vendors and no minimums. Give us a call, order before 3:00, and the product is gone that day. That is our niche.

The second division of REDA Sports Incorporated began when Scott Reda decided to buy his own brands, be his own manufacturer, and vendor. For example, he bought Patrick Soccer, Zett USA, the Louisville Slugger Apparel license, and a couple others. They are our proprietary brands. Our newest acquisition is Sergio Tachini. It is a high-end Italian tennis and golf apparel line. In this division, we are not a distributor anymore, but we are a manufacturer.

I have become responsible for the third division called RSG Interactive, and it is total e-commerce fulfillment. Consider the REDA Sports Express fulfillment discussed earlier. Put a new spin on it, and now any e-commerce site can come to us and instantly have 50,000 pieces of equipment on their site the next day.

As a key account manager, I worked by the 80/20 rule: 80 percent of your revenue comes from 20 percent of your accounts. Those 20 percent accounts were mine to ensure their contentment and generally be available to them. The key accounts want to be important, and somebody at REDA needs to reinforce that feeling. That was my job. Many of my hours were spent holding the phone to my ear while a customer yelled and complained about not receiving a shipment. I just had to say, "I'm so sorry. What can we do? What can I send you free? It'll never happen again, and so on." I also formulated and authored marketing and sales plans for each selling season. The account managers and execs anticipated accomplishments for the quarter. We also discussed appropriate programs and discount packages for each account.

I started as a key account manager and did that from July 1998 to September 1999. A significant portion of that job was cold calling new accounts or calling old accounts that were inactive. I would ask them, "How are you? What can I get for you? Why don't you use us anymore?" At the same time I called active accounts to develop and promote positive relationships. That is called relationship marketing. I might call and they would say, "I don't really need anything right now but thanks for calling." Now REDA would hopefully be the first to come to mind the next time they needed some product. I did a lot of calling, but I did not care for it.

In September 1999, I was promoted to director of service and support for RSG Interactive. My key responsibilities are development of new relationships, and I also search for people who currently sell sporting goods online. Some sites such as Value America sell computers. That is the product recognition of the company. They have tons of traffic at their site. Why not sell sporting goods?

Once we get commitments from these people I act as a public relations agent and walk them through the different areas of our business. I need to make sure packing slips and invoices are developed with their image, have all of the text they want, and make sure everything is ordered on time. I need to make sure the warehouse is in sync with the site's needs. When we get an order I coordinate it from start to finish and make sure it is done correctly. We are important to these Internet sites. The consumer's experience starts on their site with customer service and ordering and it ends with us when the product is received. If we are not doing our job it makes the site look bad. They need repeat customers, and we need to do everything we can to ensure the customers are satisfied with their order.

My biggest role model growing up was my high school basketball coach. His name is William Pensyl. From the time I was 11 playing basketball in fifth and sixth grade, he was always near. He was there as a coach but he was more to me. He often pulled me aside to see how everything was going. Every step of the way in junior high basketball he was there, constantly watching me, checking on my behavior and schoolwork, and meeting with me. As a kid I experienced the raging hormones, dating, and fights and he pulled me aside, put me in his office, and said, "Now really think about this." He talked me through it and left the choice with me. "It's your choice, but make sure you think about everything." As a freshman he put me on the varsity team where I did not know anybody. Where I am from, seventh, eighth, and ninth grades are in their own school. As a ninth grader I played varsity basketball with tenth, eleventh, and twelfth graders. Halfway through the year I started and there was a lot of animosity. He guided me through every obstacle, but it was not only basketball related. He taught me about responsibility and class. I am from a very backwoods, slate quarry town in Pennsylvania. He had rules such as mandatory tie, button down shirt, jacket or sweater, and dress pants. You sit together as a team, you leave at halftime as a team, you do everything as a team, and you act like adults or you do not play or be part of the team. He held us to high standards. When I played for him even if we lost by 20 points, he was pleased with the team's effort. I could go to practice the next day and know it was all right. We as players always wanted to win for him more than for ourselves. I learned some good life lessons from him. He was just a great person.

If I would have done anything differently in my short career I would have gone for my master's degree right after undergraduate school. You have probably heard this a zillion times. I was so excited to be done with school and I wanted to make some money so I did not consider getting my master's degree. I wanted to graduate, start work on Monday, have cash in my pocket, and not have to ask Mom and Dad for $20 to go buy a hat or something. I did not want any more tests, papers, or projects. "Let's get on with life and see what it's all about" was my attitude. Well that attitude lasted a few months. In retrospect, I should have gone to graduate school. I am only 24 years old and I have plenty of time to pursue a master's degree.

The best thing about my job is I do not know what is going to happen when I get up in the morning and go to work. I do not know who is going to call me or who is going to be our next big e-commerce partner. I do not know who I will call, what kind of orders will come through, and what kind of problems will arise. Some people would not like that at all. It makes my day go quickly because I do not know what will happen. My least favorite part is that enough hours are not in the day to get things done that need to be done and are expected to be done. The holiday season is the hottest time on e-commerce. My average day lasts 12 hours. The next morning I still have a pile of paperwork to go through and calls to make. That is tough especially now because I am married and we have a little baby.

There is stress with this job. I talk to people all day, listen to all sorts of problems, and have several bosses pulling me in different directions. I do not do anything physical; I just complain. Then I am done and I move on. I get over it and it is not a big thing. Nothing at work is worth stressing over when you look at the big picture.

I use a number of personal skills in this job. There is a lot of selling and communication. I got into this role because of my computer skills. These days every college kid surfs the net and knows how to use Excel and Microsoft Word. I was one of the few employees who had Internet experience. Early on I saw the e-commerce potential. We started with only one or two of these e-commerce clients and now have nearly 25. It is amazing because it is exploding. Communication is probably the most important skill I need in my job. I communicate with people at their level. Some of my clients are MBAs whereas some have only a high school education. I need to relate and communicate with every one.

My internships were important to me. For 4 years learning is based on books, and the professor talks and talks and talks. You read along in your book, and you do little projects here and there, but those 4 years of school could be compacted into 1 year of internship. You learn so much when you are on your own. At least in my experience, I had somebody over my shoulder at the beginning, explaining the position and expectations. You either sink or swim. I learned so much responsibility. I interacted with athletic directors, assistant athletic directors, and sports information directors. These are key people in a college community. They come to you to ask you to do something, even if it is "Can you fax this for me?" Sure, I will be the best "faxer" I can be because it pays off in the long run. Those people watch you during the internship and some day you may ask them for a job. It is all about networking.

The sporting goods industry is technologically backward. Many retailers do not have fax machines, e-mail, or Internet in their stores. It is very "old school." The people who run these stores are 60-something people who know each other across the country. They do not take kindly or easily to e-commerce. They perceive e-commerce as a threat. Once they learn that Reda Sports Express has anything to do with the Internet, these people will bang on our door and say, "You're our competition." They cannot conceptualize that we are not competing with them. They do not understand. It is foreign to them.

Here is an example. Our chief executive officer was in a meeting with the number two gentleman from a leading manufacturer, and our CEO said, "Who is doing your Internet fulfillment?" The gentleman said, "Scott, the Internet is a fad, it will be gone in less than a year." That is the number two person from a pretty successful sporting goods entity! People are scared of the Internet in the sporting goods industry. They need to open their eyes to the reality of the Internet.

Right now the trend is that every person who has a new idea is going to sell stuff online and be successful. You can sit in your house at your computer, develop your site, and sell sporting goods. We have a partner who does that. Sitting at my home computer I can go to them, and they authorize me to launch a web site. I develop it, pull products from their database, and they tell me the selling price. If somebody buys it from me, we split the profit. It is a great idea, and if you have time, you might as well do it. You have nothing to lose. What many of these people learn is that it takes millions of dollars to be successful and compete with the top sites. I think e-commerce will continue to evolve. Ten years from now a few top sites will emerge from the competition happening now to be one of them.

Providing a "one-stop shop" service will be most attractive to consumers. The top sites will be whoever can bring the most service and get that idea communicated on their page. It is not about price. It is about the whole "e" experience from start to finish. It is about customer service, timeliness, and quality of information. There is a line there. When too much information is provided, the customer says, "Heck with this, I'm going to go somewhere else." If not enough information is provided, a customer wants to know more, but does not want to call customer service. Price is lower on the list of importance. Between sites the pricing difference is pennies, which will not matter that much to the customer.

I think future managers will have to be tuned in to every area of technology. I do not know anything about data transfer, the FTP, ASCII files, or computer languages. It pains me when somebody asks me a question that I cannot answer. I hate saying, "I'll have to put you through to so-and-so." I want to answer everything. Maybe that is just me, but I want to say, "You need it, come to me." That may be a reality in less than 10 years.

As far as career opportunities for people in e-commerce, anybody can sell products or services on the Web. It is a matter of finding the right niche. Some sites sell only sporting goods, such as FOGDOG and CBS Sportsline. However, Value America and Buy.com get tons of traffic through selling computers. Now they are going to sell sporting goods and hope a percentage of that traffic will go to sporting goods. Then the team dealer markets to teams and buy in bulk. It is very fragmented and finding that niche is the key. I think there will be many jobs in the future. For every site that folds, two more will emerge. They will need people with marketing, advertising, and computer programming skills.

In contrast to what I am doing now, once the dollar signs get out of my eyes, my goal is to someday be a high school athletic director, which was my goal in college. Maybe I am striving for something I enjoy wholeheartedly. I would like to go back to school, get certified as a teacher, and then start looking at high school athletic departments. Slowly but surely those positions are becoming full-time jobs. I had such a great experience in high school; those were the best days of my life. They say college is but I had a blast in high school. I love high school sports and I know from our athletic director how to do things. I like that environment where you know every student athlete and attend every game.

I do not consider myself successful, but I have gotten a good start. When I move on from here I will have a great base. That foundation comes with responsibilities and from the experiences of doing different jobs in the 18 months that I have worked here. I have tasted every aspect of it, and I am confident that I can do just about any one of them. I am still learning on the job and how to be a manager. I am learning about delegation. I have a hard time relying on other people to do a job as well as I can. It is hard for me to part with a stack of orders on my desk. That is one of the hardest things for new managers to learn. It is also hard to be responsible for other people's actions. I am still learning and trying to grasp this concept. In life you are taught to worry about yourself. It does not matter what Johnny or Susie does, worry about yourself. Your responsibilities are defined. In the corporate world, you become responsible for Johnny and Susie, as well as the people who Johnny and Susie supervise. If they make a mistake, now as the manager, it is my responsibility, even though I had nothing to do with it. The first time I got reprimanded for somebody else's mistake I was dumbfounded. I had to think about it a long time and figure it all out because it was hard for me to understand. "I did my job correctly, she did not, so you should yell at her, not me." It does not work that way, so that is tough. Another thing young managers must learn is how the chain of command works. There is a defined chain of command. You have a boss. That boss has a boss, and you never go around him or her, even if you know your boss is clearly wrong.

I sound old when I say "work hard in school" because there is plenty of time to play. Get your schoolwork done, do those internships, and build networks. Meet as many people as you can, be polite, be helpful, ask questions, and volunteer as much you can in school. You never know who in your developing network will be impressed enough to hire you or recommend you for a position. You know how I met Scott Reda? He first became part of my network when I taught his children as a substitute teacher!

Tracy Y. Royal

Public Relations Manager
AND 1

Education:
B.S., PLANNED STUDIES: LABOR RELATIONS IN
SPORT, ITHACA COLLEGE, 1998

Career Progression:
PUBLIC RELATIONS MANAGER, AND 1, OCTO-
BER 1999 TO PRESENT

CORPORATE COMMUNICATIONS COORDINA-
TOR, NIKE, INC., 1998 TO 1999

TEAM OPERATIONS INTERN, WNBA, SUMMER
1997

SPECIAL EVENTS INTERN, WOMEN'S SPORT
FOUNDATION, AUGUST 1996 TO DECEMBER
1996

SPECIAL EVENTS INTERN, AMERICAN BASKET-
BALL LEAGUE, DECEMBER 1996

PUBLIC AND MEDIA RELATIONS INTERN, NEW
YORK KNICKERBOCKERS BASKETBALL CLUB,
MAY 1996 TO AUGUST 1996

Best piece of advice you received in regards to your career and from whom it came:
"Don't be afraid to fail. It's the best way to learn."
ERRIN CECIL, DIRECTOR OF MARKETING, AND 1

Best advice for someone aspiring toward a career in the sport industry:
"Get plenty of work experience while in college."

Quote by which you live:
"Challenges make you discover things about yourself you never really knew. They make you stretch and go beyond you own goals and ambitions."

MY NAME IS TRACY ROYAL. I am 23 years old and currently the public relations manager for the basketball footwear and apparel company, AND 1. I graduated from Ithaca College in Ithaca, New York, in 1998 with a bachelor of science
degree in planned studies and specialized in labor relations in sport. I started out
as a sport management major but decided in my sophomore year that I wanted to
learn more law and business so I switched to planned studies. A planned studies
major allows students to develop their curriculum according to their individual
wants, needs, and goals.

Ever since I could remember sports have been a part of my life. My dad was the athletic director for the IBM Country Club and during his free time he was a basketball and football coach. When I was 3 years old my parents put me into gymnastics. After gymnastics, they put me in tee-ball, swimming, bowling, tennis, baseball, softball, volleyball, and basketball. I had lessons or attended camp for every major sport possible. When it was time to narrow down my athletic interests, I stuck with volleyball, basketball, and softball. Growing up with sports in my life had an impact on my decision to study sport in college to prepare for a career in the industry.

When I first began college I did not know exactly what I wanted to do as a career. I knew it had to be in sports and hoped it would have something to do with basketball. Even now I am still not 100 percent sure. I still have thoughts of being the general manager of a professional basketball team or being a sports agent. My advisor suggested that I test the waters in many different areas of sports before settling on a specific career path. I acquired experience in college athletics, in both the league and team levels of professional sports, the not-for profit side of sports, and the sport marketing business.

One thing that drew me to Ithaca's sports management program was the staff's assistance in helping students gain work experience that prepared them for the workplace. Many schools are geared toward graduate school preparation, but Ithaca is geared toward getting students into the workforce without an advanced degree. I was also impressed with Ithaca because of its size and commitment to students. I visited the University of Massachusetts, Temple University, Ohio State University, and Michigan State University and they all had student/academic advisor ratios of approximately 100 to 1. I would have only been a number at these schools. When I began at Ithaca the ratio was approximately 25 to 1. My advisor, Dr. Wayne Blann, has the ability to sit down with his students whenever necessary to talk about career paths or class adjustments. He is very in tune with what his students do. He helped me with everything from developing my planned studies curriculum to helping me decide which job offer to take after graduation.

I began as the manager of the Cornell University men's varsity basketball team, a job I had for 3 years. It may seem a little unusual because I was not a student there, but with the schools being only 5 minutes away, it was an opportunity to gain more experience because it was a Division I basketball program as opposed to the Division III program at Ithaca. As manager I was responsible for the teams' practice schedules, travel arrangements, and game day logistics. College athletics is a great way to ease into the world of sport. It is a good combination of amateurism and business. College athletics is a major business; that is one lesson I learned.

The summer after my first season as manager, I interned for StreetBall Partners, which is the organization that runs Hoop-It-Up 3-on-3 basketball tournaments. I was the special events intern and I assisted the event manager. The event manager and I worked all of the tournaments that summer on the east coast. We did the logistics for each tournament including organizing player registration and check-in, securing special guests, and ordering food for the hospitality tents. That summer I traveled to New York, New Jersey, Pennsylvania, and Washington, D.C. It was my first internship and because the staff was so small I received hands-on work experience. One of the assistant basketball coaches at Cornell helped me get that first internship with StreetBall Partners. He knew someone there and helped me secure an interview. It is always good to have some sort of personal connection with an organization. With so many qualified applicants with similar backgrounds, getting your resume noticed is difficult. If you have someone who can get your resume noticed, it is a plus.

During one of the Hoop-It-Up events, Patrick Ewing was the special guest. The Knicks Community Affairs person accompanied him. We started talking and when he learned I was an intern, he suggested I come and intern with the Knicks. At first I thought he was joking, but he told me to send him my resume. In the spring, I sent in my resume, we talked, and he brought me in for an interview, and I got the internship. The key to going places in this business is networking! My advice to anyone pursuing a job in sport is to network. Use every opportunity to meet as many people in this business as you can. Building relationships early is key to a successful career.

That summer my internship was in the public relations department for the New York Knicks. I assisted in the writing of the press releases surrounding the draft and the media guide for the summer league 1996. For the day-to-day duties, I answered media calls and inquiries concerning the draft and free agent acquisitions. I also participated in the coordination of player appearances, a golf tournament, and various player press conferences.

After the internship with the Knicks, instead of returning to classes at Ithaca, I chose to do a semester internship. The one bad thing about summer internships is the short time period. It seems as if I spent so much time on a project or special event but rarely got to see it through to the end. Because of this, I decided to work at the Women's Sports Foundation for the first semester of my junior year. Most people wait until the last semester of their senior year to do a semester long internship with the hope they will get a job from it. I did not want to be off-campus during that time. Another option I had—which many people take—is to do their semester long internship the summer after they graduate.

I chose to do the semester long internship with the Women's Sports Foundation for several reasons. The first was my interest in women's sports, the second was I wanted the experience of working for a not-for-profit organization, and the third was the high number of Ithaca graduates who had worked there before me. They all spoke highly of the experience. Because it is such a small organization, the interns get real hands-on experience and are an integral part of the daily operation of the Foundation. We become part of the company for the time we are there because so much work needs to be done.

At the Women's Sports Foundation I was the special events intern. I worked for the director of special events and, although I worked on many aspects of the annual black-tie fund-raising event, my main responsibility was organizing the sport clinics held in conjunction with the Fund-Raising Dinner. Because it was the summer after the 1996 Olympics, the impact of women's sports was still at an all-time high. We had 22 Olympic athletes as clinicians, including the gold medal soccer team, the gold medal softball team, and the gold medal basketball team. It was an amazing experience to have 22 gold medal athletes in one room. The young girls' response to the clinics was unbelievable. They had the time of their lives and the athletes also enjoyed themselves. Conducting that clinic with no major problems or injuries was impressive to people in subsequent interviews. Someone at the Women's Sports Foundation knew someone at the now defunct American Basketball League, so I, along with several other interns, helped with the league's inaugural all-star weekend. We organized and conducted a clinic and all of the half-time festivities. For most of us it was a weekend full of networking that provided great exposure.

Looking back on my internships and work experiences, I learned the most from this one. I learned the true value of teamwork and a lot about myself during those 5 months. I realized what I was capable of doing at a time when I did not know the direction that I was headed. The reassurance was beneficial. Another reason why this was my best work experience was the friendships I made. My boss there will always be a mentor. She taught me the most important things in business are teamwork, respect, professionalism, and passion. She, along with everyone at the Foundation, was passionate about women's sports. It was cool to go to work knowing that everyone was there for a single reason. Working with something that interests you makes the internship less like work and more of an experience.

After the second semester of my junior year I did an internship with the National Basketball Association. I was placed in the WNBA Team Operations Department. It was exciting because it was the WNBA's inaugural season. The team operations department was responsible for making sure everything with the League—on and off-court—was correct. This included making sure the league's logo was presented properly, the proper signage was used in the correct arenas, and the sponsors were happy. While I was there we mailed 15,000 WNBA posters to camps and clinics across the country to get the word out about the League. We also set up clinics and player appearances as promotional tools. A couple of the player appearances I was involved in were an autograph signing session with Rebecca Lobo at Macy's department store and a clinic at the Harlem YMCA with Kim Hampton. It was eventually decided that the WNBA Team Operations Department was no longer needed, and the league began to use the resources of the NBA Team Operations Department.

It is written in each player's contract that a certain number of appearances are required for the league and with the team. In the beginning of the summer they had to do appearances and things for the league because we were trying to publicize the league. Most of our events were with the New York Liberty because the league office is in New York, but occasionally we worked with players on other teams. One of the coolest things I did at the WNBA was help set up a McDonald's commercial shoot featuring Teresa Witherspoon, Michelle Edwards, Cynthia Cooper, and Grant Hill. I picked up the players, brought them to shoot, and made sure they were comfortable.

At the end of the summer I returned to Ithaca to begin my senior year. Although I was prepared and confident to get a job because of my internships, there was still the fear of mailing resumes while living at home with my parents in the summer. During my second semester I began my job search by mailing nearly 200 resumes. I sent resumes to the directors of human resources, public relations, and marketing for each team in the NBA and NFL. The letters were very general and for the most part were not applications for any job in particular. I basically wanted to see who would bite. I got some responses, but not too many. Most of the written responses were "We got your resume. It's on file. We're not hiring right now." The people who called me were encouraging and supportive and told me that my resume looked great and that I should keep in touch. There was a work stoppage in the NBA, so any hope of working in that league dwindled with that news. I then started following up with the NFL teams.

Because most of my internship experience was basketball related, NFL teams did not have much interest. With the thought of being an agent still in the back of my mind, I decided to apply to firms that represented athletes and sport marketing companies. If I could not work with a team, I wanted to be in a position where I could work with athletes in a corporate setting, so my second mass resume mailing was to companies such as NIKE, adidas, AND 1, ProServ, and Advantage International. I sent resumes to numerous people at each company. For example, because NIKE is so large with so many different departments, I sent them eight resumes. In return I got eight "Your resume, we got it!" "Your interest, we appreciate it!" letters.

After some time, I realized the mass mailing approach was not working. It was getting my name out there but not getting me interviews. I then started a Web site to get listings of actual job openings. This method gave me some results. I got interviews with the Houston Comets and the Detroit Shock of the WNBA, Florida State University's Athletic Department, Duke University's Sports Information Department, AND 1, Career Sports Management, and Wenner Media. After weeks of interviewing, I accepted one of the positions. Although it was not exactly what I was looking for, it was in sports and it would be a stepping stone to something bigger. Weeks past, graduation arrived, and I was set. I was ready to take some time off, enjoy part of the summer, and then begin my new job.

A few days after I got home, someone in human resources at NIKE called me about an open position in the corporate communications department. The position was coordinator of corporate communications, which in actuality is a public relations assistant. Even though I had accepted a position, I could not pass up the chance to interview with NIKE. I went to New York and interviewed with a senior manager and specialist in the corporate communications department. Three days later, because they wanted to move quickly, I had a phone interview with the human resources representative from Oregon. The director of the corporate communications department then flew out from Oregon. They had narrowed it down to two people. He took me out to dinner, and 3 days later they offered me the job.

I called the company whose position I had accepted and told them I had to decline the offer. Even though the job was with NIKE, it was a tough decision. The companies and positions were different. The only similarity was the salary. As many sport professionals will say, it is hard to get rich during your early years in the sport industry. Although it depends on the specific position and the area, in general, entry-level positions in sports range from $20,000 to $30,000. I was offered jobs in Houston at $27,000 per year, in Detroit at $24,000 per year, and in New York City at $23,000 per year. NIKE made a reasonable offer of $28,000, but I negotiated a high base salary with NIKE because of my work experience.

The position with NIKE was entry level. My main responsibility was to assist the senior manager and manager in the New York office where I was located. All of the public relations managers are in charge of a category; for example, basketball, community affairs, or equipment. My managers' categories were social responsibility, apparel, retail, and cross training. If a new UV-protectant tennis shirt was available, we wrote the press release and tried to get media exposure. Overall, the three of us spent our days pitching stories to newspapers, magazines, and television news shows trying to get free publicity. The media generally like NIKE products, so it was not always a hard sell. Many people in the media like to report the bad stuff, so we tried to pitch feel-good stories about what NIKE does in the community. At that time, the media was focused on NIKE's labor issues.

The most enjoyable aspect of that job was working with athletes. When NIKE launched their interactive line, which included a new sports bra for women, I helped with the public relations and events surrounding the line. We hosted a press event where we had a couple athletes who had participated in the wear testing of the product share their thoughts and experiences. Part of my involvement in that event was working with the athletes. The least enjoyable aspect of that job was working with the media. I know it sounds strange because working with the media is a key element of public relations, but they always have deadlines and think their publication is the most important. It was frustrating because I would have 20 people wanting the story first. It was hard to keep my composure, but it had to be done.

When I reached a year at NIKE, I hit some sort of plateau and needed a new challenge. I talked to my supervisors about adding more responsibility to my position but they did not think I had enough time to handle it. I was already working between 55 and 60 hours a week. It basically came down to me asking for a promotion and them not thinking I was ready, because the coordinator position was structured as a 3-year position. Being in that position for an additional 2 years would not be good for my professional development. I was ready to advance after a year. When my supervisors disagreed, I began looking at other options.

After 1 year and 4 months I left my position at NIKE to take my current job as the public relations manager at AND 1. It was a tough decision for me, but I am happy with it. I am now responsible for the public, media, and community relations for the entire company. My day-to-day duties includes writing press releases on various topics, such as new products and community affairs efforts; pitching story ideas to local, national, and international media; and assisting in the development and execution of the company's grassroots marketing plans.

Whenever I get a chance to speak with students interested in working in sport, I tell them to be persistent and aggressive in whatever they do. If I had not sent eight resumes to NIKE, I may never have received that phone call. The human resources person saw my name come across her desk more than six times. Following through with everything you do is also important. If you meet someone, make the effort to remember his or her name. It is beneficial to write that person a note 2 weeks later saying when and where you met. It is all about building and maintaining relationships.

I am thankful that I have not encountered many obstacles in this business. For the most part, my experiences have been great. Being a woman in a male-dominated industry, I assumed sexism would be one of the problems, but I was wrong. I was in a situation where there was a female secretary trying to make her way from an administrative assistant to an assistant when I had joined her department as an intern. I was new and had fresh ideas, and she thought I was stepping on her toes and going after her job. It may sound crazy, but sometimes I think there are women in this industry who do not want to see other women succeed. Women in a male-dominated industry need to work together and help each other. Other than that one bad experience, I have had nothing but complete support from most of the women I know in sports. Throughout my career I have tried to have a female mentor and I plan to mentor young women.

My mentor now is Chrysa Chin, who is currently the senior manager of Player Programs for the NBA. She has a long history in the sport industry and has helped me in almost every aspect of my life as well as my career. Because she has been through many of the things I have or will experience, her input and support is imperative to my development as a sport professional. She has done a pretty good job.

I would describe myself as persistent, aggressive, hard working, and very focused. Those qualities come across to my coworkers. I am personable, enthusiastic, and responsive, with an ability to forge relationships and negotiate for services. To put it simply, I am a good talker. Public relations is all about communication skills and being persuasive. The most important public relations lesson I have learned is the importance of believing in the company and its product. I can do my job well if I truly believe in the product. For example, I do not watch football and have never played it, but I could work for the NFL because I believe in what the NFL does. It is easy to portray a company's mission and their goals if they are clear about the message they want to send and you know exactly what they want to convey.

As far as long-term goals, by the time I am 26, which is 3 years from now, I want to have a law degree. I want to be the director of a marketing communications department by age 30. That is my focus now. The future of this industry is that everything moves toward innovative marketing. There will not just be advertising as a department or marketing as a department or public relations as a department. It is all going to be integrated to convey a comprehensive message.

My advice to students is to be open to new ideas. Young people think that because they graduated from college they have all the answers. They do not, however. I would recommend listening carefully at every meeting and presentation and absorbing every bit of information possible. Also, learn the entire business and get as much exposure as you can. Get your name out by meeting as many people as you can, e-mailing people, offering your help for events, or volunteering in other departments. That is what I did as an intern and still do today. The most important thing I can offer is to always enjoy what you do! When you lose the passion, it is time to move on. To me, sport is all about passion for the game, passion for the idea of team, and passion for winning. With no intensity, there is no victory!

CHAPTER 11

Health and Fitness Industry

THE HEALTH AND FITNESS INDUSTRY, once considered a fad, experienced continual growth during the past 3 decades. The industry has grown from a sport-specific enterprise appealing to a select few in the 1960s, to an industry of the 21st century targeted to the masses who have adopted fitness activities as a regular part of their daily routine.

An example of the trend toward a national health consciousness was displayed in the growth of the health club industry during the 1980s and 1990s. From 1987 to 1996, the number of Americans who were health club members increased from 13.8 million in 1987 to a high of 20.8 million in 1996 (IHRSA, 1997). By 1993, nearly 43.9 million people in the United States reported they were involved in sport or fitness activities at least 100 days per year. A noticeable change in the U.S. demographics during the past 3 decades is mirrored in the health and fitness industry. Young adults aged 18 to 34 were largely responsible for the industry growth during the 1970s; however, the 35- to 54-year-old participation rates have risen by 55 percent since 1987 whereas the former age group has increased by only 20 percent (American Sports Data, Inc., 1995).

More than 48,000 fitness facilities operate in the United States, and more than 13,000 commercial clubs serve approximately 11 million of the nearly 21 million Americans who belong to clubs. According to the IHRSA report (1995), health and sport clubs represent the largest category of health/fitness clubs, whereas hotel/resort/spa facilities, member-owner clubs, apartment/condo facilities, and college/university facilities followed in terms of total numbers. About 70 percent of the commercial clubs are fitness-only facilities with fitness centers, cardiovascular equipment, and aerobics programs, with perhaps a snack bar and small pro shop. Multipurpose clubs offer most of the same amenities as the fitness-only clubs, but often add pools, gymnasiums, physical therapy centers, restaurants, and social programs. The hotel/motel and apartment complex fitness centers are usually smaller in size and have less equipment; however, they are growing entities because of the demands of business travelers and home fitness users. Corporations provide health and fitness facilities for a number of reasons. Employer wellness programs have been shown to increase morale and productivity, reduce absenteeism, and provide advantageous job recruitment and retention strategies for employees (McDonald & Howland, 1998).

Another segment of the health/fitness world is the nonprofit segment. About 39 percent of all club members exercise at nonprofit facilities (IHRSA, 1997). Organizations such as the YMCA, YWCA, Jewish Community Centers, college recreation and fitness centers, and hospital-aligned wellness centers provide competitive alternatives to consumers, often at a lower cost with nearly identical facilities and equipment. Even commercial fitness centers have realized the importance of aligning with health care organizations to provide educational programs to a health-conscious public. National and state agencies continue to support the public's growing interest in health and fitness. Insurance companies and health care organizations provide incentives for organizations to include memberships for employees to realize the benefits of regular exercise in disease prevention.

To thrive in this climate, future employees must have the attitude, skills, management expertise, and creativity to readily adapt to changes in the industry. If they can survive in that constantly changing environment, future health/fitness experts will have a satisfying career in a worthwhile, beneficial industry. The financial compensation for those interested in pursuing a career in this field can be attractive. Entry-level positions pay in the area of the mid $20,000s. As one advances within a private club or a business that is contracted out to sites, the pay increases. Middle management positions pay in mid $30,000s up to $40,000 whereas general managers and other top management positions can pay more than $60,000 a year or more. As in most sport fields it is important for the person to gain experience with low-paying entry-level positions or internships to gain the valuable experience to begin the career climb to top management positions within fitness organizations.

REFERENCES

American Sports Data, Inc. (1995). *Health club trend report*. Boston: Author.

IHRSA. (1995). *The 1995 IHRA report on the state of the health club industry*. Boston: Author.

IHRSA. (1997). *The 1997 IHRSA report on the state of the health club industry*. Boston: Author.

McDonald, M.A., & Howland, W. (1998). Health and fitness industry. In L.P. Masteralexis, C.A. Barr, & M.A. Hums (Eds.), *Principles and practice of sport management*. Gaithersburg, MD: Aspen Publishers, Inc.

Susan T. Liebenow

President/Co-owner
L & T Health and Fitness

Education:
B.S., GEOGRAPHY/GEOLOGY, MARY
WASHINGTON COLLEGE, 1971
M.S., HEALTH AND FITNESS MANAGEMENT,
THE AMERICAN UNIVERSITY, 1983

Career Progression:
PRESIDENT/CO-OWNER, LIEBENOW & TOROK,
INC., DBA L & T HEALTH AND FITNESS (FALLS
CHURCH, VA), 1996 TO PRESENT

PRESIDENT; PEOPLE KARCH INTERNATIONAL,
1995 TO 1996

SENIOR VICE PRESIDENT, PEOPLE KARCH IN-
TERNATIONAL, 1989 TO 1995

CO-DIRECTOR, DEPARTMENT OF JUSTICE FIT-
NESS CENTER (WASHINGTON, DC), 1984 TO 1988

FUND-RAISING COORDINATOR, LOMBARDI
MEMORIAL EVENT (10K RUN, BENEFIT CON-
CERT, GOLF AND TENNIS TOURNAMENTS) FOR
THE LOMBARDI CANCER RESEARCH CENTER
(WASHINGTON, DC), JUNE 1983 TO AUGUST 1983

ASSISTANT PROFESSOR AND WOMEN'S TENNIS
COACH, MOUNT VERNON COLLEGE, 1981 TO
1983

ASSISTANT MANAGER, ARLINGTON Y TENNIS &
SQUASH CLUB, SPORT & HEALTH (MCLEAN,
VA), 1981 TO 1982

EXECUTIVE ASSISTANT TO THE DIRECTOR OF
ATHLETICS, GEORGETOWN UNIVERSITY,
WOMEN'S TENNIS COACH, DIRECTOR OF MEM-
BERSHIP & RACQUET SPORTS, 1976 TO 1981

ASSISTANT PRO SHOP MANAGER, REGENCY
RACQUET CLUB (MCLEAN, VA), 1976 TO 1978

TENNIS PROFESSIONAL, WASHINGTON TENNIS
SERVICES, 1974 TO 1976

Best piece of advice you received in regards to your career:
"If you're not listening, you're not learning."

Best advice for someone aspiring toward a career in the sport industry:
"Don't be afraid to "get your feet wet;" get your foot in the door and show what you can do no matter what the job is."

Quote by which you live:
"It takes less time to do something right than to explain why it was done wrong."

LONGFELLOW

I AM CO-OWNER AND PRESIDENT OF L&T HEALTH AND FITNESS (L&T), a female-owned small business headquartered in Falls Church, Virginia, just outside Washington, D.C. L&T manages work site fitness/wellness centers and provides a variety of work site health promotion programs and services to organizations nationwide. Susan Torok, my business partner, and I founded L&T Health and Fitness in 1984. We started the business with $500 (enough to pay for incorporation), a lot of enthusiasm, excitement, and a commitment to succeed. L&T Health and Fitness now is recognized as an industry leader. We contract with Fortune 500 companies, numerous federal and other government agencies, large multinational organizations, and other businesses and organizations for the delivery of comprehensive health promotion programs. L&T programs have received top honors and industry awards, including: the Office of Personnel Management Award for the Outstanding Health Fitness Program in the Federal Government; the Association For Worksite Health Promotion Business and Industry Award; and the NOVA 7 Excellence Awards For Wellness and Health Promotion. In 1998 and 1999, L&T was listed among the top 100 fitness club organizations by *Club Industry Magazine.*

In addition to providing on-site fitness center staffing, programs, and management services, L&T brings comprehensive health education seminars, classes, health screenings, and health fairs to the work site. Our services include cholesterol, blood pressure, body composition, and cardiovascular screenings as well as health assessments (HRAs), nutritional counseling and weight loss, stress management, CPR and first-aid classes, and seminars. In short, our company tries to help people make positive lifestyle behavior changes.

I did not follow a direct career path into the health and fitness industry. Whereas today's college students can choose from a variety of programs, schools, and disciplines, my options were limited and unknown to me when I entered Mary Washington College in 1967. I chose Mary Washington for its beautiful campus, small student body, and strong liberal arts education. I did not choose it for its major in physical education, which was the only sport-related major there when I enrolled.

Although I was extremely interested in sports throughout my childhood, I was unaware of career options for women in sports or athletics. My high school had few, if any, athletic teams for girls and did not encourage girls to participate. I remember being disappointed as a 10-year-old when my brother could register for Little League and I had bowling as my only choice. Years later, I still bowl competitively and enjoy it, but it was disappointing to have so few options for competitive sports. I pursued my sports interest with my family by learning golf and tennis at an early age. Still, I never considered that a career path in sports was available to me.

I graduated from Mary Washington College in 1971 with a degree in geography/geology and a concentration in cartography. I thought I would draw maps for the rest of my life! After several years as a draftsperson and engineering technician in Charlottesville, Virginia, I realized that although I liked what I was doing, I was not passionate about my job or my career. I realized—while sitting at my drafting table every day—that what I wanted to do was teach or coach tennis. I played a lot of tennis at the time and decided I would learn to teach. Much to my parents' chagrin, I took a sabbatical from my good job with good benefits and embarked on a long and winding path that led to my current career.

I left my job as an engineering technician with the City of Charlottesville in the spring of 1974 to pursue my dream of becoming a tennis teaching pro. I went to tennis camps and tennis schools and spent every minute on the tennis courts. I found a summer job in upstate New York teaching tennis at Point O' Pines Camp for Girls, a beautiful site near Lake George with spectacular tennis facilities. I did not have much experience, but I had a lot of desire. Point O' Pines proved to be a great, but challenging experience. During the first few weeks of camp, the tennis director abruptly resigned from his position and left camp, and I was named the new tennis director to oversee a huge summer tennis program. It was a challenging summer of on-the-job training that I chalked up as a great learning experience and a test of my commitment to my new "career."

I moved to Washington, D.C., in the fall of 1974 to live with college friends and look for jobs in tennis. I found a job teaching private and group tennis lessons for an organization called Washington Tennis Services (now WTS, International) and also worked part-time at a retail tennis shop selling tennis clothes and equipment. I immersed myself in tennis and looked for opportunities to further my career. I was excited to find a job at the brand-new Regency Racquet Club in McLean, Virginia. It was a fabulous club that was voted one of the top 50 tennis facilities in the United States. Because the club was new, the employees did everything to make it successful in the early years. We had theme nights, elaborate dinners, and regular social and tennis events to promote the club. Procelebrity events brought Connors, Evert, Bjorg, and many of the top players to our club. I worked at the front desk greeting and registering members and helped manage the pro shop. The job taught me about customer service, event planning, marketing, sales, and—of course—more about tennis. I also met and worked with a mentor and friend, Sam Reed Horn.

In the summer of 1978, I saw an employment ad in the newspaper for a women's tennis coach position at Georgetown University. Although I did not have college coaching experience, I decided to apply for the job. I soon learned that the women's coach had been murdered a few weeks before the season was to begin. Because of the tragedy, Georgetown needed a coach quickly. The university was in a pinch and I was eager and available, although a little apprehensive to face my players considering the unusual circumstances.

The coaching opportunity at Georgetown was wonderful because it showed me how much I loved teaching and coaching and how much I loved sports and athletics. Although I continued some of my other part-time jobs to support myself, coaching became my passion. I spent 5 years at Georgetown and the tennis program flourished, largely because of my top players who led Georgetown to two appearances at the Division II nationals my last 2 years. It was fun and exciting to be part of a women's sports program that had been previously unrecognized on campus.

While at Georgetown, I received additional responsibilities as assistant to the director of athletics. I assisted with the marketing of Georgetown's new state-of-the-art multipurpose athletic complex, the Yates Field House, which was being built on campus. The underground facility had indoor tennis, racquetball, squash, fitness areas, and an indoor track and pool; the football field and outdoor track were on the roof. It was quite an architectural design feat at that time. I viewed my job as a great career opportunity. I assisted with membership recruitment, program development, and facility start-up. I also taught a few fitness and tennis classes and became the director of membership. It was an open-ended position that was created for me because I had the interest, some of the skills, and a great deal of enthusiasm to expand my role at Georgetown.

It was also during this time that I started my master's degree program in health/fitness management at American University. I learned about the program from Dr. Robert Karch, who came to tour the Yates Field House at Georgetown. During the tour, he told me about a new master's program he was starting at American University. The program was unique at the time because it combined courses from the business school with core courses from the health and fitness department. The program sounded perfect for me, combining my love for sports and fitness with my new job responsibilities that called for marketing, financial management, strategic planning, and other business management skills.

I started the graduate program in health fitness management in 1980 as a part-time student and continued my coaching and other job responsibilities at Georgetown. It was difficult to juggle work and school and I remember wondering if it would ever end. The master's courses were new to me with my undergraduate degree in geography/geology, so all the classes were challenging. The uniqueness of the health/fitness program at that time was the diversity of the students. An engineer, a lawyer, a salesperson, and a real estate agent were among my classmates. They were people who were excited about a fairly new concept at the time—health/fitness—and they were putting their careers on hold to explore this new area. Dr. Karch, another mentor and friend, and the people he assembled for the health/fitness management major were the strength of the program.

When I finished graduate school in 1982, I left Georgetown to work for a large commercial tennis, racquetball, and fitness club chain in northern Virginia. My primary interest was still racquet sports, but my interests and the industry were beginning to change. Clubs soon realized that you could put 50 people on a tennis court to do aerobics instead of the maximum of four playing tennis. The fitness boom was beginning and it was exciting to be part of it.

I had just been promoted to club manager when I received a call from a lawyer with the U.S. Department of Justice asking if I was interested in bidding on a contract to manage the Department of Justice Fitness Center. Sue Torok, who later became my business partner, received the same call. The lawyer had gotten our names from one of our classmates from American University. Although I was thoroughly enjoying my job at the time, the chance to bid on a fitness management contract sounded exciting and provided the opportunity to put my graduate degree to good use. Sue and I decided to write a proposal together for the management of the Justice Fitness Center. We were awarded the contract in May 1984.

In June 1984, with the help of Sue's husband and some supportive friends, we incorporated Liebenow & Torok, Inc., negotiated our first management contract; developed our initial business plan; started hiring people; set up payroll, taxes, and insurance policies; and learned to teach aerobics FAST. Our business was on the way because of our networking connections and a lot of drive and determination. That first contract was baptism by fire and an incredible learning experience. We still thank the people at the Justice Department who gave us that first opportunity to perform. They are still one of our most successful programs after 15 years.

I never had aspirations to be a business owner. I remember hearing about the high probability of small businesses failing within the first 5 years, but Sue and I did not have the time or the mentality to consider failure. Our business began to grow and we had to keep up with the growth. We had to learn about business rapidly and grow from our experiences. At the same time, we had to run a comprehensive health and fitness program for our members and teach group exercise classes, clean the floors when the cleaning people did not show up, launder towels, fix the exercise equipment, and teach people about healthy lifestyle behavior. The hands-on experiences helped me more than anything I ever did; I can empathize when employees say they do not want to clean equipment or teach aerobics, but I can also tell them that those experiences are important parts in the process of career development.

From that first contract in 1984, our company has grown dramatically in size and in the scope of services we offer to our clients. Doing business as L&T Health and Fitness, we have approximately 300 full- and part-time employees. Our management operations division provides on-site health/fitness for organizations from Maine to Georgia and from Washington, D.C. to Scottsdale, Arizona. Most of our employees are full-time health fitness professionals with either an undergraduate or a graduate degree in the field. Degrees vary greatly and include sport management, exercise physiology, health promotion, exercise science, recreation, and physical education. We also have employees with degrees in psychology and other allied health fields. All our employees must be certified in CPR and first aid and have nationally recognized certification. Part-time employees include personal trainers, group exercise or specialty class instructors, or health promotion professionals who help deliver health fairs or health education classes or programs.

L&T has a strong team of senior managers, including vice presidents who oversee our two divisions, regional directors of operations, and administrative support personnel who assist our employees and operate from our headquarters office in northern Virginia. Two people handle marketing and new business development; two people oversee human resources, payroll, billing, and accounts receivable; and four full-time people design and deliver health promotion programs and services for our wellness services division.

The growth of our company can be attributed to great employees, word-of-mouth marketing, timing, and location. We were at the right place at the right time. Our business grew initially in the federal sector in Washington, D.C. People from one federal agency would see and hear about our program at another agency. Our goal was to add one contract per year, and we did just that, all in the federal sector. Two of our programs received the prestigious Office of Personnel Management (OPM) Director's Award for the Outstanding Health/Fitness in the federal government. Federal employees were extremely excited to have affordable, professionally staffed fitness centers at the workplace and L&T was excited to have an opportunity to affect their health.

As L&T continued to grow, we realized we needed to think carefully about our growth strategy. We gradually expanded our support team so that Sue and I were no longer doing all the administrative functions such as payroll, billing, hiring, training, proposal writing, and servicing customers. We began thinking seriously about a 5-year plan, with the urging of Sue's husband, who had been in business for himself.

In 1989 Robert Karch, from American University, approached us about selling our business to become a subsidiary of a larger company called People Karch International (PKI). The new company would be a joint venture between Dr. Karch and the People Company of Japan, one of the largest sports and fitness businesses in Japan. PKI would combine the resources of Dr. Karch and People Company, a fitness management company (L&T), a child-care management company, and a software company that sold industry-leading fitness management software. People Company would provide the financial resources for start-up and acquisitions as PKI came together.

Sue and I decided to sell our company to PKI in 1989 with three goals in mind: 1) growth; 2) more opportunities and better benefits for our employees; and 3) the opportunity to work with Dr. Karch. As a well-respected industry leader and a mentor, Dr. Karch was a major factor in our decision to sell our business. PKI also included several other colleagues from American University, so we were excited to join a strong team of professionals.

A business merger requires a lot of time (for the discovery or due diligence process), good legal and financial advice, flexibility, and the ability to change the way you operate. Before PKI, Sue and I answered to each other, our employees, and our customers. We were the stockholders of the company and comprised 50 percent of the board of directors, along with my father and Sue's husband. When we sold the business, we became executives of the new company and Liebenow & Torok, Inc. became a wholly owned subsidiary of PKI. Our Japanese business partners, who remained in Japan, were the primary stockholders with Dr. Karch.

Working with the Japanese was an invaluable learning experience. As an executive of PKI and a member of the board of directors, I traveled to Japan several times to attend business meetings, observe the Japanese business culture and its growing fitness industry, tour some beautiful sites, and eat some interesting and delicious food. I was worried about being accepted as a businesswoman in a male-dominated business culture, but my Japanese hosts always treated me with respect and kindness. Although the cultures were different, we learned a great deal about business including the significance of strategic planning, the importance of precise budgeting, and the need to be accountable.

In February 1995 PKI separated into two companies: Karch International and PKI. Karch International retained the software and the rights to certain products. The fitness management and child-care business remained part of PKI. I became the new president of PKI and reported to our Japanese chief executive officer. Although this was a difficult transition for all of us, it allowed the different business segments to focus on what they did best. The split of PKI was, however, an indication that our Japanese business partners were looking to divest themselves of their U.S. holdings that included PKI. When this was apparent, Sue and I approached the Japanese about purchasing the health/fitness business back from PKI.

Buying the business back was one of the most difficult things I have ever done. PKI's fitness business had grown significantly, so the value of the business had increased substantially. We had to secure financing, change the company name, negotiate the transaction, notify customers and employees of the impending change, find office space, pack and move the office, change all tax forms and insurance policies, and continue operating the business. It was a grueling experience and one that I do not want to repeat, but it shows what you can do if you are committed to the cause. We were convinced that L&T Health and Fitness was worth buying back. In August 1996 Sue Torok and I regained ownership and control of the company we had started in 1984. We moved our offices to our current northern Virginia location and started doing business as L&T Health and Fitness.

Owning and operating a business is not for everyone. Tremendous satisfaction is derived when your customers are happy, your employees are satisfied, and your revenues are stable. At the same time, a level of responsibility and risk exists that is ever present and often uncomfortable. If a person needs a lot of guidance and direction every day, owning a business might not be right. I like charting my own destiny, making decisions, and having the independence to change direction if necessary. If you are the kind of person who is going to work as hard as you can, why not work for yourself? You can celebrate the successes and correct the mistakes.

When Sue and I started our business, there was little or no competition, or so it seemed. The industry was very young in the early to mid 1980s and there appeared to be enough business to go around. Today, as the industry has matured, considerable competition exists for every contract we seek. No real barriers exist to entry in our business, so competition ranges from a few large service providers to small companies with one or two contracts and little or no overhead.

Bidding on a management contract—even an existing contract—can be difficult. Sometimes as many as 10 to 15 competitors are vying for the contract in the early stages of the bidding process. From there, companies are screened for their ability to provide the required services and then the top companies usually get an opportunity to do a face-to-face presentation to narrow the choices. Once the final selection is made, which can sometimes take up to 6 months or longer, then contract negotiations can occur.

The bidding process can take some of the fun out of the business. With more competition, customers are selective—as they should be—in choosing a vendor. Pricing often becomes the deciding factor and many organizations select the lowest bidder. We are forced to lower prices to keep a long-term customer from switching to a new vendor. Although this can be a frustrating and difficult part of the business, it illustrates why competition is so important in business.

A management proposal can be an elaborate document, sometimes 50 pages or more including appendices and exhibits. Of the 29 proposals we submitted in 1997 for new business, we acquired seven new management contracts and finished in the top two or three in most of the other bids. It is easy to get discouraged about being the silver and bronze medalist in so many instances, but you can be proud to be among the top companies in the industry. I choose the latter, but it is difficult to be the "bridesmaid" in so many bids.

When working on a management proposal, I struggle with pricing. If the bid is too high, our proposal might get rejected immediately. If our bid is too low, we might get the contract, but be forced to lower employee compensation (salaries and associated benefits) that currently represents more than 80 percent of our total business costs. Because employee recruitment and retention have become major challenges for our industry, staff salaries must be commensurate with the job duties and requirements. Although some segments of the industry have responded with higher salaries, other segments lag behind. Employee compensation is a critical challenge that faces our industry.

One of my biggest stresses as a business owner is the threat of lawsuits. When we sold our business in 1989, I felt a sense of relief that I no longer had to feel personally (or at least 50 percent) liable and responsible for all business operations. As our society becomes more litigious, the possibility of a lawsuit is a real concern in a potentially risky business like health and fitness. Although part of the reason for setting up a corporation is to limit personal liability, considerable personal risk and responsibility still exist in running a business. A lawsuit would be time-consuming, costly, and potentially damaging to the business. Even with a sizable comprehensive liability insurance policy, which provides coverage for everything from employee theft, libel, and slander to bodily injury and death resulting from negligence, you can never think of everything that could happen.

In 15 years, we have been extremely fortunate in having only two lawsuits filed against our company. Ironically, neither case involved an accident or injury related to exercise. One case (now pending) involves libel and slander against one of our employees; the other case involved the improper delivery of chemicals by a subcontractor for a swimming pool we operate as part of our fitness center contract. Although slips and falls and exercise equipment mishaps inspire the most common insurance claims in our business, numerous other potential risks are associated with the industry.

The best defense for potential lawsuits is a well-written and well-managed risk management strategy that includes proper training and good documentation. Because our business scope is so comprehensive, our employees and managers must be knowledgeable about every aspect. These aspects include OSHA policies that cover handling blood and cleaning products; employee practices that include discrimination, wrongful termination, hiring, firing, and sexual harassment; the Americans with Disabilities Act; and copyright laws related to playing recorded music and videotapes.

I spend a lot of time considering, reviewing, preparing, and instituting policies and procedures that protect us from costly legal issues. Our insurance policy helps me sleep a little better at night, but that also must be reviewed carefully each year to assure us that we have adequate coverage.

To address risk management, L&T developed our SMART (standards manual and regulation training) handbook that guides the operations at all our sites. SMART includes policies and procedures in all areas, from equipment maintenance and cleaning to group exercise instruction and health promotion programming. Each site has the freedom and independence to develop its own health and fitness programs specific to the unique needs of the members. Our employees use SMART as an aid to guide them through policies, procedures, and certain standards that are consistent throughout our organization. Each site receives an annual site visit and written review by our risk management committee to ensure SMART compliance.

Our business success hinges on recruiting and retaining good employees. To hire and retain the best employees, we must be a good company. It is no longer enough to have a 401(k) retirement plan with matching funds, good health and dental benefits, and extensive training opportunities. In today's job market, employees are more selective about jobs, employers, and length of stay on the job. It is not uncommon today to lose an employee to a different industry, such as the technology industry, that pays significantly more. Companies that are innovative with employee training, growth opportunities, and compensation will lead the industry.

My greatest satisfaction in business comes when I get an unsolicited letter or call from a client complimenting or thanking one of our employees for making a difference in that person's life. This proves to me that we do make a difference and help people make life-changing decisions. It is also satisfying when we discover someone with a dangerous health condition through our baseline assessment process or during a health fair or health screening and the person returns to say, "Thank you, you might have saved my life." I also derive satisfaction from watching my employees grow into outstanding professionals and seeing them assume greater responsibility within our organization or within the profession.

Although employee turnover in our industry is a challenge, the positive side is the number of opportunities now available for people with a degree in health/fitness, sport management, or a related field. Jobs are plentiful in commercial clubs, corporations, hospitals or clinical settings, and community and nonprofit organizations. The focus on health care and the importance of prevention, the aging of our population, the diversity of the workforce, the lack of physical activity in our children, and the link between lifestyle and disease combine to create a plethora of opportunities in our industry. Those who are passionate about this industry can write their own job descriptions.

As I assumed more responsibility for the business, I moved from the technical side of service delivery to the conceptual side of business management. I have my American College of Sports Medicine (ACSM) standards and guidelines book in a prominent place on my bookshelf and refer to it often, but I now refer the technical questions about exercise testing or programming to my employees. My focus now is on business growth, problem solving, communication with my employees and customers, and understanding business and industry trends that affect our business.

To be a successful business owner and/or chief executive officer you have to want, and like, responsibility; make decisions and be accountable for those decisions; learn more so you can create more value for your employees and clients; and listen to and learn from your customers and your employees.

You must be a good leader and a strong communicator. As a leader, I try to remove obstacles so my employees can do their jobs better. My goal is to help my employees realize their own potential and do what they do best. A good leader should be the embodiment of what the organization represents. I have the same values for my company that I have for myself: I want the company to be respected by our employees, our customers, and our professional colleagues; I want to be recognized for our reliability, integrity, and customer service. I want every customer to feel as if he or she is our only customer. I also want our company to be known as a great place to work.

Our industry seems to be moving toward consolidation. L&T Health and Fitness has been approached about joining forces with other companies to create a stronger presence in the market. In some cases, the discussions involved an acquisition of our business; in others, a partnership involving no stock or asset exchange; and other discussions focused on creating a bigger and, hopefully, better company to take public. Should we consider another merger or even a joint venture, we know what questions to ask and what we want out of a business relationship. The biggest question is: will the employees, the customers, and the owners of L&T Health and Fitness benefit more as a result?

Mergers and acquisitions may be necessary for survival and growth as the industry continues to mature. As a trained cartographer in college, it was easy to redraw an existing map, but more difficult to map or chart new territory. Likewise, it is easy and tempting to retrace past business successes, but difficult and challenging to chart the future in this dynamic industry. The ultimate goal is clear—to help create a healthier, more productive society—but the path to that goal is crowded and undefined. This is both the challenge and the opportunity for our company, the industry and for me as a professional.

John Patrick Ringwald

General Manager
K.H.E. Fitness Inc./Hatfield Athletic Club

Education:
B.S., SPORT MANAGEMENT, ALLENTOWN COLLEGE, 1995

Career Progression:
GENERAL MANAGER, K.H.E. FITNESS INC., 1998 TO PRESENT

MANAGER, WORKOUT PLUS, 1996 TO 1998

ASSISTANT MANAGER, WORKOUT PLUS, 1995 TO 1996

PERSONAL TRAINER, WORKOUT PLUS, JANUARY 1995 TO AUGUST 1995

INTERN, WORKOUT PLUS, SEPTEMBER 1994 TO DECEMBER 1994

Best piece of advice you received in regards to your career:

"Don't talk about it, be about it." "No excuses, do the work."

FROM MY FATHER

Best advice for someone aspiring toward a career in the sport industry:

"Research positions. Do internships. Network."

Quote by which you live:

"Think big. Stay focused, and never give up."

IN COLLEGE I REMEMBER DISCUSSING WITH A PROFESSOR what I wanted to do my first or second year out of college and how much I planned on making. Some of my answers blew her away. She informed me that people out of school for a year or two do not make that kind of money and hold those types of positions. That conversation has always been a motivation for me, but then again that is my personality. I am never satisfied and I will always strive for more. I am 27 years old and I am the general manager of the Hatfield Athletic Club. The Hatfield Athletic Club has more than 3,000 members and is housed in a 25,000-square foot facility. The club is a part of the Keystone Health & Wellness Group that consists of a group of individuals who own and oversee a health club, rehabilitation center, and a nutrition counseling center. I am 4 years out of college and I have attained many of the goals that I was told were unattainable.

I decided to pursue a career in a sport-related field because I have always been involved in and loved sports. I originally went to college for business and marketing but when I transferred to Allentown College from Kutztown University, I changed my major to sport administration—thanks to my dad's advice—because it was a better avenue for me to pursue. I did not consider entering the fitness side of the sport industry until my senior year at Allentown College. Allentown is a small liberal arts college about an hour north of Philadelphia. An internship was required so I did mine at a health club in Quakertown, Pennsylvania. It was a short distance from Allentown College. I am still not sure what attracted me to do the internship with the fitness club, but in hindsight it was a good decision. I was familiar with the fitness aspect of sport because I had worked out with weights for years while playing sports. I always enjoyed the people I met at gyms. In most cases they were or had been athletes and I could relate to them. People who work out are a different niche of people. They are a very motivated group. During my internship, I found that the people working in the field were the same way. The personal trainers, sales people, and managers were all motivated people who were athletes and who loved to work out. That motivation attracted them to the field.

The only real career exploration I did while in college was the internship experience. Through that 3-month experience, I discovered that I thoroughly enjoyed the field. Through my internship experience I met one of my future business partners and one of my professional mentors, Dan Horan. Dan was my site supervisor for the internship at the health club. As I completed the requirements for my internship, Dan offered me a part-time personal training position and I accepted. I completed the internship and graduated from school in the same semester, and Dan turned my part-time position into a full-time personal training position. I was gainfully employed as soon as I graduated with my bachelor's degree. A few months later the company that operated the health club opened another facility and I was transferred to the site as assistant manager with the plan of becoming a manager once I got some experience. I did not think I was prepared to be a manager. That organization was very bare bones and did not offer much training. Any training I received came from Dan. He was a regional manager for the health club, so he was responsible for three clubs. The clubs were in Quakertown, Easton, and Harrisburg and he moved from club to club. He spent more time with me to get me prepared. He pointed me in the right direction as to what I needed to do to succeed in the fitness industry and in my position. Early on, I did not realize that a major component of this industry is sales and I had no experience or training in it. Dan helped me develop those skills. I was thrown into a position and I either would sink or swim. Looking back after 4 years, I learned to swim. While I was serving as manager of that facility, Dan Horan left the organization to pursue other avenues with two partners. They planned to open their own health club in Hatfield, Pennsylvania, which is a suburb of Philadelphia. They offered me the opportunity to open and run Hatfield Athletic Club.

I am still relatively young in terms of my career but I see myself making a career out of fitness. Ups and downs and hard times have been a part of my career but I always focus on the future. I saw there was something to aspire to so I kept working and that is especially the case with the Keystone Health and Wellness group. A lot of growth potential exists and I am getting to start at the bottom with my partners. We keep growing. Being a good weightlifter will not make you successful in the fitness business. I use the word business because the bottom line in business is to make money. Just because you know how to bench press or curl does not mean you have the business knowledge to successfully operate a health club. This view is the cause of a lot of clubs failing. Some body builders dream of owning a club, but they do not have any business experience. That is what happened to the club that was in our facility before us. I enjoy working in the private sector of the fitness industry as opposed to running a fitness facility in the nonprofit or college environments. I would not do it any other way. In the private sector, I can determine my fate. I am satisfied with the monetary rewards of my career. That is one of the reasons I got into this position. When I did my internship I did not know anything about managing or sales in fitness, but the potential monetary rewards were an incentive to stay in the industry and make it a career. In this environment the athletic competitiveness is prevalent. If I have a sales quota or goal to meet, I have confidence that I will reach it. When I do reach my goals, I like to be rewarded accordingly. If I would go to a position with a set salary I would probably be bored. In this environment there is no ceiling and there is always something for which to strive. The growth opportunities are the exciting part of the Keystone group. We are now pretty much set with our fitness facility and we look to expand into an aquatic center and martial arts facility. We also would like to expand into children's fitness. We are considering opening a little restaurant with the aquatic center and expanding our rehabilitation and chiropractic areas. That is only at this location. Once those projects are completed, we will consider purchasing or opening other locations.

I have not faced many obstacles. I do believe that I was being held back at the previous organization for which I worked. I did not like the way the owner ran his business, and if I would have stayed I would not have lasted that much longer. It was a risk when I left a club that I had opened and ran for almost 2 years. The club had already survived tough times and had experienced its growing pains. The Hatfield opportunity meant joining a group of guys who had nothing. We did not have a building to house a gym. I decided to take the risk because I believed in my partners. I believed in the ideas and I knew eventually I would "max-out" in my current position. I thought it was an opportunity I could not pass on. The time to take risks is early in a career. There is usually not as much at risk and a person is young enough to recover if things it do not work out. For me it was a calculated risk because I knew there was a great chance for success and growth. No matter what area of the sports industry, I recommend going to an organization where there is growth potential. When growth stops, decay begins.

As general manager of the Hatfield Club I oversee all aspects of the facility, but my main responsibility as general manager is generating revenue and retaining members. We have been in existence more than 2 years, so our main focus is increasing new membership sales while generating revenues in our profit centers. Having a club of 3,000 members does not happen by accident. We have done a great deal of marketing and have been proactive in creating sales to increase our membership. Our marketing efforts include using newspaper advertisement and direct mail, but referrals have been our biggest asset. People come to our club, have a great experience, and tell their friends or coworkers. We do not get involved in price promotions. From day one, we decided we did not want to sell on price. The large franchise gyms promote a $19 a month or $20 a month special rate. We do not want to compromise on the price. In regards to sales, five sales people make phone calls or are out on the road talking to people in the community including business owners and schools. The sales people introduce our club and explain our services. We try to create relationships with businesses so their employees will join but again we try to create these relationships without sacrificing on the membership price. Those relationships have enabled us to earn a good reputation in the Hatfield area. We belong to the Chamber of Commerce and we are involved with a couple of school districts. People come to our club because they hear of our great service. They do not come for a deal and we like that reputation.

The second source of revenue is the profit centers. Profit centers are any revenue source other than revenues from membership sales including sale of supplements, the use of tanning facilities, as well as offering programming such as the cardio kick-boxing and aerobic and spinning classes. To generate revenues through our profit centers we have to demonstrate a little more creativity in marketing. It is important to introduce a product and educate the members on why they should use the product but we also have to do promotions to generate sales. We do not have an accessory store but we offer a number of supplements and refreshments ranging from bottled water to Coca-Cola products. We carry a preworkout drink, a postworkout drink, and meal replacement bars. We have a small collection of clothing with our club design. I would consider revenue generation as one of the more demanding aspects of my job.

Also in my position I oversee more than 50 employees. They are full-time and part-time as well as independent contractors. There are full-time trainers, personal trainers, and sales people. There are also full-time shift managers. While on duty they do personal training, run the profit centers, and oversee the day-to-day operations. We have full-time positions in our rehabilitation and chiropractic center and a registered dietician and certified athletic trainers on staff. The independent contractors are those people who lead our aerobic and spinning classes. As a manager of employees, I focus on the bottom line. The employees know what to expect from me because I am consistent. What we do most of the time is basic and employees know right from wrong in terms of what they do. Managing people will always be a challenge. You need an understanding of people and personality types and know what makes them tick. Everybody is different and as a manager you must know how to get the most out of each individual.

I have people working for us that I know their positions are their careers. They are mostly our full-time people. I also have people working for us who view what they do as a job. Those are our part-time people and independent contractors. I relate to different employees in different ways. For the people that are here for a career I can tell them exactly what has to get done or whether they are doing a good job or not. For the people that view it as a job I have to treat with kid gloves. They have fewer responsibilities. When I am hiring people for a sales position, I look for someone who wants my job. I need someone with a driven personality who is goal oriented and has the ability to generate revenue. When I hire for other positions I look at other characteristics. I hire people who teach aerobics and who are personal trainers and people who run our kids programming. These people do not have the responsibility of generating revenue, but rather they provide the services. They will probably never want my position, but they need to have a commitment of doing their job to the best of their abilities. In regards to managing people, I deal with different areas and all different types of personalities. Although this aspect of my job is demanding, it is also the most enjoyable aspect of my job. I thoroughly enjoy seeing people with whom I work grow. It is like building a team. We started the club with five or six of us sitting at one of the owner's kitchen table with nothing but an idea. We have built this business from the ground up and hired from the ground up. It has been nice to see the people that are still here and the people who have grown with us. The mindset of operating a business like a team comes from my days as a baseball player. I try to create the team atmosphere because it breeds success.

My typical day is not the classic 9 to 5, 40-hour a week routine. Our club opens at 5:00 AM and it closes at 11:00 PM. We are open every day of the year including holidays. My typical day entails me arriving between 8:00 to 8:30 AM and doing a work out. I try to be showered and dressed and ready to work between 9:30 AM and 10:00 AM. If we have any meetings we try to do them in the morning. Usually the first hour or two of my day is getting organized from the night before or dealing with any problems that happened the night before or first thing in the morning. My primary focus is sales but that focus gets interrupted by the day-to-day operations of the club. Vendors may call to sell us products or services. Staffing problems and issues with club members arise that need to be addressed throughout the day. I usually try to head home about 9:00 PM. That depends on how our sales are going that month. Some nights I try to leave early and other nights I stay until closing. I usually work on a Saturday or Sunday two or three times a month. It is not the typical job and I tell that to potential employees right off the bat. We are in a service-oriented business and some people want to work out early in the morning and others work out late at night and on weekends and holidays. We have to meet those needs. If a person wants to get into a management position he or she is looking at 60 plus hours a week because the manager always works more hours than the employees.

January is the busiest time of the year for us primarily because of the New Year's resolutions. We get a lot of new members as well as returning members who have not been exercising. They make a commitment to get back into shape for the new year. Another reason it is busy is because of the weather. There is not much to do outside in the winter.

Conversely, summer is our down time. Many of our regular members are outside doing things or are on vacation. We do get a lot of college students who are home for the summer. We attract the college student by offering a summer-time membership as opposed to the usual year membership. We try to avoid deals or specials when it comes to price but we do offer specials to college students in the summer. They will only be in the area for 3 months, so we offer a membership to meet their needs.

Our competition is the biggest external factor that impacts our business. We try to offer more services and more quality with the service. Some clubs are more of a volume-type facility where they charge less for memberships and they offer less to members in terms of staffing, programming, and cleanliness of facility. We charge a few dollars more but think we offer more in the areas of service and quality. We do not specifically target an upscale client. We charge about $47 per month for a basic membership. People's willingness to pay depends on what their health is worth to them. Some people say they cannot afford $10 a month but they spend $80, $90, or $100 per month on all our different services because their health is important. We offer expanded hours because we have a lot of professional people in the area that like to work out first thing in the morning. When the club first started, we opened at 6:00 AM, then it was 5:30 AM, and now it opens at 5:00 AM. The same was true with our evening hours. We did close at 10:00 PM, then it was 10:30 PM, and now it is 11:00 PM. We made the decision to expand the hours based on our customer comments. Based on those comments, we met their needs. Typically, this business is about finding the new sale, but we put a great deal of attention on retention. By keeping members happy, we retain them for more than 1 year. Also, 80 percent of our sales are from referrals. If our members are happy, they tell others.

We must be conscious of external factors to keep a competitive edge. This industry changes about every 7 years. The hottest things now are some of the group programming such as the spinning and the cardio kick-boxing. If your club is the first to have it, it has an advantage on the competition. It is important to stay abreast of the latest trends in the field by reading industry magazines such as *Club Industry* and *Fitness Management*. We are also involved in the Delaware Valley Alliance that consists of 15 or 18 clubs from the Delaware Valley area. We try to meet once a month to bounce ideas off one another on current trends and new ideas. I have found it interesting that our direct competition keeps its distance. We are more than happy to open the club to anybody to show what we do and how we do it. We contact other owners in the vicinity, but since we came to this area we have affected the business of those clubs. They may think we have stolen their members, but I think we earn it through our service.

Anybody can buy a building and buy the newest equipment and throw it on the floor and call it a gym, but more is involved. People look for more. We will spend money to get the best staff to have the best club. It is the staff that makes the customers happy. Our members come in for a reason. They may come because they are overweight, they may want to get bigger, or they may want to get stronger. We make sure we have qualified people who know how to get the desired results for the members. We always try to have people available for anyone with a question or needing a program update. As long as people get results they will stay with the club. The clientele in the fitness industry has changed over the years. We cater more to the middle of the road type person who wants to lose a couple of pounds or inches and wants to tone up a bit. We are not a body builder type facility. Many clubs cater to that niche but we try to create an unintimidating atmosphere. We also want a family environment where parents can bring their children and either put them in a child care area or into a children's program such as gymnastics or karate.

As a manager, I use my personal and conceptual skills the most in executing my responsibilities. The personal skills are so important in dealing with the employees as well as the club members. I often deal with employees who are only concerned about their own needs. I have to be worried about the entire facility and the entire company and that is where the conceptual skills come into play. Employees often do not realize that what they are doing or what they are not doing impacts the whole company and affects the member. The employee may only be thinking of their own area where I have to think of what is best for the entire club. When I make decisions I keep the company goals as my priority. I consider the costs of my decisions and how they will affect our members. Often what is good for one area is not in the best interest of the entire club. The conceptual skills also are essential in dealing with the external factors. I have to plan months and years in advance. We have a business plan that contains projected quotas to meet. Planning and goal setting is essential to long-term success. If you do not plan, then you shoot in the dark. You must know where you are going and how you will get there. This is especially true in a business situation because the profit is the goal. Meeting our revenue goals is what motivates us and keeps us in business.

I do not think there is one profile of a successful sales person except that a good sales person gets results. The three owners and I all have different personalities and different approaches to sales but we are all good at selling and we get results. The key is to know your product, be enthusiastic about what you sell, and get the customer excited about the product. I have learned some lessons on the job that I wish I could have learned in school. In retrospect, I wish more time could be spent on sales and personality types. I have come to realize that everything in life is sales. It is not something people realize until they take a good look at it. You sell yourself every day. If you cannot sell yourself, you will not be able to sell anything else. I also learned through the years that many different personality types exist and understanding these personalities helps to explain people's actions. Understanding personalities is important in dealing with my employees but it also helps when I sell memberships or communicate with members. If you understand where people are coming from, you can relate to them better.

The fitness industry is not going anywhere. People will always work out. The programming will change in the future as new trends emerge, but there will always be some type of weights on the floor and cardiovascular machines. I do see the industry becoming more of a family-oriented activity. We are going in that direction. We try to make our club an all-in-one-stop for a family. The husband is in the weight area, the wife is in a cardio class, and the son or daughter is in a karate class. We have considered opening a day care facility or a children's wing. Then, a family could spend all day at the facility.

To succeed in the fitness industry in any capacity you must be able to communicate. You must be a good listener and speaker and be able to carry conversations. It is a people-oriented field. Many people look to get into the fitness field and think of it as being a trainer or as some type of instructor, but they have to communicate whether it is in a one-on-one situation or leading a class of 20. Communication is more important for those aspiring to management positions. Those people who are introverted need to work on their people skills or they will not thrive in this field. If someone has an interest in this field it is important to talk to somebody in the field. It would also be beneficial to do an internship or get a job at a fitness club to determine whether the field is right for them. It is not for everyone. Do an internship to experience it and be sure the field is for you. A sport management degree is a good degree for those seeking a management or marketing position within a facility. Clubs always need someone who can manage or generate revenue through sales and marketing. Great potential exists to make good money in this industry but it is based on the ability to generate revenue for the company. If you are just an expense for the company you are not going to go too far or last too long. But, if you can create revenue there is no limit to your earning potential. We have had some employees with an exercise physiology degree and after a couple of months here they were bored with their positions as trainers. I was lucky to find my career without much research, but I think students should do research earlier in their schooling to see what they want to do so they do not waste their time. There is nothing worse than seeing a student spend 4 years in school, and then quit a job for which their education prepared them, after 2 months.

In the profit-driven environment, it is essential that I continue to challenge myself. I challenge myself professionally by increasing my expectations. I always review and improve our goals. I am involved with a group that is never satisfied. Once we get 3,000 members we will want 4,000 members. Once we get 5,000 members we will want another facility. Once we have two facilities we will want 10 facilities. To be successful you should surround yourself with people with that type of drive and motivation. Somebody who is satisfied stops growing. For some people that is okay. I am not satisfied and neither are the people with whom I associate. I am confident we will continue to grow and meet our goals. Also, some professionals are interested in running wellness and fitness centers in institutional settings. They get a set salary, a set budget, and there is no pressure to increase membership because there is a built-in clientele. That is okay if that is what you want. But I would be bored to death.

In 10 years I would like to be in a position where I have the options to do what I want to do. Hopefully we will have a number of clubs and the business will be booming. I want to remain in business as an entrepreneur. At that time if I want to take off a day occasionally or take a weekend and go to Bermuda I can do that. I will do what it takes now so that in 10 or 20 years I will not have to any more. I would like to be in the position that if I want to stay home with my children I can or come into work for a couple of hours. I am working toward having that option.

Jody Swimmer

Owner
Swimmer Wellness Services Inc.

Education:
B.S., HEALTH AND PHYSICAL EDUCATION, UNIVERSITY OF LOUISVILLE, 1987

M.A., TEACHING/EXERCISE PHYSIOLOGY, UNIVERSITY OF LOUISVILLE

Career Progression:
PRESIDENT, SWIMMER WELLNESS SERVICES, 1993 TO PRESENT

ACADEMIC INSTRUCTOR, BELLAMINE COLLEGE, 1994

CO-OWNER AND VICE PRESIDENT, CORPORATE FITNESS SERVICES, INC., 1989 TO 1993

Best piece of advice you received in regards to your career:

"Embrace your competitors for they will make you work harder and smarter. Always be the best you can be."

MY FATHER

Best advice for someone aspiring toward a career in the sport industry:

"Identify your strengths and weaknesses; maximize your strengths and surround yourself with people who will complement you."

Quote by which you live:

"Live each day to the fullest and give and receive love every day."

I BEGAN THINKING ABOUT A CAREER IN SPORT in the early 1980s when I decided to go to college as a business major. I moved around a bit, ended up in Louisville, and decided to go into physical education. At that time I was teaching. I had always taught physical activities, such as gymnastics, horseback riding, swimming, and aerobics. By the time I moved to Kentucky I was older and needed to get at least an undergraduate degree. I considered physical therapy, but did my undergraduate work in health and physical education. I already had a minor in business from Queens College in Charlotte, North Carolina. I was establishing myself in Kentucky and started school at the University of Louisville at the same time. After finishing my undergraduate degree, I went into my master's program and was awarded a graduate teaching assistantship in the physical education department. I continued teaching and taught some 100 level and 200 level courses. I earned a master of arts in teaching from the University of Louisville in health and physical education. I continued to teach and work my way through school. I pursued the certification route for health and physical education so I could teach in Kentucky. At the same time I considered wellness and taught some of that in my physical education classes. My mentors in the school system showed me how frustrating it could be in local school systems. With my graduate studies gearing away from physical education and more into wellness, I was at the right place at the right time when Ford Motor Company called the university and wanted interns in 1985. I was two-thirds of the way through graduate school. It took an extra semester to finish my graduate work because I worked so many jobs at the·same time. I went to corporate wellness with that opportunity with Ford Motor Company. I was fortunate because I was at a good place at a good time.

As I evolved in my education I enjoyed teaching physical education, but I could not see it as a career. I liked the advanced students and the older students because they were more interested in health-related activities and wellness rather than games. I do not know how to do games. I am not that kind of person. I do not play sports like volleyball or basketball. I was always involved in individual and not team sports. I am not creative in that arena whereas many people are so it was uncomfortable. I enjoyed teaching the college students health-related fitness skills.

My parents grew up in the Depression, so they did not have access to things such as the arts, ballet, and gymnastics. They let us try those different avenues and that is how it began with me. My basic experience came from an instructor who was a physical therapist by trade, but a gymnast and modern dancer by art. I have this conglomeration in me of yoga, physical therapy, gymnastics, and ballet. I am not good at any of it, but I understand the basic skills and the appropriate steps of neuromuscular facilitation exercises. I always enjoyed the conditioning aspects of those activities, because I was not good in the art forms. As I got older I found that I was good at teaching physical conditioning activities, as well as wellness in general.

My parents are my ultimate role models. Both of my parents have always taken extremely good care of themselves. Their morals and attitudes are very fine, outstanding, and commendable. We have always had a strong work ethic in our family.

Currently, I am the owner of Swimmer Wellness Services. We operate two commercial and several corporate sites around the city of Louisville. Half of the business in terms of the revenues comes from corporate wellness receipts. Ford Motor Company is my largest client. I am the vendor for health and wellness services for the Kentucky Truck Plant in Louisville. On a daily basis I hire, fire, and supervise all employees. I have anywhere from 10 to 15 employees per month. I have five full-time employees and some part-time employees at all the different sites. I do the normal paperwork associated with any business, as well as the mail and the payroll. I also do the bookkeeping. My day generally starts at 4:00 AM because I open a site at 6:00 AM. My role now has evolved with the commercial sites so I do all the personal training that people purchase. I train clients who want personal training other than what we offer as complimentary services. I have my own clients. I oversee the management of the commercial sites. Fitness on Frankfort and Fitness in Middletown are my commercial spots. Fitness on Frankfort has been open for 4 years, and Fitness in Middletown will be open 3 years in May 2000. They are different yet similar in many ways. The commercial clubs are open 6:00 AM to 10:00 PM Monday through Friday, 7:00 AM to 5:00 PM on Saturday, and 11:00 AM to 5:00 PM on Sunday. That is about 16 hours a day during the week. On the corporate side, I have Ford Motor Company's Kentucky Truck Plant, which is open 20 hours a day, 7 days a week. We have some smaller accounts such as the Transit Authority of River City, which is the bus system. This site is open 10 hours a week. I have a chemical plant in the west end of town called Rohm and Haas, Incorporated. It is a lucrative position because a fitness center is located in the middle of the plant and programs are conducted there. Rohm and Haas is proactive with back safety and injury prevention and health. I also have a company called Bakery Chef. The owner is proactive because a small fitness center is provided and supported on-site. It is a production company with about 400 employees. Those are my commercial and corporate sites.

Mondays are typically 14-hour days because I start at 6:00 AM and work until supper. I am attempting now on Tuesday and Thursdays not to open so that I can get a little rest, get out with my dogs, or do some paperwork. Mondays, Wednesdays, and Fridays are generally my long days. Typically, I spend a good 10 to 15 hours a week at home working on the books and so forth.

I face obstacles all the time. I am a woman, but I ignore that fact. When we grew up we did not differentiate between the sexes. I do not perceive myself in that way. However, in dealing with mundane activities such as getting the roof fixed or the toilet fixed in my facility, I can be confronted with the issue of "What does she know about it?" In terms of business in the local area, I have lost corporate jobs because a man in a suit did a slick presentation. I do not perceive the world this way but some people cannot deal with a strong woman in business. I was raised to be goal driven. Sometimes when you compete with the opposite sex they are not pleased with you. Usually I ignore it. Sometimes it is funny because this attitude does not affect how I see myself or how I do business because I treat everyone equally. If you are kind, generous, and smile at me, I will always do that initially. But if you show I need to pull out a stronger side of myself, then I will do so.

Scheduling the staff is the worst part of my job. Robert Beury is my vice president, and he does the scheduling. He has a master of science in health education. He is wonderful. We complement one another. Robert helps me with the employees and the scheduling. Scheduling is a nightmare because individuals request certain hours to cover the shifts and so forth. When Robert was on his honeymoon I decided he would do the scheduling when he came back. If I do the schedule and have a problem with an employee it means more than just scheduling. It means I have to hire and fire. I delegated scheduling to Robert, and he is excited about it. He is good about documentation and he is a teacher by trade. He likes to train and help the employees improve. Two months ago I was ready to sell because I could not do it all. Scheduling took another 10 hours a month and was frustrating. I feel so much better because I have delegated it. Part of being a business owner is learning to delegate and being clear on what you need. I enjoy many things about my job; otherwise I would not continue to do it. The best part is helping people feel better about themselves. Because we are not clinical, people come to us because something occurred to make them come through our doors, whether at a corporate or commercial site. Building a name for yourself and a reputation in the community helps with business. Networking is often the source of your referrals. We have many physicians who refer us to their patients, even though we are not directly affiliated with any hospitals or clinics.

To work in this field, one needs technical skills gained from experience and education. Technical skills mean fitness testing, exercise testing, and qualifications to work with individuals postrehab as well as with those with aches, pains, and limitations. Certifications are required. Fitness professionals should have at least a health fitness instructor certification from the American College of Sports Medicine and/or the Certified Strengthening Conditioning Specialist from the National Strength and Conditioning Association. Robert and I are also medical exercise specialists from an organization lead by a physical therapist, Mike Jones, who is phenomenal. He is bridging the gap between the clinical and the nonclinical setting. Certifications and education are the criteria. When I interview, I always tell people that they may have the credentials on their resume, but they must have people skills. I do not require everyone to be bubbly, but they must have a somewhat outgoing personality. My motto is take initiative because when one takes initiative then things happen.

Technology does have an impact on the health and fitness industry. It is important to keep up with what is on the market and the latest gimmicks in cardiovascular equipment or weight training machines. However, on the other side it is nontechnical because once we start training and working with people, we invariably go to the dumb-bells and the bar-bells. That is just as basic as you can get. Basic floor exercises and flexibility activities requiring a body and maybe some assistance from a rope may be all we need. I like to strip away all the fancy stuff and get down to the essence. I think the basics are essential. When I buy equipment, from an owner's point of view, I consider maintenance. We do not buy everything with all the bells and whistles because if one part goes out it can be a big expense, thus requiring a big shutdown on the equipment. If we have a treadmill, for example, it goes faster, slower, up and down, and keeps track of mileage, time, and maybe pulse. It is pretty basic. We do not need those high-tech programs because we teach people how to interval train. Here we get back to personal service. Sometimes when people think of sport, they only think product. This part of the sport industry is a service industry. We are in a personal service industry because my clubs are small, only 4,000 square feet. We average about 500 members or approximately 2,000 visits per month per club. Ford is open 20 hours a day, so they average about 200 people a day. We have performed nearly 4,000 fitness assessments at Ford over a 5-year period. Those are good numbers. But again, it is a service industry so we need to pay attention to our client. To retain clients we must do a good job. That is what I expect my staff to do: pay attention to the client.

In terms of commercial fitness centers there will always be the big clubs and the nonprofit organizations such as the YMCA and the Jewish Community Center. Large multifaceted complex facilities will always exist. The more elaborate ones would be in the east, in California, or at a resort type situation. There has always been a place for multipurpose facilities. I think the trend will be toward smaller clubs because they are more service-oriented. They cover what you need rather than all of the stuff you may not need. You pay for what you want to use. For the next 10 years, I think small business owners like myself will continue to struggle in small cities. More educated people will exercise, as opposed to the general population perhaps. Within 10 years, though, I think we will see more people with health club memberships and not just in the wealthiest areas of the country or towns. I think job opportunities will increase because consumers will need help with basic exercise programs. Those people with degrees and education should find more opportunities because more people know they need help. The combination of sport management and exercise science degrees is the most marketable package for a recent graduate. They know how to run a facility and have the necessary science skills to work with clients.

Personal training is on the rise and people like me will hire people with degrees because they can work with the clients and keep the clients coming back. We do not push sales on individuals. My direction for the staff is to get a prospective customer to sign up for an appointment for a complimentary personal training. That is the extent of our hard sale. I do not base their salary on percentages of sales. I think employees appreciate that because they do not want to be like a car salesperson in a gym. They want to show people what they know. That is why they are in this field. They want to help people with a safe and effective exercise program. That is their motivation. If they are doing a good job they will get people to enroll. Their salary would reflect that they are doing a good job.

How do I define success? I learned an important lesson several years ago when I lost a best friend. I realized the most important thing is to be happy, to give love, and receive love every single day. It is something I remind myself of every day. If I can do that, that is success. Of course, I have to pay the bills and that makes it a lot easier. Some people are hurting and that is sad. I want to reach out, be available to people, and stop what I am doing and pay attention if somebody is needy. Sometimes that is all someone needs: attention. It may just be a little thing, but for me it is meaningful.

Every year I project my desired receipt level, and this year I made it! I will continue to project my receipts, profits, and new business. With that in mind, I may open a third location in the city. I am evolving in this business and learning more every day on how to manage it more efficiently and effectively. Two things keep me from opening a third facility: time and staff retention. On time, I would like to make some money this year because I have some things I want to do personally. On staff, I think the reason for turnover might be graduates' unrealistic expectations of a $30,000 salary. We cannot offer a 9 to 5 job. They have to work early or late and on weekends. It is a 5-day work week, but it is not necessarily Monday through Friday. That is how it is in the sport industry. When I speak to students I explain that they will have different type of schedule than their peers in different industries. That is typical of the sport industry. We work at a place where everyone goes to for fun or relaxation. I think that may be part of it. I am not saying that is across the board because I have some wonderful young people. Many of them understand what it takes to succeed.

If I were to give advice to someone who is entrepreneurial in spirit, I would say that to go into business you do not just say, "I think that sounds like a good idea." It takes energy and love of what you do. That is the essence. They need something to fall back on because money does not come out of thin air. I was fortunate. Timing is everything. I have paid for my house, I have a car, and I have taken care of personal matters. I can afford to go without money. A person needs some extra money to get started because start-ups are expensive. You do not just automatically start getting money in the door. Fitness on Frankfort did, but it was unique. Middletown was more like a real business. I have struggled for 3 years. I started in corporate fitness where there was no overhead. I had two employees. We made a go of it, gained a couple of clients, kept them going, and we are building from there. Then I received the contract for the Kentucky Truck Plant, and it was lucrative. I am fortunate to have that income each month to cover expenses. Payroll is the biggest expense. With the commercial clubs, I pay for equipment, rent, electricity, repairs, and so forth. When people say it does not cost anything to give a free membership, I want to choke them. It does cost; everything costs. To start a business, you must have energy, work hard, and have some type of resource because the most I ever made once was $30,000. People need to know that when they start off they are not going to make money immediately. It takes time for the cash flow to catch up, and then you have to work hard to keep the income higher than the expenses.

I am a control freak. I like to be in control of my positions and I have difficulty going through hoops because I am a decision maker. I was raised to make decisions. My father always said to make a decision and do something. If it is not right, fix it. I surround myself with people who make me follow the procedures when necessary. I get bored easily. A small business owner needs the ability to focus and remember what it is to be organized. There are so many things to consider when starting a business.

Should a small business owner rent or buy property? That depends on how much money is available. Renting would be the best option because up-fitting can be expensive. Up-fitting means building out your space until it can accomplish what you need it to do. When I gained the lease on Fitness on Frankfort I had to spend $30,000 to up-fit. I thought I was going to have a heart attack. This particular building had been many things. Right before I received it, it housed a florist. I was fortunate because they had updated one bathroom and had made it attractive in terms of lighting. That saved me a big expense. Some tile work was done in the front with the flooring. All I had to do was put in a bathroom, the showers, changing areas, and rubber flooring. That is minimal. Thirty thousand dollars is a bargain. Then we spent between $100,000 and $150,000 on equipment for a 4,000-square foot facility. Fitness on Frankfort was a bargain. When I opened Middletown it was in a strip mall and it was ground up, $300,000 for 4,000 square feet. I had the capital for the $30,000 up-fit on Frankfort. I had saved that money and obtained a lot of credit from a bank. I did not have to deal with the Small Business Association because I have good credit. I owned a house and my vehicle. I had small loans in the past to show my payoff abilities. For the $100,000 I needed to borrow, my father cosigned. I paid it back in a year and six months. That was phenomenal because I was paid myself, too! That was a good year because I made $30,000.

Success is always about location. I was comfortable with the area in terms of how to go retail. I have lived in the neighborhood for 15 to 16 years and watched it change to more diverse demographics with a younger population, people my age (40), and some younger families. I was comfortable with opening a facility in this neighborhood. The space was small, but it can be done if you know how to plan and design. I tried for more than 2 years to get this building. When the business before me failed, the landlords were ready to talk to me, although they wondered, "A gym in that space? How is that going to work?" They could not see it, but I could. I got married in April 1995 and in August we were finally getting ready to go on our honeymoon, which was a trip to the beach. The landlords called and said, "We want to talk to you about leasing the location." When I came back at the end of August, we negotiated it and opened for business on November 1, 1995. I put a sign in the window, "Opening November 1," missed the Yellow

Page deadline, was not in the phone book for one year, and made my minimum for overhead in the first month. Frankfort Avenue has been good to me. I also had the corporate business to fall back on when needed. I got pretty exuberant and decided in a year and a half to do the second location. My accountant did not agree with me, but I was not getting any younger and I needed to go forward.

The Middletown location makes me go to the hairdresser every month to cover up my gray. Middletown is nuevo-riche. My clients on Frankfort have just as much money or more, but they do not act like it. Middletown is in the east end of town where the people with the big corporate jobs go to live for the location. They have these great big houses sitting next to one another. The attitude bothered me so I decided not to put up with those jerks. When you have that negativity, it creates the wrong energy. I refuse to have the wrong energy created in my environment. I just kindly say, "If you aren't happy with what I have to offer, I'm sorry, this is the best we can do. Maybe you need to go down the street." It is nice to be 40 and comfortable enough to say I do not need to have every person. We are just working on making Middletown diverse and hoping that it happens. This is the first year we met my income expectations in Middletown. We are located near an expressway because it is convenient and hope we are visible to those that do not live in Middletown. It is a good location but it is taking time to get where it needs to be.

In this industry, you need to choose your niche. My father always said not to worry about competitors but to welcome them. Have them open next door because then the consumer has choices, and it makes you better. Do what you do and do it well, but do only what *you* do. Do not try to be what everybody else is. Be what you are and be good at it. I think that it is important to try things. Whatever you do, do it well. If you have difficulty, seek out people who can mentor you and teach you the skills you need to become better. Then you know you are better at the business than anything else. You have to be willing to work hard no matter what the obstacle, but in the long run, it is worth it.

CHAPTER 12

Recreational Sports

AS THE COMPLEXITIES OF LIFE CONTINUE TO CHANGE at a rapid pace, the need for recreational diversion will continue. Whether in the form of youth sport leagues, summer camps, whitewater rafting, camping in national parks, co-ed sports, the local YMCA, fitness activities, or master-level senior competitions, recreation is an important and continual aspect of life. To assist and promote the benefits of recreation, recreation professionals need to diversify their skills and training. Technology, federal and state legal issues, marketing, finance, and facility infrastructure changes present challenges to those pursuing a career in recreational sport.

The landscape of recreation is constantly changing. Demographic changes will dictate flexibility in recreation programming. U.S. recreation participants are becoming older, more racially and ethnically diverse, include more women, and are more urban. The median age for a person living in 2025 is expected to be 41, with the largest segment of population middle-aged and older. It is anticipated that approximately 81 percent of the expected U.S. population growth by 2025 will be attributed to minorities with the Latino/Latina group leading the way (Dwyer, 1994). According to the Sporting Goods Manufactures Association, 53 percent of participants in recreational fitness activities are women, which is a 33 percent increase since 1987 (Riddle, 1997).

The recreation field is broad and diverse with many segments. Community-based recreation programs cater to the local population needs. Organizations such as the local park and recreation department, YMCA and YWCA, Jewish Community Center, Boys' and Girls' Clubs, and the Boy and Girl Scouts also cater to the local population needs.

Military, outdoor, university, and therapeutic recreation are other important segments of the recreation industry. The armed services have provided a variety of recreational opportunities for military personnel and their families to encourage fitness, morale, and community. Nonprofit and for-profit organizations provide a mix of outdoor pursuits ranging from ski activities, water sports, golf, summer camps, tourist travel, and camping. University recreation centers provide a variety of activities for both internal and external publics. Students, faculty, and alumni have access to backpacking, rock climbing, skiing, canoeing and kayaking, and ropes courses for outdoor pursuits. In addition, a wide range of sports is offered at most colleges at intramural and club competition levels. Finally, recreation is increasingly used to improve an individual's physical, emotional, and mental state in the therapeutic recreation segment. Recreation used as part of the treatment or rehabilitation program may be hospital based, social service originated, state youth services directed, or even court referred.

Salaries in the recreation field vary based on the organization and the scope of the responsibilities. Entry-level positions in recreational organizations such as YMCAs pay in the low to mid $20,000s. Coordinator positions can pay in the mid $30,000s whereas executive directors can earn more than $40,000 a year. Pay in community recreation programs may not be as high but is similar. Positions in recreation at institutions like colleges and universities offer similar salaries for positions but may offer better benefit packages such as tuition waivers and retirement plans. Recreation directors at universities will earn more than those at a smaller college due to the scope and size of a university's recreation program.

Careers in recreation can provide fulfilling opportunities to work in a pleasing environment and develop a healthy lifestyle. Professionals most frequently are trained in a shortened "skills" approach or sometimes through academic degree programs. Those who wish to pursue vocations in recreation must be people and service oriented and understand the growing safety, legal, and risk management needs of a litigious and thrill-seeking society. They must adapt quickly to program needs as participant demographics change and have the willingness to partner with public, private, and government agencies to meet the needs of the community.

REFERENCES

Dwyer, J. (1994). *Customer diversity and the future demand for outdoor recreation* (General Technical Report RM-252), Fort Collins, CO: U.S. Department of Agriculture, Forest Service.

Riddle, J. (1997, February). *1997 state of the industry report.* Report presented at The Super Show, Atlanta, GA.

Bradley C. Petty

Assistant Director for Recreational Sports

North Carolina State University

Education:

B.S., CRIMINAL JUSTICE, SAM HOUSTON STATE UNIVERSITY, 1994

M.S., SPORTS ADMINISTRATION, UNIVERSITY OF SOUTHERN MISSISSIPPI, 1996

Career Progression:

ASSISTANT DIRECTOR FOR RECREATIONAL SPORTS, NCSU, 1998 TO PRESENT

COORDINATOR OF INTRAMURALS, BAYLOR UNIVERSITY, 1997 TO 1998

COORDINATOR OF INTRAMURALS, CLUB SPORTS, AND OPEN RECREATION, JAMES MADISON UNIVERSITY, 1996 TO 1997

OFFICIAL, SAM HOUSTON STATE UNIVERSITY, 1990 TO 1994

Best piece of advice you received in regards to your career:

**"Always use the POW Theory when you work.
The POW Theory: Preparation, Organization, and Work."**

STEVE REY, UNIVERSITY OF SOUTHERN MISSISSIPPI

Best advice for someone aspiring toward a career in the sport industry:

"Network and get to know administrators in the field."

Quote by which you live:

**"Treat others as you want to be treated. In any situation,
always maintain integrity and professionalism."**

I GREW UP IN HALLSVILLE, IN NORTHEAST TEXAS. I participated in sports during my junior high and high school years, but I was not a starter most of the time. I participated in football and basketball until my sophomore year, and then realized varsity sports was not my niche. I remained interested in athletics, however, as a spectator and intramural participant. I attended college at Sam Houston State University from 1990 to 1994. I went there with the basic intention of becoming a law enforcement officer. Although no one in my family was in criminal justice, I always had a general interest in the law, especially sports law, and Sam Houston had a strong academic program. I majored in criminal justice and had a minor in psychology. Although my parents were paying for my education, I called them during the spring semester of 1991 and told them I wanted to work. My only previous job experience had been in the hardware department and as a cashier at Wal Mart. I noticed in the Sam Houston State student newspaper that referees were needed in the campus recreation department, and the starting pay was $5 per game.

Despite no previous experience, I applied for the officiating position. I attended three clinics and several lectures, studied rules and mechanics, watched films and videos, and had some on-court practice. I had to understand the difference between being a spectator and a referee. As a spectator, you tend to watch the ball and cheer and sometimes yell at the referees when they make mistakes. But as an official you are in control of the game and determine its pace and tempo. You are a final judge and expected to be impartial and unbiased. At the completion of the 3-day training clinic, everyone was hired regardless of ability level. I began a weekly intramural schedule officiating the 4 major sports at that time: football, basketball, softball, and volleyball. I enjoyed working with flag football the most. When you first start as a referee, you enjoy the feeling of power and authority, and that related to my interest in majoring in criminal justice. I loved being around sports, and if I could not be a play, officiating was a great way to get involved.

Soon, the graduate assistant who oversaw the intramural program, Randall Ford, asked if I would be a supervisor. The supervisor position was a step up from the official's aspect, because they were the authority over the officials and in charge of all administrative aspects of the competitions. There was not a lot of on the field or on the court training at that time to be a supervisor. You officiated or supervised with an experienced individual two to three nights a week until you learned the job. Later that school year, Randall asked if I would like to attend some flag football officiating tournaments and perhaps referee at the regional, state, or national level. Randall told me that Steve Rey, the official's director at the national invitational flag football championships, had granted us three bids to go to New Orleans to officiate and asked if I would be interested. Despite being a rookie and an official for only one year and one semester, I was anxious and determined to do well. The first year it was a great learning experience and I enjoyed it. I learned a lot from the classroom and field training conducted by Steve Rey and associate director of officials, David Gastons from East Carolina University.

The National Flag Football competition normally begins December 27th and runs through the Sugar Bowl. It is a round robin tournament of intramural champions or individuals at universities that organize a team. We have had as many as 250 male, female, and co-ed teams. Normally all 50 states are represented, as well as teams from Mexico and military bases in Germany and Italy. The finals are normally held the day before the Sugar Bowl and the champions and runner-ups of all the divisions, with all the All-American officials, go to an exhibition game in the Sugar Bowl before the game. About 112 flag football officials across the country are assigned to crews to officiate throughout the tournament. The top 12 officials receive the All-American honor, and I was lucky to be honored with that award my first year.

The next school year, I helped with the official's clinics with all the sports. I continued to officiate and got more involved with church leagues, recreational leagues outside of intramurals, and with the prison league. With a large prison population in Huntsville, intramural championships were held in the prison league. The first year in officiating outside of the campus atmosphere was a difficult adjustment. I was used to working with people my same age and with individuals who knew me and my quality and supervision skill. However, in the church, recreation, and prison leagues I was younger than the competitors, and was expected to control games being played by experienced men. It was a challenge, but I grew fast as an official learning how to adapt and control the games.

I continued to work more tournaments, especially in basketball and softball. Officiating became a year-round experience as I went from one sport to another as the seasons changed. I loved officiating flag football and worked in tournaments in Pensacola, Texas, and west Florida. Again, I went to the nationals in New Orleans and was honored with my second All-American officiating award. Steve Rey asked me to be the referee in a training video for what was called the National Intramural-Recreational Sports Association (NIRSA). I became involved with that organization as a student member and worked on training videos for officials in several sports. Through working on videos to train officials, I met more people in flag football who became mentors to me. Bruce Maurer, number 38 in the NFL as a line judge, was an official supervisor in New Orleans and just seeing his presence, demeanor, and control influenced me to be more professional as an official. He also challenged me to consider a career in officiating. Through the videos, I became more well-known and accepted at the clinics and workshops for referees.

During my third and fourth years in college, I assumed more responsibility in the intramural department. I became the official's coordinator, a job that involved training, supervising, scheduling, and evaluating the officials. In academics, I considered changing my major to sport administration. I was advised, however, that if I changed my major it would require additional 2 years to complete that degree plan. I chose to finish in criminal justice. I decided to pursue a master's degree in sport administration and seek out a graduate assistantship that not only would pay tuition and fees, but also would provide a stipend to work in a recreational sports department. I would receive additional training and responsibility as a graduate assistant in intramurals and campus recreation, and that experience would help me in a career in the sports industry.

I went to the NIRSA national conference with the sole purpose of interviewing and obtaining a graduate assistantship. The NIRSA national conference offers presentations, workshops, training sessions for officials, and a career opportunity center. Graduate assistant positions, internship positions, and full-time positions are advertised in all recreational sports divisions including fitness, informal, outdoor, facility, marketing, intramurals, and officiating. I looked for positions in the geographical areas of my interest and for schools that had a good reputation in sport administration and sport management. I selected seven schools to interview with and received offers to all seven. I was told that if I had my SAT and GRE scores, a 3.0 grade point average, and interviewed well that an offer might be made following the interview. I received all of my offers at the convention. The best thing about the NIRSA convention is the opportunity to network with other professionals in your career field. Annually, more graduate assistantships are available than there are people to fill them. At any given time as many as 200 graduate assistantships are available that waive tuition and fees and provide stipends, sometimes as much as $10,000 a year. A graduate assistantship pays you to go to school and work, but not enough people are interested. My advice to any aspiring recreation professional is to get your degree paid for by accepting a graduate assistant position!

I narrowed my choice to two schools: the University of Southern Mississippi (USM), where Steve Rey was, and Ohio State, where Bruce Maurer was located. Both schools had super academic programs, and I knew both gentlemen very well. My choice was the University of Southern Mississippi because of the immediate response to admission in the master's degree program in sport administration. I began a 2-year commitment at USM in the fall of 1994. My duties included working with intramurals, training and supervising officials, and administrating the club sport program. I continued to officiate in church and recreational leagues, but also started high school officiating. Steve Rey, a veteran high school and college official, helped me get started refereeing high school football, basketball, and volleyball. He was the assigning secretary for softball, so I became involved with softball leagues and high school softball. I worked my way up and umpired some of the junior college softball games.

Some people think that officiating in high school can be political. The assigning secretaries often determine the number and quality of games that an official works. I have been fortunate to have had secretaries who focused on the ability and mechanics of the officials, rather than on the personalities involved. Normally a shortage of officials exists around the country. Everyone likes to yell at the officials and gripe at the officials but no one wants to be one. It is a field that you can make decent money, especially as a student or graduate student.

I enjoyed the academic program in sport administration at USM. I had good instructors and they showed me the importance of training for my field in the framework of a professional, even while I was a student. The program was flexible and let me focus on my particular area of interest and career vocation in the assignments, research, presentations, papers, and grant proposals. My academic program further prepared me for success in my career.

After 2 years at the USM, I again went to the NIRSA convention; however, this time I was looking for full-time professional positions. I went through the career opportunity center again; however fewer full-time professional positions, perhaps only 10–12 per year, were available. To secure a job you must know people, you must do quality work, and your experiences must be in a quality manner. Normally, they look at universities with high reputations of sport administration programs. Of all graduate assistants that came out of USM, they are still in the field of recreational sports. I interviewed with three different schools and accepted the job offer at James Madison University in Virginia. As the coordinator of intramural sports and open recreation I was involved in the opening of a new $18 million recreational facility, which was a big selling point for that position. I worked there for 18 months and was promoted to the sport club coordinator in charge of three different divisions—intramurals, open recreation, and sport clubs. I also was responsible for two graduate assistants, 15 supervisors, and more than 200 officials. It was a big and challenging job.

After 18 months at James Madison, Steve Rey called and told me he had been named the director of recreation at Baylor University in Waco, Texas. He asked me to join him as coordinator of intramural sports. The position was near my original home and included a higher salary, three graduate assistants, and a $30 million facility on the planning board. At Baylor, I would also have the opportunity to continue my education and pursue a doctoral degree. I began work at Baylor, but quickly discovered that a private college's philosophy could be different from public schools. A reorganization period occurred and the recreation program was moved under the student affairs division instead of the human performance and recreation division, and we reported to a different university leader. I left and went back to the NIRSA convention looking for another position. I was hired at North Carolina State as assistant director for officials, and was put in charge of the officials' program and the office staff for customer service. This is one of the first programs in the country that splits officials from intramurals. There are 2 different divisions. They do not report to the same individual and with that we could strive for the development of student officials and focus more time in their training, assessment, and evaluation. I started work at NC State on July 13, 1998.

At NC State all students are required to take two credits of physical education. The enrollment is about 28,000 students, and we have 48–50 full-time faculty and staff in the division. Our primary focus is not instruction but we do have the lecturer title because we are in the physical education division. Our primary focus is in intramural sports. Within this division, we also offer a wide variety of activities in outdoor recreation and club sports, and we have a marketing division. Last year we had 9,900 students involved in our programs, approximately 1/3 of the student campus population. I oversee approximately 20 student staff supervisors and nearly 200 officials in this department.

Our basic work schedule is 9–5 Monday through Friday. We have facility managers who supervise programs each night. We have a 400,000 square foot recreation facility with 11 basketball courts, a climbing wall, 2 indoor pools, an indoor jogging track, a fitness facility, a cardiovascular room, a sauna, gyms, an equipment checkout, and locker rooms. We also have an outdoor rental storehouse as well as 12 to 14 acres of outdoor facility space. We manage 50 club sports, which is one of the largest in the country, and we offer approximately 25 to 30 intramural sports. We also have aerobic activities each night and informal activities such as table tennis and badminton tournaments, darts, and archery. Our office hours are deceiving because from 9–5 the students are in school, but at 5:00 PM intramurals start. My typical workday is doing office administration from 9:00 AM to 5:00 PM, and then supervise and evaluate officials and supervisors from 5:00–9 PM.

To be successful in campus recreation, it is essential to have a well-rounded lifestyle. I am involved with my local church and in professional activities through NIRSA. I attend conferences and workshops to grow as a professional. I have learned that for my health and well being it is best to not work every night and to have other activities to help manage the long hours and high stress levels of my job. One of the enjoyment outlets I have is to officiate high school and college sport activities some nights and weekends.

My three ultimate professional goals are to be a director of an intramural recreational sports program,* oversee an entire campus recreation division, and rise in the leadership ranks at NIRSA to perhaps become president of the organization some day. I would like to officiate in the NFL someday. I would also love to continue my graduate education and earn a PhD. Within the next 5 years, however, I would like to be a director.

Campus recreation and intramurals continue to evolve and change as student interests change. Team competitions in flag football, basketball, volleyball, softball, and soccer have traditionally been popular. Now students are more interested in instruction, health, fitness, and wellness. Newer trends seem to show an interest in participation rather than competition in such activities as aerobics, rock

---

*Editor's note: In January 2000, Brad Petty achieved his dream ambition when he was named Director of Intramurals and Recreation at Angelo State University in San Angelo, Texas.

climbing, scuba, water aerobics, and cycling. During the past 5 to 10 years, intramural sport participant numbers have decreased, whereas outdoor adventure, fitness, and informal recreational activities have increased.

What characteristics help make a person in campus recreation, intramurals, and especially officiating successful? Professionalism, integrity, and confidence are key ingredients. For an official, professionalism exudes from your demeanor on the field, your game control, and even the way your uniform looks. Integrity deals with ruling in a consistent and fair manner at all times. Confidence is being able to sometimes make a bad call, admit your mistake, learn from it, but yet not lose the credibility or support of a coach or the participants. I believe that the collegiate game is easier to officiate than other levels of play. Despite more fans and more pressure to perform, the skill level is higher and the game is more exciting.

Intramurals is a tremendous avenue to develop the training necessary to officiate at higher levels. It takes at least 5 years to become a good official, and the earlier you start the better you will be. Officiating can be fun, rewarding, and an excellent way to earn extra money as a part-time job. College intramurals will generally pay officials $4.25 to $6.25 an hour. Junior high basically is about $35 a game, varying some from state to state. In North Carolina, refereeing junior varsity and varsity is around $65 per game depending on the sport. In Texas, however, your game fee and travel could be as much as $140 per game. Football pays the most because more fans are at the game, which nets more gate receipts. You could earn $600-$700 per person per game officiating a championship game of football in Texas 1A-5A. Junior college and small college competitions do not pay lucrative amounts. Sometimes it is $75 to $90 per game but you cover all of your travel expenses, and at times you have to drive 3 to 4 hours to the game. However, when you get into NCAA Division I officiating, you can receive as much as $600 to $700 per game.

One of the current trends in officiating is the use of the instant replay. In my opinion it should not be used because the human element is an important part of the game. The athletic contest is played by athletes and coaches who make mistakes, as well as officials who are fallible. In baseball, if a player gets a hit 3 out of every 10 at-bats the player is considered an all-star. An official however, is only as good as his or her last call and is held at a higher standard of performance. Most officials do a good job as a part-time professional, but I think it would be a good thing to hire full-time professionals to officiate in the NFL. I doubt the quality of officiating would increase greatly, however, because of the tremendous amount of training and experience of those that reach the professional levels. I would encourage all students who love athletics, but are unable to play at the elite levels, to consider becoming an official or campus recreation professional because it is a satisfying and rewarding career.

Anne Wilkinson

*Fitness Coordinator/Assistant
Facility Manager*
Temple University

Education:
B.S., SPORT ADMINISTRATION, ALLENTOWN
COLLEGE OF ST. FRANCIS DE SALES, 1995
M.S., SPORT MANAGEMENT, TEMPLE
UNIVERSITY, 1996

Career Progression:
FITNESS COORDINATOR/ASSISTANT FACILITY
MANAGER, TEMPLE UNIVERSITY, 1997 TO PRE-
SENT
MEMBERSHIP DIRECTOR, ABINGTON YMCA,
1996
ASSISTANT TICKET MANAGER (INTERN),
PHILADELPHIA PHANTOMS, 1996
ASSISTANT BUSINESS MANAGER (INTERN),
LEHIGH UNIVERSITY, 1995
RECREATION SUPERVISOR, ALLENTOWN
COLLEGE OF ST. FRANCIS DE SALES, 1993 TO
1995

Best piece of advice you received in regards to your career:

"The only way to know if you want to do something is to do it."

ROBIN HAWTHORNE, DIRECTOR OF RECREATION, ALLENTOWN COLLEGE OF ST. FRANCIS DE SALES

Best advice for someone aspiring toward a career in the sport industry:

"Be prepared to pay some dues in the beginning of your career for little pay. Do things to build your resume."

Quote by which you live:

"Hakuna Matata"

DISNEY'S *THE LION KING*

I DECIDED I WANTED TO BE INVOLVED IN THE SPORT management
field in my junior year of high school. I heard about the major being offered at Allentown College of St. Francis de Sales. Originally I was not interested in attending Allentown because my sister went there, but the sport management major
peaked my interest. I loved sports and had played them all through high school. If
I could find a way to make a career out of something I loved I was going to do it.
Currently, I am the fitness coordinator and assistant facility manager for recreation services at Temple University. My main responsibility is running the

59,000-square foot Independence Blue Cross Student Recreation Center on the Temple University campus.

As an undergraduate student at Allentown College my plan was to become the general manager of the Philadelphia 76ers. I was convinced of it and no one could change my mind. In my senior year I was hired as an intramural program supervisor for the recreation department at Allentown. That experience made me interested in recreation. The director of recreation, Robin Hawthorne, introduced me to the administrative aspect of recreation and intramural programs. I saw what she did on a daily basis and I realized it was a lot more than putting out the cones for flag football and refereeing or cleaning up after the games. That experience also opened my eyes to the career opportunities in recreation. After I graduated from Allentown in the spring of 1995, I received a graduate assistantship in the recreation department at Temple University. In this experience I saw how a large university's recreation department operated. Allentown's recreation program was well run, but was smaller because of the small size of the school. Temple had an extensive club sport program, a large and diverse intramural program, 1-day special events, and a large fitness area. My senior year at Allentown and my first year as a graduate assistant at Temple solidified my career path.

I still had lingering thoughts about working in professional sports or even college athletics. As a senior at Allentown, I completed an internship with the business manager for athletics at Lehigh University. My site supervisor, Tracey Summerfield, gave me some hands-on experience in the business side of college athletes. I reconciled tickets for home contests, printed tickets and prepared promotional materials for sport camps. This experience made me realize that college athletics was not a game—it was a product. During my first year at Temple I compared the experience at Lehigh with my experience as a graduate assistant in recreation at Temple and realized I enjoyed the recreation more than the business side.

While serving as a graduate assistant at Temple, I was also enrolled in the sport management master's degree program. Although I leaned toward the career in recreation, I decided to do my graduate-level internship in the ticket office with the Philadelphia Phantoms, a minor league hockey team in the American Hockey League. As an undergraduate I had wanted to work in professional sports, so I wanted to get an experience in the professional sport environment to make sure I was making the right decision. While working with the Phantoms I missed the actual hands-on dealings with the patrons or the clients. With the Phantoms I did a lot more behind-the-scenes work with tickets. I dealt more with the staff and I did not interact with the fan base. I missed looking at people and seeing the enjoyment that I provided to them. One of the aspects I enjoy most about what I do is the interaction with the clients. On an average day I see 1,200 people in the fitness facility. I enjoy getting to know them, even if it is just recognizing a face. The biggest joy I get is when after teaching a group fitness session, members talk to me about either fitness issues or how their day went. Getting to know them makes it worthwhile for all the behind-the-scenes work. I was not experiencing that at the Phantoms.

Even though I decided against a career in the professional sport environment, the Phantom experience was positive because I learned a great deal about problem solving and the importance of customer service. I realized that I had to be friendly even if someone was screaming at me. I had to get my point across to the person and still say no while they were screaming. That experience helps me in my current position. I run a restricted-access building. I often have to turn away students and faculty if they do not have the proper identification card. While with the Phantoms I learned how to tell a person no while also sending them away with a little bit of a positive.

I would recommend being a graduate assistant to anyone interested in getting into the recreation field. As a graduate assistant, I earned my graduate degree while gaining practical experience. This made me more marketable. I went to the National Intramural Recreation Sport Association (NIRSA) conference in Louisville, Kentucky, during my second year as a graduate assistant because it is a great conference to learn about job opportunities. I found that most job descriptions for recreation positions in the college environment listed at the conference requested a minimum of 2 years experience in the field and graduate assistantship experience was accepted. That helped me because I did not have the 2 years experience in the field but I had 2 years as a graduate assistant and I earned an advanced degree. The graduate assistantship also helped me increase my network base. When I came out of Allentown, I had a small network of administrators. They referred me to people in their network, so I adopted their networking base. I needed to create my own. In the classes at Temple, I interacted with students who were already in the field and were going back for their degree and then those students like myself trying to get into the field. I also made professional contacts through my work in the recreation department.

With the benefits came a fair amount of sacrifice. I was required to work for the recreation services department 22 hours a week and then I had classes at night. I always worked more than the required 22 hours. In return for what I did in recreation services, I received 9 credits of in-state tuition for each semester and a stipend. I was always on the go and I had very little money. My first-year graduate assistant duties involved working with the sport clubs and assisting in the main office operations. The work in the office had a business orientation. We sold facility passes and guest passes and people had to pay for the aerobics classes. All of these sales had to be tracked and reconciled. My experience at Lehigh prepared me for these responsibilities. In my second year as a graduate assistant I did publicity and promotion for the department. This was great because I enjoy marketing. Along with my recreation department graduate assistantship I secured a graduate resident assistant for the housing department my first year. I had been a resident assistant at Allentown College. I got my housing paid for and part of my meals through my graduate resident assistantship.

I finished my graduate degree and graduate assistantship at Temple in May 1997. I worked at Temple during that summer as a part-time employee and trained the incoming graduate assistant. I tried to keep my name in the mix for positions in the Philadelphia area. I also went to Colorado, Florida, and South Dakota to interview for positions I learned about at the NIRSA conference that I attended the previous spring. I was offered a job in Sioux Falls, South Dakota, and I seriously thought about taking it. It was an assistant director of recreation position and the main responsibilities were related to aquatics. I declined the offer because I didn't have a strong aquatics background other than the fact that I could swim and I wanted to live somewhere on the east coast because my family lives in the Philadelphia area.

In August of that summer I saw an ad in the newspaper for a position at the Ambler YMCA in suburban Philadelphia. I applied and was asked to interview. During the facility tour portion of the interview, I met with the youth sport director who I had met when I was working at Temple. She made me aware of a fitness director position at the Abington YMCA, which was nearby. I did not get the job at the Ambler YMCA, so I interviewed for the fitness director position at Abington. During the interview I was told that they had someone in mind for the fitness director position, but they needed a membership and marketing director and that I was qualified for the position. I interviewed for that job and was offered the job. I began working at the Abington YMCA in August 1997.

While I was with the YMCA, Temple University was working on opening its new fitness and recreation facility. As a graduate assistant I had been involved in the planning of it. I knew they would need someone to do the programming for the facility, but I figured I was not qualified for the position. They wanted somebody with the ability to teach aerobic classes, train a staff, and address fitness-related questions and problems. I was an athlete in college, but I did not have a strong exercise background. My undergraduate and graduate work prepared me for the business end of sports but not the exercise side. In December 1997, the associate director of recreation services at Temple called and asked about my availability. She told me that they still had not filled the position of running the new facility. A national search had brought in three people and all three declined the position. Even though I had not applied for it, she asked if I would send in an application before they reopened the search. This placed me in an interesting situation. The YMCA position was my first full-time job and I was excited about the opportunity, but I walked into a mess. They had not had a membership or marketing director for 8 months so I did paperwork all day to catch up. My office was in the midst of being renovated so I did not have an office or a computer of my own. After 4 months I was feeling organized when the call came. Temple offered me a position that paid more and had a better benefits package. I would be back at a university/college setting and I was offered the opportunity to open my own building. I decided to accept the position. I stopped working at the Abington YMCA on January 6, 1998 and I started working at Temple January 7, 1998. The new building opened 2 weeks later.

The facility I opened and now operate consists of three fitness floors. On the top floor is a 314-meter indoor track. The remaining two stories include areas with more than 300 pieces of equipment. The first floor is a free weight and circuit training area and has a tread wall. The second floor has cardiovascular equipment, selectorized equipment, and a stretching area. We have check-in and equipment check-out counters on both floors and an outdoor court area that is lined for volleyball and badminton and can be used for informal recreation. Four racquetball courts, an aerobic room with a spring-loaded floor, and a martial arts room with rubberized flooring are also available.

Having worked in both the university and private sector environments, I recognized differences in the environments. The YMCA had a diverse clientele. I dealt with clients ranging from 6-month-old children coming for swim lessons to a 98-year-old man taking a spinning class. Because of the variance in demographics and fitness levels it was a challenge to market our facility and programs. I enjoyed the challenge because I enjoy marketing. We did such things as 2-for-1 memberships or bring-a-friend promotions. At Temple we do not do as much marketing as I did at the YMCA. A ready-made membership base exists of students, faculty, staff, alumni, and their guests. Students pay a nominal fee that is added to the tuition bill to use the facility. The college's staff, including the faculty and administrators, is permitted to join the facility at a higher but again a nominal fee. Alumni are allowed to use the facility but at a greater fee. The only marketing I do is for special events. In one aspect the built-in membership is good because I do not have to attract clients. However, I am not challenged to attract new people to the facility.

Overcoming my lack of experience in the fitness area was a major challenge in the first year. I worked hard and I now am certified in general aerobics, yoga, and spinning. I am also certified as a personal trainer. I try to educate myself on as many fitness issues as possible. I have attended four different types of fitness conferences to learn about the different machines. Another challenge was the fact that administrators who hired me knew I was not qualified in the fitness area when I was hired, and they had a little bit of a problem viewing me as qualified once I acquired my certifications. Early on my ideas were getting shot down left and right with the phrase, "You are not qualified." To combat that reaction I made myself qualified.

For the first 18 months that my facility was open, I was the only full-time administrator in the facility. I report directly to the director of recreation services for all facility matters and I report directly to the associate director of recreation services for all programming matters. I am in charge of all group fitness programs and the special events that occur in this facility. The fitness programs, which during the regular semester involves 40 sessions offered over the course of 7 days, include yoga, all types of aerobics, spinning, circuit training, and a walking program. I have 60 students who work for me. These students must be enrolled at Temple University and they can either have a work-study grant or be part-time employees. I oversee 22 part-time group fitness leaders with different talents and who run the different sessions ranging from high impact aerobics to cardio kickboxing. I typically have 2 or 3 graduate assistants who work for me and they each work 22 hours a week in varying shifts. I also try to employ an intern every semester.

My employees are a diverse group of undergraduate students, graduate students, and fitness leaders who are sometimes independent contractors not affiliated with Temple. As a manager I communicate with the groups differently and sometimes differently within the group. The instructors are a self-motivated group who are good at their jobs. I don't really worry too much about what they do in their classes unless I see an abundant amount of comment/suggestion cards with either positive or negative comments. Every time I receive a positive one about a particular leader I let him or her know. I communicate through memos and reminders, but again I try to see them whenever I can. If I have not talked to an instructor in a while I will give a quick call to see how things are going. They may tell me about a small problem that I would not have been aware of if I had not called.

I have to watch my student workers more than the graduate assistants and instructors. We have a three-strike policy. Student supervisors, who help run this facility when I am not here, can write-up someone for being late, but they do not have the power to discipline that person. The write-up comes to me and I investigate what exactly happened. I may talk to the person to inform them of the importance of being on time. If I have spoken to this person already and the problem continues, it goes into their file as a strike. After the third strike, he or she is dismissed. We try to hire as many sport management majors as possible and we emphasize that this is practical experience to put on their resume and it will look good.

The most demanding aspect of running the facility is dealing with my student staff and patrons. Because of the schedule I do not get to see all of the student workers all of the time. We are open 16 hours a day and I usually work 8 to 10 hours. Student building supervisors are given keys to the facility and trained to handle any type of emergency situation and customer service issues. When a patron comes without identification and is irate because he or she is not allowed in the building, the student has to be strong enough not to let the person in even if the person is a regular. Those are the rules and they must be enforced. If a student comes to work out to relieve stress during finals and we do not allow them in because they have not brought their ID, they yell and scream, but obviously they have problems other than not being able to get in to the fitness center. Our student-workers are busy most of the time. We pay minimum wage and we expect them to be perfect all the time. Meanwhile their friend is getting paid the same amount but is at another department doing homework.

Usually my day is 9:00 AM to 5:00 PM. I have some flexibility with my schedule. Some days I will come in at 6:30 AM to open so I can see the morning staff. When I arrive in the morning, I walk through the facility to check on equipment or to check on any other problems. If there is a problem, I will investigate and fix it. If necessary I will call the maintenance company to get something fixed. It usually takes me about 15 minutes to walk through all three floors of the facility. After that I will reconcile my cash drawer from the night before. As mentioned we sell memberships and guest passes, and we also rent lockers and sell day locks. Reconciling is important. If things do not match up at the end of the day when I make my deposits to my associate director and I can't prove what I sold and did not sell, there is a problem. I also review the closing and opening sheets that my facility managers complete at the start and end of each day. During a regular day I spend a lot of time on the computer either proposing special events or writing evaluations of them.

The academic calendar often determines what I am doing. The busy time of year is generally the end of August and the first week of September. That is when all of the students start coming to the facility. Generally, I have a new staff so I am training my staff while also running the facility. I have to plan student's work schedules, train new workers, and refresh returning workers. The patrons ask the student behind the counter a question and expect a correct answer, but at that point in the year the student may have only worked 5 minutes. I spend a great deal of time in the facility especially at the check-in counter during those few weeks. During the year we get some ebbs and flows. For example, during exam time the facility is dead. Our staff will outnumber the amount of students in the facility. The summer is also slow and I use that time for planning for the coming year and preparing for the start of the year.

In my position I use personal skills on a regular basis and they are important. In my first semester, although I focused a great deal of time and effort on the conceptual aspects of the position such as developing long- and short- range plans and creating policy, I also worked on my technical skills by acquiring various certifications. I spent so much time that semester focusing on the conceptual and technical concerns that I did not focus on my personal skills with my staff. I could probably only name about five of the 87 students who worked for me, and I lost 95 percent of them. When I was evaluated after 3 months, I was told that I was hired for my organizational and interpersonal skills. My supervisors thought I could motivate the students and I did not. I was so focused about establishing policies and getting my fitness certifications that I let my strong interpersonal skills slide. Now I focus on my personal skills while also using my conceptual skills.

Communication is so important in regards to those personal skills. I communicate with so many different groups including patrons, student workers, and graduate assistants, and also with the other members in the recreation department on the same level as me as well as my superiors. Early on I had a problem communicating with my superiors. I think my supervisors thought they made a mistake in hiring me. In their minds, I was not doing what they thought I could do best. I was not trained for the position so I was learning the technical aspect of the job while on the job and that affected other aspects of my management including communication. The communication between us was bad, but it has gotten better. One barrier to the communication is that my building is a block away from the main recreation services office so we do not see each other on a regular basis.

To facilitate the communication with patrons, we have a comment/suggestion card system in which patrons can offer suggestions or make comments on how we can do things better. We collect the cards once a week and I read them. The patrons can put their name and number on the card so I call them back and I talk to them about their comment or suggestion. It is important to be customer-friendly. Although I have a ready-made client base I still deal with patron's comments and to try to make them happy.

In the fitness and recreation field it is important to stay in touch with current programming trends. I do a number of different things to stay up on current trends. I may be a little bit more conscientious than others in the field because I do not have the exercise science background. I am a member of several professional organizations that provide publications and certifications that enable me to remain current. I belong to AFAA, which is the Aerobic and Fitness Association of America Federation, and IFPA, The International Foundation of Personal Trainers Association. These organizations are wonderful resources. I also rely on comment cards and input from my instructors. I also may call local clubs to see what programs they offer, how they offer them, and who enrolls in the programs or classes. If enough interest exists and it is something that will be successful in our facility, I take the steps to offer the program. This involves securing an instructor, acquiring the necessary equipment, marketing the program, and making a space available. Sometimes programs that are popular in the club setting may not be as successful for us. This occurred with spinning. At the YMCA it was a popular class, but it has not been as successful for us. On the other hand, cardio kick-boxing is popular at clubs and everyone asks us to offer classes. An overall trend I see is the individualization of recreation. Aerobic classes attract large numbers, but the numbers participating in intramural sport programs are declining. People are so busy that they are not interested in waiting around for someone else or relying on nine other people for a basketball game. They are not willing to rearrange their schedule to meet with a group. They would rather work out by themselves by lifting weights, riding a bike, or getting on a stepper.

The best thing about my experience at Temple is that I can grow strong within myself and in turn that has helped me grow as an administrator. If I would leave here, I am marketable in a field that will never die. Recreation and fitness is not going anywhere. Everyone is doing it. The health and fitness field has expanded so much in recent years that a lot of career opportunities exist. I might be interested in looking beyond the college and university setting. I often feel restricted and have to scale down programs about which I am excited. It would be interesting to move to a corporate fitness center. I would also be interested in training people or giving seminars on stress management. A variety of opportunities exist and the fitness field is only going to get bigger and more important in the future.

Todd A. Sammons

General Manager/PGA Professional
Glenmary Country Club

Education:

B.S., PHYSICAL EDUCATION, UNIVERSITY OF LOUISVILLE, 1994

M.ED., SPORT ADMINISTRATION, UNIVERSITY OF LOUISVILLE, 1998

CERTIFICATE, GOLF ACADEMY OF THE SOUTH, 1989

Career Progression:

GENERAL MANAGER, GLENMARY COUNTRY CLUB, 1996 TO PRESENT

ASSISTANT GOLF PROFESSIONAL, GLENOAKS COUNTRY CLUB, 1994 TO 1996

HEAD GOLF PROFESSIONAL, CAUSEWAY GOLF CLUB, MAY TO OCTOBER 1993

GOLF PROFESSIONAL, HURSTBOURNE COUNTRY CLUB, 1990 TO 1993

ASSISTANT GOLF PROFESSIONAL, BAY HILL CLUB, 1989 TO 1990

CART ATTENDANT, SAHAL POINT COUNTRY CLUB, 1988 TO 1989

SHOP ASSISTANT, CHEROKEE GOLF CLUB, 1987 TO 1988

Best piece of advice you received in regards to your career:

"If you want to play a lot of golf, don't get into the golf business!"

MARK KEMPER, PGA PROFESSIONAL, CHEROKEE G.C.

Best advice for someone aspiring toward a career in the sport industry:

"Get as educated and experienced as you can in sport management, business, and financial affairs."

Quote by which you live:

"Trust in the Lord with all your heart and lean not on your own understanding. In all your ways acknowledge Him and He will make straight your path."

PROVERBS 3: 5,6

I UNOFFICIALLY DECIDED ON A CAREER IN SPORT in 1984. I graduated from high school in 1980 and went to work for the Bank of Louisville. After 3 years I decided that it was not what I wanted to do for the rest of my life. Sitting around at a desk and writing numbers in little boxes all day just does not excite me. I grew up in an athletic type of atmosphere, so I wanted to do something with sports. At the time I did not know exactly what in sports. My dad suggested that I get my teaching degree in physical education, so I went to the University of Louisville and started taking education classes. In my first education class some figures were on the board, and at one end was $22,000 at the other end was $29,000. I am probably exaggerating a little bit, but it was close to those numbers. I asked the teacher what those numbers meant. She said, "That's the pay scale for the Jefferson County Board of Education. That's what you're going to make the first year, $22,000, and over here to the right is what you're going to make after 30 years, $29,000." So I picked my books up, stood up, and she said, "Where are you going?" I told her I was going to drop the class.

At that point I had an opportunity to go to the golf academy in Orlando, Florida. That is when I decided to embark on a managerial career in golf. After being in Orlando, I wanted to return home so I got a job at Hurstbourne Country Club in Louisville as an assistant golf professional. I went through the normal process as far as the golf business goes and became a head golf professional. I made a couple of moves that I would not recommend. One of them was going to Maine as a head golf professional. That was a seasonal position, so I came back to Louisville and got married that fall. We decided not to return to Maine because it was a drab place. It was only good for a couple of months. July, August, and September were great. I went up in June and it was 40 degrees outside, right on the ocean. It was a beautiful place, but it is not economical. We decided at that point I should get my degree. I was on the 15-year plan, so I finished my studies at the University of Louisville. During that time I worked at GlenOaks Country Club as an assistant, and this job opened at Glenmary. I earned my master's in sport administration from the University of Louisville because I knew it would be beneficial for me.

Although a lot of positions in sport are desk positions, I prefer the part of the sport industry that allows me to be outside for a lot of the time, where I do not have to wear a tie or a sports shirt every day. Different types of sport management jobs are available. In some you work outside and in others you work in an office and never see the golf course. That is the beautiful thing about the sports world; it has a little bit of everything. Contrary to popular belief, golf professionals do not just play golf or teach all day. We play very little. We make sure that the members of this golf club have an enjoyable experience. I do a lot of office work, especially when we do not have a secretary. But I do have the opportunity to take a break and go outside on the course and talk to members. That is part of my job because customer service involves talking to the members and making sure they are happy. This job is more about customer service than golf.

The golf industry is different because people will advise you not to pursue it. If my two boys want to be golf professionals when they grow up, I will not be happy. Golf pros do not have a lot of family time. In the summer I am here a lot, although that is probably true with any sport position. I take time off when I can, but it is scarce in the summer months. As far as the golf industry goes, it is a huge commitment so a lot of people recommend against it. Some people say it takes special people to do this job. I am not a special person and I do not see myself as such. I just work hard and I like to be around golf.

I did not explore a career because I believed what the general public does about golf professionals: all they do is play a lot of golf and teach. I attended the Golf Academy of the South in Orlando, which was like a 2-year college, and learned a lot. The focus was on accounting and management. I received a Golf Course Operations and Management certificate when I graduated. It was great training to learn about the business side of the game.

Without an education I do not think I could have gone as fast or have gotten to this level. A college education to me is golden. Pursuing a master's degree is valuable, too. You experience a lot more through education. Although the education may not provide you with on-site screening or things of that nature, if you go to learn, let the material sink in, and keep your books and do not sell them it will be beneficial to you down the road. I did two internships and they are beneficial.

The golf industry is inundated. Tons of good people are getting into this field, and it makes getting a job tougher. At one time some 5 years ago, there were 21,000 Class A PGA professionals and only 8,000 jobs. That was one of the major reasons I pursued my master's so I could set myself apart from others. I needed something noticeable on my resume that is not on everybody's resume. Up until about 10 years ago, many golf professionals did not have college degrees. But in the past 10 years colleges have graduated some good people. Colleges such as Ferris State, New Mexico, and Penn State now offer golf course management. It seems like 10 years ago, when I was in school from 1984 to 1988, nobody heard about sport management degrees. Now when people graduate the competition will be tougher.

I would have a tough time saying I will be at Glenmary for 25 or 30 years, and it will not hurt me if anybody knows that. I would like a director of golf position and supervise multiple facilities on a Monday through Friday schedule for a city or a golf management company. Meadowbrook Golf Management is the corporation that manages us. I think the future of golf is headed to management companies, and that would be an excellent opportunity for sport managers. The two people I deal with from Meadowbrook travel a lot, but are home on the weekends. They spend their weeks visiting the 70 or so different facilities that they manage. They meet and sign contracts with owners, and they come in and manage their facilities. It gives a lot of direction because sport managers know the business and they slide into those positions and assist people. It sounds a lot like something like Spectacor or Ogden, the companies that manage public assembly facilities.

I have worked for a lot of good role models, and I had some favorable experiences. Jim Osborne was a great role model for me in a lot of aspects in how to do some things and how not to do some things. He was a perfectionist. He was the head golf professional at Hurstbourne Country Club. He was there for 30 to 35 years and just retired a couple of years ago. At Hurstbourne Country Club we ran 150 tournaments a year. That was a great experience for me and I learned a lot from him. He made a big deal out of mistakes, but I learned. He made me realize how important it was to satisfy the customer. Keeping good books was important, but making the customer happy is most important. Denny Thompson was also a great role model. He is the head pro at GlenOaks, and he played golf at the University if Louisville. I learned a lot from him. He arrived at the crack of dawn every morning. We had a game where I tried to beat him to work and I never did.

My main responsibility here at Glenmary is to make sure this place runs effectively and efficiently. We have a greens superintendent, and his staff takes care of all of the grounds, including the clubhouse and around the golf course. We also have a food service staff. They see me more as an administrator from the standpoint of working with personnel, and they come to me a lot and bounce ideas off of me. It is a people-oriented business, not only on the customer service side, but also on the personnel side.

I work Monday through Saturday. I try to get bookwork done during the week. The first thing I do when I get here is start on the deposits. It should be a 30-minute job but sometimes it takes me 6 hours because I have people coming in and asking questions. I cannot close my door and shut myself off from everybody. The phone rings and someone needs to speak with me. A typical day may last from 6:30 AM to 5:00 or 6:00 PM.

In the winter I try to get 2 days off a week. The workload is a lot lighter because not a lot is happening. In the winter we try to gear up for the next year. Our course is open all year. Last year it was incredible. Last year we went through the second week of December and we were packed. It becomes more difficult when that happens because we let everybody take off and only a few people are here to work. Then in the winter months and in January, we have some down time, and we take vacations. In the slower season we consider new ideas for revenue for next year. We hold a lot of meetings and do a lot of brainstorming to determine how we can improve on last year.

When we have a tournament we get the carts out and put the signs on the front of them with the hole numbers on them. When we do events we have signs, cart signs, and score cards. I print up a sheet with everybody's name in alphabetical order, and we might have 144 people. You need to be detail oriented to do that. I like it typed. I do not like it printed because handwriting is often unclear and unreadable. Cart guys stand in the parking lot to approach the cars and greet the customers. First impressions are important. These cart guys are smiling and may wipe the customers' clubs off when they get them out of the car. Then they ask for the customer's name and check in on the list that I provide to them. It is easy to find because last names are in alphabetical order. Details are important in customer service. A scoreboard needs to look nice and not be smudged where numbers run together. Rangers circulate and make sure everybody is playing quick and fast. I walk around with a rulebook in case any questions arise. Running tournaments is a lot of fun. I like playing in them, but I have a good time running them and making sure everything goes well. The compliments you receive when it is over are worth it. We probably do 75 tournaments a year.

The best part of my job is the flexibility. As the top person here I can come and go as I please as long as everything is running fine. If my wife calls and needs me to take care of the kids for a couple of hours, I can probably go home. I can do that because I have good people around me. Another good thing about my job is playing golf with members. I do not play golf with the members as much as I should. I like the amenities afforded by other clubs. If we play at other courses generally we are not charged because we are professionals. I think the most challenging part is determining what makes your membership tick. Generating the proper amount of revenue is a big concern. If we do not stay on top of our game, assess the competition, or pay attention to our customers, we could be in trouble.

In the summer we have about 50 staff members. On a full-time basis there are eight staff members. In the winter we operate with probably about 10 to 15 people. Anyone who has ever worked with part-timers knows that can be a nightmare. Trying to attract and retain part-time help can be difficult, but you must depend on them.

I am satisfied with parts of my job and I am not satisfied with others. I do not always like the hours. I must do my time in certain situations and certain places, and I can complain but in the back of my mind I know this is what it takes to get to the next level. Maybe at the next step some of that pressure and some of those hours will not be there.

I started in the golf business in 1986. I went to the golf academy, graduated from there in 1989, and through the process I got a job at a course working for Arnold Palmer. I played golf with famous people such as Stan Musial, Ted Williams, Mickey Mantle, Mickey Rooney, Donald O'Connor, and George Bush's son. It was full of glamour and it was great. You would think I made a million dollars at that kind of job but I made $12,000 a year. I left there in a couple years, and I made $14,000 a year. I came to Louisville to work at Hurstbourne Country Club, which was in the upper echelon of golf courses. I made $15,500 and I thought I got a huge raise. Four years later I made $18,500. I took that first head pro job for a ridiculously low amount of money. So I may gripe about it but it is what I wanted. You want to be a sport manager and you want to be a head golf professional. You have to pay your dues and I spent a number of years paying mine. Aspiring sport managers have to look forward to paying their dues, too.

In this business, you need people skills. Communication skills are huge. If you are weak at planning or organizing find somebody strong in those positions because it can make or break you. Tournament organization is probably my strongest point. I love doing tournaments, and I thrive on that. If I run a good tournament the players will say, "Wow, that was the greatest thing I played in. These guys really know what they're doing, let's play there again."

I think last year 486 golf courses opened and another 400 to 500 are on the slate this year, and an overwhelming number of these courses are public facilities. Private clubs are pretty much a dinosaur now. We struggle with that here because we try to make this place survive. Typical of private golf clubs, we try to open up a little more to the public. The fact that so many public golf courses are being opened accounts for where it is today. We try to become more public. I think that is probably the number one external thing that hits home here.

We must be aware of environmental issues in this business. To keep our fairways nice we must use chemicals, fertilizers, and related items and that presents environmental concerns. We must have a freestanding building to store those items. The person who sprays has to be a licensed sprayer. There are wildlife reserve concerns. On golf courses certain lines are there that you cannot touch.

I am a people pleaser. It stresses me out if one person out of 450 people is unhappy. I cannot stand it when somebody is not happy with me or something that we have done, or if we have made a mistake. When people are griping and with a legitimate complaint, that causes me a lot of stress. It is also stressful to deal with employee issues. I relieve the stress by hitting a few golf balls and being alone for a couple of minutes to assess the situation. Then I formulate a response to all the people involved to straighten out the situation.

I try to consult everybody I can consult. I do not make any decisions unless there is a clear-cut path. If I need to fire an employee, I have to make that decision, but I will consult my wife or somebody apart from the situation. I try to consult as many people when I make a decision. Then I make a decision based on what I am feeling and on the feedback I receive.

I care a lot about people yet negative situations do occur. Attitudes can become a virus and problems occur. I try to talk to people when problems exist and give them the opportunity to resolve the problems. I had a boss one time that told me if you retain bad people, not only are you doing yourself a disservice, but also you are doing a disservice to those people.

My advice to somebody wanting to get into sport management is to get your degree and go as far as you can in school. I think sport organizations look for people with college degrees and specialization in sport management or sport marketing. Education cannot be stressed enough in its importance. I used to think that you did not need to go to school to do what you want to do. My wife, however, believed in getting a degree. I did not figure it out until my master's program. It is not just the paper. If you make an effort to learn, you have an advantage. I would get my doctorate if I did not have a family and small kids, but I am 36-years-old and I have pretty well chosen my career path. If I was younger and had the opportunity to do it and keep going I think I would do it. That says a lot about the importance of education. I take more pride—this is probably goofy—in those degrees on the wall. I am proud of them, worked hard for them, and I realize how much they have helped. Do whatever you can to learn—seek out advice from different professionals and find people who are happy in what they do. Do not put the blinders on, and look at the big picture. Set some career goals. Work to achieve those goals. Determine what it is you want to do first.

Golf management companies are the future in this industry. These golf management companies are hiring the best people. I recommend signing a contract with one of these companies to manage your business and make you a profit. You sit back and pay them a little bit, but you collect money all of the time. So instead of trying to figure everything out by yourself, employ a golf management company. I think the industry is looking more for sport managers as opposed to specialized golf professionals. The PGA is big and it will keep control of putting PGA professionals into jobs, but I think those PGA professionals will need to become real sport managers.

First and foremost you need to do the best possible job you can do wherever you are. Whether that job involves putting paper clips on paper or stapling, do your best. Figure out how to use a stapler better than paper clips. Education provides the base. Do the best possible job with whatever you are given. Broaden your horizons and jump into other areas of the business. But take off the blinders.

CHAPTER 13

Sports Commissions

THE PHENOMENAL GROWTH OF SPORTS COMMISSIONS has occurred because of the popularity of sport, the lucrative economic benefits of sporting events, and the image enhancement attained by the communities hosting the events. Although the San Diego International Sports Council was the first sports commission formed in the United States in 1961, Indianapolis serves as a prime example of how a city helped change its image through sports. Indianapolis opened its Indiana Sports Corporation in 1980 to create a positive, sports-minded image for the city. By the mid 1980s, after hosting the Pan American Games, the U.S. Olympic Festival, and several U.S. Olympic trials, Indianapolis began to achieve national media recognition as a center for amateur sports. A growing reputation as the mecca for amateur sports helped Indianapolis attract such major sport governing bodies as the National Collegiate Athletic Association and the National Federation of State High School Associations to relocate their national headquarters to the city.

The anticipated economic payoff has motivated many cities to create sports commissions. The NCAA Men's 1998 Final Four Basketball Tournament netted nearly $107 million for the city of San Antonio, and Indianapolis reported a conservative net value of about $58.1 million from the sporting events they hosted in 1997. Economic benefits do not only benefit large and rich municipalities. Cities such as Macomb, Illinois (pop. 20,000), and Minot, North Dakota (pop. 37,000) have derived positive impact from their sport/recreation commissions. Minot brought seven Amateur Softball Association championships to its city and filled approximately 900 hotel rooms. The economic impact of those tournaments was estimated between $500,000 and $1.5 million for the city and surrounding area (Mullen, 1998).

Nearly half of the sports commissions in the United States are publicly funded—usually through a hotel tax—and are an arm of the convention and visitors bureau. The largest, oldest, and most successful commissions, however, are usually privately funded. A high return on investment is necessary to draw a sporting event. If a city spends $150,000 for an event that will draw 1,000 out-of-town visitors for four nights, spending $100 per day, then the yield would be about $400,000. The Return On Investment (ROI) would be better than 2-to-1, but sports commissions try to project a higher return from their efforts.

Those who pursue a career in the tourism, convention, and sports commission industry must have a variety of skills to succeed in this increasingly competitive field. Effective oral and written communication skills, knowledge of local government, marketing, finance, sales, management skills, high energy, a strong work ethic, creativity, and the ability to cooperate well with others are some of the key elements for success. Working with sports commissions can be financially rewarding. It is not uncommon for an executive director of a major sports commission to make more than $75,000 per year, whereas entry-level positions pay in the low to mid $20,000s and associate executive directors and managers earn in the mid $40,000s. Although the industry has experienced tremendous growth in the 1990s, it is expected that the growth in number of new sports commissions is expected to level off in the near future and the number of new jobs available will also decrease.

REFERENCES

Mullen, L. (1998, August 3–9). Making all the right moves. *Street & Smith's Sports Business Journal,* 1(15): 19, 28.

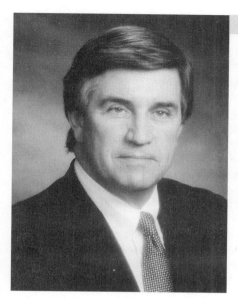

Jeffrey W. Beaver

Executive Director
Charlotte Regional Sports
Commission

Education:
A.B., RELIGION, UNIVERSITY OF NORTH
CAROLINA AT CHAPEL HILL, 1967

Career Progression:
EXECUTIVE DIRECTOR, CHARLOTTE RE-
GIONAL SPORTS COMMISSION, MAY 1999 TO
PRESENT

PRESIDENT (VOLUNTEER POSITION), NFL
ALUMNI – CAROLINAS CHAPTER, 1990 TO 1994

PLAYER, BALTIMORE COLTS FOOTBALL, INC.,
1968 TO 1970

Best piece of advice you received in regards to your career:

"Whether your responsibility is perceived as extremely important or whether it is perceived as not, just do your best—regardless!"

Best advice for someone aspiring toward a career in the sport industry:

"While there appears to be a lot of exciting things going on around you, understand straight up that it requires long hours, great patience, and hard work."

Quote by which you live:

"In life, there are no problems, just challenges."

DON SHULA

I GRADUATED FROM THE UNIVERSITY OF NORTH CAROLINA in January 1968 with a degree in religion, but interestingly enough, my first job out of college was in the sport field. I was the 15th round draft pick of the National Football League Baltimore Colts. My rookie year of 1968 was the famous year that Joe Namath and the Jets beat the Colts in Super Bowl III. I was with the organization for two years as the backup quarterback to the great Johnny Unitas and Earl Morrell. During my third year the decision to get out of football was made for me. I broke my hand in the first exhibition game of the 1970 season and a quarterback needs his hands so my time was up.

It was somewhat traumatic leaving professional football. I had gotten just enough of a taste of it to say this might not be a bad way to make a living. At the time, my wife Carol and I had no children so we were footloose and fancy free so to speak. Fortunately, we were not stupid. We knew it could be a fleeting moment and it turned out that it was one. I had worked at a bank in Baltimore during the off season and when I left the Colts I returned to my hometown of Charlotte and interviewed for positions with several banks. Entering the sport field did not enter my mind at the time because opportunities did not exist like today. I began work for what was then called North Carolina National Bank. The bank is one of many predecessor banks to what is now Bank of America. I was in investment banking for 28 years before becoming the executive director of the Charlotte Regional Sports Commission in May 1999.

When I decided to change careers I was interested in doing something associated with sport. I had a lot of questions about what the Charlotte Sports Commission was doing for Charlotte. When I approached the Commission's board of directors about employment, they were starting a search for an executive director. Even though my banking career was not directly related to sport, I was considered for the position for a couple of reasons. I am a Charlotte native and know a lot of people in the area. I had a strong background as a bond trader for most of my career at the bank. My business experience and the contacts I made have proven beneficial in my position as executive director at the sports commission. The commission is a nonprofit, privately funded organization so we depend on companies such as the Bank of America, interestingly enough, for our funding and for sponsoring events that are brought to Charlotte.

I did have some experience in the sport field, but it had been as a volunteer with the Charlotte chapter of the NFL Alumni Association. The NFLAA is a nonprofit organization that raises money for children's charities. I enjoyed that part of the work and the camaraderie of associating with former players and meeting new members. My NFL playing experience has proven beneficial. I have kept the friends that I made 30 years ago who have been helped in many ways with my new job.

The mission of the Charlotte Regional Sports Commission is to attract sporting events to Charlotte and the region with the hope that these events have a positive economic impact and a positive quality of life impact on our region. When we bid on an event such as an NCAA Championship, the city will form a Local Organizing Committee (LOC) for the event and we work with the group to produce the proposal. The proposal will be presented to the body that makes the decision on which city will host the event. An example of our mission being accomplished was Charlotte being chosen to host the 1999 and 2000 Men's College Cup, which is the NCAA Men's Division I national championship soccer game.

The games were and are played at Erickson Stadium, home of the Carolina Panthers. We have also been involved with the women's and the men's Final Four basketball championships played at the Charlotte Coliseum as well as the Atlantic Coast Conference Basketball Championship, when it is in Charlotte. In addition to attracting events, we work closely with the existing organizations in our city such as professional teams, local institutions of higher education, and local organizing committees to plan, organize, and promote their causes.

Our goal is to make sure Charlotte and the people who support our events benefit from having them here. We also help with revenue generation through sponsorships for other ancillary sporting events that we are not promoting ourselves or have not brought to Charlotte but that are worthy. An example of this would be a participation event such as a road race or bike race. We have to pick and choose those events because we do not have enough staff or time to do all the things that come across my desk. In some instances, we actually bid to bring in the event and in others we act as a support organization.

As executive director I report to the board of directors of the Charlotte Sports Commission. This board consists of prominent, high-profile citizens, many of whom have probably forgotten a lot more about sport than I know, as far as Charlotte is concerned. It is a great mix of sport people, business executives, and community leaders. The commission has a staff of four people so there is a managerial aspect to my position. My primary responsibilities as executive director include generating revenue through sponsorship and working to secure events for the city. Our director of events oversees all the events we bring to Charlotte, ranging from something as large as an NCAA championship to a small junior golf tournament. Our director of operations oversees our books. He lets me know when I can and cannot write checks and acts as our treasurer. Our director of marketing handles all of the calls for marketing opportunities, such as speaking engagements on behalf of the commission and all media relations. Our office manager handles the day-to-day dealings in the office and acts as my assistant. We have experimented with interns in the past with good results.

One of the most important traits of our organization is our ability to involve the entire staff when hosting an event. We all take responsibility and help make those events run smoothly even though our job descriptions may say otherwise. This is part of the team concept we emphasize. As a manager I try to give my people as much rope as they need to express themselves, yet I do require that we work as a team. In a business like ours, we must work closely or the right hand will not know what the left hand is doing. I realized after meeting the staff that it would be no problem promoting the team concept because my predecessor had the same ideas. People skills are extremely important whether managing my staff or communicating with the high-profile and high-energy people on our board.

Making the transition from banking to my current position was not that difficult. Both environments are competitive. I am used to competitive environments from my college and professional football days as well as my years working in investments. The sports commission environment, even though it is nonprofit, is competitive in the sense that we are constantly going against other commissions or other cities to attract sporting events. We all want the same events so naturally a high degree of competitive spirit is involved.

I am not saying I had nothing new to learn coming into my position. My learning curve has been very steep. Not only did I have to familiarize myself with the technical side of the position (i.e., making bids and submitting proposals for events), but also I had to sharpen my people skills. Furthermore, I have learned a great deal about what happens in a city relative to the Sports Commission's interests. We are basically a marketing arm for the city of Charlotte, but we are not publicly funded. I have learned to appreciate how we fit into the process of bringing events to Charlotte relative to other interests in our city and the people with whom we partner.

My eyes have been opened to Charlotte as an incredibly vibrant place. When I was with the bank I was so driven and so inwardly focused that I did not realize what was happening around me. In that sense, the change has been rewarding. When we organize an event, everyone in Charlotte benefits from it, which is a rewarding feeling. I do believe the city of Charlotte appreciates what we do, but obviously we are not the only organization that enhances the city's quality of life. A number of different organizations help put our city on the map including the Arts & Science Council, the Charlotte Center City Partners, the Charlotte Chamber of Commerce, the Convention and Visitors Bureau, the Auditorium-Coliseum-Convention Center Authority, and the Hospitality and Tourism Alliance, just to name a few. These and many similar organizations play a significant role in making Charlotte a thriving and exciting city.

The most demanding aspect of my position, without a doubt, is generating revenue through corporate sponsorships. We depend on our corporate members and sponsors for our operating budget needs. Approaching organizations about sponsoring the commission is always tough because you tend to wonder whether they are going to feel like they get what we offer in return. However, the most enjoyable aspect of my position is the interaction with the people. I enjoy getting to know those people who make things happen in Charlotte. They all have a common interest in the positive side of sports, which is something I appreciate.

When we approach a company about supporting our efforts to bring an event to Charlotte, the opportunity can be perceived in different ways. It can be approached in terms of "what's in it for them" or from the perspective of "what's in it for the city." In Charlotte, we have a large number of corporate institutions with a history of supporting both professional and amateur sports. In that sense we have a definite advantage over some cities. We have approximately 75 corporate sponsors for the sports commission whose financial support ranges from low four figures to much higher levels. Even if our sponsors are competitors, they come together to make things happen. When the corporate community deems something a good fit—particularly if it enhances our quality of life—they will all chip in and help. We ask for 3-year commitments from our sponsors. This gives us time to do significant planning for the future. Another reason I believe we are successful in Charlotte is because our region is the "Home of NASCAR." Those responsible for the success of motor sports here have drawn a great deal of attention to Charlotte and are an integral part of the reason that many organizations choose to come to our city. As a sports commission we look to strengthen our ties with groups such as Speedway Motorsports Inc., but now, we need them more than they need us. We hope, however, that we can do more with and for them in the future.

Size and scope of an event will determine the degree of support it will receive from the corporate and business communities. For instance, there are always people interested in getting involved with an ACC basketball tournament but less interested in being involved with a participation event with a lower profile. However, some people prefer to be part of something smaller and more meaningful than with a major, highly visible event.

With a budget to meet and efforts to grow our organization, revenue generation can be stressful. The stress is accentuated when someone says "no." (Nobody likes to be turned down.) It is also stressful to lose a sponsor who supported us for a number of years and then decided to go elsewhere. Stress can also raise its ugly head when we host an event such as the Men's College Cup. For example, we may make a guarantee in our proposal that a certain number of tickets will be sold. As we approach the deadline and have not sold enough tickets, the pressure to meet the guarantee is stressful.

When we host a large event we facilitate the formation and become part of a LOC. The LOC will approach our sponsors as well as other companies and ask them to help in various ways. Within the sports commission operating budget we cannot effectively run an ACC basketball tournament. We do not have the funds. Sponsorships generated by the LOC will be used to organize the event. In the case of hosting an NCAA championship we will form partnerships with local institutions of higher education, such as the University of North Carolina at Charlotte, and work as cohosts of the event. An example is the 1999 Men's College Cup in which we were equal partners with Davidson College and UNC Charlotte. Although it may seem such relationships are temporary, that is not the case. We maintain close relationships before, during, and after an event. The athletic director of UNC Charlotte serves on our board. We support her school by purchasing season tickets for one of the teams and then use those tickets to entertain our sponsors, volunteers, and members.

A typical day for the executive director of a sports commission can be a long one. I am in the office anywhere from 6:00 to 7:00 AM. I read the papers and periodicals and catch up on letters before my staff reports at 8:00 AM. My normal day ends around 6:00 PM, although it can last longer. Part of my day consists of attending meetings for various committees and boards. An example is my involvement on two committees related to the future growth of our city. I was asked to serve because of my position with the sports commission. I also do some traveling, but not too much. I will occasionally visit a local college to talk with an athletic director or travel to the site of a potential sponsor. I am fortunate because most of our sponsorship base is here in Charlotte.

Like a lot of businesses, the down time for our commission is the summer. We do not plan a lot of things during this period because we cannot depend on people being around due to vacations. People would rather attend events in the spring, fall, or winter. Our busiest time is probably between October and January and then March, April, and May. This is when most of the major sports and the events that accompany those major sports occur. October and November are busy because it is in the fourth quarter that businesses make decisions on how to spend their sponsorship money the following year. We try to work with their budget timing so hopefully we can be included in their plans.

For large events such as Final Four in basketball, the bids are prepared years in advance. Given that our board has the final say on whether we bid on a larger event such as an NCAA championship, we present the idea to the strategic planning committee of the board and determine whether the time slot fits. The board decides if we want to make the time commitment and take the potential monetary risk to make the event a reality. We follow normal business planning for the decision. For a smaller event the decision is left up to my staff and me. When we develop a bid together, we have to pay strict attention to details. It is also important to develop a strategy to align ourselves with knowledgeable and motivated partners. For example, UNC Charlotte and Davidson College bring expertise for hosting an event like a regional basketball final or the Men's College Cup. They know what it takes to do it well, they understand the risks involved, and they realize the value of doing things right.

The key to putting on a successful event is total community involvement. We do not want to take on anything here in Charlotte unless it is a first-class affair. When you are involved with any kind of national championship, the sport draws spectators. Still, we must get the total community involved. A good marketing plan is necessary to sell tickets to the right people, approach the right businesses for the right sponsorship, and find motivated volunteers who will make the time commitment. We rely on volunteers to assist in the operations of the event. Most of the volunteers are self-motivated because they come to us. We started an individual membership program called the "Team Player" that now includes about 125 members in their late 20s or early 30s. Most are having their first experience with any type of civic involvement and they love it that we are getting them involved through sport.

Sports commissions will continue to grow in importance. The Charlotte Sports Commission was formed in 1994. Previously, the city had hosted several events and our mayor realized it was the same people, volunteers, and civic groups who made the events a reality. The mayor recognized that the city needed to be more organized and proactive. Instead of waiting for groups to approach us about hosting events, we needed to find events that we wanted. As a result the Charlotte Sports Commission was formed. As sports continue to play an integral part in our society, sports commissions will continue to grow. Smaller towns will be forming sports commissions and larger cities will increase the emphasis and resources directed toward their existing sports commissions.

People always say to me that I have the "ideal job" because it requires my presence at many games and events. Yes, it is great but I am working at those events. If someone is interested in this area of sport they should enjoy people and be prepared to work long hours. An educational background in sport management would be very beneficial, but is not necessary. Personally, I have a bachelor's degree in religion; played professional football, and worked in a bank. Now I am in the sports business. Go figure! When I spoke to my children about what they wanted to study in college and pursue as careers, I always told them they will have better opportunities for success if they are well rounded. I still stand by that view.

I have not thought about the future because I have been so busy. I love what I do now, and for the most part, I loved what I did at the bank. True, I would have loved to have made it in the NFL, but I cannot complain about any three of these situations. Maybe down the road it would be fun to be involved in more of an entrepreneurial endeavor, but I am having a good time in this position and I could not begin to give that serious thought.

Success in my role as executive director of a sports commission is having the ability to constantly bring and host high-quality events on a regular basis. We do not have to do the same event over and over again, but rather offer a variety of events presented at the highest level. For example, in 1998 Charlotte hosted the University of North Carolina and North Carolina State University football game on Thanksgiving weekend. I have been told that it was the best sporting event this city has ever seen. It was successful because we had a lot of corporate partners and a lot of caring people who helped make it happen. It was not just something we did. It was something from Erickson Stadium, all the groups and organizations related to both universities and the local organizing committee. If we can continue to organize events like this, we will continue to be successful.

James A. Haynes

Marketing Coordinator
Palm Beach County Sports
Commission

Education:
B.B.A., MARKETING, UNIVERSITY OF KEN-
TUCKY, 1995

M.ED., SPORT ADMINISTRATION, UNIVERSITY
OF LOUISVILLE, 1998

Career Progression:
MARKETING COORDINATOR, PALM BEACH
COUNTY SPORTS COMMISSION, AUGUST 1998
TO PRESENT

EVENT MANAGEMENT INTERN, DISNEY WIDE
WORLD OF SPORTS COMPLEX, DECEMBER 1997
TO AUGUST 1998

ASSISTANT MARKETING MANAGER, PSIT'S
ART, 1994 TO 1995

Best piece of advice you received in regards to your career:

"Pursue a master's degree in sports administration."

JAMES HOST OF HOST COMMUNICATIONS

Best advice for someone aspiring toward a career in the sport industry:

**"Intern as much as possible while in school. It will give you
the direct experience employers are looking for in a candidate.
Pursue a master's degree in sport administration/management."**

Quote by which you live:

**"There is only one corner of the universe you can be certain
of improving and that's your own self."**

ALDUS HUXLEY

MY NAME IS JAMES HAYNES and I am the marketing coordinator for the
Palm Beach County Sports Commission in West Palm Beach, Florida. I became
interested in a career in sport while completing my undergraduate degree in business administration and marketing at the University of Kentucky. My cousin
played basketball there. After he graduated someone approached him about doing
some autograph signing sessions and basketball games around the state, and I got

involved with organizing those sessions, helping with the games, and selling T-shirts and posters. At the same time I had another cousin who was in the sport industry and he did well. At that point it all kind of came together and I knew what I wanted to do.

When I graduated from Kentucky I thought I had a verbal agreement for a job in South Florida with a sports agent. When I got there it turned out he wanted me to be in law school, and at that point I did not want to spend the next three years in law school. I started sending resumes to professional teams and event management companies across the country. I talked to some people in the sport industry and they all told me basically the same thing: go get your master's degree. I went back to Kentucky because the University of Louisville had one of the top 10 graduate programs in sport administration. I applied there and was accepted. I started the master's program in the spring and took classes in the summer and fall. Then I did an internship at Disney's Wide World of Sports Complex in Orlando, and then I accepted a position with the Palm Beach County Sports Commission.

Once I started the master's program I sought an internship. Many of the students did their internships in or near Louisville, but I did not think those kinds of internships would benefit me as much. I do not mean to diminish those organizations or the students who worked there, but my research indicated that many of them required tasks that would not benefit me. I spent probably three or four months searching for an internship while I was in graduate school. I kind of stumbled across the intensive event management training program at the Disney Sports Complex and found their internship program lasted seven months. During my internship, I joined Sports Careers, used the Sport Marketplace Directory, and sent out blind resumes to basically every place in the country. I actually started early looking for a full-time position. I started to use some of the contacts I made while I worked the events in Orlando. I just happened to meet a person I got along with pretty well, and he knew someone who knew someone, and that is how I got in at Palm Beach. One of the things I would probably change is I would have done some sport-related internships as an undergraduate. I did not understand their importance then. If I could have worked for some professional teams during the summers that would have helped me more, not only experience-wise but also networking-wise.

The sport administration program at the University of Louisville was great. The faculty was accessible because not many people were in the graduate program, and it was pretty new. We had maybe 15 graduate students when I started, so the one-on-one conversations with professors after class and during office hours gave me a chance to pick their brains and determine how they worked to get those positions. They helped me decide what to pursue in my career. I made many friends during graduate school, and we stay in touch. They all work in different sections of the industry now. The interests the students and faculty had in the various aspects of the field gave me a clear picture of the sport industry. I thought the curriculum was great. I already had an undergraduate degree in business, and the classes taught me how to apply business aspects to the sport industry.

I do not think any curriculum can prepare a student for everything that happens in the workplace, particularly in event management, but my education made me more well rounded. My education and training help me in my job today. We took sport marketing, sport finance, sport management, and legal aspects of sport, just to name a few. Those all taught me about situations I experience daily.

I have faced the normal obstacles while trying to advance. When I was an intern at Disney and considered staying, I thought I would always be seen as an intern and would not be treated with the respect I deserved. In my current job we have a very small office of 10 people, and basically we are pretty much all on the same level. We work together. If I wanted to advance someone in a position that interests me would have to leave. At this point those are the two things have kept me from advancing thus far in my career.

The cousin I mentioned earlier, Glen Cromwell, is a role model for me. He started the same way I did, sending resumes until he ended up with a company in Chicago called Pace Motor Sports. He worked his way up through the organization and landed a job with the National Hot Rod Association (NHRA). He is the national director of marketing for NHRA. I watched him constantly grinding to get ahead, putting in 80 hours a week, and doing everything he possibly could to succeed. I knew exactly that was what I wanted to do. He also helped me decide to apply to the master's program. I try to talk to him every week, and he always tells me how having a master's helps, not only now, but also in the future. He always tells me how wishes he knew that earlier. Seeing him succeed and knowing how hard he worked showed me I could reach the same level if I did the same thing. Another role model is Jim Host, the chief executive officer of Host Communications. It is kind of inspiring to see how a person from the small town of Lexington can create a company that reaches millions of people.

I would like to continue working in marketing. I like to be behind the scenes developing marketing strategies and marketing plans to reach common goals. In 5 years I would love to work in the sport marketing department of a beverage company such as Coca-Cola or Pepsi or a beer manufacturer such as Anheuser Busch. I would also love to be involved with developing sponsorship programs for Fortune 500 companies and executing those promotions across the United States.

My main responsibilities are varied. I handle all the sponsorships for the Sports Commission. We also manage a youth program that is a 501(c)(3) not-for-profit organization, so I solicit its sponsorships also. The sponsorships help us provide free clinics, camps, and services to kids. I try to solicit new sponsors and service the current sponsors contracts as well. In addition, we have a membership base that serves as a miniature chamber of commerce responsible for enrolling new members, servicing current members, and developing new ideas to offer our members. I help market and promote any event we plan with our limited budget.

The main event we host every year is the Lou Groza Collegiate Place Kicker Award that honors the top NCAA Division 1-A place kicker in college football. It is a great event. One year Sebastian Janikowski from Florida State won, and another year Martine Gramatica from Kansas State won the award. The award is named after Lou Groza, the Hall of Fame kicker from the Cleveland Browns. It is a national event that brings us a lot of exposure. Other events we have hosted include the United States Field Hockey Association National Hockey Festival, which is the largest field hockey tournament in the world. Most of the athletes are women. There is an under 16-year-old division and an under 19-year-old division, and a lot of college scouts attend to scout the high school prospects. We also have hosted the National Association of Intercollegiate Athletics (NAIA) Spring Championship Games. We brought their five spring sports into Palm Beach County all at one time. That is a multisport, multivenue event spread throughout the entire county. It was challenging but at the same time rewarding to successfully host that event. We have also hosted some water ski events, AAU events, National Police Athletic Leagues, and baseball world series. We have hosted the Sunshine State Games and the Florida chapter of the Special Olympics. The director of operations and our executive director are in charge of soliciting those types of events.

The most demanding aspect of my position is dealing with amateur sports that host just one event here. It is difficult to solicit sponsors for a one-time event, particularly if no television coverage will occur. I do not want to keep tapping my current sponsors for more money or more in-kind services for a one-time event. I also experience the frustration of not having many ticketed events. For example, I would like to have events where I have a budget to make some media buys and do other promotional activities. The most enjoyable aspect of my job is doing professional events and getting to meet sports celebrities. I have met Lee Corso and Chris Fowler from ESPN, Jack Nicklaus, and Chris Everett. That is always a neat thing for me. I do not get star struck, but it is great to shake their hand. When we host a grassroots national championship, I enjoy seeing competition at its purest. I get to see kids compete, have fun, and try to win. That is always gratifying to me.

A typical day for me is preparing for some event. I am usually on the computer most of the day typing letters to sponsors or on the phone cold-calling potential sponsors soliciting their support for an event. I continually develop new ideas to promote an event. I work with the other departments and the director of operations to coordinate promotions and other aspects of the events. For example, if the director needs some radios for an event, she wants to know what kind of deal I can negotiate with a sponsor. She turns it over to me and I start making phone calls to see what kind of deal I can make with people via trade and advertising in our programs or with on-site signage at the venue. There are always meetings and phone calls with the event owners and people who want to get involved with the event. Our office hours are 8:30 AM to 5:30 PM, and if it is a regular week with no events and its not stressful, I may come and go at those times. During events, however, I usually work more than 60 hours a week.

The pay is not great when starting a career in sport or event management. I have to remind myself to be patient and wait for my opportunity to advance. With respect to my job now, I have been compensated for my hard work, and that is gratifying. I would like to see my position broadened a little bit, allowing me to solicit event owners to sponsor more events.

I have not had the chance to manage a lot of people so I still try to feel my way through when I do have the opportunity. In another 3 or 4 years I will have a better idea of my management style. We have events requiring a high number of volunteers from the community. As far as direct subordinates, everyone in the office is pretty much on the same level. We do have a receptionist and some occasional interns. We split time supervising the interns and whoever needs them the most that week gets to use them. I am developing some managerial skills, particularly time management. For example, with the Groza Award we have time-sensitive materials that need to be sent out and returned in a certain time frame. I have to emphasize that importance to my co-workers. I am a straightforward person with respect to telling someone exactly what I want. If employees or volunteers have questions, they can ask. If someone makes a mistake I do not scream at that person. Instead I ask why it was not done correctly and what we can do to fix it. I tell them to come to my office at any time and we can straighten out any confusion or job-related issue.

The main thing relative to the external environment that impacts our operation is dealing with the volunteers. If we do a track and field meet and need young people to do things, such as rake the pits and set up hurdles quickly, they are difficult to find. Our volunteer base in South Florida consists of a lot of retirees. Many opportunities exist for volunteers at other events, but when they come to an event such as a track and field meet, sometimes I cannot always use them the way I would like. In regard to weather, most of our events are outdoor events, and there is always crisis management when inclement weather arrives before or during an event. We play it by ear at that point and try to take control of the situation. We have a backup plan and try to make sure everyone is on the same page when we execute it.

The stresses I face involve selling sponsorships. The entire process, from cultivating leads to developing proposals, making presentations, dealing with rejection, and doing follow-up, can be stressful. I constantly critique what I do and how I do it to determine whether I hit the right targets. Given that we are a government agency, our marketing budget is small. When I get the opportunity to do certain things, I have a limited budget so I constantly try to make deals with people. Sometimes I feel like I tap the well and call in one too many favors for things. That bothers me. I would like to give back a little more to our sponsors if I had the means.

Personally, I do not deal with other governmental agencies, but our executives do. We have people that deal with the Tourist Development Council, the Convention and Visitors Bureau, the Film and Television Commission, the Cultural Council, and the Board of County Commissioners. We work with them constantly as well as with facility owners to help event owners book facilities and get the best deal.

With regard to technical skills I do desktop publishing, Word, Excel, Power-Point, Internet, and e-mail. It is a necessity in this business to have computer skills. As far as personal skills, I try to reach my own personal goals and at the same time help the organization reach its goals. Conceptual skills are important, that is, the ability to see the big picture. I must be aware of what we do with an event, what our role is, how it benefits the county, and how it benefits the people in the county or the community. I also must know how we can optimize this event to make it the best it has ever been so the organizers will return the following year.

Students who want to work in a position similar to mine must work well with people. I am constantly on the phone with sponsors and potential sponsors. I need a positive attitude all the time. I cannot let potential stressors affect my day-to-day activities. If I have a couple of bad days selling and then go into another meeting with a bad attitude, it may destroy my chances with that potential sponsor. That is unacceptable. In this job one must have personal relationship skills to deal with various types of people on a daily basis. A sports background and experience in event management and marketing would help. If I hired someone for this position, I would look for someone with experience in selling. I did not have a lot myself, and so I am learning as do the job. If someone has good presentation skills, which I have, he or she is more valuable as an employee.

One of the most recent trends is the increase in the development of sports commissions. Some counties and cities consider developing a sports commission. Some entities have a separate sports commission and some operate through the Convention and Visitors Bureau with an additional sales representative for sport events. The sales representative goes out and bids on events. Sports commissions offer a wide variety of services, from giving an event a grant to pay for certain production or television costs or helping to organize and train volunteers. We are also the liaison between the event owners and the facility owners and help them book a facility with some key contacts from the commission. We have a vested interest in the success of the events, although we do not own the events. We have a say in running the events. That is where it is headed as more sports commissions get involved with their events. Sports commissions are a better option than having someone only bid on events to bring them into your county and not be further involved.

It will get more competitive to attract good events. The bottom line is the facility. If a city or county does not have a top-notch facility, it is pretty much out of contention at that point. The other major factor in winning an event is the type of preparation we can do. If we develop a good bid, have a good site visit, have a good group of people who relate well with the event owners, and can sell our county, we have a good chance of hosting that particular event. The competition is in the bid presentation.

As sports commissions continue to grow they will still make a big impact in 10 years. I think they help out facilities as well. For example, if there is a large venue without a full-time booking director and the sports commission tries to bring events to that venue, it is value added. In 10 years I do think every city in the country will need a sports commission.

Every commission will need an executive director with the conceptual skills to see the big picture. Someone who can go out and bring events into the county or city will always be needed. Graduates with sport management or sport administration degrees will be well prepared for this industry. Business skills and computer skills are also needed. Human skills and the ability to work in a team environment are mandatory.

A good Internet site can sell your city or facilities before someone even contacts you. On a good site event owners can look at your facility, look at the events you have done in the past, see what events are scheduled, and get a good feel for what your capabilities are as a sports commission. We have a good Web site and we constantly try to make improvements to make it easier for event owners to use. The Internet will also create job opportunities. In our office we actually have studied the question of whether we need a full-time Web manager. The Web site was created before I got here, but I have tried to take more control of it when possible. I do provide input on Web site content. Several mistakes and changes were necessary because the site did not look good or did not generate more traffic.

I would say that in 10 years I will still be involved in the sport industry, just not in a sports commission. I would like to get more involved in professional events or national events with more exposure. We do have some televised events in Palm Beach County, but for instance, when I was at Disney, I worked on the NFL Quarterback Challenge and with the Atlanta Braves Spring Training. I want to try to create business opportunities for people through sport.

I have thought about how to reach those goals. I think success in the sport industry—once you get in—is based on the ability to develop and maintain contacts through networking. This is not to say that I constantly look to go other places or get another job. However, in everyday conversations with people at social functions and on the phone, opportunities can arise. My next position will probably come from knowing someone. Networking is important. You never want to burn bridges. I stay in contact via e-mail or call at least once a week or once a month two or three people from the master's program. Anytime an opportunity arises to attend a function, go and exchange some business cards. I was fortunate to attend the U.S. Olympic Congress in Phoenix, Arizona one year. It was my first sport industry social event. I went to some of the dinners and networked with some of the people on the U.S. Olympic Committee. In south Florida I meet some people with the Marlins, the Panthers, and the Dolphins. I talk to people and just make sure that they remember me. That is important. Like I said, that is how I got my job. I worked with somebody who recommended me for this position because of how I worked.

I have worked hard over the past three years. I wanted to set some goals for myself, and it was not easy. I still have a stack of rejection letters from when I first tried to get internships and jobs. I occasionally refer to those letters as a motivational tool. I still have some years to pay my dues, and that does not bother me. I think my education and my contacts have helped me get to where I am today.

Students need to know basic marketing principles that apply to all industries, not just sports. It may seem as if marketing sport events would be easy, but that is not always the case. Many options exist for people to enjoy other forms of entertainment. A limited amount of disposable income is available in each household, and we need to know how to reach people in general through basic marketing principles or tactics. Applying those principles to sport is the key.

Many of the students I went to school with and meet now think working for a pro team or being an agent will be glamorous. I had a couple of interviews with a pro team for a ticketing position and decided it was not for me. People think they can get a job with a pro team making $35,000 after obtaining a master's degree. The reality is that a hundred thousand people would accept that position for $10,000 per year.

Sport administration majors can be agents without a law degree, but sport administration majors can offer sport agencies some knowledge that lawyers cannot. If they can get in with a large agency with a marketing department or financial planning department, that is where their background can set them apart. They do not think that way. They think they would rather be an agent, which is difficult to do.

For anyone coming out of an undergraduate sport administration program, I recommend going to a different school and earning a master's degree if a position is not obtained right away. I do not think they learn as much by staying in the same program. Getting my master's degree catapulted me into the industry. I am not certain what I would be doing now if I had not gotten that degree. I am not sure that I would be in the sport industry. From my experience and in talking with some other people, the master's program is the way to go.

Students also need to get as much experience as possible. I did a brief stint with a country club doing some golf tournaments in Louisville. That helped me.

The general manager of the country club was in the sport administration master's program. He needed someone to help him, I needed some experience, and it worked out well. I learned a lot and had fun putting on golf tournaments. That experience helped me get the Disney internship.

John J. Cicero

President/Chief Executive Officer
Greater New Orleans Sports
Foundation

Education:
B.S., MARKETING, LOUISIANA TECH
UNIVERSITY, 1984

Career Progression:
PRESIDENT, CHIEF EXECUTIVE OFFICER,
GREATER NEW ORLEANS SPORTS
FOUNDATION, 1997 TO PRESENT

VICE PRESIDENT OF OPERATIONS, GREATER
NEW ORLEANS SPORTS FOUNDATION, 1995 TO
1997

GENERAL MANAGER, NEW ORLEANS ZEPHYRS
BASKETBALL TEAM, 1993 TO 1995

DIRECTOR OF SPECIAL PROJECTS, GREATER
NEW ORLEANS SPORTS FOUNDATION, 1990 TO
1993

ASSISTANT GENERAL MANAGER, SHREVEPORT
CAPTAINS BASEBALL CLUB, 1986 TO 1990

Best piece of advice you received in regards to your career:

"Never align yourself with people or companies that are not of the highest quality."

TAYLOR MORRE, OWNER, SHREVEPORT CAPTAINS

Best advice for someone aspiring toward a career in the sport industry:

Be patient, work hard, be proactive and have fun, or else it is not worth it.

Quote by which you live:

"If you really want to do something, you will find a way. If you don't you will find an excuse."

MY FATHER, FRANK CICERO, WAS A COACH at the same high school, St. John's, Jesuit, for 45 years, which is now Loyola High School in Shreveport, Louisiana. He coached football for 16 years and baseball for 27 years. I grew up in a family of athletes and I played sports through high school. My brother received a baseball scholarship to Northwestern State University and later became a coach at the high school level. I played sports but did not realize I wanted to be in the management aspect until 1984, which was my senior year at Louisiana Tech University. My friends and I had taken a road trip to Dallas to see the Texas

Rangers play for the weekend. We were sitting in the left field stands and that is when I realized this is what I wanted to do for a living. It just came to me; I do not know what hit me, but without a doubt I knew my calling was in sports.

I majored in marketing with a minor in management at LA Tech. It was a business degree and I did not know what to do with a business degree. Marketing is such a vague area that nobody knows what it is. Is it sales? Is it advertising? What is it? It is all of the above. It is anything you want it to be. I started working to get into sports management. My godfather, C.O. Brocato, was a scout for the Houston Oilers at the time and he knew a lot of people in the Dallas area. I also tried to get a position with the Texas Rangers, Dallas Cowboys, and the University of Texas at Arlington (UTA). What I learned is that a ton of people want to pursue sports for a living and few jobs are available. If I wanted to do this, I would have to start at the bottom. In retrospect, not many sport management programs existed so the best experience was to work in the athletic department at Louisiana Tech. That probably would have led to a future in college athletics, although my interest was in professional sports.

Nothing was available in internships or practicums at that time, so I began working for a retail operation in Shreveport that was eventually bought out by the Dillard's Corporation. I was the last person hired before the completion of the transaction, which took about a year. After the transaction, I was the first person that was laid off. I remember it vividly because it was also the day the space shuttle crashed. It was a terrible day in my life, as I lost my job, had a flat tire, and the space shuttle crashed. However, a week later I had the job that I always wanted.

I decided that day to pursue a career in sports. I went to see Taylor Moore, owner of the Shreveport Captains Baseball Team to see whether he had any advice on getting into sport. The Captains were the Class AA affiliate of the San Francisco Giants and were opening a new stadium. The new stadium turned out to be the revitalization of minor league baseball in Shreveport. During my meeting with Taylor, I asked many questions and talked about my experience and what I wanted to do. The next day he called and offered me a position as director of group sales for the Captains.

I had no experience in the industry, but I had a sales background from working in retail and had worked my way through college as an assistant manager of a restaurant. I did have experience with customer service, however. We set records for attendance in 1986 and 1987. Attendance soared from about 25,000 people a year to eventually more than 200,000. I was with the team for five seasons and had advanced to being assistant general manager by the time I left for New Orleans. Counting Mr. Moore, there were five permanent employees, but it was one of the best experiences I have ever had because we each had to do so much. I loved it, I lived it, and on game days I was there from 9:00 AM until 2:00 AM. Everyone else who had a normal life would go home, but after I finished my business, I would review the game with our pitching coach, Marty DeMerritt. Marty was the pitching coach for the Chicago Cubs for the 1999 season. It was our way of unwinding after the event. During the off season, I did not know what to do at night because no games had to be played. Those five years were an incredible experience. To be successful in minor league baseball, you must be a little bit of everything, including detail-oriented and creative. I did everything from group sales and promotions coordination to advertising sales for television, radio, and outfield fence signs. It taught me the first rule of sales—you must know your customer. I was in the right place at the right time with the stadium coming on line. I owe a lot to Taylor Moore. He is a great leader, a great person, and taught me that you can be the good guy and still make money. He was a great member of the community. He had a lot of impact on the way I do business today and I continue to teach those philosophies to our staff at the Sports Foundation.

I began working as the director of special projects with the Greater New Orleans Sports Foundations in 1990. I was also hired as director of sales for the Olympic Track and Field Trials in 1992. That led into a wonderful experience because it was a huge event and a lot of records were set. Although the Sports Foundation had been around since 1988, this was by far our largest major event. At the time, the Foundation did not have a permanent source of funding. In 1993, I became general manager for the New Orleans Zephyrs Baseball Club. I probably would have never left the Foundation if we had been fully funded at that time. The foundation is a private, not-for-profit organization, and our mission is to attract and manage sporting events on behalf of the city and state.

I went to work as general manager of the New Orleans Zephyrs on February 15 and opening day was April 14! The franchise had been awarded but it did not have a stadium nor any employees except me. The Milwaukee Brewers were a great organization to work with because they provided players and management that understood our situation. Within two weeks I set up the office, hired staff, and we were in operation. I had experience in start-ups so I knew exactly what we needed. We played our home games at the University of New Orleans Privateer Park, a 4,500-seat stadium on Lake Pontchartrain. We finally signed the contract to play at Privateer Park 24 hours before opening day. Within two years, the club had spent more that $500,000 in upgrades to the facility.

After two years with the team, I thought the current ownership was stifling the organization. The owner was in Denver and was hands-off. He owned multiple businesses, all of which seemed to be strapped for cash. His usual business practice was to wait until the last minute until you were in the deepest, darkest corner before you paid the bills. Personally, it made it hard for me because the owner was not available. I started the business, developed the relationships, and had my reputation on the line. People I had worked with for several years were promised payment of bills, but it was always 3 to 6 months late. It was a precarious situation and it made for some uneasy times with the staff and me, but it was also an invaluable learning experience.

During that time, we lobbied quite a bit for a new stadium, but it became a political hot potato. In Louisiana, politics is a contact sport and the legislators were not going to vote for a new stadium outside the city unless a new one was voted for inside the city. After two years, I was offered a position to return to the Greater New Orleans Sports Foundation as director of events. This was December 1995 and a source of funding was in place. Doug Thornton, who is now general manager of the Louisiana Superdome, was president and chief executive officer of the Foundation at that time. He had extensive experience in the industry, but it was as a volunteer. Doug and the Foundation needed somebody to produce events—what I did best. The Super Bowl was scheduled for January 1997, and the 1996 AAU Junior Olympic Games, a 10,000-participant event, was scheduled, too.

In January 1995, we had funding to expand the offices and bring a business environment to the Foundation. Our management and sales experience distinguishes us from other sports commissions. We bid for an event, make the presentation, obtain the event, then coordinate it from the beginning to the end. The Foundation, along with then Governor Edwin Edwards and Tom Benson, owner of the Saints, led the charge to get the Super Bowl XXXI. It was designated that the Sports Foundation was going to be the host committee staff, which is the first time a sports commission acted as a staff for a Super Bowl. It was a unique situation because there was no need to set up a new office, new phone systems, or hire new staff because it was already in place. It worked out beautifully.

The Super Bowl is political and a few sports commissions have the capability to effectively run it. Indianapolis and San Antonio have the capability, but will not be awarded a game. Several cities have great people in their sports commissions, but they either do not have the number of personnel or the management focus to host the event. The Super Bowl was another huge event that put the Sports Foundation on the map. It solidified our role in the city. You learn that you must continue to prove yourself repeatedly because the mega-events come in cycles. Often it can be 5 to 10 years between the time when a city hosts another Super Bowl or an NCAA Final Four.

It makes sense for our organization to handle events like this because we have the expertise. A volunteer group does not have the experience to host an event. If the NCAA wants to talk with someone who can handle problems immediately and knows what to do, we are knowledgeable and available. It is often hard to contact volunteers because they have full-time jobs and their priorities are different. We have three clients every time we sign a contract with a national governing body: the event owner, the State of Louisiana, and the City of New Orleans. We look at events from both sides and that can become the hardest part of production. How do you make an NFL event the best event it can possibly be without damaging the city in any shape or form without taking advantage of the city? It does take more than just a great staff to organize a premium event. It takes a full effort from the organizing committee, the facility staff (usually the Superdome), the

Convention and Visitors Bureau staff, and cooperation from the city government all working together. When it comes down to who is responsible for fund raising, the administration, and daily responsibilities, it is the Foundation staff. The magnitude of these events can be a little scary sometimes but it is satisfying to know that you are in charge.

In June 1997, Doug Thornton left the Foundation to become general manager of the Louisiana Superdome. I took over on an interim basis and was made president/chief executive officer in September 1997. At first, we went through some transition. We had a highly experienced staff that did not have a mega-event in the schedule, so when the staff got offered great jobs, they left. Our media director, Greg Bensel, is now the public relations person for the Saints. Our marketing person, Carol Asher, has a successful marketing consulting business. Doug is the general manager of the Superdome. I moved up to this position. My charge now is to prepare our staff to handle the mega-events through the experience of producing smaller events.

What does the future hold for me? Several options exist for the future, but nothing in concrete. Starting my own sports management and marketing company or getting into the marketing representation of athletes are interesting possibilities. However, I love what I do and am happy with the present challenges. I am not interested in politics, and although I love professional baseball, front office jobs are time consuming and not as glamorous as perceived. It would be difficult, but not impossible, for me to relocate to another area. My roots are here. My wife is from here and we have three children. Her parents are here, and my parents live in Shreveport. The rest of my family is spread out in Louisiana.

Will there be a front office possibility if a major league baseball team moves to New Orleans? I do not think so because I do not think major league baseball will become a reality here. The size of the television market is small compared with other major league cities. Market size is important. That is why the New York Yankees get $75 million from their cable rights each year. The Seattle Mariners only get $3 to $5 million. That means the team only has $3 to $5 million to deal with for free agency. Should George Steinbrenner have to give up some of his revenues to Seattle? That is a tough question.

To be successful, you must build a baseball-owned facility that seats about 40,000 in an outdoor or retractable roof stadium. The corporate support for a new major league franchise is not here. Many of the same limitations apply to bringing an NHL or NBA team to New Orleans. It would be almost impossible for a professional baseball, basketball, or hockey team to use the Superdome because it hosts more than 250 events each year. The New Orleans Arena, however, is well suited for a professional franchise.

When I took over in 1997, we reorganized the staff. We have a full-service marketing department and sponsorship, public relations, and government relations fall under it. A full service administrative department is responsible for all financial, accounting and business operations, and office management. A full-service operations department oversees all events. Every event has the same three general areas: marketing, operations, and administration.

Under my position in the management structure are the vice presidents of marketing, administration, and operations. We have about 11 full time employees and that includes our support staff. We will expand to 25 or 26 for Super Bowl XXXVI. We have interns as needed during the season. If they have the skills and desire, we usually hire those persons part-time to handle our busy schedule in the spring and summer. The event coordinators handle the daily operations of the events. The public relations director handles all of our media, publications, press conferences, and newsletters. We have weekly staff meetings. I have an open-door policy and we talk on a daily basis, in an informal manner, about every subject, and everything we work on. E-mail has greatly changed the way we communicate with external customers, as well as internal staff.

The main industry journals we read are the *Sports Business Journal*, the foremost tabloid available on sports business, and the *Sports Business Daily*. Our best method of obtaining information about bidding on events is contacting the national governing bodies of sport, and people we know who work for them, and asking simple questions: "What do you have to bid?" Or "Would you like to bring your event here to New Orleans?" Given the hotels, the facilities, and the management group experience, we have many successful bids. We choose which events or bids to pursue based on our past experience. We have learned what events work here. The first thing we do is develop a budget and see if the event will stand alone financially. If not, can we raise the money necessary to fulfill the obligations of the bid? We also contact people who did the event the past five years and interview them. It is a process and you must look at the big picture, the number of room nights, the amount of space needed, and the amount of time needed—it has to fit together like a puzzle.

The preparation and lead time for most of the events is at least six months. We did a bid for the Tiger Woods Foundation Golf Clinic in about a week. With our experience in bid preparation we knew exactly what to do. When Tiger Woods came to New Orleans to give a clinic for underprivileged kids at the City Park's golf courses, he also conducted a workshop for parents and kids and it is a beautiful thing. We worked with the New Orleans Recreation Department, the Compact Classic, and the PGA to develop this bid. It is our responsibility to organize it. We took the operational side of building a temporary 3,000-seat venue for a golf clinic at a City Park and handled all the details concerning sanitation, sound, lights, traffic control, transportation, and other operational issues. Our database contains more than 10,000 volunteers, which is more than we need and more than we can efficiently handle. We use about 7,000 volunteers for the Super Bowl, but we have a core group of probably 200 to 300 that we use for every event.

Our role is to attract and manage sporting events to make an economic impact. The hardest thing about doing this is you usually do not get to do an event twice. However, we are fortunate that we have done the Super Bowl and the SEC Basketball Tournament twice.

There is a trend in sport to get corporate naming rights for major facilities. New Orleans is exploring selling the naming rights to the Superdome. The trend is to get as much money as you can while you can. The State of Louisiana does not want to change the name of the Superdome. That is nice but not very financially practical over the next 10 years. The Saints might come back in a few years and want to renegotiate their deal with the Superdome because it is not comparable to their competitors. They will probably ask for a new revenue stream coming from the naming rights of the Superdome. I think the Saints will go and ask for a few million dollars more a year from the state, and those monies have to be found somewhere and that may include a corporate name on the Superdome.

Many other issues and trends exist in the sport industry. One of the most important for us is the growing number of sports commissions. The coverage and visibility of the commissions have grown with the size and importance of the sporting events. The economic impact of sporting events in the community is so substantial that many cities are allocating resources to prepare bids for the mega-events. Job opportunities will continue to grow for prepared sport management graduates who desire to be a part of this exciting and challenging segment of the sport industry.

CHAPTER 14

The Academic World of Sport Management

SPORT MANAGEMENT DEVELOPED AS AN ACADEMIC DISCIPLINE because of the need for formalized training in the complexities of the sport industry. Before the initial collegiate course offerings, sport managers were generally trained on the job. These early professionals came from the business world or were former outstanding athletes who "retired" into front office administrative positions. As the business of sport rapidly grew into a major entertainment industry, the need for a new hybrid of leaders with expertise in both sport studies and business administration developed. This need led to the creation of sport administration/sport management academic programs.

Sport management programs grew rapidly during the past three decades because of the dramatic expansion of the sports industry, the interest of students in pursuing a career in sport, and the need for colleges to attract more students into their programs. According to Parkhouse (1996), the total number of sport management programs exceeds 200, with an additional 10 undergraduate and graduate programs offered in Canada. Internationally, universities offer sport management programs in Germany, Australia, New Zealand, Japan, Greece, Portugal, and England, to name a few.

To achieve a faculty position in higher education, a doctoral degree or at least a master's degree is required. However, an academic degree alone is not a job guarantee. A student must attain experience in the industry to achieve a competitive advantage in the job search for academic positions. A resume that includes work experience, volunteer experience, selling, event management, marketing, research, demonstrated oral and written communication skills, and technological expertise will distinguish a candidate among the many applicants for higher education faculty positions with similar educational training.

391

Sport management positions in academia may involve opportunities in a two-year community college or a four-year small or large, public or private college or university located in all areas of North America and internationally. Generally, faculty positions involve expectations of high quality work in three areas: scholarly activity, teaching, and service. Most enter the academic environment as assistant professors. The pay range for these positions, depending on the size of the institution, ranges from $25,000 to $35,000. Through advancement an individual can be promoted to associate professor. An associate professor can earn from $40,000 to $60,000 per year. The highest an individual in higher education can aspire to is full professor. Full professors can earn more than $60,000 per year. The key to promotion and pay increases is fulfilling the obligations of scholarly activity, teaching, and service.

The career in academia enables people to be creative and stay abreast of the latest developments in the industry. It also provides satisfaction by enriching the lives of future professionals in the field and helping to shape the future growth of the sport industry.

REFERENCES

Parkhouse, B.L. (1996). *The management of sport: Its foundation and application* (2nd ed.). St. Louis, MO: Mosby-Year Book Inc.

William A. Sutton

Associate Professor and Graduate Program Director
University of Massachusetts at Amherst

Education:
B.A., OKLAHOMA STATE UNIVERSITY, 1972
M.S., OKLAHOMA STATE UNIVERSITY, 1980
ED.D., OKLAHOMA STATE UNIVERSITY, 1983

Career Progression:
PRINCIPAL, AUDIENCE ANALYSTS CONSULTING, 1994 TO PRESENT
ASSOCIATE PROFESSOR, UNIVERSITY OF MASSACHUSETTS, 1993 TO PRESENT
VICE PRESIDENT, DEL WILBUR AND ASSOCIATES, 1990 TO 1993
ASSISTANT PROFESSOR AND PROGRAM COORDINATOR, THE OHIO STATE UNIVERSITY, 1986 TO 1990
ASSISTANT PROFESSOR, ROBERT MORRIS COLLEGE, 1982 TO 1986

Best piece of advice you received in regards to your career:

"Aim high. Seek what you want. Make adjustments as needed. Don't settle for something you don't want."

Best advice for someone aspiring toward a career in the sport industry:

"When determining your career path, it is just as important to know what you don't want to do as it is to know what you do want to do."

Quote by which you live:

"A life is not important except in the impact it has on other lives."

JACKIE ROBINSON'S TOMBSTONE.

CURRENTLY I AM AN ASSOCIATE PROFESSOR at the University of Massachusetts at Amherst. I have been there for 7 years. Before that I worked as a vice president of information services at Del Wilbur, a sport marketing firm based in St. Louis where I did consumer research and worked with teams and events. My background also includes coordinating the graduate sport management program at Ohio State, serving as assistant professor at Robert Morris College, and serving as a YMCA director.

I went to Oklahoma State from 1968 to 1972 and earned a bachelor's degree in political science. I left Oklahoma State and went back to Pittsburgh where I became involved in what I would call counseling and athletics. I did a little bit of coaching for about 4–1/2 years, went back to Oklahoma State, earned a master of science degree in recreation administration, and then stayed to earn a doctor of education in sports studies.

I started as a political scientist. When I went through college and became aware of the "politics" in government I started looking other places. My first position was as a counselor in a group home. As a counselor I worked with pre-delinquent to delinquent youth. They always wanted to be active so we formed teams and put them in leagues. First I became the coach and then I became the administrator. I enjoyed it and decided it was something that I wanted to do. But I was typecast as a political science major, so I went back to graduate school and began working at a YMCA as a program director. The YMCA was an enlightening and fulfilling experience for me. I got a feel for and sense of enjoyment from marketing. At the YMCA I was given a limited amount of United Way funds and had to earn my budget. In my first month on the job we planned for the next fiscal year. My operating budget was $43,000 in 1978 for all programming areas. I was told that I had to create a new budget for the next year and to make my projections carefully because I was accountable for them. I reviewed everything the YMCA had done, looked at the things I wanted to do, and came back to the board with a budget of $78,000 for the next year. They looked at me like I was crazy. I felt good though because I thought I was going to do about $100,000. I did not want to say that because I wanted to make sure I could accomplish my goals. I thought that with a little bit of marketing, promotion, and teaching people about the YMCA, we could hit those levels. So after a lot of debate they accepted a budget from me for $60,000, which still concerned them. We generated $111,000 and that convinced me that I had a talent for marketing. I finished graduate school, earned a master's degree in recreation administration from Oklahoma State University (OSU), and began a doctoral program in leisure counseling at OSU. I began a program in leisure counseling because it paralleled my YMCA work at that particular point in time. I had no thoughts about leaving the YMCA as a profession. I considered leaving my current YMCA job, but staying in the YMCA system. I was in the doctoral program and worked as the YMCA's executive director when a couple of things happened. First, I learned that a YMCA executive director is not a marketer; he or she is a banker. The main responsibilities are raising funds and keeping the bill collectors away. At the same time I had a professor ask me if I had ever thought about going into teaching because she thought that would be a natural place for me. I said, "No, I never thought about it," but I began to consider it. I changed from leisure counseling and created a program in sports studies combining geography, marketing, sociology, sport history, and a few law courses. It was a unique program and I was excited about it. When I finished it, I applied for some jobs and landed my first teaching job at Robert Morris College where I was fortunate to work for Steve Hardy, who gave me the marketing course to teach. I had never taught a marketing course, but I enjoyed it and started doing things. I also was responsible for internships. I decided that teaching was what I wanted to pursue as a career.

My career path is one that may be described as following my heart and my opportunities. I joke with people all the time that these words should be carved on my tombstone: "He never asked what if." I had a number of interesting opportunities and I pursued them. My family has always supported me when I pursued those opportunities. I have always liked challenges and marketing is constantly full of challenges. Marketers always have to prove themselves, and an opportunity always arises with new ideas to be creative and innovative. My path wound through a number of different things that eventually got me where I am today. I am always looking for challenges, new opportunities and new ventures, and ways to prove myself. My life has always been that way and marketing has been the way to do it.

I cannot say that I would have done anything differently. If I went back to school I would probably still be a political science major. I would probably still do the things that I have done. The YMCA was a great experience for me because it really taught me a lot.

When I first started my career I did not do any networking, but I did a lot of reading. When I discovered something that interested me, I would file it away for future reference. I went to some conferences. I would have probably found my path much quicker had I been an active networker at that time. In retrospect it is ironic because now I stress networking so much to my students. I tell them to network from day one. It is funny that it took me a while to practice what I preached, but I did not know I was preaching it initially. Probably the way I learned best was by experimentation, feeling, knowing what is right, and knowing what I wanted to do. I talked to a few professors before I got into teaching, but when I got up in front of students for the first time it felt natural to me. I had seen so many things so when I taught my classes I did not want to just be in the classroom; I wanted to make the world my classroom. I was always conscious about teaching what was relevant and making sure I knew what was relevant.

From an academic perspective I would list two role models. One was a professor, Jerry Pollinard, who taught constitutional law at Oklahoma State University when I was an undergraduate. What I respected about him was that he taught the class and made it challenging, dynamic, exciting, and fun. I did not want to miss that class. It was my favorite of all of the classes I took in college. I never missed it. It was always exciting how he captivated people, held their attention, and got them to comprehend the subject information. He was funny, witty, and intelligent. I filed that away for future reference. A second role model was John Rooney, my doctoral degree advisor, because of the way he dealt with students, tried to help students, and was a visionary. I have tried to pattern the academic part of my life after my role models.

On the practitioner side my role models are a combination of Bill Veeck, P.T. Barnum, and Pat Williams. These are people who were or are successful at what they do, but they all have one thing in common—the way they valued and dealt with people. I am a great student of watching people interact with people. That is important to me. I want everyone always to think they are important because that is the way I was treated. I read these stories about how Bill Veeck did not know Pat Williams at the time and invited him to his home. He sat and talked to him on his porch for 4 hours and listened to Pat as if he were an equal. I have always respected that and I have always tried to take all of those thoughts into my relationships, not just with my students, but also with my clients. I listen to my clients and try to interact with them on more than just a business basis. It makes for more long-term business relationships, and the same thing applies to my students. Adding that extra dimension of knowledge received from my role models has worked well for me.

Because of my drive, any obstacles I faced were overcome by either my determination or my wife Sharon's support. I would focus more and be more determined to get it done. I never perceived anything as an obstacle and said "I can't do this." I was never discouraged in my career. My philosophy was that if I could not get it one way then it would come another way, and I would try to determine other ways to get there.

I am now the graduate program director and a faculty member in the department of sports studies at the University of Massachusetts at Amherst. As a faculty member I teach the graduate marketing course, an undergraduate course on professional sport industries, and an honors course in sales and sales management. I have taught baseball and popular culture and a research course. I enjoy it. When I teach my graduate marketing course I realize it may be the only marketing course most of these students ever take. I try to teach it in such a way that it is beneficial to those students who understand marketing, but also enlightening and beneficial to those who have not taken a marketing class. I aim for the middle ground. I try to teach with the perspective that the material is not rocket science. I try to teach skills and thinking so that people are prepared to go out and be emissaries for themselves and for our program. The student pays the tuition so I have a moral obligation to give them the best possible education and to help those students who want to be helped while reaching out and attempting to help those who do not want to be helped. It is important for me to finish my day with a feeling that I made myself available and did the right kinds of things for students. I also bring a lot of the real world into the classroom. I try to teach research by having them do research, that is real research, not make-believe or pretend research. In the sales class I have them sell. I introduce them to key players in the industry and direct them to go out to observe and learn. Observation and putting things into practice are the best ways to facilitate learning. That is my personal philosophy, so I embody that in my classroom. I also believe in having realistically close relationships with students whenever possible because they need guidance. They might need a mentor, a friend, or just a good listener. I try to be all of those things. I incorporate the practitioner part of my life by helping students with an internship, having special speakers in class, or having a student call someone to talk to them. I blend that part of my life, which has added a lot to my personal fulfillment. I do things the best way I know how. I do not short-change anyone. I feel almost self-actualized in the way I do things. When I left teaching for 3 years I realized what it was about teaching that I loved and missed, yet I realized the value of the experiences I gained during my time outside the classroom. I combined those experiences when I came back. It has been successful for me, and I have been happy with it. The most demanding part of my job is helping the students outside of the classroom. The worst part is being unable to help the students outside of the classroom or being unable to help someone fulfill a dream. I find that frustrating.

I try to incorporate practitioners and practical experience in my classes. I have done it in a research context and in a sales context. What we look to do is teach the concept in the classroom, make sure they understand the concept, and then put them in a position where they can test it to see if it works, how it works—and more importantly—how they can use it. We have done things from conducting market research for teams and leagues to finding out about fan festivals, fan satisfaction and attendance, team performance, and game operations. We take that information from the research and then decide what to do about it, where the sport organization has to make the decisions and then they have to make the recommendations. We augment it with readings and do all of the proper academic framework in our formal learning situation in the classroom. Then we put it in the work place, which I think has been well received by students because that is what they want when they come to study this degree. They want the opportunity to interface with the marketplace where they hope to work.

I have seen a lot of benefit derive from the marketing plan, which looks as if it is a traditional classroom learning experience. Because I encourage the students to do real life marketing plans, they must meet people and identify a situation in that industry or business that needs to be marketed or promoted. Then they work with that group of people to promote and market that particular segment. Often it leads to a job, but at least it leads to a great learning experience in which they solved a problem. In my class now, one of my students will go to New York, take a tour of the NBA store, meet with the person responsible for the fortunes and future of the store, and try to present a fresh perspective. I have used experiences like this in the marketing class, the research class, the sales class, and event-type classes. They are time intensive, demanding, and exhausting, but they are the experiences that the students remember when they leave.

My work schedule varies. I spend time in the classroom and have office hours outside of the classroom. I do some consulting, writing, and a lot of reading during the week. I probably spend 20 to 30 hours a week on the academic side either talking to students, helping students, preparing for class, teaching class, and so forth. I spend about 10 to 12 hours per week reading about developments in the industry. I spend another 10 to 15 hours a week consulting in either paid or unpaid activities and assisting the industry.

Overall I am satisfied with my job. It frustrates me to see somebody not pulling his or her weight or not doing a job the way it should be done. We deal with our future when we deal with a student in the classroom. If we short-change the student we short-change ourselves and everyone around us. I do not like to see that. I do not see any of it in my department, but when I see it other places on campus it angers me.

Probably the most important managerial skill I have developed is becoming a good observer. In any management position you must be able to listen, observe, and understand before you talk. You should understand what it is, know how it works, and understand all of the dimensions of it. This applies to material you prepare for a lecture, a career opportunity you discuss with a student, or whether you are talking with a student. You need to know by listening and observing what happens. To me those are central skills in any management position, and they are critical to this position.

I have both a rational decision-making and an irrational decision-making process. I make most decisions with my heart. My heart sometimes influences my head, and I have tried to minimize that. I have been successful in minimizing it, but I manage by feeling. I make decisions based on how they feel, not necessarily whether they make sense. In other words, on the consulting side of my life, I may be asked to do a job for a particular client. If I do not like the way it feels or if I do not like the way I relate to this person I do not do it, even though that does not make much business sense. It makes personal sense. Probably the most important things to me are to feel fulfilled, happy, and to know that I am leading the kind of life that I want to lead.

The only stress I have in my life is when I over-commit. I would say over-commitment causes 90 to 95 percent of my stress. Do I over-commit? Yes, on a regular basis, so I have stress. What I try to do if I feel stressed when I over-commit is step back and determine what it requires to get me to the level where I am comfortable. In other words, what do I have to accomplish in the next 48 to 72 hours that will make me feel better about the way my life is now. I attack stress that way. If it means pulling an all-nighter, I pull an all-nighter. I do whatever it takes to clear that passageway. I must attack it. I cannot sit and think about it. I have to complete one of the commitments to get to that level.

If I knew someone was aspiring to a career like mine, I would tell him or her the rules of the game are research, teaching, and service. They have to decide whether they can fit into those expectations and where they want to go. The rule is, "If you can't salute the general get out of the army." If you cannot obey those kind of rules and fit into that situation then you have to assess whether other situations are a better fit. Do you need to be at a smaller, liberal arts type school or do you need to be a practitioner? What do you need to be? You have the obligation to publish or perish, and it is a fact of life. I do not think a lot of people in our discipline who love academic writing view it as their primary function. If you want to be in this profession you owe it to your students and your university to build a reputation. You owe it to yourself to become an expert in some subject. However, you cannot do it at the expense of one of the other two requirements. You cannot do it at the expense of how you treat students and how you relate to students. They must be the number one force in your heart if you are going to be good at your job. A lot of great researchers are lousy teachers and a lot of great teachers are lousy researchers. If you can do both, great, more power to you; but if you cannot, you have to decide which of the two is more important to you and work at an institution that supports that view. If I look at my own experiences, having taught at a school where research was not important and having taught at a school where research was the critical element, I was not happy at either one. Now I find myself at an institution where the blend of what is expected and what I can do is a good fit. My advice is to make sure your heart and head fit the demands and the quality of the institution.

I would describe my teaching style as caring. If I had to sum it up in one word, I do not think people have any doubt that I care. People realize that I care and what I do is important. They know I enjoy my job and I like going out beyond the norm. You could view me as a nontraditional teacher because I use a lot of different formats and environments. I do not necessarily have to be in a classroom with an overhead projector or a computer to teach someone. I use whatever is available as my lab, and I try to create unique learning that will hopefully have a meaningful impact.

When I think of trends in education I would say we are moving rapidly toward more nontraditional learning forms. We have been moving that way for 10 years, but each year it accelerates. We will do more distance learning, executive education, and service to people who cannot fit the traditional academic role. That will not change; it will always be like that. We will need to know the latest technologies and understand the industry. We will have to teach with the idea that we are not preparing students for one or even two jobs when they leave our programs. We need to understand that students graduating from sport management programs could have five or six different experiences once they leave our campus. We have to make sure they are diverse in their training and the different things that they can handle. We have to make sure the students are aware of that. We have to prepare them to be mobile.

From the practitioner side, I see continued downsizing, mergers, and diversification of large companies. The model in professional sports now is owning the building and owning at least one team, but two is better. Owners need to use their resources in that way—package all of your sponsorships and leverage your abilities to do different things in the marketplace. Family ownership is dead except for in the NFL. When teams like the Steelers are sold, that will be the end of it. We will see more conglomerations and we will be more international. Media outlets will own us. We will look for options to make sport affordable to the masses.

Students need to learn to deal with people on a variety of levels. They still need great interpersonal skills, but now they must deal with people via technology. That technology includes e-mail, Web sites, chat rooms, and everything where they are not dealing directly with the person. They must learn how to "communicate impersonally on a personal basis"—if I can say something as crazy as that. It will not be personal because they are not face-to-face, but they will need the same listening and speaking abilities even if they cannot face the people they address. They may need to be comfortable being in front of a video camera when doing part of their job and transmitting information across the globe. I see career opportunities continuing in technology, entertainment, sales, marketing, selling technology, using technology, selling entertainment, and blending more entertainment technology.

On the academic side there has been a proliferation of sport management programs in the past 10 years. More teaching jobs will be available as more business schools evolve. We will need to do some self-examination to determine where we stack up against other educational venues. Can the business schools come in and do the quality job that we do? In other words, can they devote enough people to understanding the industry or are they still going to sell it like it is Proctor and Gamble? Is that wrong or is that right? We face that challenge.

In 10 years I will be teaching and serving as a consultant. I will still do the same things because when I found out I was just doing one, I was not happy. Because I can combine the two and it has benefited everyone, I have determined that is my role and what I need to do. I have already done the quantity versus quality of life thing, and money is not the ultimate measure of happiness or success for me.

I feel successful. I have a personal level of satisfaction. I can look around and see what I have done. I have done more than I ever imagined. I see my former students as vice presidents, presidents, and athletic directors, and that shows me I have done what I was supposed to do. I have seen my name on a book and I have been the editor of a journal. I have played a leadership role in the industry. I am well received by the practitioners in the industry. I am appreciative of where I am in my profession and in life and feel a debt of gratitude to everyone who has helped me throughout my journey. To sum it all up, I point to the inscription on Jackie Robinson's tombstone: "A life is not important except in the impact it has on other lives." Although this was not meant to describe a teacher, I cannot think of better words that do.

Susan C. Brown

Associate Professor
Flagler College

Education:

B.S., PHYSICAL EDUCATION, FLORIDA STATE UNIVERSITY, 1976

M.S., SPORT ADMINISTRATION, EASTERN ILLINOIS UNIVERSITY, 1983

PH.D., SPORT MANAGEMENT, OHIO STATE UNIVERSITY, 1988

Career Progression:

ASSOCIATE PROFESSOR, FLAGLER COLLEGE, 1999 TO PRESENT

SPORT MANAGEMENT PROGRAM COORDINATOR AND ASSOCIATE PROFESSOR, WESTERN CAROLINA UNIVERSITY, 1988 TO 1998

GRADUATE ADMINISTRATIVE ASSOCIATE FOR RECREATION EDUCATION AND SPORT MANAGEMENT, OHIO STATE UNIVERSITY, 1985 TO 1988

COORDINATOR OF INTRAMURALS AND INSTRUCTIONAL PROGRAMS, ST. LOUIS UNIVERSITY, 1983 TO 1985

GRADUATE ASSISTANT FOR CAMPUS RECREATION, EASTERN ILLINOIS UNIVERSITY, 1982 TO 1983

SALES REPRESENTATIVE, KEN'S SPORTING GOODS (TITUSVILLE, FLORIDA), 1980 TO 1981

PALM BAY HIGH SCHOOL (MELBOURNE, FLORIDA), PHYSICAL EDUCATION TEACHER/ HEAD VOLLEYBALL AND SOFTBALL COACH, 1977 TO 1980

Best piece of advice you received in regards to your career:

**Not advice but rather an example set by former supervisors:
Take care of your employees!**

Best advice for someone aspiring toward a career in the sport industry:

**"Learn to sweep the floors because it will make you a better manager.
You will appreciate those who complete those tasks when you become a
manager and understand the organization as you advance."**

Quote by which you live:

"Put God in the center and everything will come together."

I INNOCENTLY DECIDED ON A CAREER IN SPORT when I was in tenth grade. It was then I decided to teach physical education, primarily because of some role models I had early on as a student. I had some physical education teachers in high school and some coaches whose influence inspired me. That is how I decided to go to Florida State University where I earned my undergraduate degree in physical education.

My first full-time teaching job was teaching physical education and coaching high school volleyball and softball at Palm Bay High School in Melbourne, Florida. They wanted to move me out of physical education into a teaching field that I had minored in college, but it was not related to sport. I decided to leave teaching and went to work full-time for a small sporting goods company as a sales representative. That added to my background in terms of experience in the sport industry. I was a sales representative both in the store and on the road and sold equipment to high schools and military bases in the area. I did that for about 10 or 11 months and decided for various reasons not to pursue it further.

Then I just stepped out of the sport industry for about a year to decide what I wanted to do with my life. That is when I decided to pursue a master's degree in sport administration from Eastern Illinois University (EIU). My graduate assistantship experience at EIU influenced my decision to enter recreational sport management. After graduation, I worked as the coordinator of intramurals in recreational sports at St. Louis University (SLU) for 2 years while starting to work on my doctoral degree part-time. I had an advisor who was a lawyer, and he was the first person to talk to me about sport law. In 1985, Columbus (Ohio) was hosting the National Intramural Recreational Sports Association (NIRSA) conference. I was introduced to Dr. Mary Daniels, who taught sport law at Ohio State. She and I started talking and she eventually offered me an assistantship to teach recreation education majors, so I left St. Louis University to attend Ohio State full-time. After taking her sport law class, I was asked to teach law to the recreation undergraduates for 2 years. That experience influenced my entire college teaching career because I consider sport law to be my specialty.

At Ohio State, I earned a degree in sport management with emphases in higher education administration and sport law. Following graduation, I took a faculty and coordinator position in sport management at Western Carolina University. I was there for 10–1/2 years. Currently, I am a faculty member in the department of sport management at Flagler College.

I do encounter two obstacles in my career. First, I teach in the area of law and do not have a law degree. Some individuals have verified that often it is the Ph.D. who teaches a better sport law class because they understand that they are teaching to practitioners and are not preparing lawyers. However, at the same time many of the lawyers do not have that perception and do not respect what we know and what we do. The second obstacle is tied to some administrators who do not take women in the sport world seriously. I have worked for male administrators and with male faculty who did not respect my background, education, training, knowledge, or experience. This is probably no different than the female in the sport business industry who has sought out a general manager's position. My sense is that as women continue to infiltrate the world of sport, value and respect will improve.

With regard to being a single female in this profession, early on in my career I put great emphasis on becoming a professional and did not pay enough attention to my personal life. My advice to a younger person entering the workforce is to develop some balance between your professional and personal life. That is something I did not do well. I was driven to succeed because I enjoyed what I did, but as I reflect on it I wish I had put a more personal balance into my life. I had been engaged briefly while living in St. Louis. Following that experience, I threw myself back into my career and the pursuit of my doctorate. Being single, however, has allowed me greater opportunity to move and pursue jobs. I was not tied down by family obligations and had more flexibility to pursue my career.

Two very strong and positive role models have influenced me. The first is Dr. David Dutler, with whom I worked at Eastern Illinois University. He was strong in paying attention to the needs of his students and his workers. He did not overwork us, was very caring, and had a personality that made him an easy individual with whom to work. That was important because from that experience I learned that nearly all employees and students are busy. Some teachers or employers like to dump responsibilities on others to lighten their own workload, but that practice can be counterproductive to organizational goals. I learned from him to respect other people's time. I try to respect students in terms of their workloads and try to understand their different perspectives and backgrounds. When I was at Eastern Illinois University, I planned on becoming a sport management practitioner. When I left, I went to work as a director of intramural programs. He influenced me greatly by showing me a lot about working in the recreational sport management field, which has been a big part of my life.

My other mentor in graduate school was Dr. Bill Sutton. I worked with him at Ohio State University. He was another professor who was understanding in terms of respecting the students and their workloads. He understood each student's different background. His area of expertise is sport marketing and he helped students not only learn concepts but also how to apply them. He would not say "Get out of my face and go somewhere else." He worked with us and helped us understand. I worked with him as a graduate assistant, too. He is a creative person and I am detail oriented so we worked well together. From that experience, I learned in any work environment, people complement each other and need to build on each other's strengths. To this day, he is supportive of former students and coworkers.

With respect to career goals, I would like to go to law school one day. I would not pursue it to become a practicing trial lawyer, but for the increased knowledge and the credibility issue mentioned earlier. I am not certain if I will pursue it because most law schools accept only full-time students. Stepping out of a job for 3 years is a little difficult financially, although not impossible. I have also wanted to get some more experience working as a practitioner, perhaps in professional golf as a tournament director. I may also open my own consulting business. Those are two things that I have not researched but I would like to do. I want to get back into writing in the area of legal issues in sport. If I could go back and do things differently, I might have earned a master's of business administration degree instead of a master's in sport administration, and I would have gone to law school earlier in my career. Instead of going straight from my doctoral program into a full-time job, I might have gone to law school. When I was at Ohio State, I could have worked on a law degree at the same time I was working on the doctoral degree.

In my current position I am an associate professor of sport management at Flagler College, where I teach two different law classes. One course is tort law and risk management and its applications to sport. The other one is statutory and constitutional law applications to sport with strong discussions in current legal issues. I also teach facility management and design, recreational sport management, and an introductory course, although not all in the same semester. The total enrollment at Flagler is more than 1,700 students. Of those students, more than 110 are sport management majors. I advise no more than 40 students and co-advise the sport management major's club that is active. The amount of committee work I am required to do on campus is limited.

The job expectations focus on teaching and service. There is no requirement to publish, but I love to write and that is why I want to continue to contribute to my field in that manner. At Western Carolina University there was a publication expectation and I dealt with the three-pronged approach of research, service, and teaching. There we had 6,700 students. Although it was not a Division I or top research institution, we still had the same expectations. We probably put more emphasis on the service component and had a more demanding teaching load than at Ohio State or any other major research institution. At Flagler College we probably have a shorter academic year than most schools. Although we start meetings in mid August, we do not start teaching until the first week of September. We are finished the third week in April, but our pay is based on a 10-month contract. Only once since starting my full-time professorate career have I taught summer classes. I have always supervised interns and used the summer to re-energize and read. Summer responsibilities almost always provide supplemental pay.

During a typical day at Flagler I am involved with teaching. I teach four classes, three on Tuesday and Thursday and one on Monday, Wednesday, and Friday. We are only required to hold one office hour for every three credit hour course, so with a 12-hour load, I am required to hold four office hours. Generally, unofficially, I hold more than that. To get back into research and writing, I am going to probably hold all of my office hours in the morning and do my research in the afternoon or vice versa depending on the day of the week. Dr. Bernadette Twardy, the chair of the sport management department, coordinates the teaching schedule, but I have selected the courses and times that I teach. The administration tries to maintain a 20-to-1 student-faculty ratio. In sport management we rarely have a class with more than 35 students, and I have had a class with only four students.

I am housed in the department of sport management. Flagler is set up with departments only. There are no colleges, schools, or divisions. Every academic unit is a department. It seems to be a good system because fewer turf issues exist compared with previous employment situations. All faculty members report directly to the department heads and the department heads report directly to the vice president for academic affairs. It is an easy environment in which to work. In my first semester, I was housed with the department of business, which was an eye-opening and pleasant experience. I began to realize that we as sport management faculty could do a lot to eliminate many of the turf issues that exist on campuses by educating business faculty about our programs. Many do not understand that we do not wear sweatsuits and teach our classes in the gym. Our situation was beneficial to me because we can now have an open and constant dialogue. I find the faculty at Flagler to be friendly and willing to share and work with each other, which is positive and somewhat unique.

Overall, I am not very satisfied with my salary. I make a comfortable living for a single person, but for what I have achieved in my career—especially my publication record and the professional positions that I have held—I should have a higher base salary. However, other issues exist to consider. For example, Florida has no state income taxes. I have a higher travel allowance than I had at previous institutions. I am the type of person who wants to contribute to the academic environment and I like working with people who respect me and respect my knowledge and years of preparation. I work best with administrators who work hard at doing everything possible to make my working environment better instead of questioning all my decisions when they have no background or experience in my field. That is probably the one negative thing that I have experienced in academia.

My teaching style is different depending on the subject. I embrace sport law. The field of sport law enamors me, and I try to display that enthusiasm when I teach my law classes. I involve the students and motivate them to think about the historical context and current issues in sport. In the first part of the semester I lecture a lot, and in the last part of the semester the students apply those notes through case law analyses, development of risk management plans, or term papers. When I teach introduction to sport management, I try to involve practitioners from the field so I encourage students to meet people and network. I probably lecture a little bit more in the other classes that I teach. I also teach a facility management class. I find that it has to be a project-oriented class or the students and I will be bored. My recreational sport management class is a mix of lecture and getting involved in running a local tournament, which the students have enjoyed.

The most demanding thing about my job is probably finding the time to do quality teaching and to maintain and advance my research agenda. It is difficult to find time for both. I accomplish more work in the morning and generally need at least one full day to be successful in the publishing arena. At a college like Flagler where teaching has to be the prime focus, it is difficult to stay focused on quality writing in a short period of time. Writing is the thing, other than the field of sport law, that keeps me energized and excited about my profession.

I have published more than 20 articles that have appeared in the *Journal of Sport Management,* the *NIRSA Journal, Sport Marketing Quarterly,* and the *Journal of Physical Education, Recreation and Dance* (JOPERD). I also was an editor for a special legal issues journal feature for NIRSA. Most recently, I was the editor for a 1999 NIRSA book titled *Managing the Recreational Sport Facility* in which I also authored a chapter titled "The Cutting Edge." Additionally, I authored the chapter "Campus Recreation" in the widely used sport management text *Contemporary Sport Management.* My presentation record includes state, regional, and national conferences/workshops for organizations such as SSLASPA, NASSM, NIRSA, and AAHPERD. Professionally, I am a member of SSLASPA (Society for the Study of the Legal Aspects of Sport and Physical Activity), NIRSA (National Intramural and Recreational Sport Association), NASSM (North American Society for Sport Management), and IAAM (International Association for Arena Managers). I probably will rejoin the Sport Lawyers Association as I try to make more of an impact on my research agenda in law. I have held leadership roles in many of these organizations. Currently, I am one of seven members of the Sport Management Program Review Council (SMPRC), the body that decides on which programs gain final "approved" status for their sport management curricula. I have also been the North Carolina state director on two different occasions for NIRSA, and I have chaired several committees for them, two of which developed new or revised publications. In 1995 I received one of the service awards as a member of the task force that rewrote the Certified Recreational Sports Specialist (CRSS) exam.

The most enjoyable part of my job always has been, is, and probably always will be, advising students. I particularly enjoy advising undergraduate students because I am helping young people who generally do not know what they want to do. They are 17, 18, or 19 years old and confused. To see them develop and grow into mature professionals is a joy. I enjoy teaching graduate students, too, as I did at Western Carolina. It is more challenging academically to teach graduate students. Some of my colleagues who teach in graduate programs believe that undergraduate students cannot get full-time jobs in the industry. This is not true. One of my former students who never attended graduate school received the 1999 Executive of the Year Award for the Florida State League. Although this is only one individual, many success stories exist. The key to being successful in this field is assertiveness, self-motivation, and persistence. Graduate students may come with more experience, but some are not willing to accept entry-level positions when they graduate. Undergraduates almost always will accept those positions and advance.

The least enjoyable part of my position is teaching classes in which I have little background or experience. For example, I was out of my element teaching a full semester of facility design and management. Although I do have considerable experience in the design and development of campus recreation facilities and have toured more than 40 such facilities, arenas and stadiums are much different. You cannot just teach seating, exits, and parking. Technology, suites, financing, floors, acoustics, and building codes are necessary topics of discussion and study. It can get very technical. Although I have a good working knowledge of many of those issues, I am not an electrician, engineer, or architect. Some of that gets left up to guest speakers if you can find any locally who have the experience in working with sport facilities. However, I do not necessarily believe that a sport management student needs to know detail in undergraduate school. Learning a working vocabulary and general concept knowledge to converse intelligently with those specialists ARE important. They will learn detail on the job.

Probably the best advice I could give somebody who wants to go into academia is to first get experience as a practitioner in some aspect of sport. Early in my career, I not only taught high school, but also I became involved in community programs and organized large softball tournaments. I learned a lot about event management. I was in charge of the set-up, operation, and follow-up for a 10-sport national championship for visually impaired persons that involved more than 400 athletes and coaches. I believe that faculty should have some understanding of sport management that is based on experience. I am an international official for the sport goalball, which is for visually impaired athletes. I have experienced the Barcelona and Atlanta Paralympics, two world championships, as well as the Australian and European Goalball Championships as an official. I understand both the large event management aspect and the volunteer side of event management. Through my travels, I have experienced sport on an international basis. All of these experiences have been shared in some manner with students in the classroom. In our field, the ability to bring on-hands experience to the classroom is essential. This is another plus that sport management professors have over business faculty.

Students who want to teach in college should not go straight through and earn a bachelor's degree, a master's degree, and then a doctorate. They need to experience sport other than just from the player's perspective, although the athlete's viewpoint is also important. I played varsity sports at Florida State University so I understand college athletics from that aspect.

Students need to conduct a good deal of research to find the best institution for them if they wish to pursue a sport management degree. I knew this field existed, but did not know how to get into it. It seems that many students experience that today even with all the technological advances we have made in promoting ourselves. When I was teaching high school in 1980, I was not happy teaching golf and team sports, so I asked the principal if I could teach a sport management class. He allowed me to teach it, so for one semester in my last year there I taught a sport management class. I chose the students—20 juniors and seniors—who thought they might want a career in sport. We brought in guest speakers and I taught them some career sport skills such as officiating. A portion of the class was similar to what most universities do now in their introductory sport management classes. I look back on that experience because it was unique. The newspapers even covered it because it was so original. I probably knew my calling a long time ago but did not know a formal way existed to get there through the colleges until I stumbled onto the sport administration program at Eastern Illinois. I am glad that it all worked out.

Additionally, sport will generally provide an avenue to supplement income. Sports officiating, scorekeeping, and lifeguarding were three ways I earned extra money while a student. Those experiences—in addition to helping pay the bills—have supported my teaching and increased my knowledge. They relate closely to aquatic management, sports information, event management, and recreation.

I have often been asked why a student should seek out a sport management degree over a business degree and what institutions I would recommend. I would reply this way. For students who want to attend an institution with a sport management degree program, there are institutions that I would recommend. To me, it is extremely important for an individual to seek out a postsecondary institution that has a sport management program that has been approved or at the least easily would comply by the Sport Management Program Review Council (SMPRC) based on the NASSM/NASPE Standards. Sometimes administrators do not want to budget the money or see the value in meeting voluntary standards. However, the NASSM/NASPE standards were originally developed by a combination of professors and sport industry professionals. Those standards have been evaluated and reevaluated. Some one who has studied in a rigorous nationally approved program with professors who are well-versed in specialty areas is ahead of a student who matriculated through a business, physical education, or science-based program. Many of these programs have chosen sport management as a program or department title because this title has proven to attract students. Potential sport management students need to do their homework and seek out the program that mixes business, marketing, law, sociology, finance, and the other required NASSM/NASPE standard areas with the application to a solid sport foundation. All of these areas must be experienced in a sport environment. Getting a degree just in business does not expose the students to the managerial or legal intricacies of sport. The sport management professional does sell a product that is often inferior and whose quality can fluctuate daily. Many in business do not understand that concept. On occasion, I have recommended that an individual with an undergraduate degree in sport management pursue an MBA degree. After doing their homework, some have told me that in discussions with business faculty, they would *not* be allowed to apply projects to the sport industry but rather to preselected businesses chosen by the professor. This is disconcerting when many believe that an MBA is superior to a master's degree in sport management. The transference of concepts to the sport industry is not easy. One *must* understand sport as a product!

To further expound on the previous topic, predicting the future of sport management education is difficult. More and more sport management programs probably will be housed and administered in the school or department of business. That will be good and bad. If the college of business faculty teaching are not in tune and do not understand sport as a product or its product extensions, that will be a detriment to the students in those programs. At the same time, I think colleges of business can offer a great deal to our students in terms of their in-depth background in marketing, finance, management, accounting, and computer information systems. I also think we are experiencing a change in the professorate in sport management. Historically, faculty members have been former physical education teachers who have broadened their scope of expertise. Now, we are seeing young professionals enter the field with a background in business, marketing, or finance coming to us with an earned master's or doctoral degree in sport management. Those are the people who will lead our profession into the future, the ones who have experience in both business and sport. The veteran faculty can draw from and share with them. That is probably one of the biggest trends in sport management education. If I were a dean or vice president hiring quality faculty for sport management—whether the program was housed in business or any other department—I would look for an individual with an experiential background in sport coupled with a strong education that had a *sport management* emphasis. I would only hire individuals with a doctoral degree and one of their degrees *must* be from an approved program or with a strong NASSM/NASPE-like curriculum. If looking for an individual in a specialty area such as sport economics or finance, I would seek an individual with at least one degree in one of those areas coupled with a strong sport management degree. A few years ago, that would have been difficult. However, it is becoming increasingly easier. If an administrator tries to fit square pegs into round holes and forces professors to teach in specialty areas such as these by just reading the textbook or attending a conference, the student will be short-changed. I believe that institutions will have to pay sport management professors the same salaries as those offered to business faculty because they would be teaching the same material. The industry of sport has surpassed many others as a multibillion-dollar industry. It just happens to be a fun and intriguing industry. Should we be paid less because we originated from the social sciences or education? We have the potential to lose many bright sport management professors to the sport industry because we are not paid a similar salary as our college of business colleagues. I often hear that the market for business professors demands that. I challenge college administrators to look at the salaries paid to sport business professionals with comparable or sometimes even fewer years of experience. Many will find that it will be enticing for some to jump into these higher paying positions particularly in sport marketing, college athletic administration, and private consulting. Some already have!

With regard to technology and the curriculum, I hope we never see total distance learning exclusively. Regardless of how many people believe that convenience should dictate the educational system of the future, nothing can replace the value of face-to-face interaction between a student and a professor. Yet, in addressing the question a little bit more in detail about essential skills in 10 years, I think the professor will need to be more open to distance learning. We may fight it but some aspect of technology and distance learning will probably become a part of all of the career positions in higher education. It is something that we cannot ignore. We will have to work with it and see where that takes us. It remains to be seen whether it is good or bad because the interpersonal relationships that are developed with students are important to the educational process. Online learning and convenience learning imply that everything must be done in such a hurry so the student can finish school and begin working. If we go the route of total distance learning at any point in time, we have lost what higher education is all about.

I had not been at Flagler long when I realized what makes it unique. We get about 35 percent of our student body from states other than Florida. We have a large international population and we have an intelligent student population with an average SAT score higher than 1100. It is a liberal arts college that probably is unique from a lot of sport management programs. We can mandate to an extent many of the classes our students take, but their general education is broad and flexible. The students can explore different courses and tend to get double majors or double minors more often than in larger schools with more rigid curricula. With our small athletic department we do not have as many opportunities for students to get college athletic experience in marketing, sports information, compliance, or facility management compared with students at a larger school. We have to go outside of the college and rely a lot on the professional sport teams in Jacksonville and Daytona Beach. We are in a unique environment in that we have several professional teams, the World Golf Village, the ATP, LPGA, and PGA Tour offices close to us that provide exciting and valuable experiential opportunities. As a smaller school, we depend a little bit more on the community to provide the student with the experiences that might be found on campus at a larger school.

At Western Carolina, we had an NCAA Division I athletic department with a lot of inside opportunities for students to gain experience through internships. However, we were in a small town and students could not work for professional teams or other organizations during their academic careers because locally none existed.

In closing, I have been asked to provide an assessment of sport management education. I have previously discussed distance learning and NASSM/NASPE standards. However, I would like to expound on the future of those standards. A mixed feeling exists among my colleagues as to the importance of those standards. Standards are a benchmark for professionalism and excellence that are often only voluntary. Many of my colleagues would not disagree that a benchmark for excellence is essential to prepare future sport managers. However, some may disagree with my opinion that we *must*—as a group of professionals—stand by these standards and promote them at every opportunity. Some believe that the professionals in the sport industry will *never* accept our standards. My position is one based on the history of educational standards. Many organizations have traditionally fought the importance of standards and whether or not they should have been written. Some of the time-honored required standards in education today had trouble getting recognized in their early formats at the beginning of the 20th century and in the early decades of the 1900s. Standards are necessary and important in *any* profession so individuals will not just do what they please without regard to what is right, just, correct, and important. The NASSM/NASPE standards are important and necessary in determining what should be taught and learned. They state that students have been exposed to various aspects of law, marketing, economics, finance, and accounting with a sport emphasis and not a combination of teaching methodology courses, an anatomy and physiology class, with one or two business classes added so they can "legitimately" call themselves "management." Sport management academicians must embrace and support these standards in their own academic institutions, but just as importantly with our industry colleagues. A time should come when general managers and college athletic administrators first seek out individuals who have matriculated through a nationally approved sport management program because of the established and time-proven standards as *the standards* by which all sport management majors and future industry professionals are judged. No, it will not happen overnight and not in a few years. Just as our sister professions in sociology, business, accounting, and law must deal with standards and the acceptance over time, so too will our professional standards endure the test of time if we band together and *believe* that what we pursue and envision in its infancy will be historically recognized as a process worth that pursuit. For those of my colleagues that have been in this profession for more than 10 years, most would surely recognize that even a few years ago, few career announcements mentioned a sport management degree as an accepted area of study. Today, many do. We are moving in the right direction. Do not give up the dream!

Dennis R. Howard

Professor of Sport Marketing, Academic Coordinator

University of Oregon

Education:
B.S., RECREATION AND PARK ADMINISTRATION, UNIVERSITY OF OREGON, 1966

M.S., RECREATION AND PARK ADMINISTRATION, UNIVERSITY OF ILLINOIS, 1968

PH.D., EDUCATION, OREGON STATE UNIVERSITY, 1975

Career Progression:
PROFESSOR OF SPORT MARKETING AND ACADEMIC COORDINATOR, UNIVERSITY OF OREGON, JAMES H. WARSAW SPORTS MARKETING CENTER, LUNDQUIST COLLEGE OF BUSINESS, 1997 TO PRESENT

PROFESSOR AND COORDINATOR - GRADUATE PROGRAM IN SPORT MANAGEMENT, OHIO STATE UNIVERSITY, 1992 TO 1997

ASSOCIATE PROFESSOR, DEPARTMENT OF RECREATION, PARKS, AND TOURISM MANAGEMENT, UNIVERSITY OF OREGON, 1982 TO 1991

Best advice for someone aspiring toward a career in the sport industry:

**"Accumulate as much sport-related experience as possible.
Certainly a specialty degree (in sport and/or business) is important
but this is a boot strap industry—individuals with the most varied
(from retail to event management) real world experience
have a tremendous advantage."**

Quote by which you live:

"The harder you work, the luckier you get."

THE FONDEST MEMORY I HAVE IS GOING TO KEZAR STADIUM in San Francisco with my dad to watch the 49ers play. That was my first real exposure to a live sporting event of any magnitude and it was totally captivating. My dad would always sit in general admission and we would be squeezed in tight, and I would come home smelling of beer with Popsicle sticks stuck to me and a new vocabulary, but it was great fun. I was 11-years-old when Willie Mays and the baseball Giants came to the Bay area, and at that impressionable age the star athletes became bigger than life to me. Then the University of California at Berkeley won the NCAA championship in basketball when I was 13, so sports was a prominent part of the landscape in my area during my childhood.

It is interesting that the literature suggests that fathers are the primary socializing agents for young boys in terms of their involvement in sports, but with me it was my mom. The happy circumstance of her overseeing the community park and recreation department for the city that I grew up in allowed me to become involved at an early age. By age 14, she had a broom in my hands and I was sweeping tennis courts, maintaining ballfields, and eventually, I became a playground director and Little League coach. At a pretty early age, not only was I actively participating, but I was also involved in the "nuts and bolts" of delivering sport and recreation services. In effect, it was as if a career path had chosen me.

My mom was anxious for me to pursue a career in parks and recreation, which I was happy to embrace at that time. I loved everything I did and that I could make a living at it was amazing. When it came time to get serious about what I was going to do, I decided to go to the University of Oregon. At the time the best recreation and parks program in the west was in Eugene at the University of Oregon. The university also had a pretty fair baseball program so it was a chance for me to move forward on my chosen career path and to also stay involved in sports. Fortunately, I was a lot better in school than I was at hitting a curve ball. I realized early that any aspirations I may have had to play baseball were not going to happen. At that point, I became serious about school and did fairly well.

When I graduated, I decided to follow my older brother Mike's footsteps and attend the University of Illinois for a master's degree in parks and recreation. The time I spent at Illinois was a real eye-opener. I was surrounded by a bunch of people who were bright, talented, and highly motivated. It was a real motivator for me because it became apparent for the first time that I would have to work hard if I wanted to amount to anything in my chosen career.

When I completed my master's degree, I returned to California to work for the City of Oakland Parks and Recreation Department as a community center director. My first center was in West Oakland followed by a transfer the next year to a larger center in the north section of the city, the part of Oakland that borders Berkeley. There was not anything that Oregon or Illinois could have done educationally to prepare me for the events that happened during the late 1960s in that area. During that period, Oakland was one of the country's centers of civil unrest and racial tension. The Black Panthers headquarters was located in my center's neighborhood, and riots were a routine activity right next door on the University of California campus. It was an amazing time, and I was exposed to a reality that I never knew existed. People came into my community center that faced many adversities, including unemployment, poor housing, and unrelenting crime. The one thing that seemed to be a lifeline to that community was its involvement in sport and recreation. It was such a positive diversion. When people came into our facility, most often the burdens they had would disappear. Along with the church, our community center was the only other beacon of positive light that existed in those neighborhoods.

It was an incredible life for 3 years. The most important realization I gleaned from that experience was the necessity of integrating our center's offerings with other community service outlets, particularly the churches in our neighborhood. Rather than depending on people coming on their own to participate in the programs offered at the center, it was necessary to be proactive by taking relevant services to the people through jointly sponsored programs delivered at churches, schools, and even nursing homes—the places where community people traditionally congregated. These institutions were and still are the key connecting points in many African American and Hispanic communities.

Almost my entire staff were minorities from the local community. I had authority by position, but in reality, I was largely dependent on those folks to show me the ropes and teach me as much as they could about the local culture that I was serving. I learned out of necessity how to appropriately delegate authority. It was mostly on the job learning. I learned a lot about myself and about the need to become a better listener and observer.

After 3 years in Oakland, I was offered the opportunity to supervise a community recreation program in Mountain View, California. Going from the inner city to what is now the heart of Silicon Valley was a huge leap. I went from a situation where people had little and public resources were strained to an area of abundance. I was there for just a year and on a career path that I thought would eventually lead me to become the director of a large city parks and recreation department somewhere in the United States. Ultimately, I thought I would like to be a city manager of a large city.

Then one day—literally out of the blue—a professor at nearby San Jose State University asked me to speak about community recreation to his undergraduate class. I spent an hour talking with the class and enjoyed myself. I do not think I was sharing much in the way of profound insights, but after I finished, the professor took me out for coffee and said that it looked like I was having a good time talking with his students. He asked if I had ever thought about teaching in a collegiate setting. I answered that I had not considered it. I did tell him, however, that in the back of my mind was this notion that some day I would return to Oregon and work on a doctoral degree. Amazingly, I received a call from the head of the recreation and physical education department at Oregon State University 2 weeks later saying that he had talked to the professor at San Jose State and heard that I may be interested in returning to Oregon to pursue my doctorate. As it turned out, 2 months before the start of the academic year, he had lost one of his faculty and was trying desperately to get a replacement. He must have been desperate because within 6 weeks of talking to that class at San Jose State, I was enrolled as a brand-new doctoral student at Oregon State and serving as an instructor within the physical education and recreation department. It was one of those crossroads decisions. In retrospect, it is probably fortunate that I did not have much time to make the decision. I had a young family, a great job, a new home, and a career path that I was satisfied with, and no intention to move. But a voice in the back of my mind said, "Hey, these opportunities don't come along very often, so jump on it!"

I spent the next 3 years focusing on my Ph.D. I completed most of my work in business and child psychology. I also had the opportunity to teach several classes so that by the time I finished my degree, I was ready to pursue a career in higher education. My first job was as an assistant professor in parks and recreation at Western Illinois University. That first year at Western Illinois was a great confidence builder. I spent the next 3 years at Texas A & M University in the department of recreation and park administration. I even had an appointment in their Agricultural Experiment Station. It was pretty heady stuff for a city boy! I was fortunate because a number of senior faculty at A & M took a personal interest in mentoring me, especially in the areas of research and scholarship. It was there that I began to understand the level of dedication and discipline necessary for someone to succeed in higher education—a full day of teaching and working with students, followed by nights and weekends conducting research and writing those papers and books essential to achieving tenure and eventually promotion to full professor. As my wife and I often say, "So much for that relaxing academic lifestyle!" You better like what you do because you will do it a lot! Also, you need a thick hide because more often than not, that paper you submitted to a key journal—the one you thought reflected your best work—will be invariably rejected for publication. Six months of work goes down the drain. Success in this business requires a surprising amount of tenacity.

My experience at A & M was a blessing in many ways. I met John Crompton who became my highly valued friend and longstanding professional colleague. We have collaborated on two books and numerous papers and articles. John was a doctoral student when I was a new faculty member at Texas A & M. He was a teaching assistant who brought a tremendous amount of management expertise from Great Britain where he had co-directed the largest recreation and sports consulting business in the United Kingdom. John's company had built state-of-the-art leisure centers and sport venues throughout Europe. Tapping his expertise was beneficial for me. We have been not only productive professional colleagues for 25 years, but also close friends.

In 1977, the University of Oregon offered me the opportunity to return to my alma mater. It was a compelling offer. My wife, Lin, and I had met as undergraduates at the University of Oregon and the campus and Eugene were special to us. I taught at the University of Oregon for the next 5 years before receiving another one of those phone calls from out of the blue, this time from Penn State University. They made such an attractive offer that my wife and I decided that along with our two children, we would head to Pennsylvania. The experience at Penn State was wonderful but brief. After little more than a year, we chose to return to

Oregon to raise our children and be closer to our families in California and Hawaii. Fortunately, the University of Oregon took me back.

In the early 1980s parks and recreation education went through a series of significant shifts. When I started in the mid 1960s, the field focused strictly on government or public parks and recreation services. That is where the jobs existed and where almost all of the instructional emphasis was placed. Over the next 10 years, however, the orientation of park and recreation curricula moved from public recreation to a greater emphasis on commercial and private recreation and then eventually to travel and tourism. I gravitated toward each of these emerging orientations and became involved in the privately funded or business side of recreation, which was then called commercial recreation. At that time, although the operation of sport services, venues, and so forth were a major part of what I taught, sport was considered to be just one part of the larger range of leisure or discretionary activities available to people. The content of my classes included financing, managing, and marketing aspects related to performing arts centers and theme parks as well as stadiums and arenas.

I did not become involved solely in sport until I went to Ohio State University in 1992. In 1991 the higher education system in Oregon underwent a traumatic period. The voters adopted a proposition called Measure 5 that reduced tax support for higher education by 40 percent. Out of what seemed a necessity at the time, central administration at the University of Oregon started looking for colleges and program areas to eliminate. Unfortunately, the unit I belonged to—the College of Human Development and Performance (historically, the HPER unit in that College was considered to be a Top Five program in the United States)—was eliminated in one massive budget cut. As this distressing news broke, I was contacted by the dean of the college of business on our campus and invited to join its marketing faculty. Over the years, I established a working relationship with a number of folks in the marketing department. Actually, for the past 15 years, I enrolled in a broad range of marketing and finance courses at Texas A & M, Penn State, and Oregon. I usually took one new class per semester. I thought it was the only way I could bring current business content into the classes that I taught. A lot of my professional writing during that period focused on integrating contemporary marketing and finance practices into the operation of public and private sport and recreation organizations. The prospect of moving to the college of business was attractive to me. However, at the same time, Ohio State had made me an offer I could not refuse, and I was discouraged with the direction that higher education was taking in Oregon.

In 1992 the graduate sport management program at Ohio State was in a bit of a funk. The program, which had begun in 1978 and had a great tradition, had been in a downward spiral since 1989. Several key faculty had left in the late 1980s, and the sport management program had floundered. Remarkably, Ohio State made a commitment to hire three new faculty, all in the same year, in an effort to reinvigorate sport management. During the recruiting process, I became part of a group interview, with the two other folks that would soon become my colleagues. They wanted to see if we could work together and get along with each other. It was a brilliant strategy because we were energized about bringing this exciting program back to its feet. I assumed the role of coordinator of the program. My background in private and commercial recreation, with a strong orientation in business, was a good fit. They hoped that I would develop closer ties with the college of business. I was not completely sure of what I was getting into, but my decision to take the job was the best professional decision I ever made. Being at a place like Ohio State, with such a tradition in sport and so many resources, allowed us to jump-start the program and immediately offer great opportunities to students. We accomplished wonderful things, and Ohio State continues to build and develop the program. It was the first time that I could commit exclusively to the sport industry, which has become my focus ever since.

Before coming to Ohio State, I knew a fair amount about intercollegiate athletics, but had a limited understanding of professional sports, particularly those aspects related to marketing and financing team operations. In the first 2 years at Ohio State I began an intensive effort to learn as much about the operation of professional sport franchises and the factors that influence their growth and development. I am still learning! I have enjoyed every aspect of this exploration process. Being at Ohio State facilitated my entrée into league offices and the opportunity to talk with general managers and marketing directors. Twelve professional sport organizations are within a 75-mile radius of Columbus so lots of opportunities exist to learn first-hand about how these organizations operated.

My goal at Ohio State was to revitalize the graduate sports marketing program. A key element of achieving that aim was to reconnect the program with its extensive alumni network. When I arrived, we had about 350 alumni, many of which were in key positions within the sport industry. For many years, no real effort had been made to connect with this valuable resource. With the help of faculty and students, we developed an alumni directory, a quarterly newsletter, and a series of events that would reconnect our alumni with what we were trying to accomplish. That became our essential network for opening the doors for fund raising and, more importantly, for creating employment opportunities and internships for our students. I spent six wonderful years at Ohio State. During that period we accomplished a tremendous amount with the help of a talented and committed faculty. From 1992 to 1997 nearly 90 percent of our master graduates found full-time employment in the sport industry. Many have established themselves as top executives in their respective sports organizations. At the same time, Ph.D. graduates from the Ohio State program seeded sport management curricula throughout North

America. They will be key players in establishing the academic integrity of sport management programs in higher education.

Ironically, shortly after I departed from the University of Oregon, one of the university's most illustrious alumni, James H. Warsaw, pledged a significant gift to the college of business to start a sports marketing program in his name. From a modest beginning in 1994, the Warsaw Sports Marketing Center quickly grew into a formidable program. Because at that time, it was the only MBA degree that offered a specialization in sports business in the west, and the demand for the program quickly outstripped the original faculty. In early 1997 the folks at the Warsaw Center called and asked if I would return and help further develop the sports business curriculum. The lure to return west once again, to this unique and exciting program at my alma mater, was irresistible. So, in July 1997, my wife and I returned to the University of Oregon. I am now officially a professor of sports marketing, and I may be the only one in the world!

Many challenges face academics in the world of sport business. The biggest challenge is keeping abreast of what is a rapidly changing industry. I spend the first hour of every day reading the *Sports Business Journal* and/or *The Sports Business Daily*. After reading these industry standards carefully, typically I will follow up with phone calls or get on the Internet to research the original source of information on the news topic. It allows me to bring into the classroom the latest information and integrate new ideas into my written work.

One aspect of this industry that has intrigued me is the current status and future prospects of professional sport in North America. The red-hot economy in the last half of the 1990s provided impetus for tremendous growth. Since 1997, 207 new sport franchises at major/minor league levels have been established. By 2002, if all the proposals for new leagues and start-up teams come to fruition, more than 620 professional teams will exist in the United States. On the one hand, more opportunities will exist for sport management graduates. On the other hand, team operators will face tremendous competition not only from other sports entities, but also from a society already glutted with thousands of other entertainment options. At some point, a serious shakeout will occur, particularly when the economy slows down. Steering through these rough waters will be a serious challenge for the graduates of sport management and sport marketing programs.

The economics of contemporary sport are spiraling out of control. The average cost of a major league stadium in 1988 was about $90 to $105 million, depending on how many amenities were added including luxury suites and club seats. By 1999 the average had risen to $250 million. The public sector used to provide the largest share of the construction capital, but now taxpayers are increasingly reluctant to pay the tab. In the past 2 years, voters defeated eight of the 12 publicly funded stadium or arena propositions. Teams have had to pay an increasing share—if not all—of the construction costs (on average, $101 million in 1999). Teams and owners often have significant debt on the facilities they operate. Instead of realizing millions of dollars in new revenue from these new facilities, many teams pay anywhere from $20 to $40 million per year just to pay off their debt obligations. In the end, they are left with a brand-new facility that provides no clear economic advantage. Teams pass the burden onto their fans by charging incredibly high ticket prices. In many venues, with ticket prices approaching $50, the average household has been priced out. It is no wonder that the average NBA and NHL teams sell more than half their ticket inventory to corporate clients, which means that the traditional bedrock fans can no longer afford to attend on a regular basis. The next generation of sport managers will be forced to confront this serious pricing challenge.

One other aspect regarding the economics of sport that I spend more time discussing in class is the notion of using "OPM" (Other People's Money). A lot of the traditional financing sources we have relied on for generations, particularly public tax sources, are drying up. It will be necessary for managers in this field to become more creative. It is imperative that our next generation of sport managers understand how to engineer joint venture agreements or public-private partnerships, as well as how to structure IPOs (initial public offerings). In addition, graduates entering this industry must be media-technology savvy. They will have to understand the "new media," the emerging convergence of television with the Internet. The interactive potential of this emerging technology in which sports will be delivered in real-time video through Web sites will revolutionize the distribution of sport. Understanding and taking advantage of this new wave of technology will be a critical competence.

Things move so fast in this field that you will always be running to catch up. That is what makes the sports industry interesting. I have enjoyed every moment of my involvement with the industry. Who would have thought when I was sitting in old Kezar Stadium as a 9-year-old that I would spend most of my adult life involved with something I cared about. I am extraordinarily lucky. I have enjoyed my career in recreation and sport management and continue to be delighted and challenged by it every day.

CHAPTER 15

Sport Marketing

SPORT MARKETING IS THE FASTEST GROWING SEGMENT of the sport industry. Mullin, Hardy, and Sutton (1993) defined sport marketing as all activities designed to meet the needs and wants of sports consumers through an exchange process. That process could entail the exchange of the consumer's money for the experience of watching a New York Yankees baseball game or running in the Boston Marathon. Sport marketing also takes on another dimension, encompassing nonsport-related companies using sport to promote its products. This may entail American Airlines paying $6.5 million per year for the naming rights on a new arena or Quaker Oats paying Michael Jordan $5 million per year to endorse Gatorade. In the case of Quaker Oats, the decision paid off as its profits doubled since signing Jordan as an endorser in 1990 (Johnson, 1998).

A person interested in a career in sport marketing can work for the marketing department of a professional major or minor league team, a college athletic department, or a professional golf or tennis event. In these environments the sport marketer tries to sell season or game tickets, luxury boxes, and sponsorship deals. They also would be involved with organizing promotions to attract and entertain fans, as well as developing advertising campaigns. If someone were involved with sport marketing for an organization geared toward participants, the marketing efforts would be directed at increasing memberships or the number of participants through price promotions, public relation events, or enhancing the place or site of the business. A common entry-level position with a professional sport organization is as an account executive in ticket sales. A person can earn up to $30,000 per year with base and meeting sales incentives. The salary range for marketing and ticket director positions can be anywhere from $40,000 to $75,000 with base salaries and incentives. Top-level positions such as vice presidents for marketing can earn anywhere from $80,000 to more than $200,000 per year.

If someone wanted to market sport products, the marketing efforts would be geared toward increasing brand awareness or enhancing product image to increase sales. This could entail signing a professional basketball player to endorse an athletic shoe or it may involve a sporting goods store offering a free pair of running shoes to people who buy six pairs in a year. Another career option is to work for a sport marketing firm that organizes events. One could also work with a company that uses sport to market its product. For example, a bank that sponsors a golf tournament needs someone to ensure the bank achieves brand awareness and uses hospitality opportunities to the fullest. The bank has the choice of acquiring the services of a sport marketing firm, or it can develop an in-house events and sponsorship department to handle the responsibilities of the golf tournament and other properties with which it is involved. Individuals interested in working on the client side of the sport marketing, whether it be for the company itself or a sport marketing firm, can anticipate making in the low to mid $20,000s in entry-level positions. Director positions can pay anywhere from the low $30,000s to as high as $50,000. Top-level executives can earn from $70,000 to more than $100,000 per year depending on the size of the company or the sport marketing agency.

Marketing is an important part of any sport organization and these organizations look for creative and motivated individuals. Career opportunities in sport marketing will increase on the property side as sport marketers look for new and innovative means to attract customers and on the client side as more companies realize the benefits of using sport to better market their products.

REFERENCES

Johnson, R. (1998, June 22). The Jordan effect. *Fortune*, 137(12): 125–138.

Mullin, B.J., Hardy S., & Sutton, W. (1993). *Sport marketing.* Champaign, IL: Human Kinetics.

Jeffrey S. Price

Vice President of Sponsorship and Events

MasterCard International

Education:

B.A., AMERICAN HISTORY, BATES COLLEGE, 1987

M.S., SPORT MANAGEMENT, UNIVERSITY OF MASSACHUSETTS AT AMHERST, 1989

Career Progression:

VICE PRESIDENT OF SPONSORSHIP AND EVENTS, MASTERCARD INTERNATIONAL, 1997 TO PRESENT

VICE PRESIDENT OF MARKETING, BIG 12 CONFERENCE, 1996 TO 1997

SPORTS MARKETING MANAGER, GATORADE, 1994 TO 1996

COMMUNITY RELATIONS MANAGER, NBA PROPERTIES, 1993 TO 1994

TEAMS SERVICES ASSISTANT, NBA PROPERTIES, 1991 TO 1992

PUBLIC RELATIONS INTERN, NATIONAL BASKETBALL ASSOCIATION, 1989

SALES MANAGER, NEW HAMPSHIRE WHITE CAPS USBL BASKETBALL TEAM, 1987

Best piece of advice you received in regards to your career:

**"This is a very small industry.
Your network is only as solid as your performance."**

GLENN WONG

Best advice for someone aspiring toward a career in the sport industry:

"Check your ego at the door when you get started in this industry."

Quote by which you live:

"Treat others as you would want to be treated."

MY MOTHER

HAVING A CAREER IN SPORTS WAS ON MY MIND when I majored in history at Bates College in Lewiston, Maine. Two things that led me to Bates College were its liberal arts education and the opportunity to play football at the NCAA Division III level. I did not have the talent to play at an Ivy League school or a Division I school, so Bates offered the opportunity to combine a strong academic background with the opportunity to play college football. I majored in history partly out of an interest in the subject, and I discovered through my studies that the liberal arts environment presented many writing and critical thinking opportunities. From that background, I developed a broad base of skills that would be beneficial in any career I chose. As I was nearing graduation in May 1987, I went through the interview process with the major companies and banks that came on campus to recruit, but I ultimately wanted to pursue a career in sport before I followed a more traditional path. My interest in sport was motivated by my desire to link a business career with my passion—sport. The prospect of marketing NBA basketball seemed a lot more exciting than marketing soap and energized my long-term vision of where my career could go. As I have grown professionally, I have seen that many similarities exist between marketing soap and the NBA, but for me there is still an emotional connection to the world of sport that cannot be found elsewhere.

Upon graduation from Bates in 1987, I contacted each of the new NBA franchises at the time: the Orlando Magic, Miami Heat, Charlotte Hornets, and Minnesota Timberwolves. I also contacted other NBA franchises, Major League Baseball franchises, and college athletic departments. My efforts were not successful because I did not have any experience or an established network. I still have all the rejection letters from the various organizations saying no positions were available. I actually began my career in sport as an advertising sales representative for a U.S. Basketball League franchise in Concord, New Hampshire, in the autumn of 1987. It was not the NBA but it was a start. During that time, I began researching graduate programs in sport management and applying to schools.

I selected the University of Massachusetts at Amherst's sport management program and started that program in the fall of 1988. At that time Ohio University and Massachusetts were the best two graduate sport management programs. I had applied to both, but Massachusetts offered me a research assistantship and an opportunity to work in the athletic department. While at Massachusetts, I was introduced to sport marketing and management in the classroom, gained practical experience, and initiated my professional network. I was a research assistant for Professor Glenn Wong and worked with him on the 2nd edition of a text he co-authored with Robert Berry titled *Law and Business of the Sport Industries: Common Issues in Amateur and Professional Sport.* I worked on chapters on labor relations and Title IX so I had a chance to delve deeply into both subject matters. I also worked in the athletic department as a sports information assistant with the men's and women's basketball, football, and men's lacrosse programs. My network was initiated because I was exposed to a number of different professionals who came on campus and the extensive network of Massachusetts' sport management alumni in the field.

During my first semester, the NBA came on campus to recruit for postgraduate and internship opportunities. From that visit, I secured an intern position in the NBA's public relations department. Looking back on my educational experiences, the combination of the Bates liberal arts experience as a foundation for my ability to effectively communicate both verbally and in writing and the educational/practical experience at Massachusetts has proved critical in my development and maturation in the sport business.

The first 2 to 3 years that I worked at the NBA were a financial struggle. I received tremendous experience working in the organization, but I did not know if I could afford to continue in the career. I made minimum wage on an hourly basis while living in New York City. My parents were both teachers and they could not necessarily support the dream I had to live in New York and pursue my career aspirations. I ate a lot of macaroni and cheese and hot dogs. It was discouraging at times because I did not know the direction of my career. This industry loses many talented individuals because there are so many people that the point of entry is difficult. Making it through the first 3 to 4 years can be an uphill battle just to survive financially.

I started with the NBA as a public relations intern in the fall of 1989 and moved from that position into a full-time role in the team services division in January 1990. In the team services division, I was responsible for sponsor asset management. I coordinated the relationship between the league sponsors and the individual teams and league events. For example, through its deal with the NBA, IBM sponsored coaches' clinics in each NBA market. It would be my responsibility to set up the coaches' clinics and work with each team's basketball staff to run the clinic. I also managed all of the sponsor assets surrounding the NBA All-Star Weekend. This included being involved with all of the events on All-Star Saturday and during the game itself.

I was in the team services division for one year before transferring to become the community relations director for the league. In that position I managed the *Stay in School* program. I worked with NBA great Bob Lanier to build the program and did everything from working with the program sponsors (IBM, Nestle, and Coca-Cola) in developing sponsor program extensions to conducting the school visits in each city that hosted an all-star game. Over the course of 3 years, Bob and I visited more than 250 schools and did presentations about life skills and the importance of education. Each year our efforts would culminate in the All-Star weekend program. NBC, TNT, and Nickelodeon would broadcast a *Stay in School* special that was part of the NBA All-Star Weekend. Along with the *Stay in School* program I coordinated the league's community relations efforts on a team level. I linked all of the NBA's national public service initiatives to the individual teams.

The final year and a half of my tenure with the NBA was as an events sponsorship sales director for NBA *Jam Session*. *Jam Session* is the interactive fan event during All-Star Weekend. In that position I was responsible for all sponsorship sales, sponsor program development, and coordination of the actual event. At that point the on-site interactive events were just beginning to grow into a major business, so I was at the beginning of the development of the NBA's program. Selling sponsorship for *Jam Session* was difficult because the league sponsors already had category exclusivity so we had to try to sell them incremental packages with *Jam Session*. I coordinated *Jam Session* at the All-Star Weekend in Salt Lake City in 1993 and in Minneapolis in 1994.

I left the NBA in 1994 to accept a position as sport marketing manager with Gatorade, a division of Quaker Oats. I worked with Greg Bradshaw there and also when he was with the Chicago Bulls. Greg and I moved up together in the industry. He was on the team side and I was on the league side. Greg moved over to Gatorade as a sport marketing manager and recommended me to his superiors as a potential candidate for a similar position. After accepting the job, Greg and I essentially split the country in half. I handled the west and he handled the east. In my position I negotiated and managed all of the team, college, conference, and grassroots sponsorship deals in the west. Our job was to reinforce Gatorade's authentic, hot and sweaty athletic performance brand equity by ensuring that Gatorade cups, coolers, towels, and products were on the sidelines at all sponsored events. We were also involved in creating promotional programs for the retail channels. The only area I was not directly responsible for was league-wide deals.

I experienced a difference going from the NBA to the sponsor or client side, but my background with the NBA exposed me to a number of different sponsors, and I understood how properties and teams worked. I translated that into an understanding of how a company like Gatorade was trying to leverage sports as a core part of its business. During my 2–1/2 years with Gatorade, I probably negotiated 150 different contracts related to our presence on the sidelines and our promotional rights. A major difference from the NBA was that Quaker Oats is a for-profit company with quarterly reports to Wall Street. The company focused on shareholder value and had specific reasons for being involved in various sports. Gatorade is a great company and it is focused on leveraging sports as a part of the essence of that brand.

When I was with Gatorade, I had some interaction with Michael Jordan because of his endorsement relationship with the company. Seeing what he did for Gatorade, I would agree with the statement that Jordan—in the business sense—was the greatest athlete of the 20th century. Jordan broke through all the clutter in the sports marketplace. His competitive drive, on-court demeanor, what he represented off the court, and the way he developed his partnerships in working with various companies such as Gatorade made the man bigger than life. He was the consummate pitch-man for Gatorade. Who better personified the competitive, hot thirsty performer than Michael Jordan? The ultimate was the day he competed against Utah in the 1998 NBA Finals when he made 37 points—sicker than a dog—and was drinking Gatorade just to function. If there was ever a moment epitomizing the functional value and authenticity of the Gatorade brand, that was it. Throughout his career, consumers perceived Jordan as being credible. He worked with products and, for the most part, you could see a direct connection between Jordan and the product. He allowed himself to have a personality whether it was Jordan with Bugs Bunny or Jordan with Larry Bird in the McDonald's commercials. All of the things he did represented his personality and enabled him to transcend basketball to be a cultural phenomenon that we may never see again. He was a professional and smart businessman and he epitomized everything about the Gatorade brand.

When you look at the sport marketing landscape, it includes companies such as Gatorade, which is a product that is a part of the game, and companies such as MasterCard, a payment services company with no real inherent association or functional association to sport. For companies such as MasterCard, sports represent an opportunity to match consumers with an affinity. The baseball enthusiast has an affinity to baseball and that will outpace other interests. Whether on the local, regional, or national level, baseball represents an interest that brings consumers together. For a potential sponsor, it creates a significant critical mass in terms of household ratings from a television perspective or on-site in the stadium. The on-site consumer will be more receptive to understanding a sponsor's messages if the sponsor is perceived to be in support of his or her team.

The basic platform of sport marketing is that a sponsor reaches a critical mass of consumers and touches them around something about which they care. Sports are an escape for the everyday person. When we look at the realities of consumers in the 21st century, they are looking for an escape. They are also looking for shared family time. MasterCard's brand positioning is "the best way to pay for everything that matters." What we have tried to do is align our involvement in sport to reinforce that position. MasterCard becomes the best way to pay for numerous things, whether it be discounts or family packages offered to fans, and also hits on the "everything that matters" platform through the emotional connection of a fan's love for the game. This is best demonstrated in the MasterCard commercial where the father takes his son to his first baseball game. Sports become a conduit to reach consumers in a way that is different than trying to reach them at other parts of their life.

I left Gatorade for my current position at MasterCard International as the vice president of sponsorship and events in 1997. Although both Gatorade and MasterCard used sport to market its product, differences existed. Gatorade could secure a tangible value when negotiating a contract. Gatorade could put cups, coolers, squeeze bottles, and towels on the sideline. Gatorade's exposure on the sideline, with an athlete drinking their product when hot and sweaty, reinforces the brand attributes and the brand image. You could equate the value of the Gatorade product being on an NFL sideline to Gatorade having a 2-minute commercial in every NFL game. The essence of creating value from the sponsorships could be built based on the dynamics of what could be delivered from the sideline. For a company such as MasterCard, the value really derives from what can we do to leverage the relationship with the sport that will reinforce the brand positioning. We have to work exponentially harder than a brand that is endemic to sport to help make the relevant connection to consumers.

It is my belief that if a company not directly related to sport is going to make a significant investment in sport sponsorship, it needs some expertise within the organization. If it is not going to commit to hiring a full staff like MasterCard, then it better secure the services of a strong integrated sport marketing agency. With the structures that are created by sport marketing firms such as Octagon and IMG where it has advertising agencies aligned with sport marketing and public relations agencies, a company may be able to leverage the property through an agency-development support mechanism. Ultimately, however, if a company is going to make a significant investment in sport sponsorship on the client side, somebody will have to make the final call on potential sponsorship opportunities, objectives, and strategies. Because of a lack of expertise, many companies enter property negotiations before determining its expectations and objectives for being a sponsor. If this is the case, the sponsorship is doomed to fail. How is the company going to measure the value of that relationship if it does not know what it wants from the relationship? If the company has not thought about how it is going to measure success before negotiating the contract, the properties will not understand what the company wants and will not know what to offer, and the company will not know how to gauge whether the dollars spent were successful at delivering measurable results.

In my position at MasterCard, I lead our integration efforts with our key properties, which are Major League Baseball and professional golf. Those integration efforts entail taking our brand positioning and ensuring that we integrate it across our properties by leveraging it in the "Priceless" advertising campaign, tying it to promotional programs, linking it to our Internet involvement, and tying it back to our members and merchants. The integration component is probably my biggest responsibility. I also oversee the execution of MasterCard's events. We do significant on-site consumer, member, and merchant hospitality activities associated with the All-Star Game and World Series in baseball; the MasterCard Colonial tournament, the British Open, the U.S. Open and the PGA Championship in golf; and the NHL All-Star Game in hockey to name a few. I negotiate our agreements with properties. Recently, I spent a lot of time thinking strategically about what sponsorship means to this organization and how does its definition reflect the nature of the agreements with our properties. The sport sponsorship and event group at MasterCard is part of a key marketing mix group. Currently, the "Priceless" advertising campaign is the engine of the brand positioning that fuels everything within the organization. Sponsorship, promotion, acceptance, and our various product development avenues are all seen as key ingredients in the overall marketing mix.

The most demanding aspect of what I do is the strategic thinking to determine how we can convey our message in a cluttered sport marketplace. How do we—as a payment services company—best develop relationships with properties such as Major League Baseball and professional golf that are going to lead to a return on our investment while reinforcing our brand position? We try to build preference and usage with consumers through leverageable programs such as the Major League Baseball All-Century Team in 1999. Negotiating in a cluttered sports marketplace makes it difficult to get a return on a dollar. When I started with the NBA, we had about eight sponsors and it was easy to help them determine the value of associating with the NBA. Now a property will potentially have 30 different sponsors at various levels and it becomes more difficult for sponsors to measure the effectiveness of their relationship with the properties. In recent years, .com companies, with a lot of IPO money to spend, have also entered the marketplace making it even more complicated and price inflated.

The great part of our integration efforts around the All-Century Team Promotional program in 1999 was that we received great consumer feedback and we obtained great research results. We had four different tracking studies including a marketing mix analysis that measured each dollar spent in marketing and what was the return for MasterCard was in gross dollar volume. The marketing mix analysis showed great return for the amount of marketing dollars spent on the project. We also tracked our advertising awareness and some key attitudinal research data, and both indicated a very successful promotion. The All-Century Team spot with Hank Aaron and Willie Mays performed as well as, if not better than, any of the other spots we have done. We also saw great upticks in usage especially in K-Mart, our retail merchant partner. We reached our critical mass and have a truly priceless program around the World Series and the All-Century Team. The integrated platform that was built has also returned value and dividends to the brand. It has become the standard by which we measure everything including a marketing integration perspective. Although this is the most taxing aspect of what I do, it is also the most enjoyable. If you can come up with something like the All-Century Team that can break through the clutter, or if you revise a relationship with a property so it has real value, you feel a sense of satisfaction. What I enjoy the most is when the strategic thinking ultimately plays out in execution.

Although I have gone from the property side with the NBA to the client side with Gatorade and MasterCard, in some ways my role has not changed. When I was on the property side, I sold the client on the benefits of being associated with the property. I am now on the client side and I still try to sell. The difference is what we sell. On the client side we try to sell the value of working with a company such as MasterCard. We bring the power of partnership, the strength of our campaign and the brand integration. We are probably in the top 10 percent of companies working with properties. Our philosophy is that we do not sit back and wait for a proposal from a property. We build partnerships that are beneficial for both sides. We do as much work as the property in preparing a strategic framework and a presentation of what we can do for the property. It is interesting because some of my skills selling on the property side have come full circle. Now we try to sell back to the property the value of working with MasterCard.

We have taken this approach to become a better long-term business partner with our properties. What we say to someone like Major League Baseball is "Here's how we're going to help you build your brand through our national 'Priceless' advertising campaign. Here's what we're going to do to build your brand through promotional programs like the All-Century team. Here's what we're going to do to extend our activity on-line to support your brand positioning. Here's what we're going to do with our members. Here's what we're going to do with our merchants." We make a case that all of that is worth exponentially more than just the dollars we will pay with our sponsorship fee.

Another difference of working on the client side of sport marketing is that it leads to a more traditional work schedule than on the property side. On the property side, you work when people are typically off, whether it is at night or on weekends. Although the client side is more traditional than the property side, if you look at the MasterCard organization, the sponsorship and event group has more nontraditional hours than people in other departments within the company. Most of our events will occur when sporting events occur and our leverage platforms may have us traveling all over the country. Although it is a more structured routine than somebody who works for the Knicks or the Rangers, it is still not the classic 9 to 5 job.

I oversee a seven-person staff and a multimillion dollar budget. As a manager I focus on three key things. One is to ensure clear communication of the company's and our group's goals, objectives, and expectations so we all work toward a common goal. It is easy to articulate goals, objectives, and expectations. The challenging part is living by them on a daily basis. One of the things that has hurt various corporate sponsorship groups is that they are perceived by other departments in the company as one that gets to play with all the toys or has the great perks, but whose function does not build business. I have tried to make sure we are perceived as adding value to the organization, whether it is from a marketing standpoint or with our customer group. First and foremost we know the goals, objectives, and priorities of the overall organization and those are translated into what we do in the sponsorship and event group. Secondly, I use good communication skills with my people and recognize that not everyone on the team is the same. You must treat people as individuals and help them to grow and develop.

Show an involvement in their career and they in turn will demonstrate commitment to the team. Finally, it is important to emphasize collaboration. Working in a cross-functional team requires time, patience, and effort. It is easy to get caught up in corporate politics and we cannot afford to do that with the assets and pieces of the marketing mix with which we are charged.

I think sport marketing—where companies look to use sport as a vehicle to market their products—is at a crossroads. An interesting dynamic exists in the marketplace. Television networks are paying 400 percent to 500 percent more for rights fees than they were 5 years ago, and they will pass those costs onto companies in the form of advertising fees. Unfortunately, the properties have the false expectation that sponsorship rights and values should increase in comparison with the rights fees they receive from the networks. Properties will have to realize that companies such as MasterCard can find other ways to reach a consumer, and we do not have to be a sponsor. We have a great campaign with the "Priceless" campaign that breaks through the clutter by the nature of the campaign and the connection to the consumers on an emotional level. If properties become fragmented, cluttered, and so expensive that companies cannot afford to buy the media in the property and the sponsorship to support it, we must make hard decisions.

If properties try to gouge the sponsors at all levels, companies will walk away saying it is not worth the investment. The .com money is fueling the rise in both advertising rights and sponsorship fees. Properties are feeling flush because .com companies have so much money that they are willing to pay anything to get a relationship like MasterCard, Budweiser, or Coca-Cola already has with the sponsor. If the properties are not willing to look at companies that have built platforms around sport as true partners and begin asking how much money is a potential sponsor bringing to the table, a company like MasterCard will walk away. I have spoken to a lot of folks on the client side and they would probably agree. We are at a crossroads and the nature of the relationship has to work for both sides. If sport sponsorship gets too expensive we will find another way to reach the consumers. If properties become too expensive and too cluttered then companies will take their money elsewhere to get a better return on the financial investment. We have a marketing mix analysis that for every one dollar spent we try to determine the return on the investment. If that model gets too far out of whack in sponsorship, that plug will be pulled. Other opportunities exist also. For example, the Internet offers a lot of ways to reach the consumer in a direct relationship.

Clutter is a concern in the sport marketplace. Clutter is created at many levels. When leagues ask for a lot of money for sponsorship opportunities at the league level and the teams sell sponsorship opportunities at the local level, clutter is inevitable. It makes it difficult for companies to develop effective sponsorship programs when confusion exists over league versus team sponsorship and national sponsorship versus local sponsorship. Clutter is also created when properties divide up categories rather than consolidating the assets behind one or two key partners. For example, Major League Baseball has MasterCard as the official card of Major League Baseball. MBNA America is the official affinity card bank. Fleet is the official bank of Major League Baseball, and John Hancock is the official financial services sponsor. It is fine for the property now because it is generating revenue from each of the four sponsors, but from a leverage standpoint on the sponsor side it creates some difficult hurdles.

It gets confusing for those of us in the industry and ultimately we are driven by what the consumer thinks and tells us. The model that Coca-Cola has developed with the NBA in which nationally Coke has linked its Sprite brand in a long-term marketing partnership with the league in exchange for rights fees is a good one. In that model, Coke invests marketing dollars internationally and also spends a significant sum on rights fees at the local level with the individual teams. A real value exists and it prevents clutter. Our consumer research has shown that consumers do not care about Major League Baseball per se. Yes, they like the World Series and the All-Star Game but their affinity is with their favorite teams. Over the past 4 years our organization has tried to reposition itself around the "Priceless" campaign by listening to consumers in terms of their thinking and values and what drives the mindset of consumers in the new millennium. The category development, along with how the marketing partnerships are structured, will determine which sponsors will benefit the most from any partnership with a property.

On the client side of sport marketing, thousands of positions exist on the corporate side of companies in America focused on sport. The reality is if somebody was in a sport management program and thinking about trying to go on the client side it will be difficult. It is more realistic to look at the sport marketing agencies that work on behalf of clients to execute and develop their sponsorship programs. If the person is interested in getting on the client side that would be a great first step. Those agencies work day-to-day with clients to help them deliver their sports programming and events. Those agencies are a great point of entry into the industry, and a person will develop an expertise in a category because each business category looks at sport differently. I was fortunate to go from the property side to the client side. Going from Gatorade to MasterCard was facilitated by the experience a big sports sponsor like Gatorade offered to somebody like Master-Card, which did not have as much familiarity or ability to develop successful sports sponsorship programs in the past. For a student interested in the corporate environment, opportunities and internships exist on the corporate side. If considering the agency route it is a good vehicle that after 2 or 3 years the next natural step would be to go to the client side.

I enjoy the client side and think many challenges exists at MasterCard. When I consider my future, a lot will be determined based on challenges facing the industry. I would love to stay on the client side whether at MasterCard or another client focused on using sport sponsorship as a way to build their brand. I do not have a crystal ball to answer how properties will react to the bigger question of the future direction of sport sponsorship. I hope I remain a strategic marketer with an expertise in sport. My expertise could take me in a few different directions, but at this point I want to remain on the client side.

In closing, I think a person goes through various phases of a business career and it is the ability to get up every morning and be motivated to enjoy what you do that will define success in a career. Since I started with the USBL in 1987, whether it was at U Mass, the NBA, Gatorade, or MasterCard, I was excited about what I did and with the prospects of what my organization was doing. I have also enjoyed being associated with people who are true visionaries. Being around Glenn Wong and his involvement in the field of sport law and working under David Stern as he reconstructed the way the NBA marketed itself and it interacted with its players, franchises, and broadcast partners were exciting and beneficial experiences.

I also measure success in terms of what I can give back. Working with the *Stay in School* Program, as well as some the programs we have done at MasterCard with the Boys and Girls Clubs have been rewarding because I gave something back. The programs that we do here are not just going to be "crass" commercial programs but we will build programs that affect "the things that matter," such as giving $500,000 to the Boys and Girls Clubs. That money enabled kids to play sports as a vehicle for life and also offered the opportunity for the kids to have fun. Doing something like that makes you feel as if you are contributing in some way to a greater good. Finally, I hope that the challenges I have faced have enabled me to leave a legacy. That is the part that I look at now. I have 13 years of great experience and I consider what I have left behind and will leave behind in the future as being important. I would like it to be a positive legacy as I work through the industry. These are the ways that I would define success in my career.

Victor S. Gregovitis

Vice President of Marketing and Broadcasting
Pittsburgh Pirates Baseball Club

Education:
B.S., SPORT MANAGEMENT, ROBERT MORRIS COLLEGE, 1986

Career Progression:
VICE PRESIDENT OF MARKETING AND BROADCASTING, PITTSBURGH PIRATES (MLB), 1997 TO PRESENT

VICE PRESIDENT OF SALES, PHILADELPHIA EAGLES (NFL), 1996 TO 1997

DIRECTOR OF TICKET SALES, CLEVELAND INDIANS (MLB), 1990 TO 1996

ACCOUNT EXECUTIVE, CLEVELAND CAVALIERS (NBA), 1987 TO 1990

GROUP SALES COORDINATOR, MINNESOTA STRIKERS (MISL), 1986 TO 1987

Best piece of advice you received in regards to your career:

"There are more opportunities in sales than in other areas of sports teams."
DR. STEVE HARDY, PROFESSOR AT ROBERT MORRIS COLLEGE

Best advice for someone aspiring toward a career in the sport industry:

"Gain experience. Start in minor leagues, you will wear many hats and learn a ton!"

Quote by which you live:

"Every morning you have to wake up and look in the mirror and ask yourself, 'Do you want to be the best or do you want to be like the rest?'"

I DECIDED TO PURSUE A CAREER IN SPORT MANAGEMENT my junior year in college. I had tried accounting, business management, and general business administration, but I had a love for sport. I decided that it was what I wanted to do and Robert Morris offered sport management as a degree program.

Robert Morris structured the sport management program so that it had a strong emphasis on the business side. I always thought that I was prepared to succeed in business, even if I did not make it in sport. At that time this was unique because other schools' focus was on physical education, which does not prepare you for the business side of sport.

I graduated from Robert Morris College in Pittsburgh with a bachelor's degree in sport management in 1986. I would not say that I did a lot of research on careers in the sport industry while in school, but I did spend time with people in the field and tried to develop a career path and set career goals on where I wanted to be at specific ages. I wanted to be in sports by 25, I wanted to be a director by 30, and I wanted to be a vice president by 35. I was fortunate I set those goals for myself.

Along with the coursework, the practical work experience I gained in college was key. I did three internships: one with the University of Pittsburgh football program, one with the Pittsburgh Pirates baseball team, and one with the Pittsburgh Spirit, a team in the old Major Indoor Soccer League (MISL). None of them were paid and in only one case did I receive academic credit. It was just a commitment to what I wanted to do. I always try to stress this to the students interested in entering the field. Those internship experiences opened doors and introduced me to people.

It was through an internship with the Spirit that enabled me to meet the general manager of another MISL franchise, the Minnesota Strikers. This meeting led to my first job in the sport industry in ticket sales for the Strikers. It was not an easy decision to take the Strikers job. It meant moving to Minneapolis from Pittsburgh where I grew up and my family was located. On top of that, the salary was low. I started at $12,000. I used to joke to myself that I made more on the mileage expense from driving tickets around Minneapolis than on my sales commission.

It was difficult seeing the friends with whom I graduated make more money than me, but I was dedicated to the career path I had established. I viewed it as an investment in my future. If someone is looking to get out of college and make $30,000 or $40,000, sports is not where it will happen.

Looking back it is easy to say it was the right decision to take the position in indoor soccer. My experience in ticket sales in indoor soccer has proven beneficial. The Strikers had a staff of only 12 people. Everyone wore so many hats at that level. Even the coaches and assistant coaches were involved in selling tickets. I paid my dues, but wearing the different hats taught me an immense amount about the sport business and the different aspects and sectors of the industry.

The biggest challenge for the Strikers was selling indoor soccer in Minnesota. People did not even know what indoor soccer was, let alone our team. I would always say it was a double sell. When you were on the phone with a potential customer, you had to educate people on indoor soccer and secondly the Strikers. With an NFL, NBA, or Major League Baseball team, there is instant recognition with the sport and team name. This helps to open up some doors and simplifies the sales process to a degree.

But in our situation, we had to be creative to attract fans in some other way. Whether it be a giveaway or special event, our goal was to have fans fall in love with our sport and our team. From indoor soccer, I learned every creative angle that I possibly could. Unfortunately, both the Pittsburgh Spirit and Minnesota Strikers eventually folded, but the experience proved invaluable as I progressed in my career.

The experience and the creative forces present in indoor soccer enabled me to land an account executive position in the ticketing department with NBA's Cleveland Cavaliers. During the interview processes, the ticket manager told me that he wanted to steal a page out of indoor soccer. The Cavaliers had witnessed how well indoor soccer had done in group sales and were interested in the kind of impact and creativity that indoor soccer did in group sales. My indoor soccer experience made me a marketable candidate for the position. With the account executive position, I sold season tickets and group packages. In the position, I did not only sell tickets for Cavaliers games, but also all events held in the arena because the Cavaliers owned the arena.

After a positive experience with the Cavaliers, I moved up the career ladder and became the director of ticket sales with the Cleveland Indians baseball club. This was an incredible experience because I was involved with the opening of Jacobs Field. I remained with the Indians from 1991 to 1996 and I was ready for my next move. That opportunity came when I was hired as vice president of sales for the Philadelphia Eagles in February 1996. The focus of that position was to sell luxury suites. I came to the Pirates in September 1997 as the vice president of marketing and broadcasting because I saw the opportunity to expand my responsibilities beyond sales. I have been fortunate because I made transitions between sports. A lot of people are unable to crossover from sports and I did that and moved up the ladder. In each experience I learned something that I could take to my next position.

I have learned that when you leave an organization—and I have crossed over quite a few—you do not want to burn any bridges. I try to stay in contact with a lot of people from my past teams as well as other teams in the leagues. I also try to reach outside of my current league to these resources when I talk about ideas we try to implement, whether it be a marketing plan or sales strategy.

As far as my career path is concerned, I do not know that I would have done a whole lot differently. I realized in college that I would not make the dean's list and that I needed to get into a competitive environment to get experience that would outweigh the dean's list. I focused on getting the experience and not on the lack of pay. This mindset lead to my career opportunities.

In my current role as vice president of marketing and broadcasting, I have six areas of concentration: ticket sales and operations, merchandising, advertising and promotions, corporate sales, premium sales, and broadcasting. In each area there is a director who reports to me. The primary focus in all of the areas is sales.

We are concerned with selling tickets, advertising and merchandise, marketing, advertising, and creating a market perception that will lead to more sales. Every year we go through a budget and revenue process and we determine our revenue goals. Our goals for the revenue side work in conjunction with our baseball department from a payroll and expense standpoint. Therefore, we must know what our revenue goals are and we need to reach them for the entire organization to work.

I am in a unique situation because I have a great ownership group and a great boss who lets us try creative things. Also, both the owner and my boss understand the sales and marketing aspect of our business. You do not always find that. When I approach the owner with an idea, he does not look at me like I am explaining something foreign; he knows what I am talking about.

As a vice president, I find myself using my conceptual skills to create the big picture and prepare long-range plans. When I was in a sales role I always worked for my next sale or looked only a month down the road. A director or a vice president in an organization really must think farther down the road than just a month. The person needs to think about where the organization wants to be 3 or 5 years down the road and how the organization will get there. With our new ballpark, we have done projections for 2000 and 2003. It just does not happen without planning.

As a vice president it is also important that I communicate with the vice presidents from the other parts of the organization for the overall good of the organization. We do an effective job of doing this with the Pirates. We have weekly meetings for vice presidents to integrate ideas across the organization. For example, if I have a marketing or promotion idea, I engage the stadium operations person in the loop early so he will buy into the idea. Lack of communication within the organization could fragment us and prevent us from achieving organizational objectives. It is vital that the whole organization is on the same page so you must look beyond your area of concentration.

My conceptual skills were developed through my experiences. For example, I look back on my experiences in indoor soccer and try to formulate concepts from those experiences. Also, I value the practice of studying other case scenarios. For example, when the Indians moved to Jacobs Field, only two major league baseball teams had moved into new parks at that time: the Chicago White Sox and the Baltimore Orioles. We spent extensive time with the staffs of those parks trying to develop a vision for our new ballpark and to overcome the obstacles and problems that those organizations encountered. I am already applying what I learned from those case scenarios, the experience of moving into Jacobs Field, and the more recent cases of teams moving into new stadiums.

Over the course of my career, I have developed several other skills that have been vital to my growth as a manager and leader. First, my personal skills have developed a lot since I started. In my first two positions I did not supervise anyone; I primarily focused on the technical skills involved in selling tickets. Now, I supervise 34 people as a manager. Different personalities exist and I must determine how to effectively communicate with them to get the most out of each individual. This is the most demanding aspect of my position.

It is also important to have a good plan that your employees think is viable. As a leader you also have to listen to your employees and incorporate their input into the plan. Motivation is also essential. It is a long season and you must create platforms and incentives. We have monthly meetings with our sales and marketing folks. Sometimes we will do it with donuts in the morning and sometimes we will do it with beer and wine after work. The old theory is if it is not broke, do not fix it, but we must challenge the employees to get to the next level. In a small market like Pittsburgh we must continue to challenge ourselves. We try to create a positive environment of teamwork and that we all strive for the same overall goal.

When a crisis arises or goals are not met, I try to remain calm. I am not a screamer. I do not become too emotional. I try to sit back and put things into perspective. I constantly remain positive. I always look for a silver lining somewhere. I stress with the directors that we cannot quit. We must pursue another angle and do everything possible to accomplish our goals.

I am fortunate to have my position and to have had advancement opportunities, but I believe a person creates those opportunities. People always call me and say, "I want a marketing job." To be honest with you, I am the only person in the Pittsburgh Pirates organization that has marketing in his or her title. People also express interest in promotions. We have one person who does promotions, but we have 10 people who sell tickets.

I have a philosophy that a college professor helped me develop. With any professional sport team, more sales people exist than anybody else in the organization. Therefore, it is easier to break into a sports organization on the sales sides than in any other area. I did not see myself as a salesperson coming out of college, but sales was my avenue to get into sports. You can prove yourself and you can learn the other areas and that is the challenge. You can be a ticket sales person and concentrate on ticket sales as your career orientation. If you want to broaden your base to understand the whole organization, you must challenge yourself and ask questions and learn from others in other parts of the organization.

The sales experience will prove beneficial if a person moves into the other parts of an organization because sport is about selling. Some people in this organization do not think they sell, but they do. Everyone in the organization sells the club from the public relations department to the stadium operations people. Successful sales entail effective people skills. We must be people-oriented to communicate with all different levels from the family of four who attends a ballgame once a year to the potential suite holder who invests big money. As an organization we must communicate across those demographics and understand the diverse groups to sell Pittsburgh Pirates baseball.

This is what I enjoy most about my position. I am a sales guy. I thrive on a sale. I love to have success. I love the challenge of trying to fill 47,000 seats on a game-in-and-game-out basis. I probably missed that a little bit when I was in the NFL. With the Eagles we had 10 games and 55,000 season ticket holders. We only had 10,000 tickets left and they were the worst 10,000 tickets in the stadium.

Baseball is a whole different realm. In baseball, I can be more creative because of the amount of seats and the number of games. We can do a lot of crazy things and try to have some success and fun with it. Also, I simply love the game. I could do a lot of worse things for a career. I come to work every day and I am involved with baseball.

In regards to sales of tickets, advertising and corporate packages, and partnerships, the off-season is probably our busiest time. Most people do not realize that. We start our sales process in September/August of the previous year, so January through April is our crunch time. We renew season tickets or sell new ones and a lot of activity occurs at that point. The off-season offers a more traditional workday, but it is still busy. When the season starts, the focus is on the implementation of the off-season efforts. In the season we are here until 10:30 or 11:00 PM.

The new stadium slated to open in Pittsburgh in 2001 will have a dramatic impact on our organization and the ticket sales. The park will be more intimate and there will be a reduction in the number of tickets and an increase in the demand. We will also have state-of-the-art amenities to deliver to our fans. I saw the tremendous impact that a new ballpark had on the sales process when I was with the Cleveland Indians when we opened Jacobs Field.

Baseball is changing and will continue to change. It used to be that a baseball game was enough to attract spectators. Now and in the future, baseball is entertainment. To increase our fan base we must attract entertainment seekers. Everywhere you go, even in elevators, people want to be entertained. A baseball game now is a huge event, and that is what we try to create. Being able to control everything in the ballpark from the people who greet the fans as they enter, to the people that sweep, to the ticket takers, and to the entertainers. All of these employees help us create the atmosphere we seek to provide.

You are also seeing the change in the designs of the new ballparks. Our new ballpark will create new revenue streams for our team through the club seating and the suites. The fans also want more amenities with the entertainment and the ballgame. The Pirates new ballpark will lead to a lot more from an inventory standpoint because we will have closed seats and suites for the first time. That means not only selling them, but also staffing them with a concierge level-type atmosphere to create a business entertainment environment. We will also have signage in the new ballpark that we will package for the first time. We are also exploring the use of smart cards or debit cards to be used at the new ballpark.

To ensure that the customer has a pleasant experience, we do annual presentations with our ticket takers even though a third party hires them. Attending a Pirates game has to be a fun and safe environment. People should have a good time if you want them to return. We want to make it an affordable family atmosphere. We are family-driven where a lot of the other sports may not be.

A change in terms of sponsorship has occurred. When we sell corporate packages, it is not sponsorship any more. It is a partnership. It must be a win/win situation for both the company and us. The relationship or partnership has to affect the bottom line of a company or they will not do it. We must be more creative in developing the packages and more attuned to what the partner desires from the relationship.

As hard as we try to create this environment, external factors sometimes detract from our efforts whereas others make our job easier. For example, the strike in 1994 was difficult because it left such a bad taste in everyone's mouth. We put that behind us and had our sales people diffuse that as much as possible. I was in a unique position during the strike because that was when we opened Jacobs Field in Cleveland. It did not have the impact on us like it did to other cities. A lot of ill-will had to be overcome. We were fortunate because we were in a new ballpark and the team was successful.

On the positive side, Mark McGwire's record-breaking 1998 year had a tremendous positive impact on our ticket sales. We were far out of first place, but sold out back-to-back games. The atmosphere was phenomenal. We had two sell outs, we won both games, and McGwire hit a home run in both games. I could not have written anything better.

In my current position, I hire employees. I prefer people with experience. It does not have to be major league experience. Working in the minor leagues is an ideal way to gain experience. Thirty major league baseball teams exist, but another 90 or 100 minor league baseball teams exist, too. An aspiring professional can learn a great deal at that level that is transferable to the major league environment.

When I hire a director such as a director of ticket sales or advertising and promotions, I look for someone who wants my job. That is the only way they will push me. If it is someone who just wants to come in and work 9 to 5, then I do not know if they have the drive that it takes. It makes me a better person if they push and challenge me in a positive way. I want someone who wants the same career path and aspirations that I do.

In turn, I believe my role is to help them grow. I am hands-off and I let them run their own departments. I tell them it is their own business from a personnel, budgetary, and revenue standpoint. I try to stay in the loop but remain as hands-off as possible. That is the only way they will grow as professionals. I let them try new horizons and yet keep motivating them in case something does not work. I would recommend one of my directors for a vice president position somewhere. I hate to lose good people, but I would hate to hold back anyone's career and I would not want anyone to do that to me.

To advance in the field you need to develop a professional reputation and a network, and you must identify positive role models. When your peers acclaim you, you will be recognized because those are the people that are credible. When I was with the Indians our ticket sales became recognized throughout major league baseball. Word spread that the Indians have a good ticket sales operation and people from other organizations called to pick our brains. In that situation, you help everyone that calls and you begin to build a network of peers, and at that point, you have created a platform.

Professional baseball is a small fraternity. One thing that I always look at when I want to develop marketing plans or ideas are my comparable markets. If I am looking for ideas I talk to a Kansas City, a Minnesota, or a Milwaukee because they face the same issues that I do in a small market like Pittsburgh. We are not competing against one another because we are in different markets so it behooves us to help each other and share ideas. We all must produce the revenues through ticket sales. That is what we absolutely must accomplish. We have our challenges because we do not have the metropolitan populations such as New York and Chicago. We always must consider that we are a small market, which requires us to be more creative.

It is also important to have role models during your career. You need someone to advise you in certain situations and analyze what you did right or wrong. If you respect the individual, the criticism or suggestions he or she provides will mean a great deal more to you. I have met some great people during my career and there are some whose opinions I consider above anybody. In each case, they were individuals who had the position to which I aspired. Learning from them enabled me to be prepared when I moved into the position. Len Komoroski, senior vice president for sales and marketing with the Eagles, was one of those people. He has worked with some model franchises and knew how to assemble a sales and marketing department. Another was Jeff Overton, the vice president of marketing and communications with the Indians. He is one of the best. I learned most of what I know in this business from him. Finally, the chief operating officer with the Pirates, Dick Freeman, is the kind of guy whose footsteps I want to follow next. My ultimate aspiration is become a vice president of business operations or a chief operating officer for a professional sport franchise. Teams are now diversified from the standpoint of having one person manage the sport side. The title is usually vice president of basketball, baseball, or football operations and one person runs the business side of the franchise.

For me to attain my future aspirations, I have to be an expert in my area of marketing and sales, but I also have to branch out into other areas of the organization. I need to gain experience in such areas as finance, public relations, and communications. Basically, I may be involved with all of the other areas of the business but I need to acquire a better understanding of them. By doing this I can see the good for the entire organization and not just for my area.

David Mitchell Wheeler

President/Chief Executive Officer
MAI Sports, Inc.

Education:
B.S., COMMUNICATIONS, INDIVIDUALIZED,
CENTRAL MISSOURI STATE UNIVERSITY, 1979

Career Progression:
PRESIDENT/CEO, MAI SPORTS, 1990 TO
PRESENT

EXECUTIVE DIRECTOR OF MARKETING,
KANSAS CITY CHIEFS FOOTBALL CLUB, 1986
TO 1990

DIRECTOR OF MARKETING, KANSAS CITY
CHIEFS FOOTBALL CLUB, 1984 TO 1986

PROMOTIONS MANAGER, KANSAS CITY
CHIEFS FOOTBALL CLUB, 1982 TO 1983

ASSISTANT DIRECTOR OF PROMOTIONS,
KANSAS CITY CHIEFS FOOTBALL CLUB, 1979
TO 1982

Best piece of advice you received in regards to your career:
"Believe in yourself and don't be afraid to slay dragons."

Best advice for someone aspiring toward a career in the sport industry:
**"Maximize your college opportunities by getting involved in
campus organizations and gaining real world experience."**

Quote by which you live:
**"This is the day the Lord has made;
we will rejoice and be glad in it."**

PSALM 118:24

BORN AND RAISED IN KANSAS CITY, I WAS ALWAYS INTERESTED in
sports as a player and fan. I was primarily a baseball player but played a little bit
of basketball and football. Following high school graduation I started playing
golf, which I still enjoy. I was the second of four children in my family, but none
of my other siblings played sport competitively. My father, however, played a
couple of years for the Chicago Cubs.

Upon completion of high school in the Kansas City area, I enrolled at Central
Missouri State University (CMSU) in Warrensburg. I attended from 1975 to
1979. During the fall of 1976, CMSU experimented with an individualized major

in which a student could meet with professors to customize an academic plan based on present and future career interests. I was the first one to graduate from the department with that degree. My degree was an individualized major in communications, with a minor emphasis in business. The technology revolution was not in full swing at that time, and although I had some coursework in radio and television, it was not my focus. I was more interested in using my communication skills in selling and marketing.

An important college event that would become a key benchmark for my career occurred at the end of my freshman year. I was appointed committee chair for our annual fraternity philanthropic effort. Previously, the fraternity had run a football from the Warrensburg campus to one of the away games and usually raised between $500 and $1,000 for a charity. I had always been encouraged to think and act "outside the box" by my parents and professors, so I decided to try something different. We planned to roll a wheelchair for Easter Seals. We wanted to do it in a high profile place, and this is where my sports interests and marketing interests collided. We rolled a wheelchair about 50 miles from Warrensburg to Arrowhead Stadium, home of the Kansas City Chiefs professional football team. We tied in a lot of the local radio stations in Kansas City and recruited a television station that supported Easter Seals to be our partner. We had public service spots on radio and television that enabled us to get the message out to the area communities. Many people knew about what we were doing because of the promotions, and we raised more than $10,000. It was a tremendous success because it was about $9,000 more than what they usually raised.

I had contacted the Kansas City Royals baseball team about being involved in the project, but at the time they were so hot that they were not receptive. The Chiefs were down a little bit at the time so they were receptive to anything that could help sell a few extra tickets and create some positive public relations. I became acquainted with Russ Cline, who was the Chiefs' promotion director. Sport marketing was in its infancy during the mid to latter part of the 1970s, and I became interested in learning about his job. Russ and I developed a relationship and I knew that I had to do everything I could to stay in contact with him. I was in the fall of my sophomore year when we met, but I stayed in touch with Russ by asking for his help on information for term papers, class selection, and other projects. I would go home on vacation and visit with him further about sport marketing issues, and I continued to work with him on projects during my junior and senior years of college.

With the help of the Chiefs, I began to use the media partners in the city and formed a lot of contacts and relationships. Most importantly, however, I obtained real life experience outside the classroom and applied it to what I was learning. One of the practical things I learned was how to send information to the media. I thought I knew how to write a press release based on the grade I received in class; however, the local Warrensburg paper would bleed its red ink pen all over the releases I wrote. It occurred to me that this person edited news releases for a living and that I could learn a lot from that person so I learned a great deal from my mistakes. My experiences in the fraternity fund raiser taught me how to schedule meetings and how to sell my program. I learned about successes, but also found out about being turned down and rejected. The "Spirit Roll" program is now about 25 years old at Warrensburg. Through that project, I developed a close relationship with the Easter Seals organization, and they appointed me to some national youth boards that gave me national exposure. I attended national conventions and continued to meet other important people. I had the opportunity to make a lot of presentations at national meetings and do real life projects from my sophomore through my senior years. After a project was completed in the fall of my senior year, Russ Cline asked me to interview for a new position with the Chiefs as assistant director of promotions. I got that position and started the day after I graduated.

The key thing I look at for somebody interested in getting into the field is what was done during college. Good solid grades are important, but we are not necessarily looking for a 4.0 grade point average. Responsible individuals who got their work done and have reasonable intelligence are important, but so are extracurricular activities. Given the countless numbers of activities on college campuses and at fraternities and sororities, I look for a student who took advantage of those opportunities for self-improvement. I want to know if the college experience was not just about getting good grades and having fun. Both of those are important, but somebody that wants to be in this business needs imagination and creativity. An involved, active student is what I seek when I hire.

I was fortunate to have several important role models and influential people in my career. One of them was Dr. Dan Curtis, who was chair of the communications department at CMSU. I had him for public speaking in my freshman year and loved him. He was open, knew how to communicate with students, and he and I had a bonding experience. He encouraged me by telling me why I *could* do the things that I wanted to try, instead of telling me all the reasons why I could not do them. He was like a spiritual father for me. He was an inspiration because of his godliness and the integrity that he displayed both professionally and personally with his wife and family. I aspired to be like him. My parents were role models, too. Looking back at my youth, when I was in 5th grade, I created a football board game. I got it copyrighted and worked real hard on it. I made lots of different presentations to companies and created prototypes and things like that for it. I never sold one game, but my parents never said it was ridiculous. They put a little bit of money behind it, and more importantly, they encouraged me and helped me pursue it.

I started with the Chiefs the day after I graduated, May 21, 1979, as assistant director for promotions. What was interesting was the good connection with media and promotion people in the city through the "Spirit Roll"; however, now I worked with them as a member of the Chiefs. I started out selling program ads, which right out of college and being a big Chief's fan, I thought things could not be any better. I quickly discovered, however, that not a lot of people in Kansas City had an interest in buying program ads for a bad football team. I was devastated thinking that I was not carrying my weight for the organization, but fortunately Russ knew how hard it was to sell program ads. I then not only got into the advertising sales, but also moved into promotion development and game/event production. I held the position for 3 years and was then promoted to promotions manager, a position I held for a year. When Russ Cline left the Chiefs to start his own sports-related company; I became the director of promotions. Then 2 years later, I became executive director for marketing, remaining in that position for the final five years of my 11-year career with the Chiefs.

My gut feeling, from early in my career, was to some day own my own company, and working with the Chiefs helped me move toward making that goal a reality. Toward the latter half of my Chiefs' experience, I started to see not only ad agencies but also sport marketing agencies begin to evolve. Key lessons I learned while working with the Chiefs included how to make the transition from just selling promotions that primarily benefited the Chiefs to promotions that were mutually beneficial. We had our pom poms, our cheerleader poster, and other various things in our promotional closet that we needed to sell. It did not matter what client it was because the proposals were basically the same driven by our needs. We used to work with the automatic typewriter where you could fill in the blank spaces with corporate sponsor names and not have to retype a proposal. As sport marketing started to take root, people had success by spending time to learn the client's business operations and objectives, whether it was a gas station or a retail grocer. From that they could develop a package that was mutually beneficial to both parties. Just as those skills started to sharpen, the ability to analyze the potential sponsors' needs became important. If you spoke to the sponsor about programs for either building its brands, image, sales, or even a secondary benefit of how to motivate employees, the dollar opportunities increased considerably. Sometimes the dollar figures increased 10 to 20 times, and at that point we knew we were onto something new and effective.

We continued to refine and create marketing partnerships versus just promotion programs. Then, on the entertainment side, one of the things that we stumbled on came from the McDonald's restaurants. McDonald's understood that it does not just sell hamburgers and french fries—it sells an experience. The Chiefs are still known for having the best fan "experience" in the NFL. We learned that we did not just sell football. Frankly, if we were just selling football, we would have had real problems because we had an average to poor team that went to one play-off game in 11 years. So we had to examine the opportunities and create something that we called the "Driveway to Driveway Experience." We thought through every touch point that we had with the person coming to the game from the time of getting into the car in the driveway to returning to the driveway after the game. We wanted the fan to tune into a good pregame show as soon as he or she got into the car. We knew the fan wanted not only good information about the game itself, but also traffic reports and game time weather reports. We were concerned with everything the fan saw and heard immediately upon entering the complex. This included friendly people directing traffic, to noticing how well the directions and signage were marked, to the parking prices, to the size of the parking spaces. Nothing was a detail too small to evaluate.

Today the Chiefs are known nationally for their tailgating experience, but that was a relatively new concept when I first worked there. It was something we worked hard to promote and develop. The Kansas City Royals, however, had a different philosophy. They were located next door and shared the same parking complex, but strongly discouraged pregame parties. You could almost get arrested for tailgating because it was a nuisance to them and it led to disruptive crowd behavior. They did not want to have people dumping their barbecue hot coals, have an occasional car catch on fire, or see people urinating in the parking lot. Those things can happen, and as management you can police it, plan how to deal with it, or promote and encourage it as a pregame celebration experience. We decided to encourage the tailgate parties and found that 60,000 to 70,000 people showed up to have a good time, and we did everything we could to provide amenities. If you have no pregame activities, so many people would show up 15 to 20 minutes before the game that it can create a severe traffic flow problem. However, if people come in waves, the flow is easier to manage. Instead of creating a problem, we decided to create an experience people would enjoy. We put out a lot of portable toilets, trash cans, and receptacles to dump hot coals as well as provided entertainment including several types of music, radio remotes, and games such as inflatable field goals to kick balls through and targets for throwing footballs. When the team began to have success, the foundation was in place for even more people to come out, and the experience became even bigger.

In addition to all the contacts I made, after the 1989 season, Russ Cline, who hired me with the Chiefs, began talking to me about other opportunities. Russ had created several sport related companies that were phenomenally successful. He owned the major indoor lacrosse league. He has now sold that but he owned it for more than 10 years and made it successful. Russ and some of his partners made tractor-truck pulls. They took them from the fields of Missouri and Kansas and created entertainment spectaculars. Instead of just having 250 farmers out in Odessa, Texas, gathering to see the event, they decided to take the tractor-truck pulls, moto-cross, and monster trucks to Arrowhead stadium and around the country. Even they were surprised at how much excitement it generated because some 50,000 to 60,000 people could attend those spectaculars. For a while it was the hot fad and they made tons of money, but now it has found its niche more in indoor facilities attracting 15,000 to 20,000 spectators. Russ also had a concert company that arranged most of the details and set up for when Michael Jackson did his world tour that opened up in Kansas City for three dates. Russ was into a little bit of everything, and he said, "Mitch, I need a little bit of help developing some sponsorship efforts behind my company." So that is how MAI Sports was created.

The business did well, but the only problem was that my heart was not in doing the tractor-truck pulls, demolition derby, moto-cross, and indoor lacrosse league events. I am grateful for the opportunity that Russ gave me, but I had this feeling that I wanted to go leverage my contacts and resources more with NFL, Major League Baseball, and NHL. I decided to buy the company from Russ. Russ and I still have a good relationship. Russ Cline and Associates continues to be active in a variety of sport ventures. He produces a lot of the Davis Cup Tennis events when they happen on U.S. soil, and he is involved in the event production behind the ESPN Extreme Games. He has sold his interests in the lacrosse leagues, the concert arm, and the moto-cross division. Russ is another one of those influential people in my life who helped me get started and encouraged me to do what I thought I needed to do. In 1992, I took over MAI Sports and it took a right hand turn to begin a new direction.

MAI Sports is in its 10th year. We are located in Overland Park in the Kansas City metro area. In the beginning our staff consisted of some of the Russ Cline support people and myself. We now have expanded to 20 full-time employees. I have a partner named Harry Campbell whose background was with Proctor and Gamble for 7 years and Sprint for 7 years. Harry is the smartest businessperson with whom I ever had the privilege of working. Because Harry comes from the consumer package goods side and I come from the property side, our strengths complement each other and are a great benefit to MAI Sports. To be successful today you must understand both perspectives. My official title is president and chief executive officer, and Harry's is executive vice president and chief operating officer.

As far as my duties and responsibilities during a typical workweek, no two weeks have ever been alike. Key things that we work on from a day-to-day standpoint are communicating the vision for the company and trying to be consistent in setting the tone and direction for the company. I spend a fair amount of time on new business development and maintaining good relationships with our business partners. In broad terms, part of new business development includes maintaining what you have and not assuming people will work with you for a lifetime. We must make sure that we maintain our relationships and do everything to over-deliver to our clients. We are always looking for new business opportunities. At any given time, I manage two or three various projects. Now that we have evolved and grown as an agency, I have more quality support people who can do a lot of the day-to-day work and a lot of the client relationship responsibilities. Various administrative functions exist and people develop our benefits and work with accounting and insurance issues that involve a lot of bureaucratic and governmental paperwork.

In retrospect, our success as an agency comes from our understanding of the client's needs in delivering products and services. Hopefully, we have not only met those needs but also exceeded them. One of the valuable lessons I learned during the last half of my years with the Chiefs was the importance of strategic thinking. Harry Campbell's experience and background with Proctor and Gamble helped us to use critical thinking strategies. Colleges and universities could do a better job in teaching critical thinking. You still find too many people, regardless of their age, that come into an organization and want direction. The person that can examine a project, assess what needs to be done, and identify the key objectives is an important person to have on staff. Strategic thinking is hard but it is a skill. Although some people seem to have a natural gift in it, it can be developed through hard work. It is a major plus in our business.

Another thing that we have tried to pinpoint is the importance of understanding the passion of the sports fan and how it translates into developing a relationship with a sponsor. The Chiefs have a reputation for having rabid fans. People who make several hundred thousand dollars per year, including doctors, lawyers, and other high-level professionals, paint their faces and put on a red headdress and go to the game. Sports fans are crazy and terribly loyal to their teams. If I am Sprint or Coca-Cola, the questions are how can I tap into that passion and—without being unrealistic—develop some of that loyalty and enthusiasm for our product? We still try to understand the passion of the sports fan so that we can apply that in a measure to our clients to help them sell their goods and services.

Another one of our objectives is to try and create passionate relationships with our clients. In our planning session for this year, we visualized what the Packer fan or Chiefs' fan looked like and we asked ourselves, "What can we do to motivate our clients to have that same level of enthusiasm about MAI?" Instead of being painted up like Chiefs or have Packers stuff in a cheese-head, what would it take to get them painted up in the MAI colors and passionately talk to others about doing business with MAI? Would one of our clients respond to an inquiry about MAI by saying "My gosh, they are fantastic, they follow up, they over-deliver, they understand detail, they're strategic thinkers, etc. etc.?" That is not the typical relationship with a sport marketing agency; however, that "passionate fan" response is what we strive for and it is our number one objective.

My management skills continue to evolve as our company and the business changes. From day one, you live the old adage, "president and chief bottle washer." I went from being an executive with an NFL team where I had a lot of support, to a company of one with the other Russ Cline companies. I had some support but still Russ was good about saying, "Hey, you're going to make or break it on your own." I had to manage the menial tasks as well as the most important ones. As the company grew, I had to delegate more responsibilities so that people thought they had ownership in the success of the business. I do a reasonably good job of saying "Here, Sue, or Larry, this is your responsibility, now go do it." Harry Campbell has been a good model for me in this particular management area, because he is excellent at it.

I think the sport marketing industry will evolve as the sport industry continues to change. The industry is taking on a lot more sophistication. If you go back to my entry into sport marketing in 1979, an awful lot of "marketers" were former players and nice guys who would sign autographs and "schmooze" with people. They often had no training or experience in the business world. Now people like Harry Campbell are the sport marketers of today with experience working in large corporations like Sprint or Coca-Cola, who have been among the best in the world at marketing their products. Harry is a huge sports fan, and although he liked working for Sprint, it is not the same thing as working in sports. The industry will continue to get more sophisticated as people, the top marketers from all industries, go to where their passion is—sport.

I tell young people that few jobs exist in sports compared with the number of people that would like to have them. Some become frustrated and say "What can I do?" If you have a job in sports, do not pass it by. At the same time, go out and get some good marketing experience. Learn why people choose toothpaste, coffee, toilet paper, or other consumer products. The perfect road is to get some good marketing experience from somebody who has one of these great training programs, such as Coca-Color or Proctor and Gamble, and get trained. If you pursue an opportunity, with say the Chiefs, and can demonstrate that you have great marketing fundamentals from working for a large marketer such as Proctor and Gamble or Coca-Cola, that experience makes you more attractive to a potential sport employer.

We have an internship program and I think most companies do. The key is always the same in an internship or practicum experience. Will somebody there expect you to just file stuff, or will you get the opportunity to work on a project? If it is just during the summer where you only get a couple of months, by the time you start to learn your job, you are finished. Students who want to pursue a sport marketing program should expect it to take 3 to 5 years to get into the business. When you are 20- to 21-years-old, 3 to 5 years seem like an eternity, but it takes that long to begin to understand the industry. Then, when you try to enter the sport industry you will be more qualified and have a better chance to be hired. Working for nonprofit organizations is also great training because you get to do a little bit of everything because they are usually understaffed. From my experience, working for organizations like the March of Dimes or Easter Seals is great training. When I see someone who has come from a nonprofit organization, I know that the person has probably gotten a lot of hands-on experience in managing projects.

Knowledge of at least the basics of technology is necessary in today's business world. You must do your own work and have a reasonable mastery of the Microsoft office products. Knowing basic PowerPoint presentation techniques can help jazz up a bland presentation. However, technology will never replace the ability to communicate effectively in both verbal and written forms. It is important to take lots of public speaking classes. People have high anxiety when it comes to those classes but a lot of their job will include selling an idea or concept. Even if you are not a "salesperson" you must sell yourself, and it might be to two people or to 20 people. You must explain key points and show what supports them. You must organize your thoughts, make a clear presentation, and do it with passion. Written communication skills are critical as well. I got a "C" grade in business writing, the best class I had in college. My papers looked like the teacher had cut his finger on it everyday because there was so much red ink on them. I wanted to strangle him sometimes, but I find myself now, 20 years later, thinking about the basic writing principles each time that I write a letter.

A trend I see is the consolidation of the media industry as it continues to put more of the integrated assets in the hands of fewer owners. Disney is a prime example of owning not only the team, but also the facilities and the airways in which they broadcast. The consumer will continue to demand more insider information and behind-the-scenes information. Technology can help deliver instant access to that information, and it is important for sport marketers to determine how to best deliver it. People want to know something that is considered inside or secretive information. Technology and the Internet almost re-invent themselves on a daily basis. Few people have the resources to keep up with them. You must determine if you want to do that, and that is not an easy decision. But the things to consider will become more complex and in many ways exciting but also challenging from the standpoint of understanding the ramifications of giving people the access that they want.

Marketing partnerships will continue to be important. Corporations are demanding it. We constantly take our valuation formulas and rework them so that when we evaluate a sponsorship that somebody wants a million dollars for, we can get a real good evaluation of what it is worth. Evaluating sponsorships and determining the return on investment varies from each corporation and each event. It varies based on the objectives and whether they are brand-building or business-building objectives. No pat answer exists to that. Sometimes just getting dollar for dollar is fine. But it goes from 1 x 1 as a minimum to ideally a 2 x 1 and sometimes you can get 3 x 1. Typically, sport properties want such outrageous dollars to be associated with their product, and they give you valuable assets kind of slowly, that their inflated numbers often make getting to 1 x 1 a major victory. Standard acceptable valuation methods exist for typical 30-second commercial spots, but when you come up with headset logos on NFL sidelines, seat backs, or scoreboard signage, a constant negotiation is hammering on those numbers.

Coca-Cola is one company that walked away from some major things that properties did not think it would, but it became more sophisticated and I think it was a key turning point for the industry. In the short term, the company told sport teams and leagues, "If you give us real value and help us achieve our objectives, we will continue to spend. Those who ignore this message, we'll walk away from." The company did what was promised and those type of major players will continue to become more sophisticated in their approach to sport sponsorship. The properties that are willing to develop long-term relationships with people who do not want to change every 3 years will have the best chance to succeed. Sport entities will have to agree to help a company market its products long term and help integrate its message to develop fan bases versus just cash.

I recommend several industry publications to students to keep up with the latest changes and trends in the industry. On the sport side the best publication is the *Sports Business Journal*. Those writers do an excellent job with their features, and they cover the news with people who understand the business, marketing, and on-the-field aspects of the programs. *Team Marketing Report* and the *Sports Business Daily* are other publications we read on a regular basis. The *Sports Business Journal* gives weekly, more in-depth articles, but we take the *Sports Business Daily* on-line to keep our finger on the pulse of the industry.

MAI has evolved into two tracks: the team league association and the corporate side where we deal with companies like Sprint and Proctor & Gamble. I would like to do more work with sport teams because that is my passion. However, the corporate side is financially more rewarding because retainer relationships allow you as a small business to enlarge faster and deeper. Most work with sport teams and leagues is driven by projects so it is constantly necessary to finish one task and work hard to replace it with another. An example of what I enjoy is something we did in 1992. We worked with the New England Patriots to help them re-invent their brand when new ownership bought the team. We worked on everything from creating new uniforms to redoing their ticket program, day of game "driveway to driveway program," and their sponsorships that were basically just selling pom-poms and team posters. We created marketing partnerships and the owner ended up selling the team for significantly more than he bought it for after only two seasons. To re-invent the brand for a team is the kind of thing that I personally enjoy above the other things we do, and I hope I get to do more of it in the future.

What are some of the keys to success in this part of the sport industry? Reasonable intelligence is one of them. You do not have to be the "sharpest knife in the drawer," but you must have reasonable intelligence. I work with some people who I believe are extremely intelligent, but it takes more than that. It takes a lot of initiative, creativity, and hustle, and the college environment gives you plenty of chances to display those abilities. Students have no excuse for not opening their eyes to the opportunities that surround them. My advice is to choose a few organizations, projects, or events and get involved and make something worthwhile happen!

CHAPTER 16

Sport Governance

EVERY LEVEL OF SPORT FROM LITTLE LEAGUE BASEBALL to the International Olympic Committee has a governance structure to create rules and ensure compliance. These self-governed organizations allow members to vote on the rules to which they must adhere. Along with member representation, a board of directors defines the mission and vision of the organization whereas various member committees investigate and present proposals for a vote by the membership. In some instances each member gets a vote, whereas in others the board votes and represents the interest of the members. Many sport organizations have executive directors as well as staffs who work to enforce the rules and conduct the daily business of the sport organization. The staff people organize championships, represent the sport organization at meetings, and provide services and education to the members.

The National Federation of State High School Association (NFHS) is the national governing body for high school sport. NFHS creates rules of play for 16 boys and girls sports for the 51 member state associations. State associations provide uniform standards for athletic competition, offer state championships, promote good sporting conduct, and ensure safe competitive environments.

NCAA is the preeminent governing body in college athletics. In its governance manual NCAA articulates 16 principles for the conduct of intercollegiate athletics. Since its inception in 1908, NCAA has addressed many issues through its governance structure. NCAA has contended with prevailing issues throughout its history including amateurism, professionalism, and eligibility. NCAA consists of member institutions, most of which belong to one of the 120 member conferences (National Collegiate Athletic Association, 1999). In most cases, an intercollegiate athletic conference consists of member institutions with the same institutional and academic missions, commitment to athletics, located in a specific geographic region.

The passage of the Amateur Sports Act of 1978 entrusted the U.S. Olympic Committee (USOC) with the coordination of all Olympic-related activity in the United States (United States Olympic Committee, 1999). Recently, the Act was amended to include the Paralympics and is now called the Olympic and Amateur Sport Act. The governance structure of the USOC includes officers, an executive committee, a board of directors, standing and special committees, an executive director, and paid staff exceeding 500. An athletes' advisory council provides athletes' opinions and advice to the board and all other USOC committees (U.S. Olympic Committee, 1999). USOC has three major functions as a governance structure. It serves as (1) a general assembly of sports bodies functioning as a congress, (2) a member services association providing common services to its members, and (3) a sports corporation handling any business-related aspects.

USOC oversees and coordinates the activities of the U.S. National Governing Bodies (NGBs). NGBs govern certain sports in the United States by regulating eligibility, rules, and championships. NGBs sanction championships, support international competition, and interact with all organizations concerned with promoting a particular sport. Examples of NGBs include US Soccer and USA Basketball.

Professional sport in the United States is owner-controlled. This structure dates back to the creation of the National League in baseball in 1876 (Helyar, 1994). The owners make up the board of governors for each league, establish the rules of play, negotiate broadcast contracts, and determine whether the league will expand and whether a franchise may relocate. Each league has an office headed by a commissioner. The league office conducts the daily business of the league.

Career opportunities in sport governance structures are available. Opportunities to work in various capacities in the NCAA offices exist as well as in individual conference offices in areas such as marketing, compliance, public and media relations, event management, member services, and sponsor relations. For more information, visit www.ncaa.org or individual conference Web sites such as www.bigten.org. Similar opportunities are available with USOC and the 39 Olympic sport governing bodies and international federations, the Pan American sport governing bodies, and the disabled sport organizations. For more information, visit www. usoc.org. Some career opportunities also exist at the various professional sport league offices. Entry-level salaries with governing structures can start in the low to mid $20,000s, whereas middle management positions pay range from $30,000 to $50,000 per year, and an executive director of a governing body can make more than $75,000 per year. The key to securing an entry-level position with a governing body is working either as an unpaid or paid intern to gain experience.

Along with the possible financial rewards, the major benefit of working with a sport governing body is the network one can establish with the member institutions and organizations. One can also gain a great deal of knowledge on the rules governing the sport both on and off the playing field.

REFERENCES

Helyar, J. (1994). *The lords of the realm: The real history of baseball*. New York: Villiard.

National Collegiate Athletic Association. (1999). *NCAA directory*. Indianapolis, IN: Author.

United States Olympic Committee. (1999). *Inside the USOC*. Available online at http://usoc.org/inside/.

Charles S. Harris

Commissioner
Mid-Eastern Athletic Conference

Education:
B.S., MASS MEDIA ARTS, HAMPTON UNIVERSITY, 1972
M.S., JOURNALISM, UNIVERSITY OF MICHIGAN, 1973

Career Progression:
COMMISSIONER, MEAC, 1996 TO PRESENT
DIRECTOR OF ATHLETICS, ARIZONA STATE UNIVERSITY, 1984 TO 1996
DIRECTOR OF ATHLETICS AND RECREATION, UNIVERSITY OF PENNSYLVANIA, 1979 TO 1984
ASSISTANT ATHLETIC DIRECTOR, ASSISTANT TO ATHLETIC DIRECTOR, ASSISTANT DIRECTOR OF SPORTS INFORMATION, UNIVERSITY OF MICHIGAN, 1973 TO 1979

Best piece of advice you received in regards to your career:

"Learn every job and don't be too big to do them if necessary."

DON CANHAM, ATHLETIC DIRECTOR, UNIVERSITY OF MICHIGAN

Best advice for someone aspiring toward a career in the sport industry:

"The future of this industry will be determined by those who find new and more efficient ways to perform mundane tasks while meeting the needs of a divergent constituency."

Quote by which you live:

"Average is not an acceptable standard."

I MADE THE DECISION TO CONSIDER A CAREER IN SPORTS while pursuing my graduate degree at the University of Michigan. I started as an undergraduate at Hampton University in journalism, which led to an employment opportunity at *Newsweek* magazine in New York. I was then offered the opportunity to enter the management program at *Newsweek* on the business side that required an advanced degree. *Newsweek* was willing to assist me to get that degree. I was admitted to several schools, decided to attend the University of Michigan, and recognized that the business side of journalism did not hold a main attraction for me. At the same time, I needed a job so I put my journalism skills to work in the media services department in the University of Michigan athletic department. I recognized quickly that it was a previously unknown career option. It was something that intrigued me and I was excited to pursue.

I went to college intending to be an athlete and decided early that I wanted to focus on being a student. At the time, Hampton University was experiencing what ultimately became a 4 and 46 losing record in football to my best recollection. My other sport was baseball, and in either my first or second year as an undergraduate, Hampton dropped baseball. It just did not work out for me athletically.

I actually worked in the media services department at Michigan for about a year. The department was in the midst of a major reorganization. The first year I was there we had a budget in excess of $1 million and had decided to add a couple of people who knew operations to the four or five person management staff. I had some experience in operational administration and volunteered to manage a couple of facilities. I started as a facility administrator, and then advanced in a year or two to the position of assistant athletic director and then subsequently to an associate director's position at the University of Michigan. From there, after 6 or 7 years, I took a job as director of athletics at the University of Pennsylvania. I was about 30 at the time. I was director of athletics and recreation at the University of Pennsylvania for 6 years, from 1979 to 1985. I then took the job as athletic director at Arizona State University in 1985 and served in that capacity until 1996.

My undergraduate education gave me a great start. Because I was not involved in athletics as a participant, I became involved in a number of extracurricular activities. I worked my way through college in the absence of having an athletic scholarship, and I developed a close relationship with athletics that way. For example, I was one of the public address announcers for the games. I did some media work and photography. I also drove a bus. I got a sense of what was required to make the pieces work behind the scenes. Having those experiences at an early stage, coupled with the background I had in journalism, made it an easy transition into operations at Michigan.

At Hampton I tried to do a lot of things myself to see something positive happen at the end of the day. That attitude, coupled with the sort of formalized training that I got from organizational behavior and industrial relations courses in the MBA, are two unique sets of experiences. Both prepared me differently, but well for my subsequent roles. The nice added element that came from Hampton is the public component of having an undergraduate degree in mass media arts. It gave me the ability to communicate with a greater comfort level than without the education. Managing a facility at Michigan that drew such enormous crowds and handling labor issues and union negotiations were invaluable learning experiences. The shear volume of issues I dealt with on a daily basis, such as interaction with television companies, accommodations for legislators, student-athlete employment, and a myriad of issues dealing with "keeping the trains running on time," was the best training I could have.

No singular barrier exists at its core, but 2 or 3 decades ago no formal degree training in sport administration existed. The University of Massachusetts program may have been the first one and then Ohio University had the second or vice versa. Basically the real barrier at the outset was if you were not a 4-year letter winner at the school where you worked, it was tough to get a job. If you had not coached for 25 years or been on the national championship team or something along that line, it was difficult. Either in real or perceived terms, that may have been an impediment. However, budgets were just beginning to increase dramatically and a growing expectation at the institutional level indicated that the people involved in managing athletic programs should have some pretty basic business background. I do not mean business in the sense of having worked in business but simply basic business practices beyond bookkeeping. An example is working with human resources issues and interacting with labor issues, which were significant in the midwest. Additionally, the early 1970s marked the time of the initiation of competitive issues related to women's athletics and related gender issues. In each case, a demand for fresh thinking was needed or—at a minimum—a need to resolve issues in a nontraditional way.

What may have been obstacles for me, not having the classic athlete or coaching background, turned into positives because I used my practical skills to overcome those initial barriers.

One of the advantages I had was that my boss at the University of Michigan was Don Canham, who was the athletic director for perhaps 25 or more years by the time he retired at Michigan. In many ways Don was a visionary in terms of what he wanted to do and what he wanted to accomplish. He had a good eye for hiring people, particularly coaches, and Coach Schembechler is a good example of that ability. He personally was not as much enamored with the idea of regularly attending Big Ten Conference or NCAA meetings so he often sent me to represent the university. Early on I had the opportunity to talk with Don Canham and get a sense of what he thought should happen at a meeting. Then in a week or two or when the next session occurred, I sat in a small room with Walter Byers, who was then the executive director of the NCAA, or Tom Jernstedt, who still serves in a senior management capacity there. Some of the people I met with included Ralph Floyd from Indiana University, George King from Purdue, Hugh Hindman from Ohio State, Paul Geil from Minnesota, Elroy Hirsch from the University of Wisconsin, Wiles Hallock (who was the commissioner of the PAC Ten), and Cedric Dempsey, who is now the executive director of the NCAA. It was at a time when most mid-level administrators did not typically get that kind of exposure. I listened to people who had a lot of influence in college athletics in informal discussions that were informative for me.

Ralph Floyd replaced a guy named Bill Orwick and went to IU to assume the athletic director's position. I remember he and George King, who was athletic director at Purdue, and Hirsch and Bump Elliott, athletic director at the University of Iowa, were helpful to me. Bump was responsible for me getting the job at Michigan in some ways. He had retired as the head basketball coach at Michigan to become assistant athletic director, then left rather abruptly to go to Iowa to be the athletic director. I was talking with Ralph who had a thing for chewing tobacco. I said, "I don't really know many people in this world who chew tobacco, but in the world of Red Oak, Virginia, where I grew up, I knew lots of people who did that." He looked at me and said, "You've got to be kidding, I'm from Cumberland." Probably 25 miles separates the two towns—what a small world. I had an advantage because these men knew Don would not attend the meetings. I had opportunities for marvelous dialogue and to get a perspective that cannot be learned unless you are in that informal environment.

With respect to my long-term goals and aspirations, I have always believed this industry is a continuum. My interest in coming to the MEAC was to make a difference at a mid–major conference that I thought was undervalued. We have a long way to go to do that, so in the sports industry I plan to make many changes. I am confident that my interest in professional sport would be minimal. I believe there is a significant body of work to accomplish at the collegiate and amateur level. I am familiar and comfortable with this area, but now I have the world's biggest job.

I am comfortable addressing my job responsibilities from both the conference and institutional level. My principal job as the commissioner is to provide back room service for the institution. Our job is to organize and administer the various aspects of competition that impact our institutions. Scheduling, development-related activities, television administration, and officiating are the principal elements. In addition, we spend a fair amount of time with marketing-related activities once we have a television package and have the other key components. At its core, the real responsibility of a commissioner's office is to put a face on the conference and increase its visibility. The relationships we develop, particularly with sponsors, drive down the real cost of administration on the individual campuses. A sponsor relationship, such as the one we have with Nike, that could reduce an institution's cost of doing business by $35,000 to $50,000 per year, is significant from a budget perspective. At the same time, the television exposure to 25 to 30 million households is equally significant because it is a tremendous recruiting tool for all of the member institutions.

At the institutional level, the job is more complex. For example, at the MEAC, I can—broadly stated—go and make sales initiatives and sales pitches to virtually anyone who is willing to listen and bring them back to the membership. Then the membership decides on whether to be involved with that sales initiative. At the institutional level any number of philosophical or practical prohibitions can keep an athletic director from doing the same thing. That becomes one of the challenges. The next level is a sort of basic notion of identification, evaluation, and subsequent selection of coaches. The next significant elements that affect on-campus athletics administration are on-campus relationships in terms of constructing, reaffirming, or in some cases revising the fundamental case for the program and its viability. In some cases it involves being the largest advocate for a program, particularly with limited or dwindling resources. It takes a different skill level to do that, particularly as it relates to alumni and those affiliated with or have a special interest in programs. I tend to characterize them as stockholders in privately held companies. Swimming people only care about swimming, track people only care about track, basketball people only care about basketball, and so forth. An athletic director has an over-arching obligation to communicate both the expectations of the institution and the program to that alumni group while recognizing his or her communication may not necessarily reflect the expectations of that constituency. At the same time, we must bring them to a general understanding of what we intend to accomplish and encourage a willingness to support it for a broader institution.

Any time you represent a collective group of individuals or campuses with the idea of ultimately having them focus on a singular target it becomes difficult. For an anecdotal example, all this week I have spent time with sponsors including new ones, renewal ones, and potential ones we hope to sign in the next few days. Some of those sponsors have had experiences with our institutions and whereas on one hand I represent them, we are unified in both purpose and goal. Some other folks can say, "Well, we had an experience with X Institution the last time, and what you're representing is not that case." So I end up having to backfill and sell at the same time. There are some demanding elements to that, but it also can be rewarding. This will be a rewarding week for us.

It is rewarding for any manager who can be responsible for an enterprise in which they have a personal interest and some background. At the same time, I have the ability to do something that will benefit the institutions and the student-athletes at those institutions. Sometimes we can do little things to enhance the conference and its members. We add a Web site and it gives kids a chance to be exposed in ways they would not be otherwise. It gives a chance to provide regular outreach to alumni at all of our institutions. Perhaps we add another television game because we have signed a new sponsor, which gives all the institutions additional exposure. All of those elements are change elements and not necessarily spectacular. Collectively, they create a mosaic that is rewarding.

To illustrate a typical week, I will describe my schedule from the last week. Last Wednesday I met with the management staff at Lowe's Hardware in North Wilkesboro, which is about a 90-minute drive. Getting an appointment with Lowe's took 6 months. I got back to work on Wednesday night. We began a cycle of weekly staff meetings, which is a 2-hour debriefing with all of the department managers covering our plans for the year. I reviewed some changes with our Web site people and then had three consecutive conference calls with three different elements of task forces who work on long-term strategic planning for our conference.

I typically check e-mail or return calls between 6:00 AM and 8:00 AM. Thursday we started with conference calls at 8:30 AM and had a staff meeting. We were done by about 2:00 PM. I then returned the next run of calls. I did general correspondence for a couple of hours. At 6:30 PM I had a dinner meeting with the Greensboro Sports Council. Friday I had two personnel related meetings here, one of which was with our benefits administrator to look at a benefits plan for our staff. Then we met with the Triad Sports Commission for lunch. Later I caught a flight to State College, Pennsylvania, to visit one of my sponsors who was there for the Penn State game. I left there on Saturday morning before the game to fly to Newark to meet with some other sponsors who were at the Kickoff Classic game in the Meadowlands. I am on the board of the Kickoff Classic, so I stayed for that game. I caught a 6:00 AM flight on Monday.

The first 2 hours of Monday were no different than the preceding Thursday or Friday. I spent an hour with our auditors in closing out the 1999 audit. Then we reviewed a couple of proposals that went out to a couple of sponsors. From 11:00 AM to 1:00 PM I met with one of a series of people we are interviewing now to handle our financial investments on behalf of the conference. I had a teleconference from 2:00 PM to 3:30 PM regarding the 1999 Heritage Bowl. From 3:30 PM to 4:30 PM I worked on general correspondence. Then I had a staff meeting regarding the 2000 basketball tournament. Tuesday I caught a 6:00 AM flight to Boston to meet with another client and spent the day there. I returned from Boston at 3:30 AM this morning. I was in here at 6:00 AM. From 6:00 AM to 8:30 AM I checked e-mail and returned calls. From 8:00 AM to 10:00 AM I had another conference call before this one [interview for this book] on some NCAA matters and it is now early afternoon.

Anyone who attaches great significance to being at home on the weekend or is only prepared to work less than about 60 to 65 hours a week will not have the appropriate temperament or sense of satisfaction from jobs in athletics. Another anecdotal example that I can give you is that, with the exception of November 27, my next open weekend is December 24. (Editor's note: The interview was done in early September.) That schedule started when we had a football kickoff activity on August 4–5. We have some activity occupying some or all of every weekend since then and I have an event on November 27, a personal commitment to be out west at a wedding.

My managerial style covers the standard run of skills. At its core, however, is the ability to plan and develop reasonable expectations with the staff and then be able to articulate them. In that sense—and this is an awkward term—I think the notion of being a "generalist manager" is important. We have eight people on the staff. Six of them have some integral responsibility for organizing our basketball tournament or any championship. I need to know what my staff does and integrate all the elements to conceive a plan so our brochure is produced on time. I have some people who do a marvelous job handling the printing, layout, and design of all our publications. I do a fair amount of the sales on the front end but someone else does fulfillment. Everything has to be coordinated with the printer and the publishing house or the mailing house to get all the material bound, stapled, collated, and mailed in time to fulfill our expectations with sponsors and to sell tickets. The notion of integrating the management element is probably the most important part, but in a small operation it is equally important to have the ability to handle all the issues related to human resources. I provide a high level of interaction to achieve the stated goals.

I establish a series of long-term goals and then have regular interaction with the department managers, coaches, or staff to understand what issues they face or anticipate. I know some pressure points to evaluate in a quantitative sense where they are in the continuum of achieving the ultimate goal. By the same token, I need to rely on individual managers to execute our goals. In both of these cases, whether at a conference or institutional level, budget management is a significant issue. Whether in the context of revenue generation or cost containment, the ability to communicate effectively, efficiently, and timely any significant variances from budget goals or expectations is a critical skill.

Students need to have an internship experience of some sort recognizing that this career will not provide tremendous personal financial rewards. It will be more of a job with personal rewards. However, the kind of remuneration discussed on the sports pages is only available to high quality, professional athletes and a limited number of high-profile coaches. Students need a clear sense that this career requires working some 50, 60, or 70 hours per week and perhaps 40 weekends a year over a large span of their professional career so they can make an informed decision. These are not jobs you can do if you do not like them. Too many variables and challenges exist.

My personal view, with respect to degree programs in sport management or administration, is that one may be better served with an undergraduate degree in sport administration to help understand the career choices. My own sense is that it can be done with less risk. An environmental set of issues benefit an undergraduate in pursuing this degree. At the graduate level a couple of opportunities exist. For a generalist manager one can rarely go wrong with a focus on business or some aspect of business administration. However, if one has achieved an undergraduate degree in sport administration and knows their real interest is in sports publications, then they can pursue a polished graduate level experience in publications. Suddenly a master's in public administration may be the most logical graduate program to pursue. It all comes from the foundation of what you discovered you want to be as an undergraduate.

I suspect we are less than a decade away from a major shakeout in intercollegiate athletics. It is not clear to me how any institution can continue to invest an additional 7 to 10 percent annually in intercollegiate athletics programs. The shakeout may come in the manner in which financial aid is administered, which can take us in those typical 40-year cycles back to the major college and the small college divisions. Some major colleges will winnow because major NCAA Division I-A programs are too expensive. That will change the shape, but not the nature of what we do. From an employment standpoint, it will provide more opportunities for more people, albeit perhaps at athletic programs with less visibility. There are 110 to 115 NCAA Division I-A football-playing institutions, of which about 75 percent lose money. As conferences begin to shift again in the next 36 months or so, the only question will be whether schools will step back. Look at any mid-major school in terms of funding in a major conference, are they going to be saying, "We can't do this any longer?" "We really just need to stop kidding ourselves and find a level, though unpopular and certainly grossly disconcerting for our alumni and perhaps some of our local constituents, where we can remain financially solvent." "Unless people are going to give us more tax money, which they clearly are not, we can't survive." Some fall-out will occur at that level.

More job opportunities will exist for sport management graduates. They may not necessarily be in intercollegiate sports, but as we look at this whole generation, a proliferation of retiring or semi-retiring baby boomers will want to make up for the time they lost trying to make either that first or fifth million. The sport industry will revolve around an active middle-aged group of people needing to be organized and managed in ways I do not think we can envision today.

The very nature of an activity held in the public forum requires anticipation of some elements of crisis management. These crises may include a snowstorm occurring when 10 teams are playing that night and all of the games matter because they affect the standings and they are televised games, or at another level if a bus turns over and 30 of your kids are on it. I want to surround myself with people who can help me communicate in a crisis. To digress for a moment, I have had both of those as well as many other incidents happen. I got a call from the state police in the middle of the night telling me a bus turned over and it had 28 of my kids on it. Many things had to happen quickly, not the least of which was putting together an information chain involving the president and other political entities at the university and in the program. In taking the leadership role, I put myself in the middle of managing an incident.

To manage an event requires a demeanor that is sensitive and compassionate but not overbearing. One must also be strong enough to ensure the appropriate data have been gathered. You will be looked to as the person who is integral to the decision-making process. Gun fights, riots in the stands, or complete brownouts in the stadium on a nationally televised game can occur. In one case at Michigan on the first cold day of the winter the plumbers actually turned off the water for all of the restrooms in the stadium and had forgotten to turn them back on. It is a problem when you have 100,000 people going to the bathroom. The main issue in crisis management is to develop a plan and mobilize the people to act out the plan.

I see interns often with an inherent assumption that they know it all. Innumerable elements are needed to bring an event to life. No level of detail is too minute or too insignificant because any one of those elements in a large and diverse activity can have a negative impact on the outcome. Students who want to enter this profession should understand that critical piece.

Jennifer L. Heppel

Director of NCAA Legislative and Eligibility Services
Big Ten Conference

Education:
B.A., HISTORY, WESLEYAN UNIVERSITY, 1990
M.B.A., SPORT MANAGEMENT, ROBERT MORRIS COLLEGE, 1993

Career Progression:
NCAA DIRECTOR OF LEGISLATIVE AND ELIGIBILITY SERVICES, BIG TEN CONFERENCE, 1998 TO PRESENT
MEMBERSHIP SERVICES REPRESENTATIVE, NCAA, 1996 TO 1998
SENIOR WOMEN'S ADMINISTRATOR, UNIVERSITY OF HARTFORD, 1994 TO 1996
BUSHNELL INTERN, EASTERN COLLEGIATE ATHLETIC CONFERENCE, 1993 TO 1994

Best piece of advice you received in regards to your career:

"Relax. It will all work out."

DAD (DAVID HEPPEL)

WHILE I WAS A HISTORY MAJOR AND AN ICE HOCKEY PLAYER as an undergraduate at Wesleyan University in Middletown, Connecticut, I never envisioned myself getting into sport management. Other than knowing there were people who worked in the Wesleyan Athletics Department, I did not know that careers existed in sport management. After I graduated from college, I did not want to do anything with my history major. My degree was in European Imperialism in the Third World and that would have geared me toward a career in foreign policy. That prospect did not interest me, so after graduation I gave myself a year to figure out what I wanted to do with my life.

I moved to Boston with some friends and started coaching the junior varsity girls ice hockey team at Buckingham, Brown & Nichols, a private school in the Boston area. I enjoyed coaching and thought I would enjoy being associated with college athletics. I started looking at graduate schools with the idea of pursuing a career in college athletics as a coach and some type of administrator. I stumbled on the idea of pursuing a graduate degree in sport management. I believe I had heard of the sport management program at the University of Massachusetts because I lived in New England at the time. I realized a graduate degree in sport management could be my foot in the door to college athletics. I did not have any contacts in sports and I needed a way to network. At that time graduate school was probably the best way so I applied and was accepted into the MBA program with a sport management concentration at Robert Morris College in Pittsburgh.

It was during one of my interviews for graduate school that I became aware of the other opportunities in college athletics besides coaching. I had mentioned during one interview that I wanted to be a women's ice hockey coach and the person kind of laughed and said there was not a whole lot of future in that. That person was wrong, but the comment did make me look beyond coaching as the only route to work in college athletics. I had this mindset because of my experience at a small NCAA Division III school. Everyone in the athletic department coached while having other responsibilities. I thought this was the only approach to a career in college athletics administration.

Ninety percent of my courses at Robert Morris were business related and four or five were sport management courses. In the business courses I molded my projects to sport. For example, in a financial control class I would use Reebok as an example as opposed to a shipping company for a project. I learned that writing in graduate school was important. Many of the people in the program had accounting undergraduate degrees and no writing background. Maybe they knew how to analyze, but they did not know how to put it on paper. My degree in history proved beneficial because I had done so much writing as an undergraduate.

While in graduate school my career orientation remained toward college athletics. I was a graduate assistant in the Robert Morris athletic department during my second year. This position was more involved with filing and busy work than actual work experience, but it did expose me to a Division I environment. I also gained practical experience by volunteering with the Pittsburgh Marathon. It was a learning experience to work with the city on the logistics of organizing the race. I also worked as a manager of a community pool to earn some money while working on my degree. To complete my degree, I needed to do an internship. I was fortunate to earn the Asa S. Bushnell Internship with the Eastern Collegiate Athletic Conference in Cape Cod, Massachusetts. ECAC is the nation's largest collegiate athletic conference with 297 member Division I, II, and III colleges and universities ranging from Maine to North Carolina. It is a conference of conferences. Within its structure are institutions from all of the athletic conferences from the aforementioned states. ECAC offers 106 championships in 22 men's and women's sports. There were three 1-year intern positions. I was the fourth choice, but one of the other finalists received an internship with the NCAA, so I received the third internship position. I have never been too upset about it being fourth choice. It does not matter how it happens, just as long as it happens.

I was comfortable going to ECAC because I knew a lot of the schools that were members of ECAC from my experience as an intercollegiate athlete in the New England area. Getting back to the New England area and living on Cape Cod were benefits, but working in a conference and being exposed to a variety of experiences from championships to sports information work to television were outstanding benefits.

My main responsibilities as the intern that year involved internal affairs, championships, special events, and publications. With internal affairs, I coordinated the ECAC scholar-athlete program; organized a seminar on emerging sports for the annual ECAC spring convention; and planned, prepared, and disseminated monthly administrative information to ECAC members. For championships, I served as the conference liaison for 14 ECAC championships, generated the tournament financial reports, and reconciled tournament expenses. I was involved with the 1993 ECAC Metro New York Basketball Challenge held at Nassau Coliseum in Long Island. I also had a chance to stay in touch with my hockey interest by coordinating highlight footage of the International Ice Hockey Federation's Women's World Championships for the Prime Network as well as serving as a feature writer on women's ice hockey for *U.S. College Hockey Magazine.*

In retrospect, I gained a great deal from the experience that has proven beneficial as I have progressed through my career. It was different than a true work experience. Yes, I learned, but the most valuable aspects were the people I met and the opportunities I was told about that exist in college athletics. As an intern, I met athletics directors and other athletic administrators at most of the ECAC institutions. Even now, 7 years later, I still keep in touch with many of those people. I also learned that many different opportunities exist in college athletics. I looked beyond my original mindset of coaching as the only avenue to working in college athletics. I also realized that many different ways exist to approach a job and still be successful.

I completed the internship and also completed the requirements for my degree in the spring of 1994, and I began my search for a position in college athletics. I applied for and was eventually named senior women's administrator at the University of Hartford in Connecticut in the fall of 1994. The pay was not great, but the opportunity was great. People looking to get into the field have to realize they will not make $50,000 with their first job. They will work for lower wages to get experience. Hartford took a risk on me because I did not have the administrative experience expected of a senior women's administrator at an NCAA Division I institution. My internship had been in a conference office and the only experience I had in an athletic department was as a graduate assistant. I had not dealt with coaches in that capacity and that was one of my main responsibilities at Hartford. In the interview process I displayed confidence that I could do the job. Also, I sold them on my willingness to learn and put in the time to do a good job. It also did not hurt that I did have the graduate degree.

The networking I did at ECAC proved valuable in securing the position. The people with whom I worked at ECAC called on my behalf and I had become acquainted with the sports information director at Hartford while I was working at ECAC. He ended up being on the search committee for the position. I never would have expected that a sports information director would help me get a job because I had no interest in being one. It shows that you never know from where assistance will come. It does not matter who the person is or what position they are in—you need to know everyone you possibly can. For example, a person may not want to coach so he or she does not spend a lot of time getting to know coaches. But coaches have a lot of influence in an athletic department.

As senior women's administrator I had administrative, compliance, and special projects responsibilities. My administrative duties included directing all aspects of student-athlete financial aid and I was the liaison to the director of student financial assistance with the university. I was also the program administrator for baseball, men's soccer, and softball. This entailed evaluating the coaching staffs, administering the program budgets, coordinating practice and competition schedules, and conducting marketing and public relations for the programs. I also assisted in the development of annual budget requests and allocations as well as strategic planning for the athletic department.

In compliance I supervised and directed the institutional compliance program, coordinated all areas of student-athlete eligibility and recruitment, and provided an ongoing rules education program for the athletic department staff, institutional administrators, faculty athletic representatives, student-athletes, and parents. The special projects I oversaw included the development of the Department Policies and Procedures Manual and the student-athlete handbook. I also served as tournament director of the 1994 North Atlantic Conference Women's Soccer Championship.

From the Hartford experience I learned how to work within the system, that is, within the athletic department as well as the university. Within the athletic department, I worked with all coaches on compliance issues, with the coaches for those sports for which I was a sports administrator, and with the athletic director. I also gained an understanding of the athletic role within the university system and the overall mission of the university by interacting with administrators outside of athletics. It is often the case that the members of the athletic department view every issue related to them as being essential, but the athletic department is only one part of the university. Therefore, as a department you have to prioritize because you will not win every battle. I viewed my role as helping the coaches succeed. If the coaches saw an obstacle to their success, I tried to help them. But I had to consider the best interests of the department and the university and determine whether the request was consistent with the mission of the department or university. If it was not, I could not do it for the coaches.

I served as senior women's administrator at Hartford for 2 years. My decision to leave Hartford was based on two rationales. First was the financial aspect. I know money should not be important, but it does matter. I was making in the mid $20,000s, and it was difficult to live off that salary. I needed to make more money for my personal well-being. The second rationale was I wanted to move on to a larger athletic department for the experience and to expand my network. Hartford is a smaller NCAA I-AAA institution. I wanted to work at a major I-A institution. Also, I already knew a lot of people in the northeast, but I did not know many people at the national level. Taking the position at the NCAA national office in membership services became a prudent career move.

The position with the NCAA meant I would concentrate more in a compliance area, but it would get me the exposure to national issues that would allow me then to move on to a larger institution. I was interested in compliance because I thought it probably would be my door into administration as a woman. A lot of institutions tie compliance to the senior women's administrator position. Also, I knew from the beginning that I did not want to do marketing and fund raising. I do not like selling. I am more interested in administrative work. I like compliance because it is organized and you do not necessarily have to take risks—you probably should not. I also like doing the research associated with compliance. That goes back to my history background.

When I first got into compliance I did not know a whole lot about it. I remember studying the NCAA manual for my interview at Hartford. I had done a little bit of compliance at ECAC, but the internship had more to do with championship administration. At Hartford I was the compliance coordinator. It turned into real on-the-job training in compliance, but sometimes that is the best training. In compliance you always learn something new, and that is one of the great things about it. Nobody knows all the NCAA rules. To succeed in compliance, you have to admit that you do not know, rather than making up an answer. This can be difficult because people expect you to have the answers. But you cannot know everything so you must say "I don't know and I will have to get back to you."

In the future, I believe the number of compliance positions will increase. But I also think that the base of experience is growing. Ten years ago you did not have many people who had experience in compliance. To a certain extent, I was a beneficiary of that when I got the job at Hartford. At that time, it was common to hire somebody who might not have had compliance experience but who was smart enough and had a desire to learn. Currently, every institution has at least one compliance person and more experienced compliance people exist.

A number of institutions do not have the resources to hire someone to handle just compliance, but larger institutions like Big Ten institutions generally have two to three people working in compliance. At smaller institutions the person may have compliance as one of their responsibilities. A common match is compliance and academic coordinator. Compliance is often a responsibility of the senior women's administrator, too. For someone starting out it might be better to be at a smaller school to tackle multiple responsibilities and gain experience in several different areas and then determine which area to pursue. By focusing solely on compliance early in a career, a person may get pigeon-holed into compliance and it may not be something they want to do the rest of their career.

Although I had several responsibilities in my position in membership services at the NCAA, my main one was rules interpretation. I assisted member institutions, conferences, student-athletes, parents, the media, and other organizations in understanding the application of NCAA legislation. I did this by responding to phone calls and through written correspondence as well as conducting in-person presentations. It was amazing how many questions arise about the interpretation of the NCAA rules. In my position I had phone duty that meant I spent 12 to 16 hours per week sitting at my desk and answering the phone. We would get almost 300 calls a day regarding rules. Anybody could possibly call. A lot of the questions were repetitive and related to the same issues. For example, I knew the transfer rules inside and out. However, a lot of the questions from NCAA member institutions tended to be more involved. For example, questions related to eligibility or fund raising and sponsorships issues were more complicated. Along with the phone duty, I also spent a fair amount time responding to letters related to interpretations.

Also in my position I served as a liaison to probably three or four different conferences. This role again entailed dealing with rule interpretations, but it involved making presentations on rules and rule changes at conference meetings as well as national organizations for admissions, registrars, and financial aid personnel. I did a great deal of public speaking. If anybody at Wesleyan had told me I would make a living giving talks, I would have laughed at them. Before this time, I had never spoken publicly in my life.

It was beneficial to have institutional experience before going to the membership services area. It gave me more credibility. Not only can I answer the question but also I can give you suggestions as to how to implement it or how to get to the bottom of the situation. Having that institutional experience before working at the NCAA was great for me. I am not saying that people at the NCAA who have not had institutional experience cannot be successful. Also, people have worked only at the NCAA level and have gone to campuses and were great because they have that national experience.

From my daily responsibilities at the NCAA I had gained a firm grasp of the NCAA rules, but I saw the experience as a stepping stone in my career. I spent the first couple of months at the NCAA trying to determine the different areas within membership services. I realized that 30 people basically did the same thing. I wanted to know how I could make a name for myself. I took the approach that I would become an expert in particular areas. To become an expert meant focusing on areas that were not perceived as the most glamorous.

For example, everybody in membership services wanted to be involved with basketball issues, but only a few could. However, nobody wanted to work with foreign student-athletes. I did a lot of work with the foreign student record consultants that dealt with all issues related to foreign student-athletes. I conducted seminars with people involved with international student-athletes. I investigated and prepared initial-eligibility waiver appeals for review by the Division I Initial-Eligibility Waiver subcommittee and assisted in the preparation of the NCAA Guide to International Academic Standards for Athletics Eligibility.

From these experiences, people began to associate me with foreign student-athletes. I also spent a lot of time working with Division III financial aid. Not a lot of people wanted do it, but I worked hard at getting to know the ins and outs of it and eventually I loved it. By creating an area of expertise, people began associating me with that area. I was not just another person that answered the phone. I shared this advice with new interns and staff members at the NCAA as well with those I came in contact with at the Big Ten. I tell them they need the experience, and they will get it in the less glamorous areas without even knowing it. The area is important to someone in the NCAA membership because otherwise we would not do it.

I loved working at the NCAA and the wonderful people in membership services. Sometimes working in membership services could get depressing with the tremendous increase in initial eligibility waivers in the fall of 1996. That year the sliding scales and 4 years of English came into play and we were not prepared to handle the volume of institutions seeking waivers on students declared ineligible by the new standard. We had a limited number of staff who were supposed to prepare every case for review by the NCAA committee overseeing this area. This was the same time that waivers for learning disabled students were increasing. It was stressful knowing that having a waiver processed was taking longer than it should and nothing that could be done about it. Great strides were made from that first year. It was impressive to see how the higher level executives at the NCAA National Office made the problem a priority, reacted to the situation, and gave the departments the necessary resources to address the problem. I credit the executives for not labeling it a nightmare to endure every year from July to November. Rather they said this is not good and we need to do something to change it for the better. I enjoyed seeing people working together to turn something from rock bottom into a positive situation in 2 years. The process was eventually modified to involve high schools in the initial eligibility process specifically related to core courses and things went smoother by the fall of 1997.

While at the NCAA, the public perception of the role of the NCAA National Office was interesting and frustrating. Most people believe that it is those who work at the National Office who make the rules. Parents of student-athletes and high school students especially have this view. When you speak to these parties you try to explain the process to them without passing the buck. This can be difficult because they want answers and no one else can provide them but the NCAA office. They get annoyed and are unpleasant. You want to bring closure to their issue but you also need to educate them on how rules are created.

They need to know that I did not wake up one morning and say, "Hey I'm gonna make this rule." An NCAA staff person does not have that power. By explaining the process that it is actually the NCAA member institutions that make decisions on rules and that the presidents have the final authority, parents seem a lot more comfortable. Sometimes this is not enough because it seems too far removed from their situation. This is where it is important to learn the intent behind the rules. People do not want to hear, "Well that's the rule." You need to explain to them why the rule exists.

It was tough reading articles that provided misinformation about the NCAA, but most often it was and still is the NCAA's policy not to respond. Sometimes after reading an article, I wanted to call a reporter who was perpetuating the myth that it was the NCAA offices that make the rules. This experience made me cynical of the media. How the NCAA operates and its rules are areas I know very well and I rarely read articles or in-depth exposes that get the rules right. It made me question why the sports reporter did not do research to get the correct information. It affected the newspaper's credibility in my eyes.

While at the NCAA I used and enhanced my technical, personal, and conceptual skills. I needed a firm grasp of the NCAA rules so my technical skills were somewhat of a given. But I developed both my personal and conceptual skills while I was there. I spent so much time dealing with people—many that I would never hear from again—that personal skills were essential. I had to rely on my ability to relate to many different kinds of people and situations. I had to learn not to take people's complaints personally. I also began to appreciate how essential conceptual skills are to compliance. I began to see how everything ties together to create what is known as college athletics. It is these rules that separate college athletics from professional sport. I realized that none of the NCAA's 33 articles and 14 operating bylaws is independent. For example, the recruiting rules are related to eligibility and financial aid and the financial aid rules are related to division membership and enforcement. Everything ties together. Although I may have to check the NCAA manual to answer a question about a rule, I reached a point that I would often know the answer based on my understanding the big picture. When people first start in compliance they think in terms of individual rules and what they are, but through time you have to look at them for more than what is written in the manual. A person needs to look at the rule and get an answer for a question related to the rule. They must interpret the rule. The more you work in it the more you realize how everything ties together.

I was with the NCAA for 2 years and I was not looking to leave when the opportunity arose with the Big Ten Conference for the position of director of NCAA legislative and eligibility services. Although I was happy at the NCAA, I could not turn down this opportunity. In my mind, the Big Ten is the best Division I conference in the country. It is the oldest and most stable conference in terms of membership. In more than 100 years only one school has left. The commissioner, Jim Delany, has a good reputation and I viewed it as a unique chance to work with and learn from him.

Although I realized coming to the Big Ten was a great opportunity, it was difficult leaving the NCAA. I left a position in which I was comfortable and knew I did a good job. I also know that if I stayed with the NCAA I could advance. I left a comfortable environment for something new and any time you do that, you are leaving a comfort zone. I had the same reaction when I left Hartford for the NCAA. During my first 5 months at the NCAA I had to convince myself I had made the right move. On paper, it was the right move, but it took awhile to get there. I went through the same thing with the move to the Big Ten. From day one I knew I had made the right move, but situations occur where I question why I left the comfort zone with my position at the NCAA.

Sometimes people are not willing to take the chance of getting out of that comfort zone and they pass on some great opportunities. Unfortunately when people get too comfortable, they can get stagnant. Issues such as geography, family concerns, and salary come into play when people consider changing jobs, but sometimes people do not look at potential career moves because they are frightened by the unknown.

My main responsibility with the Big Ten is to serve as the liaison with the compliance coordinators at the Big Ten member institutions and to coordinate rules education on the Big Ten campuses via written, electronic communication and in-person presentations. My NCAA experience gave me the knowledge of the NCAA rules as well as legitimacy with the compliance coordinators at the institutions. The compliance coordinators have the responsibility of making sure the members of the athletic staff, coaches, and student-athletes at their respective institutions follow the NCAA rules. The compliance coordinators at these schools are good. I do not view it as if I know more than they do. Rather, it is that I have the time to research an issue that they may not. Also, I am an outside voice. I am not involved in something to the extent they can get involved in it. A lot of times the compliance coordinators want confirmation on an interpretation they may have for a rule and some times they may have questions. A lot more information comes across my desk then may come across their desk. A lot of what I do is educating. I try to make sure they are kept up-to-date with the NCAA as well as conference rules.

I also serve as the primary liaison to the Big Ten Academics and Eligibility Subcommittee. This committee is responsible for all matters affecting the academic eligibility status of conference student-athletes in relation to Big Ten rules and NCAA rules. This committee is important because the Big Ten has its own rulebook, in addition to the NCAA manual. People admire us because we do have higher academic standards then any other conference. The Big Ten rules are more stringent than the NCAA because of the Big Ten degree completion requirements. Big Ten student-athletes must be enrolled in an academic program and must progress toward a degree in 5 years. For the NCAA a student needs only to complete 24 credits a year. The Big Ten also has a minimum grade point average for its student-athletes. These issues are important because if a student is ruled ineligible by Big Ten standards he or she loses his or her financial aid. People may envy us because of those academic standards, but at the same time they are not jealous of the additional set of rules and additional work that academic advisors and compliance coordinators have to deal with in terms of certifying eligibility for student-athletes. A compliance coordinator at a Big Ten institution has to worry about institutional, NCAA, and Big Ten rules and policies.

The most demanding aspect of my position is the sense of responsibility that I have for what I do. I cannot stop caring about the level of my performance because what I do affects coaches, student-athletes, and entire athletic departments. I like to remind myself of that because it sometimes is easy when you have a lot going on to say "let's do it that way" and forget about the consequences. A response like that may mean the difference between a student-athlete being eligible or ineligible or an institution breaking an NCAA or a conference rule. What I enjoy most about my position are the people that I get to work with on the Big Ten campuses. They are great. They share that level of responsibility. It would be difficult to work with somebody who did not think their job was important and that it affected a lot of people.

I have also found that a conference office offers a great work environment. It offers the best of both worlds. You are a lot more connected with institutions than working at the NCAA National Office, but you are not on call 24 hours a day as you would be working at a institution. The typical day at a conference office is still not the traditional 9 to 5 job, but it is different than being on a campus. At the conference office, I can be a lot more proactive as compared to when I was on a campus. At Hartford I constantly reacted to situations. I can remember coming into the office at Hartford in the morning with three projects I needed to get done, but it could be 3 days before I got to them because of situations that arose with students, coaches, teams, and opponents. If I needed to get a project done I either came in very early, like 7:00 AM, or stayed late. The conference office environment enables me to be more efficient. It is a small office with 22 full-time people and I do not have the constant interruptions as on a campus. Projects that should take 2 hours usually take 2 hours.

As director of legislative and eligibility services I visit campuses. It is sometimes hard to tell how I am perceived on those campuses by coaches and the athletic department staff. I think the immediate reaction from anybody within the conference is that they have to act a certain way. But a visit from a member of the conference staff is different than a visit from someone from the NCAA. We do not have an active enforcement branch in the conference office so we try to remind people of that. I am not there as an investigator. Even if I am on campus and I see something or something happens, chances are the person I am with sees it at the same time. I do not need to say anything. I know that it will get taken care of. I am not an enforcement person and I try hard not to perpetuate that perceived role.

I have enjoyed being involved in the compliance area of college athletics, and it will be interesting to see where the compliance will be in 10 years. I have no clear ideas exactly where the NCAA is headed in regards to legislation. I hope we move to more deregulation and more institutional control. I would like to see the NCAA move toward intent-based legislation. This is where an NCAA rule is in place and it is up to an institution to work within the intent of the rule.

Every time I look at NCAA convention proceedings or the legislation that is passed I wonder why we keep passing this legislation. When is somebody going to say, "OK, no legislation right now. Let's determine where we want to be." Ideally that would be great. The Big Ten has been waving that flag of deregulation for awhile. We cannot do it until we get our own shop in order, and we have got tons of our own rules that we need to take care of before we can say we did it now and let's get everyone moving in that direction.

If college athletics move toward deregulation it would place more responsibility on the institutional compliance coordinator as well as the conference office. The institution must understand the rules and legislation and have the integrity to make appropriate decisions. The way things are now, it is not so much an institution making a decision, but rather it is determining what that decision should be based on a rule. It would involve the institution understanding the intent of the rule and making a decision as to whether an action is within that intention or not. They are putting more responsibility on the shoulders of the institution. Hopefully I do not deregulate myself out of a job.

I feel lucky to be where I am in my career. I always tell people you cannot expect to get the job that you want right away. Everybody wants a job in sports, so it is competitive. To get into college athletics or compliance specifically, you must be willing to do the graduate assistantship and or the internship route. Plain and simple—you have to put your time in. To get into a specific area you may even have to volunteer to get to know it. It is not going to happen overnight.

If you want to get into college athletics administration you will need a postgraduate degree. I earned my graduate degree before I started my career in college athletics. However, I was fortunate that while I worked on my MBA as a full-time graduate student at Robert Morris, I gained experience as a graduate assistant, assisting with a marathon, and managing a community pool. Sometimes with a master's program you are a full-time student and it is difficult to do anything else. I do know people at the NCAA, conferences, and institutions without graduate degrees who have great jobs, but they have been there awhile and I do not think the master's degree was as preferred as it is now.

If a person can secure an entry-level position without a graduate degree, I say take it. But the person should make plans to earn the graduate degree at some point. If a person is interested in advancing he or she will need the graduate degree. One option is to do the degree part-time while working. This is a great option for a person who has a position on a campus. The person can take advantage of tuition waivers and earn a graduate degree part-time while working. The other option is to take a break in a career and go back full-time, but the further one gets in his or her career the harder it is to take that break. It can be done both ways, but I think it depends on the individual and the situation.

I have several ideas in regards to my future career aspirations. I have always considered being an athletic director at a smaller NCAA Division III school since I started my career. I still need more management experience. In my current position, as well as with the NCAA, I do not oversee anyone. I need to work with different kinds of sports and know the different issues related to those sports before becoming an athletic director. One of the reasons that the position with the Big Ten appealed to me is that I would work as the liaison with some coaches groups. I am getting back into a sport administration role. That was an opportunity that was not available at the NCAA. One of the benefits of being in a conference office is that so much goes on that you get an opportunity to do a lot of different things. A lot of things happen around here that I would like to be involved in that could give me that experience. I am also focusing on professional development by attending seminars related to compliance and college athletics to learn and to keep in touch with current trends and issues. I am interested in being involved with NCAA committees on the national level. I want to continue to challenge myself to excel in what I do and achieve my career goals

John D. Swofford

Commissioner
Atlantic Coast Conference

Education:
B.A., INDUSTRIAL RELATIONS, UNIVERSITY OF NORTH CAROLINA, 1971

M.ED., SPORTS ADMINISTRATION, OHIO UNIVERSITY, 1973

Career Progression:
COMMISSIONER, ATLANTIC COAST CONFERENCE, 1997 TO PRESENT

DIRECTOR OF ATHLETICS, UNIVERSITY OF NORTH CAROLINA, 1980 TO 1997

ASSISTANT ATHLETIC DIRECTOR FOR BUSINESS AND FINANCE, UNIVERSITY OF NORTH CAROLINA, 1976 TO 1980

ATHLETIC TICKET MANAGER, UNIVERSITY OF VIRGINIA, 1973 TO 1976

Best piece of advice you received in regards to your career:

To attend Ohio University's Sport Administration Master's Degree program.

HOMER RICE, THEN SPORTS INFORMATION DIRECTOR AT UNC,

LATER ATHLETIC DIRECTOR AT GEORGIA TECH

Best advice for someone aspiring toward a career in the sport industry:

"Be willing to work hard and learn the business from the ground up. My first day of my first job in sports, as a graduate assistant at Ohio University, I inventoried athletic supporters—the kind you wear, not the kind who give you money!"

Quote by which you live:

**"Go confidently into the future following your dreams....
Live the life you have imagined."**

WHILE GROWING UP IN NORTH WILKESBORO, NORTH CAROLINA, I was fortunate to have a strong, supportive family that was active in athletics. My three brothers were excellent athletes. My older brother Jim played football at Duke University from 1957 to 1959. They encouraged and motivated me as brothers often do in competitive endeavors and they have served as role models in my youth and in my career.

I played several sports at Wilkes Central High School in North Wilkesboro. I was fortunate enough to have good teammates and coaches in high school that helped me achieve success. I was a three-sport MVP, and a two-time all-state football player. Very early on, I thought I might want to be a coach after my playing days ended because I saw what a positive influence coaches had on my brothers as well as my own career. I believe my respect for the job that coaches do and the influence they have on the young people with whom they work has served me well through the years in my various administrative roles in athletics. My high school football coach, Marvin Hoffman, who is in the High School Hall of Fame in North Carolina, was a major influence on my life. He was a tremendous teacher, leader, and developer of young people not only on the field but also off the field. He encouraged and pushed me to be the best I could be in all that I did.

I grew up as a Duke fan and loved watching my brother play football for them. When I became involved in sports in high school and had some success the recruiting process began to change my thinking. The recruiting process was not new to my parents or me because we had all gone through it during my brothers' careers. I enjoyed meeting the coaches who came to visit and I realized my college choice would be difficult. While I continued to have an interest in Duke until the point I made a decision, my favorite two schools were Georgia Tech and the University of North Carolina. Coach Bobby Dodd was the coach at Georgia Tech at that time, and as it ended up, my senior year in high school was his last season at Tech. Coach Dodd decided to retire after the Orange Bowl on January 1, 1967. His decision to retire led to my decision to attend North Carolina. Academic achievement was always important in my family throughout high school, and coaches and teachers continually encouraged me to excel in my education efforts. Because of this I was also competing for the Morehead Scholarship, the highest academic scholarship at North Carolina. Although I signed a football scholarship first, I actually attended on a Morehead Scholarship.

I majored in industrial relations and psychology at North Carolina. In those days, not many educational programs in sport management existed, and the industrial relations major was similar to a business degree, but without the accounting. I wanted to pursue the business angle, but I also took some psychology courses and eventually completed a double major. My business studies provided a firm foundation for understanding the economics and finance of intercollegiate athletics. The psychology background has also been useful because much of an athletic administrator's job duties involve hiring, training, evaluating, and motivating people. I developed a deep love for North Carolina and was fortunate later to return to work there for many years. During my time at North Carolina, I played with some outstanding players during the 1969 to 1971 seasons. I played quarterback and defensive back for a successful football team that went to the

Peach Bowl in 1970. The 1971 team won the school's first-ever outright Atlantic Coast Conference championship and played in the Gator Bowl. I was named to the ACC Honor Roll and Who's Who in College Athletics.

When I first left Carolina after graduation, I spent about a year in a family business with two of my older brothers. My father had founded the business and after he passed away, my two older brothers ran it. I went to work with them for about a year, long enough to learn that it was not what I wanted to do. I called Homer Rice, the legendary athletic director who at the time was at North Carolina, and asked him if I could visit him to discuss a career in sports. During that conversation, Homer told me about the master's degree program at Ohio University. At the time, I did not know there was such a program. Only two major programs existed in the country: Ohio University and The University of Massachusetts. Ohio University had been the first program of its kind. When Homer told me about that program, it was as if someone had screwed in a light bulb in a darkroom from my career direction standpoint. Fortunately, I was accepted and went to Ohio University to complete my degree. My undergraduate studies, especially in the business aspects, served me well during my years at Ohio University. During the latter part of high school and college, I realized that I did not have a great desire to coach. I wanted to go into administration directly. It was the early 1970s, and at that point in time, we were still in an era in which most athletic administrators—at least at the collegiate level—were former coaches. The general pattern was to coach for several years and then move into administration. My desire, however, was to go directly into administration and the Ohio University program gave me a terrific avenue to do so.

As part of my academic program at Ohio University, I was required to do an internship. My internship ended up being the first 3 months of my first job as athletic ticket manager and assistant to the director of athletic facilities and finance at the University of Virginia. I actually planned to do my internship at the University of South Carolina with Paul Deitzel. I had known Coach Deitzel since high school because he had recruited me and we had stayed in touch through my days as a player at North Carolina. While I was waiting to start the internship, I received a call from Bill Cobey, who was an assistant athletic director at North Carolina. He was at an ACC meeting and told me that the University of Virginia needed a ticket manager. Apparently they wanted someone young that they did not have to pay very much. He said he thought of me. Bill put me in touch with Gene Corrigan, the athletic director at Virginia, and I interviewed for the job. Gene Corrigan still tells people that he just found me out on the street. I was there for 3 years working as the school's athletic ticket manager and assistant to the director of athletic facilities and finance.

Ticketing is a great entry-level position into sport administration because it is the base of the financial structure in a lot of ways. You must deal with the public on a daily basis, and that is always a good and challenging experience. Working at Virginia gave me the opportunity to work for Gene Corrigan, a talented and able administrator. Gene later became the ACC Commissioner, and as it would turn out, I have followed his footsteps and we have remained good friends for many years.

After working at Virginia for 3 years, I had the opportunity to go back to North Carolina as an assistant athletic director for business and finance. I handled all of the business affairs of the athletic department for 3 years. In 1979 I took on some fund-raising responsibilities. I was named the assistant executive vice-president of the Educational Foundation. My fund-raising experience would serve me well because later I became part of the leadership team that planned and executed some ambitious facility development projects. In 1980, Bill Cobey, who had followed Homer Rice as athletic director at Carolina and who brought me back to Carolina as his assistant, left college athletics to go into politics. I was then named to succeed Bill Cobey as athletic director at the University of North Carolina, my alma mater. I had become a major college athletic director at the young age of 31.

Many people helped me in my career development. Key people in athletic administration along the way strongly influenced me and were great leaders of people. People like Homer Rice, who was the athletic director at Carolina when I was playing and who sent me to Ohio University, was one of the key people. Homer has developed a number of publications and has been successful everywhere. He has meant a great deal to me—both personally and professionally—as a role model. Gene Corrigan also has contributed greatly to my career. I was fortunate in that my first job was working for someone like Gene who had all the right values, great vision, and was willing to share a lot of those kinds of things with a young guy who was at the lower end of his department. Those two guys and Bill Cobey, who hired me at North Carolina, were important. Although Bill got out of athletics shortly after hiring me in the Carolina athletic department, he did a terrific job managing an athletic program and had all the right ethics and values in my opinion. To have the opportunity to work with and be exposed to three people who are almost legends in the world of athletic administration was an amazing blessing. Not only were they superb administrators, but also they are outstanding individuals who had a lot to do with formulating who I have become professionally as well as personally.

During the 17 years I was athletic director many challenges and many successes occurred. I worked with and hired several of the top coaches and athletic administrators in the United States. During that time major changes were occurring in facilities, women's sports, television coverage, league expansion, NCAA legislation, and corporate sponsorships. One of the biggest challenges I faced was the building of the 21,572-seat Dean Smith Center because it had to be funded entirely through private means. We had to raise $35 million for a single facility. At that point in time, it was the largest single fund-raising drive ever accomplished for a facility in college athletics. It was a huge undertaking, but the university has a great deal of loyalty and a great deal of support among its alumni, faculty, and students. We built a facility that is state-of-the-art and one that will be enjoyable and functional for many years. We built the Koury Natatorium and the Kenan Football Center that were great additions to our athletic program. We were successful with the fund-raising projects and facility growth largely because of the vision and hard work of a lot of people. A major college athletic director's biggest ongoing challenge relates to finances. Because Division I programs should be financially self-sustaining, a great deal of pressure revolves around fund raising, ticket sales, corporate sponsorship, and winning.

Another area that always presents challenges is human resources and personnel. One of the tougher things we experienced was a football coaching change from Dick Crum to Mack Brown and rebuilding the football program. Fortunately, we did that successfully. We had a great deal of continuity and stability with our personnel during my tenure at UNC. One of the most important duties as an athletic director is to hire the right people. If you hire the right people you have stability, continuity, and loyalty within your program.

Success in a collegiate athletic department can be measured in a variety of ways. Abiding by NCAA rules, graduation rates of student-athletes, increased attendance, increases in fund raising and corporate giving, facility expansion, and league and national championships are a few of the measuring sticks of success. We also achieved success in women's athletics. We had success with the women's basketball program that is so popular in our league and area. The women's soccer program was recognized as one of the nation's finest, and it has contributed personnel to the U.S. World Cup and Olympic teams that have gained national and international prominence. Other sport programs developed a level of excellence. The women's programs won 18 national collegiate titles while I was there. We expanded and developed women's sports without decreasing the effectiveness of the men's programs. I am proud of the overall success of our athletic teams at UNC, and it is a testament to our outstanding staff, coaches, and athletes. During the 17 years I was the athletic director at North Carolina, Tar Heel teams claimed 123 ACC championships and 24 national collegiate titles. In the 1994–1995 season, UNC teams won an ACC-record 12 conference titles. The Sears Directors' Cup, emblematic of the collegiate all-sports champion and perhaps best overall athletic department, was won by UNC in 1993–1994, and Carolina finished in the top six during my last 3 years at the school.

Several things spurred my interest in becoming a conference commissioner. First of all, some of my colleagues at the other conference schools asked if I was interested in the position because they thought it would be a good fit. The position was in a conference that I knew well. Also the encouragement from some of the other athletic directors and faculty representatives in the league had a great deal to do with my interest in the commissioners' job. I had been doing the same thing at the same institution for 17 years, the timing seemed right, and it seemed to be the next career step for me. There were few places for which I would have left North Carolina, and working with the ACC was one of them. I was fortunate not to have to move to another area to assume a position of this nature. I did not have to uproot and go to another part of the country. It was 1 hour down the interstate, 90 minutes from where I grew up, and in the same league that I had been a part of my entire career. I knew the league and its history, its people, and its issues. My athletic director experience could benefit the league. I followed Gene Corrigan and became only the fourth commissioner in the 47-year history of the Atlantic Coast Conference in 1997.

My duties and responsibilities as a commissioner are mostly supervisory. With the help of many others, we have implemented the league's first-ever ACC student-athlete advisory committee. We have also developed comprehensive conference marketing plans for men's and women's basketball and football. We have created additional interest and television coverage by creating the ACC-Big Ten Basketball Challenge that pits schools from both conferences in head-to-head competition. Much of the foundation for our success, however, was laid by the work of talented leaders before me, and my challenge is to continue the excellence we have experienced and create new areas of achievement. Relative to being an athletic director, this job is more global in nature. It is also more corporate in nature because you are not on a campus. I do not see and deal with students on a daily basis, which is probably what I miss most in comparison of the two jobs.

My main responsibility is to oversee the daily operations of the conference office. An important aspect of my job is to maximize revenues for the member institutions. Much of the revenue production is accomplished through television contracts at our level, so I spend a great deal of time dealing with television people. We handle compliance at the conference level by helping our schools with compliance issues and rules and regulations. We run 24 championships per year at the conference level. That is a challenge and it takes a great amount of cooperation, planning, effort, and communication to effectively manage those events. We market the league through a variety of methods to reach both regional and national audiences. Our staff is talented and stable, but the management of an office this size is much different than the job I had at UNC. I have gone from having a staff of about 140 people at North Carolina to having a staff of 22 in the ACC Office. We are here to both lead and serve the conference members. More than anything else, a commissioner must have the ability to get cooperation and consensus from among the individual constituents of the conference. We have to take nine schools that are competitive with each other, put them in a boardroom, and ask them to be cooperative and make decisions in the best interest of the whole rather than in their own best interest. That can be a tricky endeavor, but one that is important for the welfare of the conference. To accomplish that, a sense of fairness and trust is critical.

Being an athletic director and a part of conference television negotiation for many years helped me tremendously in being a commissioner. I have a sense of the history of television in our league as an athletic director because I chaired the ACC television committee on four occasions. I learned television negotiation skills through watching other people. I had the opportunity to be in television negotiations and discussions with people like Gene Corrigan and Homer Rice. Tom Butters of Duke was one of the best that I have ever seen as far as television negotiations. I was fortunate to have those learning experiences and gradually participate in the negotiations and eventually play a leadership role.

At times it may appear that the television tail is wagging the athletic dog, and that may be true in some cases. Overall, however, I do not think that is the case because television cannot make you do anything. Television has been a tremendous financial boost to college athletics and has played a big part in our success during the past few decades. However, on an individual or conference basis, you have the power to decide what is in your best interest as far as television is concerned. You have to make the decision yourself, but they can make it enticing to do things that maybe you would rather not do in terms of what time you start a game and so forth. A conference has to decide whether certain rights fees are worth the changes in time or day and how those decisions affect the people playing the games and the spectators.

Corporate sponsorship in college athletics will continue to be among the leading issues of the next century. I negotiated the first NIKE sponsorship at North Carolina during my tenure as the athletic director. That was a situation in which NIKE's interest was first and foremost with the men's basketball program, and the approach we took was much broader in scope. We were glad NIKE was interested in the men's basketball program, so we leveraged their interests in the men's basketball into something that benefited the entire athletic program. In my opinion, the corporate sponsorship of the entire athletic program at UNC saved us a lot of money, provided additional publicity and national awareness, added quality products to our department, and overall was beneficial to North Carolina. The NCAA has established rules that have allowed us to control over-zealous marketing efforts by corporate sponsors and yet provide a win-win partnership with them. Ethical and moral arguments will always exist concerning the type of products and the amount of corporate involvement in amateur sports. It will be an ongoing monitoring process to maintain that delicate balance of business involvement in sport.

Many current issues continue to challenge us in intercollegiate sports. One of the continuing issues is the expansion of sport opportunities for women. When you talk about Title IX specifically, it is a legal issue with dramatic economic repercussions. Gender equity, however, is a moral issue rather than a legal issue. What it amounts to is to do what is fair and what is right in providing equal opportunities. We have come a long way in that regard particularly from a participation standpoint. There is still more to be done. If you put it solely into proportionality terms with programs that have football, you stand to maybe do more damage than improve things if you are not careful. I do not think that is what was intended when Title IX legislation was passed. Again, if you are reasonable and fair, then you can make it work. It is a huge challenge, however, because of the economics.

I have had the good fortune to be involved at the most basic level in the formation and development of the Bowl Championship Series (BCS) in college football. The whole postseason football issue in Division I-A is something that is still evolving. If you compare the old bowl system to the Alliance and the Super Alliance and now to the BCS, an evolution is obvious and it continues to make it better. The BCS is probably here to stay at least through 2006, and I say that because the PAC Ten and Big Ten have contracts with the Rose Bowl and ABC to participate in the Rose Bowl through that time. From a practical standpoint, in my opinion it creates a situation in which it is hard to go beyond the BCS until all the Division I-A conferences make themselves available for a play-off. We are solid for a while in terms of the BCS and in the first 2 years worked effectively in crowning a national champion. BCS is evolving and it will continue to evolve. I do not think we are at the end-all at this point, but I do think we are at a plateau where the only thing we will do between now and 2006 is fine-tune the BCS.

Another issue that will lead to many further discussions is the impact and success of the restructuring of the NCAA. It is still almost too soon to evaluate the new NCAA governance processes. It has been a dramatic change for the membership, and some people have adapted to it more readily than others. I still hear people say, "I wish we'd go back to the one institution-one vote system where everybody comes to the convention and deals with legislation once a year." But we are learning how to use the process in an effective way. The longer that it is in place, the more effective it will be and the more positively it will be received. It is just another part of our profession that is evolving. It is important that it works because if it does not work, the more frustration will build and the more likelihood that a part of the NCAA will branch off. I do not want to see that happen. I hope we will continue to develop and make it work, but it is a challenge because the institutions that comprise the NCAA are diverse. Some significant gaps exist, mostly related to economics and conferences' abilities to generate revenue and how that revenue is handled, shared, and distributed. That is a huge challenge to bring that kind of diversity together.

Another crucial issue in college athletics involves amateurism and its definition at the collegiate level. In the near future, a dramatic change could occur in some of our fundamental beliefs about amateurism. Right now its focus is on what the athletes do before they get on campus and what is acceptable and what is not. Should an athlete be drafted and actually be able to try it for a year and then be able to come back and play the same sport again in college if he or she failed to make it at the professional level? The amateurism issue has changed dramatically at the national and Olympic levels.

Other than the NCAA, I am a member of several professional organizations, and I have an important place in the direction of college athletics. I have been active in the National Association of College Directors of Athletics (NACDA) and was the organization's president in 1993–1994. I have found it to be an excellent organization in terms of professional development. The organization has broadened itself significantly in recent years by bringing in other organizations such as the marketing directors association, the senior women's administrators, the athletic development people, and the athletic business managers. All those organizations are now a part of NACDA. It is a very effective organization and a terrific one for young people to be involved with in terms of networking and education. The Collegiate Commissioner's Association (CCA) is an effective organization. I was aware of the organization, but I did not know how effective it was until I became a commissioner. It is streamlined. We meet about four times per year and as a group where we can relate to each other well. Little bureaucracy exists, and when we branch off into an NCAA I-A meeting, only 11 people are there. The CCA has been an effective group in the development of issues such as the BCS.

You must stay abreast of current issues and changes in college athletics. To keep up with the latest information, I recommend the NACDA magazine *Athletic Administration* and the *NCAA News*. Doing a little research and trying to find management books that have been written by people such as Homer Rice are valuable to the person considering a career in athletic administration. There has not been a lot written on the how-to's of managing the sports world, but when you can find those, they are generally worth one's time. Getting your master's degree in either business or sports administration is an excellent way to prepare for the vocation. The thing you have to do is find a way to set yourself apart from the crowd because many young people want to pursue sports administration.

Any kind of experience at the undergraduate level—however small—can be beneficial. You can demonstrate your commitment, willingness to learn, and energy. In my first day as a graduate student at Ohio University, I worked at a part-time job in the athletic department equipment room taking an inventory of jocks. No job is too small, and you must be willing to roll up your sleeves and learn from the opportunities that arise. Establish the attitude that nothing is demeaning because people watch those things and they watch the people who do the things that other people do not want to do. I read a book one time that said "the only place that success comes before work is in the dictionary." You must understand that you do not become the athletic director or the commissioner or the general manager overnight. It is a growth process, and the only way to learn it is from the bottom up.